Egypt
& the Sudan
a travel survival kit

Scott Wayne
Damien Simonis

Egypt & the Sudan – a travel survival kit

3rd edition

Published by
Lonely Planet Publications
Head Office: PO Box 617, Hawthorn, Vic 3122, Australia
Branches: PO Box 2001A, Berkeley, CA 94702, USA
12 Barley Mow Passage, Chiswick, London W4 4PH, UK
71 bis rue Cardinal Lemoine, 75005 Paris, France

Printed by
Singapore National Printers Ltd, Singapore

Photographs by

Chris Beall (CB)	Glenn Beanland (GB)	Kristie Burns (KB)
Dan Burton (DB)	Lorraine Chittock (LC)	Greg Elms (GE)
Hugh Finlay (HF)	Caroline Matthew (CM)	Damien Simonis (DS)
Paul Steel (PS)	Rob van Driesum (RvD)	Scott Wayne (SW)
Tony Wheeler (TW)		

Front cover: Ramses I Tomb, Valley of the Kings, Luxor (Dallas & John Heaton), Scoopix
Back cover: Felucca on the Nile River (CB), Retna Pictures

First Published
November 1987

This Edition
January 1994

Although the authors and publisher have tried to make the information as
accurate as possible, they accept no responsibility for any loss, injury or
inconvenience sustained by any person using this book.

National Library of Australia Cataloguing in Publication Data

Wayne, Scott
Egypt & the Sudan – a travel survival kit.

3rd ed.
Includes index.
ISBN 0 86442 191 5.

1. Egypt - Guidebooks. 2. Sudan - Guide-books.
I. Simonis, Damien. II. Title. (Series : Lonely Planet travel survival kit).

916.20455

text & maps © Lonely Planet 1994
photos © photographers as indicated 1994
climate charts compiled from information supplied by Patrick J Tyson, © Patrick J Tyson, 1994

Scott Wayne

Scott Wayne, the original author of this book, is an American who has lived, studied and travelled in the Middle East, Africa and Europe. He graduated from Georgetown University's School of Foreign Service with a degree in International Relations. He also did graduate studies at the Royal Institute of International Affairs in London and the University of Southern California. His studies at Georgetown included a long stint at the American University in Cairo and many adventures up and down the Nile. Scott is also the author of Lonely Planet's *Egyptian Arabic – a language survival kit* and *Baja California – a travel survival kit*, and co-author of *Mexico – a travel survival kit*.

Damien Simonis

Damien Simonis, an Australian journalist, has worked, studied and travelled extensively throughout Europe and the Middle East. With a degree in European languages and literature and several years' experience as a reporter and sub-editor on national daily papers in Australia, he headed for the Middle East and, later, to London, where he now lives. When Lonely Planet is not calling, Damien works for publications such as *The Guardian* and *The Sunday Times*. In addition to this guide, he has updated Lonely Planet's *Jordan & Syria – a travel survival kit*.

From Damien

Thanks are due to many individuals and organisations for their help and cooperation in putting together this edition of the book.

Much of the work on the Sudan section would not have been possible without the help, advice or simply comradeship on the road from the following (no particular order): Anthony Schierman (USA); Bernd (Germany); Elaine Wilson & Kelvin Barnsdale (UK); Nicky Spinks & Steve Burgess (UK); Jennifer Johnson (Canada) and the UNDP; Pete Last & Sue Mealing (UK); Jamie Bowden, Mark Wormald, Alistair Kerr (all UK); Father Beppe Puttinato (Italy); Fiona McDonald & Bob Affleck (Australia); Michael Wheeler (USA); Glen Christian (Netherlands) and a number of others who, whether they know it or not, have all had a hand in this. I will not quickly forget the many kindnesses shown to me and meals shared with the Sudanese people along the way.

In Cairo, Rory O'Callaghan (Ireland) and chums from the VSO opened my eyes to certain aspects of the city's life. Thanks Harry for the publicity.

Thanks are due to many people in Cairo and others met on the road for tips and companionship: Louise Hill (Aust), Kim Newman (NZ) & friends from Top Deck; John Dorman & Eileen Vaughan (Ireland); Billy Domsky (USA); all the teachers and trainers met and drunk with at ILI Sahafayeen; Melissa Verrocchi (USA) for her ideas on yachting; Amanda Reay & Simon Ward (UK); Ahmed Badawi (Egypt) & Lizzy Whitehouse (UK); C. Nisker (USA); Ayman Ahmed El Saman (Luxor) and a host of others. MEED in London, as usual, were helpful in opening up their cuttings files to me.

This Book

Scott Wayne researched and wrote the first two editions of *Egypt & the Sudan – a travel survival kit,* and Damien Simonis researched this, the third edition. Thanks to the many people who have written to us with advice, tips and travellers' tales; their names are listed at the back of this book.

From the Publisher

This book was edited by Lyn McGaurr and Jenny Missen. Proofing was done by Lyn McGaurr and Diana Saad. The mapping, design, illustrating and layout was done by Paul Clifton, with additional illustrations by Jacqui Schiff. Thanks to Rowan McKinnon and Sharon Wertheim for indexing.

Warning & Request

Things change – prices go up, schedules change, good places go bad and bad places go bankrupt – nothing stays the same. So if you find things better or worse, recently opened or long since closed, please write and tell us and help make the next edition better.

Your letters will be used to help update future editions and, where possible, important changes will also be included in a Stop Press section in reprints.

We greatly appreciate all information that is sent to us by travellers. Back at Lonely Planet we employ a hard-working readers' letters team to sort through the many letters we receive. The best ones will be rewarded with a free copy of the next edition or another Lonely Planet guide if you prefer. We give away lots of books, but, unfortunately, not every letter/postcard receives one.

Contents

THE NILE VALLEY – LUXOR **265**

THE NILE VALLEY – ESNA TO ABU SIMBEL.................................... **308**

THE SUEZ CANAL & THE RED SEA COAST **339**

ALEXANDRIA & THE MEDITERRANEAN COAST **376**

THE SINAI.. **412**

<u>THE SUDAN</u>

INTRODUCTION... **447**

FACTS ABOUT THE COUNTRY **449**

FACTS FOR THE VISITOR **467**

Map Legend

BOUNDARIES

— · — · — · — .... International Boundary
— · — · — · — .... Internal Boundary
+·+·+·+·+·+·+·+ .... National Park or Reserve
– – – – – – – – .... The Equator
· · · · · · · · · · · .... The Tropics

SYMBOLS

◎ NATIONAL .... National Capital
● MAJOR .... Major City
● Major .... Major Town
● Minor .... Minor Town
■ .... Places to Stay
▼ .... Places to Eat
✉ .... Post Office
✈ .... Airport
ℹ .... Tourist Information
◒ .... Bus Station, Transport
66 .... Highway Route Number
☾ ✝ ⛪ ✝ ...... Mosque, Church, Cathedral
∴ .... Temple or Ruin
⌂ .... Tomb
✚ .... Hospital
✳ .... Lookout
⚑ .... Camping Area
⌂ .... Hut or Chalet
▲ .... Mountain or Hill
⊢⊣ .... Railway Station
═══ .... Road Bridge
⊢⊣⊢⊣ .... Railway Bridge
⇒ ⇐ .... Road Tunnel
→) (← .... Railway Tunnel
⌢⌢⌢ .... Escarpment or Cliff
⌣ ⌒ .... Pass
ⵎⵎⵎ .... Ancient or Historic Wall

ROUTES

════════ .... Freeway
──────── .... Major Road or Highway
– – – – – – .... Unsealed Major Road
──────── .... Sealed Road
- - - - - - - ..... Unsealed Road or Track
════════ .... City Street
+++++++++ .... Railway
– – – – – – – .... Walking Track
– – – – – – – .... Ferry Route
+·+·+·+·+· .... Cable Car or Chair Lift

HYDROGRAPHIC FEATURES

.... River or Creek
.... Intermittent Stream
.... Lake, Intermittent Lake
.... Coast Line
.... Spring
.... Waterfall
.... Swamp

.... Salt Lake or Reef

.... Glacier

OTHER FEATURES

Park, Garden or National Park

.... Built Up Area

... Market or Pedestrian Mall

.... Plaza or Town Square

.... Muslim Cemetery

Note: not all symbols displayed above appear in this book

EGYPT

Introduction

Ever since Herodotus, the ancient Greek historian and traveller, first described Egypt as 'the gift of the Nile', she has been capturing the imagination of all who visit her.

The awe-inspiring monuments, left by the Pharaohs, Greeks and Romans as well as by early Christians and Muslims, attract thousands of visitors every year – but the pyramids, temples, tombs, monasteries and mosques are just part of this country's fascination.

Modern Egypt – where mud-brick villages stand beside Pharaonic ruins surrounded by towering steel, stone and glass buildings – is at the cultural crossroads of East and West, ancient and modern. While TV antennae decorate rooftops everywhere, from the crowded apartment blocks of Cairo to the mud homes of farming villages and the goatskin tents of the Bedouins, the fellahin (farmers) throughout the Nile's fertile valley still tend their fields with the archaic tools of their ancestors.

In the gargantuan city of Cairo the sound of the muezzin summoning the faithful to prayer or the mesmerising voice of Om Kolthum, the 'Mother of Egypt', compete with the pop music of ghetto blasters and the screech of car horns. And everywhere there are people: swathed in long flowing robes or Western-style clothes, hanging from buses, weaving through an obstacle course of animals and exhaust-spewing traffic or spilling from hivelike buildings.

Spectacular edifices aside, the attraction of this country lies in its incredible natural beauty and in the overwhelming hospitality of the Egyptian people.

Through everything the Nile River flows serene and majestic, the lifeblood of Egypt as it has been since the beginning of history.

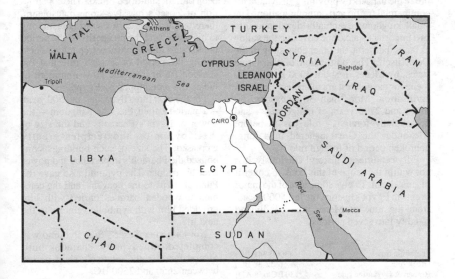

Facts about the Country

HISTORY

About 5000 years ago an Egyptian king named Menes unified Upper and Lower Egypt for the first time. No-one is quite sure how he did this, but it is known that his action gave rise to Egypt's first relatively stable dynasty of kings. Menes' powerful and civilised reign suggests that civilisation must have been developing in the Nile Valley for many centuries before this time.

The history of Egypt is inextricably linked to the Nile. Ever since the earliest known communities settled the Nile Valley, the river has inspired and controlled the religious, economic, social and political life of Egyptians. For many centuries the narrow, elongated layout of the country's fertile lands hampered the fusion of those early settlements, which held fast to their local independence. But once again it was the river, this time as a common highway, which broke the barriers by providing an avenue for commercial traffic and communication. The small kingdoms eventually developed into two important states, one covering the valley as far as the Delta, the other consisting of the Delta itself. The unification of these two states, by Menes in about 3000 BC, set the scene for the greatest era of ancient Egyptian civilisation. More than 30 dynasties, 50 rulers and 2700 years of indigenous – and occasionally foreign – rule passed before Alexander the Great ushered in a long, unbroken period of foreign rule.

Fifty centuries of history! Obviously, it is not within the scope of this book to cover it in great detail. To give some idea of the major events in Egypt's history, the last 5000 years, from the time of Menes, can be divided roughly into seven periods:

Pharaonic times	(3000-341 BC)
Greek rule	(332-30 BC)
Roman & Byzantine rule	(30 BC-638 AD)
The Arab conquest & the Mamluks	(640-1517)
Turkish rule	(1517-1882)
British occupation	(1882-1952)
Independent Egypt	(1952 onwards)

Pharaonic Times (3000-341 BC)

Little is known of the immediate successors of Menes except that, attributed with divine ancestry, they promoted the development of a highly stratified society, patronised the arts and built many temples and public works.

As you travel through Egypt, it is easy to be overwhelmed by the many names and dates of Pharaonic rule. Some of the books listed in the Facts for the Visitor chapter offer a detailed account of the long period encompassing the Old, Middle and New kingdoms.

In the 27th century BC, Egypt's pyramids began to appear. King Zoser and his chief architect, Imhotep, built what may have been the first, the Step Pyramid at Saqqara. Zoser ruled from the nearby capital of Memphis. Until his reign, most of the royal tombs had been built of sun-dried bricks. The construction of Zoser's massive stone mausoleum, therefore, was not only a striking testimony to his power and the prosperity of the period but the start of a whole new trend. It was also during the period of Zoser's rule that the sun-god Ra became the most important of the deities worshipped by Egyptians.

For the next three dynasties and 500 years – a period called the Old Kingdom – the power of Egypt's Pharaohs and the size of their pyramids and temples greatly increased. The size of such buildings symbolised the Pharaoh's importance and power over his people. The pyramid also gave the Pharaoh steps to the heavens, and the ceremonial wooden barques buried with him provided him with symbolic vehicles to the next life.

Not long after Zoser's Step Pyramid was completed, 4th dynasty Pharaohs built several more in the relatively short period between 2650 and 2500 BC.

Pharaoh Sneferu built the Pyramid of Meidum in Al-Faiyum and the Red Pyramid

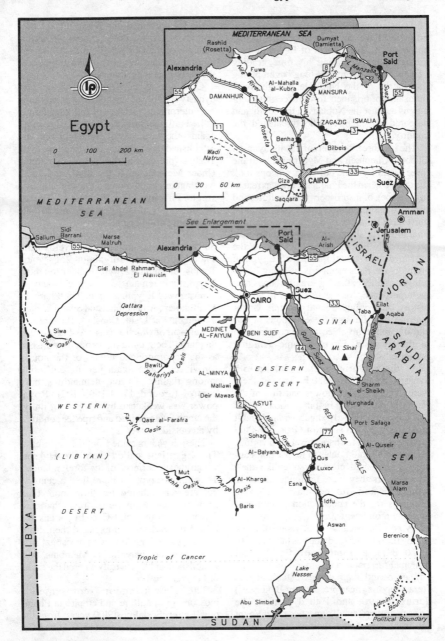

of Dahshur near Saqqara, and took royal power and the accompanying artistic and commercial development of Egypt to even greater heights. During his time, trading vessels nearly six metres long began plying the waters of the Nile. He brought back thousands of prisoners from successful campaigns against the Nubians in the south, and defeated all enemies who threatened the country.

The last three Pharaohs of the 4th dynasty, Cheops, Chephren and Mycerinus, built the three Great Pyramids of Giza. Cheops took the throne when the Pharaonic era was reaching the apex of its prosperity and culture, and if his colossal pyramid is any indication he must have been one of the greatest of all the Pharaohs. Its sheer size and mathematical precision is not only a monument to the extraordinary development of Egyptian architecture; it also suggests, as many Egyptologists believe, that the era of Cheops saw the emergence, for the first time in human history, of an organisational principle. Under his rule, and through the enormous labour and discipline involved in the construction of the pyramid, Egypt became a highly organised state.

As the centuries passed and the 5th dynasty (about 2490-2330 BC) began, there were changes in the power and rule of the Pharaohs. One of the first indications of this was the comparatively small pyramids built at Abu Sir, 12 km south of Giza. The Pharaohs had begun to share power with various high officials and nobles in the vast bureaucracies they had created, so unlike their predecessors they were no longer absolute monarchs and did not have the same resources for the construction of immense funerary monuments.

As control became even more diffused during the 6th and 7th dynasties (about 2330-2170 BC), a number of small local principalities popped up around the country, and a second capital was established at Heracleopolis (near present-day Beni Suef) during the 9th and 10th dynasties. The princes of these small dynasties ruled Egypt for many years, but their constant feudal struggles prevented any possibility of economic or artistic development. With the collapse of the Old Kingdom a state of disunity succeeded the unparalleled grandeur of the early Pharaonic dynasties.

Civil war at the beginning of the 11th dynasty finally put an end to the squabbling. An enterprising member of the Intef family rallied all the principalities of the south against the weakness of Heracleopolis, and established an independent kingdom with Thebes (present-day Luxor) as its capital. Under Mentuhotep II the north and south were again united under the leadership of a single Pharaoh. The princes of Thebes became rulers of all Egypt, and the Middle Kingdom period began.

With political order came economic stability and social and artistic development. Thebes prospered for about 250 years. Tombs and temples were built throughout Egypt; their remains can be seen today in almost every Egyptian town. The Pharaohs Mentuhotep, Amenemhet and Sesostris built monuments at Lisht, Dahshur, Hawara and Lahun – all of which are near Al-Faiyum and Saqqara. Their building frenzy diminished as the governors and nobles of the nomes (provinces) once again began squabbling among themselves and demanding more control (around 1780-1660 BC). Royal power was weakened by this lack of unity; the empire was divided and ripe for conquest by an outside power.

These invaders came from the north-east. The Egyptians called them the Hyksos, which means 'princes of the foreign lands'. They ruled Egypt for more than a century, but are remembered for little more than having introduced the horse-drawn chariot to Egypt. By about 1550 BC the Egyptians had routed the Hyksos and expelled them from power. A new kingdom, with its capital first at Thebes and thereafter at Memphis, was established and Egypt truly entered the ranks of the great powers.

The New Kingdom represented a blossoming of culture and empire in Pharaonic Egypt. For almost 400 years, from the 18th to the 20th dynasties (1550-1150 BC),

The Preparation for Life Eternal

It was death, of course, that prompted the construction of the Egyptian pyramids but the incredible amount of resources, effort and time that went into them was indicative of many aspects of life in those days. The tombs served a variety of purposes, not the least of which was to provide the final resting places of the owners and repositories for their worldly possessions.

Obviously the size and grandeur of the tombs were designed to enhance the owners' greatness in the eyes of their people during the owners' lifetimes, but their tombs also became places of worship for their subjects after the owners' deaths.

The pyramids were also a symbol of life and death, of life over death and of life after death, serving to preserve the Pharaohs in the memory of their people and to ensure the Pharaohs' continued existence in the afterlife. It was not a fear of death, or even an obsession with it, that guided the ancient Egyptians; rather it was a belief in life eternal and the desire to be one with the gods and their universe that inspired such extremes.

The pyramids were seen as an indestructible sanctum for the preservation of the Pharaohs' kas. These spirits, or life forces emanating from the gods, were the 'doubles' of living people but gained their own identities with the deaths of those people. The Pharaohs' kas would either continue to exist in their tombs – hence the need for all their worldly belongings – or would journey off to join the gods. The survival of the ka, however, depended on the continued existence of the body, so the process of mummification developed alongside the technology of tomb building.

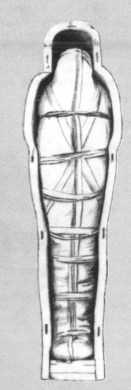

Prior to dynastic times the dead were simply buried in shallow graves on the edge of the desert and covered with sand. Because of the dry atmosphere and hot sand this practice often caused the bodies to dehydrate before the tissues decomposed and this natural method of preservation did not go unnoticed. As the ancient Egyptians changed their burial rituals and introduced coffins, the technique of mummification was developed to artificially preserve the dead bodies of those who could afford the process, as well as to preserve an incredible number of sacred birds, reptiles and other animals.

For humans the mummification process took about 70 days. The most important aspect was the removal of the vital organs and the drying of the body using a dehydrating agent called natron (a mineral of hydrated sodium carbonate). The actual wrapping of the body in bandages played no role in the preservation of the corpse.

The treatment took place in six main stages:

The brain was extracted by being broken up and removed through the nose.

The viscera (except for the heart and kidneys) were removed through an incision in the lower left abdomen. The intestines, stomach, liver and lungs were dehydrated with natron, treated with resin and stored separately in canopic jars.

The body was sterilised and the internal cavities were temporarily packed with natron and fragrant resins.

The body then underwent the main preservative treatment of being covered with natron for about 35 days.

The temporary packing was then removed; the limbs were packed, under the skin, with clay; and the body cavities were permanently packed with linen soaked in resin, bags of cinnamon and myrrh, and sawdust.

The body was then anointed with fragrant oils and ointments, the abdominal incision was covered with an amulet of the Eye of Horus, and the skin was treated with molten resin.

Finally the body was wrapped up, with pieces of jewellery and protective amulets being placed among the bandages. ■

Egypt was a great power in north-east Africa and the eastern Mediterranean. Renowned kings and queens ruled an expanding empire from Memphis, and built monuments which even today are unique in their immensity and beauty.

The temple complex of Karnak at Thebes became an important symbolic power centre for the empire. The temple seemed to grow as the empire expanded. Each successive Pharaoh of the 18th and 19th dynasties added a room, hall or pylon, with intricately carved hieroglyphic inscriptions on every wall and pillar. Some of what is known about Egyptian life during this time comes from the stories told by these inscriptions.

Significant expansion of the empire began with the reign of Tuthmosis I in 1528 BC. He grabbed Upper Nubia, and became the first Pharaoh to be entombed in the Valley of the Kings on the west bank across from Thebes. His daughter, Hatshepsut, became one of Egypt's few female rulers. A spectacular mortuary temple was built for her at Deir al-Bahri on the west bank.

Tuthmosis III, Hatshepsut's nephew, was next in line; he became Egypt's greatest conqueror. He expanded the empire past Syria and into western Asia. He built and contributed to temples at Thebes, Buhen, Amada and other locales throughout Egypt.

Empire expansion and temple/tomb building continued under the next three Pharaohs – Amenophis II, Tuthmosis IV and Amenophis III – and reached its peak in 1417 BC under Amenophis III. He built the Luxor Temple and a massive mortuary temple, of which the only remains are the Colossi of Memnon on the west bank at Luxor. During this period the country was relatively prosperous and stable.

Amenophis IV quarrelled with the priesthood of the god Amun, the leading god of Thebes, and took the name Akhenaten in honour of Aten, the disc of the rising sun. Akhenaten and his wife, Nefertiti, were so devoted to the worship of Aten that they established a new capital, called Akhetaten, devoted solely to the worship of the new god. Some historians believe that this worship represented the first organised form of

Nefertiti and Akhenaten

monotheism. Today, the scant remains of Akhenaten's capital can be seen at Tell al-Amarna, near the town of Al-Minya.

After Akhenaten's death, the priests of Thebes went on a rampage and destroyed any signs of his rule and his monotheism. This included the Temple of the Sun at Karnak. (An American archaeological team photographed the hieroglyphic inscriptions on more than 35,000 stone blocks from the temple which had been scattered around the world. From the photographs, the archaeologists were able to reconstruct the temple and learn more about the lives of Akhenaten and Nefertiti.)

Akhenaten's young son-in-law, Tutankhamun, ruled for about nine years and died just before reaching manhood. His tomb was discovered in 1922 with almost all its treasures untouched.

For the next few centuries, Egypt was ruled by generals: Ramses I, II and III, and Seti I. Like good Pharaohs and military leaders they built massive monuments, such as the temples at Abydos and Abu Simbel, and waged war against the Hittites and Libyans. However, by the time Ramses III came to power (1198 BC) as the second king of the 20th dynasty, disunity had begun to set in. The empire continued to shrink, and Egypt was subsequently subjected to attack from outsiders. This was the state of affairs when Alexander the Great arrived in the 4th century BC.

Greek Rule (332-30 BC)

Egypt was a mess when Alexander arrived in 332 BC. Over the previous several centuries Libyans, Ethiopians, Persians and Assyrians had invaded the country at different times. Alexander promptly established a new capital, which he named Alexandria after himself. After his death, Egypt was ruled by a Macedonian general, Ptolemy I, who established the Ptolemaic dynasty. Under this new dynasty, which lasted for 300 years, Alexandria became a great Greek city, housing, among other things, a famous library. The temples of Dendara, Philae and Edfu, which were built further south, are still in excellent

Cleopatra

shape, with most of their walls and roofs extant. There was a melding of the Greek and Egyptian religions.

Despite the prosperity, however, the Ptolemys' rule was not without its share of murder, intrigue and threats from abroad. While they bickered, expelled and assassinated one another, the overall weakness and instability of their reign attracted the interest of the rulers of the expanding Roman Empire. For a while, the Romans supported various Ptolemys, but this seemed to lead to more rivalry and assassination rather than peace and stability. The litany of events leading to complete Roman rule over Egypt reads like a bloody soap opera.

From 51 to 48 BC Cleopatra VII and her younger brother Ptolemy XIII together ruled Egypt, under Roman protection. Pompei, one of Julius Caesar's rivals, was sent from Rome to watch over them. Ptolemy had Pompei killed and Cleopatra banished. However, in the same year (48 BC), Caesar gave his all to Cleopatra and on arrival in Egypt threw Ptolemy in the Nile, appointing another of Cleopatra's brothers, Ptolemy XIV, as co-ruler. Cleopatra gave birth to Julius Caesar's son in 47 BC and had her brother killed in 45 BC. A year later Caesar was also assassinated. (Are you lost yet?) Marc Antony arrived from Rome, fell in love with Cleopatra, and moved in with her for 10 years of bliss, an arrangement the Roman senate wasn't too thrilled about. They declared Antony an enemy of the people and sent Octavian to deal with him. Antony and Cleopatra preferred bliss to strife. They both committed suicide in 30 BC and Egypt became a Roman province.

Roman & Byzantine Rule (30 BC-638 AD)

Octavian was the first Roman ruler of Egypt. He ruled as Emperor Augustus for a few years and made Egypt the granary of the Roman Empire. Except for a brief invasion by Ethiopia in 24 BC, Egypt was basically stable and peaceful for about 30 years.

Although the Bible tells us that Mary, Joseph and their young baby fled from Bethlehem to Egypt, where Jesus grew up before returning to Palestine to spread the word of God, it was not until St Mark started preaching the gospel, around 40 AD, that Egyptians began converting to Christianity. The Roman emperor Nero capitalised on this renewed sense of religious unity by developing Egypt as a trade centre between Rome and India in 54 AD.

A national Egyptian, or Coptic, Church was founded, despite the persecution of Christians throughout the Roman Empire during the following centuries. Egypt prospered, but by the 3rd century the Roman Empire had begun to succumb to war, famine and power struggles. In the 4th century, not long after Christianity was declared the state religion, the Roman Empire cracked in half. The eastern half became what was later known as the Byzantine or Eastern Empire. It was ruled from Constantinople (now Istanbul), while the Western Roman Empire remained centred in Rome.

The empire was too weak to rule its dominions effectively, so Egypt was left to invaders – Nubians from the south and North Africans from the west. Egypt was also left to develop the Coptic Church independently of the Byzantines. The Copts' adoption of a Monophysitic doctrine (the belief that Christ is divine, rather than both human and divine) was deemed heretical by the Byzantine and Roman orthodoxy, so they expelled the Coptic Church from the main body of Christianity. That doctrine, however, and a tradition of monasticism, greatly influenced later developments in European Christianity and are still an integral part of the Christian church in Egypt.

Aside from a few wars with Nubians, a famine and a couple of Persian invasions, life in 'Byzantine' Egypt was relatively sedate. Then, in 640 AD, the Arabs arrived.

The Arab Conquest & the Mamluks (640-1517)

The Arab conquest brought Islam to Egypt. By 642 the new Arab rulers had established Fustat as a military base and seat of government – the precursor of Cairo. Although it didn't last long as the seat of government, it grew quickly as a city of Muslims. The ruins of Fustat can still be seen just south of Cairo.

In 658 the Omayyads, an Arab dynasty based in Damascus, snatched control of Egypt and stayed until 750. During the 92 years of their rule, Islamic faith and the Omayyad Empire extended from Spain all the way to central Asia. Theological splits were inevitable in such a large empire. One of the main splits concerned the spiritual leadership of the descendants of Ali, the Prophet Mohammed's son-in-law. Two groups – the Sunni and the Shi'ite – evolved because of this dispute, and conflict between them continues today. More than 1200 years ago, this same conflict led to the downfall of the Omayyad dynasty and the decapitation of Marwan, the last Omayyad caliph, or ruler. Persian troops paraded his head around the burnt remains of Fustat. For the next 108 years Egypt was ruled by the Baghdad-based Abbassid dynasty.

The Abbassids ruled Egypt a little differently from their predecessors. They brought in outsiders, Turkish-speaking soldier slaves known as Mamluks, to protect their interests throughout the empire. One of these fighting nomads, Bayikbey, eventually gained enough power and influence to become a threat to the caliph. The caliph gave him Egypt, but Bayikbey preferred to remain in Turkey, where the caliph eventually had him killed. Bayikbey's stepson Ibn Tulun, or 'son of Tulun', was sent to Egypt as governor in his place.

Ibn Tulun wanted Egypt to be an independent state, not an Abbassid province, so he fought and defeated the Abbassids and established a dynasty. He erected one of the largest mosques in the Middle East: the Mosque of Ibn Tulun was large enough to accommodate all his cavalry – both horses and men.

After Ibn Tulun's death, Egypt was unable to keep its independence. Various leaders and invaders followed, including the Abbassids, Byzantines, Ikhshids and, finally, the Fatimids. The Fatimids came from a kingdom of rulers in north-west Africa who claimed descent from Mohammed's daughter, Fatima, and her husband, Ali. They quickly established a dynasty of independent caliphs which lasted for just over 200 years (968-1169).

Egypt flourished under the first Fatimid rulers. At the behest of the mysterious caliph Al-Muizz, a Greek named Gawhar spent four years building the new city of Cairo. Desmond Stewart writes in his book *Great Cairo: Mother of the World* that Al-Muizz:

...rule[d] mysteriously, as befitted an imam, from behind the curtain of awe. For Fatimid power was based on an idea: the sense that God allows an aspect of himself to be incarnate in an infallible ruler.

Gawhar's construction work in Cairo befitted an imam imbued with godliness, and his greatest work was the Al-Azhar Mosque. This immense structure, which resembles a fortress, became one of the world's greatest centres of Islamic studies. Today it continues to function as both a mosque and a major university. After the death of Al-Muizz, Egypt continued to flourish under his son,

Al-Aziz, but the good times ended with the rule of Al-Aziz's crazy son, Al-Hakim (996-1021).

At first, Al-Hakim ruled Egypt as an absolute monarch with beneficence and grace. A magnificent mosque was built at the northern wall of Cairo between the gates of Bab al-Futuh and Bab an-Nasr. Al-Hakim began to share his rule with a council of advisers and also attempted to understand the problems of Cairenes by touring the city on a mule and talking to his people. All of this paled into insignificance, however, when the young Al-Hakim began ruling like a lunatic.

At the age of 15 he murdered his tutor. He then decided he didn't like his advisers any more so he murdered them too. He loved the night and took to riding after dark on Moon, his pet mule, so it became illegal and punishable by death to work during the day and sleep at night.

Al Hakim also hated merchants who cheated their customers, and women. He tried to impose a 24-hour curfew on them, and when that didn't work he imposed a ban on the manufacture of women's shoes. He figured that without shoes women would not want to plod through the manure and open sewers on the streets.

This lunacy continued until one night in 1021, when Al-Hakim mounted Moon and rode off into the Moqattam Hills near Cairo. The mule was found but Al-Hakim had disappeared, never to be heard from again. He left a group of disciples who maintained the mystical belief that Al-Hakim was a divine incarnation. This group became known as the Druse. Although they still exist in Lebanon, Syria, Jordan and Israel, very little is known of their beliefs and practices, as it is blasphemous for the Druse to reveal their people's secrets to outsiders.

Over the next 150 years several Fatimid caliphs ruled Egypt. Apart from a relatively brief spate of plague and famine, and a few power squabbles, battles and wars, Egypt was prosperous. Food was plentiful in the *souqs*, or markets, and apartment buildings with as many as 10 floors (sometimes more) rose in Cairo. This prosperity, however, could not be maintained in those parts of the empire outside Egypt.

Around this time the Christians of Western Europe began a crusade to spread Christianity and rescue the Holy City of Jerusalem from the Muslims.

The Crusaders seized Jerusalem from the Fatimids in 1099. Tripoli, in Lebanon, fell in 1109 and so did several other parts of the Fatimid Empire. By 1153 all of Palestine was under Christian control, and rather than suffer a similar fate the weakened Fatimid state decided to cooperate with the Crusaders. The Muslim Seljuk dynasty of Syria was not happy about this, as the balance of power was upset – a balance which had begun to tip increasingly in their favour. So the Seljuks sent in an army led by a Kurdish warrior named Shirkoh and his nephew Salah ad-Din (known to the West as Saladin).

Salah ad-Din eventually gained control of Egypt and founded his own dynasty, the Ayyubids, in 1171. The Crusaders attacked and partly burned Cairo in 1176, so Salah ad-Din immediately began fortifying the city. He built part of the city walls and the Citadel; the latter became a small town of shops, stables and workshops. His reign marked the heyday of medieval Egypt and in 1187 he drove the Crusaders from Jerusalem.

Above all, Salah ad-Din sought power. He purchased Mamluks (whose name comes from an Arabic word for 'owned' or 'held') to assist him. Most Mamluks were Turkish mercenaries, sold by their parents when they were boys, to be trained solely to fight for the sultan. In his book *Travels through Syria & Egypt in the Years 1783, 1784 & 1785*, M Volney describes the Mamluks as follows:

strangers among themselves...Without parents...the past has done nothing for them; they do nothing for the future. Ignorant and superstitious by upbringing, they become fierce through murders, mutinous through tumults, deceitful through intrigues, corrupt through every species of debauch.

After a certain period of servitude and military service, many Mamluks were free to own land and raise families. Despite their violent nature some did choose to settle down quietly. Other Mamluks, however, began to seek positions of power and influence within the state. Their efforts brought about the demise of Shagarat ad-Durr, the last Ayyubid ruler and the first woman to reign over Egypt since Cleopatra, and ushered in more than two and a half centuries of Mamluk rule.

Two dynasties of Mamluks ruled Egypt. The Bahri Mamluks were the first: in their 132 years of rule there were more than 25 sultans. Murder, intrigue and war were rife. In between fighting and conspiring, however, the Mamluks developed a distinctive style of architecture, and several mosques were built, including those of Sultan Hassan, Az-Zahir and Qalaun.

The sultans of the next dynasty were equally given to construction. This dynasty began when a Circassian slave named Barquq seized power from the Bahri ruler, a six-year-old Mamluk. More than 21 Circassian Mamluks became sultan before Egypt fell to the Turks in 1517.

Turkish Rule (1517-1882)

Since most of the Mamluks were either of Turkish descent or from Turkey and the surrounding areas, rule over Egypt by the Ottoman sultans of Constantinople was not difficult. In fact, their rule basically consisted of collecting taxes from Egypt, while the rest of the governing business was left to the Mamluks. This continued until Napoleon invaded Egypt in 1798.

Napoleon and his army routed the Mamluk army, supposedly as a show of support for the Ottoman sultan. In reality, Napoleon wanted eventually to strike a blow at British trade in the Indian Ocean by gaining control of the land and sea routes to India. He was also keen to 'civilise' Egypt.

Napoleon established a French-style government, revamped the tax system and implemented public works projects – canals were cleared, streets were cleaned of garbage and temporary bridges spanned the Nile. Through his Institut d'Egypte he put a variety of French intellectuals to work on a

Cannon in the grounds of Fort Qait Bey, Alexandria

history of ancient Egypt and a record of the ancient monuments. The French were also responsible for the planting of new crops, establishing a new system of weights and measures, and reorganising the hospitals. However, as Alan Moorehead writes in his book *The Blue Nile*:

Everything these new conquerors proposed was a strain; it was a strain *not* to throw rubbish in the streets, *not* to bribe witnesses and officials, and it was upsetting to be obliged to undergo medical treatment where prayers had always served in the past. [The Egyptians] had been getting on very well, they felt, as they were before. They had no need for new canals, new weights and measures, and new schools...They did not believe Bonaparte's protestations of his respect for Muhammad, nor were they much impressed by his dressings-up in turban and caftan...

Napoleon's Egyptian adventure seemed doomed from the beginning. Less than a month after he arrived, the British navy, under Admiral Nelson, appeared off the coast of Alexandria. Nelson quickly destroyed the French fleet and cut off Napoleon's forces from France. A year later the British sent an army of 15,000 Turkish soldiers to expel the French from Egypt. The resulting battle at Abu Qir was a victory for the French; 5000 Turks were killed. Nevertheless, the British returned in 1801 and compelled the French to leave.

Although brief, the French occupation significantly weakened Egyptian political stability. After a period of internal strife, the headstrong Mohammed Ali became khedive (viceroy). A lieutenant in the Albanian contingent of the Ottoman army, he rose to power after the Albanian soldiers mutinied against their Turkish rulers. With Mamluk help, he temporarily expelled the British from Egypt. The Mamluk leaders, however, also posed a threat to Mohammed Ali, so he invited them to a sumptuous banquet and then had them massacred on their way home. A charming host!

Mohammed was power-hungry. He sent his troops on successful forays into the Sudan, Greece, Syria and Arabia, and by 1839 he controlled most of the Ottoman Empire. However, the British intervened again and forced him into sharing power with the sultan in Istanbul. Mohammed died in 1848 and was succeeded by his grandson Abbas, who was in turn succeeded by his son Said.

Said began implementing many government reforms and projects, foremost of which was the establishment of the railway system and the digging of the Suez Canal.

Pasha Ismail succeeded Said, and followed in his path by establishing factories, a telegraph and postal system, canals and bridges. The fledgling cotton industry of Egypt prospered as the American Civil War disrupted cotton production in America's southern states. Ismail opened the Suez Canal in 1869 and achieved political independence for Egypt in 1873. With independence, Ismail confidently spent more state money than he had. The national debt became so great that he was forced to abdicate in 1879.

British Occupation (1882-1952)
The debt and abdication brought greater British control over Egyptian affairs. With pressure from the British, Ismail's son Tawfiq reorganised Egypt's finances, and British and French controllers installed themselves in the government.

With the outbreak of WW I the Egyptian government threw in its lot with the Allies. When Turkey entered the war, and made an abortive attack on the Suez Canal, the British Foreign Office placed Egypt 'under the pro-

Allied Soldiers – WW I

tection of His Majesty', effectively terminating the suzerainty of Turkey over Egypt. The khedive, Abbas Hilmi, was deposed for his Turkish sympathies, Prince Hussein Kamil became sultan and martial law was proclaimed throughout the country.

During this time, several groups in Egypt, in particular the Ulama, or Muslim elite, and Egyptian civil servants, military officers and landowners, were disturbed by the increase in foreign influence, especially within the Egyptian government and civil service. A movement to expel Europeans from these areas evolved from a coalition of opposition groups, but the plan backfired and the British remained in such positions until 1952.

The British did, however, eventually allow the formation of a nationalist political party, called the Wafd (Delegation), and a monarchist party. The first elections were held in 1922, independence was granted, and King Fuad I was elected to head a constitutional monarchy. For the next 30 years the British, monarchists and Wafdists jockeyed for power and influence. Egypt was left in chaos following WW II and defeat in Israel's 1948 War of Independence. By 1952 only a group of dissident military officers had the wherewithal to take over the government.

Post-Revolution Egypt & Suez Crisis
The Free Officers, led by Colonel Gamal Abdel Nasser, overthrew King Farouk, Fuad's son, in a bloodless coup. The coup was quickly dubbed the Revolution of 1952. The first independent Arab Republic of Egypt was formed and Nasser, who after some manoeuvring became head of state, wasted no time in getting embroiled in international politics.

He became one of the architects of the Nonaligned Movement, an association of countries that sought to distance itself from the Western and Eastern blocs and establish a third force in world politics. Through his role in the movement Nasser criticised the West; this and his growing economic ties with Eastern Europe cost him Western assistance in building the Aswan High Dam, so he turned to the Soviets instead. As the

Western powers had given Egypt's doubtful capacity to pay a reasonable share of the costs of the dam as one reason for pulling out, Nasser nationalised the Suez Canal Company in 1956, ostensibly to raise the necessary money. The British and French, anxious to maintain some degree of control over the waterway, secretly agreed to cooperate in an attack with the Israelis, who invaded on 29 October. The French and British 'intervened' two days later, and landed paratroops at Port Said on 5 November. Despite the Soviet invasion of Hungary in the same month, the USA and Moscow found themselves on the same side just for once in opposing the Anglo-French actions, and the United Nations had little trouble urging the invaders to leave and installing a UN peacekeeping force to guarantee safe passage through the canal. Nasser became a hero, especially in the Arab world.

Six-Day War & October War
The Suez Crisis of 1956 made Nasser head of a pan-Arab nationalist movement that emphasised Arab unity. Unsuccessful attempts were made to unite Egypt, Syria and, for a short while, Yemen in a United Arab Republic. Amid a growing feeling that Egypt was getting too strong a say in Syrian affairs, Damascus pulled out of the UAR in 1961. There were further attempts at union with Syria and Iraq during the 1960s, all of them fruitless.

As Egypt's economy worsened under Abdel Nasser's 'Arab socialist' policies of nationalisation, he began diverting attention from the internal problems by emphasising Arab unity and making Israel a scapegoat. As tension increased on the Israeli-Syrian border, Nasser asked the UN force to leave the Sinai and closed the Straits of Tiran, Israel's only outlet to the Indian Ocean. Soon after, Jordan and Iraq signed defence pacts with the UAR. On 5 June 1967 Israel attacked, and in just six days destroyed the Egyptian air force, captured the Sinai and closed the Suez Canal, as well as taking the Golan Heights from Syria and the West Bank from Jordan. Despite this devastating defeat, the Egyptian people insisted that Nasser remain in power, which he did until his death in 1970. Arabs continue to revere him, and his photograph can still be found in many homes and shops.

Anwar Sadat succeeded Nasser and tried to repair Egypt's economy by becoming friendlier with the West, particularly the USA, at the expense of relations with the USSR. He also realised that to truly revitalise Egypt's economy he would have to deal with Israel – but first he needed bargaining power, a basis for negotiations. So, on 6 October 1973, the Jewish holiday of Yom Kippur, he launched a surprise attack across the Suez Canal. Although Egypt actually lost the war, thanks mainly to massive US resupply of Israeli war material, Sadat's negotiating strategy succeeded. He also managed to get back the east bank of the Suez Canal under the ensuing cease-fire terms.

Peace with Israel

On 19 November 1977, Sadat travelled to Jerusalem to begin making peace with Israel, and a peace treaty based on the Camp David Agreement was eventually signed in 1979. Most of the Sinai was returned to Egyptian control by 1982 and relations between Egypt and Israel were normalised. Egypt was immediately ostracised by the rest of the Arab world and most socialist and developing countries. The seat of the Arab League was transferred to Tunis and relations with Libya in particular – already strained (although the two countries had discussed union in the early 1970s) – rapidly worsened. By 1980, Egypt had turned the border area into a security zone and Libya had built fortresses and airfields on its eastern frontier.

For most Egyptians the treaty with Israel promised future peace and prosperity. However, radical groups of fundamentalist Muslims were opposed to the price of peace: normalisation of relations with Israel and alignment with the West (Sadat had expelled thousands of Soviet advisers and later 40 diplomats). A member of one such group assassinated Sadat during a military parade on 6 October 1981.

Mubarak in Power

Hosni Mubarak, Sadat's vice president since 1974, was sworn in as president. He has since managed, to the surprise of some, to carry out a balancing act on several fronts, abroad and at home.

In the three to four years after taking over as President, Mubarak was able, to the irritation of more hardline states like Syria and Libya, to break through Egypt's isolation in the Arab world without abandoning the treaty with Israel, although the latter's invasion of Lebanon in 1982 put relations between the two states under heavy strain. From then until late 1986, Egypt had no ambassador in Tel Aviv. From 1984, Egypt began to re-establish relations with moderate Arab countries, and used its unique position through the 1980s to promote the Middle East peace process in Israel and the Arab countries. An exception to his foreign policy success were the continued poor relations with Libya. On the superpower front he proved equally adept, reopening relations with Moscow, letting experts return, and at

President Hosni Mubarak

the same time becoming the region's second biggest recipient of US aid after Israel.

Internally, he inherited the twin problems of an economy unable to match the growing demands of an exploding population (see Economy) – violent riots over price rises in September 1984 were a sharp reminder – and the ever-present threat to secular rule posed by Islamist groups demanding rule by *shari'a,* or Islamic law. Mubarak has attempted to keep a lid on the problem with a combination of limited democracy and tolerance and heavy-handed crackdowns on purported Muslim activists. Elections in 1987 and 1990 resulted in overwhelming victory for his National Democratic Party, but opposition parties continue to protest against what they claim is electoral fraud, and the fact that elections are supervised by the Ministry of the Interior.

In October 1993, Mubarak won his third presidential term for another six years. He was the only candidate.

The Gulf War

Egypt joined Syria in throwing its weight behind the UN alliance aimed at Iraq after the latter's invasion of Kuwait in August 1990. About 35,000 Egyptian troops participated in the fighting in January and February, and despite dire warnings that the essentially pro-Western stance would bring domestic violence, Mubarak's move turned out to be an astute one. It enhanced his position as arbiter in the Middle East and as reliable partner of the West, which brought an immediate reward in the form of US$14,000 million of debt being cancelled. Relations with Libya also improved from the end of 1989 – the borders were opened and ambassadors exchanged.

Pressure at home from Islamists grew in the early 1990s, partly for the usual economic reasons never far below the surface. About 150 people, including one British tourist, were killed in violence in 1992, mostly between Islamic fundamentalists and Coptic Christians in Upper Egypt, and the Security forces carried out massive raids to round up suspects. The most spectacular involved 12,000 troops sent into the Cairo slum of Imbaba in the search for suspects in October.

The Gama'a al-Islamiyya (Islamic Association) and Jihad (holy war) groups declared war on tourism, and several groups of foreign tourists were shot at or bombed in the last months of 1992 and into 1993. At a time when the domestic economy was showing some signs of improvement, the threat to the country's single biggest foreign currency earner encouraged Mubarak to come down hard against the fundamentalists. It has also prompted the government to talk more to the Muslim Brotherhood, seen now as a comparatively moderate Islamist force. Waves of arrests led to renewed protests from human rights groups over abuses in Egypt. Amnesty International says thousands of people, mostly Islamists and other opposition figures, have been arrested under state-of-emergency laws in place since 1981. Repeated allegations of torture have been denied by the government.

Under special laws introduced in 1992, a total of 22 alleged terrorists had been sentenced to death by mid-1993.

GEOGRAPHY

Egypt is almost square in shape. The distance from north to south is 1030 km (640 miles); from east to west in the north it's 965 km (600 miles) and 1240 km (770 miles) in the south. For most Egyptians the Nile Valley is Egypt. To the east of the valley is the Eastern (Arabian) Desert – a barren plateau bounded on its eastern edge by a high ridge of mountains. To the west is the Western (Libyan) Desert – a plateau punctuated by huge clumps of bizarre geological formations and luxuriant oases.

North of Cairo, the Nile splits into several tributaries, the main two being the Rosetta and the Damietta branches. The valley becomes a delta, a wide green fan of fertile countryside, and the tributaries eventually flow into the Mediterranean. It is believed that the Delta is what remains of a Mediterranean bay that may once have extended as far south as modern Cairo.

Along the northern coast to the west of Alexandria there are hundreds of km of brilliant white-sand beaches. Some have been, or are being, developed as resorts, but a good deal of this coast is still fairly isolated. However, if you're a sun worshipper in search of the perfect beach, be careful about wandering off the beaten track. The coast from El Alamein to the Libyan border was the scene of the WW II standoff between field marshals Rommel and Montgomery. Land mines were laid throughout this area and many have still not been recovered.

To the east, across the Suez Canal, is another former battlefield – the Sinai. Terrain here slopes from the high mountain ridges, which include Mt Sinai and Mt Catherine (or Mt Katherina – the highest in Egypt, at 2642 metres), in the south to desert coastal plains and lagoons in the north. The jagged mountains and wadis (watercourses) around Mt Sinai appear to change shape and colour as the sun passes overhead, and a climb to the top offers a commanding view of this spectacle. Moses certainly chose the right mountain to climb.

CLIMATE

Egypt's climate is easy to summarise. Most of the year, except for the winter months of December, January and February, it is hot and dry. Temperatures increase as you travel south from Alexandria. Alexandria receives the most rain – approximately 19 cm a year – while far to the south in Aswan any rain at all is rare.

Summer temperatures range from a scorching 50°C (122°F) in Aswan to 31°C (87°F) on the Mediterranean coast. At night in winter the temperature sometimes plummets to as low as 8°C, even in the south.

Be prepared for the temperature extremes. Sweaters are useful in the evenings throughout the country in winter, and it can get bitterly cold in the night-time desert. It can get quite chilly in Cairo, and downright cold along the Mediterranean coast in winter – even well into spring.

Between March and June, the outstanding phenomenon is the khamsin, a dry, hot and often dusty wind that can blow in from the parched Western Desert at up to 150 km per hour.

The Sinai has unique weather. The desert is typically hot during the day and cold at night, but the mountains can be freezing, even during the day. See the Sinai chapter for further information.

FLORA & FAUNA

The lotus that symbolises ancient Egypt can be found in the Delta area, but the papyrus reed only in botanical gardens. More than a hundred kinds of grasses thrive in areas where there is water, and the date palm is to be seen in virtually every cultivable area. Along with tamarisk, eucalyptus and acacia, the imported jacaranda and poinciana (red and orange flowers) have come to mark Egyptian summers with their vivid colours.

You'll be lucky to see any mammals other than camels, donkeys, and to a lesser extent domesticated horses and buffalo. There is a variety of small desert rodents and similar animals. Bird life is richer, with 200 migrating and 150 resident types. Birdwatchers should keep their eyes open from August into winter, when many of the migratory species come to Egypt. Lake Qarun in the Al-Faiyum region is a good place to concentrate on, with birds ranging from spoonbills to marsh sandpipers present. The saltwater lagoons in the northern Delta and Lake Bardawil in northern Sinai are home to such creatures as the pink flamingo, pelicans and spoonbills.

There are 190 kinds of fish in the Nile, the most well known being perhaps the Nile perch. This is to say nothing of the underwater paradise of the Red Sea.

GOVERNMENT

The present constitution was introduced in 1971, although it has been amended since. The bulk of power is concentrated in the hands of the president, who is nominated by the People's Assembly and elected by popular referendum for six years. This term can be renewed at least once, although Mubarak decided to go for a third term in 1993. The president appoints vice presidents

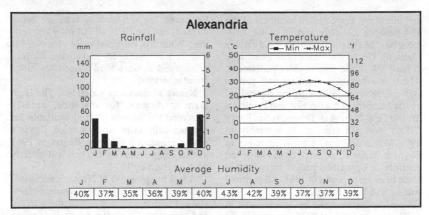

Alexandria

Rainfall

Temperature ■ Min ✖ Max

Average Humidity

J	F	M	A	M	J	J	A	S	O	N	D
40%	37%	35%	36%	39%	40%	43%	42%	39%	37%	37%	39%

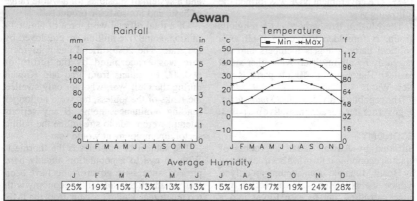

Aswan

Rainfall

Temperature ■ Min ✖ Max

Average Humidity

J	F	M	A	M	J	J	A	S	O	N	D
25%	19%	15%	13%	13%	13%	15%	16%	17%	19%	24%	28%

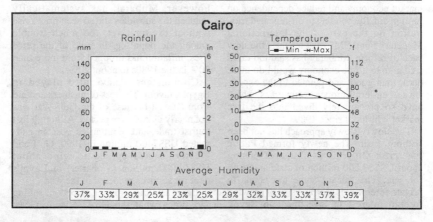

Cairo

Rainfall

Temperature ■ Min ✖ Max

Average Humidity

J	F	M	A	M	J	J	A	S	O	N	D
37%	33%	29%	25%	23%	25%	29%	32%	33%	33%	37%	39%

and ministers, as well as 10 members of the 454-member assembly and 70 of the 210-member Majlis ash-Shura (Advisory Council). Until 1990, parties had to achieve at least 8% of the vote to enter parliament, which discriminated against small parties and independents. Elections are supervised by the Ministry of the Interior, and President Mubarak's National Democratic Party (NDP) won 348 seats in the assembly in 1990. Mubarak himself admits democracy in Egypt is 'limited', although he has loosened controls on opposition parties considerably since he came to power in 1981. All political parties had been banned in 1953 and only allowed to operate again by Anwar Sadat in 1977. The government NDP was formed the following year.

The Muslim Brotherhood, as a religious group, is forbidden to present itself as a political party – it gets members into the assembly by allying itself with other small parties. The main opposition party is the New Wafd.

The republic is divided into 25 *muhafazat*, or governorates, for administrative purposes.

ECONOMY

Initiated by Anwar Sadat, a process of gradual economic reform has been continued by Hosni Mubarak, in an attempt not only to reduce the Nasserist state-run sector and huge subsidies, but to ease Egypt into a market economy and reduce dependence on foreign aid. Responding to oft-repeated frustration on the part of the International Monetary Fund (IMF) and others at the slow pace of reform, Mubarak has said too rapid a change to a free economy would do more harm than good, and pointed to the experience of eastern European economies, which have so precipitately dived into the free market whirlpool since 1989.

The slowly-slowly approach has not been without fruit. The newly formed Public Enterprise Office is in charge of putting about US$50,000 million of state assets up for sale. The sale of some top hotels to private enterprise is seen as a sign of growing foreign interest in investment in Egypt.

Exchange, tax and banking laws are being relaxed, and the E£ is all but fully convertible. What has surprised most observers is that it has managed to remain largely unchanged against hard currencies since about mid-1991.

Nasser's legacy was not all bad. The High Dam at Aswan, for instance, greatly increased the amount of land available for regular cultivation and doubled Egypt's power generation capacity. Begun in 1961 and in commission by 1971, it had already paid for itself by 1974.

A less happy result of Nasser's socialism was the growth of an enormous bureaucracy, stacked with people without anything to do, and a system of subsidies for a whole range of basic and not-so-basic products.

Of a total official workforce of about 14 million, some five million are employed by the state. The 20% official unemployment rate was exacerbated by the return of 600,000 Egyptians from Iraq and Kuwait during the Gulf War, who not only swelled the ranks of the jobless, but were no longer sending remittances home. If any serious attempt were made to streamline the public sector, unemployment would soar.

The subject of subsidies is the thorniest. With an eye to a population already hard pressed, successive governments have been loath to attack this side of the economy with too much zeal. Under pressure from the IMF, however, Mubarak has systematically reduced the subsidies and so seen prices rise without exciting, yet, too much trouble among the populace. In spite of the price rises, inflation has dropped from more than 30% in the 1980s to about 20%.

Circumstances have also played in Egypt's favour. The loss of business and aid from Kuwait because of the Gulf War was not nearly as bad as expected. Although lost tourist trade and remittances cost an estimated US$2400 million in 1990, Gulf and Western states agreed to wipe about US$14,000 million (a quarter) of Egypt's debt for services rendered in the war.

Egypt is a big exporter of cotton, selling 1½ times what the USA sells overseas.

However, the industry is facing trouble as farmers turn to other crops such as wheat, which is a popular alternative, although Egypt is still a large net importer of the grain. The growing population's demands are being aggravated by higher per capita consumption. Other important crops include various fruits, especially citrus, as well as vegetables and sugar.

The limits on available land are being pushed as far as possible, with intense crop rotation, complex irrigation (a project launched in 1992, the 'Suez Siphon', envisages diverting Nile water under the Suez Canal to the Sinai). Areas to the south-west of Alexandria, around the Delta and the belt of oases, are also targeted for greater irrigation programmes.

Industry still lags behind. Textiles account for 16% of output. Cement (although not enough for domestic needs), steel, iron, arms and vehicles (assembled under licence mainly from Fiat) are all produced.

Egypt is a net exporter of oil, and more oil and gas finds in the Western Desert have boosted hopes of continuing export profits to be made from that sector. Other raw materials mined include iron ore, manganese, phosphates, chromium and small amounts of coal. Some uranium has also been found in the Sinai.

There are plans to expand and deepen the Suez Canal to permit it to handle the biggest tankers and cargo vessels plying the world's waters. Although an expensive undertaking, it may well pay for itself. In 1990-1991, dues from commercial users of the canal amounted to US$1662 million.

A rapidly expanding sector is tourism. By the end of 1997, Egypt hopes to have increased the number of hotel rooms from 70,000 to 110,000. In 1992, just under three million tourists piled in, but the authorities were disappointed by this figure. Attacks by Islamic extremists on tourists in the second half of 1992 also put a brake on. Some tour operators pulled out, and the prospect of continued growth in tourism revenue (almost US$1000 million in 1990-1991) suddenly seemed under threat. The authorities tried, as they sent thousands of troops off on the hunt for suspects, to calm fears by saying most of the attacks had occurred in out-of-the-way places. A series of shooting and bombing attacks in Cairo and Luxor gave the lie to that claim, but the Egyptian press maintained (perhaps rightly) that Cairo was still a much safer place for a foreigner than New York or London. Published figures put tourism revenue for the first half of 1993 at anything from 25% to 75% down.

POPULATION

Egypt's population has, in a sense, become its greatest problem. Estimated at 58 million in July 1992, it is predicted by some that it will have reached 65 million by the end of 1997. With annual growth of about 2.3% (down from 2.8% in the 1980s) – something more than a million every year – it hardly seems to matter what Egypt does to improve its economic situation; the gains are always eaten up by the extra mouths to feed and people to house. The population has increased almost fivefold since 1907.

About 14 to 15 million (some estimates say 18 million) people live in the greater Cairo area and close to a further five million in Alexandria and outlying zones. One result of the rapid population growth is that half the population is now under 18 years, and the government hasn't been able to construct schools and train teachers quickly enough to keep up. Something like 99% of the population occupies only 4% of the total surface area of the country, which corresponds to the cultivable area, although various projects are in place to expand this and make it more productive.

PEOPLE

Anthropologists divide the Egyptian people very roughly into three racial groups, of which the biggest is descended from the Hamito-Semitic race that has peopled the Nile for millennia. These are the 'real Egyptians'. The truly Arab element is made up of the Bedouin Arab nomads who migrated from Arabia and who live in desert areas, particularly the Sinai. The third group are the Nubians, in the Aswan area. Of course there has been much intermingling and many other peoples have come and gone, leaving their own contributions.

Copts

The Copts number about seven million, and have long held an ambiguous position in Egyptian society. Although often subject to various forms of discrimination by the majority Muslims, and the target of Muslim fundamentalist anger in the past 40 years over economic frustration, the Copts have long provided something of an educated elite, filling many important posts in government and bureaucracy. There are ongoing attempts by the government to defuse potential conflict between Copts and Muslims (see the Religion section in this chapter), but life for Egypt's Christians is not as easy as it might be.

Bedouins

Egypt's economic problems have also begun to affect the Bedouins, the country's most isolated population group. Nearly 500,000 Bedouins survive in the harshest, most desolate parts of the Western and Eastern deserts and the Sinai. The Western Desert oases have long been slated for massive agricultural development and resettlement to ease urban overcrowding. There are also plans to increase tourism in this region. Tourism is also important to the Sinai, particularly the south-eastern coast, which is rapidly becoming a stretch of tourist resorts. With the influx of outsiders into their previously isolated domains, the Bedouins are gradually becoming more settled and less self-sufficient.

Berbers

A small number of Berbers who settled in the west of the country, particularly in and around Siwa, have retained much of their own identity. They are quite easily distinguished from other Egyptians by, for instance, the dress of the women – usually *melayas* – head-to-toe garments with slits for the eyes. Although many speak Arabic, they have preserved their own language.

EDUCATION

Although nine years of primary school education are supposedly compulsory in Egypt, and about 97% of children from six to 15 attend school, the adult illiteracy rate was estimated by UNESCO to be 51.6% in 1990. To Westerners that may seem startlingly high, but 14 years earlier the level was 61.8%! Two-thirds of Egypt's illiterates are women. (Illiteracy is not just a problem in so-called Third World countries – a recent study in the UK put the number of adult illiterates there at two million!)

Those who are literate have usually received inferior education because classes are often too large for individual attention.

Secondary education lasts for six years, beginning at 11 years of age. There are 13 universities, which are largely independent of the Ministry of Education & Scientific Research. Education is free at all levels, which is perhaps why it is not uncommon to find lawyers, engineers and other professionals spending most of their time working for their 'brother's factory' or shops in tourist areas – there is often nothing for Egypt's educated to do. Many of its professionals (and a good number of its less educated people) are compelled to seek work in other Arab countries – more than two million are said to be abroad, the bulk of them in the Gulf states, Libya and, despite harassment, in Iraq.

Males are generally subject to three years' military service, but those who complete high school do two and university students only one.

ARTS
Music

It's 5 pm. Radios throughout Egypt are turned up. A female voice is heard. At first it is soft and quiet, like a mother whispering and humming a bedtime story; then come the flutes, a gentle wailing that induces you to breathe and gyrate with the music, like a mesmerised snake. The rest of the orchestra picks up – the violins, drums, organs, and traditional wind and string instruments. You inhale deeply as the drums beat faster and the violins resound in powerful unison. The voice returns with a clear, booming resonance. The voice of Om Kolthum – the 'Mother of Egypt' – has got you by the ears.

Om Kolthum died in 1975 but her music lives on. For Westerners it epitomises and simplifies the mystery and complexity of Arabic music. As you walk down a street in Cairo or any other Egyptian city, the music lends a certain mystique to the street life. It's then, when it begins resounding in your ears, that you really know you haven't accidentally landed in a Hollywood movie studio. You have, in a sense, landed back in time.

Om Kolthum remains top of the tree, but there are many other popular names in the often parallel worlds of Egyptian and Arab music. Fareed al-Atrash, Abdel Halim al-Hafez, Fairouz and Dalida (actually French) have all left a lasting imprint on Egypt's musical heritage and that of the Arab world.

More contemporary popular music retains its essential Middle Eastern characteristics, but often betrays some vague influences of Western 'pop' – much of this is pretty awful stuff. Of course, many Westerners find it all a bit much; it appears to be an acquired taste.

Dance

Dance in Egypt can be still more alluring than the best of its music, but it is more difficult to see the real thing. Although belly-dancing shows can be seen in most of Cairo's major hotels, when watching one at such a venue you *will* think you have landed on that Hollywood set. Many of the dancers will be European or American, because it is not considered proper for an Arab woman to dance in public. Still, although the performances are usually full of Hollywood glitter and hype, the dancing is often quite authentic. A talented dancer, even if she is American, will capture your eyes with her gyrations and flowing silk scarves.

Dancing is generally considered promiscuous by Egyptians. Nevertheless, there are a few Egyptian dance troupes of both men and women that perform in Cairo, Luxor and Aswan during the winter and in Alexandria during the summer. Occasionally local

women can be seen dancing in fairly sleazy, and pretty well hidden, dives in Cairo. It comes as no surprise that the audiences are made up mainly of men, although by Western measures of the erotic, the performances are tame. As the dancer swirls around in front of a full band, with the odd inebriated local getting up to join in, a male singer croons in the background. He or a presenter usually takes care of business, raking in the cash tributes pouring in from the men in the audience. At the big hotels and nightclubs along Pyramids Rd, Gulf Arabs have been known to literally shower dancers with money. At the local places, Egyptian men, whose financial means can't match those of their cousins across the Red Sea, nevertheless are inclined to part with what for some must be sizeable sums of money.

Egyptians also dance at weddings, private parties and other family gatherings. Get yourself invited to an Egyptian wedding (which is not difficult) and you will experience Egypt and Egyptians at their best.

Belly dancer

Cinema & TV

Foreigners learning Arabic are often advised to learn the Egyptian dialect, as it is supposed to be understood in most parts of the Arab world. The reason is simple. Most of the TV shows Arabs watch and Arabic-language movies that have hit the screens over the past six decades have come from Egypt.

Om Kolthum's popularity is not restricted to Egypt: it extends across the Arab world, and in no small measure is due to her movies – often Egyptian versions of the musicals that used to pour out of Hollywood. Another famous face is that of Fareed al-Atrash, Om Kolthum's male equivalent. His voice is almost as well known and universally loved as that of Kolthum, and he was also a fine musician. Old B&W musicals starring one, the other or both regularly appear on Egyptian TV.

Literature

Egypt's most well-known writer in the West is Naguib Mahfouz, the Nobel Prize winner who has captured people's imagination with his stories, often of very ordinary lives in the poor parts of central Cairo, his stamping ground. Edward Kharrat, an Alexandrian, is another writer beginning to command more attention outside his own country. While Mahfouz takes pleasure in using the language of the people, dialect and slang, to make his characters live, Kharrat is much more of a stylist, his work informed by the classics of Arabic literature, mainly its rich tradition in poetry and the Qur'an (Koran) itself. The writings of Taha Hussein, a blind author and intellectual who spent much of his life in trouble with whichever establishment happened to be in power, reflect in great part his desire to marry the best of the West with the East. Other authors include Yusuf Idris, Tawfiq al-Hakim and Yahya Haqqi. For more on some of Mahfouz's individual works in translation, see Books in the Facts for the Visitor chapter.

Islamic Architecture

Pharaonic monuments and the work behind them are discussed at length throughout the book, but there is another side to monumental Egypt that often passes less noticed. Cairo is one of the greatest repositories in the world of Islamic, and especially medieval, architecture.

The earliest construction efforts undertaken by Muslims – more often than not mosques – inherited much from Christian and Greco-Roman models. However, various styles soon developed and owed increasingly less to their architectural forebears.

Mosques are generally built around an open courtyard, off which lie one or more *iwan* (covered halls). The iwan facing Mecca is the focal point of prayer. A vaulted niche in the wall called the mihrab indicates the kibla (the direction of Mecca, which Muslims must face when they pray). Islam does not know priests as such, but the closest equivalent is the mosque's sheikh, a man schooled in Islam who often doubles as the muezzin, who calls the faithful to prayer. At the main Friday prayers in particular, the sheikh gives a *khutba* (sermon) from the *minbar* – the pulpit raised above a narrow staircase, better examples of which are ornately decorated.

The mosque also serves as a kind of community centre, and often you'll find groups of children or adults getting lessons (usually in the Qur'an), people in quiet prayer and others simply sheltering in the tranquil peace of the mosque.

The minaret (from the word *manara*, meaning lighthouse) most often consists of a square base leading to more slender cylindrical or hexagonal stages. Most have internal staircases for the muezzin to climb (the advent of the microphone saves them that effort now) to the top.

The decoration of mosques and many other public buildings is an exercise in geometric virtuosity. As Islam frowns on the artistic representation of living beings, the art of carving out complex arabesques of vines, palms and other flora in various deceptive designs merged with a growing tradition of highly intricate decorative calligraphy. Much of the decoration along the top

Mosque at Hurghada

section in the Cairo chapter), much of it built by the Fatimid dynasty and then the Mamluks, who seemed to be passionate monument builders, from the 10th through to the 16th century.

CULTURE

Egyptians are fond of telling jokes about the government, about other Arabs and, most of all, about themselves. Every other Egyptian you meet seems to be a walking encyclopedia of jokes. One of the most common quips about themselves concerns IBM's control of Egypt:

'You know, Egypt controlled by IBM. You know, big company, IBM – 'I' for *insha-allah*; 'B' for *bukra*; 'M' for *maalesh!*' Although these three words can't completely sum up life in Egypt, they tell a lot about Egyptians: insha-allah means 'if God wills it'; bukra means 'tomorrow'; and maalesh means 'never mind', 'it doesn't matter', or 'pardon'.

This apparent nonchalance, fatalism, apathy – call it what you wish – seems to come from a centuries-old capacity for letting life flow by, a little like the Nile, in its own inevitable way. From plagues to invasion, floods to drought, Egypt and its people have seen it all, and it is as though the present generations had inherited a seen-it-all-before attitude from their forbears.

The main events of life – birth, marriage and death – and principal daily concerns – family, friends and food – are most important. The future is not, because it will not be much different from the past or present. Life goes on irrespective of lost money pouches, spilled perfume or a thousand and one other mishaps and inefficiencies. However, this is beginning to change.

Western technology and lifestyles have come to Egypt. The fellahin in the countryside, who make up the majority of Egypt's population, have begun using tractors and diesel-powered irrigation pumps in place of ploughs and ancient ox-driven water wheels.

TV programmes from the West, particularly the USA, have had an incredible impact. At the flick of a switch, a family of

end of walls is more or less stylised verses from the Qur'an. The phrase *la illah illa Allah* (there is no god but Allah), appears in a seemingly unlimited variety of designs as an integral part of decoration, fusing religious precept and the very reference to God with the art that exhalts Him.

The carved woodwork ceilings in some iwans sometimes display painstaking, again largely geometric, and graceful decoration.

The same guidelines in decoration influenced domestic building as well, and can be seen in some of the grander Ottoman residences that have survived in Cairo and other cities. The most outstanding feature of these is the *mashrabiyyah*, the intricately carved wooden screen most often used on balconies and windows to hide women while they looked out upon the goings on in the streets below them.

The biggest concentration of medieval Islamic architecture is to be found in the area known as Islamic Cairo (see the appropriate

fellahin is transported from a mud-brick house in an Upper Egypt village to places like the streets of San Francisco or the living rooms of the Ewing family in Dallas. A lifestyle of previously unimaginable luxury suddenly comes alive on a little screen in front of them and the seed of possibility, the chance of living a better life, is planted. Such images have helped feed a tide of rural migration to the already overcrowded cities, and in some cases enticed Egypt's best educated to seek that better life abroad.

TV and tractors aren't the only Western imports. Some people feel Egypt is being 'Coca-Cola-ised' by the trappings of Western life. Coca-Cola, colour TVs, VCRs and blue jeans are popular not only for what they are but, more importantly, for what they symbolise – a slice of the good life. Such material goods, and other more ambitious targets, are spawning greater motivation to succeed in one way or another, but also growing anger at the manifest shortcomings in the economy that frustrate people's attempts to improve their lot. The ranks of the frustrated *and* motivated are growing.

Egypt's Coptic Christians, estimated at around 13% of the population, seem to be one of the most motivated groups in the country, and have taken more readily to the 'Coca-Cola-isation' of Egypt. They have in any case always been an economically powerful minority and have generally found it easier to maintain close ties with Westerners and Western thought.

Some Egyptian Muslims have also welcomed modernisation, but the vast majority, the Muslim fellahin, are distressed by the possibility of sudden changes in a way of life that has remained virtually unaltered for so many centuries. Some, especially those faced with the harsh realities of being at the bottom of Egypt's socioeconomic pyramid, are turning to the extreme Islamist groups. 'Islam is the Solution' is the common cry – to precisely what, one might ask.

The impact of the trimmings on the Egyptian way of life seems, on closer inspection, not as great as all that. A desire to acquire some of the comforts high technology and diverse imports can provide is a long way short of surrendering a whole way of life and thought to another system. *Dallas* and the odd bottle of coke, however visible signs of Western 'culture', are hardly a threat to the foundations of Egyptian society.

Avoiding Offence

Although increasingly used to the antics of Westerners, Egyptians have a different code of behaviour on many subjects and find Western ways at best curious or at worst offensive. Dress is the first obvious point. Men will usually have little trouble in (long) shorts, although full-length trousers must be worn in mosques (and often in churches for that matter). Wearing singlets on sunny days may seem the most enjoyable way of dealing with the heat; choose your location. On the main tourist beaches, say in Sinai, and in big hotels men will have no trouble. Think about it in the big cities like Cairo – and wear something more modest in the smaller places. The sight of underarms and hairy legs is offensive to Muslims (and in some cases they may have a point!).

Women should pay much greater attention. Wandering around the Khan al-Khalili in short pants and a loose top is the perfect way to attract a maximum of just the kind of attention you don't want. Unless you want hands in all sorts of places, cover up. At least knee-length skirts or trousers and, in the more out-of-the-way or conservative places, elbow-length shirts. Covering your hair may help too. There is a constant stream of complaints about Egyptian men, often justified, but there's little point in attracting trouble – see also Women Travellers in the Facts for the Visitor chapter.

Alcohol is quite freely available in Egypt – getting stonkered is not a widespread national pastime, however, so it is advisable not to find yourself reeling around the streets. Just use a little common sense.

Sport

Football (or soccer to some) is king in Egypt. On the subject of imports, this is one that has been fully incorporated into most of Arab society. Of the Arab countries, Egypt is the one country with players of international capacity, and although they have yet to win a World Cup, they do at least manage to qualify. The premier teams – Zamalek and Al-Ahly – arouse greater passions, it seems, than any discussion of war or peace, secularism and religion.

RELIGION
Islam
Thousands of thin towering minarets, some as high as 80 metres, are some of the first things people notice in Egypt. Five times a day, the mosque officials known as muezzins bellow out the call to prayer through speakers on top of the minarets. Faithful Muslims follow the call and fill the mosques below for several minutes of elaborate prayers. With these prayers an Egyptian reaffirms his or her faith in Islam, the predominant religion of Egypt.

Islam shares its roots with two of the world's other major religions – Judaism and Christianity. Adam, Abraham (Ibrahim), Noah, Moses and Jesus are all accepted as Muslim prophets, although Jesus is not recognised as the son of God. Muslim teachings correspond closely to the Torah, the Old Testament and the Gospels, but the essence of Islam is the Qur'an and the prophet Mohammed.

Islam means 'submission' – submission to Allah (God). Mohammed was the last and truest prophet to deliver this and other messages from Allah to the people. He was born in 570 AD in Mecca (now in Saudi Arabia) and had his first revelation from Allah in 610. He began to preach against the idolatry that was rampant in the region, particularly in Mecca, and proved to be a powerful and persuasive speaker. He quickly gained a devoted following.

The Muslim faith was more than just a religion: it also called on its followers to spread the word – by the sword if necessary. Within two decades of the Prophet's death, most of Arabia had converted to Islam, and in succeeding centuries it spread over three continents. Mecca became Islam's holiest city because it was there that Abraham built the first shrine to Allah. The building, known as the Kaaba, is still the holiest pilgrim shrine in Islam; it contains the black stone given to Abraham by the angel Gabriel.

More than 10 years after Mohammed's death in 632 AD, his messages and revelations were compiled into the Muslim holy book, the Qur'an. No changes to that text have been permitted since 651 AD.

According to the Qur'an, faithful Muslims must carry out five acts, known formally as the Five Pillars of Faith. They must:

Publicly declare that 'there is no God but Allah and Mohammed is his Prophet'.
Pray five times a day: at sunrise, noon, mid-afternoon, sunset, and night.
Give *zakat*, or alms, for the propagation of Islam and for help to the needy.
Fast during the day for the month of Ramadan.
Make the *haj*, or pilgrimage to Mecca.

The first pillar is accomplished through prayer, which is the second pillar. Since you will probably see quite a lot of praying during your travels in Egypt and the Sudan, here is a brief description of what happens:

When Muslims enter a mosque they take off their shoes and carry them, sole to sole, in the left hand. It is considered offensive to wear shoes in the house of God. They enter with the right foot first and then wash themselves in a certain way before proceeding to pray.

Prayers are performed in one to two-minute cycles called *rek'ah*. Each worshipper faces the mihrab, the niche which indicates the direction of Mecca. In fact, the entire mosque is built so that it points towards Mecca. The first rek'ah goes something like this:

The worshipper says: *Bism-allah wisallahtu wisalaamu rasulallah allahum ergferrli zenubi waftahli abwaba rahmatik.*
Then he prays silently, and bows his head a number of times. This is followed by certain actions and prayers said aloud:
Alla-hu akbar, which means 'Allah is great'.
The first chapter of the Qur'an.
Verses from another chapter.
Alla-hu akbar.
Then he bows, kneels and places his palms on the ground, followed by his nose and forehead. The foreheads of the most faithful Muslims have a slight but noticeable indentation created by this genuflection.
'I extol the perfection of Allah the Great'
(said three times).
The worshipper stands:
Alla-hu akbar.
Back to the ground, saying the same thing as before.

That is one rek'ah, and a good Muslim performs several in a single prayer session. The rek'ah requires a lot of concentration. To create the right conditions for this, the interiors of most mosques are simple and devoid of elaborate decorations.

Visiting Mosques Before traipsing through mosques there are a few rules you should be aware of. You cannot visit during prayer time, but any other time is fine. Nor can you visit all mosques; some of those not designated by the Ministry of Tourism as 'tourist sites' are off limits. You'll know if you have stumbled into one of these because someone will probably tell you to leave.

You must dress modestly. For men that means no shorts; for women that means no shorts, tight pants, shirts that aren't done up, or anything else even remotely suggestive. Just use your common sense. Lastly, you must either take off your shoes or use the shoe coverings available for a few piastres (pt) at most mosques.

Egyptian Coptic Christianity
Before the arrival of Islam, Christianity was the predominant religion in Egypt. St Mark, one of the 12 apostles of Jesus, began preaching Christianity in Egypt in 35 AD, although it didn't become the official religion of the country until the 4th century. The word 'Copt' is derived from the Greek word for Egyptian, which the Arabs transliterated and eventually shortened to Copt. The term 'Coptic Church' originally referred to the native Egyptian Christian Church, but by the 5th century a different meaning had evolved.

Egyptian Christians split from the orthodox church of the Eastern (or Byzantine) Empire, of which Egypt was then a part, after the main body of the church described Christ as both human and divine. Dioscurus, the patriarch of Alexandria, refused to accept this description. He embraced the theory that Christ is totally absorbed by His divinity and that it is blasphemous to consider Him human. Since that time, Egyptian Christians have been referred to as Coptic Christians.

The Coptic Church is ruled by a patriarch, other members of a religious hierarchy, and an ecclesiastical council of laymen. The Coptic Church has a long history of monasticism and can justly claim that the first Christian monks, St Anthony and St Pachomius, were Copts. The Coptic language is still used in religious ceremonies, sometimes in conjunction with Arabic for the benefit of the congregation. It has its origins in a combination of Egyptian hieroglyphics and Ancient Greek. Today, the Coptic language is based on the Greek alphabet with an additional seven characters taken from hieroglyphics.

The Copts comprise about 13% of Egypt's population. The precise number has been a subject of much controversy. The Muslims and the Copts have each done a census and come up with very different figures. Muslim extremists have continuously harassed the Copts. In the late 1970s the government further Islamicised the legal system, a move that infuriated the Copts but pleased Muslim extremists. By 1981 relations between the two were very tense. A Coptic church in Cairo was bombed, and to avoid further conflict Sadat sent the Coptic pope, Shenuda III, into internal exile. He stayed at one of the monasteries of Wadi Natrun until Mubarak allowed him to return in early 1985.

Tension eased a little in the late 1980s, but again reached new heights in the early 1990s as the extremist Gama'a al-Islamiyya, which embarked on a campaign of antigovernment and antitourist terrorism, also stepped up attacks on Christians, particularly in the Dairut-Asyut area. More than 150 died in the violence in 1992.

Other Christians

Many Christian denominations are represented in Egypt by a few thousand adherents, or sometimes fewer, each. Among Catholics, apart from Roman Catholics of the Latin rite, the whole gamut of the fragmented Middle Eastern rites is represented, including the Armenian, Syrian, Coptic, Chaldean, Maronite and Melkite rites. The Anglican communion comes under the Episcopal Church in Jerusalem. The Armenian Apostolic Church has 10,000 members, and the Greek Orthodox church is based in Alexandria.

Judaism

Until 1948 more than 80,000 Jews lived in Egypt. However, with the independence of Israel and subsequent wars between the two countries, many Jews had to leave. Today, there are fewer than 500 Jews, mostly elderly, scattered through Alexandria, Cairo and Al-Minya. The marble-pillared synagogue of Cairo is open to the public (the one in Alexandria is closed) – an interesting vestige of what must once have been a thriving community.

Pharaonic Religion

The religion of Pharaonic Egypt is difficult to describe because so much about it is still unknown. The stories behind the many gods and goddesses depicted in hieroglyphics tell more about how, rather than what, ancient Egyptians actually worshipped. But Egyptologists have been able to solve a few of the mysteries and, at the very least, it is known what most of the ancient deities symbolised.

The sun shines through cloudless

skies during the day almost always in Egypt. Thus, it is no surprise that a sun-god became one of Egypt's most important deities. The sun-god was usually known as Ra; Aten was the name of the visible disc of the sun. Ra was the creator and ruler of other deified elements of nature. There was Nut, the sky-goddess, Shu, the god of air and Geb, the earth-god.

Nut was a particularly interesting goddess. She was always depicted (either as a woman or a cow) stretched across the ceilings of tombs, swallowing the sun and creating night. The next morning she would give birth to the sun.

Animals were also important to the ancient Egyptians. Several were considered sacred, especially the Apis bulls of Memphis, the cats of Beni Hasan, the rams of Elephantine (part of ancient Aswan), and the crocodiles of Kom Ombo. Animals were also often associated with various gods and goddesses; eventually many deities were portrayed in a combined animal and human form.

The human aspects of the gods were often presented like ancient soap operas. Only a few of these 'soaps' have survived Egypt's long history. One of the most celebrated starred the godly heavyweights Osiris, Isis and Horus.

Osiris was the benevolent 'ruler' of Egypt. His brother Seth, the epitome of evil, talked him into testing the inside of a crate by lying in it. Once Osiris was in the crate, evil Seth

Isis nursing Horus .

promptly locked it and tossed it into the Nile. Isis, the sister and wife of Osiris, searched all over the world until she found the crate and smuggled it back to Egypt. Seth discovered the crate, cut Osiris into 14 pieces and distributed the bits throughout the country. Loyal Isis managed to find all the pieces, built temples dedicated to Osiris, and put him back together again. Isis and Osiris then begat Horus who slew Seth. End of story.

If you wish to learn more about religion in ancient Egypt, refer to the section on Books in the Facts for the Visitor chapter.

LANGUAGE

Arabic is the official language of Egypt. However, the Arabic spoken on the streets differs greatly from the standard Arabic written in newspapers, spoken on the radio or recited in prayers at the mosque.

Colloquial Egyptian Arabic is fun, but difficult to learn. It is basically a dialect of the standard language, but so different in many respects as to be virtually like another language. As with most dialects, it is the everyday language that differs the most from that of Egypt's other Arabic-speaking neighbours. More specialised or educated language tends to be pretty much the same across the Arab world, although pronunciation may vary considerably. An Arab from, say, Jordan or Iraq, will have no problem having a chat about politics or literature with an Egyptian, but might have more trouble making himself understood in the bakery.

There is no official written version of colloquial Arabic (although there is no real reason why it could not be written with Arabic characters – Nobel Prize-winning author Naguib Mahfouz has no trouble writing out whole passages using predominantly Egyptian (or Cairene) slang).

For some reason though, foreigners specifically wanting to learn the Egyptian dialect (instead of Modern Standard Arabic, or MSA, the written and spoken lingua franca understood by most, and in fact not so far removed from the daily language of the Arab countries of the Levant) are told that it *cannot* be written, and then presented with one system or other of transliteration as a poor substitute – none of them totally satisfactory. For the student of MSA, such systems can be a hindrance rather than a help. An esoteric argument flows back and forward between those who say you should learn MSA first and then a dialect (which could mean waiting a very long time before you can converse adequately with shopkeepers), and those who argue the opposite. If you're getting a headache now, that will give you some idea of why few non-Arabs and non-Muslims embark on the study of the language.

Nevertheless, if you take the time to learn even a few words and phrases, you will discover and experience much more while travelling through the country.

Pronunciation

Pronunciation of Arabic can be somewhat tongue-tying for someone unfamiliar with the intonation and combination of sounds. Pronounce the transliterated words and phrases slowly and clearly.

The following guide should help, but it isn't complete because the myriad rules governing pronunciation and vowel use are too extensive to be covered here.

Vowels In spoken Egyptian Arabic, there are five basic vowel sounds that can be distinguished:

a	as the 'a' in 'had'
e	as the 'e' in 'bet'
i	as the 'i' in 'hit'
o	as the 'o' in 'hot'
u	as the 'oo' in 'book'

The ⁻ symbol over a vowel gives it a long sound. For example:

ā	as the 'a' in 'father'
ē	as the 'e' in 'ten', but lengthened
ī	as the 'e' in 'ear', only softer, often written as 'ee'
ō	as the 'o' in 'for'
ū	as the 'oo' in 'food'

Combinations Certain combinations of vowels with vowels or consonants form other vowel sounds (diphthongs):

aw	as the 'ow' in 'how'
ay	as the 'i' in 'high'
ei	as the 'a' in 'cake'

These last two are tricky, as one can slide into the other in certain words, depending on who is pronouncing them. Remember these rules are an outline, and far from exhaustive.

Consonants Most of the consonants used in this section are the same as in English. However, a few of the consonant sounds must be explained in greater detail.

Three of the most common are the glottal stop ('), the 'ayn' sound ('), and the 'rayn' (**gh**). These are some of the most difficult sounds in Arabic, especially for a non-native speaker, so don't be discouraged if you aren't being understood, just keep trying.

The glottal stop is the sound you hear between the vowels in the expression 'oh oh!'. It is actually a closing of the glottis at the back of the throat so that the passage of air is momentarily halted. It can occur anywhere in the word – at the beginning, middle or end.

The 'ayn' and the **gh**, or 'rayn', are two of the most difficult sounds in Arabic. Both can be produced by tightening your throat and sort of growling, but the **gh** requires a slight 'r' sound at the beginning – it is quite a bit like the French 'r'. When the 'ayn' occurs before a vowel, the vowel is 'growled' from the back of the throat. If it is before a consonant or at the end of a word, it sounds like a glottal stop. The best way to learn these sounds is to listen to a native speaker pronounce their written equivalents.

Other common consonant sounds include the following:

g	as the 'g' in 'gain' or 'grab' (Egyptian Arabic is the only Arabic dialect with this sound – the others have a 'j' sound, as in 'John'. The Egyptians have in fact

introduced an extra letter for the rare occasion when they need a 'j' sound, as in 'garage', which is pronounced as in English).

H	a strongly whispered 'h', almost like a sigh of relief.
q	a strong guttural 'k' sound. In Egyptian Arabic, often pronounced as a glottal stop. Often transcribed as 'k', although there is another letter in the Arabic alphabet which is the equivalent of 'k'. See Transliteration below.
kh	a slightly gurgling sound, like the 'ch' in Scottish 'loch'
r	a rolled 'r', as in Spanish 'para'
s	pronounced as in English 'sit', never as in 'wisdom'
sh	as the 'sh' in 'shelf'
2	as the 's' in pleasure; rarely used in Egyptian Arabic

Double Consonants In Arabic, double consonants are both pronounced. For example the word *istanna*, which means 'wait', is pronounced 'istan-na'.

Transliteration

Converting what for most outsiders is just a bunch of squiggles into meaningful words (ie, those written in the Latin script) is a tricky business – in fact no really satisfactory system of transliteration has been established, and probably never will be. For this edition, an attempt has been made to standardise some spellings of place names and the like. There is only one word for 'the' in Arabic: 'al'. (Before certain consonants, it modifies: in Arabic, Saladin's name is Salah ad-Din, meaning 'righteousness of the faith'; here, 'al' has been modified to 'ad' before the 'd' of 'Din'.) Nevertheless, 'el' is often used. This has been left only in a few circumstances such as well-known place names (El Alamein, Sharm el-Sheikh) or where locals have used it in, say, restaurant and hotel names. Riverside boulevards in Nile cities are often called Corniche el-Nil (pronounced Corniche an-Nil). Whichever way you see these little blighters spelt, either in the book or in the signs you come up against, remember that they are all the same word.

The whole business is fraught with pitfalls, and in a way there are no truly 'correct' answers. The locals themselves can only guess at how to make the conversion – and the result is often amusing. The fact that French and English have had a big influence (though the latter has all but 'conquered' the former in modern Egypt) has led to all sorts of interesting ideas on transliteration. Don't be taken aback if you start noticing half a dozen different spellings for the same thing. The high rate, among Egyptians, of illiteracy in their own language does not help.

For some reason, the letters 'q' and 'k' have caused enormous problems, and have been interchanged willy-nilly in transliteration. For a long time, Iraq (which in Arabic is spelled with what can only be described as its nearest equivalent to the English 'q') was written, even by scholars, as 'Irak'. Other examples of an Arabic 'q' receiving such treatment are souq (market), often written souk; qasr (castle), sometimes written 'kasr'; and the Cairo suburb of Doqqi, which is often written Dokki, although the Egyptian habit of swallowing 'q' and pronouncing the place 'Do'i' is a dead giveaway. In the Sudan, the 'q' is pronounced more like a hard 'g', and there are no prizes for guessing how the transliteration comes out there. It's a bit like spelling English 'as she is spoke' – imagine the results if Australians, Americans, Scots and Londoners were given free rein to write as they pronounce!

Greetings & Civilities

Arabic is more formal than English, especially with greetings; thus even the simplest greetings, such as 'hello', vary according to when and how they are used. In addition, each greeting requires a certain response that varies according to whether it is being said to a male, female or group of people.

Hello. (literally 'peace upon you')
  salām 'alēkum
And hello to you. ('and peace upon you')
  wa 'alēkum es salām

Hello/How do you do?/Welcome/Pleased to meet you.
  ahlan wa sahlan
Hello. (in response)

ahlan bīk	(to m)
ahlan bīkī	(to f)
ahlan bīkum	(to grp)

Pleased to meet you. (formal, used when first meeting)
  tasharrafna
Nice meeting you. (less formal, said as you are leaving to someone whom you have met for the first time)
  fursa sa'īda

How are you? (this is unique to the Egyptian dialect)

izzayyak?	(to m)
izzayyik?	(to f)
izzayyukum?	(to grp)

Fine. (literally 'fine, thanks be to God')

kwayyis ilHamdu lillah	(said by m)
kwaysa...	(said by f)
kwaysīn...	(said by grp)

On their own, *kwayyis*, *kwaysa* and *kwaysīn* literally mean 'good' or 'fine', but they are rarely heard alone in response to 'how are you?'

Good morning.
  sabāH al-khēr
Good morning. (in response)
  sabāH an-nūr
Good evening.
  misa' al-khēr
Good evening. (in response, also 'good afternoon' in the late afternoon)
  misa' an-nūr
Good night.

tisbaH 'ala khēr	(to m)
tisbaHī 'ala khēr	(to f)
tisbaHu 'ala khēr	(to grp)

Good night. (in response)

wenta bikhēr	(to m)
wentī bikhēr	(to f)
wentū bikhēr	(to grp)

Good bye. (literally 'go in safety')
  ma'as salāma

Excuse me.
'an iznak, esmaHlī (to m)
'an iznik, esmaHīlī (to f)
'an iznukum, esmaHūlī (to grp)

Thank you.
shukran
Thank you very much.
shukran gazīlan
You are welcome.
'afwan, al-'affu
No thank you.
la' shukran

There are three ways to say please in Egyptian Arabic, each of which is used somewhat differently:

When asking for something in a shop, for example, say:
min fadlak (to m)
min fadlik (to f)
min fadlukum (to grp)
Under similar, but more formal, circumstances (eg when trying to get a waiter's attention), say:
law samaHt (to m)
law samaHtī (to f)
law samaHtu (to grp)
When offering something to someone, for example a chair or bus seat, or when inviting someone into your home or to join in a meal, say:
tfaddal (to m)
tfaddalī (to f)
tfaddalū (to grp)
The same words beginning with 'i' (eg *itfaddal*) can be used to mean much the same thing or 'please, go ahead (and do something)'.

Small Talk
My name is...
ismī...
What is your name?
ismak ēh? (to m)
ismīk ēh? (to f)
I understand.
ana fāhem
I do not understand.
ana mish fāhem

Do you speak English?
enta bititkallim inglīzī? (to m)
entī bititkallimī inglīzī? (to f)

Yes.
aywa,
na'am (more formal)
No.
la'

One of the most useful words to know is *imshī*, which means 'go away'. Use this at the pyramids or at other tourist sites when you are being besieged by children. Do not use it on adults; instead, just say, *'la' shukran'* (no thank you).

Accommodation
Where is the hotel...?
fein al-funduq...?
Can you show me the way to the hotel...?
mumkin tewarrīnī at-tarīq lil-funduq...?
I'd like to see the rooms.
ana 'ayiz (or *'awiz*) *ashūf al-owad bita'ak*
May I see other rooms?
mumkin ashūf odda tānī?
How much is this room per night?
kam ugrat al-odda bil-laila?
Do you have any cheaper rooms?
fī owad arkhas?
That's too expensive.
da ghālī 'awī
This is fine.
da kwayyis

Getting Around
Where is the...?
fein...?
bus station for the...
maHattat al-otobīs li...
train station
maHattat al-'atr
ticket office
maktab at-tazāker
street
ash-shāri'
city
al-medīna

village	
al-qarya	
bus stop	
maw'if al-otobīs	
station	
al-maHatta	

How far is...?
  kam kilo li...?

When does the...leave/arrive?
  Emta qiyam/wusuul...?

bus	*al-otobīs*
train	*al-'atr*
boat	*al-markib*

Which bus goes to...?
  otobīs nimra kam yerūH...?
Does this bus go to...?
  al-otobīs da yerūH...?
How many buses per day go to...?
  kam otobīs fil yōm yerūH...?
Please tell me when we arrive....
  min fadlak, ullī emta Hanūsel...
I want to go to....
  ana 'ayiz arūH...
What is the fare to...?
  bikam at-tazkara li...?
Stop here, please.
  wa'if (or *hassib*) *hena, min fadlak*
Please wait for me.
  mumkin tantazarnī
May I/we sit here?
  mumkin eglis/neglis hena?
Where can I rent a bicycle?
  fein e'aggar 'agala?

air-conditioning	*takyīf hawa*
airport	*matār*
bicycle	*'agala, bīcīklēt*
boat	*markib*
camel	*gamal*
car	*sayyāra, 'arabiyya*
crowded	*zaHma*
daily	*kull yōm*
donkey	*Humār*
early	*badrī*
horse	*Husān*
late	*mut'akhar*
left side	*'ala ash-shimāl*

number	*nimra*
right side	*'ala al-yamīn*
this address	*al-'anwān da*
ticket	*tazkara*
wait!	*istanna!*
where?	*fein?*

Around Town

Where is the...?
  fein...?

bank	*al-bank*
barber	*al-Hallē'*
beach	*al-plāᵹ , ash-shaata*
citadel	*al-'ala*
embassy	*as-sifāra*
ladies' room	*twalēt al-Harīmī*
market	*as-sūq*
men's room	*twalēt ar-ragel*
mosque	*al-gāme'*
museum	*al-matHaf*
old city	*al-medīna al-'adīma*
palace	*al-'asr*
police station	*al-bolīs*
post office	*al-bōsta,*
	maktab al-barīd
restaurant	*al-mat'am*
synagogue	*al-ma'bad al-yehūdī,*
	al-kinees
university	*al-gam'a*
zoo	*Hadīqat al-Haywān*

I want to change...
  ana 'ayiz usarraf...

money	*fulūs*
US$	*dolār amrikānī*
UK£	*guinay sterlīnī*
A$	*dolār ustrālī*
DM	*mārk almānī*
travellers' cheques	*shīkāt siyaHiyya*

Shopping

Where can I buy...?
  fein mumkin ashtirī...?
How much is this/that...?
  bikam da...?
It costs too much.
  da ghālī 'awī
Do you have?
  fī 'andak?

Local Currency

The Egyptians have a collection of names for their own money, used in most everyday transactions.

pound	*guinay*
half pound (50 pt)	*nuss guinay*
quarter pound (25 pt)	*ruba' guinay*
20 pt	*riyal*
10 pt	*barisa*
5 pt	*shilling*

Numbers

English	Arabic	Pronunciation
0	٠	*sifr*, zero
1	١	*wāHid*
2	٢	*itnein*
3	٣	*talāta*
4	٤	*arba'a*
5	٥	*khamsa*
6	٦	*sitta*
7	٧	*sab'a*
8	٨	*tamanya*
9	٩	*tis'a*
10	١٠	*'ashara*
11		*Hidāshar*
12		*itnāshar*
13		*talattāshar*
14		*arba'tāshar*
15		*khamastāshar*
16		*sittāshar*
17		*saba'tāshar*
18		*tamantāshar*
19		*tisa'tāshar*
20		*'ishrīn*
21		*wāHid wi 'ishrīn*
22		*itnein wi 'ishrīn*
30		*talatīn*
40		*arba'īn*
50		*khamsīn*
60		*sittīn*
70		*sab'īn*
80		*tamanīn*
90		*tis'īn*
100		*miyya*
101		*miyya wi wāHid*
110		*miyya wi 'ashara*
1000		*'alf*
2000		*'alfein*
3000		*talattalāf*
4000		*arba'talāf*
5000		*khamastalāf*

Ordinal Numbers

first	*'awwal*
second	*tānī*
third	*tālit*
fourth	*rābi'*
fifth	*khāmis*

Days of the Week

Sunday	*(yōm) al-aHadd*
Monday	*(yōm) al-itnīn*
Tuesday	*(yōm) at-talāt*
Wednesday	*(yōm) al-arba'a*
Thursday	*(yōm) al-khamīs*
Friday	*(yōm) al-gum'a*
Saturday	*(yōm) as-sabt*

Months of the Year

East of Egypt, in addition to the Hijra (or Muslim) calendar, there is also another set of names for the Gregorian calendar. Luckily, in Egypt and west, the names of the months are virtually the same as their European counterparts and easily recognisable.

January	*yanāyir*
February	*fibrāyir*
March	*māris*
April	*abrīl*
May	*māyu*
June	*yunyu*
July	*yulyu*
August	*aghustus*
September	*sibtimbir*
October	*'uktoobir*
November	*nufimbir*
December	*disimbir*

Body Language

Walking down a crowded street, you suddenly hear what sounds like a snake hissing copious amounts of spittle in your direction. On turning around, you'll probably find someone on a bicycle is trying to get by – there are few bicycle bells in Egypt. It takes a while to get used to, but it's nothing personal.

There's another kind of hissing, which is the local version of a wolf whistle – there's everything personal about that. Arabs gesticulate a lot in conversation, and some things can be said without uttering a word. Certain expressions also go together with particular gestures.

Egyptians, like most Arabs, often say 'no' merely by raising the eyebrows and lifting the head up and back. This is often accompanied by a 'tsk tsk' noise and it can all be a little off-putting if you're not used to it – don't take it as a snub.

Shaking the head from side to side (as Westerners would to say 'no') means 'I don't understand'. Stretching out the hand as if to open a door and giving it a quick flick of the wrist is equivalent to 'what do you want?', 'where are you going?' or 'what's your problem?'. A combination of the two probably means your interlocutor has not got the foggiest idea of what you're going on about.

Getting flustered invariably excites the mirth of locals, and at the very least an admonition to slow down or take it easy (*shwayya*), along with a hand signal – palm up, all the fingers and thumb drawn together.

Guys asking directions should not be surprised to be taken by the arm or hand and led along. It is quite natural for men to hold each other by the hand and, despite what you may think, rarely means anything untoward is happening. Which is not to say it *doesn't* happen – and judging between the two kinds of situation requires some subtle thinking, or plain luck! Women should avoid such helpfulness, as more often than not it can spell trouble.

A right hand over your heart means 'no thanks' when you are offered something. When you've had enough tea, Turkish coffee or anything else to drink, you put your hand over the cup.

As the left hand is associated with toilet duties it is considered unclean and so you should always use the right hand when giving or receiving something.

Arrival in one piece is always something to be grateful for. Relieved passengers will often be heard to mutter *ilHamdu lillah 'as-salaama* – 'Thank God we arrived in safety'.

Facts for the Visitor

VISAS & EMBASSIES

All foreigners entering Egypt, except nationals of Malta and Arab countries, must obtain visas from Egyptian consulates overseas or at the airport or port upon arrival. In the UK, a single-entry tourist visa costs most Western applicants the equivalent of UK£15 (about US$22). US and Swedish citizens pay UK£10; Germans, UK£13. The big losers are the Canadians, who have to cough up UK£40. As a general rule, it is cheaper to get one on arriving at Cairo Airport (see below), but this depends on your nationality and where you apply for the visa.

Since mid-1992, South Africans have been able to go to Egypt.

Processing of visa applications varies. In the USA and the UK, processing takes about 24 to 48 hours if you drop your application off in person, or anything from 10 days to six weeks if you mail it.

You need to fill in one application form and attach one passport-size photo. If you are mailing your application, include a money order (cheques are not accepted), a stamped self-addressed envelope with enough postage to send it registered (if you are mailing it) and, of course, your passport. You must pay cash if applying in person.

The single-entry visa is valid for presentation for three months and entitles the holder to stay in Egypt for one month. Multiple-entry visas (for three visits) are also available for a little extra money, but although good for presentation for six months, still only entitle the bearer to a total of one month in the country. *Don't* get a business visa if you don't absolutely need to – they are about four times the price of a tourist visa. You must register within a week of arrival (see below).

Costs seem to vary a lot from country to country. In Jordan, for instance, it is UK citizens who come off worst, with single-entry visas costing JD40 (the best part of US$60). Canadians pay less, although still

quite enough, at JD31. Everyone else comes in at JD12. In Amman, don't go to the embassy, which is opposite the InterContinental Hotel in Jebel Amman, but down a street to the consular building just off Zahran St above 1st Circle. Applications are accepted, if you can fight your way through the crowds, between 9 am and noon, and visas are generally issued on the same day at 3 pm. You need one photo.

The consulate in Aqaba, open from 9 am to 1 pm except Friday, is much quieter and visas are usually issued on the spot. Canadians and Britons might find it useful to try here, as they might get lucky and be issued a visa for the standard JD12. You've got nothing to lose anyway! It is possible to be issued with a visa while on the ferry to Nuweiba, but the Egyptian officials make a bit of a song and dance about it, and will want payment in US$.

If you are coming from Israel, remember that you cannot get a visa on the Israeli-Egyptian border. The embassy in Tel Aviv (☎ 546-5151) is open for applications from 9 to 11 am from Sunday to Thursday. Single-entry visas cost most nationalities NIS40, and are ready to be picked up at 1 pm on the same day. Israelis pay NIS50 and must wait about a week. You need a photo. The Egyptian consulate in Eilat also issues visas.

Bear in mind that evidence of having been in Israel renders your passport useless for travel in any other Arab country. Although the Israelis generally comply with requests not to stamp passports on entry or exit (they stamp your entry card instead), you will still get an Egyptian stamp bearing the name of the border post (Taba or Rafah) – which is enough evidence if it is noticed by visa authorities of other Arab countries. Fourteen-day Sinai permits are an exception to this rule (see below).

Egypt now has an embassy in the Libyan capital, Tripoli.

In the Sudan you can obtain a visa on the

same day at the consulate in Sharia al-Gamhuriyya, Khartoum. It costs S£1550 (about US$12 at the official rate) and you need one photo.

In Greece, UK citizens pay a hefty Dr14,000, Canadians Dr10,000 and Americans only Dr2500.

If, within your one-month stay, you plan to return to Egypt after, for example, visiting Israel, Jordan or the Sudan, you should request the multiple-entry visa. Otherwise, you will have to arrange to get a re-entry visa while in Cairo (see below) or get a new visa to return.

You can get a visa on entering the country at some points. At the new terminal of Cairo Airport, where most visitors arrive, the process is simple and generally cheap. Thomas Cook or the three exchange booths you pass just before passport control will sell you the required stamps for the visa on the spot, and no photo is required. Most nationalities pay US$15 or UK£10. When you exchange money with them, they will deduct the cost of the stamps from the total amount exchanged.

However, if you are coming from Israel, you can't get a visa at the border. You must get it at the Egyptian consulate in Eilat or Tel Aviv, or elsewhere. Your passport will be stamped with the name of the Egyptian border post. You can get a visa, with much fuss, on the boat from Jordan.

Sinai

It is possible to visit the Sinai area between Sharm el-Sheikh and Taba (on the Israeli border) without a visa. You are also permitted to visit St Catherine's Monastery, but divers should note that a full visa is required to get to Ras Mohammed, south of Sharm el-Sheikh. On arrival, you are issued with an entry stamp free of charge allowing you up to 14 days in the area. If coming from Israel, you can have the stamp put on a separate piece of paper.

Valid points of entry for such visa-free stamps are Taba, Nuweiba and Sharm el-Sheikh (airport or port).

Transit & Temporary Visas

Transit and temporary visas, valid for 48 hours, used to be issued free of charge at the airport, but it appears this is no longer the case.

Registration

You must register with the police within one week of your arrival in Egypt. Most hotels will take care of this, some for a small fee. If you want to avoid the cultural experience of visiting the labyrinthine Mogamma building, let the hotel do it, although it is actually a pretty straightforward process now. The bigger hotels complete the registration formality without being asked to do so – most package tourists don't even know it happens.

The Mogamma is a mammoth government building on Midan Tahrir in central Cairo. If you have to go there, enter through the right side of the main entrance, not the left, or you will be stampeded by the exiting herd. Climb the stairs on your right and go to the window marked 'Registration'. You fill in a form and the date is filled in on your visa. The whole process takes about a minute. It is near there that you also go for re-entry visas and visa extensions. (See the Information section in the Cairo chapter.)

In Alexandria the Passport Registration Office is on Sharia Talaat Harb. Most of the main entry points, including Luxor, Aswan, Suez, Port Said, Sharm el-Sheikh and Hurghada, have passport offices where you can also register.

Visa Extensions & Re-Entry Visas

Extensions of your visa beyond the first month can be obtained for any period up to six months. Normally, you must show bank receipts proving that you've changed another US$180 for each extra month (or part thereof) you want to remain. Credit card receipts for purchases or cash advances are generally not acceptable. You need one photograph, E£12 for the extension and a modicum of patience.

If you have proof of having changed enough money, and you plan to remain in

Egypt for several months, you can pay for a few months at the one time and save yourself the repeated hassle.

The required proof of change of US$180 is a hangover from the days of an artificially fixed exchange rate and a flourishing black market. If you don't want to change the amount of money needed to cover the extension you desire, there is a way around the dilemma. You can buy Egyptian currency to the value needed, and so get the necessary bank receipt, and then simply re-exchange for hard currency. Obviously you'll lose a small amount on each exchange and commission. You will also end up with hard currency in cash, which might not suit everyone. But it is a way around the problem.

The officials keep the bank receipts, which is worth bearing in mind, as you may also need bank receipts to buy air or ferry tickets. Receipts can only be used once, so if you present some for an air ticket, you'll need more for a visa extension.

If you do not have a multiple-entry visa, it is also possible to get a re-entry visa, valid to the expiry date of your visa and any extensions, at most passport offices including the Mogamma. A single re-entry costs about E£14.

Note that there is a two-week grace period beyond the expiry date of your visa. (In other words, a one-month stay is to all intents and purposes six weeks.) If you stay beyond that, a fine of E£53 is imposed on exit, and there are also the costs and hassles of getting an extension – if you are caught at the airport in this situation, you could well have to kiss your flight goodbye.

You can get visa extensions and re-entry visas at most points of entry (eg Aswan, Luxor, Alexandria, Suez), not just in the Mogamma building in Cairo. It is often less of a hassle outside Cairo as you are not competing with hordes of people.

Egyptian Embassies

Following are the addresses and telephone numbers of Egyptian embassies and consulates in major cities around the world:

Australia
   Embassy: 1 Darwin Ave, Yarralumla, Canberra, ACT 2600 (☎ (62) 273-4437/8)
   Consulates: 9th floor, 124 Exhibition St, Melbourne, Victoria 3000 (☎ (3) 654-8869/8634)
   335 New South Head Rd, Double Bay, Sydney NSW 2028 (☎ (2) 362-3482/8, 327-5538)
Canada
   Embassy: 454 Laurier Ave East, Ottawa, Ontario K1N 6R3 (☎ (613) 234-4931/35/58)
   Consulate: 3754 Côte des Neiges, Montreal, Quebec H3H 7V6 (☎ (514) 937-7781/2)
France
   Embassy: 56, Ave d'Iena, 75116 Paris (☎ (1) 47 20 97 70, 47 20 75 97)
   Consulates: 58, Ave Foch, 75116 Paris (☎ (1) 45 00 84 64, 45 00 49 52, 45 00 69 23)
   166, Ave de Hamburg, 13008 Marseilles (☎ 91 25 04 04)
Germany
   Embassy: Konprinzen Str 2, Bad Godesberg, Bonn (☎ (228) 364000/8/9)
   Embassy branch: Berliner Str 22, Pankow, Berlin 3 (☎ (30) 482-5095)
   Consulate: Eysseneck Str 52, 6000 Frankfurt/Main I (☎ (69) 590557/8)
Greece
   3 Vassilissis Safies St, Athens (☎ (1) 361-8612/3)
Ireland
   12 Clyde Rd, Dublin 4 (☎ (1) 606566, 606718)
Israel
   Embassy: 54 Rehov Basel, Tel Aviv (☎ (3) 546-5151/2)
   Consulate: 68 Afraty St, Bna Betkha, Eilat (☎ (7) 597-6115)
Japan
   1-5-4 Aobadai, Meguro-Ku, Tokyo 171 (☎ (3) 37 70 80 22)
Jordan
   Embassy: Jebel Amman, 3rd Floor, Zahran St, Amman (☎ (6) 641375/6, 641705)
   Consulate: Al-Wahdat al-Jarbiyya, al-Istiqlal St, Aqaba (☎ (3) 316171/81)
Libya
   Al-Funduq al-Kabeer, Tripoli (☎ (21) 45940/58)
Netherlands
   Borweg I-2597, The Hague (☎ (70) 354-2000/4535)
Sudan
   Embassy: Sharia al-Gama'a, al-Mogran, Khartoum (☎ (11) 77646/7, 72836)
   Consulates: Sharia al-Gamhuriyya, Khartoum (☎ (11) 70291, 72190)
   Al-Midan al-Kabeer, El Obeid (☎ (249) 4167)
   Sharia Kabbashi Eissa, Port Sudan (☎ (249) 2036, 5910)
Sweden
   Strandvagen 35, Stockholm (☎ (8) 660-3145, 662-9603/9687)

UK
    Embassy: 26 South St, London W1Y 6DD
    (☎ (071) 499-2401)
    Consulate: 2 Lowndes St, London SW1 (☎ (071)
    235-9777)
USA
    Embassy: 2310 Decatur Place NW, Washington
    DC 20008 (☎ (202) 234-3903/4)
    Consulates: 1110 2nd Ave, New York, NY 10022
    (☎ (212) 759-7120/1/2)
    3001 Pacific Ave, San Francisco, CA 94115
    (☎ (415) 346-9700/2)
    2000 West Loop South, Houston, TX 77027
    (☎ (713) 961-4915/6, 961-4407)
    30 S Michigan Ave, Chicago, IL 60603

Foreign Embassies in Egypt

The addresses of some of the foreign embassies and consulates in Egypt are:

Algeria
    14 Sharia al-Brazil, Zamalek (☎ 341-7782, 340-
    7709).
    Visas can be obtained here and cost anything
    from nothing for Australians to E£70 for Britons.
    The visa entitles you to a one-month stay.
Australia
    5th floor, South Building, Cairo Plaza, Corniche
    el-Nil, Cairo (☎ 777900/999/273).
    Hours are 8 am to 3 pm, Sunday to Thursday.
Canada
    6 Sharia Mohammed Fahmy as-Said, Garden
    City, Cairo (☎ 354-3110).
    Hours are from 7.30 am to 3 pm, Sunday to
    Thursday
Central African Republic
    13 Sharia Shehab, Mohandiseen, Cairo
    (☎ 713291)
Eritrea
    86 Sharia Shehab, Mohandiseen, Cairo.
    Visas valid for a month are issued within 24
    hours. You need a letter of introduction from your
    embassy and two photos. Visas cost E£30, and
    you have the option of a single or multiple entry.
    If you are going via the Sudan, getting an Eritrean
    visa is quite straightforward in Khartoum, and
    costs considerably less.
Ethiopia
    3 Sharia Ibrahim Osman, Mohandiseen, Cairo
    (☎ 755133, 705372).
    People have had varying experiences here. A
    letter of introduction and two photos are required
    for visas that cost E£24. However, some people
    have been refused visas without an air ticket
    showing an onward flight.
France
    Embassy: 29 Sharia al-Giza, Giza (☎ 728649,
    728346).

This street has changed names several times, so
there are variations it's also known as Sharia Taha
Hussein, Sharia Dr Taha Hussein, Sharia el-Nil
and Sharia Bahyi ad-Din Barakat, which is actu-
ally an extension southward of Sharia al-Giza.
    Consulate: 2 Midan Orabi, Mansheya, Alexan-
    dria (☎ 482-7950). It is open from 8.30 am to 2
    pm daily, except Friday and Saturday.
Germany
    Embassy: 8 Sharia Hassan Sabri, Zamalek, Cairo
    (☎ 341-0015)
    Consulate: 5 Sharia Mena, Rushdy, Alexandria
    (☎ 545-7025)
India
    5 Sharia Aziz Abaza, Zamalek, Cairo (☎ 341-
    3051)
Ireland
    3 Sharia Abu al-Feda, Zamalek, Cairo (☎ 340-
    8264)
    Consulate: Honorary Consul, Hisham Helmy, 36
    Sharia Kafr Abdu, Rushdy, Alexandria (☎ 546-
    4686)
Israel
    Embassy: 6 Sharia Ibn al-Malek, Giza (☎ 361-
    0528). Hours are from 10 am to 2.30 pm daily.
    Consulate: 207 Sharia Abdel Salem Aref, Alex-
    andria (☎ 586-0492)
Japan
    Embassy: Cairo Centre Building, 3rd floor, 2
    Sharia Abd al-Kader Hamza, 106 Qasr al-Eini,
    Garden City, Cairo (☎ 355-3962, fax 356-3540)
    Consulate: 41 Sharia Mustapha Abu Heif, Saba
    Pasha, Ramla, Alexandria (☎ 587-9966, fax 586-
    2877)
Jordan
    6 Sharia Gohaina, Doqqi, Cairo (☎ 348-5566).
    Hours are from 9 am to noon, Saturday to Thurs-
    day. The embassy is two blocks west of the
    Sheraton Hotel. Visas cost from nothing for
    Americans and Australians to E£77 for UK citi-
    zens. You apply in the morning and come back to
    collect the visa at 1.30 pm. You need one photo.
    It is generally quite easy, and cheaper, to get a
    Jordanian visa on entering the country. At Aqaba,
    there is a police and Immigration station at the
    passenger ferry terminal, where visas are issued
    on the spot, although they can keep you waiting
    a bit. You may be denied a visa if your passport
    indicates you've been to Israel, which will be
    shown by Egyptian border stamps from Rafah or
    Taba, although some travellers have been known
    to get away with it.
Kenya
    7 Sharia al-Mohandis Galal, Mohandiseen, Cairo
    (☎ 345-3907).
    Visas valid for three months and good for travel
    in Kenya for a month cost E£26 for most Western
    nationalities. You need one photo. The embassy

is open for business from 8 am to 2 pm, but closed on Saturday and Sunday.

Lebanon
5 Sharia Ahmed Nessim, Giza (☎ 728315)

Libya
7 Sharia As-Saleh Ayoub, Zamalek, Cairo (☎ 340-1864).
It is possible to visit Libya, but generally only 10-day visas are being issued. The process requires patience. You need a translation into Arabic of your passport details, authenticated by your embassy, along with a letter of recommendation from your embassy and two photos for the application. On your first visit, they tell you they'll let you know whether or not they intend to let the application proceed, and in the meantime you can organise the translation. Even if you have a contact number, they probably won't contact you – go back after two or three weeks with passport, translation, photos and letter. If you get the thumbs up, the visa will cost E£50.

Netherlands
Embassy: 18 Sharia Hassan Sabri, Cairo (☎ 340-6434/1936)
Consulate: 3rd floor, 18 Sharia al-Hurriya, Alexandria (☎ 482-9044, 483-4210)

New Zealand
New Zealand's affairs are handled by the UK Embassy.

Sudan
Embassy: 4 Sharia al-Ibrahimy, Garden City, Cairo (☎ 354-5044)
Consulate: 1 Sharia Mohammed Fahmy as-Said, Garden City (☎ 354-5043).
The consulate is around the corner from the embassy and is open from 9 am to 4 pm (roughly) Saturday to Thursday. It's probably best to get there as early as possible. You can't miss it; there will probably be hordes of Sudanese negotiating their way past a black grill gate. You will probably be ushered straight in. Five copies of the application, five passport-size photos, and a letter of recommendation from your embassy are required before the visa can be issued. At the time of writing, it was taking anything up to a month to issue a visa. Mention of being a journalist or similar profession may not enhance your chances. They do *not* take your passport while processing your application. You pay US$50 cash (they will not accept other currencies) on receipt of the visa, which is valid for use within a month and good for a month's stay. For more details on visas and travel restrictions, refer to the Facts for the Visitor chapter in the Sudan section of this book.
Note As of mid-1993, it was reported that visas could be obtained immediately on arriving at the port of Wadi Halfa from Aswan for US$50.

Sweden
Embassy: 13 Sharia Mohammed Mazhar, Zamalek, Cairo (☎ 341-4132)
Consulate: 57 Sharia 26 July, Alexandria (☎ 483-3855, 802-5158)

Syria
18 Sharia Abdel Rahim Sabri, Doqqi, Cairo (☎ 707020)

Tunisia
26 Sharia al-Gezira, Zamalek, Cairo (☎ 340-3940).
Visas can be obtained with relatively little sweat. You need two photos. EC citizens pay nothing, others E£23. The visa is valid for use within a month and good for a month's stay.

Uganda
9 Midan al-Missaha, Doqqi, Cairo (☎ 348-5544)

UK
Embassy: corner Sharia Ahmed Ragheb and Sharia Latin America, Garden City, Cairo (☎ 354-0852). Hours are from 8 am to 1 pm, Sunday to Thursday.
Consulate: 3 Sharia Mena, Rushdy, Alexandria (☎ 546-7001/2). Hours are from 8 am to 1 pm, Sunday to Thursday; it also opens Saturday, for emergencies only.
Honorary Consul: Dr Hussein Samir, 9 Sharia al-Galaa, Suez (tel 225382)

USA
Embassy: 8 Sharia Kamal ad-Din Salah, Cairo (☎ 355-7371). Hours are from 8.30 am to 2 pm, Sunday to Thursday.
Consulate: Unit 64904, 110 Sharia al-Hurriya, Alexandria (☎ 482-1911). Hours are from 9 am to noon Sunday to Thursday.

Yemen
28 Sharia Amin ar-Rafi'i, Doqqi, Cairo (☎ 360-4806).
For a visa you will need two photographs and a letter of recommendation from your embassy. The visa costs E£17. Visas are usually issued within two days of applying, but before going ahead with the application you should check how long the visa is valid. Upon arrival you will be granted a one-month stay. The embassy is open from 9 am to 1.30 pm every day but Friday.

Zaire
5 Sharia al-Mansour Mohammed, Zamalek, Cairo (☎ 340-3662)

DOCUMENTS

The documents you need depend on where you are coming from and what you plan to do in Egypt.

Vaccination Certificate

A vaccination certificate proving that you

have been vaccinated for yellow fever and/or cholera is only necessary if you are coming from an infected area (such as most of sub-Saharan Africa and South America). Occasionally they do ask travellers coming from these areas for their certificate. To be on the safe side, it is a good idea to have these vaccinations.

Some countries, such as Kenya, require yellow fever vaccination certificates if you are coming from Egypt.

See the section on Health in this chapter for more information.

Permits

An antiquities permit is a useful thing to have, as it allows you easier access to many of Egypt's archaeological sites, especially sites usually closed to tourists. To get the permit, from the Department of Antiquities in Abbassiya, you might need a letter from the archaeology department of any university.

Travel permits are no longer required for travel westward past Marsa Matruh or to Siwa Oasis. This is a result of the easing of relations between Egypt and Libya since 1989, but it is not a guarantee, in what is after all a volatile area, that the need for permits might not be reimposed if the two countries again find themselves at loggerheads – it would not be the first time in their postwar history.

Military permits are sometimes required for travel south beyond Marsa Alam on the Red Sea coast, and may be hard to come by, particularly as long as Egypt and the Sudan continue to squabble about the Halaib region. This situation is always subject to change.

A permit is also required to visit the pyramids of Dahshur, south of Saqqara. Enquire first at the Department of Antiquities, or you could try the tourist police at the Giza Pyramids.

Student Cards

Legitimate International Student Identification Cards (ISIC) are available for E£16 (some people seem to pay E£21; it may depend on the kind of proof you present) at a booth outside Cairo University's Faculty of Dentistry. The main university entrance is straight over the Manyal Bridge. Head past the Faculty of Medicine towards the minaret and turn left – it's not hard to find; there is usually a queue of foreigners, and Egyptian students can point the way. For years, it has been notoriously easy to get a card here, but they are, loosely speaking, tightening up. A valid student card or letter from your university is required.

Failing this, a statutory declaration from your embassy to the effect that you are a student, and explaining why you don't have an ID card (eg, you lost it) might do the trick. Embassies appear to be willing to do this, at a price. The Australian embassy charges E£32 for declaration; the UK embassy E£82. Given the benefits, it is still well worth it – if it doesn't pay for itself during your stay in Egypt (and it probably will), it is perfectly legitimate for use anywhere else. You need two photos and the booth is only open from 11 am to 1 pm. It's closed on Friday. Expect a queue, and be prepared for disappointment – it seems destined not to last forever.

If this fails, travellers have reported using a whole range of cards to get student discounts for museum entry and transport, from International Youth Hostel Federation (IYHF) cards to Eurail cards. There's no guarantee, but they're all worth a try.

Business Cards

Another source of identification is a business card. A business card can also give you a certain degree of credibility in Egypt and, depending what's on it, can be a great help in obtaining assistance.

CUSTOMS

A grand total of E£100 can be imported into or exported out of the country. If you have more than this on leaving the country, there is a slim chance you might have the excess confiscated. There are no restrictions on the import of foreign currencies, although you are supposed to declare all you have when you enter. You are not supposed to take out more than you have brought in and declared.

Sometimes, Customs Declaration Form D is given to arriving tourists to fill out. You are supposed to list all cameras, jewellery, cash, travellers' cheques and electronics (personal stereos, computers, radios, VCRs, etc). No-one ever seems to be asked for this form on departure. Travellers are, however, regularly asked to declare and register their video cameras. The Egyptian government issues a list of articles which are duty-free, dutiable, prohibited or restricted. The following information comes from that list:

Duty-Free Articles

The following articles can be brought into Egypt without duty being charged: personal clothing and toiletries, equipment and tools for use during work, one bottle of liquor and 100 cigarettes.

Dutiable Articles

Customs duty will be levied on articles in excess of the duty-free allowance. Duty will have to be paid on the following items regardless of whether or not they have been used previously: cars, motorcycles and video cameras.

Prohibited & Restricted Articles

Books, printed matter, motion pictures, phonographs and materials that are considered subversive or constituting a national risk or incompatible with the public interest.

Articles for espionage or intelligence activities. (They didn't specifically say what they meant by this.)

Explosives.

Duty-Free Shops

It is possible to buy a wide range of articles duty-free, either on entering the country or within 30 days of entry. Good liquor and cigarettes are the main items worth inspection. The liquor is very expensive in the stores so it is easy to make a little profit on duty-free liquor. If you haven't already

bought some, drop into the duty-free shop when you arrive at Cairo Airport's new terminal (you'll walk past it on the left on the way to Immigration and customs). It's quite easy to resell well-known brands of whisky and cognac to the hustlers in front of the Egyptian Museum in Cairo. A bottle of Johnny Walker Red Label costs US$16. If you don't want to pick anything up on your way through the air terminal or port on arrival, there are several branches of the Egypt Free Shops Company scattered around the country. Take your passport and the air or ferry ticket you came with (the latter may not be necessary). You can buy up to US$100 worth of any item (this is the tax, not pretax, value of the item), unless of course you want to buy, say, a fridge, in which case special terms apply.

Branches can be found at:

Cairo
    106 Sharia Gamiat ad-Dowal al-Arabiyya, Mohandiseen (☎ 349-7094)
    19 Sharia Talaat Harb, Central Cairo (☎ 393-4230)
    17 Sharia al-Gomhurriya, Central Cairo (☎ 391-5134)
    Cairo Sheraton Hotel (☎ 348-8600)
Alexandria
    513 Tariq al-Hurriya (☎ 586-8546)
    16 Sharia Salah Salem (☎ 483-3429)
    Port of Alexandria (☎ 803880)
Port Said
    Sharia An-Nahda & Sharia al-Geish (☎ 238907)

It is also possible to buy duty-free in Nuweiba, in Luxor, at the Aswan High Dam (down by the dock for the Sudan steamer), in Sallum (Libyan border) and at the Aquamarina Hotel in Sharm el-Sheikh.

MONEY

Most foreign hard currencies, cash or travellers' cheques, can be readily changed in Egypt, and the process has become much easier and more flexible in the past few years. Money can be officially changed at American Express and Thomas Cook offices, commercial banks and some hotels. The hotels sometimes charge higher commissions than the other institutions.

American Express, Visa, MasterCard, JCB cards and Eurocard are good for purchases in a wide range of stores displaying the appropriate signs.

For holders of credit cards, the options have greatly increased. Visa and MasterCard are good for cash advances from many branches of Banque Misr and the Egyptian Arab-African Bank, as well as some foreign institutions like the Bank of America. Banque Misr and the Bank of America generally charge no commission for cash advances, and the limit appears to depend on the terms of your particular card. Outside the big cities and tourist hubs, cash advances are more problematic, if not impossible, so keep some travellers' cheques and/or cash handy.

Ancient Egyptian images depicted on coins

If you have an American Express card and personal cheques, American Express will cash them. If you have an American Express green card, however, you are not permitted to cash more than US$400 each 21 days without authorisation from their offices in London or the USA. You can also cash American Express travellers' cheques or use their cards to obtain hard currency. They will usually oblige you to change first into local currency and then back into the hard currency. You can obtain hard currency or travellers' cheques from American Express with a MasterCard or a Visa card, but there is a hitch. You can only get the national currency of the bank which issued your card. So if your card was issued by a British bank, you can only get UK£.

Eurocheques can be cashed at some banks. You need your Eurocheque card and passport. Always ask about commission as it can vary wildly. The Bank of Alexandria seems to be about the best, charging E£4 per cheque (you might be able to slip a couple past them), but their exchange rate is generally not so hot. Thomas Cook asks for E£7 and some banks have been known to demand as much as E£20 – so watch out! Often you will be required to cash an amount in a hard currency other than the one your account is in (usually US$).

Cheques issued on post office accounts (common in Europe) or cards linked to such accounts cannot be used in Egypt. Travellers coming from Israel, where they can be used to buy shekels, have been caught out in Egypt this way.

Most internationally recognised travellers' cheques and currencies are accepted by the main banks. In smaller places away from tourist centres, US$, UK£ and DM are probably the safest bet. Banks sometimes have a small handling charge on cheques, something in the order of 50 pt, plus E£2 or E£3 for stamps.

Whatever method you use for changing money, make sure you have your passport with you, as you'll nearly always need it.

It is also possible to have money wired from home through American Express and the Bank of America. A host of foreign banks are represented in Cairo and some in Alexandria, should you need specialised services of any kind. Check with your bank before you leave home if it has a particular partner in Cairo through which it effects money transfers.

American Express will do it through most of their branches, regardless of whether you have one of their cards or travellers' cheques. You simply need to arrange for someone back home to send whatever amount you need to a nominated office in Egypt, but enquire about their charges for this service.

See Business Hours below for opening hours of banks and other institutions.

Be careful about carrying around a lot of cash, as pickpockets are a definite problem at the more popular sights and in the big cities. See Dangers & Annoyances.

Re-Exchange

Excess E£ can be exchanged back into hard currency at the end of your stay, or during if you wish. You can sell your E£ at the various exchange places that have sprung up in the big cities since the currency was floated, sometimes at slightly better rates than those available in the few banks where it is also sometimes possible to buy hard currency.

Only the bigger branches of Banque Misr in the main centres will sell hard currency. Visa and MasterCard holders can also buy hard currency this way, sometimes directly, but more often being obliged first to buy E£ and then change. The limit appears to be only the conditions on your card and the availability of cash – one traveller took out US$1000 cash this way.

When *buying* E£, however, it's generally better to stick to the banks, as the exchange houses often offer inferior rates. The bulk of them only deal in cash too. Note that rates can vary quite a bit between banks, especially if the currency you hold is fluctuating at all on world markets. The variations seem to be minimal on the US dollar.

Currency

The official currency of Egypt is called the pound (E£). In Arabic it is called a *guinay*. A pound = 100 piastres (pt – sometimes indicated by ـ), or 1000 millims. The Arabic word for piastre is *irsh* or *girsh*. There are notes in denominations of 5, 10 (rare to nonexistent), 25 and 50 pt (useful but never in great enough supply) and E£1, 5, 10, 20, 50 and 100 (this last one will be of little help to most budget travellers). The E£50 note has only just been reintroduced. It was withdrawn after counterfeit notes were found in circulation in the mid-1980s. Be wary of the new E£50 and E£100 notes – some people tend to view them with suspicion.

Although new notes have been issued for most denominations because so much of the money was literally falling apart, you will still come across bills held together by bits of packing tape.

Coins in circulation are for denominations of ½ pt (5 millims), 1, 5, 10 and 20 pt, but the 1 pt and ½ pt coins are almost never seen. The locals have colloquial names for the coins – see Language in the Facts about the Country chapter.

Prices can be written with or without a decimal point. For example, E£3.33 can also be written as 333 pt. Some places still write prices in millims, or a combination of pounds and millims, which gives you three figures after the decimal point – it sounds confusing, but in practice it's not such a great problem.

Exchange Rates

The E£ was partly floated in 1987, so that it fluctuates in value according to economic conditions – it seems closely tied to the US$. Much to the surprise of many, the E£ has remained fairly steady since late 1990. In fact, some currencies, like the UK£, actually *fell* against the E£ in the course of 1992 and into 1993!

There seems little point in buying Egyptian currency before you leave. Aside from the fact that importing more than E£100 is illegal (even if they don't seem to check what you're carrying), you may well lose out. Thomas Cook in London was quoting a rate 15% inferior to that available in Cairo in 1993.

Exchange rates for a range of foreign currencies were as follows in mid-1993. Check with your bank for the latest rates.

Australia	A$1	=	E£2.22
Canada	C$1	=	E£2.62
France	F10	=	E£6.20
Germany	DM1	=	E£2.02
Japan	Y100	=	E£3.03
Jordan	JD1	=	E£4.90
Sudan	S£100	=	E£1.70
UK	UK£1	=	E£5.06
USA	US$1	=	E£3.33
Australia	E£1	=	A$0.45
Canada	E£1	=	C$0.38
France	E£1	=	F1.60
Germany	E£1	=	DM0.49
Japan	E£1	=	Y33
Jordan	E£1	=	JD0.21
Sudan	E£1	=	S£60
UK	E£1	=	UK£0.20
USA	E£1	=	US$0.30

Costs

Travel in Egypt is cheap, although hefty inflation and a fairly stable currency have combined to make it more expensive than it was around 1990-1991. It is still quite possible to get by on US$10 a day or even less if you're willing to stick to the cheapest end of the food and accommodation range and take 3rd-class trains packed to the hilt with screaming babies, chicken cages and half the Egyptian army.

For the most part, the amount of convenience and comfort varies according to how much you are willing to pay. Yet, even at the 1st-class level, Egypt is cheap compared to Western countries.

Until the second half of 1992, inflation was estimated at more than 30%. At the time of writing, most observers agreed it had been beaten down to about 20%, although with wages hardly moving at all, Egyptians are still taking a hiding at the shop counter. In the last two months of 1992, for instance, electricity bills shot up 30% with no prior warning – the kind of hike that leads to rising hotel charges. In addition, the usual service charge of 12% applied in restaurants and hotels has been accompanied by a 5% sales tax (said to be effectively a Gulf War tax). One odd exception is sugar. The subject of rationing in 1990, it is the one commodity that now seems to be in freefall, which must please the collective Egyptian sweet tooth.

To give some indication of daily costs, the bulk of fruit juices at stands throughout the country cost around E£1 or more, although they tend to be cheaper outside Cairo. Bottled drinks like Mirinda (an orange soda), Teem (virtually Seven-Up) and the like cost anything from 25 pt to E£1, depending of where you buy them. A one-litre bottle of the local Stella beer costs around E£3 to E£4. A 1.5 litre bottle of Baraka mineral water costs as little as 90 pt. A kg of apples, a relatively expensive fruit in Egypt, will cost E£8 to E£12. The staple snacks, *fuul* (a bean mixture) and *ta'amiyya* (fried chickpea balls) sandwiches, cost about 30 pt. A cup of tea costs 30 pt, coffee around 50 pt and a *shisha* (water pipe) 60 pt. A shoeshine is 50 pt. If you stuck largely to these, you'd get by very cheaply indeed!

In 1990, the ridiculously low entry prices to monuments were sharply increased, while in many other cases entry fees were introduced for the first time for secondary sights. The Egyptian Museum in Cairo, for instance, costs E£10 (half for students). Egyptians, it may be noted, pay much less than foreigners, sometimes as little as one-tenth. Before getting too upset, however, it should be borne in mind that, with a monthly wage of about E£100, an average Egyptian teacher with a family would find a trip to the museum at E£10 a considerable investment. The most irritating thing is that some of the smaller, and for the lay person often only moderately interesting, places have had an E£8 fee slapped on where before it was simply a matter of handing over some baksheesh (a tip) to the guardian. He still expects his baksheesh, despite the entrance fee, and this makes some of the out-of-the-way places a little too expensive by anyone's standards.

There is a severe shortage of small change in Egypt. The notes for amounts less than

E£1, which are useful for tipping, local transport and avoiding the painfully repetitious incidence of not being given the correct change, are not always easy to come by – they should be hoarded. Sometimes you're offered 'change' in the guise of boxes of matches, sweets, aspirins (at pharmacies) and the like, although more often than not they pocket the difference. The only answer is to be ruthless: when you're told there's no change, don't scrape around and find it yourself – insist that they do the scraping around, or else you'll always end up without change when you really need it. Taxi drivers are rarely going to have change if the fare can be rounded up against you. An E£8 taxi fare will often be E£10 if you don't have exactly E£8 to give the driver.

Prices

Prices change, especially with the development of Egypt's tourist industry. New hotels, resorts, restaurants and tour companies appear almost daily, which possibly means both additional price-fixing by the government in government-controlled or managed establishments, and price competition among private enterprises.

Prices are also subject to changing economic conditions – fluctuating exchange rates, an inflation rate of 20% to 30%, the rise and fall of the price of oil, the amount of interest owed on Egypt's foreign debt, etc. When comparing the prices indicated in this book, which were accurate at the time of writing, to prices during your trip, keep in mind such effects on them. Prices are not, as some travellers apparently believe, written in stone like the Ten Commandments.

On the specific subject of hotels, as a general rule there is a review of prices each year in October. One hotel manager said that a rise of around 15% was the average result, although it appears the rises are often greater. You tend to find cheaper accommodation and get more for your money outside Cairo.

Tipping

Tipping in Egypt is called baksheesh, although it is more than just a reward for having done a service properly. Salaries and wages in Egypt are much lower than in Western countries, so baksheesh is regarded as a means of supplementing income – an often essential means. For example, a cleaner in a one or two-star hotel earns only about E£50 to E£60 per month, so E£1 a day in baksheesh would mean quite a lot to him or her. Public servants generally earn only about E£100 to E£150 a month.

For Western travellers who are not used to almost continual tipping, demands for baksheesh for doing anything from opening a door to guiding you, against your will, through an ancient site can be quite irritating. But it is the accepted way of getting things done in Egypt. Don't be intimidated into paying baksheesh when you don't think the service warrants it, but remember that more things warrant baksheesh here than anywhere in the West.

In restaurants, a 12% service charge is generally already included in the bill, so tipping further is optional (the waiters don't always see it that way, and they may have a point – it is a little doubtful whether the 12% actually ends up in their pockets). The 12% also goes on to most hotel bills in the middle and upper grades, but again, lowly staff would see little of this.

Services such as opening a door or carrying your bags warrant 25 to 50 pt. A personal guide to, for example, the Egyptian Museum costs about E£5 per hour in baksheesh. A guard who shows you something off the beaten track at an ancient site should receive about E£1. Baksheesh is not necessary when asking for directions, although in Cairo there seems to be a band of professional direction-givers who ask for baksheesh practically before they have helped you down the street you never wanted to know about anyway – what you give these chaps is up to you!

In tombs and temples, if you're alone or with one or two others, the guards will whisper to you about some supposedly Pharaonic secret that they want to reveal only to you. Their English usually amounts to only a few words, which means that they can't really explain anything they're showing you.

You might be taken by the arm and shown a deteriorating panel of hieroglyphics depicting a fire, a basket of fruit or a couple of dogs. The guard will look around to make sure no-one else is listening and whisper, 'Ah food. Ah dog. Yes', and smile with conspiratorial delight. Such Pharaonic 'secrets' can cost a pound.

Unfortunately, in several tourist areas, many children have become baksheesh brats. They scream and claw at you, demanding baksheesh and pens. Many tourists give them something just to shut them up. How you handle this is up to you – there's no 'right answer' and it's unlikely that anything is going to reverse the phenomenon. If you do want to give money or gifts to impoverished children, you'll have a much greater impact by making a donation through a school, orphanage, medical clinic or any number of other social welfare organisations.

A last tip on tipping: carry lots of small change with you, but keep it separate from bigger bills, so that baksheesh demands don't increase when they see that you could supposedly afford more.

WHEN TO GO
Planning the best time to head for Egypt depends to some extent on where in Egypt you want to go. Winter is without doubt the most comfortable time to be in Upper Egypt and wandering around the sights at Luxor and Aswan. These places become insufferably hot in the summer months (June to August). The same goes for the oases.

Spring and autumn are the most pleasant times to be in Cairo, as it can get a bit nippy in winter.

The Red Sea is pleasant in winter, but many people still come in the summer as well. The Mediterranean coast is at its most popular with Egyptians in summer, which is a good reason for not being there at that time of year – the crowds can be oppressive and obviously accommodation becomes tighter. It can still be quite cool on the coast and in Alexandria as late as April however, so a sense of timing – from mid-May to mid-June -and luck with the sun will get you the advantages of warm, sunny days without the full brunt of the local summertime rush.

WHAT TO BRING
Bring sunglasses, flashlight, a collapsible drinking cup, a water bottle/canteen, sun screen (anything above factor eight is hard to find anywhere in Egypt), a hat, a flat drain stopper (not a plug), a pocket knife, two to three metres of nylon cord, plastic clothes pegs (pins), a day pack, a small sewing kit and a money belt or pouch (leather pouches can be made to order in the bazaars).

Although most toiletries can be found in Cairo, Luxor and Aswan (especially at major hotels), certain items can be expensive or difficult to find in Egypt, so you may want to bring your own contact lens solution, tampons (Tampax are about the only kind available), contraceptives (Tops condoms are available – to men – but apparently have a distressingly high failure rate; the pill is actually possible to get, but not easily), shaving cream in a can (in a tube it's readily available), or any favourite brand of shampoo or deodorant. Where you do find any of these items, they are usually fairly expensive. Women living in Egypt suggest it is better to bring your own sanitary pads and panty liners, although they are available.

TOURIST OFFICES
The Egyptian government has tourist information offices in 12 countries and throughout Egypt. The tourist offices outside Egypt are better than the ones within, with the exception of the head office in Cairo, where several languages, including English and French, are spoken by the very helpful staff. If they don't know the answer to a question they will call someone who does. They have maps of Cairo and Egypt, as well as brochures on various sites around the country. The information tends to be a bit faulty, but the photographs should give you a better idea of what you might like to visit.

Local Tourist Offices
Following is a list of the tourist offices within the country:

Cairo
Administrative Headquarters: Misr Travel Tower, Midan Abbassiya (☎ 823510, 824858)
Head Office, 5 Sharia Adly (☎ 391-3454)
Old Airport Office (☎ 667475)
New Airport Office (☎ 291-4255/77)
Pyramids Office, Pyramids Rd, near Hotel Mena House (☎ 385-0259)
Railway Station Office, Ramses Square (☎ 764214)
Manyal Palace
Al-Arish
Sharia Fouad Zikry (☎ 341016)
Alexandria
Sharia an-Nabi Daniel, just off Midan Saad Zaghloul and across from the express buses to Cairo (☎ 807985)
Airport Office (☎ 425-8764)
Marine Passenger Station (☎ 492-5986)
Misr Train Station Office (☎ 803494)
Al-Minya
Governorate Building (☎ 330150)
Aswan
Corniche el-Nil, two blocks north of the Abu Simbel Hotel, behind a small park (☎ 323297)
Hurghada
Sharia Bank Misr (☎ 440513)
Ismailia
Governorate Building
Kharga Oasis
Governorate Building (☎ 901205)
Luxor
Tourist Bazaar, across from the Luxor Temple (☎ 382215)
Marsa Matruh
Governorate Building, corner of Sharia Alexandria and the Corniche (☎ 394-3192)
Port Said
43 Sharia Palestine (☎ 223868)
Rafah
Al-Mena (☎ 300655)
Suez
Main Office, Sharia al-Qena (☎ 221141)
Port Tewfiq (☎ 223589)

Overseas Reps

Following is a list of Egyptian tourist offices outside the country:

Australia
At the time of writing, plans were afoot to establish a tourist office in Australia, but it was not yet known where.
Austria
Aegyptisches Fremdenverkehrsamt, Elisabeth Str 4, Pornringhof, 1010 Vienna (☎ (1) 587-6633)

Canada
Egyptian Tourist Authority, Place Bonaventure, 40 Frontenac, Montreal, Quebec H5A 1V4 (☎ (514) 867-4420)
PO Box 304, Montreal, H5A 1V4
France
Bureau de Tourisme, Ambassade de la RAE, 90 Ave des Champs Elysées, Paris (☎ (1) 45 62 94 42)
Germany
Aegyptisches Fremdenverkehrsamt, 64A Kaiserstrasse, 6 Frankfurt/Main (☎ (69) 252319)
Greece
Egyptian State Tourist Office, 6th floor, 10 Amerikas St, Athens 10671 (☎ (1) 360-6906)
Italy
Ufficio Informazioni Turistiche, 19 Via Bissolati, 00187 Rome (☎ (6) 482-7985)
Japan
Egyptian Tourist Authority, Akasaka 2-Chome Annex, M-S Akasaka 2 Chome, Minato Ku, Tokyo (☎ (3) 58 90 65 31)
Spain
La Toree de Madrid, planta 5, oficina 3, Plaza de España, 28008 Madrid (☎ (1) 578-1732)
Sweden
Egyptian Tourist Office, Drottnin 99 Atan 65, 11136 Stockholm (☎ (8) 102548)
Switzerland
Office du Tourisme d'Egypte, 9 Rue des Alpes, Geneva (☎ (22) 732-9132)
UK
Egyptian Tourist Authority, 168 Piccadilly, London W1 (☎ (71) 493-5282)
USA
Egyptian Tourist Authority, 630 5th Ave, Suite 1706, New York, NY 10111 (☎ (212) 332-2570)
Egyptian Tourist Authority, Suite 215, 83 Wilshire Boulevard, Wilshire San Vincente Plaza, Beverly Hills, CA 90211 (☎ (415) 653-8815)
Egyptian Tourist Authority, 645 North Michigan Ave, Suite 829, Chicago, IL 60611 (☎ (312) 280-4666)
Egyptian Tourist Authority, 5858 Westheimer, 307, Houston, Texas 77057 (☎ (713) 782-9107)

USEFUL ORGANISATIONS
Disabled

A tour company specialising in tours, accommodation and sightseeing in specially equipped buses for the disabled is Etams Tours (☎ 745721, 752462), at 99 Sharia Ramses, Cairo. They also have information on which of the better hotels claim to have facilities catering to the disabled.

BUSINESS HOURS

Banks

Banking hours are from 8 or 8.30 am to 2 pm from Sunday to Thursday. Many banks in Cairo and other cities open again in the evening from 5 or 6 pm for two or three hours, largely for foreign exchange transactions. Some of them also open on Friday and Saturday for the same purposes. Banque Misr at the Nile Hilton in Cairo is open 24 hours, and there are banking services open 24 hours at the new terminal of Cairo Airport. Foreign banks are shut on both Friday and Saturday. During Ramadan, banks are open between 10 am and 1.30 pm.

Exchange Offices

The main advantage these have over banks is that they are generally open right through the day.

Government Offices

Most government offices operate from about 8 am to 2 pm, Sunday to Thursday, but tourist offices and the Mogamma are exceptions. The main tourist office in Cairo is open seven days a week from 9 am to 7 pm (and often later if demand requires it). For registration at the Mogamma in Cairo, see the Information section of the Cairo chapter.

Shops

Generally, shops have different hours at different times of the year. In summer most shops are open from 9 am to 1 pm and from 5 to 8 pm. Winter hours are from 10 am to 6 pm. Hours during Ramadan are from 9.30 am to 3.30 pm and from 8 to 10 pm. There are no real hard and fast rules however, and even on Fridays, it is not uncommon to see shops open for much of the day.

HOLIDAYS

Egypt's holidays and festivals are primarily Islamic or Coptic religious celebrations. Because the Islamic, or Hijra ('flight', as in the flight of Mohammed from Mecca to Medina in 622 AD), calendar is 11 days shorter than the Gregorian (Western) calendar, Islamic holidays fall 11 days earlier each year. Thus 1 January 1992 was 26 Gamada at-Taniyya (the Egyptian rendering, see Language) 1412 AH. The 11-day rule is not entirely strict – the holidays can fall from 10 to 12 days earlier. The precise dates are known only shortly before they fall, dependent upon the sighting of the moon. The Hijra (or Higra in Egyptian Arabic) calendar has 12 lunar months, which are:

1st	Moharram
2nd	Safar
3rd	Rabei al-Awal
4th	Rabei at-Tani
5th	Gamada al-Awal
6th	Gamada at-Taniyya
7th	Ragab
8th	Sha'aban
9th	Ramadan
10th	Shawal
11th	Zuu'l Qeda
12th	Zuu'l Hagga

Islamic Holidays

The following is a list of the main Muslim holidays:

Ras as-Sana
New Year's Day; celebrated on 1 Moharram.
Mulid an-Nabi
Birthday of the prophet Mohammed; celebrated on 12 Rabei al-Awal. The streets of Cairo are a feast of lights and food on this day.
Ramadan
The ninth month of the Islamic calendar, Ramadan is considered the fourth of Islam's five fundamental pillars of faith. For the entire month, faithful Muslims fast from dawn to sunset in order to gain strength against evil spirits. No food and water are allowed until sunset. The *iftar*, or breaking of the fast, occurs the moment the sun has set. Try to attend an iftar at an Egyptian family's home. Everyone counts the minutes and seconds until it's time to eat, then chicken bones, scraps of bread and pieces of vegetables fly as the family descends upon the feast dish. You need to be quick – a feast for 10 is consumed in less than 10 minutes.
Eid al-Fitr
The end of Ramadan fasting; the celebration lasts from 1 to 3 Shawal.

Table of Holidays

Hejira Year	New Year	Prophet's Birthday	Ramadan Begins	Eid al-Fitr	Eid al-Adha
1414	21.06.93	30.08.93	12.02.94	15.03.94	21.05.94
1415	10.06.94	19.08.94	01.02.95	04.03.95	10.05.95
1416	31.05.95	09.08.95	22.01.96	22.02.96	29.04.96
1417	19.05.96	28.07.96	10.01.97	10.02.97	18.04.97
1418	09.05.97	18.07.97	31.12.98	31.01.98	08.04.98
1419	28.04.98	07.07.98	20.12.99	20.01.99	28.03.99
1420	17.04.99	26.06.99	–	–	–

Eid al-Adhah
The time for Muslims to fulfil the fifth pillar of Islam, the pilgrimage to Mecca. Every Muslim is supposed to make the haj at least once in his or her lifetime. This special period for making the haj lasts from 10 to 13 Zuu'l Hagga. The holiday period is also known as Bairam.

Ramadan It is more difficult to travel around Egypt during Ramadan than during the rest of the year. Almost everything closes in the afternoon or has shorter daytime hours; this does not apply to businesses that cater mostly to foreign tourists, but some restaurants and hotels may be closed the entire month of Ramadan.

Transportation schedules, which are usually erratic even at the best of times, become even crazier and sometimes it is more difficult to buy reserved seats. *Never* travel during Eid al-Fitr, which marks the end of Ramadan. All of Egypt is travelling at that time, so practically all buses and trains are dangerously crowded – especially on the last day of the *eid*, or feast, when everyone is returning home.

Coptic Christian Holidays
These are a mixture of religious and commemorative holidays.

Christmas
7 January
Epiphany
19 January
Annunciation
23 March

Easter
celebrated on different dates each year
Sham an-Nessim (Sniffing the Breeze)
A special Coptic holiday with Pharaonic origins. It falls on the first Monday after the Coptic Easter and is celebrated by all Egyptians, with family picnics and outings.

Other Holidays
The following are also public holidays:

New Year's Day
1 January
Union Day
28 February
Sinai Liberation Day
25 April
May Day
1 May
Evacuation Day (the day the British left Egypt)
18 June
Revolution Day
23 July
National Day (a day of military parades and air displays)
6 October
Suez City & National Liberation Day (commemoration of the Suez Crisis)
24 October
Victory Day
23 December

CULTURAL EVENTS
Cairo Film Festival
Usually held in late autumn every year, the festival is a veritable feast of modern (although not always the latest) cinema, and most of it is uncensored. The films are shown in several cinemas, and the *Egyptian Gazette* always carries details. The screenings are

generally more expensive than usual cinema performances, and often it is necessary to buy tickets in advance. Although the censors are supposed to keep the scissors off (they retain the right to reject films outright, but are more lenient than usual for the occasion), they have been known to chop the odd scene.

Cairo Book Fair

The satellite town of Nasr City plays host to the growing book fair around February every year. A host of new releases in various languages is presented, but for travellers it probably doesn't have much more interest than would, for instance, the annual Frankfurt Book Fair in Germany. After Cairo, the fair usually moves up to Alexandria.

POST & TELECOMMUNICATIONS
Post

The Egyptian postal system is slow but eventually most mail gets to its destination. Letters are slow in coming and going; postcards are even slower; and packages...well, bring out the camel express. Receiving and sending packages through customs can cause tremendous headaches, but there is generally little problem with sending letters and postcards to most destinations – it's just, like so many things, a matter of time. They can take anywhere from four to 10 days to get to the UK and one to three weeks to get to the USA or Australia. It takes about the same time for a letter to arrive from the USA or Australia, although waits of more than a month are not as uncommon as you might wish. Letters seem to take one to two weeks from Europe.

Postal Rates Postcards and letters up to 10 grams cost 55 pt to Arab and some African countries and 80 pt to all other countries, although sometimes 70 pt seems to suffice for postcards. Stamps are available at post offices, and some souvenir kiosks, shops and newsstands and the reception desks of some major hotels. Stamps bought outside the post office generally cost a little more than their face value.

Sending Mail Post offices in Egypt are open from 8.30 am to about 3 pm every day except Friday. The GPO at Midan Ataba in Cairo is open from 7 am to 7 pm, seven days a week (at least in theory; it is wise not to leave it until the last minute on Fridays and holidays). Sending mail from the post boxes at major hotels instead of from the post offices seems to be quicker. If you use the post boxes, blue is international airmail, red is internal mail and green internal express mail.

Packages Packages going by normal sea mail or airmail normally have to be sent from the GPO, although in Cairo they can only go from the huge post office branch at Midan Ramses. As an indication of fees, a parcel to Australia costs E£32.50 per kg for airmail; E£16 to the UK. Sea mail rates are lower (and arrival times impossible to guess).

There is usually a long and complicated process of customs inspection and form filling to be withstood – don't close the parcel until the procedures are over. Most curio shops will send your packages for a fee. See the Information section in the Cairo chapter for more details about the formalities.

Express Mail Service It is possible to send a letter of up to 100 grams by EMS. There are several branches of this service around the main cities. In Cairo there is one across the road from the poste restante of the GPO. Such a letter to the UK would cost E£26 and arrival is 'guaranteed' by the following day. Parcels can also be sent by EMS. Ten kg to Australia costs E£321 and takes at least three days to arrive; the same parcel to the UK would cost E£221 and apparently take only two days.

Receiving Mail Mail can be received at American Express offices or at the poste restante in most Egyptian cities. American Express offices are the better option if you have an American Express card or travellers' cheques. In Cairo, have mail sent to the head office: American Express, 17 Sharia Mohammed Bassiuni, Cairo, Egypt. Mail sent to other American Express branches in Cairo is generally forwarded to the central office. More often than not, they won't ask to see American Express cheques or cards, but simply your passport. Unfortunately, the service is not perfect, as some mail does not seem to get through.

The poste restante in Egypt functions remarkably well. If you plan to pick up mail there, have the clerk check under Mr, Ms or Mrs in addition to your first and last names. The main poste restante section is at the GPO – in Cairo it's through the last door down the side street to the right of the main entrance.

Some embassies will hold mail for their nationals, but check this first with your representatives.

If you receive a package, you'll probably get a card telling you to pick it up from the GPO or one of the other main branches. It'll all be written in Arabic, so you'll need to get help making head or tail of it. As anyone who has tried it will attest, having a package sent to you in Egypt is slow torture – you could wait in vain for months.

Telecommunications
Telephone The phones in Egypt can be a test of one's patience, but they're a lot better than they used to be – the introduction of card phones is the most hopeful sign yet.

In 1986 the Egyptian government began the process of revamping the system. Lines

and connections are still being upgraded around the country. Many numbers have changed and more will follow. In Cairo the situation is especially confusing because not all parts of the city have been converted to the new numbering system. See the Cairo Information section for more details. A lot of number changing has been going on throughout the rest of the country too, with similar confusion resulting.

Local telephone calls cost 10 pt with pay phones – if you can find one that works. Calls can be made from cigarette kiosks, major hotels and telephone offices (local calls generally for 50 pt, although some hotels will charge E£1). There are a few pay phones around, but the bulk of them are just outside telephone offices. There are a few pay phones in the lobby of the Nile Hilton in Cairo. Telephone office locations are mentioned throughout the book.

The big news is the gradual introduction of phonecards. As these spread and queues shorten, much of the present stress may be taken out of the process. Increasingly, when you go to a telephone office (known as the *centraal*), you will simply be sold phonecards (one of 30 units for E£33 and another of 15 units for E£16.50) – you get approximately the same amount of time you would for a call placed through the exchange, but can simply call direct anywhere in Egypt or internationally at the special orange phones. There is no three-minute limit if you call this way. Dial 00 and the country code for international calls.

Otherwise, you pay for the call in advance at the telephone office. You can either use one of the booths in the office or have the operator call you at a private number. From smaller towns, you can find yourself paying for a call, only to be told that a line out cannot be obtained and that you must pay 45 pt for having taken up their precious time! Some private lines have direct connections to international lines.

There are different rates for day (8 am to 7.59 pm) and night (8 pm to 7.59 am) calls, and there is a three-minute minimum (unless you are using a card). Three-minute calls to

[Handwritten annotation at top: FROM IN COUNTRY USE "0" i.e. 02 = CAIRO FROM OUT COUNTRY, DROP 1ST ZERO]

the USA cost E£23.50/18 for the first three minutes at the day/night rates respectively; to Australia, E£33.50/25; the UK, E£20.50/15.55; to Germany, E£20.60/15.70. Each extra minute costs from about E£5 to E£10, depending on where you are calling and at what rate. Collect calls cannot be made from Egypt.

In Cairo, the central telephone and telegraph offices at Sharia Adly, Midan Tahrir, Sharia Ramses and Sharia Alfi Bey are open 24 hours a day, seven days a week. Other telephone offices are generally open from 7 am to 10 pm.

Calling from hotels is generally more expensive, although some dispense with the three-minute minimum. One quote in 1993 was E£13 a minute to Australia and E£11 a minute to the UK. The Nile Hilton in Cairo charges E£38 for the first three minutes to Australia and E£12.75 for every minute afterwards; and E£25 to the UK and E£8.50 per extra minute. Some of the middle-range hotels with international lines charge still more.

Some of the dialling codes for Egyptian cities are: Cairo, 02; Alexandria, Marsa Matruh, 03; Al-Faiyum, 084; Beni Suef, 082; Luxor, 095; Aswan, 097; Hurghada, 065; Port Said, 066; Ismailia, 064; Suez, Sharm el-Sheikh, St Catherine, Nuweiba, Dahab & Taba, 062. *[Handwritten: COUNTRY CODE 20]*

Telex & Telegraph Telegrams in English or French can be sent from the telephone and telegraph offices in central Cairo. The rates to the UK and Europe are 66 pt per word and to Australia 76 pt a word.

Telex machines are available at the telephone and telegraph offices on Sharia Adly and Sharia Alfi Bey, and at major hotels. Rates vary.

Fax Fax machines are available for sending and receiving documents at the main telephone and telegraph offices in the big cities, at most five-star hotels, and at some of the smaller hotels as well. A one-page fax to the UK costs about E£13.55 and E£20.15 to Australia. Hotel rates are quite a bit more.

The minimum from the Nile Hilton to the UK is E£34.50, and E£51.25 to Australia. You can also send and receive faxes at some EMS offices. Receiving costs E£3 per page.

TIME

Egypt is two hours ahead of GMT/UTC and daylight saving time (beginning on 1 May) is observed. So, without allowing for variations due to daylight saving, when it's noon in Cairo it is: 10 am in London; 5 am in New York and Montreal; 2 am in Los Angeles; 1 pm in Moscow; and 7 pm in Melbourne and Sydney.

ELECTRICITY

Electric current is 220 volts AC, 50 Hz. Alexandria and the Cairo suburbs of Maadi and Heliopolis used to have current of 110 to 120 volts, 50 Hz, but they all seem to have been brought into line. Wall plugs are the round, two-pin European type. Bring adapter plugs and transformers if necessary; travel-size transformers are difficult to obtain in Egypt.

LAUNDRY

There are a few self-service laundries around Cairo. Another option is to take your clothes to one of Egypt's many 'hole-in-the-wall' laundries where they wash and iron your clothes by hand. The process is fascinating and entertaining to watch. The *mukwagee* (ironing man) takes an ancient iron which opens at the top, places hot coals inside and then fills his mouth with water from a bottle on the table. The water is sprayed from his mouth over the clothes as he vigorously irons. Most hotels can organise to have your washing done.

Your last option, and the most common, is to do your own laundry. You can buy powdered laundry soap throughout Egypt. Bring a nail brush for scrubbing, a flat rubber stopper for the sink and some nylon cord and clothes pegs (pins) for hanging up your wet clothes.

WEIGHTS & MEASURES

Egypt is on the metric system. Basic conversion charts are given at the end of this book.

BOOKS

The following is a short list of books which can further introduce you to Egypt and the Egyptians. Most can be found at bookshops in Egypt or in the library and bookshop of the American University in Cairo. Outside Egypt, many of them can be ordered through local bookshops.

People & Society

Shahhat: An Egyptian, Richard Critchfield, Syracuse University Press, 1984. Critchfield lived and worked for an extended period in a west bank village near Luxor to write this in-depth portrait of a young man named Shahhat and his life in an Egyptian village.

Egypt: Burdens of the Past, Options for the Future, John Waterbury, Indiana University Press, 1978. This book is an excellent comprehensive portrayal of Egyptian society by a leading scholar of North Africa.

An Account of the Manners & Customs of the Modern Egyptians, Edward Lane, first published 1839; reprinted by the State

Mutual Book & Periodicals Service, New York, 1986. Lane's wonderful classic continues to offer insight into the traditional Arab culture of Egypt.

Journey to the Orient, Gerard de Nerval, first published in the 19th century and now distributed by Kampmann & Company, Moyer Bell Ltd, Mt Kisco, New York (1986 reprinting). This book will prime you for exploration of the mysteries of Egypt.

The Other Nile, Charlie Pye-Smith, Penguin Books, 1987. A highly readable and incisive account of a leisurely ramble up the Nile through Egypt and into the Sudan, where internal strife stopped the author going any further. He contrasts the trip with an earlier one he made right through the Sudan and Ethiopia in the mid-1970s.

The Hidden Face of Eve: Women in the Arab World, Nawal El-Saadawi, Zed Press, 1980, and Beacon, 1981. This, the first of the author's numerous works to be translated into English, considers the role of women in world history, Arab history and literature, and contemporary Egypt. Nawal El-Saadawi is a psychiatrist, feminist, novelist and writer of nonfiction. She is the founder and president of the Arab Women's Solidarity Association. All her books, many of which have been translated into several languages, are well worth reading for the insight they provide into the lives of women in the Arab world.

Khul-Khaal: Five Egyptian Women Tell their Stories, edited by Nayra Atiya, The American University in Cairo Press, 1991. The life stories of five contemporary Egyptian women from a variety of backgrounds. Fascinating information for anyone interested in understanding Egyptian life.

Women in Egyptian Public Life, by Earl A Sullivan, The American University in Cairo Press, 1987, gives a different insight again into what some extraordinary women have achieved in Egypt.

Monks and Monasteries in the Desert, by Otto Meinardus, The American University in Cairo Press, 1989, offers information on a little discussed aspect of Egyptian religious life that could be of interest.

Siwa Oasis, by Ahmed Fakhry, The American University Press, 1990, takes a close look at a part of Egypt that is really quite un-Egyptian.

Fiction

Midaq Alley, Miramar and *The Thief & the Dogs*, Naguib Mahfouz, The American University in Cairo Press. These novels, by Egypt's first Nobel Prize-winning author, provide insightful perspectives on life in Egypt. *Midaq Alley* portrays a poor back-alley neighbourhood in Islamic Cairo. The book focuses on the life of a girl who gets engaged to the local barber but becomes a prostitute while her fiancé is off earning money for their future together. *Miramar* presents a microcosm of Egyptian society through the story of a young girl from the countryside who flees to Alexandria to avoid an arranged marriage. The relationships she develops with her neighbours in the city form a revealing picture of life in a fairly typical urban neighbourhood in Egypt. *The Thief & the Dogs* is a critical, somewhat cynical, psychological study of a man who was wrongfully imprisoned for several years and then set free. His new life becomes a symbolic quest for justice.

Mahfouz, who has written 40 novels and short story collections and 30 screenplays, was awarded the 1988 Nobel Prize in Literature for works that many compare to those of Dickens or Balzac. According to the Swedish Academy, his works are 'rich in nuance – now clear-sightedly realistic, now evocatively ambiguous...his work speaks to us all'.

Arab & Islamic History

For those wanting to become generally acquainted with the wider Arabic-speaking world, there are several books to recommend. Philip Hitti's work, *History of the Arabs* (Macmillan paperback), now regarded as something of a classic and highly readable, is one.

A more recent but equally acclaimed work is Albert Hourani's *A History of the Arab Peoples* (Faber, 1991). Peter Mansfield has written several very readable works, including *A History of the Middle East* (Penguin, 1992) and *The Arabs* (Penguin, 1990).

If it's weightier stuff you're after, or a pretty comprehensive reference source (although it's weak on more recent history) not just on the Arabs but on the whole Muslim world, you could try delving into the two hardback or four paperback volumes of *A Cambridge History of Islam*.

Egyptian History

The Penguin Guide to Ancient Egypt, William J Murnane, Penguin Books, 1983. Murnane has given us one of the best overall books on the life and monuments of ancient Egypt. There are plenty of illustrations and descriptions of almost every major monument in the country.

The British Museum Book of Ancient Egypt, British Museum Press, edited by Stephen Quirke and Jeffrey Spencer, gives an authoritative overview of Ancient Egypt, but is surprisingly short on plans and diagrams of monuments.

Sakkara and Memphis, Jill Kamil, Longmann, 1985, is full of plans, photos and descriptions of these sights.

Luxor, also by Jill Kamil, Longmann, 1989, may also be of interest.

The Ancient Egyptians: Religious Beliefs & Practices, Rosalie David, Routledge & Kegan Paul, 1982. This is one of the first books to trace the evolution of religious beliefs and practices in ancient Egypt. It is a very thorough and comprehensible treatment of a complex subject.

The Gods & Symbols of Ancient Egypt, Manfred Lurker, Thames & Hudson, 1984. This is an illustrated dictionary which offers brief explanations and descriptions of the most important aspects of ancient Egypt. It can be helpful in understanding some of the hieroglyphics.

Discovering Egyptian Hieroglyphics, Karl Theodor Zangich, also published by Thames & Hudson, explains in depth the Egyptians' ancient system of writing, which long baffled the modern world before the Rosetta stone helped shed light on it.

Top: Cairo skyline from Zamalek (GB)
Middle: Walls of a village in central Egypt (RvD)
Bottom: Desert nomads (GB)

Top: School children, Asyut (DS)
Middle: Camel dealer smoking a home-made pipe, Aswan (KB); Nubian woman,
Elephantine Island, Aswan (KB); Camel trader peeks through his tent, Aswan (KB)
Bottom: Men play backgammon in a neighbourhood cafe, Cairo (KB)

The Blue Nile and *The White Nile*, Alan Moorehead, New English Library, 1982, and Random House, 1983. Both books are classics which cover the history of the Nile during the 19th century. *The Blue Nile* deals with the period 1798 to 1856; *The White Nile* is concerned with events from 1856 to the end of the century. Moorehead's detailed descriptions of events and personalities are superb. These two should definitely be read.

In Search of Identity, Anwar Sadat, Harper & Row, 1979. Sadat's autobiography is a good introduction to the events leading up to and following Egypt's 1952 Revolution.

Great Cairo: Mother of the World, by Desmond Stewart, The American University in Cairo Press, 1981. This covers 55 centuries of Cairo's history; the descriptions of the many diabolical rulers are wonderful.

Nagel's Encyclopedia Guide to Egypt, Passport Books, National Textbook Company, Illinois, 1987. This is an expensive but extremely thorough guide to Egypt's ancient monuments.

The History of Egypt, P J Vatikiotis, Johns Hopkins University Press, Baltimore, 1986. This is one of the best books on the history of Egypt. It emphasises the 19th and 20th centuries with a focus on political and social development since 1805 and the 'new social order' that has evolved since the 1952 Revolution.

A Short History of Modern Egypt, by Afaf Lutfi al-Sayyid Marsot, Cambridge University Press, Cambridge, 1985. For a more concise history of Egypt from 639 AD read this book, which is by one of Egypt's foremost historians. It offers a great introduction to Egyptian history.

Travel Guides

The Blue Guide, Veronica Seton-Williams & Peter Stocks, W W Norton, 1988. This

Egyptian Zodiac

massive tome is one of the most comprehensive guides to Egypt. It describes every place of even the slightest historical interest and has excellent sections on Egypt's natural history. However, it is a bit heavy to lug around in a backpack.

Alexandria: A History & A Guide, E M Forster, Michael Haag Ltd, 1985. First published in 1922, this is still one of the best guides to the sights and history of Alexandria.

Cairo: A Practical Guide, The American University in Cairo Press. Almost every bit of practical information from auctions to toy shops is contained in this guide. The maps are some of the best you will find.

Guide to Egypt, Michael Haag Ltd, 1987. A fairly comprehensive guide with plenty of detail about the monuments and their place in history, as well as practical information for getting around.

Let's Go Israel & Egypt, St Martin's Press. Put together by Harvard Uni students, the Let's Go series provides plenty of background info, tells you about things to see, places to stay, etc, and is updated annually. This one also covers Jordan.

Egypt, The Nile and *Cairo* are three separate books done by Insight Guides, APA Publications. Put together by a team of specialists, they are intended less as practical guides than as colourful journey companions in essay style – which they are.

Egypt – A Traveller's Anthology, compiled by Christopher Pick, John Murray, 1991, is a collection of literary tid-bits from some of Egypt's more illustrious visitors.

Al-Fustat, by Wladislaw B Kubick, The American University in Cairo Press, 1988, is a slim volume dealing with the Muslims' first settlement in what would one day come to be known as Cairo.

Coptic Egypt, by Jill Kamil, contains a guide to the Coptic Museum as well as providing an introduction to the history and life of the Copts.

The Citadel of Cairo, William Lyster, The Palm Press, traces the history of the most visible feature of Cairo's landscape.

Language

Those who want a comprehensive guide to Modern Standard Arabic or colloquial Egyptian Arabic should check at the American University in Cairo Bookstore for the latest textbooks. Otherwise, Lonely Planet's phrasebook, *Egyptian Arabic – a language survival kit*, should suffice. It's small enough to easily fit in your pocket.

Bookshops

Cairo and Alexandria have several English-language bookshops where you can find most of the books mentioned here. For addresses refer to the Cairo and Alexandria sections.

MAPS

Michelin map No 954 covers Egypt, the Sudan and the Sinai. The Sudan section is excellent but there are better maps on Egypt and the Sinai. The best is published by Kümmerly & Frey, a Swiss company. It covers all of Egypt and the Sinai, on a scale of 1:950,000, and sells for about US$9. They also do a separate map of the Sinai and a

pictorial (but fairly useless) map of the Nile, for about US$7.50.

Another map publisher, Freytag & Berndt, publishes a map which includes a plan of the Great Pyramids of Giza and covers all of Egypt except the western quarter on a scale of 1:1,000,000.

The Macmillan Publishers *Map of Egypt* has a 1:1,000,000 map of the Nile Valley and a small map of all Egypt, plus good maps of Cairo and Alexandria, and a variety of enlargements, temple plans and the like for around US$7. The map of Egypt itself is not much to write home about.

Clyde Surveys, of England, has an excellent map of eastern Egypt. It covers the Nile region from the coast to Aswan, and has detailed maps of Cairo, Alexandria, Luxor and Thebes, and the Great Pyramids of Giza, with notes in English, French and German. It is entitled *Clyde Leisure Map No 6: Egypt & Cairo*.

The Bartholomew *World Travel Map of Egypt* is also quite good, although it is very inaccurate in the Sinai. The scale is 1:1,000,000. It costs about US$7.50.

Falk does a detailed map of Cairo, with a small Alexandria addition and booklet packed with details about the two. But you have to appreciate Falk's style of unravelling map – you either like it or you hate it. It costs about US$8.50.

GEOprojects in Beirut does a map of Egypt with city maps of Cairo and Alexandria, but at more than US$9 – outside Egypt – it is not a good buy.

There is an expanding plethora of maps of Cairo or Cairo suburbs available in the better bookshops in the city. Some are OK, others pathetic and most of little interest to the traveller passing through.

Palm Press is producing a series of maps covering parts of Islamic Cairo designed by the Society for the Preservation of the Architectural Resources of Egypt (SPARE). The first couple were a little amateurish, but it is hoped later versions will be better.

MEDIA

By Middle Eastern standards, the press in

Egypt suffers under a moderate level of censorship. Under President Mubarak, the reins have been loosened somewhat, and there is some reasonably lively debate in the papers and magazines. Total freedom there is not. Watching the news on TV (in whatever language it appears – Arabic, English or French) shows more graphically some of the parameters – you can only take so much of Egyptian political talking heads, especially that of the president.

Newspapers & Magazines

The *Egyptian Gazette* is Egypt's daily English-language newspaper. It is difficult to find outside of Cairo and Alexandria, and the news coverage can be pretty mediocre. That is due, in part, to government censorship. At the very least, though, it gives you some idea of what is happening in Egypt and the rest of the world. The Saturday issue is called the *Egyptian Mail*. The French language equivalents are the daily *Journal d'Egypte* and Sunday's *Progrès Dimanche*. All are good entertainment for lovers of typos and quirky expressions.

The *Egyptian Gazette* can be useful for listings info, with TV and radio programmes and the main cinema performances in Cairo and Alexandria. The times for the cinema are rarely shown, as the performances generally take place at the same time each day (see Entertainment in the Cairo chapter).

Since mid-1990, a weekly summary of the Arabic-language daily, *Al-Ahram*, has been providing some decent competition for the daily English-language stalwarts. The English can be a little awkward.

Cairo Today, another English-language publication, is a monthly magazine that covers a variety of subjects including the arts and sport in Egypt. Feature articles regularly focus on different parts of Egypt. Every issue has a guide to nightlife in Cairo, Alexandria and a few of the main tourist destinations.

Of less interest is the bi-monthly *Places in Egypt*, which until recently was simply a freebie distributed at hotels. There are occasionally some informative pieces about, well, places in Egypt.

The *Middle East Times* is a weekly English-language newspaper that offers quite good coverage of events and issues in Egypt and the rest of the Middle East.

The *Middle East Observer* is also found at newsstands in Cairo, but it covers mostly news about African and Middle Eastern financial markets, so it really isn't much use to travellers.

Almost every major Western newspaper and news magazine can be found in Cairo and Alexandria, including *Newsweek* and *Time*. They're available in major hotels and at a few newsstands and bookshops. In Cairo they tend to be a day old, and you can even find a selection as far away as Aswan, where they are usually two or three days old.

For the latest international news there are wire service teletype machines in the lobby of the Cairo Sheraton. It's on the opposite bank of the Nile from Midan Tahrir. The news printouts are hung on a bulletin board next to the machines. The Nile Hilton also has wire service teletype machines.

Radio & TV

The most interesting development in Egypt is the arrival of satellite TV. Some of the hotels have it, even those towards the lower end, and it has revolutionised viewing possibilities. The local offering, apart from some good old movies, was and remains painful. One wonders what the effect of totally uncensored Western viewing in a wide array of languages is having on a population that until recently was used to pretty anodyne, and often plain awful, stuff. On the local channels there are daily English-language programmes.

This is also the case with radio. Check the *Egyptian Gazette* for the latest programme information. Normally, the news can be heard in English on FM95, radio frequency 557 kHz, at 7.30 am, 2.30 pm and 8 pm. This is the European-language station and in addition to English it has programmes in French, German, Italian, Spanish and Greek.

BBC and Voice of America (VOA) broadcasts can be picked up on medium wave at various times of the morning and evening.

The BBC can be heard on about 1320 kHz, and VOA on 1290 kHz. Radio Monte Carlo sometimes has English and French-language programmes in addition to its Arabic broadcasts – it can be picked up on medium wave bands in the evening.

TV news in English is usually shown at 8 pm and in French at 7 pm. Several American and British TV series appear on Egyptian TV. At the time of writing, *The Bold and The Beautiful* was *the* big hit in Egypt. Usually the programmes are shown with Arabic subtitles, but some are dubbed. Some great Hollywood classics appear on Channel 2 at around 11 pm. TV during Ramadan is throat-slitting, for most Westerners anyway.

FILM & PHOTOGRAPHY
Egypt is full of opportunities for great photography. Early morning and late afternoon are the best times to take photographs. During the rest of the day, the sunlight can be too bright and the sky too hazy and your photos will look washed out. There are a few remedies for this: a polarisation filter will cut glare and reflection off sand and water; a lens hood will cut some of the glare; Kodachrome film with an ASA of 64 or 25 and Fujichrome 50 and 100 are good slide films to use when the sun is bright.

Film
Colour print processing costs from E£1 to E£2 plus from 50 to 60 pt per print depending on film size. B&W processing is not recommended, but colour processing is usually adequate for nonprofessional purposes. Film generally costs as much as, if not more than, it does in the West, so you may as well bring it with you. If you do buy in Egypt, check the expiry dates. There are quite a few labs and one-hour processing places in the big cities and tourist centres.

At a new Kodak store in Cairo's Sharia Adly, Kodacolor Gold 100 (36 exposures) costs E£11.70, Kodacolor 200 (36 exposures) E£17.55, and Kodacolor 400 (24 exposures) E£12.45. For Kodachrome 100, 200 and 400 slide film, you'll pay E£21.70, E£25.20 and E£29.30 (all 36 exposures).

Symbol of the Sun

Developing a roll of slide film costs about E£12. Polaroid instant passport photos cost around E£9 for four.

Expatriates have recommended this place for developing colour prints and slides. Another place that has been recommended for developing film is Actina Photo Stores, at 4 Sharia Talaat Harb, near Midan Tahrir.

If you're having problems with your camera and desperately want to have it fixed, you could try Misr 2000, 6 Sharia Alfi – opposite the Alfi Bey Restaurant.

Photography
Cameras and lenses collect dust quickly in Egypt. Lens paper and cleaner are difficult to find, so bring your own. A dust brush is also useful.

Be careful when taking photos of anything other than tourist sites, the Nile, the Suez Canal and beaches. It is forbidden to photograph bridges, train stations, anything military, airports and other public works. Signs are usually posted. You can take photos of the interior of mosques, temples and a few tombs, although at an increasing number of sites the government now charges E£5 or E£10 for the privilege. The situation is worse if you want video film; a standard charge for the right to shoot video is E£150!

It can sometimes be tricky taking photos of people, so it's always better to ask first. Children will almost always say yes, but their parents or other adults might say no. Some Muslims believe that by taking photos of children you might be casting an 'evil eye' upon them. Similar attitudes sometimes apply to taking photos of women, especially in the countryside. Egyptians are also sensitive about the negative aspects of their country. It is not uncommon for someone to yell at you when you're trying to take photos of things like a crowded bus, a donkey cart full of garbage or a beggar – so exercise discretion.

HEALTH
Travel health depends on your predeparture preparations, your day-to-day health care while travelling and how you handle any medical problem or emergency that may develop. While the list of potential dangers can seem quite frightening, with a little luck, some basic precautions and adequate information, few travellers experience more than upset stomachs.

Don't forget that you should always see your doctor for medical advice before heading off for a trip overseas.

Travel Health Guides
There are a number of books on travel health: *Staying Healthy in Asia, Africa & Latin America*, Volunteers in Asia. Probably the best all-round guide to carry, as it's compact but very detailed and well organised.
Travellers' Health, Dr Richard Dawood, Oxford University Press. Comprehensive, easy to read, authoritative and also highly recommended, although it's rather large to lug around.
Travel with Children, Maureen Wheeler, Lonely Planet Publications. Includes basic advice on travel health for younger children.

Predeparture Preparations
Health Insurance Get some! You may never need it, but if you do you'll be very glad you got it. There are many different travel insurance policies which cover medical costs for illness or injury, the cost of getting home for medical treatment, life insurance and baggage insurance. Some protect you against cancellation penalties on advance purchase tickets should you have to change travel plans because of illness. Most travel and insurance agents should be able to recommend a policy, but check the fine print before you decide which one to take out.

Medical Kit It is always a good idea to travel with a small first-aid kit. Some of the items which should be included are: Band-aids, a sterilised gauze bandage, Elastoplast, cotton wool, a thermometer, tweezers, scissors, antibiotic cream or ointment, an antiseptic agent (Dettol or Betadine), burn cream (Caladryl is good for sunburn, minor burns and itchy bites), insect repellent and multivitamins.

Don't forget water sterilisation tablets or iodine, antimalarial tablets (if you feel the need for them), any medication you're already taking and contraceptives, if necessary.

Recommended traveller's medications include diarrhoea tablets, such as Lomotil (although some medical experts warn against it) or Imodium, paracetamol for pain and fever, and a course of antibiotics (check with your doctor). Erythromycin is recommended for respiratory, teeth and skin infections and is a safe alternative to penicillin. Metronidazole (Flagyl) is recommended for the treatment of amoebic dysentery and giardia. Again, check with your doctor before leaving home.

Most of these items, other than contraceptives, water sterilisation tablets and insect repellent, are readily available in Egyptian pharmacies at considerably lower prices than in the West.

General Precautions Make sure your teeth are in good shape before you leave home. If you have an emergency, however, there are English-speaking dentists in most of Egypt's cities and towns. In Cairo, consult your embassy.

If you wear eyeglasses, carry a second pair or at least a copy of your prescription in case of loss or breakage.

Public toilets are bad news: fly-infested, dirty and stinky. Some toilets are still of the squat-over-a-hole-in-a-little-room variety. Always carry a roll of toilet paper with you; it's easy to buy throughout Egypt.

Vaccinations
These should be obtained before you arrive in Egypt. However, if you have to get a vaccination in Egypt, buy a sterilised syringe at a pharmacy and go to the government

Public Health Unit, at the back of the lobby of the Continental Savoy Hotel in Midan Opera, Cairo.

The recommended vaccinations are cholera (there is some dispute about the worth of this one), typhoid, yellow fever (only needed if coming from an infected area) and tetanus. You might also consider gamma globulin for protection against infectious hepatitis if you plan to be in Egypt for more than two months. Check out the new hepatitis A vaccine, Havrix. It's not cheap, but if you travel a lot in dodgy places, three shots over a year give you 10 years' protection. You should check with your doctor for up-to-date details.

In London, there are several places where you can get advice and vaccinations. Trailfinders (see under Air in the Getting There & Away chapter) has an inoculation centre, as does British Airways at its Victoria Station office. The Travel Clinic of the Hospital for Tropical Diseases (☎ (071) 637-9899) at Queen's House, 180-182 Tottenham Court Rd, is open from 9 am to 5 pm for consultations and shots. You can also buy such health-related travel gear as mosquito nets and water filters. The clinic runs a recorded-info line on specific destinations (☎ (0839) 337733). The problem with all these is that some of the shots can be quite expensive. If you are resident in the UK and on the National Health Service, ask your GP what shots he or she can do for you – many will either be free or cost UK£3 to UK£4 for the prescription. Compared with, say, UK£25 for a shot of Havrix, the saving is obvious, although the process is a little more laborious.

If you are in Melbourne, Australia, the Travellers' Medical & Vaccination Centre (☎ (03) 650-7600) can help you.

A pre-exposure rabies vaccine is advised for people planning an extended stay or on working assignments.

Food & Water

Tap water in Egypt's cities is generally safe to drink. It is so heavily chlorinated that most microbes and other little beasties are annihilated. Unfortunately, the excessive chlorination can sometimes be hard on your stomach. If the tap water makes you feel sick it is possible to buy bottled water. Make sure that the bottles have been properly sealed before you pay for them, as there used to be a scam of refilling them with tap water.

In the countryside the water is not so safe. You should only drink tap water which has been boiled for at least 10 minutes. Simple filtering won't remove all dangerous organisms, so if you can't boil water it should be treated chemically. Chlorine tablets (Puritabs, Steritabs or other brand names) will kill many but not all pathogens. Iodine is very effective in purifying water and is available in tablet form (such as Potable Aqua), but follow the directions carefully and remember that too much iodine can be harmful.

If you can't find tablets, tincture of iodine (2%) or iodine crystals can be used. Two drops of tincture of iodine per litre of clear water is the recommended dosage; the water should then be left to stand for 30 minutes. Iodine crystals can also be used to purify water but this is a more complicated process, as first you have to prepare a saturated iodine solution. Iodine loses its effectiveness if exposed to air or damp, so keep it in a tightly sealed container. Flavoured powder will disguise the taste of treated water and is a good idea if you are travelling with children.

There are also a few common-sense precautions to take with food in Egypt. You should always wash and peel fruits and vegetables and avoid salads. Egyptians sometimes fertilise their fields with human excrement and this waste has a way of sticking to the produce. The food isn't always well washed before it reaches your plate. If you can't wash or peel it, don't eat it. On the other hand, many travellers have eaten salads regularly in Egypt with few ill effects. If you think that you are particularly susceptible to stomach troubles, then you should avoid salads.

Meat is safe as long as it has been thoroughly cooked. If you favour raw meat, keep in mind that conditions in Egypt can make the meat a nice and tasty home for worms. Your stomach and intestines are an even better habitat. Similar precautions should be taken with fish, which is more perishable than meat.

Avoid milk that hasn't at least been boiled; the same goes for cream. Milk in sealed cartons is usually imported and safe to drink because it has been pasteurised and homogenised. Most processed and packaged ice cream is safe.

Avoid anything raw, especially shellfish.

Contaminated food or water can cause dysentery, giardia, hepatitis A, cholera, polio and typhoid – all of which are best avoided! The UK Travel Clinic's advice in any case of doubt, and it is sound, is 'cook it, peel it or leave it'.

Medical Problems & Treatment
Common Ailments Almost every traveller who stays in Egypt for more than a week seems to be hit with Pharaoh's Revenge, more commonly known as diarrhoea. There is usually nothing you can do to prevent the onslaught; it is simply your system trying to adjust to a different environment. It can happen anywhere. There is no 'cure', but following certain regimens will eventually eliminate or suppress the problem. Avoid taking drugs if possible, as it is much better to let it run its course.

The regimen to follow is fairly basic: drink plenty of fluids but not milk, coffee, strong tea, soft drinks or cocoa. Avoid eating anything other than dried toast or, perhaps, fresh yogurt. Yoghurt is recommended by Egyptians, but it's not absolutely convincing as a remedy.

If you are travelling, it may be difficult to follow this path. That is when Lomotil, Imodium, codeine phosphate tablets, a liquid derivative of opium prescribed by a doctor, or a medicine with pectin (like kaopectate) can be useful. Lomotil is convenient because the pills are tiny, but it tends to clam your system up so that nothing, including the nasties causing the problem, can get out. If you are still ailing after all of this, then you might have dysentery. See a doctor.

Breathing can sometimes be troublesome in Egypt. I know that sounds odd because, of course, you have to breathe. However, the lack of humidity, the contrast of heat outside and air-conditioning indoors, and the abundance of dust can aggravate your eyes, nose and throat. Eyedrops and throat lozenges can be helpful, although you can survive without them while travelling through Egypt. During hot periods, try not go in and out of air-conditioned rooms too frequently or you'll catch a cold – which is particularly miserable when the weather is hot.

Dysentery This is, unfortunately, quite common among travellers. There are two types of dysentery, characterised by diarrhoea containing blood and lots of mucus. Seek medical assistance if you have these symptoms.

Bacillary dysentery, the most common variety, is short, sharp and nasty but rarely persistent. It hits suddenly and lays you out with fever, nausea, cramps and diarrhoea but, as it's caused by bacteria, it responds well to antibiotics.

Amoebic dysentery, which, as its name suggests, is caused by amoebic parasites, is much more difficult to treat, is often persistent and is more dangerous. It builds up more slowly, cannot be starved out and if untreated will get worse and permanently damage your intestines. Metronidazole (Flagyl) is the recommended drug for the treatment of amoebic dysentery; it should be taken under medical supervision only.

Hepatitis This is a liver disease caused by a virus. There are two types – infectious hepatitis (Type A) and serum hepatitis (Type B). Type A, the more common, can be caught from eating food, drinking water or using cutlery or crockery contaminated by an infected person. Type B can only be contracted by having sex with an infected person, by using the same syringe or having a contaminated blood transfusion. Symptoms appear 15 to 50 days after infection (generally around 25 days) and consist of fever, loss of appetite, nausea, depression, lack of energy and pains around the base of the ribcage. Your skin turns yellow, the whites of your eyes turn yellow to orange and your urine will be deep orange or brown. Do *not* take antibiotics.

There is no cure for hepatitis except complete rest and good food. You should be over the worst in about 10 days but continue to take it easy after that. A gamma globulin injection is said to provide protection against Type A for three to six months, but its effectiveness is still debatable. More certain is the new vaccine, Havrix. Two shots give protection for a year. A third shot within six months to a year takes it to 10 years.

Cholera This can be extremely dangerous, as it is very contagious and usually occurs in epidemics. The symptoms are: very bad but painless watery diarrhoea (commonly known as 'rice-water shits'), vomiting, quick shallow breathing, fast but faint heart beat, wrinkled skin, stomach cramps and severe dehydration.

Do not attempt to treat cholera yourself – see a doctor immediately. Cholera vaccinations are valid for six months and if you're revaccinated before the expiry date it is immediately valid. The vaccine doesn't give 100% protection but if you take the usual precautions about food and water as well you should be safe.

Polio This is another disease spread by unsanitary conditions and found more frequently in hot climates. There is an oral vaccine against polio – three doses of drops taken at four to eight week intervals. If you were vaccinated as a child you may only need a booster. Once again, take care with food and drink while travelling.

Typhoid Typhoid fever is a dangerous infection which starts in the gut and spreads to the whole body. It can be caught from contaminated food, water or milk and, as its name suggests, the main symptom is a high temperature. Another characteristic is rose-coloured spots on the chest and abdomen which may appear after about a week. Two

vaccinations, a month apart, provide protection against typhoid for three years. Seek medical assistance if you think you've been infected.

Malaria Malaria is spread by mosquitoes. The disease has a nasty habit of coming back in later years – and it can be fatal. You must start taking precautions before you travel. Although malaria is uncommon in Egypt, you should exercise caution in rural areas of the Nile Delta, the Al-Faiyum region, the Nile Valley and the Western Oases, particularly from June to October. Sleeping near a fan (mosquitoes hate fast-moving air) and using insect repellent are usually adequate; antimalarial protection has not always been regarded as essential.

The disease is common in the Sudan and becomes more so the further south you travel. Common symptoms are: headache, fever, chills and sweats.

According to the World Malaria Risk Chart published by the International Association for Medical Assistance to Travellers (IAMAT), malaria is 'present' in Egypt. You should consult your doctor about the latest recommended methods of prevention. Note that Fansidar is no longer recommended as a prophylactic.

The IAMAT chart also indicates that June to October is the period of highest risk for contracting malaria. However, the risk here is quite low compared to in the Sudan.

In the Sudan, malaria is present in both urban and rural areas all year. There are chloroquine-resistant mosquitoes that carry falciparum malaria – the most dangerous strain – so special precautions are essential. According to the IAMAT:

It is mandatory to remain in well-screened areas after sunset and to use mosquito bednets at night. Wear light-coloured clothing that covers most of your body. Do not use perfume or aftershave lotion. Use mosquito repellents (containing DEET) on your body and pyrethrin insecticides to spray the room at night.

This advice is also pertinent to travellers in Egypt: just avoid getting bitten, regardless of malaria risk. Mosquito coils are available throughout Egypt.

Yellow Fever A serious, often fatal, disease transmitted by the mosquito. It is caused by a virus that produces severe inflammation of the liver. Yellow fever is entirely preventable. It requires one injection, at least 10 days before departure, which is valid for 10 years.

Bilharzia Bilharzia, also called schistosomiasis, is prevalent in Egypt. The Nile and Nile Delta are infested with the bilharzia parasite and the microscopic snail which carries it; both prefer warm, stagnant pools of water. Do not drink, wash, swim, paddle or even stand in water that may be infested. The parasites – minute worms – enter humans by burrowing through the skin. They inhabit and breed in the blood vessels of the abdomen, pelvis and sometimes the lungs and liver. The disease is painful and causes persistent and cumulative damage by repeated deposits of eggs.

The main symptom is blood in the urine, and sometimes in the faeces. The victim may suffer weakness, loss of appetite, sweating at night and afternoon fevers. If you have contracted bilharzia, you will begin noticing these symptoms anywhere from one to four weeks after contact. Treatment is possible, so see a specialist in tropical medicine as quickly as possible.

Do *not* swim in the Nile! If you must, do it in the middle, where the risk of being infected is much lower than along the banks.

Rabies If you are bitten, scratched or even licked by a rabid animal and do not start treatment within a few days, you may die. Rabies affects the central nervous system and is certainly an unpleasant way to go. Typical signs of a rabid animal are: mad or uncontrolled behaviour, inability to eat, biting at anything and frothing at the mouth. If you are bitten by an animal, react as if it has rabies – there are no second chances. Get to a doctor and begin the course of injections that will prevent the disease from developing. Remember that a pre-exposure rabies vaccine is now available.

Meningococcal Meningitis Sub-Saharan Africa is considered the 'meningitis belt', but there are recurring epidemics in other places, including the Nile Valley. The disease is spread through close contact with people who carry it in their throats and noses, spread it through coughs and sneezes, and may not be aware that they are carriers.

This very serious disease attacks the brain and can be fatal. A scattered blotchy rash, fever, severe headache, sensitivity to light and neck stiffness that prevents forward bending of the head are the first symptoms. Death can occur within a few hours, so immediate treatment is vital.

Treatment is large doses of penicillin given intravenously or, if that is not possible, intramuscularly. Vaccination offers good protection for over a year, but you should also check for reports of current epidemics.

Tetanus Tetanus is a killer disease, but it can easily be prevented by immunisation. It is caught through cuts and breaks in the skin caused by rusty or dirty objects, animal bites or contaminated wounds. Even if you have been vaccinated, wash the wound thoroughly.

Sexually Transmitted Diseases Sexual contact with an infected person spreads these diseases. While abstinence is the only 100% preventative, use of a condom is also effective. Gonorrhoea and syphilis are the most common of these diseases, and sores, blisters or rashes around the genitals, discharges or pain when urinating are common symptoms. Symptoms may be less marked or not observed at all in women. The symptoms of syphilis eventually disappear completely but the disease continues and can cause severe problems in later years. Treatment of gonorrhoea and syphilis is by antibiotics.

There are numerous other sexually transmitted diseases, for most of which effective treatment is available. However, there is no cure for herpes and there is also currently no cure for AIDS. The latter is common amongst heterosexuals in parts of Africa. Using condoms is the most effective preventative.

AIDS can also be spread through infected blood transfusions (most developing countries cannot afford to screen blood for transfusions) or by dirty needles – vaccinations, acupuncture and tattooing can potentially be as dangerous as intravenous drug use if the equipment is not clean. If you do need an injection buy a new syringe, as suggested in the Vaccinations section.

Coping with the Heat

Protect yourself against the heat of the sun in Egypt and the Sudan. It is difficult, especially in Egypt, to gauge how quickly you are losing body water, because the climate is dry. Headaches, dizziness and nausea are signs that you have lost too much water and might have heat exhaustion. To prevent this, take a bit of extra salt with your food, drink plenty of fluids and wear a hat and sunglasses. The salt helps keep you from getting dehydrated. Incidentally, the caffeine in coffee and tea also contributes to dehydration.

Sun screen will prevent the sun from frying your skin. Wearing pants and long sleeves is cooler than shorts and short sleeves because your body moisture stays closer to your skin. Lastly, remember that when you're on the beach or in the water you will burn quite quickly, so wear a shirt while snorkelling or swimming.

Prickly Heat Prickly heat is an itchy rash caused by excessive perspiration trapped under the skin. It usually strikes people who have just arrived in a hot climate whose pores have not yet opened sufficiently to cope with greater sweating. Keeping cool and bathing often, using a mild talcum powder or even resorting to air-conditioning may help until you acclimatise.

Heat Exhaustion Dehydration or salt deficiency can cause heat exhaustion. Take time to acclimatise to high temperatures and make sure you get sufficient liquids. Salt deficiency is characterised by fatigue, lethargy, headaches, giddiness and muscle cramps and in this case salt tablets may help. Vomiting or diarrhoea can deplete your liquid and salt levels. Anhydrotic heat exhaustion, caused by an inability to sweat, is quite rare. Unlike the other forms of heat exhaustion, it is likely to strike people who have been in a hot climate for some time rather than newcomers. You will stay cooler by covering up with light, cotton clothes that trap perspiration against your skin than by wearing brief clothes.

Heat Stroke This serious, sometimes fatal, condition can occur if the body's heat-regulating mechanism breaks down and the body temperature rises to dangerous levels. Long, continuous periods of exposure to high temperatures can leave you vulnerable to heat stroke. You should avoid excessive alcohol or strenuous activity when you first arrive in a hot climate.

The symptoms are feeling unwell, little or no sweating and a high body temperature (39°C to 41°C). Where sweating has ceased, the skin becomes flushed and red. Severe, throbbing headaches and lack of coordination will also occur, and the sufferer may be confused or aggressive. Eventually the victim will become delirious or convulse. Hospitalisation is essential, but meanwhile get patients out of the sun, remove their clothing, cover them with a wet sheet or towel and fan continually.

Fungal Infections Hot weather fungal infections are most likely to occur on the scalp, between the toes or fingers (athlete's foot), in the groin (jock itch or crotch rot) and on the body (ringworm). You get ringworm (a fungal infection, not a worm) from infected animals or by walking on damp areas, like shower floors.

To prevent fungal infections wear loose, comfortable clothes, avoid artificial fibres, wash frequently and dry carefully. If you do get an infection, wash the infected area daily with a disinfectant or medicated soap and water, and rinse and dry well. Apply an antifungal powder like the widely available Tinaderm. Try to expose the infected area to air or sunlight as much as possible and wash all towels and underwear in hot water as well as changing them often.

Bugs, Bites & Cuts

Cuts of any kind can easily become infected, especially in the hot months, and should always be treated with an antiseptic solution. Walking on the coral along the Red Sea coast is to be discouraged – it does the coral no good at all, but if you must, wear shoes – coral cuts are notoriously slow to heal as the coral injects a weak venom into the wound.

Trekkers in desert areas should keep an eye out for scorpions, which often shelter in shoes and the like and pack a powerful sting. Snake bites are also a possibility. Wrap the bitten limb tightly, immobilise it with a splint and seek medical help. (If possible keep the dead snake for identification.) Tourniquets and sucking out the poison are now comprehensively discredited.

Bedbugs & Lice Bedbugs live in various places, but particularly in dirty mattresses and bedding. Spots of blood on bedclothes or on the wall around the bed can be read as a suggestion to find another hotel. Bedbugs leave itchy bites in neat rows. Calamine lotion may help.

All lice cause itching and discomfort. They make themselves at home in your hair (head lice), your clothing (body lice) or in your pubic hair (crabs). You catch lice through direct contact with infected people or by sharing combs, clothing and the like. Powder or shampoo treatment will kill the lice and infected clothing should then be washed in very hot water.

Women's Health

Gynaecological Problems Poor diet, lowered resistance due to the use of antibiotics for stomach upsets and even contraceptive pills can lead to vaginal infections when travelling in hot climates. Keeping the genital area clean, and wearing cotton underwear and skirts or loose-fitting trousers will help to prevent infections.

Yeast infections, characterised by a rash, itch and discharge, can be treated with a vinegar or even lemon juice douche or with yogurt. Nystatin suppositories are the usual medical prescription. Trichomonas is a more serious infection; symptoms are a discharge and a burning sensation when urinating. Male sexual partners must also be treated and if a vinegar douche is not effective medical attention should be sought. Flagyl is the prescribed drug.

Pregnancy Most miscarriages occur during the first three months of pregnancy, so this is the most risky time to travel. The last three months should also be spent within reasonable distance of good medical care, as quite serious problems can develop at this time. Pregnant women should avoid all unnecessary medication, but vaccinations and malarial prophylactics should still be taken where possible and if recommended by your doctor.

Doctors & Hospitals

There are hospitals throughout Egypt. Most of the doctors are well trained and often have to deal with a greater variety of diseases and ailments than their Western counterparts. On the other hand, most medical facilities are *not* well equipped and, consequently, it is not unusual for diagnoses to be inaccurate. If you need an operation, don't have it here. London or other European cities are only a few hours away by plane.

Before you leave for Egypt or the Sudan it is worthwhile writing to the International Association for Medical Assistance to Travellers, or IAMAT, for their worldwide directory of English-speaking doctors. Doctors who belong to this organisation charge fair and reasonable standard fees for their services. The fees are set by IAMAT. Their membership addresses are:

Canada
    40 Regal Rd, Guelph, Ontario N1K 1B5

New Zealand
    PO Box 5049, Christchurch 5
Switzerland
    57 Voirets, 1212 Grand-Lancy, Geneva
USA
    417 Center St, Lewiston, NY 14092

In Cairo there are IAMAT centres at the following locations:

Central Cairo
    13 Sharia Wakf al-Kharboutly (☎ 284-1375/6/8/9, 243-4653); coordinator Dr Nabil Ayad al-Masry
    11 Sharia Imad ad-Din (☎ 916424); coordinator Dr Samir B Bassily
Maadi
    87 Rd 9 (☎ 350-3105, 351-0230); coordinator Dr Sherif Doss
Heliopolis
    1 Midan Roxy (☎ 258-2729); coordinator Dr Amin Iskander Fakry

The British, Canadian and US embassies can also help you find a doctor.

WOMEN TRAVELLERS

Egyptians are conservative, especially about matters concerning sex and women; Egyptian women that is, not foreign women.

Most Egyptian women don't wear veils but they are still, for the most part, quite restricted in what they can do with their lives. They do not have the same degree of freedom, if any at all, that Western women enjoy. Egyptian men see this not as restraint and control, but as protection and security – many of the women seem to see it that way too. For many Egyptians, both men and women, the role of a woman is specifically defined: she is mother and matron of the household, and it is this which the men seek to protect – they don't want their wives to have to work. Ironically, in maintaining this position a woman actually works very hard. Even if she can afford domestic help and doesn't do any household work herself, her husband's view is still that she should not have to work for a wage. It is *his* role to provide for the family.

It is difficult for Westerners to make balanced judgements about a whole social structure they little understand. It certainly appears that any Egyptian women wanting to go beyond the family roles allotted to them are going to have a very hard time. On rare occasions outstanding and determined individuals – almost exclusively in the upper classes – succeed in carving out some such niche for themselves. The vast majority continue to be raised in and embrace the traditional roles. This is an important consideration – women take the division of roles as seriously as men. And the men are quick to assert that, within the family, women have far greater power than is at first apparent.

Premarital sex is a taboo subject, although, as in any society that disapproves of what is considered promiscuous activity, it happens. Nevertheless, it is still rather the exception than the rule – and that goes for men as well as women. The presence of foreign women presents, in the eyes of some Egyptian men, a chance to get around the local norms with greater ease. That this is even possible is heavily reinforced by distorted impressions gained from Western TV and, it has to be said, the behaviour of some foreign women in the country.

The belief that the Western woman is ready and willing to hop into bed with the nearest male has produced in some Egyptian men the belief that they are all candidates for immediate gratification by any Western woman who walks down the street. At the very least, pinching bottoms, brushing breasts or making lewd suggestions seem to be considered by some perfectly natural means of communication with the unknown foreign woman.

Which brings us to the subject of dress. Away from the Sinai beaches, Egyptians are, to a greater or lesser degree, quite conservative, especially about dress. The woman wearing short pants and a tight T-shirt is, in some people's eyes, confirmation of the worst views held of Western women. And don't think this goes for women alone. In places less used to tourists, the sight of a man in shorts and singlet is considered offensive. Count the number of Egyptian men in shorts.

Obviously, any potential harassment will

usually be directed at women. This, by all reports, can range from bottom-pinching to flashing and masturbating in front of the victim (this is rare). Serious physical harassment and rape are not significant threats in Egypt.

You can travel independently if you follow a few tips: avoid direct eye contact with an Egyptian man unless you know him well; try not to respond to an obnoxious comment from a man – act as if you didn't hear it; be careful in crowds where you are crammed between people, as it is not unusual for crude things to happen behind you; if you're in the countryside (off the beaten track) it's often a good idea to wear a scarf over your hair; and, most of all, be careful about behaving in a flirtatious or suggestive manner – it could create more problems than you ever imagined.

Generally, if you're alone or with other women, the amount of harassment you get will be directly related to how you dress: the more skin that is exposed, the more harassment you'll get. As hot as it gets in Egypt, you'll have fewer hassles if you don't dress for hot weather in the same way as you might back home. Unfortunately, although dressing conservatively should reduce the incidence of any such harassment, it by no means guarantees you'll be left alone.

An entire book could be written from the comments and stories of women travellers about their adventures and misadventures in Egypt. Most of the incidents are nonthreatening nuisances, in the same way a fly buzzing in your ear is a nuisance: you can swat him away and keep him at a distance, but he's always out there buzzing around.

Here are a few comments and tips from women travellers:

Wear a wedding band. Generally, Egyptian men seem to have more respect for a married woman (this seems not always to work; sometimes Egyptians assume you are not really married).

Expect to be asked out constantly to discos and offered to be shown around Cairo.

Be wary when guys at the pyramids want to take you riding. A guy'll ride really close to you and grab your horse, among other things. After the ride he apologises and asks, 'You want to stay at my house?'. When this happened to me I said 'No', and told him he was crazy. If you tell these guys that they are dirty old men, they will just laugh at you.

Egypt isn't the place for a full suntan.

The Egyptian man sees the Western woman as an exotic object usually associated with sex. He will try anything in order to be able to conduct a conversation or, better yet, have a drink or a meal with her. This leads to endless calls of 'Hello, I love you', 'You're beautiful', etc. On any stroll you may wish to take, if you decide to chat with an Egyptian man, expect many personal questions and perhaps offers of marriage...If you don't wish to be friendly with any of the many men who approach you on the street, ignore them and, if that doesn't work, be blunt and say 'I want to be alone'. This is usually enough to leave you in peace.

If you need help for any reason (directions, etc), ask a woman first. Egyptian women are very friendly and will not threaten or follow you. Lastly, do not be overly fastidious about Egyptian men. Many of them are very kind and sincerely interested in simply conversing with someone from another country.

From a woman traveller

Another recommendation for women travellers is to befriend an Egyptian girl. Apart from having someone totally nonthreatening to show you around, you will probably also learn much more about life in Egypt from her. Many speak at least some English from high school. Some travellers have, however, reported that this is easier said than done.

Lastly, if you need any more information and tips, refer to an article by Ludmilla Tüting titled 'The Woman Traveller', which has appeared in both *The Globetrotters Handbook* and *The Traveller's Handbook*. Another good source of information and tips, particularly the section on travel in Middle Eastern countries, is a British book entitled *The Guidebook for Women Travellers*.

See the Books section in this chapter for details of books which offer insights into Egyptian women's lives.

DANGERS & ANNOYANCES

Egypt is generally a safe place to be, although a growing wave of violence directed by Islamists at tourists and the authorities in what appears to be an attempt to overthrow the present regime has added a degree of uncertainty to travel.

This aside, the amount of violent crime of any kind is negligible compared with its incidence in many Western countries. That may be due to a heavy-handed Security regime or the nature of Egyptian society, or more probably a combination of both. This does not mean it does not exist at all, and common sense dictates you don't take anything for granted. In all, even taking the low risk of terrorist attack into account, Cairo is a much safer place to wander around at night than, say, New York.

Terrorism

What began as one or two isolated incidents in 1992 took on all the signs of a concerted campaign against tourism in early 1993 and then seemed to subside again as Islamists turned their attention to killing police. A bomb blast in early March in a central Cairo café often frequented by travellers brought home the risk to many with greater force than the several attacks on tour buses had until that point. Subsequent blasts at the Egyptian Museum and on the road to the pyramids rammed the message home further – violence that had been confined largely to Upper Egypt was now possible anywhere.

Although the bulk of the attacks has been directed against the Security forces (which have carried out repeated raids in areas as far apart as Aswan and the Cairo suburbs of Shubra and Imbaba), members of al-Gama'a al-Islamiyya have declared attacks on the tourist industry (and hence on tourists) to be a legitimate strategy in the fight to establish an Islamic state.

The authorities have embarked on a campaign to reassure the world as to how safe Egypt is, but the danger of being caught in the cross-fire, however statistically slight, should at least be borne in mind. Many people are going one step further and staying away in droves – tourism in 1992-1993 was at least 20% down.

Drugs

Marijuana and hashish are fairly freely available in certain places around Egypt where travellers gather – most notably Aswan and Dahab. Harder drugs are also in circulation at Dahab. Remember that the authorities take a dim view of drug use and do not feel overly indulgent towards anyone caught with the stuff – Westerners have been arrested in Dahab. Use common sense and try to be discreet. If you are not interested in smoking and are trying to organise yourself into a group for a felucca ride, say, from Aswan, it might be an idea to find out what the intentions of the other passengers are. If it makes you uneasy, it'll be a bit late once you're sailing. Penalties for smuggling and dealing include 25 years' jail or death by hanging.

Theft

Petty crime can be a problem. Pickpockets like money. In fact, some like it so much they are brave and deft enough to search your pockets while standing in front of you on a crowded bus – and you probably won't even realise what's happening until it's too late.

Be careful about carrying money and valuables in a day pack or handbag. Razor blades work wonders on bags when the dastardly perpetrator is standing behind you in a queue or on a crowded bus. Passengers on the bus from Midan Tahrir to the pyramids are a favourite target for these stealthy fingers. Money belts and pouches around your neck keep your money where it belongs. Another protective measure is to carry travellers' cheques; they can be replaced if stolen or lost.

Hawkers

In the bazaars you expect it, but the chitchat in the streets of central Cairo can be a real pain. Take a large dose of patience combined with firmness. Foreigners wandering around in ones and twos inevitably win 'instant' friends who often coincidentally have a papyrus 'factory' they'd like to show you.

Everyone works out their own strategy for reducing this to a minimum. Try to smile and just walk on by. Some people try mumbling words in what they hope will be a little-known language – but it's amazing how many languages these guys seem to latch on to, even if only in a limited way.

Women, as already mentioned, will have to be prepared to deal with possible harassment, ranging from declarations of love to lightning gropes. Not everyone encounters this sort of thing, but there is little point in pretending it doesn't happen.

The unfortunate thing about all this is that often people are just being genuinely friendly and curious. It can be hard to know what you are dealing with and inevitably some locals feel offended by the apparent brusqueness of their foreign guests. Keep an open mind and remember that Egyptians, like the bulk of Arabs, take hospitality to strangers seriously.

RESPONSIBLE TOURISM

As long as outsiders have been stumbling upon or searching for the wonders of Ancient Egypt, they have also been crawling all over them, chipping bits off them or leaving their own contributions engraved on them. It is forbidden to climb the pyramids at Giza, but people still do it, and local 'guides' will make 'exceptions' for people willing to pay a little baksheesh for such privileges. When visiting the monuments, consider how important it really is for you to climb to the top of a pyramid or take home a bit of stone belonging to a Pharaonic column. You wouldn't get away with anything like it at the Tower of London, so why here?

The natural wonders of the Red Sea parallel (many would even say surpass) the splendours of Egypt's pyramids, but again care is needed if the delicate world of coral reefs and fish is not to be permanently damaged. Divers and snorkellers should heed the requests of instructors *not* to touch or tread on coral. If you kill the coral, you'll eventually kill or chase off the fish too.

Rubbish: there's lots of it in Egypt, and tidy town awards do not feature here. Quite a deal more of the refuse – plastic mineral water bottles for instance – is actually recycled in many ways, so don't be too quick to point an accusing finger at the Egyptians. However, there is no doubt that inadequate waste disposal and little regard for the environmental issues that have become so popular in the West in the past 20 years produces some ugly sights. Try not to add to them. Possibly the worst thing to happen environmentally in Egypt lately is the discovery of the plastic cup. Coke stands are springing up all over the country and selling the drink in these wasteful containers. It's probably a losing battle, but why not stick to the cheaper bottled stuff? You have a drink and hand the bottle back – much cleaner.

WORK

More than 40,000 foreigners live and work in Egypt. That figure alone should give you some idea of the immense presence foreign companies have in the country. It is possible to find work with one of these companies if you are committed and motivated. Begin your research before you leave home. *Cairo: A Practical Guide*, published by The American University in Cairo Press, has lists of all foreign companies operating in Egypt. There's also a directory listing all foreign companies, subsidiaries and representatives in Egypt that's available in most hotel bookshops (eg the Nile Hilton). If you know some Arabic, you will definitely be in an advantageous position. Once you have an employer, securing a work permit through an Egyptian consulate or, in Egypt, from the Ministry of the Interior, should not be difficult.

In addition to working for foreign companies, there are also many opportunities for teaching English as a second language. The Institute of International Education (☎ (212) 883-8200) has information on teaching opportunities abroad. Contact them at 809 United Nations Plaza, New York, NY 10017.

The first preference should be the recognised schools. They pay better and are usually better equipped and have some interest in the progress of their students. The down side is that you will need a qualification. The RSA Teaching English as a Foreign Language (TEFL) Preparatory Certificate is the minimum requirement. If you have that and some experience, try the British Council (☎ 345-3281) at 192 Sharia el-Nil, the Center for Adult & Continuing Education (☎ 354-2964) at the American University in Cairo (AUC), or the International Language Institute (ILI) (☎ 346-3087) at 3 Sharia Mahmoud Azmy, Sahafayeen. (The ILI has another office (☎ 666704) on Sharia Mohammed Bayoumi, in Heliopolis.) They are always on the look-out for part-time teachers, with the RSA TEFL certificate the minimum qualification. Only UK citizens can get full-year contract packages at the British Council, but other nationals often work part time. A teacher with the RSA certificate and no experience could expect E£583 a month for six hours' work a week in mid-1993. This was expected to rise about 15% from late 1993. Most teachers generally work double or more. Pay at the other places is lower.

If you have no qualification or experience, you could try the International Living Language Institute (ILLI) (☎ 748355) at 34 Sharia Talaat Harb, which is often looking for teachers of English, French and German as second languages. You will work hard and not earn much, but it's better than nothing. Another one to try might be the British Language Institute (☎ 347-0481) at 54 Sharia al-Mahrousa in Sahafayeen.

Several schools in Cairo and Alexandria are listed in *Cairo Today*. Some of them are what the trade knows as 'cowboy outfits' – you work hard for little return and often with only minimal interest taken in the progress of students. Check with recognised institutions such as the AUC and British Council for advice.

The British Council and, above all, the ILI run RSA certificate and diploma courses throughout the year.

Another possible source of work for English speakers is in copy-editing or writing on one of the various English-language publications in Cairo. *Al-Ahram*, *Cairo Today* and *Places in Egypt* sometimes

have openings, or at least may be interested in freelance contributions. The pay is nothing terrific, and they are at pains to make clear that beginners need not apply.

If you look European and want to earn a few extra pounds in Egypt while you're travelling, you can appear in Egyptian TV commercials or even in films, as the local advertising agencies are always looking for Western faces. For what can sometimes boil down to a few minutes' work you can earn as much as E£50 – not bad at all.

Notices for cameo parts in commercials and TV soap operas are sometimes put on the bulletin board at the Oxford Pensione, and people have been known to be offered this kind of work by middlemen plying Sharia Talaat Harb. Beware of shysters.

ACTIVITIES
Diving
Many visitors to Egypt rarely have their heads above water. Small wonder, as some of the best scuba diving and snorkelling in the world is to be found along the Red Sea coast. It is a boom sector of the country's tourism industry.

The pick of the crop is with little doubt along the south coast of the Sinai peninsula, from the Straits of Tiran to Ras Mohammed, a marine nature reserve on the tip of the peninsula. A plethora of diving schools in Na'ama Bay and nearby Sharm el-Sheikh offer every possible kind of course, from PADI, NAUI and CMAS beginners' courses (around US$300) through to the most advanced levels. Also on offer are numerous packages for experienced divers, or you can do a lot on your own. Away from the expensive resort atmosphere, there are other possibilities further north, such as in Dahab. Or you can cross the Gulf of Suez and head down to Hurghada.

Studying at the American University

The American University in Cairo (AUC) is one of the premier universities in the Middle East. The campus, on Midan Tahrir, is in the heart of Cairo. The curriculum, and half the faculty of 160, are American and accredited in the USA. Four types of programme are offered.

The AUC offers both nondegree and summer-school programmes. The nondegree programmes are designed primarily for American university students who wish to take their third year of studies in Egypt. Any of the regular courses offered can be taken. Popular subjects include Arabic Language, Arab History & Culture, Egyptology, Middle East Studies and social science courses on the Arab world. Up to 15 unit hours can be taken per semester at the undergraduate level.

Summer programmes offer similar courses. The term lasts from mid-June to the end of July. Two three-unit courses can be taken and several well-guided field trips throughout Egypt are usually included.

The largest programmes at the AUC are for bachelor's and master's degrees; they offer more than 20 subjects ranging from Anthropology to Teaching English as a Foreign Language.

The AUC is also home to the Arabic Language Institute. This independent wing of the university offers intensive instruction in Arabic language at beginner, intermediate and advanced levels. There are courses on both colloquial Egyptian Arabic and Modern Standard Arabic (MSA). There have been some complaints from students in this programme because they wanted most of their course work in colloquial Egyptian Arabic, but found the programme emphasised classical written Arabic. (For information about MSA and colloquial Egyptian Arabic, see Language in Facts about the Country.)

Others simply found the course content uninspired. Apparently, you must specify what you want and insist on it. In 1993, the intensive courses cost US$300 a term (72 teaching hours), the nonintensive (36 hours) US$150 and a year-long certificate programme US$750.

Applications for programmes with the Arabic Language Institute and undergraduate and graduate studies at the university are separate. Specify which you want when requesting an application form. A current catalogue and programme information can be obtained from: The Office of Admissions, The American University in Cairo, 866 United Nations Plaza, New York, NY 10017-1889; or you can write to PO Box 2511 in Cairo (☎ 354-2964, extension 5011/12/13). Tuition in 1993 was US$7560 for the year, and US$1885 for the summer.

Egyptian Universities

It is also possible to study at Egyptian universities such as Al-Azhar, Alexandria, 'Ain Shams and Cairo. Courses offered to foreign students include Arabic Language, Islamic History, Islamic Religion and Egyptology. For information on courses, tuition fees and applications, contact: The Cultural Counsellor, The Egyptian Educational Bureau, 2200 Kalorama Rd NW, Washington DC 20008. In London, contact the Education and Cultural Office at the embassy (☎ (071) 491-7720).

Language Programmes

If the AUC programmes do not appeal, you might want to try the British Council (☎ 345-3281), at 192 Sharia el-Nil. It appears to be the most popular place to do a range of intensive and other courses in colloquial Egyptian Arabic and MSA, having inherited the mantle from the International Language Institute (ILI) (☎ 346-3087) at 3 Sharia Mahmoud Azmy, Sahafayeen, as favourite training ground for diplomats, journalists and others when a whole group of teachers moved from the ILI to the Council in the early 1990s. The ILI has another office

(☎ 666704) on Sharia Mohammed Bayoumi, in Heliopolis.

For details of other places to learn Arabic in Cairo, refer to the Activities entry in the Cairo Information section.

HIGHLIGHTS

Tourism is a major component of the Egyptian economy, and the country offers a rich variety of attractions, from Pharaonic ruins through the underwater wonders of the Red Sea to the wild beauty of blossoming oases surrounded by thousands of km of harsh desert.

The first thing to spring to mind when evoking images of Egypt are the **pyramids**. These extraordinary testimonies to the power and science of the ancient Egyptians are still without doubt one of the world's great attractions. But perhaps because they are such a familiar image, some people are touched by a slightly uneasy feeling of disappointment – the feeling of overpowering elation at finally seeing them does not always come and the hordes of tourists and hustlers don't help.

Perhaps any disappointment felt makes the discovery of Cairo's other, less universally known, wonders all the more satisfying. The tumbledown medieval labyrinth of so-called **Islamic Cairo** is for many the most powerfully evocative of places the foreigner encounters. Here the modern and the centuries-old melt together in a breathtaking way unknown in many other cities with histories approaching the length of Cairo's. Where medieval city centres of Europe have been carefully preserved and sanitised, here you get the feeling that, apart from the addition of cars, radios and electricity, little has changed over the centuries. Even the most touristy parts of the **Khan al-Khalili** are not completely bereft of this chaotic magic.

Of all the Pharaonic gifts to the present, the collection of sites from **Luxor** south to **Abu Simbel** is not to be missed. Bathed in the bright light of the winter sun (summer is oppressively hot), the temples of Luxor and in particular **Karnak** tower above their admirers. The west bank offers everything from the **Valley of the Kings** and other tombs to startling monuments such as the **Temple of Hatshepsut**. You could easily spend many days exploring all there is to be seen here. Abu Simbel is as impressive for the salvation work done to move it out of reach of the rising waters of **Lake Nasser** as for its own grandiose dimensions.

For those left cold by the big cities or monument-gazing, the seascape of the **Red Sea** may be the high point – there are numerous places along the coast, from Hurghada to the Sinai towns, from where the extraordinary beauty of the area's sea life can be enjoyed. Most divers seem to agree that the area around Sharm el-Sheikh and Ras Mohammed in the south of the Sinai peninsula offers the cream of the country's diving. Some just prefer the easy tranquillity of hanging around **Dahab**.

The **oases** present a unique escape from the madding crowds and frenetic tourism. There's not a helluva lot to do, but that can be the whole pleasure of being there in the first place. Despite its growing popularity, **Siwa** is probably still the pick of that crop.

ACCOMMODATION

Accommodation in Egypt ranges from cheap to expensive and rough to luxurious. There are hotels, pensions, youth hostels and a few camping grounds.

The majority of travellers seem to fly first to Cairo, arriving in the late evening or early morning. For most, the first Egyptians they meet on arrival at the new or old terminal in Cairo will be the infamous 'tourism officials', usually sporting an official-looking badge that says 'Egyptian Chamber of Tourism' or something similar, who will usher you through customs and gladly help you find a hotel room 'free of charge'. Many travellers think they are government officials because they approach them in the customs and passport control areas. Wrong!

After shunting you through officialdom, they will take arrivals in the old terminal to a row of shabby little travel-company offices on one side of the arrivals hall to arrange accommodation; arrivals at the new terminal are put into taxis and sent to a hotel.

These touts do offer what could be a useful service, especially during the high season – calling hotels for you to arrange rooms – but they are quite devious about it.

No matter which hotel you ask for, they usually say something like, 'No, that hotel is no good', 'I know they don't have rooms, I just called them for another foreigner', 'That hotel is very expensive', or 'It is impossible to get a room for that price'. They'll tell you prices have quadrupled and all sorts of other porkies.

When they finally do book a room for you, it will usually be at a hotel that isn't, as they claim, in or near central Cairo, but across the river in the neighbourhoods of Doqqi, Giza or Mohandiseen. In addition, the rate you are quoted may be higher than the hotel's usual rate because the tout's commission is included.

If you really wish to have them help you find a room, then insist on making the call yourself and offer to pay 25 to 50 pt for the call.

Camping

Officially, camping is allowed at only a few places around Egypt: in Cairo, at Giza near the pyramids; on the Mediterranean coast at Sidi Abdel Rahman; at Hurghada almost on the beach; and at Luxor and Aswan. Outside the plots specifically set aside for camping, almost all the land is either desert or cultivated fields. At the official sites facilities tend to be rudimentary.

Youth Hostels

Hostels are among the cheapest places to stay in Egypt, although you can find the odd hotel that outdoes them. There are 15 recognised by the International Youth Hostels Federation (IYHF), located in Cairo, Alexandria, Port Said, Aswan, Asyut, Damanhur, Marsa Matruh, Al-Faiyum, Ismailia, Hurghada, Luxor, Tanta, Sharm el-Sheikh, Sohag and Suez and they generally range in price from about E£3 to E£8. The one in Ismailia has beds as expensive as E£18 – it's virtually a hotel. Having an IYHF card is not absolutely necessary, as nonmembers are admitted. A card will save you about E£1 or E£2. The youth hostels tend to be noisy, crowded and a bit grimy. Reservations are not usually needed.

The Egyptian Youth Hostel Association office (☎ 758099) at 7 Sharia Dr Abdel Hamid (near Cinema Odeon), Cairo, can give you the latest information.

Hotels

At the five-star end of the price range are hotels representing most of the world's major chains: Hilton, Sheraton, Holiday Inn, Marriott, Jolie Ville and the Meridien. Prices at these hotels typically start at about US$100 per night, not including a series of taxes and service charge coming to about 20%. There are also a few privately owned Egyptian hotels in this range. Note that, although all five-star and many much cheaper hotels still quote prices in US$, it is usually no problem paying in E£.

In the next price range – four stars – there are mostly Egyptian hotels managed and owned by a government organisation, the Egyptian Hotels Company, or private groups of Egyptian and/or foreign investors. These hotels range upwards in price from about E£100 per night and add similar charges and taxes. Standards are still fairly high at this price.

Next come the three-star hotels. They are generally clean, comfortable and good for someone who wants most of the comforts of the fancier hotels but doesn't want to spend as much money. Rooms cost from E£50 to E£100 per night.

Taxes and service charges may be only two of the 'extras' that get added on to your final bill. Egyptian hotels are very keen on giving you breakfast but it's often 'compulsory' rather than included. Sometimes you are charged extra for the fridge and TV in your room as well. In this way you can take an ordinary double room, add E£4 each for two breakfasts, E£2 for the fridge you never used and E£2 for the TV you never turned on, whack 12% service on the whole lot and then 5% sales tax and possibly a government tax on top of that, and your E£30 room suddenly costs you E£50 a night.

The two, one and no-star hotels form the budget group. Often the ratings mean nothing at all, as a hotel without a star can be as good as a two-star hotel, only cheaper. You can spend as little as E£10 per night for a clean single room with hot water or E£40 plus for a dirty double room without a shower. Pensions are in this range and tend to be fairly good. Generally the prices quoted include any charges and quite often a meagre breakfast. A word on hot water (and remember, in the top half of the country this can be a consideration in winter). Most hotels will tell you they have it. The truth ranges from no, in fact, they don't have it, through a trickle of lukewarm water dripping antagonisingly over your shivering body to hot showers, but only at a certain time of day. Don't take assurances of steaming hot baths at face value. On the plus side, more and more hotels seem to be installing electric water heaters – something worth looking out for when viewing the bathroom – which seem to be a reasonable sign that there really is hot water.

You get what you pay for – and the great Egyptian budget bed is one of the delights found not always exclusively at the very bottom rung. A thin mattress and nice hard planks can be the perfect combination for acquiring a sizeable backache. Also, many bottom-end establishments seem to be economising on sheets, putting either one or sometimes even none between you and blankets that may never have been washed since they were acquired. A sleeping sheet is a good antidote.

A note on payment. Some hotels in the three-star range and upwards still quote prices in US$. Generally there is no problem paying in local currency, but some hotels still demand a bank receipt as proof of official exchange, an anachronism left over from the days of fixed exchange and a booming black market. If this is going to be a pain you can live without, ask first if the hotel you are looking at still requires such proof. Most hotels quoting prices in dollars will accept most credit cards, particularly Visa, MasterCard and American Express. Even many smaller places will accept credit cards.

Note Residents in Egypt are often entitled to something closer to the local rate for rooms in the bigger hotels. Yes, there is one rate for foreigners and another for locals. If you are a resident, make a point of asking about resident rates, as they entail a considerable saving.

FOOD

Egyptian food varies from exotic to mundane, and sampling the various types of Egyptian food should be part of the adventure of your visit. Be open-minded, don't look at the kitchens, and remember that you can have a uniquely great meal here for very little money.

Egyptian restaurants often include a 12% service charge at the bottom of the bill, but the money probably goes into the till rather than the waiter's pocket. If you want to tip the waiter you have to add the baksheesh afterwards.

Appetisers

Fuul and ta'amiyya are unofficially the national staples of Egypt. Fuul is fava beans, with a variety of things such as oil, lemon, salt, meat, eggs and onions added to spice it up. Ta'amiyya is a concoction of mashed chickpeas and spices fried into little balls, similar to felafel. A fuul and ta'amiyya sandwich on pita bread with a bit of tomato makes a tasty snack or light lunch.

It's also popular to substitute *tahina* for fuul in pita bread sandwiches. Another national staple, tahina is a delicious sesame spread spiced with oil, garlic and lemon. In addition to putting it on ta'amiyya, you can also order a plate of tahina to eat as a dip with pita bread. With a couple of sandwiches, pita bread, a plate of tahina and some fruit from the market, you have a decent meal for about 50 pt.

Hoummos and *baba ghanoug* are two other popular spreads which can be eaten in the same way as tahina. Hoummos is a chickpea spread which is especially tasty with a bit of oil and a few pinenuts on top. Baba ghanoug is a mix of mashed eggplant and tahina.

Sandwich stands also serve – you guessed it – the *sandweech*. However, they aren't quite sandwiches as you and I know them. Most Egyptian sandweeches are small rolls with an equally small piece of meat, cheese or *basturma*, a smoked meat which resembles pastrami. Nothing else. Add some mustard to perk it up. Other popular sandwiches include grilled, crumbed or fried *kibda* (liver) served with spicy green peppers and onions; *mokh*, or crumbed cows' brains; and tiny shrimp.

Shawarma is also good for sandwiches and is the Egyptian equivalent of the Greek *gyros* sandwich. Throughout Egypt you will see the shawarma spits with rotating legs of lamb. Hot strips of lamb are cut from the spit and placed in a pocket of pita with tomatoes to make a sandwich fit for pigging out on.

Another appetiser which you will often be served is *torshi*, which is a mixture of pickled vegetables such as radishes, carrots and cucumbers. They look somewhat strange and discoloured but taste great if they're pickled properly.

There are several other quick, cheap dishes available, such as the following. *Fiteer* is a cross between pizza and pastry and is served at a place called a *fatatri*. It's flat and flaky, and contains sweet things like raisins and powdered sugar, or something spicy like white cheese, ground meat or eggs.

One fiteer is almost filling enough to be an entire meal.

Shakshooka is a mixture of chopped meat and tomato sauce with an egg tossed on top. You must taste this; the combination is delicious. It's rather like a Spanish omelette with meat.

Makarone is a clump of macaroni baked into a cake with ground meat and tomato sauce inside and *pashamel* (white sauce or gravy). It is very filling and costs from 50 pt to E£1.

Mahshi are various vegetables such as vine leaves (in summer), cabbage (in winter), tomatoes, and white and black aubergines, usually stuffed with minced meat, rice, onions, parsley, green herbs and, sometimes, tomatoes.

Main Dishes

Kofta and *kebab* are two of the most popular dishes in Egypt. Kofta is ground meat peppered with spices, skewered and grilled over a fire just like shish kebab. Kebab is similar, but the meat isn't ground. Grilled tomatoes and onions are also served. Both dishes are ordered in Egyptian restaurants by weight.

Molokhiyya is also very popular and is one of the few truly Egyptian dishes. It's a green, slimy, delicious soup made by stewing a strange leafy vegetable, rice and garlic together in chicken or beef broth.

Firakh, or chicken, is something you'll probably be eating quite often. It is usually grilled or stewed and served with a vegetable. Takeaway spit-roasted chickens are available from many small restaurants for about E£3.50 to E£5 depending on the weight. They are easy to spot – just look for a case of brown spinning chickens.

Grilled *samak* (fish) is tasty. The best fish comes from the Mediterranean and south Sinai coasts. The restaurants along the Mediterranean serve their fish by the kg. You choose it yourself from a large ice tray near the kitchen and the price usually includes a salad, bread and dips like tahina and baba ghanoug. Remember, fish spoils quickly in the summer heat. Before ordering your fish, be sure that it's fresh. It shouldn't smell like

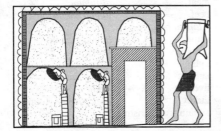

the inside of a locker room and shouldn't feel spongy.

Another grilled dish is *hamam*, or pigeon. Pronounce the word carefully because another 'm' makes the word *hammam*, which means bathroom. Hamam is served grilled on charcoal or sometimes stuffed with *freek* (wheat stuffing). It's also served as a stew cooked with onions, tomatoes and rice or freek in a deep clay pot known as a *tagen*.

Another popular dish is *kushari*, a combination of noodles, rice, black lentils, fried onions and tomato sauce. Each item is cooked separately and piled high in the windows of kushari joints, which are never street stands because the tomato sauce spoils quickly in the sun. A bowl of kushari is healthy and very filling and costs only about 50 to 75 pt. The fried onions are usually extra.

For those who find themselves on long train or bus rides, it is also essential to know about bread and cheese – the easily transportable staple of the traveller. Bread, including pita, is called *aysh*. In Egypt aysh also means 'life'. Egyptians say that life without aysh isn't life. Most of the aysh which you'll see and eat is *aysh baladi*, also called country bread or pita. The other main type is called *aysh fransawi*, or French bread (for obvious reasons).

There are also two main types of cheese: *gibna beyda*, or white cheese, which tastes like Greek feta; and *gibna rumi*, or Roman cheese, which is a hard, sharp, yellow-white cheese. Imported processed French cheeses such as Ki-Ri and La Vache qui Rit are also quite common.

Here are some more food words which could be helpful as you eat your way around Egypt:

Soup

soups	*shurba*
lentil soup	*shurbat 'ads*
chicken soup	*shurbat firakh*
tomato soup	*shurbat tamatim*

Fish & Shellfish

fish	*samak*
Nile perch (try it grilled)	*ishr bayad*
flatfish	*samak musa*
red mullet	*mourgan*
fried fish	*samak maklee*
crab	*kaboria*
prawns, shrimps	*gambari*
squid	*calamari*

Vegetables

aubergine	*badingan*
cabbage	*khroumbe*
carrots	*gazar*
cauliflower	*arnabeet*
green vegetables	*khudrawat, khudar*
green beans	*fasooliyya*
lentils	*'ads*
maize	*durra* (try it charcoal grilled from a sidewalk vendor)
okra	*baamiyya*
peas	*baseelah*
potatoes	*batatas*
turnips	*lift*
dry green wheat	*fareek*

Salad Items

salad	*salata*
cucumber	*khiyaar*
garlic	*tum*
lettuce	*khass*
onion	*bassal*
green winter pepper	*sabanekh* (great source of iron)
hot pepper	*shattah*
sweet pepper	*filfil*
tomato	*tamatim, uta*

Meat & Poultry

meat	*al-luhum*
beef	*lahma kanduz, lahma ba'aree*
camel	*lahma gamali*
chicken	*firakh*
kidney	*kalawi*
lamb	*lahma danee*
liver	*kibda*
turkey	*deek roumee* (found mainly at Christmas)
veal	*lahma beetalu*

Desserts

cornflour pudding	*mahalabiyya*
ice cream	*ays krim*
semolina cake	*basboosah*
Turkish delight	*malban*
milk dish with nuts, raisins & wheat	*bilaylah*
flaky pastry & nuts in honey	*baqlawah*
shredded wheat, pastry with nuts	*atayf*
pastries dipped in rosewater	*zalabiyyah, lomet al-addee*
cornflour pudding with nuts & cream	*om ali*
stringy pastry with honey & nuts	*kounafa*
baked rice & milk pudding	*ruz bi laban*
flaky pastry with nuts & honey or cheese	*ghoulash*

Fruit

fruit	*fawakah, fak-ha*
apricots	*meesh-meesh*
apples	*tooffah*
bananas	*mohz*
dates	*balah*
figs	*teen*
grapes	*einab*
guavas	*guafa*
limes	*limuun*
mangoes	*manga*
oranges	*burtuaan*
peaches	*khukh*
pears	*kumitrah*
pomegranates	*rumman*
strawberries	*farawleh*
tangerines	*yusuf affandi*
watermelons	*batteekh*

Miscellaneous Items

bread	*aysh, khubz*
pita bread	*aysh baladi*
butter	*zibda*
cheese	*gibna*
cream	*ishta*

eggs	*bayd*
jam	*murabbah*
honey	*asal*
milk	*laban*
mint	*nana*
salt	*malh* (pronounced almost as 'malha')
sugar	*sukkar*
yoghurt	*zabadi*
water	*mayya*
watermelon seeds	*lib* (roasted, a national passion)

DRINKS
Tea & Coffee

Shay and *ahwa* – tea and coffee – head the list of things to drink in Egypt. Both are usually made strong enough to be major contenders for the title of most caffeinated drink in the world.

Tea is served in glasses at traditional Egyptian cafés and in teacups at Western-style restaurants. At cafés, the tea leaves are boiled with the water. Unless you enjoy chomping on tea leaves, wait until they settle back down to the bottom. Tea bags are appearing in the Western-style places.

If you don't specify how much sugar you want, two or three big teaspoons of sugar will be automatically plopped into your glass. If you only want a bit of sugar in your tea, ask for *shay ma'a shwayya sukkar*. If you don't want any sugar at all ask for *shay min gheer sukkar*. Egyptians are always amazed that Westerners don't like as much sugar as they do. Try *shay bi-nana* (mint tea) or *shay bi-laban* (tea with milk).

If you ask for coffee, you will probably get *ahwa turki* (Turkish coffee), which is served throughout the Middle East. It bears a strong resemblance to mud and it's quite a surprise to find your spoon doesn't actually stand up in it. Don't be deceived by the size of the tiny porcelain cups; this coffee is *very* strong. Let the grains settle before drinking it, in small sips. As with tea, you have to specify how much sugar you want if you don't want to suffer an overdose. *Ahwa ziyadda* is for those who seek the ultimate sugar and caffeine high – it is extra sweet. *Ahwa mazboota* comes with a moderate amount of sugar but still fairly sweet and *ahwa saada* is without sugar. Egyptians drink the latter when a relative or close friend has died.

Western-style instant coffee is called Nescafe. It comes in a small packet with a cup of hot water.

Another popular hot drink is *hoummos ash-shem*, which is made from boiled chickpeas, tomato sauce, lemon and cumin.

Fruit Juices

On practically every street corner in every town throughout Egypt there is a juice stand, where you can get a drink squeezed out of just about any fruit or vegetable you want. Standard *asiir*, or juices, include:

banana	*mohz*
guava	*guafa*
hibiscus	*karkaday*
lime	*limuun*
mango	*manga*
orange	*burtuaan*
pomegranate	*rumman*
strawberry	*farawleh*
sugar cane	*asiir asab*
tamarind seed	*tamr hindi*
tangerine	*yusuf affandi*

Other Nonalcoholic Drinks

Soft drinks are extremely popular in Egypt and most major brands are sold here, including Coca-Cola, Sport Cola, Seven-Up, Fanta, Schweppes and Pepsi. Schweppes drinks come in various fruit flavours such as orange, lemon, mandarin and apple. If you drink at the soda vendor's stand, you won't have to pay a deposit on the bottle. Soft drinks are cheap – only 25 to 35 pt – but it's not unusual to pay as much as E£1 in hotels and at tourist sites. The short squat bottles cost about 50 pt each and don't have to be returned. Cans of drink can cost as much as E£1 each, though, because the can isn't re-usable. Diet soft drinks are becoming quite popular in Egypt, especially Diet Coke, Pepsi and Seven-Up. Remember that when it's hot, a soft drink will not quench your thirst. In fact, if anything, the sugar in it will make you more thirsty.

Sahleb is a sweet, milky drink made from rice flour, grapes, coconut and various nuts, including hazelnuts and pistachios. Cheap juice stands sell a simpler version.

A few other *mashrubat*, or drinks, which you might encounter are:

carob	*carob*
cocoa	*kakaw*
aniseed	*yansun*
licorice	*arasus*
caraway seed	*karawiyya*

Tap water is generally safe to drink throughout Egypt. However, some travellers prefer to begin drinking it gradually rather than immediately. See the Health section in this chapter for more details.

Alcohol

Egypt also has several indigenous alcoholic beverages. The beer, which to most palates is a little on the watery side, is called Stella, and is served in huge one-litre bottles, costing E£3 to E£4. There is also Stella Export, which comes in smaller bottles, has double the alcohol content of regular Stella and also costs more, at E£5.50 in liquor stores and anywhere up to E£15 in restaurants and hotels. Few things (available) can beat a cold bottle of Stella on a hot day. Be wary of expiry dates, however. In spring and autumn, a dark beer, a bit like stout, sometimes makes an appearance. They have given it the German name Märzen Bier. It seems a

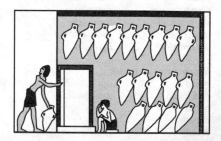

bit of a rarity, but anyone who likes beer who has tried it has sung its praises – at least it's different.

A nonalcoholic beer called Birelli (or Bireel) is also available, but it seems to be little more than a concoction of hops and soda water. It's often used as a prescribed remedy for people with kidney stones.

Try the Egyptian wines too. One of the best medium-dry white wines is called Gianaclis Village; it comes from a village of the same name in the Nile Delta. A good dry white wine is Patalomai. A sweeter wine is Reine Cléopatra. There's only one type of rosé wine – Rubis d'Egypte – and it's pretty awful. For red wines, the best dry one is Omar Khayyam, the best medium-dry is Gianaclis Château, and the sweetest is Nefertiti. They don't exactly compare with Western wines, but they aren't too bad. Most come from the Gianaclis vineyards in the Delta.

There is also an odd-tasting sweet liqueur, Abu Simbel, which contains iron – recommended by some as an agent against anaemia!

For hard liquor, you can get quite expensive Western brands in the major hotels and some nightclubs, but the Egyptians, apart from creating their own series of drinks with labels that look almost like the real McCoy (Black Jonny for instance!) to fool whomever will be fooled, also do a few honest, if not high-class, drops. A couple of brandies are available, including Vat 20 and its stronger relative Vat 84. There is also an Egyptian version of *araq* or *raqi* (the Greek version is ouzo) called *zibiba*. You can get it in the small liquor stores and some supermarkets like Sunnys. Most drinks are cheaper if you buy them in the liquor stores. Stella is about E£3.50 and you get a deposit back on returning the bottle.

ENTERTAINMENT
Cinemas
It is quite possible to catch a good and recent mainstream movie in either Cairo or Alexandria. Cinemas fall roughly into two categories – those showing the kind of movies you might want to catch at home and others showing either local product or the Terminator-Bruce Lee genre that seems to appeal a lot to male audiences in the Arab world. Those in the latter category generally cost less – from E£2 to E£3 depending on where the seats are. The others are screened in a handful of cinemas and usually subtitled, not dubbed, in Arabic. A seat costs E£5 in the stalls or E£7.50 in the balcony. Going to the local cinemas can be a cultural experience in itself – the chattering audience and sweets vendors sometimes combine to make so much noise you can hardly hear the film. This is generally not the case at the more expensive movie houses.

Discos, Nightclubs & Bars
Most of the discos of the Western variety are in the middle to top-range hotels, although a lot of them may not appeal much as there can be rather a lot more picking up going on than simply dancing and having a good time. Nightclubs of this variety are often pretty disappointing and tacky.

In Cairo and a few other tourist centres it is possible to see belly dancing. You can do this the expensive way and go to a hotel floorshow or, say, one of the places on Pyramids Rd, or you can hunt around for one of the local establishments, which is a more authentic if not so glittering experience. There is also an assortment of bars around. See the Cairo Entertainment section for more details.

THINGS TO BUY
Egypt is a budget souvenir and kitsch-shopper's paradise. Hieroglyphic drawings of Pharaohs, queens, gods and goddesses embellish and blemish everything from ashtrays to engraved brass tables. Jewellery, leather, woodwork, basketry, copperware, brassware, ceramics and alabaster and, of course, the ubiquitous papyrus are just some of the possibilities. Although markets abound all over the country, there is no doubt that the greatest range is to be found in Cairo, especially in the medieval labyrinth of Islamic Cairo. The Khan al-Khalili is the

heart of the shopper's paradise, but often the source of the greatest rip-offs.

Benetton and the trendy Paris chain Naf Naf have got stores in Cairo, Alexandria and a few other spots, and some travellers have described going on spending sprees to pick up items they could never afford at home. The products are locally made to the stores' European designs and specifications.

Jewellery

Gold and silver jewellery can also be made to specification for not much more than the cost of the metal. A cartouche with the name of a friend or relative spelled in hieroglyphics makes a great gift.

Although gold shops are concentrated in the centre of the Khan al-Khalili, gold can be bought all over Islamic Cairo. It is generally sold by weight. Buying gold and jewellery is always a little fraught. The Assay Office in Birmingham, UK, says that hallmarking for

gold of at least 12 carats and silver of 600 parts per thousand or more is compulsory in Egypt – verifying this is another matter. The hallmark contains a standard mark showing where a piece was assayed and a date mark in Arabic. In the end, however, the office can only recommend that customers 'buy things they like, but only if the price is such that it won't worry them if their purchases turn out to contain less gold or silver than they thought'. Foreign goods cannot be resold, in the UK at least, unless they are first assayed there. Storekeepers have an irritating habit of weighing the gold out of sight. Insist that they put the scales on the counter and let you see what's happening. This doesn't eliminate the chances of cheating, but does reduce them. Another precaution may be to check the day's gold prices in the *Egyptian Gazette*.

Much the same cautionary rules apply to silver and other jewellery. An endless assortment of rings, bracelets, necklaces and the like can be found all over Islamic Cairo. Hunt around, and beware of the 'antiques' made to look so. A lot of attractive stuff can be had for very little.

Papyrus

You can pick up cheap bits of poor quality papyrus all over Egypt for virtually nothing (a distressing number of well-heeled visitors part with ridiculous sums of money for garbage). Look long and hard at what you are getting. Good papyrus will not be damaged by rolling and the quality of designs varies from the sloppy machine print to masterful hand painting. The name Dr Ragab has long been associated with papyrus, and he has 'institutes' and shops all over the country. His stuff is expensive however. One alternative is Said's Delta Papyrus Centre, in Islamic Cairo. See the appropriate entry in the Islamic Cairo part of the Cairo chapter.

Cotton Goods

Since cotton is one of Egypt's major crops it is no surprise that cotton clothing is very popular. Cotton shirts, pants and *galabiyyas* (the loose gowns worn by many Egyptians) can be made to your specifications. Many

The best thing about souvenir hunting in Egypt is not the souvenirs. They are secondary to the excitement of the expedition up and down the back alleyways of the bazaars, past pungent barrels of basil and garlic and through medieval caravanserais. Take your sense of humour and curiosity with you, and if you want to buy something, be prepared to bargain for it; it is expected.

Everyone seems to have a different bargaining strategy. Don't show too much interest in the thing that you want to buy. Start the bargaining with a price much lower than you are really prepared to pay and then barter up to that point. When you state your first price the shopkeeper will inevitably huff about how absurd that is and then tell you his 'lowest' price. If it is still not low enough, be insistent and keep smiling. Tea might be served as part of the bargaining ritual; accepting it doesn't place you under obligation to buy. If you still can't get your price, just walk away. There are hundreds of shops in the bazaars. ∎

Cairene tailors can work from photographs of the clothing. The area between Al-Azhar and Bab Zuweila in Cairo is teeming with shops selling ready and tailor-made galabiyyas. You can also try at the village of Kerdassa, near the pyramids. T-shirts abound all over the country.

A lot of travellers have found it extremely cheap to have suits and other clothes tailor-made in Egypt. Although the prices can be ridiculously low by Western standards, the risk remains that the items will simply fall off your back.

In and beyond the covered bazaar south of Bab Zuweila in Islamic Cairo you can pick up some beautiful cotton wall hangings, cushion covers and similar items. Some of the more intricate Islamic designs on big items take a week's work or more and can cost as much as E£1000. Mostly the work and prices are far more moderate (a typical cushion cover will go for E£15 to E£20), and fierce bargaining remains the first rule. You can also buy the printed appliqué material so often used to decorate booths and stands for major festivals, and especially during Ramadan. The masters' work seems to be concentrated at the southern end of this part of the market. Look closely at the stitching.

In Dahab, in Sinai, cotton trousers and printed shirts are quite popular. A pair of light, simple trousers will cost around E£8. The Bedouins also make up traditional clothing for sale. Canvas bags are also cheap and popular, usually around E£5 depending on size and quality.

Fezzes
There are only two fez shops left in Cairo, just south of Al-Azhar on Sharia Muizz li-Din Allah. Introduced by the Turks and once worn as a sign of having made it in society, hardly anybody wears the red *tarboosh* any more. Bargaining may get you one for E£5.

Tapestries & Carpets
As with a lot of items, you can find carpets and rugs all over the place, but if you have time and happen to be in the pyramids area, it would be an idea to visit some of the carpet and tapestry schools along the Saqqara Rd.

Leather
Leather is another popular buy. Generally you will be offered items in the soft leather of gazelle hide. The material is generally not bad, and sometimes very good, but watch out for the workmanship, which can be anything from flawed to nonexistent. Although it does not apply to everything, it is not unheard of to find your new leather jacket falling to pieces. You can get every conceivable kind of leather bag, clothing and wallets.

Copperware & Brassware
Plates, coffee pots and a variety of other objects make nice gifts, and are often fairly cheap, going for as little as a few pounds for something small and basic. Engraved trays and plates start at around E£15, depending on their intricacy and age. Watch for the quality of any engraving work and don't set too much store by claims that the object in your hand is a hundred years old – more often

than not it rolled off the production line a couple of weeks ago.

Basketware
Especially good in Al-Faiyum, basketware is a cheap but awkward souvenir. Many of the baskets are nicely decorated and often sturdy and well made. For some reason, a bunch of polyglot young girls hangs around the Tell al-Amarna site in Upper Egypt trying to flog this kind of thing to tourists as soon as they get off the Nile ferry bringing them from the other side of the river! You can pick up a big basket for as little as E£5.

Inlay & Woodwork
Along with papyrus, inlaid backgammon boards and jewellery boxes are a popular buy. So long as you don't believe the stories about them all being done with mother-of-pearl, they make an attractive and typically Egyptian souvenir.

Spices
Every conceivable herb and spice, and many you will never have heard of or seen, can be bought in most markets throughout the country. Generally they are fresher and better quality than any of the packaged stuff you'll find in the West, and four to five times cheaper. How much cheaper will depend on your bargaining. Try not to think the first offer you're made sounds terrific by standards at home, and push the price down.

Things to Avoid
Unfortunately, ivory is also sold in Egypt's souvenir shops. Most of the ivory comes from the Sudan and Kenya, where the elephant populations are being decimated to meet tourists' demands for ivory jewellery, trinkets and bookends. Perhaps, if people stop buying ivory, the elephant slaughter will also end. The slaughter prompted former US President George Bush to initiate a ban on all ivory imports to the USA and to call for similar bans in other countries. Ivory brought into Australia without a permit from Australian National Parks & Wildlife *and* the country of origin will be detained by customs.

Getting There & Away

However you're travelling, it's worth taking out travel insurance. Work out what you need. You may not want to insure that grotty old army surplus backpack – but everyone should be covered for the worst possible case: an accident, for example, that will require hospital treatment and a flight home. It's a good idea to make a copy of your policy, in case the original is lost. If you are planning to travel for a long time, the insurance may seem expensive – but if you can't afford it, you certainly won't be able to afford to deal with a medical emergency overseas. Check out the details. In most cases you need to pay extra to cover you for 'dangerous sports' such as diving. Also, you often need to pay a surcharge for expensive camera equipment and the like.

If you're heading to Egypt or the Sudan from Europe, you have the choice of either flying direct or going overland to one of the Mediterranean ports and taking a ferry to North Africa. If you're coming from any other continent, it can sometimes be cheaper to fly first to Europe, and then make your way to Egypt, than to fly direct. There are also the overland combinations of bus, taxi and ferry from other countries in Africa, and from Jordan, Kuwait, Saudi Arabia, Israel and Libya.

Whichever route you take there is always the inescapable search for the cheapest ticket and the certainty that no matter how great a deal you find, there's always someone out there with a better one.

AIR

Travellers thinking of booking flights from Cairo should note that some airlines and travel agents still demand to see bank receipts proving you exchanged money in the bank. This is not really a big problem, as there is no black market anyway. It can be a hassle if you need the receipts to get a visa extension, but there are ways around this (for details of which see Facts for the Visitor).

To/From the USA & Canada

The *New York Times*, the *LA Times*, the *Chicago Tribune* and the *San Francisco Examiner* produce weekly travel sections in which you'll find any number of travel agents' ads. Council Travel and STA Travel have offices in major cities nationwide.

The magazine *Travel Unlimited* (PO Box 1058, Allston, Mass 02134) publishes details of cheap air fares.

In Canada, Travel CUTS has offices in all major cities. The Toronto *Globe & Mail* and the *Vancouver Sun* carry travel agents' ads. The magazine *Great Expeditions* (PO Box 8000-411, Abbotsford BC V2S 6H1) is useful.

The cheapest way from the USA or Canada to the Middle East and Africa is usually a return flight to London and a bucket-shop deal from there.

A Round-the-World (RTW) ticket including a stopover in Cairo is a possibility. Check the travel sections of Sunday newspapers for the latest deals.

EgyptAir flies from New York and Los Angeles to Cairo. Advance purchase and youth fares are available. The cheapest advance purchase tickets are for a maximum stay of one month. You must stay in Egypt a minimum of six days and a maximum of two months. The youth fare is valid all year, but you must be between 12 and 26 years old and book at least 72 hours in advance. The advance purchase fares from New York and Los Angeles are US$1270 and US$1634 respectively. EgyptAir has no connections to Canada.

Lufthansa has connections to Cairo via Frankfurt from 12 cities in the USA, including Anchorage, Chicago, Los Angeles, New York, San Francisco and Seattle. Advance purchase and youth fares are available. From Los Angeles, the cheapest return fare is US$1634, and entails a minimum stay of seven days and a maximum of two months. The cheapest one-way ticket from Los

Air Travel Glossary

Apex Apex, or 'advance purchase excursion', is a discounted ticket which must be paid for in advance. There are penalties if you wish to change it.

Baggage Allowance This will be written on your ticket: usually one 20 kg item to go in the hold, plus one item of hand luggage.

Bucket Shop An unbonded travel agency specialising in discounted airline tickets.

Budget Fare These can be booked at least three weeks in advance but the actual travel date is not confirmed until seven days prior to travel.

Bumped Just because you have a confirmed seat doesn't mean you're going to get on the plane – see Overbooking.

Cancellation Penalties If you have to cancel or change an Apex ticket there are often heavy penalties involved; insurance can sometimes be taken out against these penalties. Some airlines impose penalties on regular tickets as well, particularly against 'no show' passengers.

Check In Airlines ask you to check in a certain time ahead of the flight departure (usually one to two hours on international flights). If you fail to check in on time and the flight is overbooked, the airline can cancel your booking and give your seat to somebody else.

Confirmation Having a ticket written out with the flight and date you want doesn't mean you have a seat until the agent has checked with the airline that your status is 'OK' or confirmed. Meanwhile you could just be 'on request'.

Discounted Tickets There are two types of discounted fares – officially discounted (see Promotional Fares) and unofficially discounted. The cheapest fares often have drawbacks, like flying with unpopular airlines, inconvenient schedules, or unpleasant routes and connections. A discounted ticket can save you things other than money – you may be able to pay Apex prices without the associated Apex advance booking and other requirements. Discounted tickets only exist where there is fierce competition.

Full Fares Airlines traditionally offer 1st-class (coded F), business-class (coded J) and economy-class (coded Y) tickets. These days there are so many promotional and discounted fares available from the regular economy class that few passengers pay full economy fare.

ITX An 'independent inclusive tour excursion' (ITX) is often available on tickets to popular holiday destinations. Officially it's a package deal combined with hotel accommodation, but many agents will sell you one of these for the flight only. They'll give you phoney hotel vouchers in the unlikely event that you're challenged at the airport.

Lost Tickets If you lose your airline ticket an airline will usually treat it like a travellers' cheque and, after inquiries, issue you with another one. Legally, however, an airline is entitled to treat it like cash, so that if you lose it, it's gone forever. Take good care of your tickets.

MCO A 'miscellaneous charge order' (MCO) is a voucher that looks like an airline ticket but carries no destination or date. It is exchangeable with any IATA airline for a ticket on a specific flight. Its principal use for travellers is as an alternative to an onward ticket in those countries that demand one, and it's more flexible than an ordinary ticket if you're not sure of your route.

No Shows 'No shows' are passengers who fail to show up for their flight, sometimes due to unexpected delays or disasters, sometimes due to simply forgetting, sometimes because they made more than one booking and didn't bother to cancel the one they didn't want. Full-fare passengers who fail to turn up are sometimes entitled to travel on a later flight. The rest of us are penalised (see Cancellation Penalties).

On Request An unconfirmed booking for a flight – see Confirmation.

Angeles is US$1452. From New York, the same two tickets are US$1270 and US$1088 respectively.

To/From the UK

London is one of the best centres in the world for discounted air tickets. The price of RTW tickets, especially, is about the best available anywhere and tickets can be had for well under UK£1000, although Cairo is not a very common stop on such a ticket and may lift the price considerably.

For the latest fares, check out the travel page advertisements of the Sunday newspapers, *Time Out*, the *News & Travel Magazine (TNT)*, *City Limits* and *Exchange & Mart*. All are available from most London newsstands. A good source of information on

Open Jaws A return ticket where you fly out to one place but return from another. If available, this can save you backtracking to your arrival point.

Overbooking Airlines hate to fly empty seats and since every flight has some passengers who fail to show up (see No Shows), airlines often book more passengers than they have seats. Usually the excess passengers balance those who fail to show up but occasionally somebody gets bumped. If this happens, guess who it is most likely to be? The passengers who check in late.

Point-to-Point This is a discount ticket that can be bought on some routes in return for passengers waiving their rights to stop over.

Promotional Fares These are officially discounted fares like Apex fares, available from travel agents or direct from the airline.

Reconfirmation At least 72 hours prior to departure time of an onward or return flight, you must contact the airline and 'reconfirm' that you intend to be on the flight. If you don't do this the airline can delete your name from the passenger list and you could lose your seat. You don't have to reconfirm the first flight on your itinerary or if your stopover is less than 72 hours. It doesn't hurt to reconfirm more than once.

Restrictions Discounted tickets often have various restrictions on them – advance purchase is the most usual one (see Apex). Others are restrictions on the minimum and maximum period you must be away, such as a minimum of 14 days or a maximum of one year. See Cancellation Penalties.

Round-the-World An RTW ticket is just that. You have a limited period in which to circumnavigate the globe and you can go anywhere the carrying airlines go, as long as you don't backtrack. These tickets are usually valid for one year, the number of stopovers or total number of separate flights is worked out before you set off and they often don't cost much more than a basic return flight.

Standby This is a discounted ticket where you only fly if there is a seat free at the last moment. Standby fares are usually only available on domestic routes.

Tickets Out An entry requirement for many countries is that you have an onward or return ticket – in other words, a ticket out of the country. If you're not sure what you intend to do next, the easiest solution is to buy the cheapest onward ticket to a neighbouring country or a ticket from a reliable airline which can later be refunded if you do not use it. Also, see MCO.

Transferred Tickets Airline tickets cannot be transferred from one person to another. Travellers sometimes try to sell the return half of their ticket, but officials can ask you to prove that you are the person named on the ticket. This is unlikely to happen on domestic flights, but on an international flight tickets may be compared with passports.

Travel Agencies Travel agencies vary widely and you should ensure you use one that suits your needs. Some simply handle tours while full-service agencies handle everything from tours and tickets to car rental and hotel bookings. A good one will do all these things and can save you a lot of money, but if all you want is a ticket at the lowest possible price, you really need an agency specialising in discounted tickets. A discounted ticket agency, however, may not be useful for other things, like hotel bookings.

Travel Periods Some officially discounted fares – Apex fares in particular – vary with the time of year. There is often a low (off-peak) season and a high (peak) season. Sometimes there's an intermediate or shoulder season as well. At peak times, when everyone wants to fly, not only will the officially discounted fares be higher but so will unofficially discounted fares, or there may simply be no discounted tickets available. Usually the fare depends on your outward flight – if you depart in the high season and return in the low season, you pay the high-season fare. ■

cheap fares is the magazine *Business Traveller*.

Most British travel agents are registered with Association of British Travel Agents (ABTA). If you have paid for your flight to an ABTA-registered agent who then goes out of business, ABTA will guarantee a refund or an alternative. Unregistered bucket shops are riskier but also sometimes cheaper.

The Globetrotters Club (BCM Roving, London WC1N 3XX) publishes a newsletter called *Globe* that covers obscure destinations and can help in finding travelling companions.

One of the most reliable London agencies is STA (☎ (071) 937-9962), at 74 Old Brompton Rd, London SW7; 117 Euston Rd, London NW1; and 38 Store St, London

WC1. Another is Trailfinders (☎ (071) 938-3366, (071) 938-3939), at 42-50 Earls Court Rd, London W8 (and an office around the corner at 194 Kensington High St, London W8). The latter also offers an inoculation service and a research library for customers.

The Africa Travel Shop (☎ (071) 387-1211), at 4 Medway Court, Leigh St, London WC1, caters to the growing number of travellers interested in Africa. It is ABTA bonded, has a free video library and can organise overland safaris and most other travel requirements.

Its best 1993 low season fares include a UK£199 return fare with British Airways, with a 35-day maximum stay. Regular return tickets without restrictions (valid for a year) include UK£315 with Air France. Turkish Airlines have a regular one-year return ticket via Istanbul for UK£235 to UK£250, depending on which bucket shop you go to. Sudan Airways have a similar ticket via Khartoum, which seems like the long way around to get to Cairo. If all goes well, it takes 12 hours (!) to get to Khartoum from London and could mean an equally long wait (if not longer) for a connection to Cairo. All this for UK£220. The bulk of these tickets involve long delays between connections, and sometimes overnight stays.

Travellers planning to head further into Africa might be advised to get a ticket to, say, Nairobi in Kenya with a stopover in Cairo. Air fares are generally expensive within Africa. The Africa Travel Shop has one-way tickets to Nairobi with a stop in Cairo for UK£295 – much better than anything you'll find in Cairo.

STA offers charter flights return to Cairo for UK£199 in the low season with a minimum stay of seven days and a maximum of three months. Short-stay trips with charter airlines can be cheaper still, at around UK£175 for two weeks, with a UK£15 increment for each extra week you want to stay.

For shorter trips, it is worth looking into package trips or combined air fare and hotel deals. Charters to Luxor and leaving from Cairo, with accommodation in two to three-star hotels, can come to about UK£350 for two weeks.

The cheapest, but most unpredictable, way to fly to Cairo from London may be for free as a courier for DHL or another air courier service.

To/From Europe

Germany One of the most popular European carriers for flights between North Africa and the rest of the world is Lufthansa German Airlines. If your trip is originating in Germany, or if you wish to stop over in Germany before or after visiting Egypt, Lufthansa and its charter subsidiary Condor offer some of the most frequent connections with flights to and from Egypt. There are direct scheduled flights from Frankfurt to Cairo and Alexandria. During the high season (October to April), there are several flights weekly to Sharm el-Sheikh.

In Munich, a great source of travel information and equipment is the Därr Travel Shop (☎ (089) 282032) at Theresienstrasse 66, D-8000, Munich 2. Aside from producing a comprehensive travel equipment catalogue, they also run an 'Expedition Service' with current flight information available.

In Berlin, ARTU Reisen (☎ (030) 310466), at Hardenbergstr. 9, near Berlin Zoo (with five branches around the city), is a popular travel agency.

Netherlands Amsterdam is a popular departure point. Some of the best fares are offered by the student travel agency NBBS Reiswinkels (☎ (020) 620-5071). They have seven branches throughout the city. Their

Top: Old men smoking shisha outside a cafe, Old Cairo (KB)
Left: Tables set for the break-fast during Ramadan, Cairo (KB)
Right: Pyramids seen through hotel window, Giza (KB)

Top: Nubian women washing clothes in the Nile, Aswan (KB)
Middle: Woman selling fruit, Cairo (DS); Village guard in traditional dress, Egypt (KB);
Young boys, Mut, Dakhla Oasis (DS)
Bottom: Imbaba camel market, Cairo (DS)

fares are comparable to those of London bucket shops. NBBS Reiswinkels has branches in Brussels, Belgium, as well.

Greece Bucket shop agencies around the Plaka and Syntagma Square in Athens charge about the lowest fares you can find for flights from Athens to Cairo. Fantasy Travel at 10 Xenofontas St (near Syntagma Square), Speedy Ways Travel Agency and Lin Travel (☎ 322-1681), at 39 Nikis St, have been recommended by travellers. From Cairo, the one-way flight with EgyptAir or Olympic Airways costs E£450 (student fare).

Turkey A similar crowd of bucket shops is also clustered around the Sultan Ahmet area of Istanbul.

France Paris is not a bad place to organise a trip to Egypt from. It seems to abound with Egypt and desert specialists. You might try Monde de l'Egypte et du Proche Orient (☎ 43 20 76 37), 20, rue des Fosses-Saint-Bernard, 75005 Paris, or Voyageurs en Egypte et au Proche Orient (☎ 42 86 17 87) at 12, rue Sainte-Anne, 75001 Paris. Two other places worth looking at, particularly if you are looking for something more organised on the ground or desert expeditions are Explorator (☎ 42 66 66 24), 16, Place de la Madeleine, 75008 Paris, and Déserts (☎ 46 04 88 40), 6 et 8 rue Quincampoix, 75004 Paris.

To/From Israel

Air Sinai and El Al regularly fly between Cairo and Tel Aviv for about E£520 one way (and double return). El Al offers a 'Cairo extension' fare for half the regular price if you fly into Tel Aviv with them from somewhere else. If you have the time, however, travelling overland between Egypt and Israel is much cheaper and more adventurous.

To/From Jordan

There are regular flights with Royal Jordanian and EgyptAir between Cairo and Amman, but there is no discounting. Amman to Cairo is JD80 (about US$120) one way and double return. Going the other way, the fare is E£400. There are no student reductions.

For the jet-setter, the Egyptian al-Massria air company runs small planes between Aqaba and Sharm el-Sheikh (US$120 one way) and Hurghada (US$180 one way) four days a week. If you're coming from Aqaba, they can arrange the visas if you want.

In Aqaba, ask at the bigger hotels or call Mr Hussein (☎ 316570).

To/From the Sudan

Flights on a variety of airlines leave Khartoum every day for Cairo. Sudan Airways flies between Khartoum and Cairo. The flight from Cairo costs E£1247 one way or double return (!). The youth fare is E£793 one way. From Khartoum there are regular flights. Sudan Airways has seven a week, EgyptAir two and Air France, KLM and Lufthansa all stop in Cairo en route to Europe. The one-way adult fare for all of them is about US$240. Air France and KLM offer student reductions of about 40%. Check with your agent if a Civil Aviation Permit is required on any of the European airlines for the trip *to* Khartoum. It is certainly required for the flight from Khartoum (see Khartoum Getting There & Away for more details).

To/From Tunisia

Tunis Air and EgyptAir offer student discounts on flights between Cairo and Tunis, but that doesn't make it cheap. The one-way fare is E£625. If you're over 31, it will come to E£1100. Consult the offices of each airline for the latest information.

To/From Africa

As you will have gathered from the information on flights to Tunis and Khartoum, there is nothing cheap about travelling by air between African capitals. About the best you can do to Nairobi is E£1375 with Kenyan Airways. The flight to Addis Ababa in Ethiopia is E£1495.

To/From Australia & New Zealand

Some of the best fares from Australia to Cairo are offered by STA. Fares start at A$1130/1870 one way/return from Melbourne or Sydney, and A$1045/1720 one way/return from Perth. RTW fares with a stopover in Cairo start from A$2199. All fares vary according to season. STA has offices throughout Australia.

Along with STA, Flight Centres International are a major dealer in cheap air fares. Check the travel agents' ads in the Yellow Pages and ring around.

To/From Asia

Cheap tickets to Cairo are available in Hong Kong and Singapore, usually as part of an RTW ticket. From Bangkok, EgyptAir offers a one-way fare of around US$1011. Investigate bucket shop deals on EgyptAir and other airlines in Hong Kong and Bangkok.

Arriving & Leaving by Air

Egypt has several airports but only six are international ports of entry: Cairo, Alexandria and, increasingly, the 'international' airports at Luxor, Aswan, Hurghada (Al-Ghardaka) and Sharm el-Sheikh. Most air travellers enter Egypt through Cairo. The other airports tend to be serviced from outside Egypt by charter and package deal flights in the high season only.

EgyptAir, Air Sinai and ZAS have internal flights linking at least nine destinations. See the Getting Around chapter.

Cairo The airport is 25 km, or a 45 to 60 minute drive, from central Cairo. There are two terminals – old and new – about three km apart, and plans to build a third. Most of the world's major airlines fly through the new terminal. Check out the duty-free stores on your arrival or departure, as they supposedly offer some of the best deals in the world on perfumes and liquor. Refer to the Getting Around section in the Cairo chapter for notes on airport transport.

At the new terminal there are banking facilities (no cash advance on credit cards though) at the Thomas Cook branch and exchange offices for several banks. They are right next to each other and their rates vary a little, so check them all out. They can also issue stamps for a visa (see Visas & Embassies in Facts for the Visitor). Similar banking facilities are present in the old terminal too.

There is also a tourist information office, supposedly manned 24 hours a day, and a post office in the departure lounge. Next to it is a telex and telegraph office, and phones (including card phones) are also available.

The Avis and Hertz rentacar companies have booths in the arrivals hall.

There is no left-luggage facility. Outside the old terminal is a lost-and-found booth.

Warning On arrival at Cairo Airport, if you're not with a group, the chances are that you will be approached in the baggage-claim area by a man or woman with an official-looking brass or laminated badge that says 'Egyptian Chamber of Tourism' or something similar. Such people are not government tourism officials, they are hotel touts. See the Accommodation section in the Facts for the Visitor chapter for more details of their operating methods.

Alexandria The international airport in Alexandria is much smaller than in Cairo. Only Lufthansa and Olympic have direct flights between, respectively, Frankfurt and Alexandria, and Athens and Alexandria.

Luxor & Aswan Charter companies fly directly from Europe, especially Germany, to Luxor International Airport, and increasingly also to Aswan. The charter flights are often part of package deals that include discounted accommodation at hotels such as the Jolie Ville and the Sheraton, among others.

Hurghada & Sharm el-Sheikh There are similar charter flight packages between these Red Sea spots and European destinations, also invariably part of package deals. The Egyptian airline ZAS also runs flights from Cairo to Frankfurt and vice versa via Hurghada.

Buying a Plane Ticket

The plane ticket will probably be the single most expensive item in your budget, and buying it can be an intimidating business. It is worth putting aside a few hours to research the state of the market and check around the many travel agents hoping to separate you from your money. Start early: some of the cheapest tickets have to be bought months in advance, and some popular flights sell out early. Talk to other recent travellers – they may be able to stop you making some of the same old mistakes. Look at the ads in newspapers and magazines, consult reference books and watch for special offers. Then phone round travel agents for bargains. (Airlines can supply information on routes and timetables; however, except at times of inter-airline war they do not supply the cheapest tickets.) Find out the fare, the route, the duration of the journey and any restrictions on the ticket. (See Restrictions in the Air Travel Glossary.) Then sit back and decide which is best for you.

You may discover that those impossibly cheap flights are 'fully booked, but we have another one that costs a bit more...'. Or the flight is on an airline notorious for its poor safety standards and leaves you in the world's least favourite airport in mid-journey for 14 hours. Or they claim only to have the last two seats available for that country for the whole of July, which they will hold for you for a maximum of two hours. Don't panic – keep ringing around.

Use the fares quoted in this book as a guide only. They are approximate and based on the rates advertised by travel agents at the time of going to press. Quoted airfares do not necessarily constitute a recommendation for the carrier.

If you are travelling from the UK or the USA, you will probably find that the cheapest flights are being advertised by obscure bucket shops whose names haven't yet reached the telephone directory. They sell airline tickets at up to a 50% discount where places have not been filled, and although airlines may protest to the contrary, many of them release tickets to selected bucket shops – it's better to sell tickets at a huge discount than not at all. Many such firms are honest and solvent, but there are a few rogues who will take your money and disappear, to reopen elsewhere a month or two later under a new name. If you feel suspicious about a firm, don't give them all the money at once – leave a deposit of 20% or so and pay the balance when you get the ticket. If they insist on cash in advance, go somewhere else. And once you have the ticket, ring the airline to confirm that you are actually booked onto the flight.

You may decide to pay more than the rock-bottom fare by opting for the safety of a better-known travel agent. Firms such as STA, who have offices worldwide, Council Travel in the USA or Travel CUTS in Canada are not going to disappear overnight, leaving you clutching a receipt for a nonexistent ticket, but they do offer good prices to most destinations.

Once you have your ticket, write its number down, together with the flight number and other details, and keep the information somewhere separate. If the ticket is lost or stolen, this will help you get a replacement.

It's sensible to buy travel insurance as early as possible. If you buy it the week before you fly, you may find, for example, that you're not covered for delays to your flight caused by industrial action.

Air Travellers with Special Needs

If you have special needs of any sort – you've broken a leg, you're vegetarian, travelling in a wheelchair, taking the baby, terrified of flying – you should let the airline know as soon as possible so that they can make arrangements accordingly. You should remind them when you reconfirm your booking (at least 72 hours before departure) and again when you check in at the airport. It may also be worth ringing round the airlines before you make your booking to find out how they can handle your particular needs.

Airports and airlines can be surprisingly helpful, but they do need warning. Most international airports will provide escorts from check-in desk to plane where needed, and there should be ramps, lifts, accessible toilets and reachable phones. Aircraft toilets, on the other hand, are likely to present a problem; travellers should discuss this with the airline at an early stage and, if necessary, with their doctor.

Guide dogs for the blind will often have to travel in a specially pressurised baggage compartment with other animals, away from their owner, though smaller guide dogs may be admitted to the cabin. All guide dogs will be subject to the same quarantine laws (six months in isolation, etc) as any other animal when entering or returning to countries currently free of rabies, such as Britain or Australia.

Deaf travellers can ask for airport and in-flight announcements to be written down for them.

Children under two travel for 10% of the standard fare (or free, on some airlines), as long as they don't occupy a seat. They don't get a baggage allowance either. 'Skycots' should be provided by the airline if requested in advance; these will take a child weighing up to about 10 kg. Children between two and 12 can usually occupy a seat for half to two-thirds of the full fare, and do get a baggage allowance. Push chairs can often be taken as hand luggage.

LAND
Your Own Transport
It is possible to bring your own vehicle to Egypt, but you will need a *carnet de passage en douane* and your own insurance. An International Certificate of Motor Vehicles may be required. In addition, you may be required to buy compulsory insurance on entering the country, valid for one to three months. Don't be surprised to be hit for 'service' fees as well, but pay attention as rip-offs are not unheard of. Depending on the engine capacity of the vehicle, fees for Egyptian number plates can be as high as E£600, although their application is haphazard. Another rule that does not seem to be universally applied is that foreign vehicles must leave from the

same point at which they entered the country – not much good to most overland travellers. If you are coming by sea, check with the ferry company that you are covered for any letters of guarantee that may be required by customs. If you are staying for more than six months, proof of payment for road tax and customs duties, refundable on departure, is supposedly required.

The Egyptians themselves give conflicting advice on whether or not diesel-powered vehicles may enter the country, and people wishing to bring in 4WD cars should check at an Egyptian embassy first.

The UK Automobile Association requires a financial guarantee for the carnet, which effectively acts as an import duty waiver, as it could be liable for customs and other taxes if the vehicle's exit is not registered within a year. The kind of deposit they are looking at can be well in excess of US$1000. The carnet itself costs UK£57.50 to UK£67.50 in the UK, depending on the number of countries you want to cover (up to 25). It is essential to ensure that the carnet is filled out properly at each border crossing, or you could be up for a lot of money. The carnet may also need to have listed any more expensive spares that you're planning to carry with you, such as a gearbox.

Obviously, you will need the vehicle's registration papers, and an international driving permit.

Bringing in a motorcycle can pose added hassles, as a special permit is supposedly required from the '26th Group, Military Intelligence' in Heliopolis, Cairo. This has not stopped motorcyclists from getting their vehicles in. Check with the embassy before departure, but don't be surprised if they seem to know nothing.

To/From Israel
There are two crossing points between Egypt and Israel. The more popular one is at Taba, on the Gulf of Aqaba coast near the Israeli resort town of Eilat. The second is via Rafah and the Gaza Strip.

Egyptian visas can be obtained from the embassy in Tel Aviv or the consulate in Eilat.

For more information see the section on Visas in the Facts for the Visitor chapter. No visa is required for most nationalities entering Israel.

There is an Israeli exit tax of NIS31.30 at Taba, followed by an Egyptian entry fee of E£16.75. It's possible to pay the first in US$, but the Egyptian fee has to be paid for in E£ (you can change at the Taba Hilton). There are no taxes going the other way.

At Rafah, the Egyptian exit tax is E£16 and entry fee E£7. The Israelis have no entry fee but a hefty exit tax of US$25 or the equivalent in NIS.

Bus Several tour operators run buses directly between Cairo and Tel Aviv, Jerusalem and Eilat.

A bus for Tel Aviv leaves from in front of the Cairo Sheraton Hotel at 5.30 am every day but Saturday. Misr Travel sells one-way tickets for E£85 (return E£130), while many of the others charge just that little bit more (like E£95). Misr Travel's head office (☎ 393-0100) is at 1 Sharia Talaat Harb, but you're more likely to notice their office at No 7. They have other offices scattered around town. You can also book the tickets through Travco (☎ 342-0488), 13 Sharia Mahmoud Azmy, Zamalek.

The East Delta Bus Co has a bus to Tel Aviv at 8 am on Mondays and Wednesdays for US$20. You must book ahead at the Sinai Terminal in Abbassiya, Cairo.

There seems to be a wider choice of possibilities coming from Israel. Mazada Tours (☎ 544-4454), 141 Ibn Gvirol St, Tel Aviv (50 metres from the Egyptian embassy), has buses to Cairo from Tel Aviv, Jerusalem, Eilat and Nazareth. They all cost US$25 via Rafah and US$30 via Taba. Round trip tickets cost from US$35 to US$50, depending on the route.

Nizza Tours & Travel (☎ 510-2832), 75 HaYarkon St, Tel Aviv, has buses from Tel Aviv and Jerusalem for US$25 one way and US$38 round trip.

Both companies also have offices in Jerusalem. Mazada can also be contacted at the Cairo Sheraton Hotel (☎ 348-8600).

As prices vary, it is worth hunting around. Other travel agencies in Tel Aviv include: Galilee Tours (☎ 546-6622), 42 Ben Yehuda St; United Tours (☎ 754-3412), 113 HaYarkon St, and Neot Hakikar (☎ 225151), 78 Ben Yehuda St.

You can also contact them in Jerusalem: Mazada Tours (☎ 255453), 24 Ben Sira St; Nizza Tours & Travel (☎ 304880), Beit Rimonim, 208 Jaffa St; Galilee Tours (☎ 383460), Centre 1, 43 Yirmiyaha St; and Neot Hakikar (☎ 699385), 36 Keren Hayesod St.

Check around the hostels, particularly in Tel Aviv, as they sometimes have cut-price tickets.

Remember that there are *no* bus services on Saturday.

As a rule, passengers transfer from an Egyptian to an Israeli bus (or vice versa) on crossing the border. None of the quoted fares includes border taxes.

Bus & Service Taxi It can be considerably cheaper, although more involved, using local transport. Buses and service taxis operate from Cairo to Rafah (see Cairo Getting There & Away). A service taxi to Rafah costs E£15 (E£12 to Al-Arish, from where buses go to or near the border for E£1 to E£2). Service taxis operating *from* the border to destinations in Egypt tend to demand higher fares (E£17 to Cairo). The Egged bus No 362 to Tel Aviv, which leaves the Israeli side at 3 pm, costs NIS19, making the trip worth about US$13. There is a bus to Taba from Cairo, but it won't save you anything. You could try going first to Suez (E£4.50 by service taxi), and picking up the Taba bus from there (E£17). On the Israeli side, the local bus No 15 from the border to Eilat costs NIS5 (a taxi is NIS20). The Egged bus from Eilat to Tel Aviv costs NIS34. For more local transport information and possibilities, and border crossing formalities, see the Taba and Rafah Getting There & Away sections.

To/From the Sudan
There are three potential ways to travel overland from the Sudan to Egypt, but they're not

very practical, and probably impossible, for foreign travellers – unless you're already a practised camel herder or have your own 4WD vehicle.

The camel herders, following an age-old caravan route known as Darb al-Arba'een, or the 40 Days Road, bring their camels up from western Sudan through the desert to Aswan, where they sell them. With a bit of negotiation and an adventurous spirit, you might be able to join a caravan.

If you have a tough 4WD vehicle, it may be possible to drive up from the Sudan along the Red Sea coast. The border is seldom crossed, and at the time of writing, special permission was required to travel the stretch in Egypt between Marsa Alam and Bir Shalatayn.

People determined to drive into the Sudan, or at least get their vehicles in, can try to negotiate for a boat to transport them from the docks at the High Dam, south of Aswan, to Wadi Halfa. In March 1993, some people took two cars and two trail bikes across this way for E£5000. There have been reports that more regular car ferries are planned.

To/From Libya

There are direct buses running between Cairo and Benghazi and Tripoli from the Midan Ulali station in Cairo. Tickets cost E£125 and E£230 respectively. See the Cairo Getting There & Away section for more details. You can also get buses to the same destinations from Alexandria. A more laborious, but cheaper, alternative would be to get local transport (buses, trains or service taxis) to Sallum and a service taxi to the border. From there you can get Libyan transport heading west. See the Sallum entry.

SEA & RIVER
To/From Europe

Adriatica Lines operates a ferry between Venice, Bari, Patras (Greece), Heraklion (Crete) and Alexandria. Their Venice office can be contacted through Adriatica di Navigazione (☎ 29133), 1412 Zattere. Other agencies for Adriatica Line include: Serena Holidays (☎ (071) 373-6548), 40 Kenway Rd, London SW5 0RA; Extra Value Travel (☎ (212) 758800), 437 Madison Ave, New York, NY 10022; Ilion Shipping Agencies (☎ 429-1389), 85 Akti Miaouli, Piraeus; Creta Travel Bureau (☎ 227002), 2-22 Epimenidou St, Heraklion; Menatours (☎ 740864), 14 Sharia Talaat Harb, Cairo; and Menatours (☎ 809676), Midan Saad Zaghloul, Alexandria.

There are other companies that operate ferries or other kinds of boats from Limassol (Cyprus) to Port Said, and from Lattakia (Syria) to Alexandria. They then have connections beyond Limassol and Lattakia to such places as Haifa (Israel), Piraeus, Rhodes and Turkey. For more information see the Alexandria and Port Said Getting There & Away sections.

To/From the Sudan

Steamer The most common way of travelling between the Sudan and Egypt is by steamer from Wadi Halfa up Lake Nasser to Aswan. Generally there is no timetable for the steamer, although if you're lucky there may be two a week – generally it is more like one every week to two weeks. For more details on this, refer to the sections on Wadi Halfa and Aswan. Heading into the Sudan, the problem can be getting a connecting train on to Khartoum – delays of a week or so are not unheard of. The alternative is some very rough desert riding in buses and trucks. Again, see the Wadi Halfa section for more details.

To/From Jordan

Ferry There are car ferries between Nuweiba, in Sinai, and Aqaba, Jordan's only port. You can reach the Nuweiba port directly by bus from Cairo's Abbassiya Sinai terminal. The trip takes about eight hours and costs E£45 to E£50. Some buses for Cairo, Ismailia and the Delta from Nuweiba wait for the arrival of the boat. In Aqaba, the ferry terminal is a few km south of the town centre. A taxi from the terminal to the centre costs JD1, but they'll try for more. There used to be a service to Suez too, but this was stopped in 1990.

There are two sailings a day each way. From Nuweiba they are supposed to leave at 11 am and 4 pm, and from Aqaba at noon and 6 pm. The trip costs more from Egypt (US$26) than the other way (US$18 plus a 200 fils charge), although the Jordanian port tax evens things up. It is impossible to pay for the ticket, which you buy in a small booth near the departure gate, in Egyptian currency. If you don't have the dollars, there are four banks clustered near the departures gate. In Aqaba, tickets can be bought from the Arab Bridge Maritime Co and numerous travel agents, some of whom will accept Jordanian currency, in which case you pay JD13.500. Tickets can generally be bought for either passage on the day of travel.

The trip is meant to take three hours, but can often take much longer. Occasionally a southerly wind blows up that can oblige ferries coming to Nuweiba to wait until it subsides, but the problem is more likely to be chaos at one port or the other. Although some travellers have reported the luxury of travelling on a near empty boat, the more common experience is of ferries packed beyond capacity. Be prepared for a trip that could last as long as eight hours. The worst time is around the time of the haj, when traffic on both sides is swelled by hajjis (pilgrims) heading to and from Mecca in Saudi Arabia. At the peak of this period, they sometimes put on two extra boats. Foot passengers should have little problem getting a ticket, but spare a thought for the thousands of families from across North Africa waiting sometimes for days to get their cars on a boat.

There is a E£2 departure tax from Nuweiba and a port departure tax from Aqaba of JD6. There is an Egyptian consulate in Aqaba and visas are issued with relatively little fuss on the same day.

Bus & Ferry You can book a ferry and bus combination ticket from Cairo or Alexandria through to Aqaba or even on to Amman if you wish. From Cairo, the trip to Aqaba is US$23 plus E£40.20. You can also book a ferry and bus right through to Cairo at the JETT bus office in Aqaba. The ticket costs

US$43, but you can pick up Cairo-bound buses on arrival at Nuweiba anyway. Remember that it is generally cheaper to pay for each leg as you go than to get a ticket for the whole trip.

To/From Saudi Arabia & Kuwait

Ferry There are direct ferries taking about three days between Suez and Jeddah. Frequency varies, but getting a berth during the haj, the pilgrimage to Mecca, is virtually impossible. The price of berths ranges from E£145 deck class to E£255 for 1st class. You can get information at Misr Travel agencies, or buy a ticket directly in their office in Port Tewfiq, Suez.

Bus & Ferry In the same way that passage can be booked straight through to Aqaba and Amman, you can purchase tickets through to many destinations in the Gulf, either at the Abbassiya Sinai terminal, or a couple of the other terminals in Cairo or in Alexandria. The fare to Riyadh is E£210 and US$26, and to Kuwait E£358 and US$26.

Arranging passage from Jeddah in Saudi Arabia to go to Egypt can be somewhat complicated and expensive. In Jeddah tickets are sold by the Red Sea Shipping Company, on Mina'a St across from the service taxi stand, and by Misr Travel on Al-Malek Abd al-Aziz St in the commercial centre across from the Corniche. It's possible to buy a combination bus/ferry ticket that will take you from Jeddah and Riyadh via Aqaba and Nuweiba all the way to Cairo.

Buses depart Jeddah at least three times a week from the international bus terminal on Ba'ashan St, next to the SAPTCO terminal and across from the GPO. In Riyadh, tickets can be bought from most of the agencies near the SAPTCO terminal, just off Al-Bathaa St. Finding someone around these terminals who speaks English can be difficult, if not impossible.

A bus travels from Kuwait across Saudi Arabia to Aqaba, Jordan. From Aqaba you can take the ferry to Nuweiba and then a bus to Cairo.

TOURS

There are any number of tour possibilities to Egypt, and a plethora of agents dealing with everything from Nile cruises to overland safaris or diving trips. Figure out what kind of tour you want to do, or what area of Egypt you want to cover. A charter package to Sharm el-Sheikh won't do much for the Islamic architecture buff. On the other hand, the diving along the Nile is not the best either. If there is an Egyptian Tourist Authority in your city, it may be a good place to start. They should at least be able to provide you with brochures giving you an idea of what's where – don't fall for all the gushing propaganda though! They will usually have the names of several travel agents dealing with tours, and possibly save you time looking for more specialised tour operators (such as for diving in the Sinai).

Some of the cheapest air fares with charter aircraft also come with short stays (see Air earlier in this chapter).

It should be remembered that the programmes on such trips are usually fairly tight, leaving little room for roaming around on your own, but they take much of the hassle off your plate. It pays to shop around. Check itinerary details, accommodation, who does the ticketing, visa and other documentation footwork, insurance and tour conditions carefully.

Nile Cruises & Other Packages

Many of the packaged trips to Egypt include a stint on one of the approximately 190 cruis-ers operating up and down the river. These vessels come in all shapes and sizes, but the big floating hotels ('flotels') seem to dominate. These beasts roam up and down the river in such numbers that smaller vessels, and feluccas especially, have to pay careful attention not to be capsized. There's something worrying about being asked in the dead of night by a felucca captain for a pocket flashlight to shine on the sail, in the hope of not being rammed by a cruiser – they are in fact not supposed to sail after dark.

The Nile Cruise Centre (☎ (071) 924-3999, fax (071) 924-3171) at 2 Cinnamon Row, Plantation Wharf, York Place, London SW11 3TW, claims to be the only specialist of its kind, and offers advice on a range of cruises and one-off charters.

The Imaginative Traveller, which has offices around the world, including in the USA, the UK, Australia, Canada, New Zealand and South Africa, offers various programmes of differing duration in Egypt. Costs vary depending on season and country of departure, but a typical two-week trip starting in Cairo and including five days on a felucca can come to UK£295 excluding air fare.

Jasmin Tours (☎ (0628) 531121), High St, Cookham, Maidenhead, Berks SL6 9SQ, runs numerous tours to Egypt, mostly including cruises. Their 17-day guided tour on the former paddle steamer *Memphis* may be a more homely alternative to the characterless flotels, but will cost up to UK£2000. Several organisations run such vessels.

A well-known name in Middle East and African touring is Bales, based at Bales House, Junction Rd, Dorking, Surrey, RH4 3HB (☎ (0306) 885991). They offer a wide range of tours, again the bulk of them involving cruises. They have combined air and land trips to the ancient sights, an excursion to Siwa Oasis and other tours combining Egypt with Jordan or even Kenya. They have an escorted budget tour starting at UK£455 (low season) for eight days.

There are many Cairo-based tour operators with offices in several countries around the world, including the Egypt Travel Centre, Sphinx Tours and Gaz Tours, to name a few. With these you can also organise shorter cruises locally, rather than fully organised tours from abroad (see the Getting Around section for more details on organising tours within Egypt).

Adventure & Overland Safaris
The increasingly popular mode of travelling through Africa and Asia seems to be by overland truck. These are not everyone's cup of tea, as you spend a lot of time with the same group of people, travelling, camping and cooking. There are treks as long as 30 weeks or more covering Africa from top to bottom, but once you've paid up, you're stuck with it, whether you like your travelling companions (or they like you!) or not. Organisers of these tours do take much of the hassle out of the bureaucratic footwork, helping out with visas and dodging a lot of the cross-border hassles. Egypt often features as a leg on one of these trips.

London, again, is teeming with places that organise such excursions. One is Top Deck, which has branches in Sydney and Auckland as well. The Africa Travel Shop (see the Air section in Getting There & Away, above) is another. Check the papers and magazines like *TNT* for others.

Some of them also offer off-the-beaten-track (or even not so far off-the-beaten-track) trips to Egypt alone. For trips to the Sinai, you might want to contact Wind Sand & Stars (☎ (071) 433-3684) at 2 Arkwright Rd, London, NW3 6AD. They offer climbing and walking tours in the Sinai, as well as bird-watching and snorkelling in the Red Sea.

There are a number of similar specialists based in Paris (see To/From Europe in the above Air section).

Diving Tours
It is possible to organise diving holidays to the Red Sea. The UK-based Twickers World Ltd (☎ (081) 892-8164), 22 Church St, Twickenham TW1 3NW, offers a range of tours to Egypt, Israel, Jordan and Syria, including one and two-week diving holidays. There are other organisations that can do similar trips, including beginners courses.

LEAVING EGYPT
For Westerners at any rate, leaving Egypt is generally painless. You'll become aware of this at borders or the Nuweiba and Aswan boat terminals as you are ushered past queues of agonised locals with their mountains of belongings.

Luggage is given a cursory check, if checked at all, and at passport control you will have to fill out an exit form before having your passport stamped. Exit fees seem to vary. On leaving Aswan for the Wadi Halfa steamer, Nuweiba for the Aqaba boat or crossing the Libyan border, there is a E£2 exit fee.

There is no exit fee at the Taba crossing into Israel, but at Rafah you pay E£16.

There is no airport departure tax.

Getting Around

Egypt has a very extensive public and private transport system. If you don't suffer from claustrophobia, and have plenty of patience and a tough stomach, you can travel just about anywhere in Egypt for relatively little money.

AIR

In Egypt, air fares are about average by international standards, but probably out of the range of most low-budget travellers. There are two kinds of fare too, one for foreigners and one for Egyptians. One guess who pays more. The one-way air fare from Cairo to Aswan is E£393 and E£283 to Luxor; it's E£168 for the 40-minute flight to Alexandria. In general, it is only worth flying if your time is very limited.

If you do have to go by plane, EgyptAir flies from Cairo to Marsa Matruh, Alexandria, Hurghada (Al-Ghardaka), Sharm el-Sheikh, Al-Arish, Luxor, Kharga Oasis, Aswan and Abu Simbel.

During the high season (October to April), many of these flights are full. In 1989, EgyptAir had to rent Kuwaiti and Yugoslavian planes (with crews) to meet domestic flight demands.

Air Sinai (to all intents and purposes EgyptAir by another name) has flights from Cairo to Sharm el-Sheikh (Ras Nasrany) and Taba (Ras an-Naqb). For God only knows what reason, they charge US$ for these flights, and don't muck around. One way to Sharm costs US$96, and US$100 to Taba! Mind you, at E£323 one way to Sharm, EgyptAir's own fare boils down to the same thing.

In 1989 a small charter company called ZAS began competing with EgyptAir (and Air Sinai). It now covers most major domestic routes and has some international flights as well. Prices vary little from those of its rivals. The Cairo to Aswan stretch costs E£388 one way.

BUS

Buses service just about every city, town and village in Egypt. Ticket prices are generally comparable with the cost of 2nd-class train tickets. Intercity buses, especially on shorter runs and in Upper Egypt, tend to become quite crowded, and even if you are lucky enough to get a seat in the first place, you'll probably end up with something or somebody on your lap. It's one way to meet Egyptians!

Deluxe buses travel between some of the main towns. For instance, the Arab Union Transport and West Delta Bus companies run deluxe ('Super Jet') buses between Cairo and Alexandria daily. Similar services are being extended to other parts of the country, and air-conditioned, comfortable buses run between Cairo, Ismailia, Port Said, Suez, St Catherine's Monastery, Hurghada and Luxor. Tickets cost a bit more than on standard buses but they're still cheap. The bulk of buses running south of Cairo along the Nile tend to be more basic. Information about these buses will be given in the appropriate sections.

Often tickets for buses on the same route will vary according to whether or not they have air-con, video or any other 'luxuries'. There are no student discounts on bus fares.

A king in his chariot

A direct bus between Cairo and Aswan will cost E£35 to E£45, and E£8 to E£15 between Cairo and Alexandria. The direct buses from Cairo to Sinai destinations tend to be disproportionately expensive.

Tickets can be bought at windows at the bus stations or, often, on the bus. Hang on to your ticket until you get off, as inspectors almost always board the bus to check fares. It is advisable to book tickets, at least on very popular routes (such as to the Sinai from Cairo) and those with few buses running (out to the Western Oases from Cairo), a day or two in advance. Where you are allowed to buy tickets on the bus, you generally end up standing if you don't have an assigned seat with a booked ticket.

On short runs there are no bookings and it's a case of first on best seated.

You may find you end up with a fistful of tickets – each one has a certain amount printed on it, and the fare is made up of a combination of these.

The issue of timetables is a vexed one. Some lines are more reliable than others, but any specific departure times mentioned should be taken with a pinch of salt.

The basic buses can be grimy, dusty affairs, and their drivers occasionally seem a little too confident of their skills, but generally they do the job. On the other hand, buses with video, although cleaner, faster and more comfortable, are a serious threat to your ear drums. An overnight ride from Cairo to Luxor with nonstop Egyptian and Indian movies at high volume is great headache material.

TRAIN

Trains travel along more than 5000 km of track to almost every major city and town in Egypt from Aswan to Alexandria, although the system needs substantial investment for modernisation. However, the timetables are a little more reliable than those for the buses. A timetable for the main destinations, in shoddy English, is updated every year (valid to June 30) and occasionally actually available for E£1.

Classes
Services range from relatively cheap (compared to the USA and Europe) 1st-class wagons-lits (cars with deluxe sleeper compartments) through 1st class sitting, 2nd class air-con and 2nd class ordinary to the ridiculously cheap 3rd-class cars.

Wagons-Lits Trains with wagons-lits are the most comfortable and among the fastest in Egypt. The cars are the same as those used by trains in Europe and only sleeper compartments are available. Two wagon-lit trains used to travel between Cairo, Luxor and Aswan every day, but at the time of writing the number had dropped to one.

Wagon-lit trains are air-conditioned, and each compartment has hot and cold water. There are lounge cars, and dinner and breakfast are served in the compartments. A double compartment costs about E£242 one way, per person, including the sleeper ticket, meals, service and taxes. If you get a return ticket, it's E£222 each way. For a little more, you can fly.

Bookings can be made at the reservations office (☎ 755922, 752476) to the left of the car park next to the Ramses Station main building – just follow the blue-on-yellow signs marked 'Res. Office'. Take your passport.

Other Classes Regular night trains with and without sleeper compartments and meals included leave every day and cost much less than the wagons-lits, but for some time now the 1st-class sleepers have not been available to anyone but Egyptians and Sudanese.

To Luxor, the 1st-class sitting fare is E£38 (student E£25). Reservations must be made in advance at Ramses Station in Cairo. They also go to Aswan. You can usually buy hot meals in 1st class for E£11, or E£4.50 for bread, jam and cheese – if that sounds too expensive, you're probably right, so you may want to flout the rules and bring your own.

The fastest trains are the sleek Turbos that run between Cairo and Alexandria nonstop four times a day.

Always check the timetables posted at stations – if you can make head or tail of them – for the latest train schedules.

If you have an International Student Identification Card (ISIC) discounts as high as 50% are granted on all fares except those for wagons-lits. Some travellers report getting a 50% discount with International Youth Hostel Federation cards and Youth International Educational Exchange cards. It is possible to travel from Cairo to Aswan for E£2.90 if you have an ISIC and are willing to take a beating in the 3rd-class cars.

TAXI

Travelling by 'ser-vees' taxi (you'll occasionally hear them referred to rather quaintly as *bijoux* – don't let the French deceive you; they're generally anything but 'jewels'!) is the fastest way to go from city to city. In most places the service taxis and their drivers congregate near bus and train stations. Each driver waits with his Peugeot 504 taxi (or increasingly Toyota microbus) until he has six or seven passengers; he won't leave before his car is full unless you and/or the other passengers want to pay more money. If you want to go somewhere these taxis don't usually go, you can either hire a whole taxi for yourself or coax other travellers into joining you.

Service taxi rides can be a little hairy at times. Most of Egypt's main Nile road has only two lanes, so one ambling donkey cart can cause an immense traffic jam. This prompts everyone to try passing everyone else, even though the oncoming traffic usually prevents a clean, smooth pass. It's a modern joust where, fortunately, the jousters usually miss each other. Occasionally they don't, however, and the metal scraps of past accidents litter the roadside all over the country.

MICROBUS

A slightly bigger version of the service taxi is a van that would normally take about 12 people. More often than not they cram on as many as 22 – it can be done, but it is not very comfortable. These run on fewer routes than

the service taxis, and generally cost the same. There are several types variously known as *meecrobus* (microbuses), *meecro*, *baas* or service taxi, depending on whom you ask. Increasingly, microbuses are being used as service taxis for the simple reason that they can carry more people.

On either microbuses or service taxis, travellers are frequently charged extra for luggage; it's up to you whether or not you want to argue about it. Don't take it personally, the same applies to Egyptians. This is one advantage of the big buses, where luggage is dumped in the hold.

PICK-UPS

Toyota and Chevrolet pick-up trucks cover a lot of the routes between smaller towns and villages off the main roads. The general rule is to get 12 inside the covered rear of the truck, often with an assortment of goods squeezed in around feet on the floor. After that, it's a matter of how many can and want to scramble on to the roof or hang on at the rear – it's remarkable how many people you can get on to them if you try!

CAR & MOTORBIKE
Road Rules

Driving in Cairo is a crazy affair, so think seriously before you decide to rent a car there. However, driving in other parts of the country, at least in daylight, isn't necessarily so bad. It would be great to have a car – or better still a 4WD – in the Sinai, where the traffic is very light and there are lots of fascinating places to visit.

Motorcycle would be an ideal way to travel around Egypt. The only snag is that you have to bring your own and the red tape involved is extensive. Ask your country's automobile association and the Egyptian embassy about regulations. You must ride very carefully because the roads are often sandy and pocked with potholes.

For more information on road rules, suggested routes and other advice, it might be worth picking up a copy of *On the Road in Egypt – A Motorist's Guide* by Mary Dungan Megalli (The American University in Cairo

Press), available at least at the Lehnert & Landrock bookshop in Cairo.

Petrol is readily available. Normal, or *benzin aadi*, costs 80 pt a litre. *Mumtaz*, or super, is more expensive at 90 pt a litre. Forget about lead-free.

Warning Driving at night is a particularly hazardous exercise, especially outside well-lit areas. Headlights are often not used or, if at all, only to warn oncoming traffic with a blinding flash. It should be noted that going as a passenger in a private car, service taxi or even bus at night can be risky. There seem to have been a few too many fairly gruesome nocturnal meetings; in late 1992, a busload of schoolchildren was virtually decapitated when a charging bulldozer with raised scoop managed to sheer the top off the bus, which had been left standing in the middle of the highway in the Sinai without headlights on by the driver while he relieved himself.

Rental

Several car rental agencies have offices in Egypt, including Avis, Hertz and Budget. Their rates are on a par with international charges and finding a cheap deal with local dealers is virtually impossible – anything less than E£60 a day would be exceptional, and you'd want to read the fine print. An international driving permit is a good idea, although not always necessary for drivers over the age of 25.

Avis (☎ 354-7400; fax 356-2464) has its main office at 16 Sharia Ma'mal as-Sukkar, Garden City, in Cairo. It also has offices at the Hotel Meridien (☎ 989400), Nile Hilton (☎ 766432), Cairo Airport (☎ 291-4266), Heliopolis Sheraton (☎ 291-0223) and Meridien Heliopolis (☎ 290-5055). In Alexandria their office is at the Cecil Hotel (☎ 807055). The cheapest deal they will do is E£150 a day for a 1989 Fiat Nova Regatta, including insurance and the first 100 km. Every km after is 60 pt.

Budget Rent-a-Car has offices all over the place, including at Cairo's new airport terminal (☎ 291-4266). Head office (☎ 340-0070) is at 5 Sharia al-Makrizi, Zamalek, in Cairo.

Some of the Cairo offices include 85 Rd 9, Maadi (☎ 350-2724); 1 Sharia Mohammed Ebeid, Heliopolis (☎ 291-8244); the Semiramis Hotel (☎ 355-7171) and the Ramses Hilton (☎ 758000). They have an office in Alexandria (☎ 597-1273) too. Their cheapest car is also a Nova Regatta (1988 model). Including insurance and 100 km, you'll pay about US$40. Unlimited km takes it to US$50.

You can contact Hertz (☎ 347-4172) at 195 Sharia 26th of July, just into Mohandiseen, in Cairo. Their cheapest car is a Fiat 128, which costs US$26.50 a day plus US$5 daily insurance and 100 free km. Each km extra costs 15 cents. Taxes are chucked in on top, so ask what the final price comes to. Unlimited km comes only if you hire a car for at least three days, in which case the rate is US$35.50 plus insurance and taxes.

Starco (☎ 393-1682; fax 392-1205), 1 Midan Talaat Harb, seems to specialise in Mercedes (the cheapest is US$79 a day), but you can also hire an autocaravan for US$120 a day on unlimited km with a three-day minimum. It costs slightly less for a week. The charges are subject to various taxes, so if you feel you can afford this sort of deal, make sure the terms are clear before you set off. If your licence is valid for at least a year, you don't necessarily need an international driving permit.

Max Rent Cars (☎ 347-4712/3), 27 Sharia Lubnan, Mohandiseen, will rent out 1992-1993 Toyota Starlets for US$41 a day including insurance and 100 free km. A week's rental costs US$268. Extra km cost 14 cents. They only rent cars with unlimited km when bookings are made from overseas.

White Line Co (☎ 341-1505), 2 Sharia Taha Hussein, Zamalek, won't rent cars for less than a week, but appear to be about the cheapest place available. A Fiat 128 costs E£60 a day (E£420 a week) with 100 free km and 40 pt a km on top. Check their insurance provisions carefully, as this aspect of things seems a little dodgy.

Best Car (☎ 700300), 54 Sharia Syria, Mohandiseen, seems to be one of the worst deals around. They charge E£120 a day for a Dogan (1992) with 100 km and 75 pt for each extra km. They also don't seem keen to hire out cars for less than a week and claim to want E£1000 for insurance!

BICYCLE

Bicycles are a practical way of getting around a town and its surrounding sites. In most places, particularly Luxor, you can rent a bicycle quite cheaply; prices start at around E£5 per day. Bicycles are, however, somewhat impractical for travelling long distances. The biggest problem is the possibility of getting flattened by one of Egypt's crazy drivers, who are not the slightest bit accustomed to cyclists on the roads.

HITCHING

It is easy to hitch in Egypt, but drivers are used to being paid for giving you a ride. You'll probably not save very much money by hitching, but it could be a good way to meet people. On the other hand, in Egypt, as elsewhere, hitching can be a dangerous practice, especially for women travellers. Just because we say it's possible does not mean we recommend it.

CAMEL

Yes, it is actually possible to travel around Egypt by camel. While the more intrepid travellers will probably want to buy their own 'ship of the desert', there are easier and less costly alternatives.

Camels are brought, in caravans, from the Sudan to Egypt's two main camel markets at Daraw, near Kom Ombo, and Imbaba, near Cairo. If you're serious about owning your own, note that the camels are cheaper at Daraw, as it's closer to the end of the caravan route. They can cost as little as US$400 there, while in Imbaba the price rises to as much as US$1000 per animal. This US$ price, of course, depends on the current exchange rate. In 1993, a medium-size camel was selling for E£1200 at Imbaba, while a bigger one was E£3000. Note that you might not be buying a great pedigree: the bulk of camels on sale are destined for the slaughterhouse.

Once you've purchased your camel you then have to buy a proper saddle and appropriate kit bags. It all gets somewhat costly and complicated. It would be a good idea to try and get hold of an article by Rene Dee called 'Travel by Camel', which appeared in *The Traveller's Handbook*.

If you're less adventurous (or more sensible!) there are easier and less physically and financially draining ways to realise your camel fantasies. It's easiest to hire a camel for a couple of hours and take a tour around the pyramids at Giza or the temple complex at Saqqara. A guide usually accompanies you. It is also easy to arrange a camel safari in the Sinai from near Nuweiba and Dahab.

More information about such treks is given in the Sinai chapter.

DONKEY

Donkeys are a very popular means of transport and you'll see them everywhere in Egypt except, perhaps, in restaurants. *Don't* buy one of these critters. They are cheap enough to rent for a couple of hours, or a few days, for getting you around some of Egypt's ancient sites.

BOAT

Felucca

The ancient sailboats of the Nile are still the most common means of transport up and down the river. Sunset is one of the best times to take a felucca ride, but you can arrange a few hours' peaceful sailing at any time from just about anywhere on the Nile.

The best trip to make, however, is the journey between Aswan and Esna, Edfu or Kom Ombo; this takes from one to three days. See the Aswan Getting There & Away section for more information on how to arrange a trip.

Yacht

It is possible to take a yacht into Egyptian waters and ports. There are 12 designated ports of entry, including Alexandria, Port Said, Sharm el-Sheikh, Suez, Dahab, Nuweiba and Ismailia. A Security permit is required to enter the Nile River, and transit fees of US$10 per person and US$20 for the yacht need to be paid to negotiate the Suez Canal. These and other fees are liable to change.

You will need all the usual documentation for the yacht, plus six copies of the crew list. You will also need valid visas and a raft of other bits of paper, including health certificate, customs list of yacht's equipment and insurance policy (for the Suez Canal). You can get visas on arrival in your first port.

It is also possible to shelter in other 'nonentry' ports, but you cannot go ashore.

Fuel is available in all ports of entry, and navigational charts in Alexandria, Port Said and Suez (ask for 'Marinkart'). There are nine yacht clubs in Egypt. For more details, contact your own yacht club before heading for Egypt.

Before departing, a departure permit has to be obtained from the Coast Guard and you are supposed to leave within 24 hours of obtaining it.

If you want to get a lift on a yacht around Egypt or heading elsewhere, it can be best done in Suez. For more details, see the Suez section.

LOCAL TRANSPORT

To/From the Airport

The great majority of visitors to Egypt come through Cairo Airport. You will be hassled no end to take a taxi or limousine for inflated prices – if you accept, triple check what they think you have agreed to pay, as there is an irritating tendency to nod at what you say and hit you with an out-of-the-world fare later on. Despite claims that the official fare to central Cairo is E£28, ruthless bargaining can get them down to E£15. The aforementioned hotel touts are also in cahoots with the drivers, solemnly shaking their heads at suggestions of paying less than the 'official fare' and declaring that there is no bus.

In fact there are quite a few buses and minibuses to various points in Cairo from the old terminal, and several from the new terminal. See the Cairo Getting Around section for more details.

There are a couple of limousine services that run between the airports and destinations in the capital, for about E£30 to E£50.

From Alexandria Airport there are several buses and minibuses to Midan Orabi in the centre of town. A taxi should cost E£10, but you'll often be hit by demands for as much as E£20.

Bus

Cairo and Alexandria are the only cities in Egypt with their own bus systems, although neither one ever seems to have enough vehicles. If this is your first visit to a developing country, it will probably be the first time you have ever seen buses as crowded as these.

You may find it more tempting to photograph than ride them, but this tends to anger the locals, who object to being treated like a tourist sight – so perhaps you should consider your reasons for doing so.

Local buses seem to awaken an unusual level of energy in Egyptians. Typically laid back to the point of being aggravating, seemingly always prepared to wait until tomorrow to get something done, Egyptians, and Cairenes in particular, seem not to be able to get on to that bus fast enough. Stampeding the entrance before the thing has even slowed down, there can be an almighty lot of pushing and shoving to barge on – even when hardly anyone is using that particular service. In summer it is advisable not to get crowded buses. There are times when, crammed up the back with exhaust fumes billowing around you and ever more people squeezing on, asphyxiation seems perilously close.

Minibus & Microbus

More comfortable and slightly more expensive are government-run minibuses, which also only run in Cairo and Alexandria. Increasingly, they are facing competition from privately owned and usually unmarked microbuses. For the average traveller, the latter are difficult to use, as it is quite unclear where most of them go. The exception is the run from Midan Tahrir in Cairo to the pyramids. Most of the smaller cities and towns have similar microbuses doing set runs around town. The distinction between what is a minibus and what is a microbus is not easy to extract from the locals. For the sake of clarity, only the government-run services in Cairo and Alexandria will be referred to as minibuses – the rest are microbuses.

Metro

Cairo is the only city in Egypt (indeed in Africa) with a metro system. It's a single line of 33 stations that stretches for 43 km from the southern suburb of Helwan to Al-Marg near Heliopolis. The five stations in central Cairo are the only ones underground. At least two more lines are planned, one between Shubra and Giza. Feasibility studies are being done for an underground train line in Alexandria.

The metro is fast, inexpensive (30 pt from Midan Tahrir to Ramses Station) and usually not crowded. It seems to have significantly reduced traffic in central Cairo.

Tram

Cairo and Alexandria are also the only two cities with tram systems. Alexandria's trams are relatively efficient and go all over the city but they also get quite crowded. Cairo's trams (actually known to Cairenes as the 'metro' – confused?) are similar, but only three lines remain.

Taxi

There are taxis in most cities in Egypt. The most common and cheapest are the black and white taxis in Cairo and the black and orange ones in Alexandria. Almost all of them have meters but most of the meters don't work, so you have to pay what you think is right and be prepared to argue and bargain. The best method for paying is to get out of the cab when you arrive at your destination, stick the money through the front passenger's side window and walk away.

If you have to argue the price with the driver and he seems to be trying to cheat you, then just mention the police, and the taxi driver will probably accept your price to avoid any hassle. Don't be intimidated by the driver's yelling; it's usually just an act to get you to cough up more money. If he agrees with you about seeing the police, then the fare you offered is probably too low. Sometimes, as one traveller reports, the driver may even jump out of the car, rip open his shirt like Superman and pound on his chest. Fortunately, this latter tactic is rarely used.

Don't be afraid to hop out just after getting in if, as sometimes happens, the driver names too high a fare. Simply tell him what you are prepared to pay and demand to be let out if he does not accept.

The taxis sometimes marked 'Special' charge more than other taxis; these are almost always Peugeot 504s that can hold up to seven passengers. The advantage of these taxis is that you can get a group together and commandeer one for a trip to the pyramids or Saqqara for less than a black and white taxi might charge.

Whichever type of taxi you choose, if you're uncertain about the fare, then first consult a local or, as a last resort, negotiate the price before you get in. For long trips, such as to the pyramids or the airport, the driver will usually insist on first setting a fare. If possible, however, the best strategy whenever you take a taxi is to pretend that you know the fare, and pay after you've left the taxi.

When you want a taxi, stand where a driver can see you and wave your arm. When he slows down, yell out your destination so that, if he feels like it, he can stop for you. It's quite common to share a taxi with other passengers.

TOURS

There are numerous possibilities for organising tours in Egypt. As with those organised outside the country, the most popular tend to involve Nile cruises.

Top-of-the-range cruises can be booked through the Nile, Sheraton and Oberoi hotels. A single bed, meals and sightseeing for about four days costs around US$700. Some of the operators at this level include: Hilton Nile Cruises (☎ 740880); Cairo Hotel/Nile Tours (☎ 340-0675), 23B Sharia Ismail Mohammed; Oberoi Hotels & Misr Travel Co (☎ 247-0077), Misr Travel Tower Abbassiya; Presidential Nile Cruises (☎ 340-0517), 13 Sharia Marashli, Zamalek;

Travcotels (☎ 340-0959), 112-116 Sharia 26th of July, Zamalek; and Sonesta Nile Cruises (☎ 262-8111), Sonesta Hotel, At-Tayaran, Nasr City.

A host of Cairo travel agencies organise less luxurious tours of a similar duration. Many such agencies, including Misr Travel (☎ 393-0100), Sphinx Tours (☎ 778799) and Eastmar Travel (☎ 753147), cluster around Sharias Qasr el-Nil and Talaat Harb and Midan Talaat Harb.

Misr Travel has a lengthy programme of other less costly, if also not quite so romantic, tours, including four-day trips to the New Valley (read oases) and a series of full-day excursions to Luxor (flying), Alexandria, Al-Faiyum and Wadi Natrun.

There is also a long list of possible one and half-day sightseeing tours of Cairo itself. All those listed on their main brochure require a minimum of six people. However, each day of the week they have a sightseeing tour taking in different parts of the city, which single tourists can sign up for. They all cost between US$35 and US$45.

Cairo

Cairo is a seething, breathing monster of a city that swallows new arrivals and consumes those who return. All are destined to be captured and captivated in some small way by its incredible past and vibrant present. There are few, if any, cities in the world where the clash between old and new, modern and traditional, and East and West is more evident. Tall, gleaming hotels and office buildings overlook streets where cars and buses rumble and weave past donkey carts and their stubborn drivers. Less than one km from a computer store and supermarket in central Cairo there are mud-brick houses where goats still wander through 'living rooms' and water is obtained from spigots down the street. This is not something the authorities are totally happy with, and shanty towns on the edge of Greater Cairo and Giza became the particular object of municipal attention in early 1993, with vows to either rehouse people or bring basic utilities to them.

Cairo is still the heart of Egypt and is allegorically called the Mother of the World. Since its rise in the 9th century, under Ibn Tulun, Egyptians have known Cairo as Al-Qahira, which means 'the victorious', and Misr (or Masr), which also means 'Egypt'. For Egyptians it is the centre of the country and has been attracting them in increasing numbers for centuries. No-one is sure how many people have been drawn in from the countryside, even over the past few years, but the city has grown to mammoth proportions. Estimates of Greater Cairo's population hover at 15 million or more – roughly a quarter of Egypt's total.

The massive and continual increase in the number of people has overwhelmed the city. Housing shortages are rife; buses are packed to the hilt; snarled traffic paralyses life in the city; and broken pipes spew water and sewage into the streets. Even the rare burst of rain is enough to cause streets to run with muck. Everything is discoloured – buildings,

buses and footpaths are brown and grey from smog and desert dust.

Amidst this chaos, the city government is trying to do what it can. An underground rail line with 33 stations, including five in central Cairo, has alleviated traffic problems – although for the first-time visitor that may be hard to believe. New lines are planned. Satellite suburbs such as Nasser City, 6 October City and 10 Ramadan City have been, or are being, built to alleviate housing shortages, although people have not been as quick as was hoped to move to them. There have even been somewhat futile attempts to ban donkey carts from the city streets.

HISTORY

The oldest reminder of Cairo's ancient beginnings is to be found in Fustat and what is now known as Old Cairo, south of the modern city's centre. Not far from here Seth and Horus are supposed to have engaged in combat. Around 500 BC, the Persians turned the area into a fortress, known as Babylon, and were later replaced by the Ptolemys, Romans and finally Byzantines.

The local Byzantine commander, Cyrus, allowed himself to be lured out of the city into battle against the invading Muslim Arab forces of Amr ibn al-As near Heliopolis in 640 AD. After his victory, Amr established himself at Fustat, outside the Christian city. The Christian and Jewish inhabitants, as People of the Book, were treated reasonably, and in the following two centuries Babylon and Fustat melded as the administrative centre of an important granary for the new Muslim world order.

Ibn Tulun, appointed by the caliph in Baghdad as governor of Egypt, eventually exploited internal weaknesses in the caliphate to establish his virtual independence and overrun Syria. After his death in 884, Syria was lost, but Egypt's autonomy within the Muslim world was untouched. Ibn Tulun left behind him one of the great monuments of the Islamic world – the mosque named after him south of what is now called Islamic Cairo.

In June 969, the Fatimids, coming from the west, conquered Egypt. These Ismaili Shi'ites rejected the Sunni Abbassid caliphate in Baghdad and claimed the moral leadership of the whole Muslim world. The general Gawhar determined that a new city should be built north of Fustat. The area, it is said, was pegged out and labourers waited for a signal from Moorish astrologers, who were to ring bells attached to the ropes marking off the area when the right moment came. A raven landed on the rope and set off the bells, however, with the planet Mars (al-Qahir) in the ascendant. So work began and, to avoid evil, it was decided to call the city al-Qahira (Cairo): it became the capital of an independent empire stretching from North Africa and Sicily to Yemen. Fatimid rule soon degenerated. One of its more odd-ball products was Al-Hakim, who banned the production of women's shoes to make women stay indoors and then later banned daytime work, because he liked staying up at night and thought everyone else should too. He disappeared one night on his mule Moon, but as a divine character became the focus of what is now known as the Druse faith. He left an elegant mosque in the north of the Fatimid city, inside the two remaining medieval city gates in the north, Bab an-Nasr and Bab al-Futuh.

In 1171, Salah ad-Din (known to the Crusaders and later to the West as Saladin), restored Sunni rule in Cairo and established a new dynasty, the Ayyubids. This was a welcome change to Cairenes after the last days of confused Fatimid rule, in which, fearing the city would fall to the advancing Crusaders, they destroyed the city of Fustat in a kind of policy of scorched earth – for nothing, as it turned out. Salah ad-Din went on to bring most of Syria under his control and break the back of the Crusader kingdoms in Palestine, symbolised by his capture of Jerusalem. It was Salah ad-Din's idea to erect a defensive wall enclosing Cairo and Fustat together, and he established the citadel that dominates the city still.

His dynasty met its end in 1250, when the Mamluks, a Turkish slave-soldier class, took the reins of power. To them are owed a great many of the monuments remaining in what today is called Islamic Cairo. Their rule was colourful and often bloody. There was no real system of succession, and every change of power usually involved an orgy of blood-letting.

Mamluk rule lasted until the arrival of the Ottoman Turks, who incorporated Egypt into their empire in 1517. Cairo's days as a great imperial centre were at an end.

The growing influence of the French and British in the 19th century, despite continued nominal Ottoman rule, left its imprint in the part of Cairo that lies between the Nile and Islamic Cairo, and on the island of Zamalek. Mohammed Ali, the Albanian trooper who became the virtual sovereign of Egypt, left behind him the great mosque, in a gaudy Turkish style, that still dominates the citadel.

Cairo was the headquarters of British operations during WW I, and Commonwealth troops brought a colourful, if not terribly reputable, dimension to Cairo life while on leave in the war years. Already in the early years of the century, Cairo was attracting increasing numbers of Egyptians from elsewhere in the country, but the pace of growth picked up rapidly after WW II. Today, the sprawling city is bursting at the seams, with a population vaguely estimated at 15 to 18 million.

The most spectacular recent event in the lives of Cairenes, and one that demonstrated again how far Egypt has still to come, was the earthquake that hit the city in October 1992. More than 500 people died and 800 buildings were flattened. Another 10,000 were badly damaged and almost 800 schools were damaged beyond repair. Many of the city's monuments were also damaged. The government's slowness to rehouse the thousands of homeless led to violent demonstrations. Indeed, accusations run rife that most of the international aid sent to help deal with the disaster has ended up where it

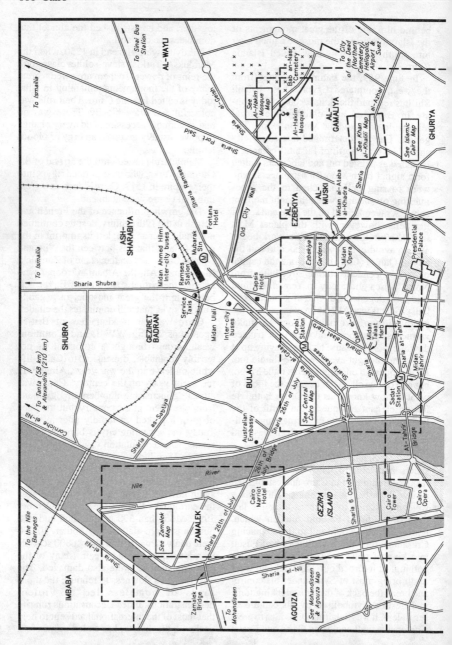

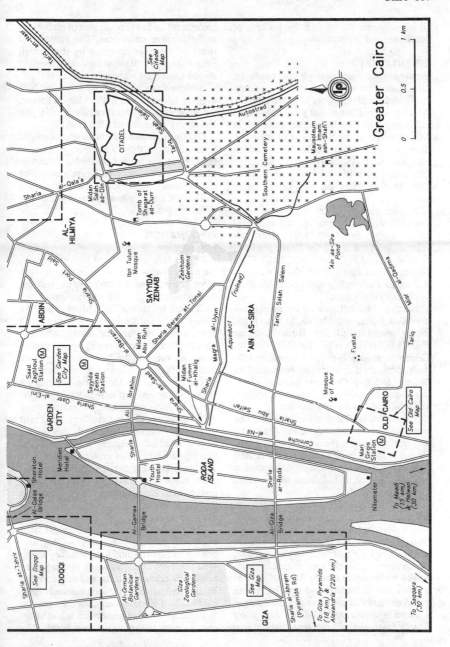

Greater Cairo

so often seems to – lining the pockets of politicians and bureaucrats.

ORIENTATION

Finding your way through the chaos is, remarkably, not as complicated as you may first think, and Cairo is a great city for walking around because it's not too spread out. Almost all travellers find themselves in Midan Tahrir at the beginning of their trip through Egypt. From Midan Tahrir north-east to Midan Talaat Harb and Ezbekiya Gardens you will find most of Egypt's Western-style shops and many of the budget hotels.

Further east there are some of Cairo's poorer districts, the market and medieval neighbourhoods of Al-Muski, Darb al-Ahmar and the City of the Dead. South of Darb al-Ahmar is the ancient Citadel. Continuing farther east towards the airport you will enter Heliopolis, also called Masr al-Gadida or New Cairo.

North of Midan Tahrir are the neighbourhoods of Bulaq and Shubra. In the 1800s, under Mohammed Ali, Bulaq became Cairo's industrial centre. Today, it's one of Cairo's most densely populated areas and the industrialisation has spread northward to Shubra. Much of the recent Islamist unrest has its source in this area. Ramses Station is at the junction of the two districts.

West of Midan Tahrir is Gezira Island, the home of Cairo's elite, including diplomats and one of Egypt's foremost soccer teams. On the northern end of Gezira is the central Cairo district of Zamalek, with its embassies, modern apartment buildings and a large private sports club.

Across the river from Gezira Island are, from south to north, the districts of: Giza, which stretches to the edge of the desert; Doqqi (often written Dokki), which has the rest of Cairo University and the zoo; Agouza; Mohandiseen, which was originally conceived by President Gamal Abdel Nasser as a district of engineers; and Imbaba, where camel herders still come to hawk their wares.

Heading south from Midan Tahrir along Sharia Qasr al-Eini, the first district you come to is Garden City, an area of embassies and expensive residences. The convoluted street pattern was designed by the British early this century to allow a quick, defensible escape from their embassy.

Bridges from Garden City cross the Nile to Roda Island, home to the Manyal Palace, the Nilometer, the Meridien Hotel, and Cairo University's Faculty of Medicine.

Old Cairo, famous as the Coptic centre of Cairo, is about three km south of Garden City. Eight km further on is the district of Maadi, home to many of Egypt's wealthier citizens and several thousand expatriates.

That's Cairo. Follow the maps and you shouldn't get lost.

INFORMATION
Registration

All foreigners are required to register with the police within seven days of their arrival. Most hotels, even the cheap ones, will get your passport registered for you, sometimes for a small fee (about E£2). More expensive hotels do it automatically, without even being asked. A triangular stamp, which is usually placed next to the Egyptian visa in your passport, with the date filled in by hand, indicates that registration has been done.

You can go to the Mogamma building on Midan Tahrir yourself to register. The registration is usually a simple procedure taking only a minute or two, but at other times a visit to this government behemoth can be an adventure and a frustrating lesson in Egyptian bureaucracy. This extraordinarily ugly 14-storey building houses 18,000 bureaucrats from 14 ministries and 65 other government departments. It is estimated 20,000 people try to squeeze in and out of the place every day.

The registration office is on the 1st floor in a booth marked – what else? – 'Registration'. You fill in a small form and they stamp your passport. Sometimes you may be asked to go to window 45, at the end of a corridor leading left from the booth marked 'Registration' – the process remains the same.

If you need any other service, ask at Information, next to the registration booth. The

Mogamma offices are open (for registration only) Saturday to Wednesday from 8 am to 4 pm; on Thursday from 8 am to 2 pm; on Friday and holidays from 10 am to 1 pm, and every evening from 8 to 10 pm (summer) or 7 to 9 pm (winter). These hours are, however, apt to change, especially during Ramadan.

For anything other than registration, the Mogamma is open only from 8 am to 2 pm every day but Friday.

On the ground floor, in room 99, there's a small photo studio – Studio Mogamma Tahrir – where you can get four passport-size colour photographs for E£15. If you really only need B&W photographs, though, one of the photographers in front of the Mogamma will use an antique box camera to copy your passport photo or other photo and make four copies for only E£3. It's worth buying the photos even if you don't need them just to watch the photographer open and close little hatches on the box and expose the film.

Visa Extensions

You also get visa extensions from the Mogamma building (see Registration for the opening hours), although this can take longer than registration. You need bank receipts showing you have changed US$180 for every month you want to stay, and one passport size photo. Go to window 42 and ask for the form (E£5.75) and fill it in. Then go to windows 22-27 to process it. They'll shunt you to window 28 to pick it up and pay E£6.10.

Re-Entry Visas

Once again, go to the Mogamma building (see the above Registration section for opening hours). Start at window 42 and pay for the appropriate form (65 pt). Fill it in and go to windows 17 and 18. It will take about an hour to process. The re-entry visa's validity will extend to the limit of your visa or extension. It costs E£13.10.

Tourist Offices

The head office of the Ministry of Tourism (☎ 391-3454), 5 Sharia Adly, is about half a block west of Ezbekiya Gardens, near Midan Opera. The staff in the front office are usually extremely helpful, although they have their off days. If they can't find the answers to your questions in their sparse but colourful tourist brochures or notebooks, they will call someone who does know. It's open every day: usually from 8.30 am to 7 pm, but only from 9 am to 5 pm during Ramadan. You can leave messages under the glass on the main desk.

Cairo International Airport's new terminal has a tourism office (☎ 291-4255/77) just after customs control; so does the old terminal (☎ 667475). The new terminal one should be open 24 hours, but don't bank on it. Don't be fooled by the so-called tourist officials who approach you to book hotel rooms; see the Accommodation section in the Facts for the Visitor chapter for more on these airport hotel touts.

There's also a tourist office (☎ 385-0259) at the pyramids; it's on Pyramids Rd (also known as Sharia al-Haram), on the left just after the junction with the Desert Rd to Alexandria. It's usually open from 8.30 am to 5 pm every day. There is another small office at the Manyal Palace.

Misr Travel (☎ 393-0010), the official Egyptian government travel agency, is at 1 Sharia Talaat Harb.

Money

Changing money has become much easier and more flexible in the past few years. In addition to the many foreign banks that have branches in Cairo, the main Egyptian banks are also reasonable places to change money. Cash advances in E£ are available at the Bank of America and at many branches of Banque Misr and the Egyptian Arab-African Bank (which sometimes seems to go by the name of the Arab-African International Bank) if you have a Visa card or MasterCard. Some branches of Banque Misr will give you the advances in foreign currency. The only limits are those on your card and the availability of cash at any given momemt. Money can be wired through the following banks in Cairo:

Bank of America
106 Sharia Qasr al-Eini, Garden City (☎ 354-7508). It is open from 8.30 am to 2 pm, Sunday to Thursday, but only from 10 am to 1.30 pm during Ramadan.

Barclays International
Banque du Caire, 12 Midan ash-Sheikh Yusuf, Garden City (☎ 354-0686). Personal banking services are available, but the office specialises in corporate banking. Mail must be addressed to PO Box 2325, Cairo.

Lloyds Bank Group
44 Sharia Mohammed Mazhar, Zamalek (☎ 340-6437). Personal and corporate banking facilities are available.

Citibank
4 Sharia Ahmed Pasha, Garden City (☎ 354-0938). It is open from 8.30 am to 2 pm Sunday to Thursday.

Misr America International Bank
8 Sharia Ibrahim Neguib, Garden City (☎ 756341). This is the head office of an Egyptian bank that is affiliated with the Bank of America.

Most Egyptian banks, including Banque Misr, have the same morning hours (8.30 am to 2 pm), but also open for a couple of hours from 5 or 6 pm. Some open on Saturday too. There are Banque Misr exchange offices at the Nile Hilton and outside Shepheard's Hotel that are open 24 hours a day.

American Express American Express has several offices in Cairo. They can provide US$ cash for US$ travellers' cheques, exchange money, cash personal cheques or sell travellers' cheques. An American Express card is necessary for cashing personal cheques. Travellers' cheques or hard currency can be purchased with American Express cards or MasterCard.

You should change money for a visa extension at a commercial bank, although this rule is subject to change. Without the right kind of receipt, your application can be knocked back. American Express issues two different kinds of receipts, one for those involving the purchase of Egyptian currency, and another for transactions resulting in the purchase of foreign currency. The latter are no good for visa extensions or buying air tickets. The former are good at least for air tickets.

There are American Express offices at:

Central Cairo
Egypt Head Office, 17 Sharia Mohammed Bassiuni (☎ 764244)
15 Sharia Qasr el-Nil, between Midan Tahrir and Midan Talaat Harb (☎ 750426). It is open from 8.30 am to 6 pm, but only from 9 am to 4 pm during Ramadan. The client letter service is closed on Friday, and open until 5 pm on other days.

Ramses Hilton
1115 Corniche el-Nil, Garden City (☎ 773690, 744899)

Nile Hilton
Corniche el-Nil (☎ 765810, 764342)

Sheraton Hotel
Sharia el-Nil, Doqqi (☎ 348-8937)

Cairo Marriott
Sharia Gezira, Zamalek (☎ 341-0136, 340-6542)

Hotel Pullman Maadi Towers
Rd 18, Maadi (☎ 350-7817)

Meridien Heliopolis
51 Sharia Oroubal (☎ 290-9157/8)

Semiramis Hotel
Corniche el-Nil, Garden City (☎ 354-0613/4)

Cairo International Airport
(☎ 670895)

Thomas Cook Thomas Cook has four offices in Cairo, and a foreign exchange counter at Cairo International Airport (☎ 244-3149, fax 201-6378). The offices are at:

Central Cairo
17 Sharia Mohammed Bassiuni (☎ 574-7183, fax 762750)
5 Sharia Latin America, Garden City (☎ 357-2331, fax 354-9322)

Maadi
88 Rd 9, Station Square (☎ 351-1438, fax 350-2651)

Mohandiseen
Shops 9 & 10, Sharia 26th of July (☎ 346-7187, fax 342-1530)

Heliopolis
7 Sharia Baghdad (☎ 291-9024, fax 291-6215)

Exchange Offices A growing number of exchange offices is springing up around Cairo. They generally deal only in cash transactions. Here you can exchange your E£ for hard currency. There is no need to present bank receipts to do this. You can then use the hard currency to buy travellers' cheques at Banque Misr branches or American Express.

The only advantage over the Banque Misr branches that also sell hard currency is the sometimes slightly better rate and longer opening hours.

Post

Cairo's GPO, in Midan Ataba near Midan Opera and the Ezbekiya Gardens, is open from 7 am to 7 pm, supposedly seven days a week (be wary on Fridays and public holidays). The poste restante is around the corner to the right of the main entrance, through the last door of the building, opposite the EMS fast mail office, and is open from 8 am to 6 pm (Fridays and holidays from 10 am until noon only). EMS is open from 8 am to 7 pm every day but Friday, and also has a fax service. Branch post and EMS offices close between 2 and 3 pm.

To send a package you must go to the office at Midan Ramses; it's the huge, squat building to the north of the railway station, and is open every day but Friday from 8 am to 1 pm only. Set aside a couple of hours for this process, bring your passport and a strong sense of the absurd. Do not seal your package before letting a customs official see the contents.

Go to the 2nd floor and find room 23 to pick up form 13 (E£5). You'll notice it's all in Arabic. Go back towards the stairs and turn right into the big hall. Turn left and get someone to help you fill it in. You'll then be pointed in the direction of some desks. In between eating and chatting, they'll ask you questions, look at the items to be sent, fill in forms and eventually send you back to the counter, where you'll buy revenue stamps for E£2. You'll probably be sent down to the 1st floor to find someone who will actually lick the stamps and apply them to various bits of paper, upon which you'll be directed to whence you came. There, two or three more people will need to countersign everything and add a few more unintelligible marks to empty spaces. You then pay E£2 to have the parcel wrapped or, in the case of bigger ones, sewn up with cloth – bring your own cardboard boxes if you think you're going to need them.

Then back to the counter to fill in a few more customs forms, have the parcel weighed and pay for it. Airmail to the UK and Australia costs E£16 and E£32.50 a kg respectively. Sea mail to both is E£8.35. Sometimes they will tell you there is no sea mail. It's very difficult to make any sense of it at all. Parcels of more then 20 kg will not be accepted. Nor should they be bigger than one metre long, wide and deep.

You may have to get export licences or have goods inspected, depending on what they are. It's risky, but you're probably better off trying to get it through first time rather than going through the hassle of tracking down the right authorities. Printed matter must supposedly go through the censors. Audio and visual material has to be checked by the censorship authorities at 58 Sharia Qasr el-Nil. Al-Azhar University has a department that likes to inspect religious books, and foodstuffs and medicines also need clearance. The total worth of the goods being sent must not exceed E£250.

The easiest way to send a package is to pay someone else a small fee and have them do it for you. Some shopkeepers will provide this service, especially if you've bought the article in their bazaar. It should include obtaining an export licence, packaging and mailing.

There are also post office branches at: Cairo International Airport (in the departures section); on Midan Falaki; in the grounds of the Egyptian Museum; and at Ramses Station. You can only send packages from the Midan Ramses branch. Hours are 8.30 am to 2 pm, except Friday.

For more details of postage rates, see Post & Telecommunications in the Facts for the Visitor chapter.

In addition to the EMS fast mail service, you could try DHL (☎ 355-7301), which has its head office at 20 Sharia Gamal ad-Din Abu al-Mahasin, Garden City; Federal Express (☎ 355-0247), 1079 Corniche el-Nil, Garden City; Middle East Courier Service (☎ 245-9281), 1 Sharia Mahmoud Hafez, Heliopolis; and TNT Skypak (☎ 348-8204), at 33 Sharia Doqqi, Doqqi. Most of them have several offices. These courier services are also possible sources of free or discounted air tickets to various destinations outside Egypt, because they often need couriers to transport their packages.

Telecommunications

Telephone Since 1986, Cairo has been revamping its telephone system and changing the numbering system. It's hard to know which parts of the city have changed and which haven't, and which will and which won't. Some parts of the same street, for example, have new numbers while others don't. Those places that have changed generally now have seven-digit numbers, while those that have not have retained numbers of six digits or less. Often the first digit or two of the old number has been dropped and replaced by two or three new ones, but this is not a strict rule. Many numbers in the up-market Zamalek area have lost, say, an initial 8, replaced by 34. The rest of the number remains unchanged.

There seem to be few rules, however, and if you are having trouble, you may need to get help to track the number down. The tourist offices may help, otherwise try *Cairo: A Practical Guide*. At the time of writing the latest available edition was from 1988, long overdue for a revamp. If there isn't one, an alternative is the small but up-to-date Blue Pages telephone directory, which you can find in the American University in Cairo Bookstore and maybe some hotels – it is, however, pretty limited. There's also a Cairo 'yellow pages' telephone directory, available at most of the major hotels. As a last resort, you can ask someone to look up a number in the multivolume Egyptian telephone directory.

Local telephone calls cost 10 pt in pay phones. The public phones (which come in a variety of colours, including steel grey, yellow and green) are usually in front of telephone offices, in metro stations, and in the lobbies of major hotels, and often don't work.

Many kiosks and small shops have telephones for public use, for 50 pt per local call. The Nile Hilton, right by Midan Tahrir, has a bank of pay phones for which they sell 50 pt tokens. Small hotels usually allow guests to use their phones for 50 pt to E£1.

Long-distance calls can be made from some home phones, but most are made from hotels or telephone offices. Many hotels, but not the very cheap ones, have direct international lines, but they'll charge more than the telephone offices (sometimes as much as double). At either place the connections are usually quite good. It's impossible to make collect calls from Egypt.

Card phones (look out for the orange phones) are increasingly coming into use. Otherwise, calls booked at telephone offices must be paid for in advance. They can either be taken in a booth at the office or directed to an outside number such as a private home or hotel. If you opt for the latter, keep the receipt just in case you need a refund for an incomplete call.

There are telephone offices in several places around Cairo, and most have a few card phones; just look for the sign with a telephone dial on it. There's an office on the north side of Midan Tahrir, in Sharia Adly near the tourist information office, in Sharia Alfi Bey, in Sharia Mohammed Mahmud in the Telecommunications building and on Sharia 26th of July in Zamalek. All main telephone offices are open 24 hours a day. Branch offices are open from 7 am to 10 pm.

For information on rates, see the Post & Telecommunications section of the Facts for the Visitor chapter.

Telegram & Fax Telegrams can be sent from most of the telephone offices. The charge for a telegram is 66 pt per word to the UK and 76 pt per word to Australia. Each word in an address is also counted. Faxes can be sent from the telephone offices on Sharia Adly (to

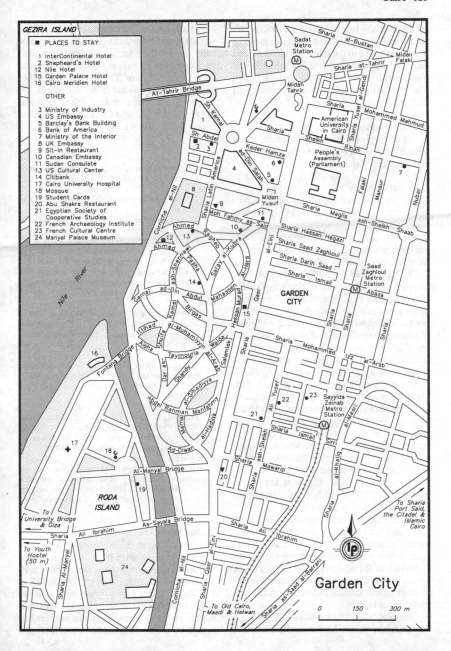

the right of the office and up the stairs) and Sharia Alfi Bey. As a pointer to the range in prices, one page to the UK costs E£13.55 and E£20.15 to Australia. Most larger hotels will also provide this service, but at greater cost. The Nile Hilton has a minimum charge of E£34.50 for a fax to the UK.

Foreign Embassies
A list of foreign embassies in Cairo, along with consulates elsewhere in Egypt, is in the Facts for the Visitor chapter.

Cultural Centres
There are several cultural centres in Cairo sponsored by other countries. Most run libraries, show films and stage various lectures, exhibitions and performances. They are great places to catch up on the latest news from home or to watch a free movie or video.

The American Cultural Center (☎ 357-3436) is at 4 Sharia Ahmed Ragheb, Garden City, opposite the UK embassy. The library holds more than 200 periodicals and 10,000 books, and shows *Worldnet's MacNeil/Lehrer News Hour* Monday to Friday from noon and the CBS *Evening News* Monday to Friday from 1 to 1.30 pm. On Sunday at noon there is the hour-long ABC *News Weekly Highlights*, repeated on Monday at 3 pm. Used-book sales are also arranged occasionally. The reading rooms are open from 10 am to 8 pm on Monday and Wednesday, and from 10 am to 4 pm the rest of the week except on Saturday and American and Egyptian holidays, when they're closed.

The British Council Library (☎ 345-3281), which is in a villa near the circus grounds at 192 Sharia el-Nil, Agouza, carries most major daily and weekly newspapers. It has more than 35,000 books and 148 periodicals, and the reading rooms are open daily, except Sunday, from 9 am to 1.50 pm and from 3 to 8 pm. Library membership costs E£35 or half for students at the Council. The Council offers an extensive range of classes in English and Arabic, and occasionally puts on films and plays.

Germany's Goethe Institut (☎ 759877), 5 Sharia Abdel Salam Aref, near the Cleopatra

Hotel and Midan Tahrir, presents interesting seminars and lectures in German on Egyptology and other topics. There are also performances by visiting music groups and special art exhibits. The library has rather erratic hours, so phone first.

There are quite a few other cultural centres, a full list of which you can find in *Cairo Today*. They include:

Canada
  Canadian Embassy, 6 Sharia Mohammed Fahmy as-Said, Garden City (☎ 354-3119)
France
  1 Madrassat al-Huquq al-Fransiyya, Mounira (☎ 354-7679)
  27 Sharia Sabri Abu Alam, Midan Ismailia, Heliopolis (☎ 663241)
  Both centres regularly put on films, lectures and exhibitions, have libraries open to the public (call to check hours, as they are all over the place) and run French and Arabic-language courses. Get news and views from the French-speaking world via the satellite TV station TV-5.
Italy
  Istituto Culturale Italiano, 3 Sharia as-Sheikh Marsafy, Zamalek (☎ 340-8791). The centre puts on films and organises lectures. There is also a library.
Japan
  Japanese Cultural Centre, 2 Sharia Abdel kader Hamza, Garden City (☎ 355-3962). The centre is open from 9 am to 2 pm daily except Friday and Saturday.
India
  Information Service of India, 23 Sharia Talaat Harb (☎ 393-3396). If you don't have Lonely Planet's *India – a travel survival kit*, this is the next best source of information on India.
Netherlands
  Netherlands Institute of Archaeology and Arabic Studies, 1 Sharia Mahmoud Azmy, Zamalek (☎ 340-0076). The institute usually has lectures every Tuesday evening, except in summer.

Travel Agencies
The area around Midan Tahrir in central Cairo is teeming with travel agencies. One that has been recommended and seems fairly efficient is De Castro Tours (☎ 574-3144), at 12 Sharia Talaat Harb. They have a wide range of destinations and offer student discounts on many fares. They are not terribly fussed by the business of bank receipts, and

will accept credit cards for payment where the airline concerned also does.

Just down the road is Norma Tours, which touts itself as being a cheap air-fare specialist. Unfortunately though, one thing about Cairo is that it is no London bucket shop scene. This does not mean you shouldn't hunt around, but don't expect huge differences or amazing deals.

Bookshops & Newsstands
One of the best English-language bookshops in Egypt, and probably the whole of the Middle East, is the Anglo-Egyptian Bookshop. It has an impressive range of works on Egypt, the Middle East and a whole lot of other things besides.

For English speakers, the American University in Cairo (AUC) Bookstore, inside the university entrance on Sharia Mohammed Mahmud, carries an excellent selection of books in English, including a wide range of books and guides about life in Egypt. The bookstore also carries many Lonely Planet titles (including this book), periodicals and newspapers from Europe and the USA. It opens from 8.30 am to 4 pm Sunday to Thursday and from 10 am to 3 pm on Saturday. It's closed on Friday and in August. There is also a much smaller branch at the new AUC College on Sharia Mohammed Sakeb in Zamalek.

If these fail to satisfy, the next stop might be the predominantly German-language Lehnert & Landrock, 44 Sharia Sherif. It carries a reasonable selection of books on Egypt in German, English and French, and maps too.

A reasonable, but not brilliant, possibility is Shourouk, on Midan Talaat Harb and at 3 Sharia al-Bursa al-Gedida, off Sharia Qasr el-Nil. They have books, mainly in English and French, on Egypt, including some translations of contemporary Egyptian authors such as Mahfouz – although you are better off at the AUC Bookstore for his works. In front, there are several major news magazines and newspapers.

In front of Groppi's on Midan Talaat Harb is one of the better newspaper and magazine

stands in Cairo. It carries the most recent editions of major newspapers and magazines from around the world, including *Time, Newsweek*, the *Times* and the *International Herald Tribune*. You can also find most of the English-language Cairo publications here. Another good place to look for a wide range of newspapers and magazines is along Sharia 26th of July in Zamalek.

Across the street from Groppi's at 15 Sharia Qasr el-Nil is L'Orientaliste, one of only three bookshops in the world specialising in Egyptology. L'Orientaliste has an excellent collection of antiquarian books and prints of 19th century Egypt.

Nearby in Midan Talaat Harb, Madbouly (or Madbouli) bookshop has a limited collection of books in English, French and German.

For a reasonable collection of English literature, check out the bookshop at the International Language Institute at 3 Sharia Mahmoud Azmy, Sahafayeen.

If it's books in French you're after, head straight for the Maison des Livres on Sharia Qasr el-Nil, just by Sharia Sherif. It's the best.

With a dusty range of Italian books (plus a reasonable smattering of books in other languages) and a good selection of Italian newspapers, the Mengozzi bookshop across the road from the Café l'Américaine on Sharia Talaat Harb is probably the only place to go.

There are quite a few other bookshops around town, and also in most of the big hotels, but none match the ones already listed.

In early 1993, a Cairo institution was eliminated. The 50-year-old flea market at Ezbekiya Gardens, off Midan Opera, was 'cleaned up' – completely removed. Here, for years, Cairenes and outsiders alike had been able to forage through masses of all sorts of books, sometimes turning up some real gems. As one local lamented in February, as the last of the market traders were obliged to ship out, 'You should know that a whole era of Cairo history is coming to an end in front of us'.

For the latest wire service news reports, check the wire copy in the lobby of the Sheraton Hotel in Giza, or across from the business centre in the Nile Hilton.

Medical Services

Hospitals There are three hospitals in Cairo with more modern facilities than most of Egypt's other hospitals: Cairo Medical Centre (☎ 258-0525) in Heliopolis; Anglo-American Hospital (☎ 340-6162/3/4/5), next to the Cairo Tower in Zamalek; and As-Salam International Hospital (☎ 363-2195), Corniche el-Nil, Maadi, which has 24-hour facilities. It has another branch at 3 Sharia Syria, Mohandiseen (☎ 346-7061/66).

24-Hour Pharmacies There are a number of pharmacies in Cairo that operate day and night. These include the Zamalek (☎ 340-2406) at 3 Sharia Shagarat ad-Durr, Zamalek; Isaaf (☎ 743369) on the corner of Sharia Ramses and Sharia 26th of July; the New Pharmacy (☎ 350-8404) on 87 Rd 9 in Maadi; and Maqsoud (☎ 245-3918), which is at 29 Sharia Mahmoud Shafik in Heliopolis.

Almost anything can be obtained without a prescription from Egypt's pharmacies.

Doctors & Dentists Enquire at your embassy for the latest list of recommended doctors and dentists or consult *Cairo: A Practical Guide* published by The American University in Cairo Press.

There are International Association for Medical Assistance to Travellers (IAMAT) centres at:

Central Cairo
  13 Sharia Wakf al-Kharboutly (☎ 284-1375/6/8/9, 243-4653); coordinator Dr Nabil Ayad al-Masry
  11 Sharia Imad ad-Din (☎ 916424); coordinator Dr Samir B Bassily
Maadi
  87 Rd 9 (☎ 350-3105, 351-0230); coordinator Dr Sherif Doss
Heliopolis
  1 Midan Roxy (☎ 258-2729); coordinator Dr Amin Iskander Fakry

It might also be worth contacting SOS Assistance (☎ 717553), especially if you are considering a long stay in Egypt. They can be contacted care of Cairoscan, 35 Sharia Suleiman Abaza, Mohandiseen, and for US$140 a year claim to offer full medical cover in case of emergency, including a flight out to the country of your choice under their SOS MEDEVAC scheme. Call for more information.

Vaccinations Vaccinations against cholera, yellow fever, tetanus, hepatitis, and a few other diseases are available at the Mogamma building and the former Hotel Continental. At the Mogamma building on Midan Tahrir, go to the public health section just inside the entrance on the left side. One traveller who got vaccinations here claimed that the 'place looked dirty, but they do use sterile needles'. However, it is always safest to take your own syringe.

At the old Hotel Continental, on Sharia al-Gomhurriya facing the Ezbekiya Gardens, is the International Vaccination Centre; it's at the back of the lobby on the right side. They give you the standard yellow International Certificate of Vaccination card free. If you are getting a yellow fever vaccination, keep in mind that protection doesn't become effective until 10 days after vaccination. The centre is open from 10 am to 1 pm and 6 to 7 pm, seven days.

Emergency
Some important numbers in Cairo are:

Ambulance
  Cairo Ambulance Service (☎ 123, 770123/230); possibly slow
  Giza (☎ 720385)
  Heliopolis (☎ 244-4327)
  Maadi (☎ 350-2873)
Police
  Central (☎ 13)
  Emergency (☎ 122, 757987)
  Tourist Police (☎ 126)
Fire
  all districts (☎ 125, 391-0466/0115/0777/0727)

Film

Kodak has several stores in Cairo, including a new one on Sharia Adly, across the road from the Hotel Select. The city centre and suburbs like Zamalek, Heliopolis and Maadi are dotted with places that will process film and where you can buy most kinds of film and video tape.

There are numerous places to have passport photos done, too, but if you are having trouble finding one of them, try the place under the Hotel Ismailia in Midan Tahrir. It is nothing special, but will do the job. Film is generally no cheaper in Egypt than in the West. For more details, see Film & Photography in the Facts for the Visitor section.

Central Cairo

Most travellers begin their Egyptian experience in the vicinity of Midan Tahrir and Sharia Talaat Harb. It's the bustling, noisy centre of central Cairo where you'll find an amazing variety of shops as well as most of the budget hotels and eating places, banks, travel agencies and cinemas. Central Cairo also has a number of museums, art galleries, markets, gardens and scenic views of the Nile (see map page 170).

Egyptian Museum

This museum is in a huge building a little north of Midan Tahrir. Also called the Museum of Egyptian Antiquities, it should not be missed. In fact, it's a good idea to visit this place at least twice – at the beginning of your visit to familiarise yourself with Egypt's ancient history, and at the end to understand better all you have seen throughout the country.

More than 100,000 relics and antiquities from almost every period of ancient Egyptian history are housed in the museum. This vast collection was first gathered under one roof in 1858 by Auguste Mariette, a French archaeologist who excavated the temples of Edfu, Dendara, Deir al-Bahri, Amun (at Karnak in Luxor) and a few others. The place

is virtually bursting at the seams, and hardly the last word in modern museum techniques. The word is around that there are vague plans to build a new museum out near the pyramids, but it will probably be quite a while before that happens.

The exhibits are arranged chronologically from the Old Kingdom to the Roman Empire. Each room could easily be a museum in its own right; if you spent only one minute at each exhibit it would take more than nine months to see everything. The sheer number and variety of things to see, while fascinating, is quite overwhelming. To help you deal with this labyrinth there are a couple of guidebooks available.

A Guide to the Egyptian Museum, a 300-page list of the museum's artefacts, is available at the museum's ticket window or the gift shop for E£5. It's organised by catalogue number rather than by room, with little description of each item. The *Blue Guide* is a costlier alternative but it describes the museum room by room in excellent detail. *The Egyptian Museum Cairo – Official Catalogue* has been out of print for more than a year. There are two other alternatives that more or less fill the gap. *Egyptian Museum Cairo*, by Dr Edouard Lambelet (Lehnert & Landrock), is published in English, French and German, and has a fairly extensive and generously illustrated description of the main objects of interest, identified by room and catalogue numbers. It sells for E£65. A less ordered version of the same thing is put out by the French publishers Hachette, and is called *The Egypt of the Pharaohs at the Cairo Museum*, by Jean-Pierre Corteggiani (E£75).

Admission to the museum is E£10, or E£5 for students with a student card. It's open from 9 am to 5 pm daily but closes between 11.15 am and 1.30 pm on Friday. Cameras have to be left at the front desk unless you wish to pay an extra E£10 for permission to use one in the museum. Use of a video camera costs E£100. There are official guides who will take you around for about E£5 per hour.

The following is an abbreviated guide to

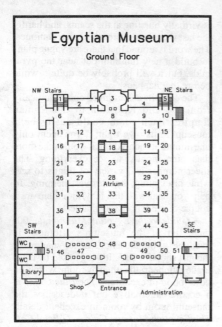

Egyptian Museum
Ground Floor

from the tombs of Pharaohs far greater than Tutankhamun.

The king's decaying mummified body, the outer of three mummiform coffins, and the huge stone sarcophagus are all that remain in his tomb. The rest of his funerary treasures, about 1700 items, are spread throughout 12 rooms on the 1st floor of the museum. The rooms and the best relics are:

Rooms 3 & 4

Gold is the glittering attraction of these rooms, which feature an astounding collection of jewellery, including the 143 amulets and pieces of jewellery found amongst the wrappings on the king's body, and a pair of gold sandals which were on the feet of the mummy. The two innermost coffins of Tutankhamun's tomb, one of gilded wood and the other of solid gold, have been moved from Room 4 to Room 3, which used to be exclusively reserved for jewellery. The centrepiece of the room, also shifted from Room 4 next door, is Tutankhamun's legendary and exquisite mask of beaten gold inlaid with lapis lazuli and other gems.

some of the most popular exhibits. If you wish to learn more about a particular period or set of antiquities, it is best to refer to more specialised works on Egyptology. The American University in Cairo Bookstore and the Anglo-Egyptian Bookshop both have a range of books on the subject.

Tutankhamun Without doubt, the exhibit that outshines everything else in the museum is the treasure of the comparatively insignificant New Kingdom Pharaoh Tutankhamun.

The tomb and treasures of this young king, who ruled for only nine years during the 14th century BC, were discovered in 1922 by English archaeologist Howard Carter. Its well-hidden location in the Valley of the Kings, below the much grander but ransacked tomb of Ramses VI, had prevented tomb robbers and, later, archaeologists from finding it any earlier. The incredible contents of his rather modest tomb can only make one wonder about the fabulous wealth looted

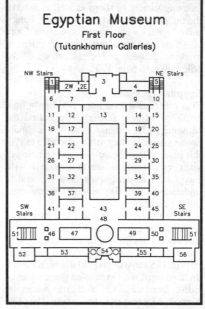

Egyptian Museum
First Floor
(Tutankhamun Galleries)

Tutankhamun & his Sister/Wife

It has been replaced in Room 4 with a magnificent Roman-era crown made of gold. It was discovered in 1989 around Qasr Dush, in the southern end of the Kharga Oasis.

Among the jewellery on display in Room 3, which dates from the 1st dynasty to the Byzantine period, there are some exquisite pieces made in the 12th dynasty using gems such as lapis lazuli, amethyst and turquoise.

Rooms 7, 8 & 9

The gilded wooden shrines that fitted inside each other and held the gold sarcophagus of Tutankhamun at their centre are in these rooms.

Room 15

King Tutankhamun's bed befits a Pharaoh; it is covered with sheet gold, with string stretched across the frame, and accompanied by several less costly beds. Beautifully rigged model ships, to be used by the Pharaoh on his voyage through the afterworld, are also found in this room.

Room 20

Here you can see some exquisite alabaster jars and one chalice in particular, in which a small light has been inserted to demonstrate the delicacy of its translucent artwork.

Room 24

Here you will see the originals of the papyrus paintings that you find in bazaars throughout Cairo. More can be seen in Room 5, in the stairwell leading up to the Tutankhamun exhibits.

Room 25

The most interesting item in this room is Tutankhamun's wooden throne. Covered with sheet gold, silver, gems and glass, the wooden throne has winged cobras and lions' heads on the arms and the back; it is decorated with the famous scene of Tutankhamun's queen placing her hand on his shoulder.

Room 30

A gilded bronze trumpet is the feature of this room; it was once 'played' in 1939.

Rooms 40 & 45

Exhibits in these rooms include a board game (Room 45, Case 189) with ivory playing pieces that resembles checkers or draughts, a beautifully carved wooden clothes chest and the statue of Anubis, the dog who was the god of mummification, found in Tutankhamun's tomb.

Akhenaten For those interested in the Pharaoh who set up Ancient Egypt's first and last monotheistic faith, Room 3 on the ground floor contains statuary and artefacts

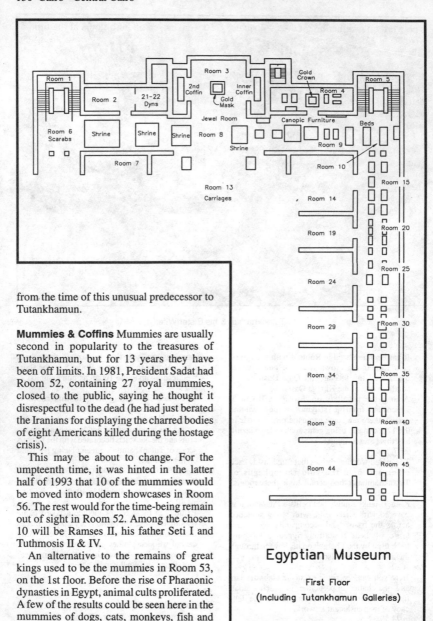

Room 1
Room 2
21-22 Dyns
Room 6 Scarabs
Shrine
Shrine
Shrine
Room 7
Room 3
2nd Coffin
Gold Mask
Inner Coffin
Jewel Room
Room 8
Shrine
Gold Crown
Room 4
Room 5
Canopic Furniture
Beds
Room 9
Room 10
Room 13 Carriages
Room 14
Room 19
Room 24
Room 29
Room 34
Room 39
Room 44
Room 15
Room 20
Room 25
Room 30
Room 35
Room 40
Room 45

Egyptian Museum

First Floor
(Including Tutankhamun Galleries)

from the time of this unusual predecessor to Tutankhamun.

Mummies & Coffins Mummies are usually second in popularity to the treasures of Tutankhamun, but for 13 years they have been off limits. In 1981, President Sadat had Room 52, containing 27 royal mummies, closed to the public, saying he thought it disrespectful to the dead (he had just berated the Iranians for displaying the charred bodies of eight Americans killed during the hostage crisis).

This may be about to change. For the umpteenth time, it was hinted in the latter half of 1993 that 10 of the mummies would be moved into modern showcases in Room 56. The rest would for the time-being remain out of sight in Room 52. Among the chosen 10 will be Ramses II, his father Seti I and Tuthmosis II & IV.

An alternative to the remains of great kings used to be the mummies in Room 53, on the 1st floor. Before the rise of Pharaonic dynasties in Egypt, animal cults proliferated. A few of the results could be seen here in the mummies of dogs, cats, monkeys, fish and other animals, until it too was closed. There is no word on whether or not they will again go on view. Rooms 46 and 47 on the 1st floor contain the royal coffins of several New Kingdom Pharaohs.

Statues & Palettes There are thousands of statues and statuettes in the museum from almost every period of ancient Egyptian history.

Room 47 on the 1st floor is lined with sarcophagi and statues. Check out the centre exhibit cases, which have several interesting statuettes from the Old Kingdom period. These include a hunchback, a dwarf, and figures engaged in everyday activities such as plucking birds, kneading dough and baking.

Room 42 on the 1st floor contains the Palette of Narmer, possibly the oldest record of a political event and one of the most significant items in this room. It describes, in a series of pictures and symbols, the unification of Upper and Lower Egypt for the first time by King Narmer. Narmer was probably another name for Menes, the founder of the 1st dynasty.

Solar Barques Solar barques were wooden boats placed in or around the tombs of Pharaohs. They were symbolically important as vessels for transporting the Pharaoh's soul over the sea of death beneath the earth. Two of these barques are on the ground floor in Room 43, just inside the entrance. Both are from the 12th dynasty (1990-1780 BC); one comes from the Pyramid of Senusert III in Dahshur and the other from the Colossus of Senusert III at Karnak in Luxor.

Greco-Roman Artefacts Apart from a reasonable collection of statuary, the Greco-Roman period in Egypt is perhaps most curiously represented by a collection of portraits in Room 14, most of them found in the Al-Faiyum area, dating from 60 AD to 230 AD. A collection of Greco-Roman era coins is located in Room 4 on the ground floor.

Note that, in addition to those rooms already mentioned as closed, Rooms 49 and 50 were closed on both floors at the time of writing, as were the south-east stairs and Rooms 2, 55 and 56 on the 1st floor.

Entomological Society Museum
This museum, at 14 Sharia Ramses, houses an excellent and well-preserved collection of the birds and insects of Egypt. It's open from 9 am to 1 pm daily except Friday, and also from 6 to 9 pm on Saturday, Monday and Wednesday.

Post Office Museum
The Post Office Museum is on the 2nd floor of the GPO on Midan Ataba. There are collections of old stamps and displays of the history of Egypt's postal service. It's open from 9 am to 1 pm except Friday.

Cairo Puppet Theatre
Also on Midan Ataba, this theatre presents colourful puppet shows. Although the presentations are in Arabic they are still worth seeing, as most of the actions are self-explanatory. Just behind it is a theatre for modern experimental works in Arabic.

Egyptian National Railways Museum
A sign outside the main entrance to Ramses Station leads you to the museum at one end of the station. This well-organised museum displays the history of railways and railway-related architecture in Egypt. On the ground floor are locomotives once used by Egypt's 19th century rulers.

A beautifully preserved locomotive built in 1862 for Princess Eugénie on the occasion of the opening of the Suez Canal still has its original upholstery and oil lamps. The museum is open daily except Monday from 8 am to 1 pm. Admission is E£1.50, or E£3 on Fridays and holidays.

Western Cairo

Gezira Island
Opera House Just over At-Tahrir Bridge on Gezira Island is the Opera House (☎ 342-

0589, 341-2926), which is far from being a mere house. It's a US$30-million arts complex that includes a museum, library, art gallery, and music halls with modern technical equipment and superb acoustics. The complex was built using traditional Islamic designs, visible in both the geometric layout of the courtyards and the styles of the windows and doors. The main music hall and opera house have hosted groups from all over the world, including theatre groups from the USA and dance troupes from Spain and Portugal. There's always something happening here; check *Cairo Today* and the *Egyptian Gazette* for the latest details, or go down and pick up a programme.

Museum of Modern Art This museum, recently moved from Doqqi and now housed in an impressive new building in the grounds of the Opera House, will give you some idea of contemporary culture and changing life in Egypt. The museum is open from 10 am to 1 pm and 5 to 9.30 pm, except Friday and Monday, when it is closed. Admission is E£10, or E£5 for students.

Cairo Tower One of the best places for a panoramic view of Cairo is the 185-metre-high tower. Early in the morning, when you can usually see the pyramids at Giza, or late afternoon are the ideal times for taking photographs. There's a revolving restaurant on top which is a bit expensive by Egyptian standards, but there's also a cafeteria where you can have the same revolving view of Cairo with much cheaper drinks. The entrance fee for the tower, if you're going to the top, is E£4. Hours for the viewing area are 9 am to midnight, daily. You might find a bit of a queue at dusk.

Mohammed Mahmoud Khalil Museum This museum, at 1 Sharia ash-Sheikh Marsafy, is opposite the entrance to the Gezira Club. The collection includes several sculptures by Rodin, a surprisingly rich collection of French paintings, largely Impressionists, and contemporary works by Egyptian artists. There's also a varied

display of ceramic works. The house, once belonging to the Egyptian royal family, is named after the person who was president of Egypt's Friends of the Arts Society in 1940. The contemporary exhibits offer an interesting insight into the minds of modern Egyptians. The museum is open from 9 am to 2 pm, and admission is E£1, or 50 pt for students.

Gabalaya Park & Aquarium Gabalaya Park, near Sharia al-Gezira, includes an aquarium. This cute place, where the fish inhabit aquariums built into tunnels that look like they were once bomb shelters, seems to be practically unknown to foreigners. Even if fish don't interest you, the park is still worth a visit for the respite it offers from the chaos of Cairo. It's open from 8.30 am to 3.30 pm seven days a week and costs 50 pt to get in.

Centre des Arts Just to the right of Sharia 26th of July as you come off the bridge from central Cairo is this tiny haven of modern art. There are works from all over Europe, but there's not all that much to it. It's free and open every day but Friday from 10 am to 1.30 pm and again from 5 to 7 pm.

Moukhtar Museum This museum, also known as the National Centre for Fine Arts (☎ 340-2519), is on the left side of Sharia At-Tahrir, just before you cross Al-Galaa Bridge to Doqqi. Moukhtar (1891-1934) was the sculptor laureate of Egypt, and this museum contains most of his major works. It is open from 10 am to 1 pm and 5 to 9 pm daily, except Monday, when it is closed. The entrance fee is E£2, or E£1 for students.

Doqqi, Agouza & Imbaba
Agricultural & Cotton Museums This complex (☎ 360-8682) in Doqqi is off Sharia Wizarat az-Ziraa, at the foot of the overpass on Sharia 6th of October. The Agricultural Museum contains lots of stuffed animals and exhibits that show life in Egyptian villages. The Cotton Museum has displays of the history of cotton production in Egypt. Both

are open from 9 am to 2 pm, except on Monday (although the Cotton Museum apparently closes half an hour earlier on Friday). As with one or two other things not considered to be likely tourist targets, there is no foreigners' admission price. Consequently you can get in for 10 pt.

Cairo Circus This small big top is at the foot of Zamalek Bridge, off Sharia 26th of July in Agouza, between the British Council and the Balloon Theatre. There rarely seems to be anything going on, but check with the tourist office or *Cairo Today* to see if there are performances.

Camel Market The camel market, or Souq al-Gamaal, is just off Sharia Sudan, near the Imbaba airstrip. It is the largest of its kind in the country. Amongst the growing urban sprawl the market looks rather like a mirage – which is probably why it's one of the most interesting things to see in this part of Cairo.

The majority of the camels are brought up the 40 Days Road from the Sudan to Aswan by camel herders from western Sudan. Then

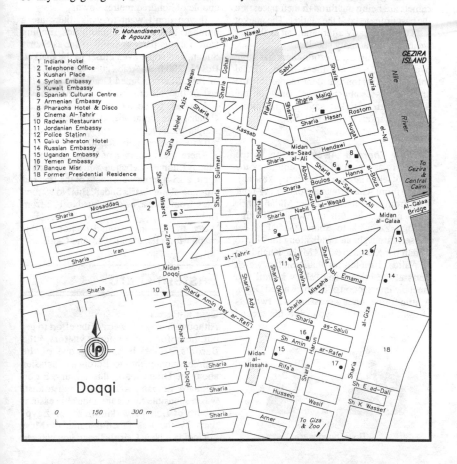

1 Indiana Hotel
2 Telephone Office
3 Kushari Place
4 Syrian Embassy
5 Kuwait Embassy
6 Spanish Cultural Centre
7 Armenian Embassy
8 Pharaohs Hotel & Disco
9 Cinema Al-Tahrir
10 Radwan Restaurant
11 Jordanian Embassy
12 Police Station
13 Cairo Sheraton Hotel
14 Russian Embassy
15 Ugandan Embassy
16 Yemen Embassy
17 Banque Misr
18 Former Presidential Residence

Doqqi

0   150   300 m

they are crammed into trucks in Aswan for the 24-hour journey to Imbaba, where they're sold or traded for other livestock such as goats, sheep and horses. If you're interested in buying a camel, smaller ones cost about E£1200 while the bigger models are E£3000. In addition to those from the Sudan, there are camels from various parts of Egypt (including the Sinai, the west and the south) and sometimes as far away as Somalia. They are sold for farm work and for slaughter – yes, your kofta is probably camel meat. Early Friday and Monday mornings, when bargaining activity is greatest and camels are being put through their paces, are the best times to be at the market. The market lasts until the early afternoon, but as the day wears on, the activity subsides.

For a long time a question mark has hung over whether or not there is an official entrance fee for tourists to the market, but the practice has established itself and you are issued with a ticket saying, in Arabic, Imbaba Market. It costs E£1.50.

Getting There & Away Getting to the market is as much of an adventure as the market itself. The easiest way is to take a taxi, but the more scenic route is a one to 1½-hour walk from central Cairo. From Midan Tahrir walk across the 6th of October Bridge through Zamalek to Sharia Gamal Abdel Nasser, turn right and walk along the Nile to Midan Kit Kat (also called Midan Khalid ibn al-Walid). Turn left on Sharia Sudan, which starts at the midan, and follow it until you meet the intersection of Sharia Ahmed Orabi. A little further on is a crossing over two sets of train tracks. When you cross the second

set of tracks, turn left and follow them for about 10 minutes to another crossing. Cross and veer right, then take the first left. The market is about five minutes' walk up on your left (and can be missed if you are distracted by all the other market activity around and outside it).

You can cut some time off the walk by turning left from the Nile at Sharia 26th of July (before Midan Kit Kat), heading up to Sphinx Square and then veering left up Sharia Ahmed Orabi. Walk the length of this street, turn left into Sharia Sudan and the first of the rail crossings is off to your right a couple of hundred metres down.

If you don't want to walk, there are a number of buses and minibuses running from various parts of Cairo as far as Sharia Sudan, and some even closer to the market. Bus No 200 from Ataba goes via Sharia 26th of July, Sharia Ahmed Orabi and up to the last of the rail crossings mentioned above. Ask where to be let off for the Souq al-Gamaal. An unnumbered minibus does a similar route, leaving from just by the same rail crossing for Ataba for 60 pt.

There are a number of buses running to Midan Lubnan (Lebanon Square), which is about a 15-minute walk south of the first rail crossing along Sharia Sudan. Bus No 99 runs there from Ataba, as does bus No 172 from Abbassiya.

See the Getting Around section in this chapter for a list of buses around Cairo.

Eastern Cairo

Qasr al-Baron
Although it may not warrant the effort to get out here for shorter term visitors, 'the Baron's Palace' is certainly one of the weirder monuments to European fantasies about the Orient. Early this century, Baron Edouard Empain, a Belgian industrialist, was responsible for creating the chic eastern suburb of Heliopolis (known to the Egyptians by the less fanciful name of Masr al-Gedida – New Cairo). Today you can see

Royal headgear

the results of his work in some elegant if pretentious Moorish-style architecture. The *pièce de résistance* was his own residence, an Indian Palace – the last thing you'd expect to see in Egypt. Now disused, it lies on Sharia al-Uruba – you can see it off to the left coming in from the airport.

October War Panorama

About two km further in towards the city, also off to the left, is the 1973 October War Panorama. Built with help from North Korean artists, this memorial to the 'victory' of 1973 over Israelis occupying the Sinai is quite an extraordinary propaganda effort. Outside the central building is an array of Egyptian and captured Israeli tanks, artillery and warplanes.

Inside the cylindrical building at the centre, you climb two flights of stairs past a roll call of the fallen into the panorama room. A revolving dais carries the audience around a quite remarkable three-dimensional mural depicting the breaching of the Bar Lev line on the Suez Canal by Egyptian forces and the initial retreats by the Israelis, including the taking of the canal town of Qantara. A stirring commentary recounts the heroic victories but is short on detail on the successful Israeli counterattacks that pushed the Egyptians back before both sides accepted a UN-brokered cease-fire. The Sinai was eventually 'liberated' – but by negotiation six years later.

It's closed on Tuesday. Admission is E£8 for foreigners, and performances, usually with an Arabic commentary, begin at 9.30 and 11 am and 12.30, 6 and 7.30 pm. Groups can request a performance with an English commentary.

Islamic Cairo

Islamic Cairo (a more appropriate name would be Medieval Cairo, given that the area is no more nor less Islamic than any other part of Egypt, but this appears to be the convention) is replete with medieval mosques, apartment buildings, and the greatest density of people in the country – and probably the Middle East.

An unhappy feature today is the evidence of the extent to which the whole area was shaken by the earthquake in October 1992. Few buildings of historical significance escaped damage. Before climbing any minarets, it would be as well to try to ascertain how badly they were hit.

It is easy to get lost in this district. In the back alleyways and streets of neighbourhoods with names like Darb al-Ahmar and Baatiniyya you'll suddenly find yourself back in the Cairo of six or seven centuries ago; in a time when donkeys and camels transported people and goods, buildings were like shaky wooden pyramids, and exotic foods were hawked from pavement stalls. Be prepared for this passage to the past because it hits all your senses.

Splendid mosques and imposing buildings still loom over narrow, crowded streets and bustling squares; the sweet, pungent aromas of tumeric, basil and cumin drift from open barrels, mix with the offensive odours of livestock, and grab at your nose like invisible fingers; and people go about their daily business as they have done, it seems, forever. This could be the medieval Cairo of Ibn Tulun or Salah ad-Din, except that the age-old aromas now mingle with petrol fumes as donkeys and camels compete with cars for space; and an awful lot of poverty offsets the grandeur of the architecture throughout what was once the intellectual and cultural centre of the Arab world.

Your tour can begin anywhere in the area, but the following describes two different walking tours. They are by no means an exhaustive guide to all the monuments, but rather a selection of the more important ones. A closer examination of the more than 150 buildings of historical interest in the area would involve weeks, if not months, of exploring a labyrinth of nooks and crannies. You may therefore want to buy a specialised guide. *A Practical Guide to Islamic Monuments in Cairo*, by Parker & Sabin (The

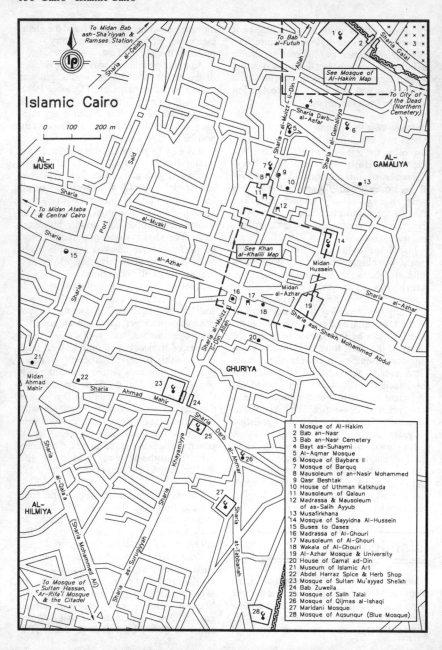

Islamic Cairo

1 Mosque of Al-Hakim
2 Bab an-Nasr
3 Bab an-Nasr Cemetery
4 Bayt as-Suhaymi
5 Al-Aqmar Mosque
6 Mosque of Baybars II
7 Mosque of Barquq
8 Mausoleum of an-Nasir Mohammed
9 Qasr Beshtak
10 House of Uthman Katkhuda
11 Mausoleum of Qalaun
12 Madrassa & Mausoleum
   of as-Salih Ayyub
13 Musafirkhana
14 Mosque of Sayyidna Al-Hussein
15 Buses to Oases
16 Madrassa of Al-Ghouri
17 Mausoleum of Al-Ghouri
18 Wakala of Al-Ghouri
19 Al-Azhar Mosque & University
20 House of Gamal ad-Din
21 Museum of Islamic Art
22 Abdel Harraz Spice & Herb Shop
23 Mosque of Sultan Mu'ayyad Sheikh
24 Bab Zuweila
25 Mosque of Salih Talai
26 Mosque of Qijmas al-Ishaqi
27 Maridani Mosque
28 Mosque of Aqsunqur (Blue Mosque)

American University in Cairo Press), is packed with detailed explanations and maps of the monuments. It's available at the American University in Cairo Bookstore. The Society for the Preservation of the Architectural Resources of Egypt (SPARE) is putting out a growing series of maps covering the area. For those with lots of time and keen to get to know the less celebrated monuments, these are a great aid.

As you begin your exploration of this part of Cairo, carry lots of small change for baksheesh. You'll need it for tipping guards and caretakers, who will expect baksheesh if you ask to see something special, such as a minaret. Also note that any given opening times should be interpreted as only a rough guide, as caretakers are as apt to close up shop early as they are to open up late, depending on mood.

WALKING TOUR 1

The first walking tour begins at Midan Salah ad-Din at the foot of the Citadel, in front of the mosques of Sultan Hassan and Ar-Rifa'i. Lots of buses go there from different parts of Cairo – for details, see Getting To/From the Citadel further in this section.

There are several interesting monuments to visit in the area, apart from the Citadel. Around it you can you can visit the Mosque of Sultan Hassan, Ar-Rifa'i Mosque, an open-air market, Ibn Tulun Mosque, Gayer-Anderson House, the Mausoleum of Shagarat ad-Durr, and the Mausoleum of Imam as-Shafi'i.

Mosque of Sultan Hassan

The mosque is to the left of Sharia al-Qala'a if the Citadel is behind you. It was built between 1356 and 1363 AD, during the time of Mamluk rule, with stones that historians believe were taken from one of the Great Pyramids of Giza. Originally the mosque was a *madrassa*, or theological school, and each of the four iwans, or vaulted halls, surrounding the central court served as classrooms for each main school of Sunni Islam. The interior is typically devoid of decoration to make it easier for worshippers to concen-

trate on prayers. Hundreds of chains which once held oil lamps still hang from the ceiling of each iwan. Behind the iwans is the mausoleum. The southernmost of the two minarets is the second highest in Cairo, after that of the new Al-Fatah Mosque near Ramses Station. Try to visit this place in the morning when the sun lights up the mausoleum portion of the mosque; the effect is quite eerie. The mosque is open seven days a week from 8 am to 5 pm (6 pm in summer), but is closed to visitors during the midday prayers on Friday. Entrance is E£6, or half for students.

Ar-Rifa'i Mosque

Just across Sharia al-Qala'a from the Mosque of Sultan Hassan is this 19th century imitation of a Mamluk-style mosque. The Princess Dowager Khushyar, mother of the khedive Ismail, had the mosque built in 1869 to serve as a tomb for herself, her descendants and future khedives. Members of modern Egypt's royal family, including King Farouk, are buried here – as is the Shah of Iran, whose casket was paraded through the streets of Cairo from Abdin Palace to the mosque in 1980, with President Sadat, the shah's family and Richard Nixon leading the cortege. Hours and tickets are the same as for the Mosque of Sultan Hassan. For a little baksheesh, you can see the tombs of Egypt's royals and the shah.

After visiting these two mosques, walk south-west down Sharia ash-Sheikhun and Sharia as-Salibah away from the Citadel to the Ibn Tulun Mosque. Keep your eyes open along the way. You will pass a 15th century *sabil-kuttab* (public fountain-cum-Qur'anic school) – this one named after Sultan Qaitbey. Just before it is a prison – the sight of faces and hands pressed up against the bars of prison trucks is enough to make you not want to transgress any law here! You then pass between the **Mosque of Sheikhu** on the right and, opposite it, the **Khanqah of Sheikhu**. Both were built by a Mamluk army commander, in 1349 and 1355 respectively. Just off on the right is the 19th century **Sabil-Kuttab of Um Abbas**, which houses the

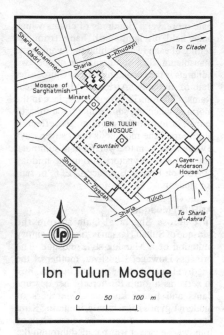

Ibn Tulun Mosque

0   50   100 m

and in the morning you can usually see the Great Pyramids of Giza. The admission fee for both the mosque and the minaret is E£3, or E£1.50 for students, plus baksheesh for slippers to put over your shoes in the mosque – if you don't want to just take your own off, that is.

Gayer-Anderson House

This museum is immediately adjacent to the Ibn Tulun Mosque, and you can get to it from the outer court of the mosque, to the left of the main entrance.

The house is also called Bayt al-Kritliyya, which means 'house of the Cretan woman'. It is actually two houses, one dating from the 16th century and the other from the 18th. The house was named after a British major, John Gayer-Anderson, who occupied and restored it between 1935 and 1942. In 1942 he bequeathed the house and exotic furnishings to Egypt for use as a museum. Each room has a different exotic theme – the Persian Room, the Queen Anne Room, the Chinese Room, the Mohammed Ali Pasha Turkish Room and the Harem Room of Amina Bint Salem al-Gazzar.

Most of the rooms have windows with intricately carved wooden mashrabiyyah screens, which enabled the women of the harem to discreetly observe the goings-on of

Centre for Art & Life. The centre, once serving as a small museum on the island of Roda, now seems only to house bureaucrats. You pass another small 15th century mosque before arriving in the big square containing the huge Ibn Tulun Mosque. Turn left and the entrance is on your right.

Ibn Tulun Mosque

This is one of the largest mosques in the world. Ibn Tulun was sent to rule Cairo in the 9th century by the Abbassid Caliph of Baghdad. He had the mosque built in 876, with an inner courtyard large enough for most of his army and their horses. The 13th century fountain in the centre continues to provide water for washing before prayers.

After wandering around the massive courtyard, you should climb the spiral minaret (see map of Ibn Tulun Mosque) – if they take away the scaffolding that's been in place since the earthquake in 1992. The views of Cairo from the top are magnificent

Ibn Tulun Mosque

any male visitors without being seen themselves. Hours are 8 am to 4 pm seven days a week. It closes from noon to 1 pm on Friday. Admission is E£8, or E£4 for students. Taking photos will cost you another E£10.

When you leave Gayer-Anderson House turn right on the street parallel to the Ibn Tulun Mosque and walk to Sharia Tulun. Turn left and walk the short distance to the intersection with Sharia al-Khalifa, then turn right. Sharia al-Khalifa becomes Sharia al-Ashraf, and you continue walking down this street into a district called the Southern Cemetery. This is the beginning of a vast Muslim necropolis which stretches all the way to the suburb of Maadi, about five km south. After about 250 metres you will come to the Mausoleum of Shagarat ad-Durr on the left.

Mausoleum of Shagarat ad-Durr

Built in 1250, this is a small simple tomb which has Byzantine glass mosaics gracing the prayer niche. The most interesting thing, however, is the story of the woman whose remains are entombed here (see below).

Mausoleum of Imam ash-Shafi'i

This mausoleum is two km south of the Midan Salah ad-Din, in the Southern Cemetery. To get there, walk south from the Citadel along Sharia Mabarrat Mustafa Kamel to Tariq Salah Salem. Turn right and then left off the square into Sharia al-Qadiriyyah, which becomes Sharia Imam as-Shafi'i. The mausoleum is a little over one km further on.

You can also take bus No 405 from Midan Salah ad-Din, get off before it turns left towards the Moqattam Hills, and walk the remaining distance down Sharia Imam as-Shafi'i. You can't miss the building, as it has a large red, blue and gold dome topped by a bronze boat.

If you don't want to visit the mausoleum, you can proceed directly to the Citadel from Midan Salah ad-Din.

Imam ash-Shafi'i, a descendent of an uncle of the Prophet, was the founder of the Shafi'ite, one of the four major schools of Sunni Islam. Regarded as one of the great Muslim saints, he died in 820 and his mausoleum – the largest Islamic tomb in Egypt is the centre of a great annual moulid, or birthday festival, held in his honour.

In the 12th century Salah ad-Din founded the first madrassa on the same site to counter

---

Shagarat ad-Durr

Shagarat ad-Durr was a slave from a nomadic tribe who managed, albeit briefly, to become the only female Muslim sovereign in history. She secured this position fairly easily and in the process instigated Mamluk rule, which was to last for the next 200 years; however, she came to a very nasty end.

Salih Ayyub, the last ruler of the Ayyubid dynasty, married Shagarat ad-Durr at a time when the soldiers of the 7th Crusade had taken control of Damietta, in the Nile Delta. Knowing that Ayyub was sick and dying, the Crusaders were prepared to wait out his death and attack Cairo when the government collapsed. So when he died in 1249, Shagarat ad-Durr hid his corpse, and for three months managed to pretend that he was still alive and passing on orders to his generals through her. She waited for her son to come back from Mesopotamia and take control, but when he did return he proved to be a weak ruler, so she had him killed.

She then declared herself Sultana of Egypt and ruled for 80 days – the only woman to rule over Muslims until Queen Victoria. But the Abbassid Caliph of Baghdad refused to recognise her position, so she married a Mamluk, the leader of her slave warriors, and ruled through him. When he decided that he needed an extra wife, Shagarat ad-Durr had him killed and threw his second wife into prison. When the Mamluk warriors discovered Shagarat ad-Durr's part in the assassination, she offered to marry their new leader but was imprisoned instead. She was eventually turned over to her husband's second wife who, along with several other women, beat Shagarat ad-Durr to death with wooden clogs. They hung her body from the side of the Citadel as food for the dogs. What was left of her was salvaged and entombed. ∎

the influence of the Shi'ite Muslim sect of the Fatimid dynasty he had overthrown. It became a centre of Shafi'ite missionary work. Today most Muslims in Cairo are Shafi'ite, and Shafi'ite Sunni Islam is also predominant in much of the Saudi peninsula, Malaysia and East Africa.

The Citadel

A spectacular medieval fortress of crenellated walls and towers perched on a hill above Midan Salah ad-Din, the Citadel was home to most of those who ruled Egypt during a period of about 700 years.

Today the Citadel is a complex of three mosques and four museums. From Midan Salah ad-Din, walk east along Sharia Sikkat al-Maghar. The road leading to the entrance goes off to the right, about 100 metres past the intersection with Sharia Bab al-Wazir. You can also enter from Tariq Salah Salem, on the south side.

Salah ad-Din began building the Citadel in 1176 to fortify the city against the Crusaders, and over the centuries it has been modified and enlarged with the palaces and buildings of subsequent rulers and governments.

Mohammed Ali, one of the last rulers to reside in the Citadel, actually levelled most of the buildings of the Mamluk period to build his own mosque and palace. And it was in a narrow rock-hewn passage near one of the Citadel's front gates that he sealed his control over Egypt with the massacre of the Mamluks.

On 1 March 1811 he treated the Mamluk leaders to a day of feasting and revelry, at the end of which they were escorted from the Citadel through a narrow lane. Mohammed Ali's troops sealed both ends of the passage, trapping all 470 dinner guests. Only one managed to escape; the rest were massacred from the wall above.

The Citadel

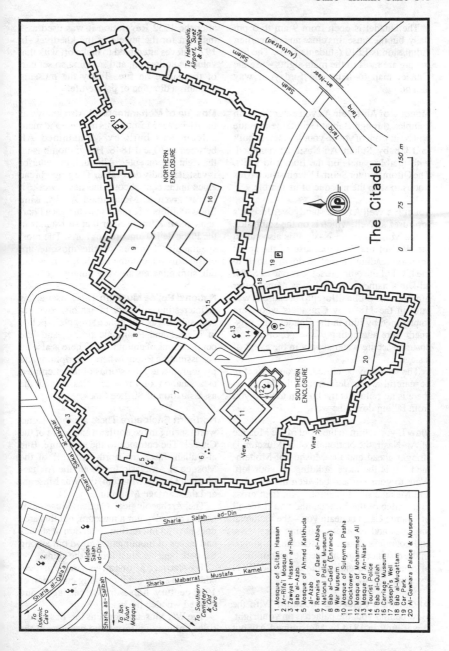

The Citadel

NORTHERN ENCLOSURE

SOUTHERN ENCLOSURE

To Heliopolis, Suez, Airport, & Ismailia

Salah Salem (Autostrad)

an-Nasr

Tariq

0   75   150 m

Sharia Sikkat al-Mehgar

Midan Salah ad-Din

Sharia Salah ad-Din

Sharia Mabarrat Mustafa Kamel

Sharia as-Salibah

To Islamic Cairo

Sharia al-Qala'a

To Ibn Tulun Mosque

To Southern Cemetery Cairo

VIEW

VIEW

1 Mosque of Sultan Hassan
2 Ar-Rifa'i Mosque
3 Zawiyat Hassan ar-Rumi
4 Bab al-Azab
5 Mosque of Ahmed Katkhuda al-Azab
6 Remains of Qasr al-Ablaq
7 National Police Museum
8 Bab al-Gadid (Entrance)
9 War Museum
10 Mosque of Suleyman Pasha
11 Mosque of An-Nasir
12 Clocktower
13 Mosque of Mohammed Ali
14 Tourist Police
15 Bab al-Qullah
16 Carriage Museum
17 Joseph's Well
18 Bab al-Muqattam
19 Car Park
20 Al-Gawhara Palace & Museum

The Citadel is open from 9 am to 5 pm daily, but the museums close an hour earlier. Admission is E£10 (students E£5). The following are most of the main sights – use the Citadel map to help you find your way around.

Mosque of An-Nasir As you enter the main complex through Bab al-Gedid, the mosque will be in front of you to your left. It was built in 1318 by Sultan An-Nasir Mohammed, with marble panels on the floor and walls. The Ottoman ruler Selim I later instructed his troops to strip the mosque of its marble.

Joseph's Well A tower stands over Joseph's (or Yusef's) Well, which is on the south side of the Mosque of An-Nasir. It is also called the Well of the Snail because of the spiral staircase leading 88 metres down a shaft to the level of the Nile. Yusef was one of Salah ad-Din's names. The well was named after him (not the biblical Joseph) because it was built in the 1180s by Crusaders who were imprisoned by him in the Citadel. The prisoners were attempting to escape, or at least ensure a secure water supply in the event of a siege.

The well may be closed; if you can get in be careful when descending the stairs, as there is no railing at the bottom to keep you from falling down the well.

View If you return to the front of the Mosque of An-Nasir, the National Police Museum is straight ahead and the Mosque of Mohammed Ali is the large building on your left. Walk to your left and between the museum and Mosque of Mohammed Ali, then cross to the edge of the parapet, and you'll see all of Islamic Cairo beneath you – the medieval mosques and minarets, winding alleyways, and countless shaky, ramshackle buildings. In the distance you can see the tall buildings of central Cairo and, sometimes, the Great Pyramids of Giza.

Al-Gawhara Palace & Museum With the view behind you, the palace is on your right. It was built in 1814 by Mohammed Ali, but after the 1952 Revolution it was used as a museum for the jewels of the khedives. In 1972 thieves attempted to make off with that valuable collection, and in doing so set part of the palace on fire. Today the museum contains a diorama of palace life.

Mosque of Mohammed Ali Also known as the Alabaster Mosque, this mosque and mausoleum was built by Mohammed Ali between 1830 and 1848. His gilt tomb is on the right as you enter. Although the interior is vast, it is badly decorated. The gingerbread clock in the central court has never worked; it was given to Mohammed Ali by King Louis-Philippe of France in return for a Pharaonic obelisk from Luxor that still stands in the Place de la Concorde in Paris. The most spectacular features of the mosque are outside: its huge dome and half-domes and tall, slim minarets are very impressive.

National Police Museum This museum has an interesting collection of exhibits covering such subjects as 'the police struggle', 'police in Islamic and Pharaonic times', and 'the confiscations of antiquities'. There is also an Assassination Room, where descriptions and photographs tell the stories of the attempted assassination of President Nasser and the assassination of Sir Lee Stack.

Northern Enclosure There are three sights worth seeing in the northern enclosure of the Citadel. The entrance to the enclosure, Bab al-Qullah, faces the north-east side of the Mosque of An-Nasir. Inside are the Archaeological Garden Museum, the War Museum and the Carriage Museum.

The Archaeological Garden Museum is neither a garden nor a museum, but this area does have an interesting collection of statues and pieces of monuments spread out among the park benches. Just follow the signs.

The Carriage Museum, next to the garden, contains a small but interesting collection of 19th century horse-drawn carriages and painted wooden horses.

The War Museum contains lots of swords, rifles, military uniforms and cannons in the various exhibits detailing Egypt's military history, from Pharaonic times through the Greco-Roman and Islamic periods to the present. There is also an extensive display on Egypt's modern conflicts with Israel, especially its 'victorious' encounter in the 1973 Yom Kippur war.

Getting There & Away There are several buses to various parts of the city from the small bus station next to Midan Salah ad-Din, or you can pick up one of the numerous other passing buses or minibuses. Bus No 173 starts and terminates at Midan Tahrir and passes the citadel en route. Bus No 160 from Midan Ramses (the bus stop in front of the main train station) passes the Citadel and Midan Tahrir on its way to the pyramids. Bus No 174 also goes to Midan Ramses. Another bus operating between the Citadel and the pyramids is the No 905. The No 404 from Ataba passes the Citadel and goes on to Midan Tahrir. Two other buses to Ataba are the No 951 and the No 801. The No 54 minibus goes to Midan Tahrir and the No 57 to Ataba.

You can now either catch one of these or a taxi out of here or continue to the next part of the walking tour.

From the Citadel to Al-Azhar

This part of the walking tour takes you through one of Cairo's oldest and poorest districts. It is called Darb al-Ahmar, which means 'red road'. It almost seems like time stopped here several centuries ago; poverty and conservatism have kept the district isolated from many of the changes, both good and bad, that other parts of Cairo have experienced.

An alternative to starting your exploration at the Citadel would be to come down the other way from the Al-Azhar Mosque. The following section, which is written as if you are starting at the Citadel, describes some of the main sights.

Leave the Citadel by the main entrance and go downhill and left into Sharia Sikkat al-Maghar, then take the first right on to Sharia Bab al-Wazir, the 'street of the gate of

the vizier'. About 550 metres up the street on the east side there is a unique mosque – the Mosque of Aqsunqur.

Mosque of Aqsunqur Also called the Blue Mosque, this was built in 1347 and then rebuilt in 1652 by a Turkish governor, Ibrahim Agha, who added the blue tiles on the walls. Agha imported the decorated tiles from Damascus, but apart from making the mosque unique in Egypt they do little for the aesthetics of the place.

Behind the mosque you can see part of Salah ad-Din's city walls, which run from north to south and have largely been covered with rubbish and tumbledown buildings. Across the street from the mosque there is a Turkish apartment building which dates from 1625 and is still inhabited. However, unless by some strange stroke of luck you happen to know one of the inhabitants, this building is not open to tourists.

Admission to the mosque costs E£3, and E£1.50 for students. It is open from about 9 am to 5 pm.

Maridani Mosque Continue walking up Sharia Bab al-Wazir another 350 metres as it becomes Sharia at-Tabbanah. The Maridani Mosque will be on your left where a small street, Sharia Sikkat al-Maridani, meets Sharia at-Tabbanah. Built in 1339, the mosque is one of the oldest buildings in the area.

Several styles of architecture were used in its construction: eight granite columns were taken from a Pharaonic monument; the arches were made from Roman, Christian and Islamic designs; and the Ottomans added a fountain and wooden housing. There are several other decorative details inside. The lack of visitors, the trees in the courtyard and the detailed wood panelling make for a peaceful spot to stop. There is no official entry ticket, but someone will probably expect baksheesh.

Hammam Bashtak Before pursuing this walk north, you may want to double back a bit down Souq as-Silah to the only baths in

Cairo open to women. The place is not the most inviting of baths, but it's the only choice women have. For E£15, you can have a massage and bath from 11 am to 5 pm (hareem – women only). From 8 pm until 10 am the following day it opens to men. Men pay E£10. The baths are open seven days a week.

Mosque of Qijmas al-Ishaqi
Back up past the Maridani Mosque, Sharia at-Tabbanah changes name again and becomes Sharia Darb al-Ahmar. The beautiful little Mosque of Qijmas al-Ishaqi is about 200 metres north of Maridani Mosque, on the other side of the street. Qijmas was Master of the Sultan's Horses and took charge of the annual pilgrimage to Mecca. His mosque is one of the best examples of architecture from the 15th century Burgi Mamluk period.

The plain exterior of the building is quite deceiving, as inside there are beautiful stained-glass windows, inlaid marble floors and stucco walls. The floor under the prayer mats in the eastern iwan is a fantastic marble mosaic. Ask the guard to lift the mat for you.

Mosque of Salih Talai
This small but intriguing building, 150 metres further up on the left, is one of the best examples of the Fatimid style of architecture, with strangely shaped arches, classical columns and wooden beams. The mosque is directly opposite Bab Zuweila, one of the original city gates. Ask the guard to show you up to the roof, as the views of the surrounding neighbourhood are great. The guard will expect some baksheesh; 50 pt should be appropriate.

Sharia Khayamiyya
This is the 'street of the tentmakers', which intersects Sharia Darb al-Ahmar at the Mosque of Salih Talai. About 400 metres further south, it becomes Sharia as-Surugiyyah, the 'street of the saddlemakers'. Part of this thoroughfare is a wooden arcade that has stood for several centuries. Medieval apartments with mashrabiyyah screens on the windows jut out over the street. The tentmakers here make the appliqué panels used throughout Egypt on the ceremonial tents that are set up for funerals, wakes, weddings and holiday celebrations. This is also the best place to buy hand-sewn cushion covers and wall hangings; shop around, and note that the real masters seem to be at the southern end of the arcade and just after it.

Bab Zuweila
Of the original 60 gates of the medieval city of Cairo, Bab Zuweila, built in 1092, is one of only three that remain. The other two, Bab an-Nasr and Bab al-Futuh, were built at about the same time, and even as recently as the late 19th century were used to close off the city. Bab Zuweila, the southern gate, was also often the site of public executions. The last Mamluk sultan, Tumanbay, was hanged here three times – he survived the first two attempts! You can climb up to the top of the gate through the adjoining Mosque of Sultan Mu'ayyad Sheikh.

Mosque of Sultan Mu'ayyad Sheikh
This was built between 1416 and 1420 by the Burgi Mamluk Mu'ayyad Sheikh, a freed Circassian slave who eventually rose through the ranks of the Mamluks to become Sultan of Egypt. Mu'ayyad had a drinking problem before becoming sultan, and his fellow Mamluks considered beatings and incarceration just therapy for such a weakness. Mu'ayyad was imprisoned on this site and vowed that one day he would replace the prison with a mosque. Although it's not a terribly impressive building there is a magnificent view of Cairo from its minaret, which is on top of Bab Zuweila, not the mosque.

If you climb the minaret, be careful on both the first set of stairs, where the wooden railing is very shaky, and on the second set, which is steep and very dark in parts. The guard will insist on giving you a tour and showing you the entrance to the minaret. This is not necessary, but be careful if you refuse his offers of assistance or don't give him baksheesh, you may find the door locked when you want to get back out.

The entrance fee is E£3 (E£1.50 for students), with an additional E£1 of baksheesh to the guard for showing you the minaret.

Turkish Hammam In front of the Mosque of Sultan Mu'ayyad Sheikh there is a small door which leads to an old Turkish bath house. There is no sign – just head for the blue-tile entrance. It was undergoing repairs at the time of writing, which it looked like it could do with. The surly chap in charge was not keen to give away what his post-repairs prices would be, but the men-only joint looked so gungy that you'd really want to think twice.

Said Delta Papyrus Centre A little further up on the same side of the street is one of the best places to buy your papyrus souvenirs, the Said Delta Papyrus Centre (☎ 512-0747). Said learnt his craft from the famed Dr Ragab, and some of his work is stunning. The papyrus is made in, as the name suggests, the Delta. The shop is up on the 3rd floor. On the ground floor is a huge shoe shop. Most people who come here are led by someone, who Said claims gets a 40% commission. At any rate, the posted prices appear to be negotiable.

Abdel Harraz Spice & Herb Shop For another change from mosques and minarets, go back through Bab Zuweila onto Sharia Darb al-Ahmar, turn right, and walk another 400 metres. The street changes name again, to Sharia Ahmed Mahir. On the right side, one block before the Museum of Islamic Art, there is a very special shop which has everything imaginable in the way of herbs, spices and exotic concoctions.

Museum of Islamic Art With the treasures of the Pharaohs being the main objective of most tourists to Cairo, this museum, which has one of the world's finest collections of Islamic art, is rarely crowded. The museum, established in 1881, is on the north side of Midan Ahmed Mahir, where Sharia al-Qala'a, Sharia Port Said and Sharia Ahmed Mahir all meet.

Some exhibits are arranged chronologically to show the influence of various eras, such as the Fatimid, Ayyubid or Mamluk periods, on Islamic art in Egypt; others are in special displays dealing with a particular subject. The latter include collections of textiles, glassware, calligraphy, tapestries and pottery from throughout the Islamic world.

The intricate woodwork in the collection of mashrabiyyah window screens is among the best you will see in Egypt. There is also one room of inlaid metalwork, another with a collection of magnificent Oriental carpets, an exhibit of medieval weapons and suits of armour, and a collection of superb illuminated books and ancient Qur'anic manuscripts. There is also a modest coin collection.

The museum is open seven days a week from 9 am to 4 pm, except from 11.30 am to 1.30 pm on Friday, which is prayer time. Admission is E£8, or E£4 for students, and the entrance is actually at the side. Labelling is in Arabic, English and occasionally in French, and you can purchase a very weighty and serious-looking catalogue in French. There is a cafeteria in the grounds.

Back to the City Centre
This is the end of the first walking tour through Islamic Cairo. You can return to Midan Tahrir by walking the 1½ km west along Sharia Sami al-Barudi, Sharia al-Bustan and Sharia at-Tahrir.

WALKING TOUR 2
The second walking tour around Islamic Cairo begins at the Al-Azhar Mosque and University. The first set of things to see is south of Al-Azhar Mosque, back towards Bab Zuweila, and the second set takes you from the mosque to Bab an-Nasr.

Al-Azhar & Khan al-Khalili
Al-Azhar Mosque & University The oldest university in the world, and one of the first mosques, Al-Azhar was built in 970 AD for the study of Qur'anic law and doctrine.

There are more than 80,000 Islamic

manucripts in its libraries. While the basic curriculum in theology has changed very little since the time of the Mamluks, the university has expanded to cover subjects such as medicine and physics as well as foreign languages.

Courses in Islamic theology sometimes last as long as 15 years, and the traditional Socratic method of teaching with one tutor and a small group of students is still practised. Over 4000 students from all over the Islamic world receive free board and tuition and live all year on mats around the courtyard of the mosque. On the eastern side there is also a Chapel of the Blind, which accommodates blind students. Like many other buildings throughout the area, the university was badly shaken by the earthquake in October 1992. Some repair work is now under way.

The university is open daily from about 9 am to 7 pm except on Friday, when it is closed from 11 am to 1 pm. This seems to be fairly flexible, and it seems quite possible to get in as late as 10 pm. Admission is E£3, and for a little extra the guard will show you up the minaret for a great view of the complex. Women must cover their heads with scarves.

Wakala of Al-Ghouri This ancient caravanserai, at 3 Sharia as-Sheikh Mohammed Abdul, just around the corner from the Al-Azhar Mosque, is excellently preserved and now serves as a cultural centre. It was built in 1505 as a merchants' hotel. The merchants would sleep in rooms above where their animals were stabled, and business would be carried out in the courtyard around the fountain.

The courtyard now serves as a theatre and concert hall; the hotel rooms house a permanent exhibition of peasant and Bedouin crafts, and workshops for teaching traditional crafts are held there. The *wakala* is open from 9 am to 5 pm daily except during Ramadan, when it's open from 9 to 11 am and 2 to 4 pm. The entrance fee is E£3, and half for students.

Madrassa & Mausoleum of Al-Ghouri Opposite each other, at the intersection of Sharia al-Muizz li-Din Allah and Sharia al-Azhar, are two of the last great Mamluk structures built before the Ottomans took control of Egypt. Al-Ghouri, the penultimate Mamluk sultan, went all out to ensure that he left his architectural mark on the city. During his 16 years of rule he managed, quite well, to perpetuate the Mamluks' reputation for being thieves, murderers and tyrants. His madrassa, though elegant and peaceful, was apparently partly built from materials extorted or just simply stolen from other buildings.

Al-Ghouri, who was killed in a battle against the Turks near Aleppo in Syria when he was well into his 70s, is not entombed in his mausoleum. The body which is there is that of his successor, the almost-lucky Sultan Tumanbay, who was hanged three times from Bab Zuweila before the rope held together long enough to kill him.

The madrassa and mosque complex, on the north-west corner, was badly jolted by the October 1992 earthquake. The mausoleum is fronted by a sabil-kuttab and now serves as a youth and cultural centre. Inside the library is a beautifully carved dome. You can also see an enchanting display of the *raqs ash-sharqi*, or Sufi dancing, every Wednesday and Saturday night from 8 pm for free. The two buildings were once connected by awnings over the market street between and known collectively as the Ghouriyya.

House of Gamal ad-Din This restored upper-class 16th century merchant's house is worth visiting. It is at 6 Sharia Khushqadam, which runs east off Sharia al-Muizz li-Din Allah, just south of Sharia al-Azhar. Enter through the mammoth wooden door and continue into the courtyard through the foyer, where horses used to be tied up. Then call out for the guard, who will show you around. Don't miss the beautiful mashrabiyyah and stained-glass windows of the 'business room'; when the sun shines through them, the effect is brilliant. The house is open from 9 am to 5 pm, and admission is E£3, or E£1.50 for students.

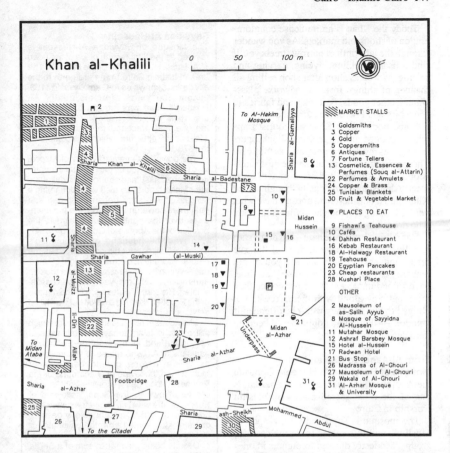

Khan al-Khalili

0   50   100 m

To Al-Hakim Mosque

Sharia al-Gamaliyya

Sharia - Khan - al - Khalili

Sharia al-Badestane

Sharia   Gawhar   (al-Muski)

Sharia al-Muizz li-Din Allah

To Midan Ataba

Footbridge

Sharia   al-Azhar

Sharia   al-Azhar

Sharia   ash-Sheikh   Mohammed   Abdul

Midan Hussein

Midan al-Azhar

Underpass

P

To the Citadel

MARKET STALLS

1 Goldsmiths
3 Copper
4 Gold
5 Coppersmiths
6 Antiques
7 Fortune Tellers
13 Cosmetics, Essences & Perfumes (Souq al-Attarin)
22 Perfumes & Amulets
24 Copper & Brass
25 Tunisian Blankets
30 Fruit & Vegetable Market

▼ PLACES TO EAT

9 Fishawi's Teahouse
10 Cafés
14 Dahhan Restaurant
16 Kebab Restaurant
18 Al-Halwagy Restaurant
19 Teahouse
20 Egyptian Pancakes
23 Cheap restaurants
28 Kushari Place

OTHER

2 Mausoleum of as-Salih Ayyub
8 Mosque of Sayyidna Al-Hussein
11 Mutahar Mosque
12 Ashraf Barsbey Mosque
15 Hotel al-Hussein
17 Radwan Hotel
21 Bus Stop
26 Madrassa of Al-Ghouri
27 Mausoleum of Al-Ghouri
29 Wakala of Al-Ghouri
31 Al-Azhar Mosque & University

Khan al-Khalili To reach this famous bazaar, return to Sharia al-Muizz li-Din Allah, turn right and walk north past the Madrassa of Al-Ghouri, then continue along Sharia al-Muizz li-Din Allah to Sharia al-Muski.

After you have finished roaming through the bazaar, stop at the famous Fishawi's teahouse a few steps off Midan Hussein. It's a colourful place where you can chat with the locals, puff on a shisha (water pipe), or just sit and soak up the atmosphere. People have been doing just that there for more than 200 years.

The Khan is one of the largest bazaars in the Middle East, if not the world. It stretches from Sharia al-Muski, between Sharia Port Said and Midan Hussein, up Sharia al-Muizz li-Din Allah and Sharia al-Gamaliyya, to the Mosque of Al-Hakim.

The bazaar began as a caravanserai built in 1382 by Garkas al-Khalili, Sultan Barquq's Master of Horses. When the Ottomans gained control of Egypt, the caravanserai changed from a fairly simple inn where caravans rested and a little trade was carried out to a fully fledged Turkish bazaar which attracted traders and customers from throughout the world.

Today the Khan is an immense conglomeration of shops and markets. As you wander through the labyrinth of narrow streets you'll find artisans building, dyeing, carving and sewing, as well as shop after shop selling all manner of things from woodwork, glassware, leather goods, perfumes and fabrics to souvenirs and Pharaonic curiosities.

Some parts of the Khan are tourist traps where anxious and aggressive shopkeepers try to get as much of your money as they can. These people are some of the greatest salespeople and smooth talkers you will ever meet. Almost anything can be bought in the Khan, and if one merchant doesn't have what you're looking for, then he'll find somebody who does.

Bargaining is the rule here – but don't start haggling until you have an idea of the true price, and never quote a price you're not prepared to pay. Most of all, take your time, have some fun, accept the tea or coffee they offer and play along with them. You're not obliged to buy and they won't be offended if you don't – though no doubt they'll keep up the sales pitch.

From Al-Azhar to Bab an-Nasr

Mosque of Sayyidna Al-Hussein Opposite the Al-Azhar Mosque, next to the bazaar, is one of the most sacred places of Muslim worship in Cairo.

The mosque is supposedly only open to Muslims, and this seems to be the case for groups. Modestly dressed foreigners in ones and twos seem to have little trouble getting in outside prayer times. The best time to visit it is during Ramadan, when the breaking of the fast each evening is a major event. The square in front of the mosque comes alive with festive celebrations when all the restaurants lay out their food.

Al-Muski This bazaar stretches on both sides of Sharia al-Muski (which is also called Sharia Gawhar) between Sharia al-Muizz li-Din Allah and Sharia Port Said, one block in and parallel to Sharia al-Azhar. Almost always jammed with a solid moving mass of people, Al-Muski is the bazaar where the

---

Sayyidna Al-Hussein

The Mosque of Sayyidna Al-Hussein is revered as the final resting place of the head of Al-Hussein, grandson of the Prophet. The area of Islamic Cairo from here north to the city gates is known as Al-Gamaliyya. In 1153, almost 500 years after his death, Al-Hussein's head was brought to Cairo in a green silk bag and placed in the Fatimid mosque that preceded this more modern 19th century structure, which was completed in 1878.

The powerful Omayyad family of Mecca, who were supported by the Prophet's favourite wife, had assumed control of the caliphate after Mohammed had died without naming a successor. As Islam began to spread and gain more power in the world, the tribal tensions over the rights of succession to the position of the Apostle of God also grew. Ali, who was the husband of Mohammed's daughter Fatima, put himself forward as the natural successor, claiming the right by marriage. When he was passed over he took up arms against the Omayyads, but was assassinated. His son, Al-Hussein, a blood relative of the Prophet, then led a revolt but was killed in battle.

Their deaths resulted in the schism which still exists in Islam today. The followers of Al-Hussein and Ali became the Shi'ites, or partisans of Ali, who refuse to acknowledge as caliph anyone but descendants of Mohammed, believing only someone of the Prophet's blood has the divine right to succession. However the Sunni, followers of Sunna, or 'the way', still have the power and the majority, and have banned any descendants of Mohammed from the caliphate for all time.

Despite being the mausoleum of a Shi'ite martyr, the shrine of Al-Hussein is one of the main congregational mosques in Cairo. Even the president of Sunni Egypt prays there on special religious holidays. ■

---

locals shop for things like bolts of colourful cloth, plastic furniture, wedding portraits, toys, spices and food. Although Al-Muski is less exotic than Khan al-Khalili, it's still interesting to wander through.

Souq al-Attarin A true delight for all the senses is the Souq al-Attarin, or spice bazaar, where dried and crushed flowers and fruit add their aromas to those of saffron, cinnamon, ginger, pepper, cloves, and other exotic or easily recognisable spices. The bazaar is just off Sharia al-Muizz li-Din Allah, south of Sharia al-Muski.

Sharia al-Muizz li-Din Allah Also called the Steet of the Coppersmiths (Sharia an-Nahassin), Sharia al-Muizz li-Din Allah is the thoroughfare which takes you north out of Khan al-Khalili. During the times of the Fatimids and Mamluks it was the major avenue through the heart of Cairo, and it was along this street that parades of pilgrims marched on their return from Mecca. It is still easy to imagine how life may have been here several centuries ago.

Madrassa & Mausoleum of as-Salih Ayyub The madrassa is just off Sharia al-Muizz li-Din Allah, on a small alley on the right about 125 metres north of Sharia al-Muski. The entrance is marked by an arch but there is not much left to see. The mausoleum can be entered by going back to Sharia al-Muizz li-Din Allah and turning right. The door, below the dome on your right, will probably be locked, but there will be someone around who can find the keeper, for the usual bit of baksheesh.

The madrassa and mausoleum were built in the 13th century by the last sultan of Salah ad-Din's Ayyubid dynasty. As-Salih Ayyub died before his complex was finished, so it was completed by his wife, Shagarat ad-Durr, who became one of Egypt's few female rulers. During the following Mamluk period the complex became Cairo's central court. Executions were conveniently carried out just outside the doors, on Sharia al-Muizz li-Din Allah.

Mausoleum of Qalaun There is a hospital, madrassa and mausoleum in this late 13th century complex opposite the Mausoleum of as-Salih Ayyub. Qalaun, one of the most successful Mamluk sultans and also one of the longest-lived (1220-1290), founded a dynasty which lasted nearly a century. The whole complex was built in about a year from 1284 to 1285.

A *maristan*, or hospital and insane asylum, has stood on this site for more than 700 years, but a modern facility has been built within the boundaries of the original. Sultans like Qalaun built the facilities that enabled enlightened care for the sick and insane. Hospitals and separate clinics were established, and even delicate surgery such as the removal of cataracts was performed here.

The interior of the mausoleum is beautifully decorated, especially near the entrance, and once your eyes become accustomed to the soft rainbow effect of sunlight through the stained-glass windows the tomb seems to be much larger than it is. Mashrabiyya screens, inlaid stone and carved stucco add to the overall feeling of peace and tranquillity that pervades the entire Qalaun complex. Entry is E£3 or E£1.50 for students, and also entitles you to wander around the Mausoleum of an-Nasir Mohammed. A guide will inevitably be on hand to take you up the minaret if you want – remember the baksheesh. Opening times seem to be flexible – about 9 am to 6 pm.

Hammam as-Sultan Qalaun Just off to the side from the hospital part of the Qalaun complex is a men-only hammam, also known as Hammam an-Nahassin, open from 9 am to 7 pm. A bath and massage costs you E£15, and you are bound to be invited to participate in extracurricular activities.

Mausoleum of an-Nasir Mohammed Except for the facade, doorway and courtyard, there is very little left of this 14th century tomb. It is just north of the Mausoleum of Qalaun, in Sharia al-Muizz li-Din Allah. It was one of several public works projects undertaken by Qalaun's son, an-Nasir Mohammed, who also built the Mosque of an-Nasir in the Citadel and the aqueduct from the Nile. His 40-year reign marked the pinnacle of Egyptian culture and prosperity under the Mamluks.

The Gothic doorway was taken from a church in Acre, which is in present-day

Israel, when an-Nasir and his Mamluk army ended Crusader domination there in 1290. Not many people visit the mausoleum; an-Nasir is actually buried in his father's tomb next door. Opposite is a Turkish-era *sabil* or fountain.

House of Uthman Katkhuda Katkhuda was an 18th century city official who built his house from a 14th century palace. His house is opposite the tomb of Qalaun, on a small street which runs east from Sharia al-Muizz li-Din Allah. The doorway is about half way down on the left side and you either knock or go upstairs and ask for someone to show you around. Baksheesh is expected, but wait until you have seen all you want to see.

Despite Katkhuda's renovations the house is still a fine example of Mamluk domestic architecture, and what's left of the decor of the spacious interior shows the influences of both the 14th and 18th centuries. One of the best things about the house is that there won't be hordes of tourists around. In fact you may be the only one there, and the view from the roof is fantastic.

Mosque of Barquq This mosque is just north of the Mausoleum of an-Nasir Moham-med, in Sharia al-Muizz li-Din Allah. Barquq, the first Burgi Mamluk sultan, came to power like most of the Mamluks through a series of plots and murders. His beautifully restored mosque, with its black and white marble entrance way and silver-inlaid bronze door, was built in 1386 as a madrassa. The colourful ceiling over part of the inner courtyard is supported by four Pharaonic columns made of porphyry quarried from near the Red Sea coast. Barquq's daughter is buried in the splendid domed tomb chamber, which is decorated with marble walls and floors and stained-glass windows, while the sultan himself rests in his mausoleum in the City of the Dead. Admission is E£3 and half for students. For the usual consideration, you can go up to the top of the minaret, but you may want to think about it twice. Since the October 1992 earthquake, many of the build-ings in this area have become pretty dodgy.

One Cairene architect suggests the smartest thing you can do on getting to the top is head straight back down again before it topples over! This may be overstating the case, but the minaret was visibly damaged by the quake.

Hammam as-Sultan This seems a slightly better bath house than the one just down the road. It's open 24 hours a day and also costs E£15. The entrance is marked by an old sign engraved in stone. The doorway is directly opposite a shop with a big sign reading Saad al-Khananky, just north of the Mosque of Barquq.

Qasr Beshtak Only a small part of this splendid 14th century palace remains. It's on Sharia al-Muizz li-Din Allah, just north of the Mosque of Barquq on the east side, and was built on the foundations of an earlier Fatimid palace. The Emir Beshtak was a very wealthy man who was married to the daugh-ter of Sultan an-Nasir. When he built this palace in 1334 it had five storeys, each with running water. Climb up on to the roof for a beautiful view south along Sharia al-Muizz li-Din Allah.

Sabil-Kuttab of Abdul Katkhuda Also on Sharia al-Muizz li-Din Allah, where the street forks, is a sabil-kuttab built in 1744 by Uthman Katkhuda's son, Abdul. The porches of the *kuttab*, a Qur'anic school for children, overhang the street on both sides of the fork. The kuttab is still used as a local school. The remains of the great sabil (a covered public drinking fountain) are underneath, and behind the kuttab is a 14th century apartment building. Note the exquisite Turkish ceramic work inside the fountain.

Bayt as-Suhaymi This superb merchant's house, built in the 16th and 17th centuries, is one of Cairo's greatest houses. To find it, turn right on Sharia Darb al-Asfar, which runs east off Sharia al-Muizz li-Din Allah. It's No 19, on the left; just knock on the big wooden door. The house is in rather decrepit condi-tion and only partially furnished but it has a peaceful and elegant atmosphere that invites you to linger as long as possible. Mashrabiyya screens, lattice windows, beautiful tiling and arched galleries abound. Ask the self-appointed guides to show you the women's bedroom and the harem reception room which overlooks the garden courtyard. Admission is E£3, or E£1.50 for students.

Bab al-Futuh One of the original 60 gates of medieval Cairo, Bab al-Futuh (the Gate of Conquests) is at the end of Sharia al-Muizz li-Din Allah. It was built in 1087, and through it thousands of pilgrims returned from Mecca. Of the three remaining gates of Cairo, Bab al-Futuh has the most interesting interior. Wide stonecut stairs lead to a large room with a high ceiling. Various additions and alterations have been made to the gate, including some by Napoleon, which also explains the names carved into the stone of two of the wall's towers, the Tour Junot and the Tour Perrault.

There are narrow slits, just wide enough for arrows, cut in the sides of the room, and along the tunnel which leads to Bab an-Nasr. Soldiers were once housed in this tunnel while awaiting their next battle.

There's a wonderful view of the Fatimid wall, Bab an-Nasr, and the minarets of the Mosque of Al-Hakim. You can walk along the wall linking the two gates and the roof and one minaret of the mosque. Admission is E£3, or E£1.50 for students. The caretaker usually sits in front of a café opposite the gate.

Bab an-Nasr Still attached to Bab al-Futuh by a tunnel inside the old wall, this is the Gate of Victory. Look for the hole over the entrance. Boiling oil was poured through this aperture to discourage unwelcome visitors from entering the city. Wandering through the passageways between the gates is quite an eerie experience. Climb the stairs to the roof and the minaret of the adjoining Mosque of Al-Hakim. Outside the gate and walls you can see the vast City of the Dead, with its tombs stretching for several km across the

horizon. On the other side, walk across the roof to the Mosque of Al-Hakim.

Mosque of Al-Hakim The haunting mosque of the ruthless and paranoid Al-Hakim has rarely been used as a place of worship. Completed in 1010, it has been used as a prison for Crusaders, as one of Salah ad-Din's stables, and as a warehouse by Napoleon. It has been largely repaired by members of the Ismaili sect of Shi'ite Islam, who claim the Fatimids as their religious ancestors and the Aga Khan as their spiritual leader.

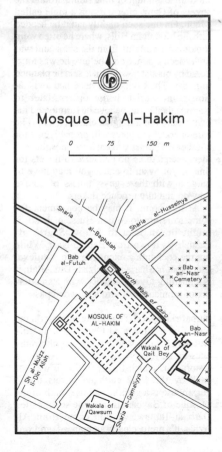

Mosque of Al-Hakim

Al-Hakim was the third of the Fatimid caliphs, who ruled with absolute political, religious and military authority. His name means 'he who rules at the command of God', which was something he professed to do, with complete disregard for anyone but himself, so that he's ranked close to the infamous Caligula in the dreadful treatment of his subjects. He restricted the free movement of women, Jews and Christians around the city; ordered decapitations for the slightest offences, sometimes out of mere personal dislike; incited riots which resulted in huge sections of the city being burnt; and spent an inordinate amount of time riding around the streets of Cairo after dark on a mule called Moon. On one such nightly jaunt he headed into the Moqattam Hills, where he often went looking for portents from the stars, and was never seen again. Some believe he was murdered by his sister, whom it is said he planned to marry. The Copts believe he had a visitation from Christ, while others, later to become the Druse, believe he formulated his own version of a religion akin to Islam. The caretakers of the gates will probably ask for another E£3 to let you enter the mosque, but there seems to be no evidence of tickets for this. If you want to enter, you may have to bargain with these guys, unless of course they do actually produce tickets.

At this point, it may be convenient for some to return to Midan Hussein. If so, it might be an idea to follow Sharia al-Gamaliyya down from Bab an-Nasr. While not the enchanting excursion into Medieval Cairo that is Sharia al-Muizz li-Din Allah, it is a bustling hive of activity, with a smattering of remnants of Cairo's crowded past.

Musafirkhanah Of particular interest on the way down Sharia al-Gamaliyya is this Ottoman palace, whose name loosely translates to 'travellers' caravanserai'. Although restoration, which began in 1986, was set back by the 1992 earthquake, this lavish guesthouse is a gem. It's a little south of the Mosque of Baybars II in a side street called Darb at-Tablawi (if you come from Al-Azhar, it's pretty clearly signposted) and was built between 1779 and 1788 by a wealthy merchant from Al-Faiyum, Mahmoud Muharram. It was later bought by Ibrahim, the son and short-lived successor of Egypt's independent-minded 19th century ruler, Mohammed Ali. A later successor, Ismail, was born here. Mahmoud Badeer, the son of one of the house's employees, is keen to show you around.

The central attraction is what is claimed to be the biggest mashrabiyyah in the world, jutting out from the *haramlik* (women's quarters) above a courtyard and garden where the royal family enjoyed plenty of dancing and festivities – so the women of the house could watch, but not join in, the fun. The male equivalent of the haramlik, the *selamlik*, is the first main room in the building to the left when you enter. You can also see a couple of private bath and sauna rooms – the coloured glass in the roof is original, as is most of the exquisite carved mahogany employed in the ceilings and the stained glass. This place is often overlooked, but well worth a detour. Admission is E£3, or E£1.50 for students, and opening hours flexible. Mahmoud says he is happy to open the place to visitors coming outside the loosely prescribed official hours of 9 am to 5 pm.

City of the Dead

The City of the Dead, or Northern Cemetery, is a vast Mamluk necropolis inhabited by hundreds of thousands of Cairenes, both dead and alive. The dead are still buried there in tombs which date from the 12th century, while the living exist in what amounts to little more than a huge shanty town amongst the impressive marble tombs of Mamluk sultans and nobles.

On Friday and holidays visitors flock here to picnic and pay their respects to the dead. Sometimes you can see an entire family feasting on top of a tomb and, wandering around this area, you often have to remind yourself that, yes, you are in a cemetery.

The City of the Dead begins outside and to the right of Bab an-Nasr and Bab al-Futuh, and stretches away to the north and also around to the east – it's actually the eastern part most people want to visit. As you leave Bab an-Nasr turn right down Sharia Galal and walk about half a km east; cross Sharia Mansuriyya and dogleg to your left and right before continuing down to the multilane highway, Tariq Salah Salem. When you cross this, you're in the cemetery. Head in and turn right at the first main tomb you see – the Mausoleum of Barquq is then a couple of hundred metres down to the right and left. Ask anyone for Barquq if you feel lost. There's something odd about sitting down to a cup of tea and game of cards among the tombstones, but there's no evidence that the locals feel strange about it at all.

Mausoleum of Barquq

You will be able to see the minarets of this mausoleum, 1½ km from Bab an-Nasr, long before you cross into the City of the Dead. From the outside the effect of its domes is reduced by the surrounding architecture but the interior of these high vaulted structures is quite splendid. The building was completed in 1411 and the tomb chambers contain the bodies of Barquq, who was moved from his mosque, his sons and the women of the family. Don't miss the beautiful marble minbar, or pulpit. For a little baksheesh the caretaker will take you up the northern minaret; there is a magnificent view of Cairo, including the necropolis. Admission is E£3, and the guardian tires of keeping the place open after about sundown.

Mosque & Mausoleum of Sultan Barsbey

The interior of the decorated dome and the mosaics on the floor and minbar are the highlights of this edifice, which was completed in 1432. It is 50 metres down the road from Barquq's tomb, on the left side, and contains several other tombs, including one of Amir Ganibak al-Ashrafi, whom Barsbey bought as a boy. He stayed loyal to his master, even joining him for a stint in jail, and was rewarded later when Barsbey became sultan by being made an amir. Keep an eye open for the wooden minbar in the mosque, which is the first building you enter.

Look for the guard or have one of the children in the area find him; he'll let you in for E£1 of baksheesh – although he'll probably start higher and insist it's for a 'ticket'.

Mausoleum of Qait Bey

Completed in 1474 and rated as one of the greatest buildings in Cairo, Qait Bey's tomb is also featured on the E£1 note. The exquisite dome and the finely tapered minaret, with its three intricately decorated tiers, stand out among the mausoleums in the area. The splendid, refined interior is equally beautiful.

Sultan Qait Bey, a prolific builder, was the last Mamluk leader with any real power in Egypt. He ruled for 28 years and, though he was as ruthless as the Mamluk sultans before him, he had a reputation for fairness. He also had a great love of beautiful architecture. The tomb contains the cenotaphs of Qait Bey and his two sisters, as well as two stones which supposedly bear the footprints of the Prophet. You must go through the same baksheesh procedure here.

Back to the City Centre

From the Mausoleum of Qait Bey you could walk back to Midan Hussein. Cross Tariq Salah Salem and head for the Ad-Darasa bus station (use the footbridge over the highway as a landmark). From here just head down the main road leading out on the left side of the station. Or you can get bus No 961, which will take you to Midan Ataba via Midan Hussein, and then on to Midan Ramses passing by the Windsor Hotel. Bus No 190 goes to Imbaba, and follows a similar route into town. Minibus No 66 goes to Midan Tahrir on its way to Bulaq ad-Dakrur, on the western limits of the city. Minibus No 10 goes to Midan Ataba and Midan Ramses.

Southern Cairo

Roda Island

Roda Island is south of Gezira Island. In the 13th century, Sultan as-Salih Ayyub built an immense fortress here for his army of Mamluks. The fortress had barracks, palaces, mosques and more than 50 towers. Various sultans used the facilities until the 18th century, by which time other, stronger fortresses in Egypt had replaced this one. Today the island is home to an eclectic palace built in the early 20th century, the Nilometer, a couple of pleasant riverside restaurants and several thousand Cairene apartment dwellers.

Manyal Palace Museum The Manyal Palace Museum is on your left after you take Sharia Ali Ibrahim across the canal to Roda Island.

It was built in the early part of this century as a residence for Prince Mohammed Ali Tewfiq. The government converted it into a museum in 1955. Apparently the prince couldn't decide which architectural style he preferred for the palace, so each of the five main buildings is different. Indeed, the first of the them, known now as the Reception Palace (which you enter on your right just inside the main entrance – you have to buy a ticket first at a booth further inside the grounds), is itself a combination of several. The ceramics and some of the ceiling woodwork is exquisite. The styles include Persian, Syrian, Moorish and Ottoman.

After you enter the palace grounds, walk along the path on the right to the Mosque of Mohammed Ali and the hunting museum of the royal family. The hunting museum was added to the complex in 1962 to house King Farouk's huge collection of stuffed animal trophies. This is not a place for animal lovers. The heads of several hundred gazelles line the walls along with a variety of other animals shot by the royal family, and there's also a strange table constructed from elephant ears. The butterfly collection is extremely colourful.

Return to the path leading from the palace entrance and follow it to the other buildings. The Residence Palace is the next one you will see. Each room is ornately decorated with hand-painted geometric shapes – a traditional design in Islamic art. Several of the doors are inlaid with carved pieces of ivory,

and the windows feature intricate mashrabiyyah screens.

There is rather an odd view from one of the bedroom windows on the 2nd floor. You can see over the fence into the swimming pool area of Club Méditerranée, which now occupies half of the palace grounds. It's a bit of a surprise while touring rooms steeped in the art, history and traditions of Islam to be suddenly yanked back to the 20th century with views of scantily clad Club Med vacationers!

The largest building contains Mohammed Ali's fascinating collection of manuscripts, clothing, silver objects, furniture, writing implements and other items dating from medieval times to the 19th century. A self-appointed guide likes to show you around this part of the museum object by object. If you don't want his services let him know.

The palace is open daily from 9 am to 4 pm, and admission is E£5, or E£2.50 for students. Photography permits are E£10.

Nilometer This interesting ancient monument is on the southern tip of Roda Island. Built in the 9th century to measure the rise and fall of the Nile, it helped predict the state of the annual harvest. If the Nile rose to 16 cubits, approximately equal to the length of a forearm, this would hold great promise for the crops, and the people would celebrate.

The conical dome was added when the Nilometer was restored in the 19th century. The measuring device, a graduated column, is well below the level of the Nile in a paved area at the bottom of a flight of steps. The admission fee is E£3, or half for students. Save yourself some trouble and approach it down the east side of the island. You can't get to it coming down the west side.

Old Cairo
Originally a Roman fortress town called Babylon, this part of Cairo was of great importance to the early Christians. Egypt was one of the first countries to embrace the new Christian faith in the 1st century AD. The fortress was built about 900 years before the Fatimids founded Cairo, on a then-stra-

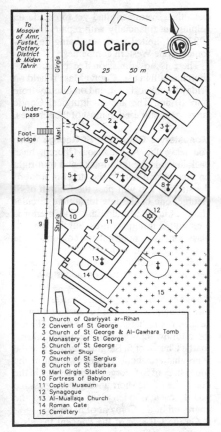

Old Cairo

To
Mosque
of Amr,
Fustat,
Pottery
District
& Midan
Tahrir

0   25   50 m

Under-
pass

Foot-
bridge

Girgis

Mari

Sharia

1 Church of Qasriyyat ar-Rihan
2 Convent of St George
3 Church of St George & Al-Gawhara Tomb
4 Monastery of St George
5 Church of St George
6 Souvenir Shop
7 Church of St Sergius
8 Church of St Barbara
9 Mari Girgis Station
10 Fortress of Babylon
11 Coptic Museum
12 Synagogue
13 Al-Muallaqa Church
14 Roman Gate
15 Cemetery

by the Copts but by the Jews and later the Muslims who lived in the area. At one time there were 20 churches and a synagogue there. The Christian monuments of Old Cairo that have survived the centuries are still very important to the Copts. There are also several mosques in the area, and Cairo's small Jewish population still worships at the ancient synagogue.

Getting There & Away Old Cairo is 5½ km south of central Cairo. To get there you can take either a bus, a taxi – ask for Masr al-Qadima – or the metro from Midan Tahrir (get off at Mari Girgis Station, which is above ground); the metro only costs 30 pt from Midan Tahrir and is by far the easiest way to get there.

Several buses run past Midan Tahrir on their way to the terminus by the Mosque of Amr – Nos 135 and 814 among them.

The slow way, but perhaps more pleasant if you have the time, is to get a water bus from near the Radio & Television building, just north of the Nile Hilton. Ask for the Masr al-Qadima water bus and make sure it's going all the way to the terminus, as many only do a few stops. It takes about 50 minutes and costs 25 pt. From the landing head straight in from the river and veer right. You'll soon see the metro station, and there's a bridge over the tracks just to the north of it, which leaves you in front of the Church of St George.

Fortress of Babylon The main remaining part of the fortress, built in 30 AD by Emperor Augustus, is a tower that was part of the waterside Roman battlements. The tower originally overlooked an important port on the Nile before the river shifted course, and excavations directly below the tower have revealed part of the ancient quay, several metres below street level.

Coptic Museum The fortress's tower now marks the entrance to the tranquil courtyards and lush, verdant gardens of the Coptic Museum. The museum building is paved with mosaics and decorated with elegant

tegic point on the Nile. The river has since shifted its course about 400 metres west.

The development of Coptic Christianity, and the monastic tradition it adopted after Paul of Thebes chose a life of solitude in the Egyptian desert, greatly influenced early European Christianity. But for Egypt the Christian period was merely one of transition from Pharaonic times to the Islamic era. During the several centuries that Christianity did predominate in Egypt, this town, only five km south of where the Muslims would later build their city, became quite a metropolis. It was considered a holy place not only

mashrabiyyah screens from old Coptic houses, and is bright and airy. Its exhibits cover Egypt's Christian era from 300 to 1000 AD, showing the Pharaonic, Greco-Roman and Islamic influences on the artistic development of the Copts. It is the world's finest collection of Coptic religious and secular art. The icons and textiles are particularly interesting, and there are also splendid examples of stonework, manuscripts, woodwork, metalwork, glass, paintings and pottery.

The October 1992 earthquake badly damaged the south side of the museum, which takes in some excavated remains of the old fortress. That part of the museum is closed for repairs.

The museum is open from 9 am to 4 pm from Sunday to Thursday, and from 9 to 11 am and 1 to 4 pm on Friday. Admission is E£8, or E£4 for students. You must leave your bag and camera outside in a booth, unless you want to pay E£10 to take some snaps.

Al-Muallaqa Church Dubbed the Hanging Church, this is one of the oldest Christian places of worship in Egypt. It was built on top of one of the old fortress gatehouses with its nave suspended over the passage. Dedicated to the Virgin Mary and properly known as Sitt Mariam, or St Mary, it is also one of Cairo's most beautiful churches.

Just inside the entrance, through a doorway in the walls just south of the Coptic Museum, there is an interesting 10th century icon of the Virgin and the Child. The inner courtyard is adorned with icons and the interior of the church, renovated many times over the centuries, is quite beautiful. In the centre, standing on 13 slender pillars that represent Christ and his disciples, is a beautiful pulpit which is used only on Palm Sunday every year. One of the pillars is darker than the rest, symbolising Judas.

Like many buildings in the area, the church suffered in the earthquake that hit Cairo in October 1992. The quake rocked the foundations and cracks are evident in the north wall. Scaffolding is keeping part of the inside standing. According to church offi-

cials, the government had yet to decide on helping out financially with repairs in mid-1993, and limited work was being done by some private Western companies.

There is no admission fee because the church is still in use. Coptic Mass is held on Friday from 8 to 11 am and on Sunday from 7 to 10 am. The ancient liturgical Coptic language is still used in most of the services.

Monastery & Church of St George When you leave the Al-Muallaqa Church, head back towards the train tracks and turn right on Sharia Mari Girgis, the street in front of the station. You will pass the Church of St George, one of the few remaining circular churches in the Middle East. The interior is a bit gutted from past fires, but the stained-glass windows are bright and colourful. The monastery next door is closed to the public, but it can sometimes be entered if you ask permission at the church or monastery.

Convent of St George This is an especially interesting place to visit because of a rather strange ritual that is practised there. To get there follow the sign on Sharia Mari Girgis for the Church of St Sergius and descend the stairs that are about 25 metres north of the Monastery of St George, on the right. On the other side of the short underground passage you'll see a wooden door leading to the courtyard of the Convent of St George.

On the left side of the convent there's a small room still used for the chain-wrapping ritual, in which visitors are welcome to participate. Remove your shoes before entering. The chains are symbolic of the persecution of St George during the Roman occupation. A nun oversees the wrapping and says the requisite prayers while standing next to a 1000-year-old icon. Several of the nuns speak English and are thrilled when you ask them questions about their beliefs. Photographs are permitted.

Church of St Sergius To get to St Sergius, also called Abu Serga, leave the Convent of St George by the same door you entered, turn left and walk down the lane to the end. Pass under the low archway on the right and enter the church on the left side.

This is supposedly one of the places where the Holy Family rested after fleeing from King Herod. Every year, on 1 June, a special mass is held here to commemorate the event. At the turn of the century this little church, which dates from the 10th century, was the most important pilgrimage spot in Old Cairo for visiting Christian tourists. There are 24 marble columns lining the central court, and a series of 12th century icons above an iconostasis (a partition screen bearing icons) depicting the 12 apostles.

Church of St Barbara To get to this church, also known as Sitt Barbara, turn right as you leave the Church of St Sergius. When you get to the end of the alley turn left, and the Church of St Barbara is in front of you. This church is dedicated to the saint, who was beaten to death by her father for trying to convert him to Christianity. The church, which is similar to the church of St Sergius, was restored during the Fatimid era. St Barbara's relics supposedly rest in a small chapel to the right of the nave, and the remains of St Catherine, after whom the famous monastery in the Sinai was named, are also said to rest here.

Ben Ezra Synagogue This synagogue, one of the oldest in Egypt, is a few metres south of the Church of St Barbara. Turn left when leaving the church and enter the first gate on your left, marked by a Star of David. Although there is no rabbi, and services are rarely held, it is used by the 42 Jewish families that reside in the area.

Set in a shady garden, it was built on the site of a 4th century Christian church, which the Copts had to sell in the 9th century to enable them to pay taxes to Ibn Tulun for the construction of his mosque. The synagogue, named after a 12th century Rabbi of Jerusalem, Abraham ben Ezra, was severely damaged by Arabs after the 1967 war with Israel, but it has been almost completely renovated.

There are also many legends about the synagogue. It is said that the temple of the prophet Jeremiah once stood on the same spot and that Jeremiah is actually buried under a miracle rock in the grounds. There is also a spring which is supposed to mark the place where the Pharaoh's daughter found Moses in the reeds, and where Mary drew water to wash Jesus.

Mosque of Amr

This mosque is a few blocks north of the Fortress of Babylon but isn't all that interesting. The original mosque, of which nothing remains, was the first place of Muslim worship built in Egypt. It was constructed in 642 AD by the victorious invader Amr, the general who is said to have founded Fustat on the site where he had pitched his tent. However, according to Coptic history books, the mosque was built over the ruins of a Coptic church. There couldn't have been much left of those ruins, as the first structure is said to have been made of palm branches and leaves. The site witnessed a series of replacements as the mosque was rebuilt and extended several times under the Umayyad and Abbassid dynasties. The core of the present mosque structure probably dates back to 827, although much of the mosque has been restored quite recently. Admission is E£3, or E£1.50 for students. Don't forget to take off your shoes before entering the mosque.

Pottery District

Behind the mosque, nestled beneath smouldering mounds that are actually workshop roofs and kilns, is a community of potters. You can wander around and watch them make and fire pottery vessels and utensils.

Fustat

This was where Cairo first rose as a city. To get there from Old Cairo, head north up Sharia Mari Girgis till you see the Mosque of Amr on the right. Take Sharia 'Ain as-Sira, just south of the mosque, over a crossroad and then go left along a short lane to the Fustat site.

The site has been excavated by an archaeological team from the American University in Cairo. Although the remains are scanty, you can make out traces of alleyways, houses, wells and water-pipe systems surrounded by a low wall. Part of the original wall of Cairo has also been restored here. Several families in the area make pottery.

Fustat started out in about 640 AD as a tent city, a garrison town for the conquering Muslim army. It became the first Islamic capital in Egypt and for three centuries it continued to grow and prosper. At the height of its glory, before the conquering Fatimids founded the neighbouring city of Cairo in 969 AD, Fustat had a water supply, sewerage and sanitation facilities far superior to anything that was known in Europe before the 18th century.

The city was destroyed and abandoned in 1168 to prevent it falling into the hands of the invading Crusader, King Amalric of Jerusalem.

Giza

The Giza district begins opposite the west side of Roda Island and stretches 18 km westward to the Great Pyramids. Most of the things of interest are either near the Nile or at the western end of Pyramids Rd (Sharia al-Ahram – but invariably called Sharia al-Haram by the locals. *Haram* means pyramid; *ahram* is the plural, which nobody ever seems to say or even fully understand). For the mere pittance of 10 to 25 pt you can have the bone-crushing experience of riding buses No 904, 905 and 160 (which pass by Midan Tahrir) almost all the way to the pyramids. They will drop you at or near the turn-off to the Desert Rd to Alexandria, just short of the Hotel Mena House Oberoi on Pyramids Rd. From Ramses Station you can take bus No 30 to Midan Giza for 10 pt, and then bus No 3 to the pyramids. You can also get bus No 913 to the Sphinx entrance. It passes through Tahrir on the way from the suburb of Shubra. Buses are much easier to take in the other direction, from the pyramids to central

Cairo, because they start off empty; get a seat near the front so you'll be able to get out more easily.

A much more practical and comfortable alternative is to take a minibus. They leave from in front of the Mogamma building; the fare to the pyramids is 35 pt. Look for No 83 or the men standing next to minibuses and shouting 'haram, haram', which means 'pyramid, pyramid' (why they use the singular is anyone's guess).

There are also privately run microbuses from just near the No 83 minibus. They are far more frequent and cost you 50 pt. You can also get one from Midan Giza for 25 pt.

Another way to get through Giza and out to the pyramids is to take a taxi, which should cost about E£10, although you may have to bargain with the driver to get this price. Ask locals for the latest estimate.

Some of the public transport may leave you at Saqqara Rd, so you will have to walk

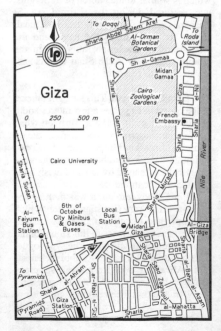

Pyramids of Giza

It was not an obsession with death, or a fear of it, on the part of the ancient Egyptians that led to the construction of these incredible mausoleums; it was their belief in eternal life and their desire to be one with the cosmos. A Pharaoh was the son of a god, and the sole receiver of the ka, or life force, that emanated from the god. The Pharaoh, in turn, conducted this vital force to his people, so in life and death he was worshipped as a god.

A pyramid was thus not only an indestructible sanctum for the preservation of a Pharaoh's ka, nor simply an incredible, geometric pile of stones raised over the mummified remains of a Pharaoh and his treasures to ensure his immortality. It was the apex of a much larger funerary complex that provided a place of worship for his subjects, as well as a visible reminder of the absolute and eternal power of the gods and their universe.

The age of the pyramids lasted only a few hundred years. Egypt's first pyramid, in Pharaoh Zoser's mortuary complex at Saqqara, was a 62-metre-high marvel of masonry completed in the 27th century BC. It was a product of the technical brilliance of Imhotep, the Pharaoh's chief architect. This was the first time stone had been used to such an extent and with such artistry and precision. Imhotep's architectural genius changed the face of Egypt. Less than 100 years after his tribute to his Pharaoh there arose from the sands of Giza the perfection of the Great Pyramid of Cheops.

The mortuary complexes of Cheops, Chephren and Mycerinus, who were father, son and grandson, included the following: a pyramid, which was the Pharaoh's tomb as well as a repository for all his household goods, clothes and treasure; a funerary temple on the east side of the pyramid; pits for the storage of the Pharaoh's solar barques, which were his means of transport in the afterlife; a valley temple on the banks of the Nile; and a causeway from the river to the pyramid. The entrance passageways face north towards the Pole Star, as do those in all 80 royal pyramids found in Egypt; the tomb chambers inside face west, towards the Kingdom of the Dead; and the mortuary temples outside face east, towards the rising sun.

The pyramids and temples at Giza were built from stone quarried locally and from the Moqattam Hills. Napoleon estimated that there would be enough stones in the three main pyramids alone to build a wall, three metres high, all around France. ■

the rest of the way to the pyramids – about 15 minutes away. On the way, you'll pass the tourist office, where you can check on the official rates for horse and camel rides (about E£8 per hour, or E£40 per person for the ride to Saqqara). However, it's not uncommon for prices to be higher or lower. The tourist office is otherwise extremely low on information. It is open from 8 am to 5 pm daily, except Friday, when it open from 9 am to 4 pm. The entrance is up the hill and off to the left. If you find someone steering you into the unmistakable stench of a stable, backtrack fast – ignore all the jabbering about them being able to get you into the pyramids area without a ticket.

The other entrance is by the Sphinx. Most people seem to exit this way. The road down to it is off to the left (facing west), just before the turn-off for the Desert Rd.

There's an admission fee of E£10 (E£5 for students) for the site. To enter the Great Pyramid of Cheops you pay another E£10 (half for students) and the same again to visit the Solar Boat Museum, which closes at 3.30 pm. The pyramids close about 4 pm, but the site is open from about 7 am to 8 pm.

The best times to visit are at sunrise, sunset and night. During the day it can get very hot and crowded, and the hazy sky makes it difficult to take photographs.

Pyramids Road

The road to the pyramids, also called Sharia al-Ahram, was built in the 1860s so that Empress Eugénie could travel the 11 km from Cairo in her carriage. The road was another in a long list of public works projects initiated by Khedive Ismail. However, it wasn't paved until US president Jimmy Carter visited the pyramids. The khedive also had a palace (now the Cairo Marriott Hotel) built for the empress, so that she would have a place to stay while attending the ceremonies for the opening of the Suez Canal. Pyramids Rd intersects Sharia al-Giza about 500 metres south of Cairo Zoo.

Before you go to the pyramids, you might want to first turn left at Midan al-Galaa from Sharia at-Tahrir, into Sharia al-Giza, to see a couple of interesting buildings. The first big building on your left after you pass the Cairo Sheraton is the Russian embassy, which has perhaps lost most of its aura since the hammer and sickle were traded in for the Russian version of the red, white and blue. What was the official residence of the President of Egypt is next to it. It's being converted into some sort of arts authority, but you can still see the graceful old building through the gates. About one km further south along Sharia al-Giza you will see the entrance to the zoo. The buses to the pyramids pass by here.

Great Pyramids of Giza
The ancient Greeks considered the Great

Pyramids to be one of the Seven Wonders of the World. They are Egypt's most visited monuments, and among the world's greatest tourist attractions. For centuries the Great Pyramids of Giza have intrigued and puzzled visitors and, even in the 20th century, it is difficult to stand before them and not be overwhelmed. For 4½ millennia, surviving the rise and fall of great dynasties and outlasting Egypt's many conquerors, they have shared the desert plateau of Giza with other monuments: smaller attendant pyramids, some for royal wives; rows of mastabas, the tombs of 4th and 5th dynasty princes and nobles; and the imposing figure of the Sphinx.

Getting Around Every visit to the Great Pyramids includes a stroll, or sometimes a run, through a veritable obstacle course of hustlers, souvenir shops, alabaster factories, papyrus museums, and self-appointed, and usually unwanted, guides. A common tactic

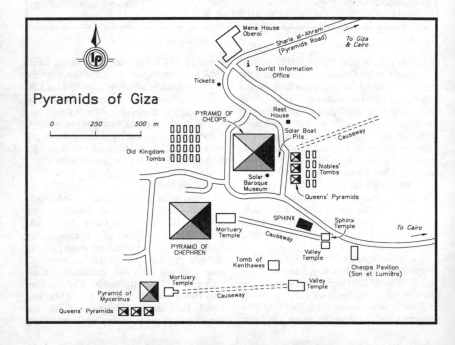

Top: The Sphinx & Pyramid of Chephren, Giza (CB)
Left: Pyramid & copt graveyard, Giza (GE)
Right: A camel smiles after a sunrise ride around the pyramids, Giza (KB)

Top: Pyramids at sunrise, Giza (KB)
Middle: The Pyramids at Giza (GB)
Bottom: Camel and rider by the pyramids at sunset (PS)

The Sphinx & the Pyramid of Chephren

they employ is to pretend, with all the pompous officious bombast they can muster, to be employees demanding to see your tickets – don't give them to these people whatever you do – the real ticket inspectors near the ticket booth are a much friendlier, more laid-back bunch, because they don't want anything from you. Above all, don't despair; escape from this maddening onslaught is possible.

The best strategy is just to ignore them, although this is not always easy. An alternative is to hire a horse or camel and gallop, glide, or jolt through the desert around the pyramids. There are stables near the tourist office on Pyramids Rd.

You can also try approaching one of the many camel and horse owners around the pyramids. Some people would suggest avoiding these people altogether. If you are burning to get on one of these critters and do

not have the time to explore the stables outside the area (a little way south of the entrance by the Sphinx), bargain fiercely and be sure of what you have agreed on. Stories abound of people getting on to their mounts and being led around for all sorts of unwanted extras and then being charged accordingly. Not a few people have found themselves paying ridiculous amounts of money to be let *off* camels. *Don't* hand your cameras over to these people for that shot of you on the camel – one person reportedly paid US$100 cash to get his camera back! A horse or camel should not cost more than E£8 an hour. Women should take care, as the animal-owners are not beyond trying to exploit a position of power.

The best time to go for a ride is at sunset, ending at the Cheops Pavilion just as the sound & light show illuminates the pyramids and the Sphinx.

Great Pyramid of Cheops This great pyramid, the oldest at Giza and the largest in Egypt, stood 146.5 metres high when it was completed around 2600 BC. After 46 centuries its height has been reduced by only nine metres. Approximately 2½ million limestone blocks, weighing around six million tonnes, were used in the construction. It supposedly took 10 years to build the causeway and the massive earth ramps used as a form of scaffolding, and 20 years to raise the pyramid itself. The job was done by a highly skilled corps of masons, mathematicians, surveyors and stonecutters as well as about 100,000 slaves who carried out the backbreaking task of moving and laying the stones. The blocks had to be exactly placed to prevent excess pressure building up on any one point and causing the collapse of the whole structure.

Although there is not much to see inside the pyramid, the experience of climbing through such an ancient structure is unforgettable. The entrance, on the north face, leads to a descending passage which ends in an unfinished tomb (usually closed) about 100 metres along and 30 metres below the pyramid. About 20 metres from the entrance, however, there is an ascending passage, 1.3 metres high and one metre wide, which continues for about 40 metres before opening into the Great Gallery, which is 47 metres long and 8.5 metres high. There is also a smaller horizontal passage leading into the so-called Queen's Chamber.

As you ascend the Great Gallery to the King's Chamber at the top notice how precisely the blocks were fitted together. Unlike the rest of the pyramid, the main tomb chamber, which is just over five metres wide and 10 metres long, was built of red granite blocks. The roof, which weighs more than 400 tonnes, consists of nine huge slabs of granite, above which are another four slabs separated by gaps designed to distribute the enormous weight away from the chamber. There is plenty of air in this room, as it was built so that fresh air flowed in from two shafts on the north and south walls. Entry costs E£10 (half for students).

Climbing the outside of the Great Pyramid has been a popular adventure for centuries. It is officially forbidden, and there is a strong school of thought that suggests it does nothing for the pyramids themselves. If you decide you want to do it, there are enough 'guides' to show you the way: make sure you follow one, because each year a few people fall off and are killed. It takes about 20 minutes to get to the top and it's quite a climb, as many of the blocks are taller than you are. The view of Cairo and the surrounding desert from the summit is magnificent.

Back on the ground, around the pyramid, are five long pits which once contained the Pharaoh's boats. These solar barques may have been used to bring the mummy of the dead Pharaoh across the Nile to the valley temple, from where it was brought up the causeway and placed in the tomb chamber. The boats were then buried around the pyramid to provide transport for the king in the next world. One of these ancient wooden vessels, possibly the oldest boat in existence, was unearthed in the 1950s. The sacred barge was restored and a glass museum built over it to protect it from damage from the elements.

On the eastern side of the pyramid are the Queens' Pyramids, three small structures about 20 metres high, which resemble little more than pyramid-shaped piles of rubble. They were the tombs of Cheops' wives and sisters.

Pyramid of Chephren South-west of the Great Pyramid, and with almost the same dimensions, is the Pyramid of Chephren. At first it seems larger than his father's, because it stands on higher ground and its peak still has part of the original limestone casing which once covered the whole structure. It is 136.5 metres high (originally 143.5 metres).

Although the chambers and passageways are less elaborate than those in the Great Pyramid, they are also less claustrophobic. The entrance leads down into a passage and then across to the burial chamber, which still contains the large granite sarcophagus of Chephren.

One of the most interesting features of this pyramid are the substantial remains of Chephren's mortuary temple outside to the east. Several rooms can be visited, and the causeway, which originally provided access from the Nile to the tomb, still leads from the main temple to the valley temple.

Pyramid of Mycerinus At a height of 62 metres (originally 66.5 metres), this is the smallest pyramid of the three. Extensive damage was done to the exterior by a 16th century caliph who decided he wanted to demolish all the pyramids.

Inside, a hall descends from the entrance into a passageway, which in turn leads into a small chamber and a group of rooms. There is nothing particularly noteworthy about the interior, but at the very least you can have the adventure of exploring a seldom-visited site.

Outside are the excavated remains of Mycerinus' mortuary temple and, further

east, the ruins of his valley temple, still lying beneath the sand.

The Sphinx Legends and superstitions abound about this relic of antiquity, and the mystery surrounding its long-forgotten purpose is almost as intriguing as the sight of the structure itself. Known in Arabic as Abu al-Hol, which means 'the father of terror', the feline man was called the Sphinx by the ancient Greeks because it resembled the mythical winged monster with a woman's head and lion's body who proposed a riddle to the Thebans and killed all who could not guess the answer.

Carved almost entirely from one huge piece of limestone left standing in the quarry from which Cheops had the stones cut for his pyramid, the Sphinx is about 50 metres long and 22 metres high. It is not known when it was carved but one theory is that it was Chephren who thought of shaping the rock

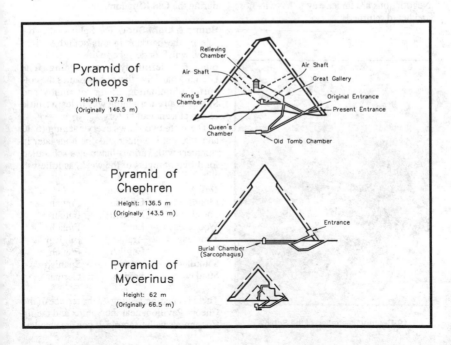

Pyramid of Cheops
Height: 137.2 m
(Originally 146.5 m)

Relieving Chamber
Air Shaft
Air Shaft
Great Gallery
King's Chamber
Original Entrance
Present Entrance
Queen's Chamber
Old Tomb Chamber

Pyramid of Chephren
Height: 136.5 m
(Originally 143.5 m)

Entrance
Burial Chamber (Sarcophagus)

Pyramid of Mycerinus
Height: 62 m
(Originally 66.5 m)

into a lion's body with a god's face, wearing the royal headdress of Egypt. Another theory is that it is the likeness of Chephren himself that has been staring out over the desert sands for so many centuries.

One legend about the Sphinx is associated with the fact that it was engulfed by sand and hidden completely for several hundred years. The sun-god Ra appeared to the man who was to become Tuthmosis IV and promised him the crown of Egypt if he would free his image, the Sphinx, from the sand. The stelae (stone tablets) found between the paws of the Sphinx recorded this first known restoration.

During the period of the Ottoman Empire the Turks used the Sphinx for target practice, and its nose and beard, which are now in the British Museum, fell off. A team of American and Egyptian archaeologists is restoring parts of the Sphinx, most obviously now at the base. The scaffolding that scarred its face for the past few years has now been removed. Negotiations are under way to have its nose and beard returned.

19-Century Illustration of the Sphinx

Tomb of Khenthawes This rarely visited but imposing structure, opposite the Great Pyramid and north of Mycerinus' causeway, is the tomb of the daughter of Pharaoh Mycerinus. Khenthawes became queen of Userkaf and founder of the 5th dynasty. The tomb is a rectangular building cut into a small hill. You can go down a corridor at the back of the chapel room to the burial chambers, but the descent is a bit hazardous, so be careful.

Cemeteries Around the pyramids are private cemeteries with several rows of tombs organised in a grid pattern. Most of the tombs are closed to the public, but those of Qar, Idu and Queen Mersyankh III, in the eastern cemetery, are accessible, although it's sometimes difficult to find the guard who has the keys.

The Tomb of Iasen, in the western cemetery, contains interesting inscriptions and wall paintings which show life and work during the Old Kingdom.

Sound & Light Show The Sphinx takes the role of the narrator in this sound & light show, which is designed with the tourist in mind but definitely worth seeing. The booming narrative that accompanies the colourful illumination of the pyramids and Sphinx is an entertaining way to learn a little of Egypt's ancient history.

There are two shows every evening (6.30 and 7.30 pm in winter and one hour later in summer) with various languages scheduled for different nights of the week, as follows:

Day	1st show	2nd show
Monday	English	French
Tuesday	French	Italian
Wednesday	English	French
Thursday	Arabic	English
Friday	English	French
Saturday	English	Spanish
Sunday	French	German

There is open-air seating on the terrace of the Cheops Pavilion, near the Sphinx and facing Chephren's valley temple. If you are wandering around the area behind the Sphinx around dusk, you may find you can get a reasonable look at the performance without paying a cracker – you'll have to walk bold as brass when exiting though. Admission costs E£10. During Ramadan, depending on the time of year in which it falls, performance times can be different. If you are unsure, call 385-2880, 385-7320, or the tourist office.

Ride to Saqqara If you're after adventure you could rent a camel, donkey or horse for the ride across the desert to Saqqara. This trip is not really for inexperienced riders. By the end of the day you will have spent about six or seven hours atop a horse or camel and a few more hours roaming around the sites at Saqqara.

The trip takes about three hours each way, and costs about E£30 for a horse and E£40 for a camel, although people have been charged as much as E£100. Don't forget that a camel can carry two people.

Cairo Zoo
The zoo is near Cairo University, between Sharia Gamiat al-Qahira (Cairo University St) and Sharia al-Giza; it is worth a visit, especially if you've had an overdose of ancient tombs and medieval mosques. The animals aren't the healthiest, but it's still pleasant to get away from the Cairo chaos and walk around the grounds. Avoid the zoo on Friday, Saturday and holidays, when it becomes extremely crowded. There's a restaurant on an island in the centre of the park. Hours are 9 am to 5 pm and admission costs 15 pt. Just to the north is the small but comparatively well kept Orman Park.

Dr Ragab's Pharaonic Village & Papyrus Institute
About 20 minutes' walk south of Al-Giza Bridge in Giza, this floating excursion into a world of people dressed up as ancient Egyptians is only for those with money to burn. For E£25 (students E£10), you can float down the 'canal of mythology' and try to imagine you've been thrown back a millen-

ium or two. It's open from 9 am to 4 pm in winter, and until 9 pm in summer.

Further north, near the Cairo Sheraton, is Dr Ragab's original Papyrus Institute. Here you can see some displays on this ancient art, as well as buy some of the doctor's work. It's open from 10 am to 7 pm.

Kerdassa
Many of the galabiyyas, scarves, rugs and weavings sold in the bazaars and shops of Cairo are made in this village near Giza. To get there, head down Pyramids Rd towards the pyramids, turn right at the Maryutia Canal (just before the obelisk), and follow the road to the village. The minibus from Midan Tahrir to the pyramids begins and ends its trips at the junction of the canal and Pyramids Rd, and a local microbus does the stretch along the canal for 25 pt. Many tourists visit this village in search of bargains, so it's probably no longer the great place it once was for special deals. You can also get bus No 116 en route from Midan Giza to Kerdassa.

The camel trail across the Western Desert to Libya begins in Kerdassa. If you're looking for an incredibly challenging adventure join a caravan here – but it's definitely only for the experienced!

Harannia
If it's carpets and the like you want to look at while you're in the area, it may be worth heading down here. Just next to the Motel Salma is the Wissa Wassef art school. Here children from the age of eight begin learning the art of weaving tapestries, and eventually become proficient enough to sell their work. The school was actually founded in 1942 in Old Cairo, but had to shut down because of the war. Its founder, Ramses Wissa Wassef, ran it until his death in 1974, when it got its present name. About one hundred artists work here now. A lot of the work features rural scenes, Pharaonic motifs or flora and fauna. It's worth a visit just to see how they create some beautiful pieces on the loom. A microbus from the corner of Pyramids Rd and Saqqara Rd heading to Abu Sir will drop

you there for 25 pt. It's the same stop as for the Motel Salma.

ACTIVITIES
Language Courses
For information on the most recognised organisations offering Arabic lessons in Cairo, namely the AUC, British Council and ILI, refer to Activities in the Facts for the Visitor chapter. Arabic lessons are also offered through cultural centres. The French Cultural Centre (☎ 354-7679), 1 Madrassat al-Huquq al-Fransiyya, Mounira, offers various courses of quite a high standard.

The Goethe Institut (☎ 759877), 5 Sharia Abdel Salam Aref, also offers relatively inexpensive Arabic lessons, but generally concentrates on not overly demanding courses in colloquial Egyptian Arabic.

The Egyptian Centre for International Cultural Cooperation (☎ 341-5419), 11 Shagarat ad-Durr, Zamalek, offers courses in classical Arabic. Intensive courses over 12 weeks cost US$110 and normal courses over the same period US$55. Contact Mrs Abla Ghoneim any day between 10 am and 1 pm.

Check the magazine *Cairo Today* for a list of other organisations that offer Arabic courses, but be wary of quality and cost.

Felucca Rides
Feluccas are the ancient broadsail boats seen everywhere up and down the Nile. Taking a felucca ride while you're in Egypt is an absolute must; there's no better way to see the Nile, especially at sunset. If you don't have the time or inclination to spend five days on one between Luxor and Aswan, the next best thing is to hire one in Cairo and take a leisurely cruise for a few hours. It costs about E£10 per hour to hire a felucca (along with its captain). This rate is, of course, subject to haggling and could be higher or lower depending on your negotiating (or arguing) skills. Feluccas congregate at several quays along the river, but one of the most popular departure points is in Garden City, opposite the Meridien Hotel. Others are

Feluccas on the Nile

along the south-east end of Gezira, between 6th of October and At-Tahrir bridges, and in Maadi.

Dive Clubs
The Cairo Divers Group organises monthly diving trips, rents equipment and offers plenty of information on the dive sites. The club meets on the first Monday of each month at the Semiramis InterContinental Hotel. Annual membership fees for divers are E£40. For more information, call Magdy Hanna (☎ 352-4216).

The Maadi Divers is another group. They organise trips and sell and rent equipment as well. Call Magdy al-Araby (☎ 352-6375).

The British Sub-Aqua Club, also in Cairo, offers BSAC and PADI certification and instruction. Members meet on the third Monday of each month.

Diving equipment is available at Scubatec (☎ 668243), at 9 Sharia Dr Hassan Aflaton, Heliopolis; and Scuba Plus (☎ 340-7860), 1B Sharia as-Sayed al-Bakry, Zamalek.

Horse-Riding
Certainly popular with some expatriates, a horse ride out by the pyramids, especially in

the evening, can be a great way to fully escape the clamour of Cairo and vent some pent-up aggro. But avoid the hustlers in and around the entrances to the pyramids. If you head south of the entrance by the Sphinx (turn right on your way out) you'll come across several stables. MG has been recommended by some, but look around a little. You can also organise lessons.

Hammams

There are several old Turkish baths functioning in Islamic Cairo. These are mostly men-only institutions working virtually round the clock, and some are definitely no-go areas for people not interested in more than just a scrub down and massage. If you'd like to try your luck, see the Islamic Cairo section for the location and details of some individual bath houses. It has to be said, however, that if you have the opportunity to try out bath houses in Damascus or Aleppo (in Syria) or Istanbul (in Turkey), do so. The Cairo hammams tend to be dingy and not overly inviting places.

Sufi Dancing

On Wednesday and Saturday nights at 8 pm you can treat yourself to a display of *raqs ash-sharqi*, or Sufi dancing. The troupe performing in the Madrassa of Al-Ghouri in Islamic Cairo does the dancing as a cultural performance (although it is supposed to be a form of ecstatic mystical dance) and has toured overseas. The performance is free. See the appropriate entry in the Islamic Cairo section for more information.

Alternatively, you may be lucky enough to witness a *zikr*, or Sufi ceremony and dancing, at one of the Sufi mosques around Islamic Cairo and the City of the Dead. There tend to be more from October to April, as this seems to be when the bulk of *moulids* (saints' feast days) take place. The moulids, or in some cases weekly zikrs, generally take place around a mosque containing the remains of a venerated saint. Occasionally the ecstatic dancing takes a more extreme turn, with people pushing needles and skewers into parts of the face (nose, cheeks)

and withdrawing them again leaving no trace and apparently feeling no pain. Such a sight is, however, more of an exception than the rule.

Swimming

Finding a place to go for a swim is not easy in Cairo. There are a few private clubs about, but generally membership is required. You could also try some of the big hotels, which charge from around E£20 to as much as E£140 – the latter being the price for two at the Nile Hilton. Club Med has a E£45 lunch and pool package (see Places to Eat).

One place expatriates use a bit is the Atlas Zamalek Hotel in Mohandiseen, near Midan Sphinx. Entry to the pool costs E£10.

If you can be bothered going all the way out to the Moqattam Hills, the Bel Air Hotel has a decent-size pool that you can use for E£20. Most of the bigger hotels have pools.

PLACES TO STAY
Places to Stay – bottom end

Cairo is full of inexpensive hotels and pensions. The prices can be deceiving, because they aren't always accurate indicators of the hotel's quality, and because prices can sometimes be negotiated. So consider the room rates given as estimates; although they were obtained directly from the hotels, travellers have reported paying different prices for the same accommodation.

The Manyal Youth Hostel on Roda Island is one of the cheapest places to stay in Cairo. A couple of hotels in central Cairo just undercut it.

Unless otherwise indicated, the prices quoted include breakfast. Don't have great expectations about these breakfasts. They usually consist of no more than a couple of pieces of bread, a chunk of frozen butter, a dollop of jam, and tea or coffee. Beyond this, you have to pay extra. The cheapest prices are around E£5 to E£10, for a bed in a share room (not usually more than four beds).

The more expensive hotels usually quote prices in US$. In most cases, however, there is no problem paying in E£.

Central Cairo The *Golden Hotel* (☎ 392-2659), 3rd floor, 13 Sharia Talaat Harb, is in a great location – between Midan Tahrir and Midan Talaat Harb. It was once something of an institution among travellers, but it has deteriorated over the years and gets few recommendations. All that can be said is that, outside youth hostels, it is about as cheap as you'll find. The polish has long worn off the wooden furniture and floors, bed bugs are rife, the odd cockroach has been seen loitering, and the elevator is usually broken. A double costs E£12, a single (sometimes little more than a tiny cell) costs E£7. If you want a hot shower, you pay E£2 extra – don't expect much there either. The use of a refrigerator is included. There is no breakfast. Few travellers have anything good to say about the place, although some persist with it. At the time of writing, there were rumours that some refurbishing was planned – it could certainly do with it.

Just around the corner from the Casablanca restaurant, in the market street, are two cheapies right next to each other on the 5th floor of a building with a corridor filled with sacks of cement and debris. The *Tawfikia Hotel* (☎ 755514) has beds for E£5. For E£1 more, you can get a bed in the *Safary Hotel* next door. This place is especially popular with Japanese travellers, and if you want to leaf through Japanese comics, this is the place to do it. It seems a tad better than its neighbour, but there's not much in it. Travellers seem to like both of them though, and they are not as squalid as the Golden Hotel.

The *Oxford Pensione* (☎ 758172), 32 Sharia Talaat Harb, opposite the Hotel des Roses, has been another long-time favourite way-station. You've heard of five-star ratings – well this hotel gets a five-roach rating. Despite the cockroaches, bed bugs and dirty bathrooms, the Oxford is still popular with a lot of hard-core trans-Africa travellers. Information about working in Cairo and travelling through Africa is still readily available here. There are 32 rooms, and singles/doubles cost E£15/23. A bed in a share room costs E£8.

The *Hotel Beau Site* (☎ 392-9916), 5th floor, 27 Sharia Talaat Harb, is actually down a small alley just off Sharia Talaat Harb. Reports about this hotel are mixed. A few travellers have said it is an interesting place to stay, and more than one 'star' has been discovered here by Cairene advertising agents on the hunt for foreign faces for local TV commercials. One traveller who asked the tourist police about this was told that the agents are really thieves in disguise who lure travellers into the desert and steal their belongings, but this story sounds far-fetched for Cairo.

Rooms range from OK, but dark and dusty, to darker and dustier. At E£15 for a single and E£23 for a double, it's not totally unreasonable.

The *Pensione de Famille* (☎ 574-5630) in Sharia Abdel Khaliq Sarwat, just off Sharia Talaat Harb, is cheap and basic, but not bad for the price. The building itself should have been condemned years ago and the beds are a little lumpy, but at E£8/14, you can't go too far wrong. You can use the kitchen to cook in if you want.

One that has been open since 1991 right on Midan Tahrir (at No 1) is the *Ismailia House Hotel* (☎ 356-3122), on the 8th floor. It has become quite popular with travellers. In its favour are that the bright, whitewashed rooms are clean, the linen is regularly changed, and the breakfasts include a boiled egg. This already puts it streets ahead of a lot of the competition. They also have satellite TV in the lounge and, perhaps best of all, several bathrooms, all with electric water heaters ensuring hot showers. The rooms vary in quality, and have little or no furniture. Singles, a few of which are pretty dingy, cost E£25 – a bit steep. Doubles come at E£40 and are the best value. A bed in a share room (a double with two extra rickety beds crammed in) costs E£12 to E£15, depending on the room. You can sleep in the hall for E£10. If you end up with one of the better rooms, it's very good value, and it's hard to argue with the location.

The same people have also totally renovated the *Hotel Petit Palais* (☎ 391-1863), at

45 Sharia Abdel Khaliq Sarwat. It is done out in similar style and has the standard satellite TV and breakfast with a boiled egg. Beds in triples start at E£15 and doubles go up to E£40 (singles E£20). The bathrooms are new and spotless, and unlike at the Ismailia, each room has hot water in the sink.

The *Tulip Hotel* (☎ 393-9433, 392-2704) on the 3rd floor, 3 Midan Talaat Harb, is right on the midan, but is not the good value it once was. There is a range of rooms, with and without bathrooms, from about E£20 to E£40. The rooms with balconies are lighter and cooler than the inside rooms. The rooms are OK, and at least they have a bit more furniture than those at the Ismailia, but the beds tend to be as soft as planks.

The *Gresham Hotel* (☎ 762094, 759043), 3rd floor, 20 Sharia Talaat Harb, has slipped a bit in its rating, largely because its prices don't seem to have changed much. If you stay two nights or more, singles/doubles without bath are E£25/35. (Often a lone guest will get a double for the single price.) With bath they are E£35/45. Given the way the prices in some other cheap hotels have tended to rocket in the past couple of years, this is now pretty good value. There is a fairly cosy bar that closes about 1 am – you can buy drinks to take to your room if you wish.

The *Hotel des Roses* (☎ 393-8022) is on the 4th floor, 33 Sharia Talaat Harb, near the junction with Sharia Abdel Khaliq Sarwat. Again, they have gone a little overboard with prices. A single/double with bath and breakfast is E£23.10/31, which is OK but not brilliant. The bathrooms are big and clean. The dining room is well lit, so you can see your breakfast in the mornings (if you really want to). Try to get a room on the top floor along the balcony, as the views of Cairo are great.

The *Hotel Select* (☎ 393-3707), 8th floor, 19 Sharia Adly, is next to the heavily guarded synagogue. The rooms seem to have been reorganised and the rate is a simple E£10 per person in a share room – although you may end up with only a fairly well-used mattress on the floor. This is one of the many places offering trips to the Giza and Saqqara pyra-

mids, as well as Memphis. The E£20 is for transport only without guide, and the stories about these trips, which quite a few hotels in this range organise, have often been negative, so forewarned is forearmed.

Across the road, in the alley by the Kodak shop, is the *Panorama Palace Hotel* (☎ 392-9127), at 20B Sharia Adly. Like so many Cairo hotels in this range, it is a little on the musty side, but the rooms are acceptable. Prices range from E£15 for a bed in a share room to E£40 for a double with bathroom. They also do the trip to the pyramids, for E£15.

The *Anglo-Swiss Hotel* (☎ 751491), 6th floor, 14 Sharia Champollion (on the corner), is generally clean and comfortable and, for the price, a reasonable deal. In the mornings, a team of workers cleans and polishes the floors and furniture. It costs E£22 for a big single, E£17 for a more pokey one, E£16 per person in a double and E£14 each in a triple. There is hot water in the morning. The elevator occasionally breaks down. During the winter, the hotel is sometimes booked up by groups.

The *Pensione Suisse* (☎ 746639), in Sharia Mohammed Bassiuni, just west of Midan Talaat Harb, has a collection of double and triple rooms, all of which seem to cost E£15 with breakfast. If you're alone, that's not overly good value – if there are three of you in one room, it's definitely one of the better deals in town.

The *Hotel Viennoise* (☎ 574-3153), 11 Sharia Mohammed Bassiuni, is a little west of the Pensione Swiss. It is not representative of anything related to the beautiful city of Vienna. Big, dusty single rooms with hot water are E£13.50, and doubles E£18.50. Some of the rooms are indeed huge and have balconies.

The *Pensione Roma* (☎ 391-1088), 169 Sharia Mohammed Farid, near the junction with Sharia Adly, is tucked away in a side alley and is still about the best of the budget hotels. The entrance is easy to miss, but you'll be pleasantly surprised by the reception area. All the rooms have shiny hardwood floors and beautiful antique furniture.

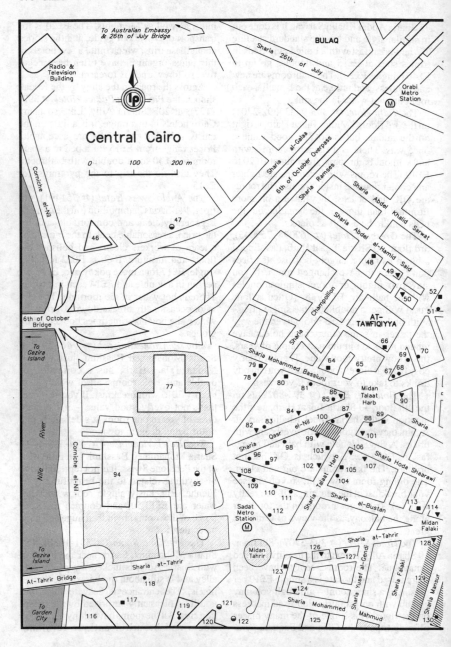

Central Cairo

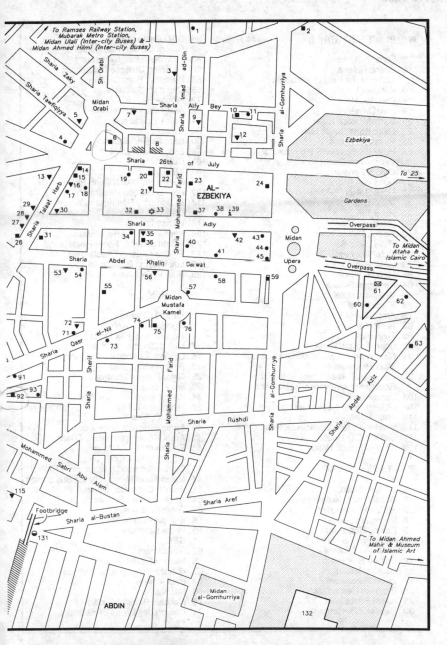

■ PLACES TO STAY

2 Luna Park Hotel
6 Grand Hotel &
   Valley of the Kings Restaurant
10 Windsor Hotel
14 Claridge Hotel
15 Hotel Minerva
20 Samar Palace Hotel
22 Cairo Khan Suites Hotel
23 Pensione Roma
24 Hotel Continental & International
   Vaccination Centre
26 Oxford Pensione
31 Hotel des Roses
32 Hotel Select
36 Panorama Palace Hotel
37 Hotel Tee
46 Ramses Hilton
48 Odeon Palace Hotel
52 Hotel Beau Site
55 Hotel Montana
59 Hotel Petit Palais
63 New Rich Hotel
64 Pensione Suisse
66 Gresham Hotel
75 Plaza Hotel
79 Anglo-Swiss Hotel
80 Hotel Viennoise
89 Tulip Hotel
92 Cosmopolitan Hotel
94 Nile Hilton & Taverne du Champs de
   Mars Restaurant
97 Cleopatra Palace Hotel, Valentino's
   Restaurant & Kowloon Restaurant
103 Lotus Hotel
105 Golden Hotel & Juice Stands
113 Amin Hotel
116 Semiramis InterContinental Hotel
117 Garden City House
123 Ismailia House Hotel

▼ PLACES TO EAT

3 Coffee House
5 Casablanca Restaurant
7 Alfi Bey Restaurant
8 Ice cream places
9 Peking Restaurant
12 Ali-Hassan al-Hatti
13 Cafe l'Amèricaine
16 Bambo Restaurant
21 Saigon Restaurant
27 Zeina Restaurant
28 Brazilian Restaurant
29 Amira Restaurant
30 Excelsior Restaurant

35 GAD Restaurant
42 Groppi Garden Restaurant
49 Coin de Kebab Restaurant
50 Fu Shing Chinese Restaurant
53 Kentucky Fried Chicken
56 Cap d'Or Cafeteria
72 Wimpy Bar
82 Arabesque Restaurant
84 Caroll Restaurant
86 Groppi's
90 Lappa's Restaurant
99 Estoril Restaurant
101 Cafè Riche
102 Wimpy Bar
106 Felfela Sandwich Take Away
107 Felfela Garden Restaurant
114 El Domuaty Restaurant &
   Cafeteria Horea
115 Wimpy Bar
124 Kentucky Fried Restaurant
126 Fatatri at-Tahrir Fiteer Restaurant
127 El-Tahrir Kushari Restaurant
128 Lux Kushari Restaurant
129 Budget Eats Area

OTHER

1 Karim I Cinema
4 Mengozzi Bookshop
11 Telephone & Fax Office
17 Metro Cinema
18 Lehnert & Landrock Bookshop
19 Palmyra Nightclub
25 Cairo Puppet Theatre
33 Synagogue
34 Kodak shop
38 Telephone Office
39 Tourist Office
40 Anglo-Egyptian Bookshop
41 Arab-African International Bank
43 EgyptAir
44 Big EgyptAir Office
45 Cairo International Automobile Club
47 Midan Abdel Minnim Riyadh Bus Station
51 French Consulate General
54 Anglo-Eastern Pharmacy
57 Turkish Airlines
58 Banque Misr
60 Poste Restante
61 GPO
62 Fire Station
65 Madbouli Bookshop
67 Pakistan International Airlines
68 Iraqi Airlines
69 Naf Naf
70 National Bank of Sudan
71 Maison des Livres Bookshop

73	'Disco' Nightclub	104	Lufthansa German Airlines
74	Libyan Arab Airlines Office	108	British Airways
76	Benetton	109	Sudan Airways
77	Egyptian Museum	110	Goethe Institut
78	Italian Embassy	111	Papyrus Centre
81	Thomas Cook Office (money exchange & travel office)	112	Telephone Office
		118	Ministry of Foreign Affairs
83	Royal Jordanian Airlines	119	Omar Makram Mosque
85	Newsstand	120	Mogamma
87	Air France	121	Microbus to Giza & the Pyramids
88	Shourouk Bookshop	122	Minibus Terminal &
91	Olympic Airways		Buses to Cairo University,
93	Cairo Stock Exchange		Giza & the Pyramids
95	Bus Terminal	125	American University in Cairo
96	TWA	130	Telephone Office
98	KLM	131	Midan Falaki Tram Terminus
100	American Express	132	Presidential Palace

Single/double/triple rooms without a bath are E£18/34/43. Doubles and triples with bath go for E£37/50, and a room with four beds can be had for E£56.50. It is best to make reservations here, especially during the high season, because a few adventure travel companies have discovered it. Singles are hard to get, as students often take them for extended periods.

The *Luna Park* (☎ 918626, 904592), 65 Sharia al-Gomhurriya, between Midan Ramses and Midan Opera, is a good clean place for the budget traveller. Each room is supplied with soap, towels, toilet paper, and a sink with hot and cold water. A small café and bar are attached to the hotel. Singles/doubles are E£12/21.

The *Plaza Hotel* (☎ 392-1939), 8th floor, 32 Sharia Qasr el-Nil, is next to the Galion children's store, near Midan Mustafa Kamel. It's a clean place with occasional hot water, and at E£7.50 per person in share doubles or triples, is one of the better value places in town. It is becoming increasingly popular with long-term and trans-Africa travellers.

The *Hotel Tee* (☎ 391-1002) at 13 Sharia Adly, near the synagogue, has small single/double/triple rooms for E£25/35/40 with baths, hot water and dirty carpets. They even provide towels and toilet paper. Doubles and triples without bath are E£5 cheaper. The hotel has a bar.

Hidden in an alley off Sharia 26th of July, just across the road from the Grand Hotel, is the entrance to the *Hotel Minerva* (☎ 392-0600/601/602). It has big clean rooms and cold showers that are cleaned every day. The elevator is broken, but don't be discouraged by the dark, gloomy staircase. Most rooms have wooden floors and Queen Anne furniture. Double rooms are E£11.

Over the road and in another back lane near the Saigon restaurant is the *Samar Palace Hotel* (☎ 392-9611). They'll probably be surprised to see anyone come in, as the sign is in Arabic only. They seem a little reticent about taking on foreigners, although single white males seem OK. For E£12.30, you can have a crumbling double that looks like an earthquake victim.

The nearby *Claridge Hotel* (☎ 393-7776, 392-5261), near the corner of Sharia Talaat Harb and Sharia 26th of July, seems to have lifted its game. It has a range of big rooms, singles and doubles, with prices varying according to size and whether or not you want a room with bath. Most of the rooms have attractive (if dusty – but what isn't in central Cairo?) balconies. Singles range from E£13.70 to E£21.50, doubles come for E£27.25 to E£33 and triples are E£36.70 to E£42.

The *Hotel Montana* (☎ 392-8608/6264), 7th floor, 25 Sharia Sherif, is another low-cost hotel bordering on the middle range. Singles/doubles with bath come at E£30.50/45.50 and without for a few pounds less. A triple with air-con costs E£67. It has a restaurant upstairs and is quite adequate, although not outstanding.

The *Amin Hotel* (☎ 393-3813), 38 Midan Falaki, Bab al-Louk, has fully carpeted rooms all with fans and some with bathrooms. The shared bathrooms tend to get somewhat messy. Single rooms with/without a bath are E£15/13.50, and doubles with/without a bath are E£19/17.50.

The *New Garden Palace Hotel* (☎ 356-4365), in a street just behind Sharia Qasr al-Eini in Garden City, is five blocks south of Midan Tahrir and has singles/doubles for E£35/45. There is a restaurant and bar, and hot water in the ensuite bathrooms, but the whole place is kind of grubby and run down, and there is not that much to recommend its location.

Around Midan Ramses The *Everest Hotel* (☎ 574-2707/2688/2506) on Midan Ramses is in the tallest building opposite Ramses Station. Its 80 rooms are on the 14th, 15th and 16th floors, and the reception desk, restaurant and cafeteria are on the 15th floor. The rooms are cheap and dusty. Singles/doubles without a bath cost E£10.20/16. The low prices, its proximity to the train station, and the fantastic views from the balcony have made this a popular place, but the deteriorating condition of some of the rooms has begun to discourage people from staying here. And that's not all.

Some of the blood-curdling stories to come out of here should be enough to keep people away, even if the chaos of the area is not. One woman traveller reported that she and her friend were bludgeoned by an intruder and that, when the police came, the management claimed they were lesbians who had done it to each other. The same traveller went on to claim that the Australian embassy later told them they were investigating the 'suicide' of another Australian national there!

Zamalek There are two places worth investigating here, not far to the south of Sharia 26th of July. It's a leafy and relatively peaceful area not that far from the centre of town, and with most of the facilities you may need nearby (phone, post and banks).

The *Mayfair Hotel* (☎ 340-7315), 9 Sharia Aziz Osman, has singles/doubles without bath for E£14/24, or E£25/35 with. They also have a few triples. It seems to be popular with Poles, and got a good write-up in *Cairo Today* back in 1991. Breakfast is E£2 extra. The showers are hot and long, but the standard Egyptian bed (nice and hard) is a slight drawback. It's right by the Sunnys supermarket, something of an institution among expats for the range of goodies you can find there that seem not to exist elsewhere.

Two blocks down and to the right along Sharia Salah ad-Din is the *Zamalek Pension* (☎ 340-9318), which is really heading into the middle range of places. It has clean, comfortable singles/doubles for E£30/60. It is not bad for what you get. The great thing about both is that they get you out of the hassle of central Cairo without really taking you that far away.

Roda Island The *Manyal Youth Hostel* (☎ 840729), 135 Sharia Abdel Aziz as-Saud, is near the Manyal Palace. It's in reasonable nick with clean toilets, although the beds are nothing great. Sheets (hm!) and blankets are provided in dorm rooms sleeping six people each. There are no rooms for couples or families. Mosquitoes and cats are plentiful enough to ensure constant companionship of a sort. Breakfast is included. It's only a 30-minute walk from Midan Tahrir, and costs E£6.60 with IYHA membership card, E£7.60 without. Take any bus passing by the Manyal Palace, get off at the University Bridge and head about 100 metres down the riverside street.

Camping The *Motel Salma* (☎ 384-9152) is next to the Wissa Wassef carpet school in Giza. It is owned by an Egyptian with a Swiss-German education. Camping costs E£7 per person with your own tent or campervan, or you can get a two-person cabin for E£30, a four-person one for E£40, or the same with your own shower for E£50. There are cold and hot showers and the toilets are fairly clean. The restaurant is way over the top. Breakfast costs E£6 (E£10 if you want an omelette!), soft drinks are E£1.50, Stella beer E£6 and main meals about E£20. Overland tour companies use this camping ground, which has views of the pyramids from the back area. If you have your own vehicle and/or tent, it might just be worth it for the views (the cabins are claustrophobic and stuffy), otherwise not.

To get there, take a service taxi (microbus) for Abu Sir down the Saqqara Rd from Pyramids Rd. It's about four km in, but ask where to be let off, as the signs can be a bit misleading and someone in the taxi will know the best place to alight. Be prepared for a mosquito attack at sunset.

Places to Stay – middle

Central Cairo The *Garden City House* (☎ 354-4969, 354-4126), 23 Sharia Kamel ad-Din Salah, Garden City, is around the corner from the American embassy, opposite the Semiramis Hotel. Look for the small sign outside the 3rd floor and the bronze plaque at the front of the building. This hotel has long been a favourite among Egyptologists and Middle East scholars, although it's looking a bit dusty now, and some travellers have reported it not worth the money. Singles/doubles start at E£37/67, and include breakfast and one other meal (lunch or dinner), whether you want it or not. The bathrooms have electric water heaters, which should guarantee hot showers. It is best to make reservations. Better rooms can be found for lower rates at other hotels, but you can't beat this hotel's location and sometimes fascinating guest list.

The *Lotus Hotel* (☎ 750966/627; fax 921621), 12 Sharia Talaat Harb opposite Felfela Garden, is one of the best hotels in this price range. The elevator to the reception desk is reached through an arcade which almost faces Sharia Hoda Shaarawi. The rooms are clean and comfortable. You'll pay anything from E£39.97 for a single without a bath to E£49.57 for one with bath and air-con. Doubles range from E£45.77 to E£64.96, and triples from E£77.93 to E£81.18.

There's a restaurant, bar and a quasi-sundeck on the top floor. The hotel seems to have particular favour with French tour groups.

The *Cosmopolitan Hotel* (☎ 392-3663/3845; fax 393-3531) is in Sharia Ibn Taalab, just off Sharia Qasr el-Nil. It is an upper-middle range hotel that's quite popular with various tour groups, so getting a room here can sometimes be difficult. It has beautifully plush old rooms with dark lacquered furniture, central air-conditioning, and tiled bathrooms with tubs. Some rooms have balconies and there's a wonderful old open elevator. Singles/doubles cost US$38/48 and despite the hotel's very central location it's surprisingly quiet. It's one of those places with lots of the fast-disappearing 'old world charm', although sometimes the service is a little more Third World.

The *Odeon Palace Hotel* (☎ 767971, 776637), 6 Sharia Abdel al-Hamid Said, is about 1½ blocks north-west of Sharia Talaat Harb. It is an upper-middle range hotel, but lacks the old Victorian character of the Cosmopolitan. The rooms are quite clean and comfortable. Each has a minifridge, TV, telephone and air-conditioning. Single/double rooms are US$36/46. All credit cards are accepted here. You can pay in E£, but they still demand bank receipts (a hangover from the days of artificially fixed exchange rates and a flourishing black market) as proof of change.

The *Grand Hotel* (☎ 757509/700/747; fax 757716), 17 Sharia 26th of July, at the intersection with Sharia Talaat Harb, has clean and comfortable rooms with hardwood floors and antique armoires. You'll find a wide variety of rooms, with and without bathrooms or air-conditioning. Singles/doubles start from E£112/145, including breakfast and all the nefarious taxes that are tacked on. They have international direct phone and fax lines. The Valley of the Kings

Restaurant on the 1st floor has a great view over the busy streets below and an exotic-looking fountain in the centre. The food is quite good.

Unfortunately the hotel's staff are not always as communicative as they should be and they are notoriously bad about taking messages or putting through phone calls.

The *Cleopatra Palace Hotel* (☎ 759900/923), just back from Midan Tahrir on Sharia al-Bustan, has had some pretty scathing reports. They seem to have more trouble with hot water than some much smaller establishments, and if you don't like toenails and pubic hair in your bed, this is not the place to stay. Maybe it's not as bad as all that. Singles/doubles cost US$49/63, breakfast and taxes included.

The *New Rich Hotel* (☎ 390-0145; fax 390-6390), 47 Sharia Abdel Aziz, near Midan Ataba and the GPO, is a relatively new hotel with singles/doubles for E£42/57, including shower and air-conditioning. The staff at the front desk are not overly welcoming.

The *Windsor Hotel* (☎ 915277; fax 921621), 19 Sharia Alfi Bey (near Ezbekiya Gardens), was once a great place with lots of class and comfort, but it has deteriorated. The Windsor has an interesting history. During the time of the Ottoman Empire it was the private bath house of the Turkish leaders; it was used to house Russian engineers during the construction of the Aswan Dam; and it was set on fire during the 1952 Revolution because it was the British Officers' Club.

The British comedian Michael Palin stayed here when making his BBC *Around the World in 80 Days* series. The busboy will probably show you the very table he sat in at the restaurant and bar.

Several travellers have written to complain about the Windsor. One claimed to have been charged double rates, and another said their room had bed bugs. There is a wide variety of rooms, with and without bath or shower, with prices ranging from about US$21.40 for a single with shower to US$40.30 for a 'luxury' double.

Around Midan Ramses The three-star *Fontana Hotel* (☎ 922321, 922145), Midan Ramses, is on the other side of the footbridge (east) as you leave the train station. The location is hardly inviting, but the views from the clean single/double rooms (E£57/84) are impressive. The linen is clean and the beds soft. There's even a swimming pool and disco on the 8th floor.

The two-star *Capsis Palace Hotel* (☎ 754219/188/029), 117 Sharia Ramses, is conveniently situated near the train station and intercity bus terminals (Midan Ulali and Midan Ahmed Helmi). The rooms are small and nothing special, but there are hot showers with towels and soap and noisy air-conditioning. Single/double rooms are a bit much at E£42/62.

Islamic Cairo *Hotel al-Hussein* (☎ 918089), in Midan Hussein, is right in the thick of things in Islamic Cairo, right by the Khan al-Khalili bazaar. The rooms are clean and well maintained, and the restaurant on the roof has a fantastic view of medieval Cairo. Singles and doubles with bath and views over the square are E£36/46, including breakfast. Small rooms without bath or view are E£25/35. Air-conditioning, a telephone and hot water are included, but a TV or fan is extra.

Diagonally across from it is the *Radwan Hotel* (☎ 901311, 900427). It has quite OK rooms without such hot views for E£25/35 with breakfast and bath. Be aware that in either of these places you're almost sure to be woken by the early calls to prayer.

Zamalek Given the competition, the *New Star Hotel* (☎ 340-0928; fax 340-1865) on Sharia Yehia Ibrahim, a couple of blocks north of Sharia 26th of July, might be worth the few extra dollars. This three-star place has single/double/triple suites for US$40/46/54. The rooms are practically the size of small apartments, with kitchenettes, sparkling bathrooms, air-conditioning, colour TV, reception rooms and very clean bedrooms. Downstairs is the Angus Brasserie – 'the only typical Argentinian Steakhouse in

Egypt'. There are a few other middle to upper-middle level hotels scattered around Zamalek.

Giza & Doqqi The *Indiana Hotel* (☎ 349-3775/3774, 714503), at 16 Sharia Hasan Rostom, has clean and comfortable singles for US$36 and doubles for US$45. Some rooms have TVs and refrigerators. Ask for one at the front, as the rooms at the back are pretty pokey. The beds are nice and big. If you've got to be on this side of the Nile, it's not a bad location.

Places to Stay – top end

Almost all the world's major hotel chains have hotels in Cairo. Their prices, standards and amenities are usually on a par with their hotels in other countries. Most of these hotels distribute detailed brochures about their facilities and amenities. If your local travel agent doesn't have current information, check the *International Hotel Guide*, which can be found in major libraries. Most agents should also be able to check the current rates and package deals.

A few of the more expensive hotels are interesting to visit and pleasant places in which to seek refuge from the chaos and cacophony of Cairo's streets. Prices given are generally exclusive of taxes and breakfast.

Central Cairo The centrally located five-star *Shepheard's Hotel* (☎ 355-3800/3900) was recently renovated and has all but lost its British Empire atmosphere, which in any case was a bit artificial, since the original, burnt down during the 1952 Revolution, was in fact located in Midan Opera. Founded in 1841 by an Englishman, Samuel Shepheard, it was one of the first European-style tourist hotels in Cairo. It was renovated in 1891, 1899, 1904, 1909 and 1927. After its destruction, the new version was built on the Nile in 1957. During the British occupation of Egypt, the original hotel and its rooftop terrace bar were favourites with British military officers and administrators. Alas, it's a little difficult to imagine all this now that the new hotel is nowhere near its original location. Singles/doubles fronting the Nile go for US$97/120, while those at the back cost US$75/90. There is a buffet breakfast for E£11.

Right across the road from Shepheard's is the *Semiramis InterContinental Hotel* (☎ 355-7171), one of the newest and best hotels in Egypt. It's right on the Nile and the rooms and amenities in this large hotel are exactly what you would expect from the lines of Mercedes and even Rolls-Royces parked outside. Singles/doubles are US$120/145, singles with a view of the Nile can go up to US$190 and there is are suites with costs heading up towards the sky.

The *Nile Hilton* (☎ 767444, 765666; fax 760874), on the Corniche el-Nil, also has terrific views across the Nile. It is very centrally located, backing on to Midan Tahrir right by the Egyptian Museum, and is one of the most popular hotels with Westerners, but don't expect it to be up to the standard of Hiltons in other countries. It was one of Egypt's first five-star hotels and the rooms are large and clean although the plumbing is unreliable. Prices for the better single/double rooms are about US$145/173.

Just north of the Nile Hilton, and also right by the river, is the newer *Ramses Hilton* (☎ 777444; fax 757152), 1115 Corniche el-Nil. Rooms start from US$120 for a standard single to US$2030 for a three-bed suite.

A cheaper alternative to the big names is the new *Cairo Khan Suites Hotel* (☎ 392-2015; fax 390-6799) on the corner of Sharias 26th of July and Mohammed Farid. Comfortable but smallish singles/doubles with the usual facilities cost US$60/77, but they seem keen to do deals. The suites come with kitchenettes. They even have a dental clinic.

Zamalek The *Cairo Marriott* (☎ 340-8888; fax 340-6667) is in Sharia al-Gezira, just south of the 26th of July Bridge. It is in a palace built in 1869 by Khedive Ismail to accommodate Empress Eugénie during the opening of the Suez Canal. The hotel, with 1250 rooms, is 19th century elegance at its best: polished marble floors, engraved brass lamps and ornately carved mashrabiyyah screens. Have a Stella beer in the garden next to the swimming pool. Single/double rooms are US$130/145, plus taxes. Roy's restaurant has Mexican food on Sunday, Monday and Tuesday evenings.

Another one due for completion in 1993, but well short of making that date, is the *Forte Grand*, a 500-room cylinder on Sharia Gezira.

Roda Island, Gezira Island & Doqqi The *Cairo Meridien Hotel* (☎ 262-1717), Corniche el-Nil, Roda Island, is right on the river, and the views are magnificent. Spacious single/double rooms with all facilities are US$110/140.

The views from the Meridien are matched only by those from the *El Gezira Sheraton* (☎ 341-1555), right across the river from the Meridien at the southern end of Gezira Island. Singles/doubles start at US$90/96

before taxes. The *Cairo Sheraton* (☎ 348-8600), across the river in Doqqi, is a smidgin cheaper.

Giza The *Hotel Mena House Oberoi* (☎ 383-3444/3222) is the closest hotel to the pyramids, but it is a long way from the other places of interest in Cairo. It's one of the grand old hotels of the world, with an abundance of elegance and opulent Oriental decor. It has played an important role in Middle East history as a base for the British in WW II and the site of peace negotiations between Egypt and Israel. Prices are about US$125/155 for single/double rooms, plus taxes.

There are several other top-range hotels near the pyramids, some along the Desert Rd. They include the *Forte Grand Pyramids Hotel* (☎ 383-0383), the *Pyramids Park Sofitel* (☎ 383-8666) and the *Siaq Pyramids Hotel* (☎ 385-6022, on Saqqara Rd). Among the four-star jobs, which tend to stretch along Pyramids Rd back towards central Cairo, are the *Europa Cairo Hotel* (☎ 621100), the *Green Pyramids Hotel* (☎ 537619) and the *Hotel Les 3 Pyramides* (☎ 582- 2223).

PLACES TO EAT

Eating in Cairo can be a real treat. There are thousands of cafés, teahouses and market stalls where you can find exotic or plain food and where it's easy to have a very filling meal for less than E£10. On the more expensive side there are plenty of restaurants serving European dishes and places where you can get Western imports like hamburgers, pizzas and donuts.

Breakfast

Almost all the major hotels offer all-you-can-eat breakfast buffets, some of which are fairly good deals, if you are sick of the budget hotel food.

The *Nile Hilton* has a buffet from 6 to 10.30 am for E£15 (continental breakfast) and E£30 (all-you-can-eat hot and cold buffet). The latter is a wonderful treat, particularly after a long, dusty tour around Egypt. They serve everything from freshly

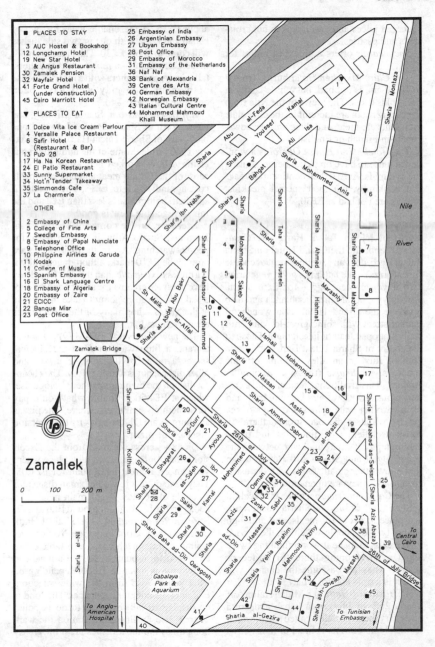

squeezed juices and cornflakes to hot croissants and pastries.

Shepheard's offers a breakfast buffet for E£11.

The *Cairo Meridien Hotel* buffet, from 7 to 10.30 am, is not bad, but a little costly at E£24 plus taxes. The views of the Nile from the dining room are incredible, the chocolate croissants are great, and there are free newspapers in French or English.

The *Hotel Mena House Oberoi* is a wonderful place to have breakfast before touring the pyramids. At E£9 their continental breakfast is skimpy, but their special breakfast buffets are not bad at E£30.

Budget Eats
North of Midan Talaat Harb The *Casablanca*, opposite the Grand Hotel on Sharia Talaat Harb, does an excellent meat or cheese fiteer (pizza) – the latter is a good vegetarian dish if you can eat egg – for E£6. Sharia Tawfiqiyya, beside the Casablanca and also opposite the Grand Hotel, is a wonderful market street with some great-looking fruit stalls that operate until late at night. Close to the corner of Sharia Talaat Harb and Sharia 26th of July, in an alley running off this street, is *Ash-Shams* (the sign is only in Arabic). This traditional teahouse is a colourful place, with waiters hustling back and forth carrying water pipes and trays of tea glasses while in the background there's a constant clatter of domino tiles and backgammon pieces. In a small lane between the Grand Hotel and Sharia Alfi Bey you can find a few other small stands with the usual cheap eats – they are open quite late.

The *Café l'Américaine*, at the intersection of Sharia 26th of July and Sharia Talaat Harb, is a place to avoid for meals, and although it's not bad for people-watching, the service is so bad as to make it worth thinking twice about even stopping there for coffee or dessert. They also assume the change you expect is a tip – and for what?

Ali Hassan al-Hatti, at 8 Midan Halim (off Sharia 26th of July), is a kebab and kofta place. Try their speciality called *moza*, which is roast lamb on rice. A meal of moza costs

about E£15. A reasonable meal for two of kebab and kofta with one or two side dishes will come to about E£30. The place is one of those Cairo gems – a relic with chandeliers, tall mirrors and waiters with a reserved sense of humour who may well have been employed 40 years ago.

Alfi Bey Restaurant, Sharia Alfi Bey, one block north of Sharia 26th of July and one block east of Sharia Talaat Harb, has a relaxing 1940s style. Some of the numerous staff claim to have worked here since the '40s! Most of their main meat and chicken meals cost around E£11 to E£13, but a plate of spaghetti bolognaise is less than E£2 and the mixed vegetable stew is good.

Excelsior, on the corner of Sharia Talaat Harb and Sharia Adly, is a great place for people-watching. Again, the main dishes are around the E£10 mark, although generally it is a bit less expensive than the Alfi Bey. They have great ice creams for a few pounds – not a bad idea if you're about to take in a movie at the Metro – but many of the meat dishes are overcooked.

The new *Bambo* (☎ 392-5179) pizza restaurant, a little way up from the cinema, serves a range of Italian-style pizzas and other dishes, but is a little pricey. The cheapest dish on the menu is spaghetti bolognaise, which at E£4.50 is double what you'd pay for something similar elsewhere. The pizzas and burgers are OK though – try their version of a calzone pizza.

Directly across the road from the Excelsior is the *Amira*, a bright new place where you can get a great lentil soup for E£1.05. They have quite a few other small dishes for a couple of pounds. Their main meals like kebab and kofta come for around E£6 to E£7.

Zeina Restaurant, 34 Sharia Talaat Harb, is next to the Oxford Pensione. You can get a simple meal of chicken, vegetables, rice and bread for around E£10, but a meal can easily cost as much as E£20, depending on what you choose from the wide selection. Eating at the counter is cheaper. The food is on display so all you need to do is point. There's also an English menu on the wall. Sometimes the meat dishes are a bit greasy but the makarone is fairly good and filling. One serving makes a great lunch. The shawarma sandwiches are also good and inexpensive, and there's a fair selection of traditional Egyptian pastries.

The *Coin de Kebab* (or Kebab Corner) is about one block off Sharia Talaat Harb, near the Odeon Palace Hotel (see the Central Cairo map). You can get excellent kebab and tahina here. Just opposite the synagogue in Sharia Adly is *GAD*, which serves fairly cheap, decent meals.

If you wander into the arcades linking Sharia Adly and Sharia 26th of July near the EgyptAir office, you'll find some great sweet and ice-cream shops.

South of Midan Talaat Harb The *Felfela Garden* (☎ 392-2751/2833), 15 Sharia Hoda Shaarawi, just off Sharia Talaat Harb, is one of the better all-round restaurants in Cairo, although its enormous popularity with locals and foreigners alike means there are quite a few dishes you could get elsewhere for less. This is the original Felfela Restaurant, founded in 1963 by Madame Amina Zaghloul as a small vegetarian restaurant serving mostly fuul and ta'amiyya. A vegetarian, she started the restaurant because she was dismayed by the lack of clean, inexpensive vegetarian restaurants in Cairo. To earn a four-star government tourism rating, she eventually had to add various meat and poultry dishes such as pigeon and kofta.

Your dinner of fuul, ta'amiyya, tahina, and tea can cost as little as E£10, especially if you come with a small group and share various dishes. Try the desserts: om ali, a pastry baked with milk, raisins and nuts; baked rice with milk; and the 'Felfela cocktail' of ice cream, rice pudding and nuts. Check out the fish and turtles in the aquariums. Overall,

this is a good, very reasonably priced restaurant for sampling typical Egyptian dishes. You can also get a beer here. The Felfela chain is spreading, and you can find it in Sharia Ahmed Orabi, Mohandiseen, along Pyramids Rd, on Roda Island and in Maadi.

Felfela Sandwich Take-Away, just around the corner from the main restaurant, has excellent ta'amiyya, shawarma, kofta and fuul sandwiches, most costing around E£1.25.

At the stand outside *Lappas* you can get good little burgers and sausages for around E£1 to E£2. Go to the cashier inside first, tell him what you want and pay, and then take the receipt to the cook outside.

The *Pizzeria* at the Nile Hilton serves good small pizzas (12 types) and various Italian dishes such as spaghetti carbonara. It's moderately priced, but really heading out of the budget range. The pizzas go for about E£10 to E£15. It's off to the right of the outdoor café and open from noon to 2 am.

At 166 Sharia At-Tahrir, east of Midan Tahrir, is *Fatatri at-Tahrir*, an excellent place for fiteer – E£6 for small ones, E£8 for medium and E£10 for large. The savoury ones have cheese or meat, green peppers, tomato, egg and olives. The sweet ones contain raisins, syrup and coconut icing.

Just west of it and a little further east along Sharia at-Tahrir, right by the Midan Falaki tram terminus, are two equally good kushari (lentils, rice, noodles and fried onions) places, the *El-Tahrir* and *Lux*. A big serve of the stuff costs from E£1 to E£2.

El Domuaty is a cheap restaurant on the north side of Midan Falaki. Look across the tram tracks for the pale orange awning at the foot of the blue pedestrian overpass. They serve fuul, ta'amiyya, pickled vegetables, a reasonable lentil soup and tahina, for under E£1 an item. Next door is one of the better Cairo coffee houses, *Cafeteria Horea*, where you can have a game of chess with your shisha, and even get a Stella beer.

The block of Sharia Mansur that stretches from Midan Falaki to Sharia Mohammed Mahmoud has a wonderful variety of cheap eats possibilities. It's easy to find Sharia

Mansur, as the pedestrian footbridge over the disused Midan Falaki tramlines is on the street. There are several small, nameless restaurants and an interesting market. This area is a great place to introduce yourself to Egyptian food and shopping strategies. The market does not cater at all for tourists, and is a real sensory experience.

There's everything from sandwich places to fiteer restaurants, juice stands (where most freshly squeezed juices come for about E£1), bakeries, fuul and ta'amiyya stands and kushari restaurants. Or you can get fuller meals of chicken, kebab or kofta for E£3 to E£4. One of the better places is *Cafeteria el-Shaab*, about half way along Sharia Mansur. You can get a serve of makarone and potato stew for E£2.

When you've finished eating, there are several local cafés along Sharia Mansur where you can relax over a coffee and shisha and observe the antics in and around the market.

The market on Sharia Mansur is in a converted warehouse just off the street. Each stall and shop in the market specialises in something different like eggs, fruit or flowers. Watch out for the huge hunks of meat that the meat man hangs on high hooks. You probably won't see them until something wet and red drips on you. Most prices are posted, but it's not uncommon to bargain. Go early in the morning before the stench of old meat and chicken gets too strong. Shopping here, or at least having a look around, is an adventure everyone should have at least once, if only to get a taste of daily life in Cairo.

Round the corner on Sharia Mohammed Mahmud there's a 24-hour sandwich shop across the street from the old Bab al-Louk Station, near the Telecommunications building. Sandwiches of basturma, cheese and olives or egg cost about E£1.50.

A bakery a couple of doors along from the sandwich shop sells small loaves of French bread or hot pieces of pita straight from the oven for about 15 pt. The almond cookies are good, but the pastries are only for those looking for intense sugar highs.

Garden City On Sharia Latin America the *Sit-In Restaurant* (π 554341) serves everything from shrimps at E£18 to hot dogs and sausages for around E£3. They're at No 1 (look for the big Donald Duck sign across from the British embassy and just south of the US embassy).

Islamic Cairo *El Hussein Restaurant*, right in Khan al-Khalili in Islamic Cairo, is a rooftop restaurant in the hotel of the same name, near the Mosque of Sayyidna Al-Hussein. The views of the Citadel and surrounding area are great and compensate somewhat for the lousy food. During Ramadan this is one of the most popular places in the area.

There are a couple of places right on the square by the Mosque of Sayyidna Al-Hussein. They serve a tasty half kg of mixed meats, salad and soft drinks for two for E£24 – a bit pricey, but the food tastes good. In the next street, which runs off Sharia al-Muski, there is a popular teahouse and *Egyptian Pancakes*, which has excellent pancakes.

The *Dahhan* is popular with Egyptians. A big plate of moza with salad, tahina and a soft drink costs about E£12. You get limited views of the bustle around you from upstairs.

Roda Island Just 100 metres south of the Youth Hostel is another of the expanding chain of *Felfela* restaurants. The food is more or less the same as in the other places, and the riverside location is perfect for a relaxing beer. There are one or two other places in a similar vein as you continue down the same street.

Doqqi & Mohandiseen This is not really budget territory, but if you happen to be near Sharia Ahmed Orabi, about half way between Midan Sphinx and Sharia Sudan, there is yet another *Felfela* next to the Omar Effendi department store.

The *Radwan* restaurant on Sharia Doqqi, just near Midan Doqqi, is quite a pleasant little place. It serves the usual sort of food, but at decent prices. Across the road and north of Sharia At-Tahrir is a good kushari place.

Cafés & Tearooms

Groppi's, on Midan Talaat Harb, used to be one of the most popular places in Cairo for sipping coffee, munching on baqlawa, and watching a unique assortment of people troop in and out. However, the management changed and it's not quite like it used to be. Their display of cakes and sweets is positively mind-blowing. There is also a *Garden Groppi's* on Sharia Adly, opposite the tourist office.

Café l'Américaine, mentioned above for its lousy food, is not such a bad café, but is shabbier than Groppi's.

Western Fast Food

There are several *Wimpy* bars in Cairo where you can partake of the Egyptian version of these very British hamburgers. It costs a little more to eat in and the takeaway menu is shorter than the eat-in one. The average burger costs E£3.50 and is quite edible. They have strange ice-cream desserts if you are eating in, going for about E£4 a piece. If you really can't live without a Wimpy burger, you can find them on Sharia Taha Hussein in Zamalek, Sharia Medinat Mohandiseen in Doqqi, Sharia Gamiat ad-Dowal al-Arabiyya in Mohandiseen and on Pyramids Rd in Giza. In central Cairo there are Wimpys on Sharia Hoda Shaarawi near Midan Falaki, on Sharia Talaat Harb, not far from Felfela, and on Sharia Sherif. There are a couple of other Western-style takeaway places near the Wimpy bar in Sharia Hoda Shaarawi.

There are 56 *Kentucky Fried Chicken* places all over Egypt, and they seem to be spreading like wildfire. There's a good half dozen in Cairo offering the Colonel's usual menu. There's one in Sharia al-Batal Ahmed Abdel Aziz in Mohandiseen (right next to the Wimpy), one just opposite the AUC and one on Sharia Abdel Khaliq Sarwat just off Sharia Talaat Harb in central Cairo. Other 'branches' are in Maadi, Heliopolis and Nasser City. A chicken fillet burger is E£3.80

and a Family Bucket (15 pieces of chicken) E£27.95. Some of them even do home delivery.

If you happen to be in a totally fast food mood and tucking in at the Wimpy bar, Kentucky Fried Chicken or Chicken Tikka in Mohandiseen (all next to each other from the corner of Sharia Gamiat ad-Dowal al-Arabiyya down Sharia al-Batal Ahmed Abdel Aziz), you could finish off with dessert in the *House of Donuts* across the road. This new establishment offers a whole range of donuts every bit as good as anything you'll find in the West – at a price. A couple of donuts and soft drinks will set you back about E£10.

The *Pizza Hut* is not making such great inroads, but there are a few around. There are two in Doqqi, one opposite the AUC and next door to Kentucky Fried, one at 38 Sharia al-Ahram in Heliopolis, in Sharia Abu al-Feda in Zamalek, in Giza, in Maadi and along Pyramids Rd.

In a similar vein is *Pizza Inn*, with restaurants at 10 Sharia Syria in Mohandiseen, 13 Sharia al-Khalifa al-Mamoun in Manshiyyat al-Bakry, in Heliopolis and along Pyramids Rd.

In Zamalek, just around the corner from Sunnys supermarket, you can get a good takeaway pizza, or chicken, for E£10 to E£15 at *Hot 'n' Tender*. There are several other local imitations of this not-so-fast pizza restaurant scattered around suburbs like Maadi, Mohandiseen and Heliopolis.

Most of these places also do home delivery, if you can't get up the energy to go out – not an uncommon situation in the madness of Cairo.

Restaurants

Central Cairo *Fu Shing* (☎ 756184), 28 Sharia Talaat Harb, is actually in a lane; look for the sign on the main street. It is one of Cairo's few Chinese restaurants, and it has a menu in English. For about E£20 you can get a full meal that could include chop suey, shark fin soup and various fried noodle dishes. For those worried about authenticity, they work out your bill on an abacus.

The *Valley of the Kings Restaurant* (☎ 757509), on the 1st floor of the Grand Hotel, 17 Sharia 26th of July, has a great view over the busy streets below and an exotic-looking fountain in the centre. The food is quite good. There are a couple of cafés there too, where you can get a decent cup of hot chocolate and two pieces of marble cake for E£3.50, while watching the chaos in the market below on the other side of the street.

The *Caroll Restaurant* (☎ 746434), 12 Sharia Qasr el-Nil, is a popular place for European and Egyptian food. It's opposite the American Express office. They do a wide range of meat and fish dishes for E£20 plus. Some of the pastas are very good and filling and considerably cheaper. The service is particularly friendly and the place has a pleasing atmosphere with just a touch of class.

Across the road is *Estoril*; the address is 12 Sharia Talaat Harb, although it's actually in a lane next to the American Express office. Meals are a combination of French and Middle Eastern food and cost E£15 to E£24. Dishes include grilled beef, veal cutlets, roasted chicken and prawns. On the cheaper side, try their cannelloni: for E£5.50, it's very good.

Taverne du Champs de Mars (☎ 740777), on the ground floor of the Nile Hilton, is a great bar that's good for lunch and dinner. The entire interior was transported from Belgium and reassembled.

Arabesque, 6 Sharia Qasr el-Nil, between Midan Talaat Harb and Midan Tahrir, is the only restaurant in Egypt which is also an art gallery. It's a small gallery, but sometimes there are interesting works displayed. The food is mediocre at best and seems quite overpriced for what you get, which isn't much. What you're really paying for, apparently, is the pleasant Oriental decor and not the food.

Paprika (☎ 749744), 1129 Corniche el-Nil, just south of the Radio & Television building, serves various European dishes, including pizza. It's open from noon to midnight. Radio and TV personalities like to hang out here.

The *Peking* (☎ 912381), 14 Sharia al-Ezbekiya, near Sharia Mohammed Farid, serves Cantonese food for about E£18. It's not bad, although some of the dishes seem to have been 'Egyptianised' in one way or another. They have another restaurant in Mohandiseen.

The *Kowloon* (☎ 759831) in the Cleopatra Palace Hotel, Sharia al-Bustan (near Midan Tahrir), is a popular Korean and Chinese restaurant that serves dinner from 7.30 to 11.30 pm. In the same hotel is *Valentino's*, a friendly Italian restaurant.

The *Evergreen*, near the Lotus Hotel, contains a couple of restaurants and the English-style *Robin Hood* bar, which serves a ploughman's lunch. It's run by a Briton from the Isle of Wight.

Zamalek Zamalek is generally not the cheapest part of town for anything, but there are some good places to track down. If you are staying here, don't want to cope with the chaos across the river but can't afford the more expensive restaurants, there are a few ta'amiyya stands and coffee shops.

The *Four Corners* (☎ 341-2961, 340-7510), 3rd floor, 4 Sharia Hassan Sabri, is a real treat – four restaurants in one. One is a classic French restaurant called *Justine* that serves typical *haute cuisine*; another is *La Piazza*, which has an international menu with Italian pasta specialities; the third is *Matchpoint*, an American-style snackbar and bar with American sports videos and music; and the fourth is *Max's*, a disco for couples only.

Angus, in the New Star Hotel building, Sharia Yehia Ibrahim, specialises in Argentine dishes, particularly steaks.

El Patio, at 5 Sharia as-Sayed al-Bakry, is part of the same small restaurant chain and has reasonable pasta dishes at around E£15 and good desserts. Count on about E£30 per person. This used to be a good place for a drink, but alcohol seems to have been struck from the menu now.

La Charmerie is anything but charming. They have fairly ordinary food on offer and very expensive drinks. If you are unfortunate enough to stumble in on one of their 'reggae' nights, you'll be hit with a E£5 cover charge that they won't tell you about until you're leaving. They only serve Stella Export (the expensive Egyptian beer) and add on all possible taxes.

The *Ha Na* Korean restaurant serves high-quality food in generous helpings. For E£20 a head you will get an authentic and satisfying meal that would cost four times as much in a place like London.

Mohandiseen *Le Chalet* (☎ 728488) restaurant, downstairs from the chic Swissair Restaurant at 10 Sharia an-Nakhil, serves European-style food in a pseudo-Swiss coffee shop atmosphere.

The *Tandoori* (☎ 348-6301) at 11 Sharia Shehab, just off Sharia Gamiat ad-Dowal al-Arabiyya, serves tandoori chicken, kema (a curry of minced lamb with potatoes and peas) and jhinga (curried prawns cooked in a special sauce). A meal costs about E£25 per person. No alcohol is served.

Papillon (☎ 347-1672) is a popular Lebanese restaurant on Sharia 26th of July, about 200 metres up from Midan Sphinx on the right. They have a wide range of Oriental dishes, some of them a pleasing variation on Egyptian cuisine. Try the kofta khoshkhash, the usual minced meat cooked on skewers, but in this case served on a very tasty tomato sauce base.

Prestige at 43 Sharia Geziret al-Arab is, as its name indicates, one of Cairo's chic restaurants. Actually, it's two restaurants in one: a dapper, romantic (when the lights and rock music are turned down) pizzeria on one side; a full Italian restaurant with cloth serviettes and candles on the other. The pizzeria serves various types of individual pizzas for around E£10. Beer is served inside only. The Italian restaurant is more expensive, but at E£20 and up for a main course is still reasonable by international standards.

For a culinary leap north, you could head a few doors up to No 38 for the Alpine atmosphere of the *Tirol Restaurant*, where an array of dishes seems to have the stamp of approval from Cairo's Austrian community – you may even see a few getting around in lederhosen. It's not cheap though – reckon on about E£30 for a main.

The *Taj Mahal* (☎ 348-4881) is at 15 Midan Ibn Afaan, just across Sharia Ibn al-Waleed from the Singapore embassy. It is one of the best restaurants in Cairo. You'll walk away feeling stuffed and satisfied with the tandoori chicken, papadums, curried vegetables and other typically Indian foods. An average meal costs about E£40.

You'll find a decent Korean and Chinese restaurant called *Paxy's* in the basement of the Amoun Hotel on Sphinx Square. A good meal from an extensive menu will cost you about E£30 to E£40 a head – a little on the expensive side.

The *Peking Chinese Restaurant* (☎ 349-9086) has opened a branch at 26 Sharia al-Ataba in Mohandiseen (see above).

Gezira Just south of At-Tahrir Bridge, across from the Opera House, is an outrageously priced 'singing restaurant' called the *Kaser el-Nil*. The food is nothing special and the singing you could live without. Rather, go outside and down the stairs. You can sit right by the river and the Stella costs a fairly standard E£4.50.

Roda Island & Garden City You may not ever be able to afford to stay at a Club Med, or even want to, but a day by the pool and access to their full buffet lunch might be just the ticket if you're hot, hungry and feeling like a splurge. It's not a bad deal at E£45. The Club is just behind the Manyal Palace.

At *Abou Shakra*, 60 Sharia Qasr al-Eini (about 1½ km south of Midan Tahrir), you will find some of the best kofta and kebab in Cairo. The guy who opened the place in 1947, Ahmed Abu (or Abou) Shakra, was known as the 'the King of Kebab'. To get there from Midan Tahrir, walk or take any of the buses heading south for Manyal Bridge and beyond and get off when they turn right. A half-order is plenty of food for one person. The prices are moderate to high, and a 12% service charge is added. A kg of kebab costs E£31. One speciality, pigeon stuffed with

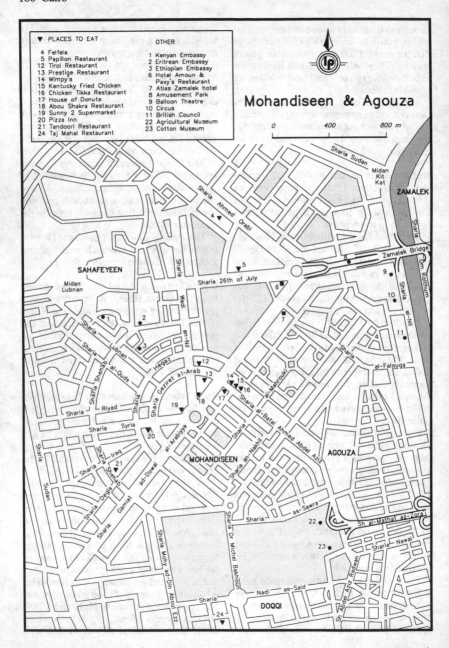

PLACES TO EAT

4 Felfela
5 Papillon Restaurant
12 Tirol Restaurant
13 Prestige Restaurant
14 Wimpy's
15 Kentucky Fried Chicken
16 Chicken Tikka Restaurant
17 House of Donuts
18 Abou Shakra Restaurant
19 Sunny 2 Supermarket
20 Pizza Inn
21 Tandoori Restaurant
24 Taj Mahal Restaurant

OTHER

1 Kenyan Embassy
2 Eritrean Embassy
3 Ethiopian Embassy
6 Hotel Amoun &
  Paxy's Restaurant
7 Atlas Zamalek hotel
8 Amusement Park
9 Balloon Theatre
10 Circus
11 British Council
22 Agricultural Museum
23 Cotton Museum

Mohandiseen & Agouza

rice with chips, costs E£11. There are several salads and a cheaper takeaway service. There are a few cheap eating places and teashops just around here.

They recently opened another restaurant in Sharia Gamiat ad-Dowal al-Arabiyya, Mohandiseen.

Maadi *The Seahorse* (☎ 988499), opposite As-Salam Hospital on the Corniche el-Nil, is a seafood restaurant right by the Nile. It's open from 12.30 pm to 1.30 am.

The *Peking Swiss Chalet* (☎ 351-8328) at 9 St 151 does particularly tasty Chinese food and is not outrageously priced, with most mains starting at below E£20. If you have a spare E£17, you might like to try the Irish coffeee – its fiery preparation is quite a performance.

Giza *Andrea's Chicken & Fish Restaurant* (☎ 851133), 60 Sharia Maryutia, is one km from Pyramids Rd, opposite Saqqara Rd. It is usually a bit overrun by tour groups.

Felfela Village (☎ 383-0574) is down the road and across the canal from Andrea's. However, it's not quite as easy as that, as it's on the other side of the canal and there's no bridge. If you're at one and decide you'd rather be at the other, you'll have to walk back to Pyramids Rd or get one of the service taxis (of the microbus variety) that run up and down each side of the canal.

If you're after a packaged Middle Eastern atmosphere with everything that is supposedly exotic, then this is the place. This restaurant and circus has everything: dancing horses, camel rides, acrobats, snake charmers, and a playground and small zoo for the kids. However, despite the kitsch tourist atmosphere, this place seems to be more popular with Arabs than Westerners, which in itself is a reason for coming here.

Come here with a group, because massive amounts of traditional Egyptian food are served. Try the paper-wrapped baked meat and tomatoes or the baked rice and chicken. The show is only on Sunday, Wednesday and Friday, and starts about 1.30 pm. With a meal, it'll cost about E£40.

A couple of other ones on the same side of the canal as Felfela are *La Bonita* and *The Farm Singing Restaurant*.

Just on the turn-off for the Desert Rd from Pyramids Rd is an overpriced fish restaurant called *Christo* (☎ 383-3582). They have set menus ranging from E£22 to E£40, plus service charges. The fish is OK, but ignore the sign about anything being cooked in the Greek way – this place is all Egyptian, down to the women baking your meal's bread in the corner.

Restaurant el Dar (☎ 385-2289) is on Saqqara Rd, about six km from the junction with Pyramids Rd (a couple of km past the Motel Salma). It's better to come here with a small group because of the great amount of food they serve. The restaurant is outdoors under thatched roofs in a pseudo-Egyptian village atmosphere, also with women baking bread in the corner.

Half way between the bus stop and the Sphinx entrance to the pyramids is a small place called the *China Restaurant*. Clustered around it are a few of the usual stands selling ta'amiyya and the like.

All the big hotels around Giza and out along the road to Alexandria have various restaurants catering to most tastes, if not most budgets. The *Moghul Room* Indian restaurant at the Mena House Oberoi Hotel is an expensive place but popular with expatriates for a special treat.

Floating Restaurants A series of floating restaurants is moored up near the Gezira Club in Zamalek. Heading north from At-Tahrir Bridge, the first one you meet is the *Al-Safina*, where a main meal at lunch will cost about E£25 and the same about E£40 for dinner with a show, which starts about 9 pm.

Next up is a more modest place with an open top-deck café. It's called *Ali ad-Din*. An average dish here will cost around E£15 to E£20.

Up past the Casino an-Nahr and the 6th of October Bridge is the *Omar Khayyam Restaurant*, which is aboard a houseboat on the Nile, opposite the Gezira Club in Zamalek.

It's a fairly formal place with a full Oriental grill.

Le Pacha 1901 (☎ 340-6730) is the last of the Gezira crowd, and is relatively new. All up, there are nine restaurants on board.

In Garden City, not far from the US embassy compound, is the *Al-Laila*. A quite reasonable meal of traditional kebab or chicken with salads and drinks will cost about E£30. It is very pleasantly located.

The *Scarabee* and its more modern and luxurious stablemate, the *MS Aquarius* (☎ 354-3198), are moored alongside Corniche el-Nil, next to Shepheard's Hotel. The first sails at 8.15 pm for a two-hour dinner cruise with entertainment that costs E£45 excluding drinks. The second leaves at about 10 pm for a similar deal costing E£60 a head. There are also lunch-time cruises. It is safest to book ahead.

The *Kamar el Zaman* is moored on the west bank of Roda Island, just south of the Al-Gamiat Bridge.

The *Nile Pharaoh* and *Golden Pharaoh* (☎ 738855/959/914), at 31 Sharia el-Nil in Giza, are flashy cruising restaurants. Call for departure times and reservations.

ENTERTAINMENT
Nightclubs with floor shows, Western-style discos and movie theatres with English-language movies abound in Cairo.

Nightclubs
There are two categories of nightclub. The ones usually patronised by foreigners are generally fairly expensive and often include a lavish feast, folkloric dance performances, belly dancers and Arabic music. Expect to spend at least E£20 just to watch the show. All the major hotels have floor shows, as do many of the overpriced clubs along Pyramids Rd. Note that cover charges and other costs usually have taxes tossed on top at the end.

These are interesting, but more so are the little places catering mainly to Egyptians – although it has to be said these latter can be tacky to sleazy. The *Palmyra*, on Sharia 26th of July, is run by someone who has come to be known as Madame Monocle because, well, she really does get about the place holding up said monocle in order to keep an eye on proceedings. This place has the full Arab music contingent, belly dancers from about 1 am to 4 am and occasionally other acts like acrobats. There is an entry charge of E£3. Around the Palmyra are a couple of other similar nightclubs, one of them called the *Miami*. They all have their good and bad nights – sometimes they're full, on other occasions hardly anyone seems to be there.

Another similar but much smaller place on Sharia Qasr el-Nil, a short way down from the Plaza Hotel and simply calling itself a disco, has a similar line-up only tackier. They have also introduced an appalling and obligatory E£40 meal on top of their cover charge.

Just down from the Cairo Khan on Sharia Mohammed Farid is an even tackier place with virtually no charm at all – the *Honolulu* – half the time there's only an appalling 'disco' going on here.

You might want to pop into the *Shahrazad Night Club* – a belly dancing and drinking hole near the Alfi Bey Restaurant, but it's not as entertaining as the Palmyra.

Discos
Discos are discos – lots of bright, twirling lights and loud music. They vary greatly in quality, and entrance prices generally start at around E£25, which sometimes includes a drink or two. Most places close by 3 am.

Jackie's at the Nile Hilton is interesting if you can get in. It's a private club where, in dark corners at candle-lit tables, Egyptian couples momentarily forget their conservatism and get a bit cosy. Outside on the street, such displays of affection are scorned.

The *Atlas Zamalek Hotel disco* in Mohandiseen is a popular place. Tables often have to be reserved, but it is possible to get in without booking ahead. It generally costs about E£30 (which includes two drinks), and the crowd is an interesting mix of Westerners and trendy, wealthy Egyptians.

The *MS Universe*, a boat moored on the Nile a little way north of the Meridien Hotel end of Roda island, also has a disco. Sometimes it's free, others they charge E£35 – the music is not always too hot.

Another popular but much less exclusive disco is sponsored every Thursday at *Hotel Longchamp*, next to the Cypriot embassy, by a loose-knit group known as the African Students of Cairo. They play a combination of African, reggae and soul music.

There's a string of discos and nightclubs along Pyramids Rd, most of them pretty expensive and tacky. You could try the *Vendome Blow Up Disco*, the *Palma* or the *Aly Baba*, within a km of each other about 10 minutes' drive from the pyramids back towards town.

Bars

If you're missing the typical pub or bar scene, then try *Pub 28* in Zamalek, a pseudo-British pub with a mixed crowd. You can get a meal here too and prices are moderate.

The *Odeon Palace Hotel* off Sharia Talaat Harb has a terrace bar that usually stays open 24 hours. Quite a few hotels have bars. The *Windsor Hotel* has a particularly atmospheric one that a lot of locals use. Talk to Mahmoud, the 1955 Mr Egypt who still boasts rock-hard biceps and a particular liking for being in group photos with patrons – ask to see his photos. The *Gresham Hotel* in Sharia Talaat Harb has a small cosy bar. Places like this are generally open until about 1 am. In the big hotels, there are places to avoid and others that are quite reasonable. You can sit in the garden bar of the *Marriott Hotel* and sip a Stella for normal prices, but *Harry's Bar* has a E£25 minimum charge. There is a bar in the *Ramses Hilton* and also one on the 2nd floor (avoid the 1st floor bar) in the *Cairo Sheraton* in Doqqi, where you can drink with no minimum charge. The *Taverne du Champs de Mars* at the Nile Hilton is not a bad place for a drink, and the E£11.80 minimum charge is not too onerous. Stellas cost E£5 and the flow of peanuts is endless.

You can drink in some restaurants and not at others, and there doesn't seem to be any obvious rule on this.

For those looking for the authentic Egyp-

tian pub scene at the bottom rung, there is a string of out-of-sight places where foreigners are a surprising and rare addition to the clientele. They are mostly simple drinking establishments and don't go out of their way to advertise themselves. Some double as brothels or tacky pick-up joints. One such bar is on the *Corniche el-Nil*, by the 26th of July Bridge. Another, the *Cap d'Or Cafeteria* (most of these places call themselves cafeterias) is a typical spit-and-sawdust representative of the species. It's on Sharia Abdel Khaliq Sarwat.

Another, the *Arizona*, is just opposite the Alfi Bey Restaurant. Women can get in here, but may feel uncomfortable. Drinking is done downstairs, while other transactions are carried on upstairs. Another tacky joint is the *Pussy Cat*, in a lane around the corner from the Alfi Bey. A few metres east of the same restaurant is another nameless drinking place. There are a few others nearby, such as the *Cafeteria Port Tewfik* on Midan Orabi and the *Cyprus Cafeteria* a little way up Sharia Orabi on the right.

Just opposite the entrance to the Grand Hotel is a fairly awful escort bar (not to be confused with the rather pleasant café next to it). You can get Stella and spirits at most of these places, and you'll be served plates of beans and salad to munch on while you drink.

Squashed in between the Felfela restaurant and takeaway on Sharia Talaat Harb is the very simple *Stella* bar, which has been there for 30 years. It's a typical lively *baladi* bar, but women may not feel at home, especially if they have to go to the loo – it must be the smallest *pissoir* in the world.

The more you look, the more of these places you'll turn up – half the fun is in discovering them. A clue to another area to look in is just east of Midan Opera. Happy hunting.

If it's alcohol to take home you want, you can buy it in some of the so-called supermarkets and the occasional liquor store. One such place is next to the Rivoli Cinema on Sharia 26th of July, just west of the Grand Hotel.

Cinemas

Going to a movie in Cairo can be an interesting and inexpensive cultural experience. Most foreign-language movies have subtitles in Arabic, but because the audience doesn't have to listen to the soundtrack they often talk all the way through the movie. The same applies to the multitude of hawkers plying the aisles with buckets of soda bottles, boxes of candy and trays of small sandwiches.

Don't be surprised if a scene in a movie suddenly disappears. Censorship is common in all movies except those shown at the Cairo International Film Festival in autumn, and even then it's been known to happen. The same five censors who decide which parts of a movie millions of Egyptians won't see also scrutinise music tapes, video cassettes, books, magazines and anything else which they feel might not be appropriate for local consumption.

Some cinemas are better than others, and show reasonably up-to-date movies that cost more than those in many of the picture houses around town specialising in the *Terminator* style of movie that seems so popular with the local lads (few Egyptian women are seen at the cinema, particularly the cheaper ones). They also seem to attract a far less rowdy bunch than the cheaper cinemas, and it can be just like going to the movies at home – well, almost.

The *Egyptian Gazette* carries advertisements for the better cinemas, which in Cairo include the Karim I and II on Sharia Imad ad-Din, the El-Tahrir, not far on from the At-Tahrir Bridge in Doqqi, the Cine at-Tahrir, further on from the El-Tahrir and the Normandy in Heliopolis. Movies at these cinemas cost E£5 in the stalls and E£7.50 in the balconies (tickets to the cheaper movie houses cost E£2 to E£3). There are generally five screenings a day at Egyptian cinemas, at roughly the same times: 10 am, 1 pm, 3 pm, 6 pm and 9 pm. There are sometimes midnight screenings on Thursday and Saturday.

Opera, Music & Dance

The Cairo Opera House at the bottom end of Gezira can be a real treat. Well-known international troupes from all over the world sometimes perform here for prices that would be unheard of in the West. Some of the locally performed stuff (Cairo Opera Ballet Company and Cairo Orchestra) can be quite reasonable too. Check with the Opera House (☎ 341-2926) for what's on while you're in town. Jacket and tie are required, but less well dressed travellers have been known to borrow them from staff. There are often music recitals of varying quality at the AUC's Ewart Hall. Entry is often free or next to it. Enquire at the AUC's information booth in Sharia Sheikh Rihan.

Hash House Harriers

All over the world where expatriates gather, a branch of the British-initiated running and drinking fraternity forms. The Cairo branch has people from all over the place, including a lot of locals, who meet on Fridays for a run and a bit of a get-together afterwards. You can try calling John Hoppe (☎ 259-0803), but check in the *Cairo Today* listings section for the latest contacts.

THINGS TO BUY

The Things to Buy section in the Facts for the Visitor chapter outlines some of the Egyptian shopping possibilities. If it's available anywhere in Egypt it will be available in Cairo.

For regular, run-of-the-mill tourist souvenirs the sprawling Khan al-Khalili bazaar is definitely the place to head for. The confusing maze of alleys is packed with places selling brassware, inlaid boxes, T-shirts, papyrus paintings and every possible souvenir of a visit to Egypt. Unfortunately a great deal of it is simply tourist junk, cheap and amusing bits of souvenir kitsch but nothing more. You'll find the same sort of items in the tourist shops in the major hotels.

Although they're mass produced in such numbers that you soon become heartily sick of them, the papyrus paintings make attractive and easily packed little gifts. They're certainly clearly Egyptian.

The Egyptian Museum has a great series

of posters including a fine one of Tutankhamun's tomb. They're available from the shops just inside the museum entrance but you'll often find them cheaper at other outlets, such as the Lehnert & Landrock bookshop on Sharia Sherif.

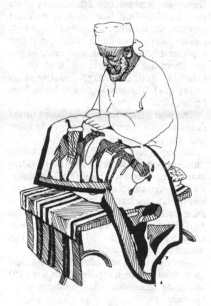

Benetton and Naf Naf have opened outlets in Egypt, and a few travellers have reported filling their luggage with European-designed items made in Egypt at prices well below those in Europe.

In addition to the usual postcards and the like, some bookshops sell some very attractive reproduction prints of drawings done in Cairo and Egypt by several 19th century artists and draughtsmen.

GETTING THERE & AWAY
Air

EgyptAir flies between Cairo and several places within Egypt, including Hurghada, Sharm el-Sheikh, Luxor, the Kharga Oasis, and Aswan. Fares are fairly reasonable by international standards but a lot more expensive than surface transport. A one-way ticket to or from Luxor costs about E£283, Sharm el-Sheikh E£325 and Alexandria E£168.

There are a lot of travel agencies clustered around Midan Tahrir. One, De Castro Tours (☎ 574-3144) at 12 Sharia Talaat Harb, has been recommended by some travellers and has a wide range of flights on offer, many of them with considerable student discounts. They don't seem too concerned about getting bank receipts indicating official exchange either. Another claiming to offer cheap flights is Norma Tours (☎ 760062), at No 10 Sharia Talaat Harb.

EgyptAir has a big barn-like office on Midan Opera open seven days a weeks from 8 am to 8 pm and another office on Sharia Talaat Harb open the same hours. For more international air-fare details, see the Getting There & Away chapter.

Most airlines that operate in and out of Egypt will only sell you air tickets if you can show them bank receipts that prove you officially changed enough money for the ticket. They will also keep the receipts so you can't reuse them for visa extensions. This is not a rigid rule. Some airlines have never worried about receipts and since the anti-black market measure is an anachronism, it is not overly difficult to find airlines and agents who don't require them, should you not have one on you for any reason. It is possible to pay for airline tickets with a credit card, but not all airlines and agents accept them.

You can call Cairo Airport for flight information (☎ 291-4288/99). The addresses of airlines which operate in and out of Cairo are:

Air France
  2 Midan Talaat Harb (☎ 574-3516/479/624)
Air India
  1 Sharia Talaat Harb (☎ 393-4864/73/75)
  Cairo International Airport (☎ 966756)
Air Sinai
  Nile Hilton Hotel (☎ 760948)
Alitalia
  Nile Hilton Hotel (☎ 574-3488)

Austrian Airlines
Nile Hilton Hotel (☎ 574-2755)
British Airways
1 Sharia Abdel Salam Aref (☎ 759977, 762914)
Bulgarian Airlines
13 Sharia Qasr el-Nil (☎ 393-1211)
Czechoslovak Airlines
9 Sharia Talaat Harb (☎ 393-0395)
EgyptAir
Nile Hilton (☎ 759771)
Reservations (☎ 747-4444)
Cairo International Airport (☎ 244-5982)
6 Sharia Adly (☎ 922444)
Flight information (☎ 872122)
El Al Israel Airlines
5 Sharia Mazriki, Zamalek (☎ 341-1795)
Ethiopian Airlines
Nile Hilton Hotel (☎ 574-0603)
Garuda Indonesia Airways
17 Sharia Ismail Mohammed, Zamalek (☎ 340-1948)
Hungarian Airlines (Malev)
12 Sharia Talaat Harb (☎ 753111)
Japan Airlines (JAL)
Nile Hilton Hotel (☎ 574-7233)
KLM (Royal Dutch Airlines)
11 Sharia Qasr el-Nil (☎ 574-7004)
Kenya Airways
Nile Hilton Hotel (☎ 762494)
Lufthansa German Airlines
9 Sharia Talaat Harb (☎ 393-0366)
Olympic Airways
23 Sharia Qasr el-Nil (☎ 393-1459/277)
Singapore Airlines
Nile Hilton (☎ 762702)
Sudan Airways
1 Sharia al-Bustan (☎ 747145)
Trans World Airlines
1 Sharia Qasr el-Nil (☎ 749900, 757256)
Turkish Airlines
3 Midan Mustafa Kamal (☎ 390-8960/1)
ZAS Airlines
Sharia Gamal ad-Din Abu Muhassin, Garden City (☎ 290-7840/1/2)

Bus

Cairo has several long-distance bus stations. For buses to Alexandria, the Delta, Marsa Matruh, Hurghada, Luxor and Aswan, there is a fairly new station just around the corner from the Ramses Hilton along Sharia al-Galaa. Although some people will tell you that this area is all part of Midan Tahrir, the swirl of streets and overpasses in front of the various booths is actually called Midan Abdel Minnim Riyadh. It seems one helluva

place to put a bus station – there's no room for it.

Heading around from the Ramses Hilton, the first booths you come across are booking offices for the East Delta Bus Co's international services. You can book tickets to destinations as far afield as Tunis, Istanbul, Damascus, Amman, cities throughout Saudi Arabia and the Gulf. None of these are direct services, but involve transferring to national carriers. Remember that it is cheaper (often considerably) to pay each leg locally as you go. There are also direct buses to Tripoli (Monday and Thursday) and Benghazi (every day). The buses actually leave from Midan Ulali.

The next office has regular buses to the Cairo satellite towns of the 6th of October and 10th of Ramadan cities.

Next up is the Upper Egypt Bus Co, which runs its luxury buses from here (with video, air-con and toilet) to Luxor (8.30 pm daily; E£35); Aswan (5 pm daily; E£50) and Hurghada. This last trip takes six hours, and there are five departures – at 9 am, noon and 3, 10.30 and 11 pm. You can also get these same buses from the Ahmed Hilmi bus station behind Ramses Station.

Moving along, you come to the Middle Delta Bus Co, which services Tanta (E£5.25) and some other smaller destinations along the route.

Next is the Arab Union Transport Company. Its mega-comfy 'VIP Super Jet' buses will whisk you to Midan Saad Zaghloul in Alexandria for E£15. There are 25 daily departures, starting at 5 am and finishing at 9 pm. Arab Union has nine daily services to Port Said (E£13; three hours). The first leaves at 6 am, the last at 4 pm, and it stops to pick up passengers in Heliopolis on the way. The daily bus for Marsa Matruh (summer only) costs E£30 and leaves at 8 am. The trip takes about five hours.

Last in line is the West Delta Bus Co. It has 31 services running to Alexandria. The 'Golden Arrow' (as-sahim ad-dahabi) buses, with video, air-con and on-board toilet, cost E£12; the ordinary buses cost E£6 or E£8, depending on how clapped out they

Top: Busy scene at Midan Tahrir, Cairo (KB)
Left: Detail of ornate building facade, Old Cairo (DS)
Right: Cinema advertisement, Cairo (DS)

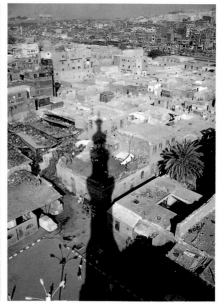

Top: Mosque of Al-Hakim, Cairo (SW)
Left: Mosque of Mohammed Ali, The Citadel, Cairo (GB)
Right: Minaret casts a shadow across the City of the Dead, Cairo (CB)

are. The first bus leaves at 5.30 am and the last at midnight. It has a no-frills bus to Marsa Matruh at 8.45 am for E£15 all year round. In summer, there are two or three extra luxury buses to Marsa Matruh for E£25, leaving around 7.15 and 7.45 am.

To/From the Nile Delta, Suez Canal & Red Sea Big yellow buses of the East Delta Bus Co leave from Midan Ulali (see the northern end of the Greater Cairo map) for Mansura (E£6.50) and Damietta (E£11). They leave about every half hour from 6 am to 6 pm. As you enter from Sharia Ramses, the ticket office for these two destinations (and Libya) is on your right.

Further on, and off to the left, there are buses to Port Said (from E£8 to E£12, depending on comforts; departures every hour), Ismailia (E£5.50, departures every half hour) and Suez (E£5, departures every half hour).

The Upper Egypt Bus Co runs buses to Hurghada, Port Safaga and Quseir from the Ahmed Hilmi terminal, which lies behind platform 11 at Ramses Station. The five Hurghada services leave at 9 am, noon and 3, 10.30 and 11 pm. The 9 am and 3 pm services go on to Port Safaga. There is a bus for Quseir at 7 am and 10 pm. The fare to Hurghada is E£24 or E£30 (air-con and video).

To/From Upper Egypt Buses with the Upper Egypt Bus Co for destinations such as Al-Minya, Asyut, Luxor and Aswan leave from Ahmed Hilmi Station. These tend to be the cheaper no-frills green buses, not the all-mod-cons type leaving from Midan Abdel Minnim Riyadh. Buses to destinations such as Al-Minya and Asyut run every half to one hour from about 6 am to 6 pm.

To/From the Sinai All buses to the Sinai leave from Abbassiya Station (commonly known as the Sinai Terminal), just off Midan Abbassiya. These buses are considerably more expensive than those in the rest of the country. Six buses run to Sharm el-Sheikh at 7.30 and 10 am, 2, 4 and 11.30 pm, and

midnight. The 7.30 am and midnight buses go on to Dahab, and all buses stop at a few places such as El-Tor. The 9 am bus to Nuweiba goes via St Catherine's, and the 11 pm one goes on to Taba. There are three buses to Al-Arish – at 8 am and 3.30 and 5.30 pm. The first of these goes on to Rafah, on the Israeli border. Ticket prices (it is irritating to note that foreigners pay between E£10 and E£20 more than Egyptians) vary. The daytime buses to Sharm el-Sheikh cost E£30 or E£35, while the two late-night services are E£50. The Dahab leg on these costs an extra E£5. The day bus to Nuweiba costs E£45 (E£40 to St Catherine's) and the night bus E£50 (E£15 extra to go all the way to Taba). The bus to Al-Arish costs E£25, and E£35 to Rafah.

Note that it is generally considerably cheaper to travel first to Suez and pick up other transport from there. See the Suez Getting There & Away section.

To/From the Western Oases & Al-Faiyum Buses travel daily to the Western Oases (or Al-Wadi al-Gedid, 'New Valley') from a small Upper Egypt Bus Co station at 45 Sharia al-Azhar, a few blocks east of Midan Ataba – look out for the small white-on-green sign. Daily buses to Bahariyya cost from E£9.20 to E£14.20, depending on whether or not they have air-con and/or a video. The trip takes about six hours (take some food and water, as sometimes the oasis buses don't stop anywhere useful for breaks). One of the daily services to Bahariyya goes on to Farafra, except on Wednesday. The 7 am bus on Sunday, Tuesday and Friday goes all the way to Dakhla and costs E£22.

There are three daily buses to Dakhla via Asyut and Kharga, but supposedly only one actually stops at Kharga. It takes about 12 hours and costs E£20 to E£28, depending on the bus. One bus at 10 am goes to Kharga only, takes nine hours and costs E£15.

The buses stop at Midan Giza on the way, at the 6th of October City minibus stop where the overpass forks and Pyramids Rd (Sharia al-Ahram) begins.

Buses for Al-Faiyum leave from the station at Midan Ahmed Hilmi and a separate station at Midan Giza. For the latter, continue past the minibus stop until you reach Sharia Sudan. The bus lot is on the other side of the railway line. Buses cost E£2.50.

For more details of specific times and fares from Cairo, see the Getting There & Away sections for each oasis.

To/From Israel Buses to Tel Aviv and Jerusalem usually depart daily, except Saturday, from the Cairo Sheraton at about 5 am. The one-way fare varies, depending on where you purchase the ticket, but is around E£85 with Misr Travel and Travco. See the Getting There & Away chapter for more details.

The East Delta Bus Co has buses from the Sinai Terminal in Abbassiya in Cairo at 8 am on Mondays and Wednesdays. It costs US$20 (you can't pay in E£).

To/From Jordan & the Gulf It is possible to book a ticket from Cairo through to Aqaba in Jordan, or even beyond to Saudi Arabia and other Gulf destinations. You can book the ticket at Midan Ulali or Midan Abdel Minnim Riyadh, but the bus for the Cairo-Nuweiba leg leaves from the Sinai Terminal at Midan Abbassiya. The bus and boat to Aqaba cost E£40.20 plus US$26. Note that tickets bought in Jordan coming the other way are cheaper. It is also possible to buy tickets for Saudi Arabia at the Sinai Terminal itself. The one-way trip to Riyadh is E£210 plus US$26. The fare to Kuwait is E£358 and US$26.

To/From Libya The East Delta Bus Co runs a daily service to Benghazi, in Libya, from Midan Ulali (you can also book the ticket at the Midan Abdel Minnim Riyadh office). The booking office is on the right as you approach from Sharia Ramses. One-way tickets cost E£125. The bus leaves at 9 am and takes about 18 hours. On Monday and Thursday the bus continues for another 18 hours to Tripoli. That ticket costs E£230. Make sure you have a visa.

Cheaper tickets are available with the

Hebton bus company at 305 Sharia Shubra, Midan al-Khalifawi, Shubra, or at their offices behind the car park east of Midan Opera. Departure times are unreliable.

To/From Tunisia, Algeria & Morocco If you have the visas and want to book a bus ride right across North Africa, you might also try the Hebton company. They have irregular services running across Libya and all the way to Morocco. The buses are basic, and generally cater for Egyptian workers in those countries.

Train

Ramses Station, on Midan Ramses, is Cairo's main train station. Everything and everyone seems to be moving all at once, and at first it can be a bit confusing trying to buy tickets from the right window. There is a tourist office with tourist police just inside the main entrance on the left. Note also that among the phones, further inside on the left, are a few card phones. In a secondary entrance further to the right is a small post office and, next to it, the left-luggage area (marked 'cloak room'). It is open 24 hours a day, seven days a week, and the service costs E£1 per piece. Outside the main entrance is a colour passport photo machine – four photos cost E£5. (The fun part is that someone has to manually make the thing work!) A bit of a pain for those who do not read Arabic is that the electronic departure indicators are all in Arabic only.

Sometimes, representatives of the Tourist

Friends Association roam around the station, and they will help you buy tickets. The Friends will probably find you before you find them if you look lost enough. They're quite sincere when they say they only want to help you and practise their English. They will show you their official papers to prove that they are legitimate and not asking for baksheesh.

One advantage (for a change) of being a woman here is that you go straight to the head of the queue for train tickets.

If you have an International Student Identification Card you are eligible for a discount of up to 50% on all tickets, except those for wagons-lits. Other forms of student or quasi-student identification have sometimes been successfully used by travellers.

There are at least five classes of train: 1st class deluxe (wagons-lits); 1st class ordinary; 2nd class with air-con; 2nd class ordinary; and 3rd class. Not all trains have all classes, so make sure you know when the next train is going with your class of ticket (it would be a shame to waste a 1st-class ticket on a 2nd-class trip).

Wagons-Lits The wagon-lit office is in a separate building south of the car park on the left side of the main building. Follow the blue-on-yellow signs saying 'Res. Office'. The spacious office is on the 1st floor and is unlikely to be crowded – although the price for Egyptians is half that for foreigners, few could afford it. This is the only kind of sleeper available to foreigners and there is now only one train a day, which travels to Luxor and Aswan. It costs E£242 one way, or E£222 each way if buy a return ticket, and includes all meals. There is no student reduction. The price is the same for Luxor and Aswan, even if you only want to go as far as Luxor. If you want to do both, you have to use the Luxor to Aswan leg within 72 hours. You need to book two or three days in advance. From Cairo, the train leaves at 8 pm and arrives at Luxor about 6 am and at Aswan four hours later. The return train leaves Aswan at 3.45 pm and Luxor at 8 pm and arrives in Cairo at 6 am.

To/From Southern Destinations The overnight trains to Luxor and Aswan are the ones most commonly taken by foreigners. They are among the best trains in Egypt. Even for sit-up tickets you'll need to book at least a day, and probably two days, in advance.

There are five express overnight trains from Cairo to Luxor and Aswan. The slowest of them is No 88, which makes quite a few stops. No 84 is the wagon-lit train. Trains Nos 886, 82 and 86 make hardly any stops outside Luxor and Aswan. They leave at 7, 7.30 and 8.30 pm respectively. Where stops are made, they can last for up to 45 minutes. Heading north, the respective trains are No 89 (slowest of the express trains), No 85 (wagons-lits), and Nos 887, 83 and 87.

Now that there are two tracks as far as Luxor, train timetables have become more reliable than in the past. Work is continuing to extend the second track to Aswan, which will see an end of trains shunting backwards to small sidings to allow others coming in the opposite direction to pass.

First-class seat tickets for destinations south of Cairo are bought at an office along platform 11. There are eight windows and each one deals with specific trains having 1st-class cars. The destinations and train numbers are written up in Arabic on the windows, although the system does not seem to be rigorously applied. In addition to Luxor and Aswan, this is where to get tickets for such places as Asyut, Al-Minya and so on. You can also buy 2nd-class air-con tickets at these windows.

The 1st-class fare from Cairo to Aswan is E£47 and the student fare E£30.50 (2nd class E£26.50/20). To Luxor, the full fare is E£38 and the student discount E£25 (2nd class E£22/16.50). It appears these fares can vary a little depending on whether or not you're on one of the faster trains (about E£3 to E£4 more for the faster ones).

A lot of people have reported an odd, and slightly suspicious, practice. Sometimes passengers have been told they cannot buy tickets all the way to Aswan, but that they must pay for as far as, say, Edfu, and worry about the rest later. They then find themselves paying rather a lot for another ticket on the train to complete the journey. It all seems a bit mysterious, and it's difficult to see who gets what out of it.

To/From Northern Destinations For 1st-class tickets to Alexandria, Marsa Matruh and the Nile Delta, head for the windows directly in front of you when come in the main entrance, past the tourist office and the telephones. The window at the far left is for same-day sales; each of the others is for advance bookings for particular trains. For 2nd-class tickets, walk past the 1st-class ticket windows outside and across to the next office. Same-day ticket sales are made at the far right end counter, while the other counters each cover advance bookings for certain trains. Rules are made to be broken, and even armed with all this information, you'll still probably be shunted from window to window. It happens to the locals too, so keep cool.

The best trains running between Cairo and Alexandria are the Turbos. They make only one stop, at Sidi Gaber Station in Alexandria, and take two hours and 10 minutes. Second class in this train is about as good as 1st class in most others. You can't mistake the train – it looks a little like the French TGV (although it's not quite as fast!). Turbos Nos 905, 917, 921 and 927 leave Cairo respectively at 8.10 am and 2 , 4.25 and 7.15 pm. It is more expensive than other trains and the student discount is not very high. First and 2nd class cost E£20.70 and E£12.40. Other trains, which can take anything up to four hours, depending on the number of stops, cost E£15 and E£9.40 in 1st and 2nd class respectively. They call at Tanta and Damanhur on the way.

To/From Eastern Destinations Four trains make the trip from Cairo to Port Said. They leave at 6.25 and 11.40 am, and 2.50 and 6.45 pm. The trains stop at Zagazig, Ismailia and Qantara, and take about 4½ hours. There are six other trains for Ismailia. Those making the fewest stops leave at 5.35 and 8.45 am. The 2nd-class fare to Port Said and Ismailia

is E£10.50 and E£7.40 respectively. Third-class tickets are E£2.20 and E£1.50 respectively.

Six trains leave for Suez from 'Ain Shams station, in the west of the city. This is particularly awkward for most people, so stick to the buses and service taxis.

Third Class Third-class tickets for all destinations, including Alexandria, Luxor and Aswan, can be bought at the row of windows next to the wagon-lit office, between the car park and platform eight. Be prepared for a battle to buy tickets for popular destinations.

Some examples of 3rd-class full/student fares to or from Cairo are:

Alexandria	E£2/1
Al-Minya	E£2.30/1.20
Aswan	E£5.80/2.90
Asyut	E£3.20/1.70
Beni Suef	E£1.20/0.60
Esna	E£5/2.60
Ismailia	E£1.50/0.80.
Port Said	E£2.20/1.30
Kom Ombo	E£5.60/2.80
Luxor	E£4.80/2.40
Port Said	E£2.20/1.30
Qena	E£4.50/2.30
Sohag	E£3.80/1.90

Service Taxi

Cairo's service taxis depart from various places around the city. By Ramses Station, they stretch around from the Midan Ulali bus station up to the train station. They depart for Mansura, Qantara, Damietta (Ras al-Bar), Alexandria (E£8), Suez (E£4.50), Ismailia (E£5), Port Said (E£8), Al-Arish (E£12, five hours) and Rafah (E£15, six hours). Fares are determined by the distance travelled, so keep an eye out for what others pay to get the set price.

Service taxis for Alexandria also leave from in front of Ramses Station and the Nile Hilton (E£8.50 to E£10). Taxis for destinations in and around Al-Faiyum leave from the Faiyum bus stop at Midan Giza (E£4). Note that sometimes 'service taxis' are in fact microbuses.

The service-taxi station at Midan Ahmed Hilmi covers the Delta area. There are regular departures for Mansura (E£8), Tanta (E£5), Zagazig (E£4) and other destinations.

Sacred barque

GETTING AROUND

Getting around Cairo can be a confusing and frustrating experience, but several modes of transport are available. Buses are the most common form of transport for the majority of Cairenes, but minibuses are equally popular, less crowded, and increasingly prevalent. Taxis are everywhere at any time of the day or night. There's a partially underground metro train service between Helwan and Al-Marg, near Heliopolis, and there's also a waterbus that travels the Nile from Maadi to Qanater, north of Cairo. Several tram lines (confusingly, Cairenes also call trams 'metros') run in eastern parts of the city. Private donkey carts and horse-drawn carriages continue to weave through the streets and alleyways, along with an occasional camel laden with goods for the market.

To/From the Airport

If you arrive at the new airport terminal, don't believe the taxi drivers when they tell you there is no bus. There is at least one an hour to Midan Tahrir (No 422) for 25 pt, which leaves from in front of the snack stand in the car park in front of the terminal. Other buses from various other parts of Cairo also stop here, and many of them serve as a shuttle to the old terminal, from where you have a wider choice of buses and minibuses into the centre.

Otherwise you can get a taxi. The 'official price' is E£28. This is also rubbish. Ignore pleas about expensive petrol. The maximum you should pay is E£20, and the drivers can be bargained down to E£15. It is generally less torment when catching a taxi to the airport.

Most international air carriers use the new terminal. EgyptAir uses the old terminal, and a few other airlines sometimes have their flights assigned there too, so on departure you should double check which one you need.

From the old terminal, there are several ways to get to central Cairo. You can get a taxi for around E£15 to E£20, depending on your bargaining skills. It seems that the closer you are to the arrival hall, the higher the taxi fare. Keep your cool, walk away to the bus stops and let them come to you with their offers.

Bus No 400 (25 pt) and minibus No 27 (50 pt) depart frequently round the clock; they leave from the lot in front of the old airport terminal. Going to the airport, you can take the same bus (No 400) from the central Cairo terminal behind the Nile Hilton, or minibus No 27 from the stands in front of the Mogamma building. Note that on all the buses you are likely to be charged extra for the space your luggage takes up (this is not strictly legal, but try arguing about it!).

There are a few limousine taxi services that operate between both terminals and various destinations in Cairo. Bank Naser Limousine (☎ 506-0426) will take passengers to central Cairo for E£32.50 and to Alexandria for E£69. The more luxurious Limousine Misr (☎ 285-6721) charges E£52.50 to or from central Cairo.

It is possible to get a bus to destinations beyond Cairo directly from the airport. The Arab Union Transport Co has 14 buses to Alexandria from the new and old terminals. Buses leaving before 4 pm cost E£20, those afterwards E£25. The last service leaves at 8.45 pm. The Upper Egypt Bus Co, the East Delta Bus Co and the West Delta Bus Co have booths at the old terminal with occasional departures for destinations all over the country.

For more information about arrival details, see the Accommodation section in the Facts for the Visitor chapter.

Bus

If you're really planning on squeezing in and out of Cairo's crowded buses, you may want to try to get your hands on the booklet that lists all the city's bus and minibus routes. It is sold at some newsstands and is called the *Daleel an-Naql al-Aam*. It's in Arabic only, and is not always easy to get a hold of, but could make life easier for the dedicated supporter of public transport.

Riding a bus in Cairo requires more than just the slippery eel-like qualities necessary for claiming your space. Route numbers are usually indicated in Arabic numerals (sometimes in English also) on small signs behind the windscreen and on painted signs on the side of the bus. You have to be able to recognise the numerals quickly, because the buses hardly stop. They roll into the station, sometimes already full, and a few seconds later roll out the other side, seemingly with even more passengers and less space. If there are lots of people waiting for the bus, the strategy for boarding is to push, shove and grunt. Watch your wallets and money pouches because it is during this crunch that a lot of things tend to disappear. Once you're on the bus, try to squeeze your way up towards the front door, which is the exit. At some point during the trip, a man will somehow manage to squeeze his way right down the bus to sell you your ticket, which is usually 10 pt or, increasingly, 25 pt.

There are two parts to Cairo's main bus terminal, which is in the area around Midan Tahrir. Directly in front of the Nile Hilton, buses leave for Islamic Cairo, Heliopolis, Cairo Airport, Shubra, Bulaq, Zamalek, Agouza and Mohandiseen. A lot of buses heading out to Zamalek, Doqqi and beyond slow down or sometimes even stop to set down and pick up passengers as they pass between the Nile Hilton and the Mogamma

on Sharia at-Tahrir. This, by the way, is also a convenient place to pick up a taxi.

The other part of the main bus terminal is in front of the Mogamma building. Most of the buses from there are actually passing by from other stops and heading down Qasr al-Eini, Manyal and Roda Island before crossing the river and heading out towards Giza, the pyramids and other destinations.

This is also where the minibus station is. Minibuses run to Giza and the pyramids, the Citadel, the City of the Dead, Maadi and places like Doqqi and Mohandiseen in the west of the city. Taking a minibus is one of the best ways to travel. It costs only 25 to 50 pt (depending on your destination) for a seat. Passengers are not allowed to stand and crowd each other (this rule is frequently overlooked), and each minibus leaves as soon as every seat is taken. A minibus is easily recognised by its smaller size and orange and white stripes (sometimes a black and red one).

There are other bus terminals worth noting. Midan Ataba, which is just east of the Ezbekiya Gardens, has plenty of buses going out to the Citadel, and some heading from there on to Tahrir, Manyal and Giza.

There is a smaller terminal in front of Ramses Station, although if you're just trying to get into the centre of town, you're better off taking the metro.

The bus terminal at Giza has buses going to the pyramids, the airport and the Citadel. Next to it is a microbus stand. You can also get to the pyramids from here for 25 pt.

Following is a list of some of the bus numbers and their destinations. One word of caution. Sometimes bus route numbers change (usually the high numbers indicate new numbers) without any other change taking place. Cairenes say this is little more than a ruse to put up fares – new route number, higher fare. This seems to be borne out by the facts. More often than not the fare on buses with higher numbers is 25 pt. The 10 pt fare is slowly on the way out. If you're worried that you're being done, look at your ticket – you'll need to know Arabic numerals – and the most prominent figure you'll see is the fare. Note that some buses servicing the old and new airport terminals occasionally have fares higher than the 25 pt fare. Some numbers have an oblique stroke in front of them – corresponding to those bus numbers with a stroke *through* them.

Note that some of the information overlaps, for ease of use from bus stations and various sites in the city. Some information also appears in the relevant sections. If you want to find out something specific, you could try your luck calling the Greater Cairo General Transport Authority (☎ 830533).

To/From Midan Tahrir – Nile Hilton terminal

No 422	Midan Tahrir – Midan Roxy – Cairo Airport (new terminal)
No 400	Midan Tahrir – Midan Roxy – Cairo Airport (old terminal)
No /400	Midan Tahrir – Abbassiya
No /24	Midan Tahrir – Midan Ahmed Hilmi – Shubra
No /50	Midan Tahrir – Midan Roxy – Heliopolis
No 36	Midan Tahrir – Sharia Port Said – Al-Amiriyya
No 16	Midan Tahrir – Galaa Bridge – Agouza
No 99	Midan Tahrir – Agouza – Sharia Sudan – Midan Lubnan
No 128	Midan Tahrir – Abbassiya – 'Ain Shams
No 66	Midan Tahrir – Sharia Port Said – Mosque of Al-Azhar & Khan al-Khalili
No 35	Midan Tahrir – Abbassiya

To/From Midan Tahrir – Mogamma terminal

Minibus No 27	Midan Tahrir – Cairo Airport (old terminal)
Minibus No 24	Midan Tahrir – Midan Roxy
Minibus No 52	Midan Tahrir – Maadi
Minibus No 54	Midan Tahrir – Sayyida Zeinab – Citadel
Minibus No 82	Midan Tahrir – Midan Nadi ar-Rimayya
Minibus No 83	Midan Tahrir – Pyramids

To/From Midan Ataba

No 99	Midan Ataba – Midan Lubnan
No 200	Midan Ataba – Sharia 26th of July – Sharia Ahmed Orabi – Imbaba (Camel Market)
No 904	Ad-Daraasa – Midan Ataba – Midan Tahrir (Mogamma) – Pyramids
No 404	Midan Ataba – Citadel – Midan Tahrir (Nile Hilton)
No 951	Midan Ataba – Citadel
No 801	Midan Ataba – Citadel
Minibus No 57	Midan Ataba – Citadel
Minibus No 48	Midan Ataba – Zamalek
No 930	Midan Ataba – Qanater

To/From Ramses Station

No 30	Ramses Station – Midan Giza
No 160	Ramses Station – Citadel – Midan Tahrir (Mogamma) – Manyal – Giza Pyramids
No 174	Ramses Station – Citadel
Nos 210, 212	Ramses Station – Qanater

To/From Midan Giza

No 3	Midan Giza – Pyramids
No 30	Midan Giza – Ramses Station
No /116	Midan Giza – Kerdassa
No 949	Midan Giza – Cairo Airport (old & new terminals)

To/From Zamalek

No 13	Midan Falaki (nr Bab al-Louk) – Midan Tahrir – Zamalek – Sharia Abu al-Feda
Minibus No 48	Midan Ataba – Zamalek
Minibus No 49	Midan Falaki – Midan Tahrir – Gezira – Zamalek
Minibus No 47	Midan Ramses – Zamalek

To/From the Pyramids

No 904	Ad-Daraasa – Midan Ataba – Midan Tahrir (Mogamma) – Pyramids
No 905	Citadel – Midan Tahrir (Mogamma) – Qasr al-Eini – Manyal – Pyramids
No 3	Midan Giza – Pyramids
No 160	Ramses Station – Citadel – Midan Tahrir (Mogamma) – Manyal – Pyramids
Minibus No 83	Midan Tahrir (Mogamma) – Doqqi – Pyramids

To/From the Citadel

No 173	Midan Tahrir – Citadel
No 174	Ramses Station – Citadel
No 905	Citadel – Manyal – Giza – Pyramids
No 404	Midan Ataba – Citadel – Midan Tahrir (Nile Hilton)
No 951	Midan Ataba – Citadel
No 801	Midan Ataba – Citadel
Minibus No 57	Midan Ataba – Citadel
Minibus No 54	Midan Tahrir (Mogamma) – Citadel

No 800	Abbassiya – Ramses Station – Giza
No 48	Abbassiya – Midan Ataba
No 922	Abbassiya – Maadi
No /400	Abbassiya – Midan Tahrir

Other Routes

No 913	Sphinx (Abu al-Hol) – Midan Tahrir – Shubra
Minibus No 77	Ad-Daraasa – Midan Tahrir – Doqqi – Bulaq ad-Dakrur

Increasingly Cairenes are using private microbuses (as opposed to the public minibuses) to get around. Destinations are unmarked in any language, so they are hard to use, except for those travelling to the pyramids from next to the minibus station in front of the Mogamma for 50 pt.

Metro

Cairo's metro system is a single line of 33 stations that stretches for 43 km from the southern suburb of Helwan to Al-Marg, near Heliopolis. The five stations in central Cairo are the only ones underground. The Central Cairo map shows entrances to the main underground stations. Another line is planned between Shubra and Giza.

The metro is fast, inexpensive and usually not too crowded. It costs 30 pt to ride up to nine stops; 50 pt up to 16 stops; 60 pt up to 22 stops; 70 pt up to 28 stops; and 80 pt to ride the length of the line. If you're going to be in Cairo for a long time and using the metro on a regular basis, it might be worth enquiring about weekly or monthly passes. The service closes about 11.30 pm.

Men should note, to save themselves red faces, that the first carriage is reserved for women only.

Tram

The bulk of Cairo's trams (known to Cairenes, confusingly for outsiders, as 'metros') have been phased out. Only three lines run in the north-east of town, merging at Midan Roxy in Heliopolis, and coming from Nozha, Merghany and Abdel Aziz Fahmy.

The trams are as cheap, and often as crowded, as the buses. Until mid-1993 they ran into central Cairo, but the lines behind the Egyptian Museum have been torn up.

Taxi

A taxi is one of the most convenient ways to get around Cairo. Fares should be no more than E£3 for a cross-town ride of up to about 30 minutes (short hops are less), although you'll often have to fight not to be charged much more. The best way to check the latest fares is to ask a local.

If possible, don't set the price unless the ride is especially long, such as from central Cairo to the airport (E£15 to E£20) or the pyramids (about E£10). Wait until you arrive at your destination, get out of the car, pay the driver through the window, and walk away. Sometimes the driver will yell for more money or even (rarely) jump out of the car, rip open his shirt like Superman and pound on his chest. If he adopts the latter technique then it's possible you really have underpaid him!

For more information on the different sorts of taxis and how to flag them down, see the Getting Around chapter.

Waterbus

Two waterbuses leave from the Maspero landing in front of the big, round Radio & Television building (see Central Cairo map) and go north as far as the Nile barrages and Qanater. One stops en route at Imbaba, not far from the camel market. Other waterbuses go south and stop near Cairo University, Old Cairo and Maadi. The fare costs only 10 to 15 pt.

Car

If you're crazy enough to want to battle the traffic in Cairo, there are several car rental agencies in the city, including the 'big three' – Avis, Hertz and Budget. Their rates and terms vary and change. See the Getting Around chapter for more details.

Around Cairo

The region around Cairo offers some of Egypt's most interesting attractions, including the ancient tombs and pyramids of Saqqara, Al-Faiyum – one of the world's largest oases – and the medieval monasteries of Wadi Natrun. Most of the destinations described in this chapter can be visited on day trips from Cairo.

MEMPHIS

Memphis, once the glorious Old Kingdom capital of Egypt, has almost completely vanished. It is believed that the city was founded around 3100 BC, probably by King Menes, when Upper and Lower Egypt were first united. It had many splendid palaces and gardens, and was one of the most renowned and populous cities of the ancient world. Like most Egyptian cities with any degree of importance, Memphis also had its own deity, the all-powerful creator-god Ptah, who formed the world with words from his tongue and heart.

Even as late as the 5th century BC, long after Thebes had taken over as capital of Egypt, Memphis was described by the Greek historian Herodotus as a 'prosperous city and cosmopolitan centre'. Its enduring importance, even then, was reflected in the size of its cemetery on the west bank of the Nile, an area replete with royal pyramids, private tombs and sacred animal necropolises. This city of the dead, centred at Saqqara, covers 30 km along the edge of the desert, from Dahshur to Giza.

Centuries of annual floods have inundated the city with Nile mud, while other ancient buildings and monuments have long since been ploughed over and cultivated by the fellahin. Today there are few signs of the grandeur of Memphis: in fact, it's extremely difficult to imagine that a city once stood where there is now only a small museum and some statues in a garden. The museum contains a colossal limestone statue of Ramses II, similar to the one which stands at the centre of Midan Ramses in Cairo. This one, however, is a lot more neglected and damaged.

In the garden there are more statues of Ramses II, an eight-tonne alabaster sphinx, the sarcophagus of Amenhotep and the alabaster beds on which the sacred Apis bulls were mummified before being placed in the Serapeum at Saqqara. The museum is closed for restoration, but you can still see the statue from just outside – and pay for the privilege. Admission is E£7 and half for students. It's open from 9 am to 5 pm. There is an extraordinarily overpriced cafeteria across the road where you could swear they are growing the oranges prior to making you a fruit juice.

Getting There & Away

Memphis is 24 km south of Cairo and three km from Saqqara. The cheapest way to get there from Cairo is to take the 3rd-class train from Ramses Station at about 10.20 am from platform eight to Al-Manashy, and get off at Al-Badrashein village; the trip takes about two hours (that's right – two hours to go 24 km!) and costs 35 pt. From the village, you can either walk for about half an hour, catch a Saqqara microbus for 25 pt or take a taxi.

Rather than catch the slow train, you could just as easily go via Helwan on the metro and get a boat across the Nile to Al-Badrashein. See the Saqqara Getting There & Away section for more details of transport into and out of this area.

One way of getting to Memphis is to gather six or seven people and hire a service taxi (Peugeot 504) for about E£50 to E£60 for a day trip that also includes Saqqara.

SAQQARA

When Memphis was the capital of Egypt, during the Old Kingdom period, Saqqara was its necropolis. Deceased Pharaohs, family members and sacred animals were ceremoniously transported from Memphis to be permanently enshrined in one of the

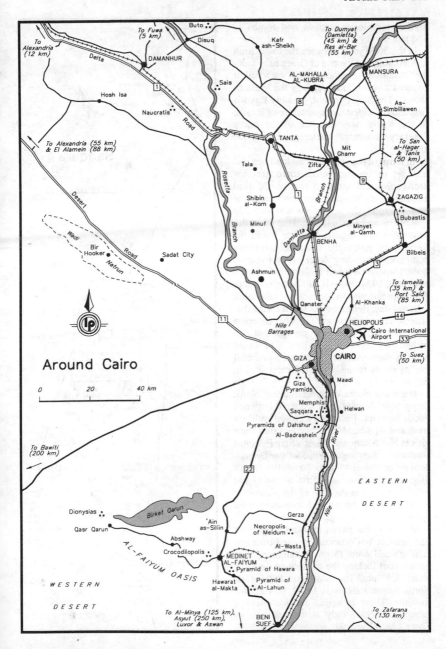

Around Cairo

0   20   40 km

To Alexandria (12 km)

To Fuwa (5 km)

Buto

Disuq

Kafr ash-Sheikh

To Dumyat (Damietta) (45 km) & Ras al-Bar (55 km)

Delta

DAMANHUR

Sais

AL-MAHALLA AL-KUBRA

MANSURA

Hosh Isa

Naucratis

8

As-Simbillawen

To Alexandria (55 km) & El Alamein (88 km)

Rosetta Branch Road

TANTA

Mit Ghamr

To San al-Hagar & Tanis (50 km)

Tala

Zifta

Desert Road

Wadi Natrun

Bir Hooker

Sadat City

Shibin al-Kom

1

Damietta Branch

9

ZAGAZIG

Bubastis

Minuf

Minyet al-Qamh

Ashmun

BENHA

Bilbeis

3

To Ismailia (35 km) & Port Said (85 km)

Qanater

Al-Khanka

11

Nile Barrages

HELIOPOLIS

Cairo International Airport

44

33

GIZA

CAIRO

To Suez (50 km)

Giza Pyramids

Maadi

Memphis

Saqqara

Helwan

Pyramids of Dahshur

Al-Badrashein

To Bawiti (200 km)

22

River Nile

EASTERN DESERT

3

Dionysias

Birket Qarun

Gerza

Qasr Qarun

'Ain as-Sillin

Necropolis of Meidum

Abshway

Al-Wasta

Crocodilopolis

MEDINET AL-FAIYUM

AL-FAIYUM OASIS

Pyramid of Hawara

Hawarat al-Makta

Pyramid of Al-Lahun

WESTERN DESERT

To Al-Minya (125 km), Asyut (250 km), Luxor & Aswan

BENI SUEF

To Zafarana (130 km)

myriad temples, pyramids and tombs at Saqqara.

In the 3000 years between the foundation of Memphis and the end of Greek rule under the Ptolemies, the necropolis grew till it covered a seven km stretch of the Western Desert. The Step Pyramid, possibly Egypt's first and the oldest stone structure of its size in the world, was just one of the many funerary monuments and temples built in the area.

In terms of the value of what has been and has yet to be uncovered, there are few archaeological sites in the world that compare with Saqqara; yet, apart from the Step Pyramid, the necropolis was virtually ignored by archaeologists until the mid-19th century, when Auguste Mariette found the Serapeum. Even the massive mortuary complex surrounding Zoser's Step Pyramid wasn't discovered and reclaimed from the sand until 1924, and it is still being restored. A worthwhile visit to Saqqara will take more than one day. Because of its size it seems that other visitors are few and far between, apart from the organised tour groups that are rushed through in the mornings. You'll find here, in the middle of the desert, a peaceful quality rarely found at other ancient sites in Egypt.

The main places of interest are in North Saqqara, with other sites scattered between South Saqqara, Dahshur (a closed military area) and Abu Sir. Most travellers start their visit in North Saqqara (Zoser's Step Pyramid area) and, if they are up to it, continue by taxi, donkey or camel to Abu Sir and/or South Saqqara. However, ask first at the ticket office, which is at the base of the plateau of North Saqqara, about which monuments are open.

Most of the pyramids and tombs at Saqqara can be 'officially' visited between 7.30 am and 4 pm (5 pm in summer). The guards start locking the monument doors at about 3.30 pm. The admission fee for all North Saqqara sights is E£10, or E£5 for students. There is a E£5 fee for using a camera, collected only at the entrance to Zoser's Step Pyramid.

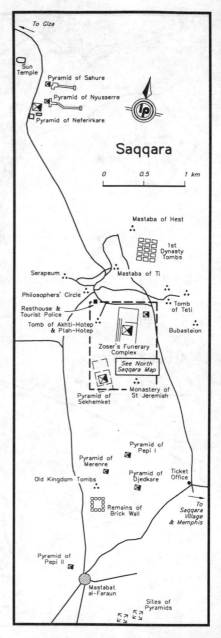

Step Pyramid

When it was constructed by Imhotep, the Pharaoh's chief architect, in the 27th century BC, the Step Pyramid of King Zoser was the largest stone structure ever built. It is still the most noticeable feature of Saqqara. Imhotep's brilliant use of stone, and his daring break with the tradition of building royal tombs as underground rooms with the occasional mud-brick mastaba (the flat tomb superstructure common at the time), was the inspiration for Egypt's future architectural achievements.

The pyramid began as a simple mastaba, but Imhotep added to it five times. With each level of stone he gained confidence in his use of the new medium and mastered the techniques required to move, place and secure the huge blocks. This first pyramid rose to over 62 metres, in six steps, before it was sheathed in fine limestone.

The Step Pyramid dominates Zoser's mortuary complex, which is 544 metres long and 277 metres wide and was once surrounded by a magnificent bastioned and panelled limestone wall. Part of the enclosure wall survives, to a height of over 4.5 metres, and a section near the south-eastern corner has been restored, with stones found in the desert, to its original 10-metre elevation. In the enclosure wall, the many false doors which were carved and painted to resemble real wood with hinges and sockets allowed the Pharaoh's ka, or attendant spirit, to come and go at will.

For the living there is only one entrance, on the south-eastern corner, via a vestibule and along a colonnaded corridor into the broad Hypostyle Hall. The 40 pillars in the corridor are the original 'bundle columns', ribbed to resemble a bundle of palm stems. The walls have been restored, but the protective ceiling is modern concrete. The roof of the Hypostyle Hall is supported by four impressive bundle columns and there's a large, false, half-open ka door. Here you will be accosted by a bevy of 'guides' eager to show you around.

The hall leads into the Great South Court, a huge open area flanking the south side of

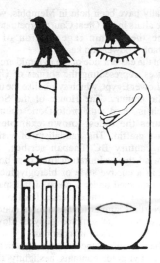

Zoser's Cartouche

the pyramid, with a rebuilt section of wall featuring a frieze of cobras. The cobra, or uraeus, was a symbol of Egyptian royalty, a fire-spitting agent of destruction and protector of the king. A rearing cobra, its hood inflated, always formed part of a Pharaoh's headdress.

Near the frieze is a shaft that plunges 28 metres to the floor of Zoser's Southern Tomb, which is similar in decoration to the main tomb beneath the Step Pyramid. Originally, it probably stored the canopic jars containing the Pharaoh's preserved internal organs.

In the centre of the Great Court are two stone altars representing the thrones of Upper and Lower Egypt. During the 30th year of a Pharaoh's reign it was traditional for him to renew his rule by re-enacting his coronation. In a ritual called the Heb-Sed Race, he would sit first on one throne and then on the other to symbolise the unification of Egypt. He would also, during the five-day jubilee, present all the provincial priests with gifts, obliging them to recognise his supremacy over their local gods. The jubilee would actually have been held in Memphis, while these altars in the Great Court perpetuated in stone the cosmic regeneration of the Pharaoh's power and ka.

On the eastern side of the pyramid are two 'houses' representing the shrines of Upper and Lower Egypt, which symbolise the unity of the country. The House of the South, which is faced with proto-Doric columns, features the oldest known examples of tourist graffiti. The vandalism of visiting 12th century BC Theban scribes, who scrawled their admiration for Zoser on the wall in a cursive style of hieroglyphics, is now protected under a piece of transparent plastic just inside the entrance. The House of the North is similar to its southern counterpart, except that sculpted papyrus flowers grace the capitals of its columns.

The Serdab, a stone structure right in front of the pyramid, contains a slightly tilted wooden box with two holes drilled into its north face. Look through these and you'll have the eerie experience of coming face to face with Zoser himself. Inside is a life-size, lifelike painted statue of the long-dead king, gazing stonily out towards the stars. Although it's only a copy (the original is in the Egyptian Museum), it is still quite haunting. Serdabs were designed so that the Pharaoh's ka could communicate with the outside world. The original entrance to the Step Pyramid is directly behind the Serdab, but is closed to the public.

Pyramid & Causeway of Unas

What appears to be a big mound of rubble to the south-west of Zoser's tomb is actually the Pyramid of Unas, the last Pharaoh of the 5th dynasty. This is one of the easiest pyramids to visit at Saqqara, which means if there's a tour group in the area it will probably be crowded. The entrance is on the north face along a 1.4-metre-high passage.

Only 350 years after the inspired creation of the Step Pyramid, and after the perfection of the Great Pyramids of Giza, this unassuming pile of loose blocks and dirt was built. In fact, despite the tomb's exterior, it marked the beginning of a trend in design. Until

Unas' time (24th century BC), pyramid interiors had been unadorned – so while the outside of his tomb looks more like Zoser's than Cheops', the inside is of immense historical importance.

In 1881, Thomas Cook & Sons sponsored the excavation of the tomb by Gaston Maspero, who found the walls covered in hieroglyphs. Carved into the huge slabs of white alabaster, these so-called Pyramid Texts are the earliest known examples of decorative writing in a Pharaonic tomb chamber. The texts record the rituals, prayers and hymns that accompanied the Pharaoh's burial to enable the release of his ka, and list the articles, like food and clothing, necessary for his existence in the afterlife.

Part of the one km causeway, which ran from the east side of the Pyramid of Unas, has been restored. On either side of it more than 200 mastabas have been excavated and there are several well-preserved tombs, some of which can be visited. The beautiful tomb of the 5th dynasty princess Idut, who was probably a daughter of Unas, is next to the southern wall of Zoser's complex. On the walls of its 10 chambers are colourful scenes of oxen, gazelle, ibex, hippopotamuses and other animals. The Mastaba of Queen Nebet and the Mastaba of Mehu are also beautifully decorated; and the Tomb of Nebkau-Her, which may be closed, is worth visiting if you can gain access.

Egyptologists debate whether the huge, sculpted boat pits, made of stone and located south of the causeway, actually held the royal barges which took the Pharaoh on his journey to the afterlife, or whether they merely represented these solar boats. Nothing was found when the 40-metre-long crescent-shaped trenches were excavated.

Persian Tombs

The tombs of three Persian noblemen, just south of the Pyramid of Unas, are some of the deepest subterranean burial chambers in Egypt. The entrance is covered by a small inconspicuous wooden hut, to which a guard in the area has the key. If you don't have your own torch he will lead you the 25 metres

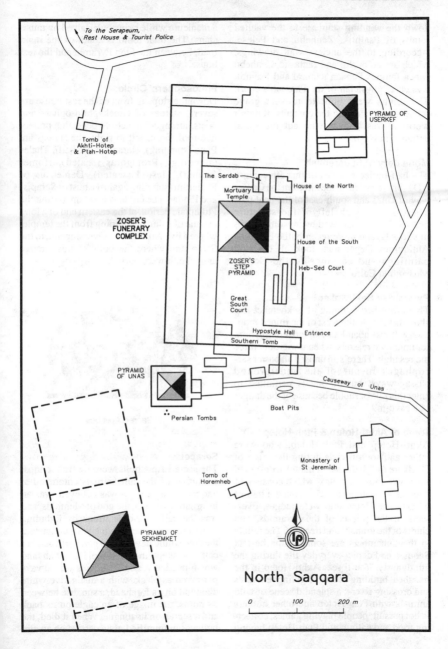

To the Serapeum,
Rest House & Tourist Police

Tomb of
Akhti-Hotep
& Ptah-Hotep

PYRAMID OF
USERKEF

ZOSER'S
FUNERARY
COMPLEX

The Serdab

Mortuary
Temple

House of the North

House of the South

ZOSER'S
STEP
PYRAMID

Heb-Sed Court

Great
South
Court

Hypostyle Hall   Entrance

Southern Tomb

PYRAMID
OF UNAS

Causeway of Unas

Boat Pits

Persian Tombs

Monastery
of St Jeremiah

Tomb of
Horemheb

PYRAMID OF
SEKHEMKET

North Saqqara

0   100   200 m

down the winding staircase to the vaulted tombs of Psamtik, Zenhebu and Pelese. According to the ancient wall drawings, which are colourful and fantastic, Zenhebu was a famous Persian admiral and Psamtik was chief physician of the Pharaoh's court. The tombs were built to prevent grave robbers from stealing the contents. It didn't work: it was thieves who cut the spiral entrance passage.

Monastery of St Jeremiah

The half-buried remains of this 5th century AD monastery are up the hill from the Causeway of Unas and south-east of the boat pits. There's not much left of the structure because it was ransacked by invading Arabs in 950 AD, and more recently the Egyptian Antiquities Department took all the wall paintings and carvings to the Coptic Museum in Cairo.

Pyramid of Sekhemket

The unfinished Pyramid of Sekhemket is a short distance to the west of the ruined monastery. It was abandoned before completion, for unknown reasons, when it was only three metres high. There's an unused alabaster sarcophagus in one of the underground passageways, but no-one is permitted to enter this pile of rubble because of the danger of a cave-in.

Tomb of Akhti-Hotep & Ptah-Hotep

Akhti-Hotep and Ptah-Hotep, who were father and son officials during the reign of Djedkare (a 5th dynasty Pharaoh), designed their own tomb complex, which consists of two burial chambers, a chapel and a hall of pillars. The Hotep duo were judges, overseers of the priests of the pyramids, and chiefs of the granary and treasury. The reliefs in their chambers are some of the best at Saqqara and depict everyday life during the 5th dynasty. You'll see: Akhti-Hotep in the marshes building boats, fighting enemies and crossing rivers; a splendid scene of wild animals with Ptah-Hotep and other hunters in hot pursuit; people playing games, collecting food and eating; and Ptah-Hotep having

a manicure while being entertained by musicians. The dual tomb is south of the main road, between the Step Pyramid and the rest house.

Philosophers' Circle

Down the slope in front of the rest house are several statues of Greek philosophers and poets, arranged in a circle beneath a protective roof. From left to right, the statues are Plato (standing), Heraclitus (seated), Thales (standing), Protagoras (seated), Homer (seated), Hesiod (seated), Demetrius of Phalerum (standing against a bust of Serapis) and Pindar. The circle was set up, during the Ptolemaic period, at the eastern end of a long avenue of sphinxes running from the temple, where a live Apis bull was worshipped, to the Serapeum, where the bulls of this strange animal cult were buried.

Sacred Apis bull

Serapeum

The sacred Apis bulls were by far the most important of the cult animals entombed at Saqqara. The Apis, it was believed, was an incarnation of Ptah, the god of Memphis, and was the calf of a cow struck by lightning from heaven. Once divinely impregnated, the cow would never again give birth and her calf was kept in the temple of Ptah and worshipped as a god. The Apis was always portrayed as black, with a distinctive white diamond on its forehead, a sun disc between its horns, the image of an eagle on its back and a scarab on its tongue. When it died, the bull was mummified, then carried on an alabaster bed to the subterranean galleries of the Serapeum at Saqqara, and placed in a huge sarcophagus.

The Apis catacombs date from the 13th century BC, when Ramses II began the first gallery, which reached a length of 68 metres. In the 7th century BC Psammetichus I cut a new gallery, which was extended by the Ptolemies to a length of 198 metres, and used till around 30 BC. Twenty-five Apis were embalmed and stabled in perpetuity here in monolithic granite coffins weighing up to 70 tonnes each. Only one mummified bull, now in the Cairo Agricultural Museum, was found when the Serapeum was excavated.

Until 1851, the existence of the sacred Apis tombs was known only from classical references. Having found a half-buried sphinx at Saqqara, and following the description given by the Greek historian Strabo in 24 BC, the French archaeologist Auguste Mariette began digging, and uncovered the avenue of sphinxes leading to the Serapeum. His great discovery sparked the extensive and continuing excavation of Saqqara. In 1856 Mariette wrote that he'd been so profoundly struck with astonishment on first gaining access to the Apis vaults, five years before, that the feeling was still fresh in his mind. Only one chamber, walled up during the reign of Ramses II, had escaped the notice of tomb robbers. Finding it intact, Mariette wrote:

The finger marks of the Egyptian who had inserted the last stone in the wall built to conceal the doorway were still recognisable on the lime. There were also the marks of naked feet imprinted on the sand which lay in one corner of the tomb chamber. Everything was in its original condition in this tomb where the embalmed remains of the bull had lain undisturbed for 37 centuries.

The entrance to the Serapeum is near the rest house, on the main road, west of the Philosophers' Circle. It's very likely you'll experience the same feeling as Mariette, for this place is definitely weird and gets stranger still as you wander along galleries lit only by tiny lanterns that cast a murky light over the vaults and the enormous, macabre black sarcophagi they contain. The largest sarcophagus, at the end of the main gallery, was carved from a single piece of black granite and is covered in hieroglyphs.

Mastaba of Ti

This tomb, or mastaba, is one of the main sources of knowledge about life in Egypt towards the end of the Old Kingdom. Ti, an important court official who served under three Pharaohs, collected titles like his kings collected slaves. He was Lord of Secrets, Superintendent of Works, Overseer of the Pyramids of Abu Sir, Counsellor to the Pharaoh and even Royal Hairdresser. He married a woman of royal blood and the inscriptions on the walls of his tomb reveal that his children were rated as royalty. One of the best reliefs depicts Ti standing regally on a boat sailing through papyrus marshes, while others show men and women at various jobs like ploughing, ship-building, reaping grain and feeding cranes. The tomb, discovered by Mariette in 1865, is a few hundred metres north of the Philosophers' Circle.

Tombs of Teti, Mereruka & Ankhma-Hor

The avenue of sphinxes excavated by Mariette in the 1850s has again been engulfed by desert sands, but it once extended as far east as the Tomb of Teti. To get to this somewhat weathered tomb now, you must follow the road from the rest house, heading a little to the north once you've passed the Step Pyramid. The interior is often closed to the public but is worth seeing if you can get in.

Nearby is the Tomb of Mereruka, which has 30 rooms, many with magnificent wall inscriptions. Egyptologists have learned a great deal about the wildlife of ancient Egypt from these drawings. As you enter the tomb, notice on one of the walls the large-mouthed, sharp-tusked hippopotamuses. The Tomb of Ankhma-Hor, a little further east, contains some very interesting scenes depicting 6th dynasty surgical operations, including toe surgery and a circumcision.

Mummified Animals

Excavations in this area have also uncovered several temples. They include the Anubieion, sacred to the jackal-headed Anubis, god of embalming and the dead, which has a gallery for dogs; the Bubasteion, sacred to the cat-goddess Bastet, which is filled with mummified cats; as well as other galleries with thousands of mummified birds and monkeys.

Abu Sir

The three pyramids of Abu Sir, at the edge of the desert, surrounded by a sea of sand dunes, formed part of a 5th dynasty necropolis. There were originally 14 pyramids at Abu Sir. Those that remain are mostly just mounds of rubble and are closed.

Pyramid of Neferirkare Neferirkare's tomb is one of the best in the area and stands 45 metres high. It now resembles Zoser's Step Pyramid but, like the Giza pyramids, originally had an outer casing of stone.

Pyramid of Nyuserre Though the most dilapidated of the three, the Pyramid of Nyuserre has a causeway that runs to what's left of his mortuary temple to the south-east.

Pyramid of Sahure This is the most complete and the northernmost of the group. The entrance is open but it's only half a metre high – you have to crawl along for about two metres through Pharaonic dust and spider webs to get into the Pharaoh's tomb. The remains of Sahure's mortuary temple still stand nearby. From his pyramid, on a clear day, you can see as many as 10 pyramids stretching out before you to the horizon.

Other Monuments

North of the temple there are several interesting monuments, including several mastabas and the Tomb of Ptahshepses, who was a court official and relative of King Nyuserre. If you happen to be going to Abu Sir by camel, horse or donkey across the desert from Giza, then stop off at the 5th dynasty Sun Temple of Abu Ghorab. It was built by King Nyuserre in honour of the sun-god Ra. The huge altar is made from five big blocks of alabaster and once served as the base of a large solar obelisk. Very few travellers ever make it this far off the beaten track.

Mastabat al-Faraun

The oldest structure in the South Saqqara area is the unusual mortuary complex of the 4th dynasty king Shepseskaf, believed to be a son of Mycerinus. Shepseskaf's tomb is neither a mastaba nor a pyramid. The Mastabat al-Faraun, or 'Pharaoh's bench', is an enormous stone structure resembling a sarcophagus topped with a rounded lid. The complex once covered 700 square metres and the interior consists of long passageways and a burial chamber. It is possible to enter the tomb if you can find a guard.

Southern Pyramids

The pyramids of the 6th dynasty Pharaohs Pepi I, Merenre and Pepi II, who made the move to South Saqqara, have been cleared of sand and feature some interesting hieroglyphic texts. The crumbling southernmost pyramids, built of sun-dried bricks, belong to 13th dynasty Pharaohs.

Pyramid of Pepi II A little north of the Mastabat al-Faraun is the pyramid of this 6th dynasty Pharaoh, who allegedly ruled for 94 years. Pepi II's tomb contains some fine hieroglyphs. The ruins of his mortuary temple, which was once connected to the pyramid by a causeway, can also be explored. Nearby, to the west, are the remains of the pyramids of Queen Apuit and Queen Neith.

Pyramid of Djedkare North of what's left of Pepi II's valley temple is the tomb of Djedkare, a 5th dynasty Pharaoh. Known as Ahram ash-Shawaf, or 'pyramid of the sentinel', it stands 25 metres high and can be entered through a tunnel on the north side.

Getting There & Away

Saqqara is about 25 km south-west of Cairo and three km north-west of Memphis. If you are coming from Memphis, take the Giza road north, then turn west about half a km after Saqqara village and the desert site will be straight ahead. If you're coming from Cairo or Giza, you have several options. Refer to the Memphis Getting There & Away section for details on the train. The train from Cairo to the village of Al-Badrashein also goes to Dahshur; a taxi from either to North Saqqara should cost about E£5.

Bus One of the cheapest ways of getting to Saqqara without going via Memphis is to take a bus or minibus (10 to 35 pt) to the Pyramids Rd (see Giza Getting There & Away) and get off at the Maryutia Canal (Saqqara Rd) stop. From the canal, you can get a microbus to Abu Sir (50 pt), from where you can pick up another to Saqqara and on to Saqqara village for 25 pt.

Metro, Boat & Microbus If you want to go via Memphis, a fairly quick way from the Midan Tahrir part of town is to take the metro to the end of the line, Helwan (60 pt), a microbus (don't believe it if you're told there are none) for 25 pt from the station to the boat landing (ask for the *markib lil-Badrashein* – 15 pt) and another microbus to Saqqara village, from where it's about a three-km walk to the Saqqara ticket office, or you may get a lift with an Abu Sir-bound microbus. If you want to visit Memphis along the way, just hop off the Saqqara village microbus and pick up another when you want to go on. There is usually a fair amount of traffic – the odd service taxi and microbus, along the Saqqara to Abu Sir road, which is a very colourful bit of Egyptian countryside to travel through. The easiest way to get to the Abu Sir pyramids is to get one of these microbuses from Saqqara.

From Al-Badrashein, by the way, there are sometimes direct microbuses to Giza.

Taxi A taxi from Giza to Saqqara should cost about E£15. There are plenty of taxis available for the return journey. The odd service taxi also passes by from Saqqara to Giza for E£2 a head.

Camel The most adventurous, although physically strenuous, option is to hire a camel, donkey or horse and cross the desert from the Great Pyramids of Giza to Saqqara. This takes at least eight hours for a round trip so make sure you're prepared for it. Unless you're accustomed to it, that amount of time spent on an animal will make sitting down rather difficult for a few days.

Animals can be hired from the stables near the Hotel Mena House and the Giza pyramids. See also the Horse-Riding section in the Cairo chapter for more details.

Getting Around

If you haven't already crossed the desert from Giza on your own beast of burden, the ideal way to visit the sights is to hire a camel, horse or donkey at North Saqqara.

They can be hired at the rest house near the Serapeum in North Saqqara. A trip around North Saqqara should cost, after bargaining, E£4 for a camel or horse. Many of the animals wear blanket saddles emblazoned with the logos of various foreign tour operators and airlines, so don't be surprised to see a camel flying past with a Lufthansa or TWA sign on its side.

DAHSHUR

If you want to go to Dahshur, first check with the tourist office in Cairo to see if you still need permission from the Ministry of the Interior offices in Abbassiya (Cairo), as Dahshur is considered a military zone. The tourist police at the Giza pyramids may be able to help, but there is no guarantee of this. If it all seems too much trouble, take heart in the fact that you can see them in the distance from Saqqara.

This southern extension of the necropolis of Memphis is a field of royal tombs, about 3.5 km long, just west of the village of Dahshur.

The Bent and Red pyramids were both built by Pharaoh Sneferu, the father of Cheops and founder of the 4th dynasty. Why Sneferu had two pyramids, and possibly a third at Meidum, is a mystery that has not been altogether solved by Egyptologists. If the purpose of a pyramid was to be a container for the Pharaoh's ka, then why would one Pharaoh with one ka need more than one tomb?

The other two dilapidated pyramids at Dahshur, which belong to 12th dynasty Pharaohs Amenemhet III and Sesostris III, are less interesting and really only for those with pyramid fever. Around all the pyramids there are also the customary tombs of the members of the royal families, court officials and priests.

Bent Pyramid

This is the most conspicuous of the four pyramids at Dahshur. Although its rather strange shape seems to suggest otherwise, this tomb and the Pyramid of Meidum, also built (or at least completed) by Sneferu, demonstrate the design transition from step pyramid to true pyramid.

For some reason, though, just a little over half way up its 105-metre height, the angle of its exterior was reduced from 52° to 43.5°, giving it its distinctive blunt shape. The reason for the change in design is not known, but perhaps it was believed the initial angle was too steep to be stable. If it was considered unsafe it could explain why Sneferu

built another tomb only two km away, the so-called Red Pyramid, which rises at a constant angle of 43.5°.

Most of the Bent Pyramid's outer casing is still intact and it is unique in having two entrances. Nearby are the remains of the mortuary temple and further north are the ruins of Sneferu's valley temple, which yielded some interesting reliefs.

Getting There & Away

See the Saqqara Getting There & Away section for details. You can get a microbus to Dahshur along the road from Abu Sir or from Saqqara village.

HELWAN

Helwan, an industrial suburb of some 40,000 people, is about 25 km south of Cairo. At one time this was probably quite a pleasant place, but as a factory city it grew quickly and is now probably the most polluted area in Egypt. There are, however, a few unique things that are almost worth seeing.

Japanese Gardens

Strange as it may seem, Helwan is home to the only Japanese gardens in the Middle East. Although most of the grounds are scruffy and overgrown with weeds, and the once-grand duck ponds now have more squawking human bathers than quacking ducks, it is still obvious that this was once a magnificent place. It's worth seeing if only to check out the row of red Buddhas – probably one of the last things you expect to see in Egypt. To get to the gardens, head east (left from in front of the train station) for about 500 metres – they are at the end of the street. Admission is 50 pt and, believe it or not, they want another 50 pt for photography.

Wax Museum

Helwan's Wax Museum, which depicts Egypt's history from Ramses II to Nasser in not awfully lifelike tableaus, is a little on the pitifully dusty side, but it's easy enough to get to if you're in the area. Displays include the death of Cleopatra, Roman soldiers stabbing Christians with spears, a man being hanged, scenes of peasant life and Nasser's leadership of the 1952 Revolution. Fans whir at the feet of the figures to keep them cool, although most of them look as if they've already melted once and been remoulded. The unlabelled depiction of a public hanging is a little distasteful, and some of the figures languishing in dungeons look as if they have accumulated four or five centuries' dust. The caretaker usually insists on guiding you through the museum. It's open from 9 am to 5 pm and admission costs E£1, or 50 pt for students, plus a 50 pt tip for the caretaker. To get there, get off the metro one stop before the end of the line, at 'Ain Helwan. The museum is just outside to your left. You could also walk from the Helwan station – it's about 20 minutes north – just follow the tracks.

Getting There & Away
The easiest way to get to Helwan from Cairo is to take the metro from Midan Tahrir station to Helwan, which is the end of the line (60 pt). It takes a little over half an hour.

For details of getting from Helwan to Saqqara, see the Saqqara Getting There & Away section above. Note that the reverse procedure may be a little tricky, as there does not always seem to be any transport waiting at the Helwan side of the Nile from the boat landing.

Getting Around
If you don't feel like walking around Helwan you can take a *hantour*, or horse-drawn carriage, from the station to both the Japanese Gardens and the museum.

AL-FAIYUM
About 100 km south-west of Cairo is Al-Faiyum, Egypt's largest oasis. The region of Al-Faiyum is about 70 km wide and 60 km long, including the lake known as Birket Qarun. Home to more than 1.8 million people, it is an intricately irrigated and extremely fertile basin watered by the Nile via hundreds of capillary canals.

The region was once filled by Birket Qarun, which is fed by the Bahr Yusef, or

'river of Joseph', a tributary that leaves the Nile at Dairut. The lake, which lies 45 metres below sea level, now occupies only about one fifth of Al-Faiyum, on the north-western edge.

The Pharaohs of the 12th dynasty reduced the flow of water into the lake and reclaimed the land for cultivation by regulating the annual flooding of the Nile. The oasis became a favourite vacation spot for Pharaohs of the 13th dynasty, and many fine palaces were built. The Greeks later called the area Crocodilopolis, because they believed the crocodiles in Birket Qarun were sacred. A temple was built in honour of Sobek, the crocodile-headed god, and during Ptolemaic and Roman times pilgrims came from all over the ancient world to feed the sacred beasts. Al-Faiyum has been called the garden of Egypt: lush fields of vegetables and sugar cane, and groves of citrus fruits, nuts and olives produce abundant harvests; the lake, canals and vegetation support an amazing variety of bird life; and the customs, living conditions and agricultural practices in the mud-brick villages throughout the oasis have changed very little in centuries. All this tradition and fertility, however, surrounds the rather grimy Medinet al-Faiyum, or 'town of the Faiyum', which sadly is a microcosm of everything that is bad about Cairo: horn-happy drivers, choking fumes and dust, crowded streets and a population of more than 350,000.

Orientation
The bulk of the hotels and useful offices are gathered around the water wheels in the centre of town by the canal. The bus and taxi stations, unfortunately, are all a bit of a hike from the centre.

Information
Tourist Offices There are tourist offices by the water wheels in Medinet al-Faiyum (open – supposedly – from 8 am to 3 pm seven days a week), at 'Ain as-Siliin and about half way along the road between Beni Suef and Medinet al-Faiyum. The people in the office near the wheels don't speak much

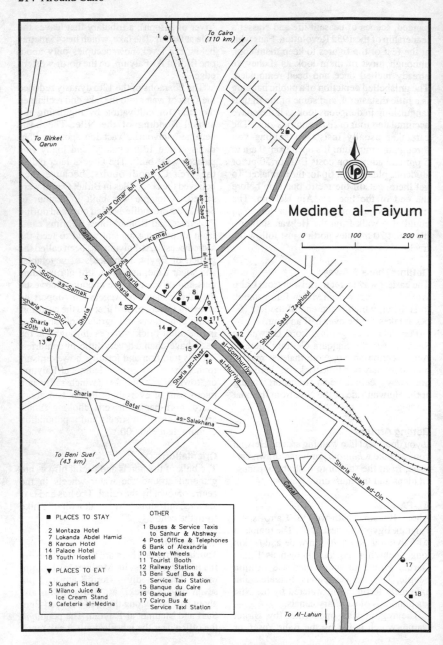

Medinet al-Faiyum

0   100   200 m

To Cairo
(110 km)

To Birket
Qarun

Sharia Omar Ibn Abd al-Aziz

Sharia as-Saad

Kamel

Mustapha

Sharia

al-Ali

Sh' Souq as-Samak

Sharia as-Shut

Sharia
20th July

Sharia Saad Zaghloul

al-Gomhuriya

al-Hurriya

Sharia an-Nasr

Sharia
Batal

as-Salakhana

To Beni Suef
(43 km)

Sharia Salah ad-Din

To Al-Lahun

■ PLACES TO STAY

2   Montaza Hotel
5   Lokanda Abdel Hamid
8   Karoun Hotel
14 Palace Hotel
18 Youth Hostel

▼ PLACES TO EAT

3   Kushari Stand
5   Milano Juice &
    Ice Cream Stand
9   Cafeteria al-Medina

OTHER

1   Buses & Service Taxis
    to Sanhur & Abshway
4   Post Office & Telephones
6   Bank of Alexandria
10 Water Wheels
11 Tourist Booth
12 Railway Station
13 Beni Suef Bus &
    Service Taxi Station
15 Banque du Caire
16 Banque Misr
17 Cairo Bus &
    Service Taxi Station

English, but they can direct you to the train, bus or service taxi station. They also have an unclear map in Arabic.

Money Close by one another across the canal from the tourist office are the Banque Misr, the Banque du Caire and, on the same side as the tourist office, the Bank of Alexandria. You can't get cash advances on credit cards. They keep the usual hours.

Post & Telecommunications A 24-hour-a-day phone and telegraph office is also located by the canal. There is a post office in the same building, open from 8 am to 2 pm and closed on Friday.

Water Wheels
Four functioning models of the actual water wheels still in use around Al-Faiyum (in total, there are about 200 dotted around the oasis) can be seen opposite the tourist office. Irrigation water has to be obtained from the Nile rather than from Birket Qarun, as the lake is salty.

Al-Faiyum Market
This is an interesting local market which sells fruits, vegetables, and household goods such as huge aluminium pots and copper pans. You won't get hassled here – no-one speaks English.

Hawara Pyramid & Labyrinth
About 10 km south-east of Medinet al-Faiyum, on the road to Beni Suef, is the dilapidated 58-metre mud-brick Pyramid of Amenemhet III. His once vast mortuary complex is now nothing but mounds of rubble, and even his temple, which had quite a reputation in ancient times, has suffered at the hands of stone robbers. Herodotus said the temple was a 3000-room labyrinth that surpassed even the pyramids; while Strabo claimed it had as many rooms as there were provinces, so that all the Pharaoh's subjects could be represented by their local officials in the offering of sacrifices. In 24 BC, Strabo wrote:

...there are long and numerous covered ways, with winding passages communicating with each other, so that no stranger could find his way in or out of them without a guide. The roofs of these dwellings consist of a single stone each, and the covered ways are roofed in the same manner with single slabs of stone of extraordinary size, without the intermixture of timber or any other material.

The area was also used as a cemetery by the Greeks and Romans, who here adopted the Egyptian practice of mummification. Now, all that remains are pieces of mummy cloth and human bones sticking through the mounds of rubble. There's also a crocodile cemetery north-east of the pyramid. Entry is E£8, or E£4 for students. The official opening hours are 7 am to 5 pm.

Getting There & Away The buses between Beni Suef and Medinet al-Faiyum pass through Hawarat al-Makta, from where it's a short walk to the pyramid. Just ask the driver to let you off.

Pyramid of Al-Lahun
About 10 km south-east of Hawara, on the Nile side of the narrow fertile passage through the desert that connects Al-Faiyum to the river, are the ruins of a small mud-brick pyramid. Once cased in limestone, it was built by Senusert II back in the Middle Kingdom period around 1885 BC. This monument is definitely off the beaten track. Although there's not much of it left, you can climb to the top for a great view of the surrounding area. The people in the neighbouring village will probably be so surprised to see you that they'll invite you to tour their fields and houses. The hitch is the entry price slapped on a couple of years ago – E£8 and half for students.

Getting There & Away You can probably hitch from Beni Suef or Medinet al-Faiyum to the dirt road leading to the village of Al-Lahun; or take the local bus between the two cities and tell the driver where you want to stop.

Pyramid of Meidum

Standing beyond the vegetation belt, about 32 km north-east of Medinet al-Faiyum, is the ruin of the first real pyramid attempted by the ancient Egyptians. The Pyramid of Meidum is impressive, although it looks more like a stone tower than a pyramid, rising abruptly as it does from a large hill of rubble. This is one case, however, where the apparent state of disrepair was not caused by time or centuries of stone robbers, but was actually the result of one instantaneous accident. The pyramid began as an eight-stepped structure; the steps were then filled in and the outer casing was added, forming the first true pyramid shell. However, there were serious design flaws and sometime after completion (possibly as late as the time of the Ptolemaic rulers in the last centuries before Christ's birth) the pyramid's own weight caused the sides to collapse, leaving just the core that still stands today.

The pyramid was started by King Huni, but completed by his son Sneferu, the founder of the 4th dynasty. Sneferu's architects obviously learnt from the mistakes that eventually led to the disaster of Meidum, as he also built the more successful Bent and Red pyramids at Dahshur, and his son Cheops built one of the Great Pyramids at Giza.

Entrance to the site is E£8 (half for students). Ask the guard at the nearby house to unlock the entrance of the pyramid for you. You can follow the steps down 75 metres to the empty underground burial chamber.

Getting There & Away It is actually much easier to get to the pyramid from Beni Suef, about 45 km to the south, than from Medinet al-Faiyum. Get a pick-up from Beni Suef to al-Wasta for 75 pt (45 minutes). From there take another to Meidum village (35 pt), from where you'll have to walk a couple of km – unless you can get a ride.

Alternatively, you could get one of the service taxis or buses running between Beni Suef and Cairo and ask to get off at the Meidum turn-off, from where you still have about six km to go. The reverse of this is probably the easiest way to get back to Beni Suef (or go on to Cairo for that matter), just flag down a service taxi or hitch a ride.

'Ain as-Siliin

The spring waters and gardens here, about 18 km north-west of Medinet al-Faiyum, are a pleasant place to hang around for a little while, although there is really not much to do. The spring water itself is sweet to taste and is said to help in the prevention of arteriosclerosis because of the traces of titanium found in it. There is a crowd of cafés and little stores for water, biscuits and the like. It costs 25 pt to get in.

Getting There & Away From Medinet al-Faiyum, get a Sanhur service taxi or bus from the station in the west of the town (35 pt) and tell the driver where you want to get off.

Birket Qarun

This is another pleasant enough spot where there is really nothing to do, except sit at one of the beachside cafés or hire a boat for a trip out on the lake for about E£5 an hour.

There appears to be a E£2.20 (half for students) charge for wandering on to the beach, where, by the way, people don't seem to do any swimming. The 'ticket' looks a little dubious.

Getting There & Away To get here, take a Sanhur to Shakshouk pick-up (40 pt). When you see the lake and Auberge du Lac, you've arrived; get off wherever you choose. It's easy enough to get another pick-up going either way along the south bank road.

Qasr Qarun

The ruins of the ancient town of Dionysias, once the starting point for caravans to Bahariyya Oasis in the Western Desert, are just near the village of Qasr Qarun at the western end of Birket Qarun.

The Ptolemaic temple is just off to the left of the road shortly before the village, and was erected to the god of Al-Faiyum, Sobek, in the fourth century before Christ. It was partly restored in 1956. You can ask to go

19-century Nile River scene

down to the underground chambers and climb up to the top for a view of the desert, the sparse remains of Ptolemaic and Roman settlements and the oasis. Entry is E£8 (half for students).

Getting There & Away Getting out here is a bit of an ordeal, considering the relatively small distances involved. From Medinet al-Faiyum, take a service taxi or pick-up to the town of Abshway, a bit of a local transport hub (there are even buses to Cairo from here), for 50 pt (one hour) and from there another the 40 km on to Qasr Qarun (E£1, Two to three hours on poor roads).

If you're coming from the lake, you can get to Abshway from Shakshouk (50 pt).

Places to Stay
There are a few places to stay in Al-Faiyum. The *Youth Hostel*, down by the Cairo bus station, almost two km from the centre of Medinet al-Faiyum, is almost the cheapest – E£2.10 with IYHA card and E£4.10 without for a bed in a room of six. The building looks like it's been bombed out.

The cheapest, and stinkiest, is the fairly horrible *Karoun Hotel*, opposite the Cafeteria al-Medina. It has doubles for E£3, and

there's even a cold shower. Much lower you cannot go.

Trying hard to meet the same grimy standards is the *Lokanda Abdel Hamid* (just 'Hotel' in English). It's just around the corner facing the canal and has doubles for E£5 and triples for E£9. They do have hot water.

The *Montaza Hotel* (☎ 324633), almost a km north of the centre, has fairly good singles/doubles with bath and fan for E£15.20/23.20, including breakfast. The beds are of the hard variety. Follow the smaller canal north to the first bridge and take the first left and then right after it.

More comfortable and in an easier location is the *Palace Hotel* (☎ 323641). It has good, clean singles/doubles for E£20/40 with breakfast. The showers are a little temperamental.

Further out of town past the Montaza is the *Queen Hotel* (☎ 326819).

In 'Ain as-Siliin, you can get a rock-hard bed in the so-called *chalet* for E£31 with breakfast. It's not a bad place, but nothing great for the money they ask.

There are several expensive hotels out on the lake, spaced out over a few km. The one you pass first is the four-star *Auberge du Lac*. World leaders met at the original hotel on this site after WW I to decide on the borders of the Middle East; it later served as King Farouk's private hunting lodge. It's not cheap, but you could have a Stella beer in the Churchill Bar or splurge on a big lunch.

Further south are the *Oasis Hotel* and the *Panorama Shakshouk Hotel*, three-star joints that are none too cheap either. A double in the latter costs E£183, including all taxes, breakfast and dinner. They have a swimming pool built out over the lake.

Camping It is possible to camp at the lake, but watch out for the mosquitoes. Bring mosquito repellent, as the nasty little critters get a bit thick sometimes. Also prepare your nose for the slightly offensive smell of the lake; it is possible to get used to it.

Places to Eat
Aside from the standard fuul and ta'amiyya and kushari stands (there's a good one in Sharia Mustapha Kamel, not far in from Sharia al-Hurriya), there's the *Cafeteria al-Medina* in Medinet al-Faiyum, built around the water wheels, which serves shish kebab and a few other meat and chicken dishes. It's hellishly expensive, charging about E£20 for a generous but unoriginal meal. The big hotels at Birket Qarun all have restaurants and there are several at 'Ain as-Siliin.

The *Milano* juice shop does good juices, and the neighbouring ice cream stand doesn't do a bad job either. Get a bucket of vanilla and mango ice cream for E£1.

Things to Buy
Throughout Al-Faiyum, especially at 'Ain as-Siliin, you will see lots of colourful basketware and rugs. The baskets come in all shapes and sizes and cost as little as E£1 for the simplest ones. The rugs are made in cooperatives in and around Medinet al-Faiyum. If you're interested in visiting the cooperatives, ask at the tourist booth for locations. Also available are little flutes for E£1 or E£2.

Getting There & Away
Bus Buses leave regularly from the station in the east of town for the Ahmed Hilmi station behind Ramses train station in Cairo. The bus costs E£2.50 and takes about two hours. It stops at the Giza bus and service-taxi station on the way. Coming from Cairo, you're better off getting on at Ahmed Hilmi. They can get pretty full in the high season.

Buses for Beni Suef leave from a separate station in the south of the town and cost E£1 (one hour).

Train For the 3rd-class train buff, there are five daily departures from Medinet al-Faiyum to Cairo for E£1.30. Its progress must be so slow as to be barely perceptible – it takes more than four hours.

Service Taxi Service taxis leave from the bus stations. To Giza, in Cairo, they cost E£4; to Beni Suef E£1.25.

Getting Around
For details of how to get to the various sights around the oasis, see the respective entries. In Medinet al-Faiyum itself, there are green and white minibuses between the western and eastern bus stations and the centre of town *(wust al-balad)* for 25 pt.

WADI NATRUN
Wadi Natrun is a partly cultivated valley, about 100 km north-west of Cairo, that was important to the Egyptians long before the Copts took refuge there. The natron used in the mummification process came from the large deposits of sodium carbonate left when the valley's salt lakes dried up every summer.

A visit to the monasteries of Wadi Natrun should explain the endurance of the ancient Coptic Christian sect. It is the desert, in a sense, that is the protector of the Coptic faith, for it was there that thousands of Christians retreated to escape Roman persecution in the 4th century AD. They lived in caves, or built monasteries, and developed the monastic tradition that was later adopted by European Christians.

In Wadi Natrun alone there were once more than 50 monasteries, built as fortresses to protect the isolated communities from marauding Bedouins. The focal point of the monasteries was the church, around which were built a well, storerooms, a dining hall, kitchen, bakery and the monks' cells. The whole complex was surrounded by walls about 14 metres high and four metres thick, and guarded by the keep – a tower which also served as an internal fort during sieges. While only four of the monasteries survived the Romans, the Bedouin raids and the coming of Islam, the religious life they all protected is thriving. The Coptic pope is still chosen from among the Wadi Natrun monks, and monasticism is experiencing a revival, with younger Copts again donning hooded robes to live within these ancient walls in the desert.

You can visit the monasteries as a side trip en route between Cairo and Alexandria or as a day tour from either city. Before you make the journey, however, you should check with the Coptic Orthodox Patriarchate. In Cairo the Patriarchate (☎ 825863, 821274) is next to St Mark's Church, 222 Sharia Ramses, Abbassiya; in Alexandria it's on Sharia al-Kineesa al-Kobtiyya (Coptic Church St), one block behind Sharia an-Nabi Daniel. As a general rule, you can visit all but Deir Abu Makar (Makarios).

If you want to stay overnight, you must first call the monasteries' Cairo residences: Deir al-Anba Bishoi (☎ 924448); Deir as-Suriani (☎ 929658); Deir al-Baramus (☎ 922775); Deir Abu Makar (☎ 770614). Women are generally not allowed to stay overnight at the monasteries and if men wish to do so they need written permission from one of these residences. If you can't stay at one of the monasteries then you'll have to either camp or return to Cairo or Alexandria. You can generally get a simple meal of fuul or the like at the monasteries. It costs nothing, but a small donation wouldn't hurt.

Deir al-Anba Bishoi

St Bishoi founded two monasteries in Wadi Natrun, this one (which bears his name) and the nearby Deir as-Suriani. Deir al-Anba Bishoi – a great place to watch a desert sunset – contains the saint's body, which is said to be perfectly preserved under a red cloth, and the remains of Paul of Tamweh, who made quite a name for himself by committing suicide seven times. The monks there claim that it is not uncommon for St Bishoi to perform miracles for true believers.

Deir as-Suriani

Deir as-Suriani, or the 'monastery of the Syrians', is named for the many Syrian monks who once lived there; it's about 500 metres north-west of Deir al-Anba Bishoi. There are several domed churches in the gardens and courtyards of this tranquil monastery. Ask the monks to show you St Bishoi's private cell where he stood for nights on end with his hair attached to a chain dangling from the ceiling. It was during one of these marathon prayer vigils that Christ is said to have appeared and allowed Bishoi to wash His feet and then drink the water.

Deir Abu Makar (Makarios)

This monastery is south-east of Deir al-Anba Bishoi. Although structurally it has suffered worst at the hands of raiding Bedouins, it is perhaps the most renowned of the four monasteries, as over the centuries most of the Coptic popes have been selected from among its monks. It is the last resting place of many of those popes and also contains the remains of the '49 Martyrs', a group of monks killed by Bedouins in 444 AD. It is also the most secluded of the monasteries, and permission even to visit must be organised in advance.

Deir al-Baramus

The most isolated of the Wadi Natrun monasteries is that of St Baramus, which is across the desert to the north-west. It's probably the best one to stay at if you can get to it, and have permission, as it's a little less austere than the others. The special feature of its church is a superb iconostasis of inlaid ivory.

Getting There & Away

From Midan Abdel Minnim Riyadh in Cairo, near the Ramses Hilton, you can get a West Delta Bus Co bus to Wadi Natrun for E£2.75

every hour from 6.30 am. From there you have to negotiate for a taxi to head either to Deir al-Anba Bishoi and Deir as-Suriani or the other way to Deir al-Baramus. You can always try to hitch.

If you have your own vehicle and you're coming from Cairo, take Pyramids Rd (Sharia al-Ahram) through Giza and turn onto the Desert Rd just before the Hotel Mena House. At about 95 km from Cairo (just after the rest house) turn left into the wadi, go through the village of Bir Hooker and continue on, following the signs indicating the monasteries. The first one is Deir al-Anba Bishoi, Deir as-Suriani is about half a km to the north-west, Deir Abu Makar is a few km via a paved road to the south-east, and Deir al-Baramus is quite a hike through the sands to the north-west.

THE NILE DELTA

If you have the time, it's well worth the effort to explore the lush, fan-shaped Delta of Egypt between Cairo and Alexandria. This is where the Nile divides in half to flow north into the sea at the Mediterranean ports of Damietta and Rashid (Rosetta). The Delta is also laced with several smaller tributaries and is reputedly one of the most fertile and, not surprisingly, most cultivated regions in the world.

The Delta region played just as important a part in the early history of the country as did Upper Egypt, although few archaeological remains record this. While the desert and dryness of the south helped preserve the Pharaonic sites, the amazing fertility of the Delta region had the opposite effect. Over the centuries, when the ancient cities, temples and palaces of the Delta were left to ruin, they were literally ploughed into oblivion by the fellahin. The attraction of this area, then, is the chance of coming across communities rarely visited by foreigners, where you can gain a little insight into the Egyptian peasant farmer's way of life.

Although service taxis and buses crisscross the region from town to town, the best way to get off the beaten track and wander through this incredibly green countryside is

Nile Kingfisher

to hire a car. Along the back roads and canals you can visit the quaint farming villages that thrive amongst the fields of cotton, maize and rice. Theoretically, you're not supposed to leave the main roads, but in the unlikely event of you being hassled by the police you can always say you're lost.

Nile Barrages (Qanater)

The Nile Barrages and the city of Qanater (which simply means barrages) lie 16 km north of Cairo where the Nile splits into the eastern Damietta branch and the western Rosetta branch. The barrages, begun in the early 19th century, were successfully completed several decades later. The series of basins and locks, on both main branches of the Nile and two side canals, ensured the vital large-scale regulation of the Nile into the Delta region, and led to a great increase in cotton production.

The Damietta Barrage consists of 71 sluices stretching 521 metres across the river; the Rosetta Barrage is 438 metres long with 61 sluices. Between the two is a one-km-wide area filled with beautiful gardens and cafés. It's a superb place to rent a bicycle or a felucca and take a relaxing tour.

The town of Qanater, at the fork of the river, is officially the start of the Delta region.

Getting There & Away To get to the barrages from Cairo you can take a river bus for 50 pt from the water-taxi station in front of the Radio & Television building (Maspero Station), just north of the Ramses Hilton. The trip takes about two hours. A faster but less relaxing way to get there is by taking bus No 930 from Ataba bus station or Nos 210 and 212 from the bus lot in front of Ramses train station.

Zagazig

Just outside this town, founded in the 19th century, are the ruins of Bubastis, one of the most ancient cities in Egypt. There's not much to see in Zagazig itself, but as it's only 80 km north-east of Cairo it's an easy day trip to the ruins. The train heading for Port Said from Cairo takes about 1½ hours to Zagazig and a service taxi takes about one hour. There are buses to Zagazig from Cairo, Alexandria, Ismailia and Port Said (E£5). There is even a direct service from Nuweiba connecting with the ferry from Aqaba in Jordan.

Bubastis The great deity of the ancient city of Bubastis was the elegant cat-goddess Bastet. Festivals held in her honour are said to have attracted more than 700,000 revellers, who would sing, dance, feast, consume great quantities of wine and offer sacrifices to the goddess. The architectural gem of Bubastis was the Temple of Bastet, sited between two canals, surrounded by trees and encircled by the city, which was built at a higher level to look down on it. The temple was begun by Cheops and Chephren during the 4th dynasty, and Pharaohs of the 6th, 12th, 18th, 19th and 22nd dynasties made their additions over about 17 centuries. Herodotus wrote:

Although other Egyptian cities were carried to a great height, in my opinion the greatest mounds were thrown up about the city of Bubastis, in which is a temple of Bastet well worthy of mention; for though other temples may be larger and more costly, none is more pleasing to look at than this.

The temple is now just a pile of rubble, and the most interesting site at Bubastis is the cat cemetery 200 metres down the road. The series of underground galleries, where many bronze statues of cats were found, is perfect for a bit of exploration.

Tanis

Just outside the village of San al-Hagar, 70 km north-east of Zagazig, are the ruins of ancient Tanis, which many believe to be the Biblical city where the Hebrews were persecuted by the Egyptians before fleeing through the Red Sea in search of the Promised Land. It was certainly of great importance to a succession of powerful Pharaohs, all of whom left their mark through the extraordinary buildings or statues they commissioned, and for several centuries Tanis was one of the largest cities in the Delta.

Tanis covers about four sq km, only part of which has been excavated. The monuments uncovered date from as early as the 6th dynasty reign of Pepi I, around 2330 BC, through to the time of the Ptolemies in the 1st century BC. The excavation of the city so far has revealed sacred lakes, the foundations of many temples, a royal necropolis and a multitude of statues and carvings.

Although it's less impressive than other archaeological sites in the country, the Egyptian government has been promoting Tanis as a tourist destination for the past few years.

Tanis Sphinx

Tanta

Tanta, the largest city in the Delta, is 90 km from Cairo and 110 km from Alexandria. There's nothing much of interest there, although it is a centre for Sufism, a form of Islamic mysticism. A mosque in Tanta is dedicated to Sayyid Ahmed al-Badawi, a Moroccan Sufi, who fought the Crusaders from there in the 13th century and then went on to assist in the defeat of Louis IX at Damietta.

In this area of the western Delta, although there are no actual structural remains, are the sites of three ancient cities. North-west of Tanta, on the east bank of the Nile, is Sais, Egypt's 26th dynasty capital. Sacred to Neith, the goddess of war and hunting and protector of embalmed bodies, Sais dates back to the start of Egyptian history and once had palaces, temples and royal tombs.

West of Tanta, about half way along the road to Damanhur, is the site of Naucratis, an ancient city where the Greeks were allowed to settle and trade during the 7th century BC. The city of Buto, east of Damanhur and north of Tanta, was the cult centre of Edjo, the cobra-goddess of Lower Egypt, always represented on a Pharaoh's crown as a uraeus.

Getting There & Away All Alexandria to Cairo trains except the Turbos stop here. Service taxis from near the Midan Ahmed Hilmi bus station cost E£5. Middle Delta Bus Co buses from near the Ramses Hilton cost E£5.25. There are buses and service taxis from Alexandria too.

Mansura

At the centre of Egypt's cotton industry is Mansura, one of the most important cities in the Delta. The best thing about a visit to Mansura is the chance to taste the city's delicacy – buffalo milk ice cream.

Mansura is known as the 'city of victory' for the part it played in Egypt's early Islamic history. In 1249, the Egyptians retreated from the coast and set up camp at Mansura after the Crusader forces, under Louis IX of France, had captured the Mediterranean port of Damietta. When the Crusaders decided to

make their push inland, they charged straight through the Muslim camp, only to be cut down on the other side of Mansura by 10,000 Mamluk warriors. Louis himself was captured and ransomed for the return of Damietta.

Getting There & Away There are regular train connections with Cairo and a service taxi from Midan Ahmed Hilmi costs E£8. The bus from Midan Ulali costs E£6.50.

Damietta (Dumyat)

Once a prosperous Arab trading port, Damietta's fortunes suffered greatly with the construction of the Suez Canal and the subsequent development of Port Said. During the Middle Ages, its strategic position on the north coast of Egypt, at the mouth of the Nile, meant it was regularly being threatened by foreign armies. Over the centuries it was taken by the Germans, English and French, and defended by, among others, Salah ad-Din and Mohammed Ali. When it wasn't being attacked by marauding Crusaders, Damietta (Dumyat to the locals) was doing a roaring trade in coffee, linen, oil and dates, and was a port of call for ships from all over the known world. There is not much to see, but it is the easiest place from which to go on to Ras al-Bar, about 12 km to the north. There are buses from Midan Ulali in Cairo every half an hour for E£11 from 6 am to 6 pm. Regular buses to Port Said take about an hour and cost E£1.50.

Ras al-Bar

The small town of Ras al-Bar, north of Damietta, is right at the point where the eastern branch of the Nile meets the sea, 170 km north-east of Cairo. It is a pleasant beach resort, and if you're planning on staying anywhere in the Delta region this would be the best choice.

The town is actually spread over both banks of the Nile. The bulk of the local people live on the eastern side. The bulk of the hotels, restaurants and so on are on the west side, which is actually a tongue of land, with the Nile on one side and the Mediterranean on the other. Little motor ferries connect the two halves, weaving in between the flocks of deep-blue fishing trawlers.

There are other quiet little beach resorts to the west of Ras al-Bar at Gamasa, Baltim and Al-Burg.

Information The post and telephone offices are on Sharia Mahmoud Talaat, a couple of blocks north of the big mosque where buses and microbuses to Damietta terminate.

Places to Stay & Eat The place is crawling with hotels and private villas, but outside the summer season most of them are closed. Most of the streets are numbered rather than named, and the easiest thing to do is wander along the Nile-side road and duck in to the side streets wherever you see a hotel that might look OK. The *Families Hotel*, a block north of Sharia Mahmoud Talaat, costs E£10 a night. Further up, on the road next to the Nile, the *Dar al-Abyad Hotel* (the name, as with many of the smaller places, is in Arabic only), costs E£15 for a double.

Other OK hotels a bit higher up the price scale are the *Marine an-Nil* and the *Marine Ras al-Bar*, both on Sharia Mahmoud Talaat, and the *Hotel Mobasher*, which is closer to the point where the Nile spills into the sea.

There are numerous restaurants along the Nile, and on the point is one called *High Garden*. As you work your way back along the Mediterranean side, there are a couple of other restaurants, one with a sometimes-full seawater pool. Along the beach you can hire parasols and deckchairs.

There are at least two listed hotels at Baltim, both charging E£8/10 a night for singles/doubles. They are the *Baltim Beach Hotel* and the *Cleopatra Touristic Hotel*.

Getting There & Away Buses leave Cairo for Damietta every half an hour, and from there you can get another bus for 50 pt. Wine-red microbuses also cost 50 pt, but drop you about two km away from the main bus station in Damietta. In summer there are supposed to be regular buses direct from Cairo, for which you need to book ahead.

The Nile Valley – Beni Suef to Qus

The ancient Greek traveller and writer Herodotus described Egypt as 'the gift of the Nile'; the ancient Egyptians likened their land to a lotus – the Delta being the flower, the oasis of Al-Faiyum the bud and the river and its valley the stem. Whichever way you look at it, Egypt is the Nile. The river is the lifeblood of the country and the fertile Nile Valley is its heart. And whether you journey down the valley by felucca, train, bus or plane you'll discover that even an outsider cannot ignore the power of the Nile and the hold it has always had over Egyptian life.

Rain seldom falls in the Nile Valley, so the verdant stretch of land, ranging from a couple of metres to a few km wide on either side of the river, is rendered fertile only by the winding Nile as it makes its way through the barren desert. The countryside is dotted with thousands of simple villages where people toil, day in day out, using tools and machinery modelled on designs thousands of years old. Even the region's large towns and cities, like Al-Minya, Asyut, Luxor and Aswan, are in some ways merely modernised extensions of these villages.

Travelling south from Cairo you pass through a world where ancient and medieval monuments almost seem to be part of the present. From Saqqara to Luxor, while you marvel at the remarkable history of the Pharaonic tombs and their builders, you'll realise that the daily labour and recreation of the fellahin in the 20th century differs very little from the images depicted in the wall paintings of the ancient monuments. The colourful scenes of Egyptians building, hunting, fighting, feasting, harvesting and fishing more than 2500 years ago are repeated daily on the banks of the Nile and in the valley's fertile fields.

BENI SUEF

Beni Suef is a provincial capital 130 km south of Cairo. Even with a population of 150,000 and a few multistorey buildings it isn't a big town, but is typical of the large Egyptian country towns that are basically overgrown farming villages. There are more donkey carts and hantours in the streets than cars and buses. While there's nothing of particular interest in Beni Suef itself, it is a good base for visiting Al-Faiyum, and probably the best point from which to visit the Pyramid of Meidum (see under Al-Faiyum).

Information

There is a 24-hour telephone and telegraph office in the train station building, a post office just past it, and yet another telephone office after it. Just before the post office is a little tourist police booth. The Bank of Alexandria has a branch just off Midan al-Gomhurriya.

Places to Stay

The *Semiramis Hotel* (☎ 322092, 324607) is the two-star premier establishment in town and has good singles/doubles with bath, TV and breakfast for E£29.50/39.50. Without the ensuite bath, they are E£24/32. It has six singles and 24 doubles.

Across the train tracks and close to the bus and service-taxi stations is the *Hotel Rest House* (☎ 325572). It's a bit musty, but has pretty reasonable singles/doubles with bath for E£10/15. There's no breakfast, but the hot water system is pretty good.

A block back from the square in front of the train station is the *Hotel El Bakry*. Its singles/doubles with bath are E£15/17 (E£13/16 without). The price includes breakfast, but it's a rowdy place.

On the square itself is the *Hotel Dishasha* (just 'Hotel' in English). They seem rather odd here, and not overly willing to take guests. Singles/doubles, if you can and want to get in, are E£12/20.

Places to Eat

There's not an awful lot to choose from food-wise. The Semiramis, Rest House and

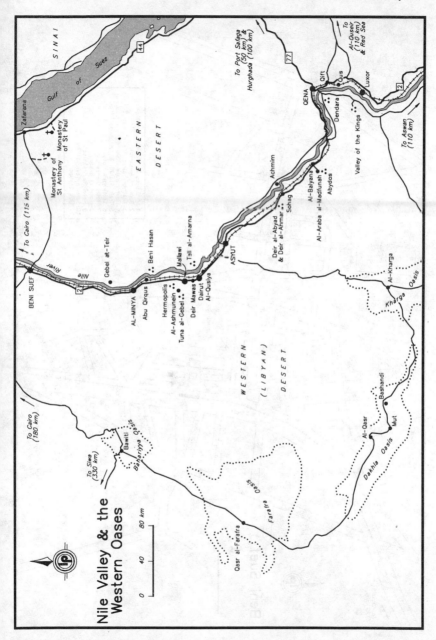

Nile Valley & the Western Oases

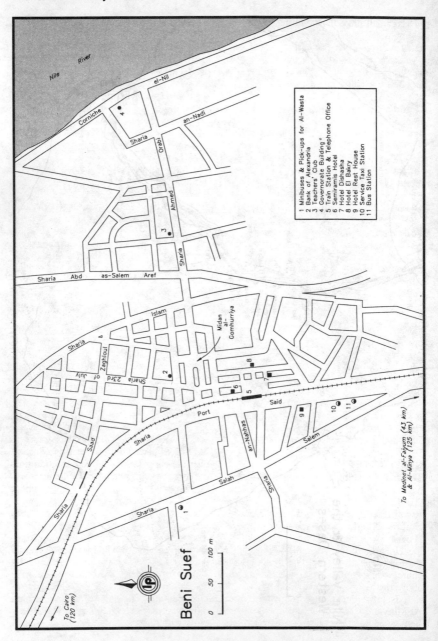

Beni Suef

1 Minibuses & Pick-ups for Al-Wasta
2 Bank of Alexandria
3 Teachers' Club
4 Governorate Building*
5 Train Station & Telephone Office
6 Semiramis Hotel
7 Hotel Dishasha
8 Hotel El Bakry
9 Hotel Rest House
10 Service Taxi Station
11 Bus Station

Nile River

Corniche el-Nil
Sharia an-Nadi
Sharia Orabi
Sharia Ahmed
Sharia Abd as-Salem Aref
Sharia Islam
Sharia Zaghloul
Sharia 23rd of July
Midan al-Gomhurriya
Sharia 2
Sharia Saad
Sharia Port Said
Sharia an-Nahhas
Sharia Salah
Sharia Salem

To Cairo (120 km)
To Medinet al-Faiyum (43 km) & Al-Minya (125 km)

0   50   100 m

El Bakry all have their own restaurants. A filling meal of kebabs, rice, potatoes and salad will cost you E£7 at the Rest House. The same will cost you about E£10 at the Semiramis. Otherwise, there are a few fuul and ta'amiyya stands about.

Getting There & Away

Beni Suef is a departure point for the trek across the desert to the Monastery of St Anthony, which is about 150 km east, near the Gulf of Suez. You'd really need your own truck or 4WD to make this journey, as it might be difficult to hire a service taxi in Beni Suef for the whole trip. But you might be able to get close taking the Hurghada bus.

Bus Buses run from about 6 am to 6 pm to Ahmed Hilmi station behind Ramses train station in Cairo for E£3.50. The trip to Al-Minya costs E£3 and the one-hour ride to Al-Faiyum E£1. There is also supposed to be one bus a day to Hurghada.

Train There are frequent connections north to Cairo and south to Al-Minya for the same prices either way: E£9.80 in 1st class; E£6 in 2nd class with air-con; and E£2.60 in normal 2nd class.

Service Taxi The station is next to the bus station. Prices are posted in Arabic. The trip to Giza costs E£3.75 and to Al-Faiyum it's E£1.25. The drivers also claim to go to Helwan for E£3.75.

GEBEL AT-TEIR

The main feature of this small Christian hamlet, 93 km south of Beni Suef, is Deir al-Adhra – the 'monastery of the Virgin'. Established as a church/monastery in the 4th century AD by the Byzantine empress Helena, it was built on one of the sites where the Holy Family supposedly rested while fleeing Palestine. Gebel at-Teir and its church are perched on a hill 130 metres above the east bank of the Nile.

It is much more quickly reached from Al-Minya, 25 km to the south, than from Beni Suef. Get a service taxi or microbus from Al-Minya to Samalut for 60 pt. From there, take a pick-up to the Nile river landing for 25 pt, where you can take the car ferry for E£1 or the felucca for the same. On the other side is a pick-up going to Deir al-Adhra, but you may find yourself paying about E£1 to get it moving, as there are not always a lot of passengers going that way. When you arrive, ask for the *kineesa*, or church, and someone will appear with the keys and give you a short tour. There are some interesting 400-year-old icons inside.

AL-MINYA

They call it the 'bride of Upper Egypt' *(Arous as-Sa'id)*, as Al-Minya more or less marks the divide between Upper and Lower Egypt. A semi-industrial provincial capital 247 km south of Cairo, it is a centre for sugar processing and the manufacture of soap and perfume. There are several hotels, which make this a convenient place to base yourself for day trips to the Pharaonic tombs and temples of Beni Hasan, Tuna al-Gebel and Hermopolis.

There's not much to see or do in town, except just walk around and meet some of the friendly local people, most of whom will be extremely interested in whether or not you're married. The tree-lined Corniche along the Nile is a pleasant place for a picnic or a ride in a hantour. The town has a big Christian population and is part of the belt of towns where clashes between Christians and Muslims (usually said to be fundamentalists) have taken place with increasing frequency over the early 1990s – although feuding of the sort has long been a part of the territory.

If you haven't already felt the tension caused by the sectarian violence and occasional pot shots taken at tourists in the area, you may start to here. The high profile of troops and military police, the constant checkpoints along the highway up and down the Nile, and the anxious assertions by officials and others that there are no problems and that tourists are well liked combine to give a slight feel for the troubles of which most visitors, thankfully, never have any direct experience.

Information

Tourist Office There's a tourist information office (☎ 320150) at the corner of the Corniche (also known as Sharia Ramadan and Sharia el-Nil at this point) and Sharia Abdel Monem. The guy here is very helpful – particularly if you speak French, as his English is not so hot. He can help you with the latest information on getting to the Beni Hasan tombs, Tell al-Amarna, Hermopolis and Tuna al-Gebel. Hours are 8.30 am to 8.30 pm daily except Friday.

Money The Banque Misr branch on Midan as-Sa'a actually does Visa card cash advances – it takes some time though. There are a couple of other banks marked on the map for cash and travellers' cheque transactions.

Post & Telecommunications The new post office is around the corner from the tourist office and is open every day but Friday from 8 am to 2 pm. The telephone office – the usual madhouse – is across the road from the entrance to the train station.

Museum

The museum behind the tourist office has been closed for years, but a brand new one is due to open on the east bank of the Nile in 1994, in the context of the town's twinning with the German city of Hildersheim. The small museum in Mallawi, south of Al-Minya, has also been closed, and the artefacts of the two are being sorted for eventual combined display in the new museum.

Zawiyet al-Mayyiteen

This is a large Muslim and Christian cemetery across the river from Al-Minya, near the ferry landing. Its name means 'corner of the dead'. The cemetery consists of several hundred mud-brick mausolea stretching for four km from the road to the hills. It is said to be one of the largest cemeteries in the world. You can walk there from the centre of town. Head south along the Nile for about a km to the bridge and cross over. Ask from there; it's not far.

Places to Stay

The cheapest place in town must be the *Majestic Hotel* (☎ 324212). A three-bed room costs E£6.60. If you're on your own, they'll let you have it for E£5.50 – but there's little to attract you to this dusty, depressing place.

The *Ibn Khassib Hotel* (☎ 324535) is in an ageing building on a side street near the train station. It has 12 doubles and six singles, all with high ceilings and Victorian-style furniture. Bathrooms/showers are crammed together. Single/doubles with breakfast, dinner, air-con and bath are a bit pricey at E£50/60. Without bath or dinner, they come down to E£34.25/43.75. They have a restaurant and bar. Tour groups sometimes use this hotel and you might be able to get a ride to some of the sights outside the town.

The *Beach Hotel* (☎ 323207) is a clean, pleasant place down near the river. At E£20/30 for a single/double without bath, it's quite OK, but not breathtaking. All the rooms there have full carpeting.

Just back a block towards the train station, with no sign, is the *Amoun Hotel*. Very often, someone will lead you there. For E£12 you can have a comfy bed in a room to yourself with hot water. Breakfast is E£3.

The *Hotel Seety* (☎ 323930), 71 Sharia Saad Zaghloul, is half a block south of the train station. It looks seedy from the outside, but several of the rooms are clean, comfortable and airy, and they are, at E£8/10 without bath and E£10/11 with, pretty cheap. The best part is a central living room full of antique furniture and an out-of-tune piano.

The *Savoy Hotel* (also called the *Hotel Savoy*) (☎ 323270) is directly across from the train station. It has large, clean rooms with very high ceilings for E£20/30/36. Bathrooms are near the rooms.

The *Touristic Lotus Hotel* (☎ 324541) is on Sharia Port Said, about a 10-minute walk from the train station. It's a modern brown structure with a restaurant on top, which serves simple meals such as chicken, salad, oily vegetables and chips for about E£12. It's popular with German groups and pretty reasonable. Singles/doubles should cost

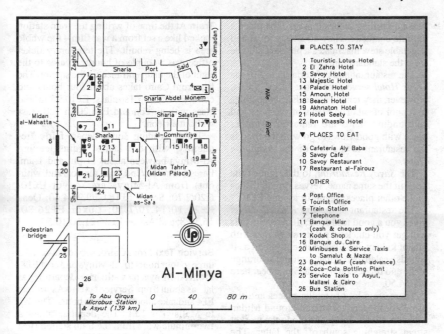

PLACES TO STAY
1 Touristic Lotus Hotel
2 El Zahra Hotel
9 Savoy Hotel
13 Majestic Hotel
14 Palace Hotel
15 Amoun Hotel
18 Beach Hotel
19 Akhnaton Hotel
21 Hotel Seety
22 Ibn Khassib Hotel

PLACES TO EAT
3 Cafeteria Aly Baba
8 Savoy Cafe
10 Savoy Restaurant
17 Restaurant al-Fairouz

OTHER
4 Post Office
5 Tourist Office
6 Train Station
7 Telephone
11 Banque Misr (cash & cheques only)
12 Kodak Shop
16 Banque du Caire
20 Minibuses & Service Taxis to Samalut & Mazar
23 Banque Misr (cash advance)
24 Coca-Cola Bottling Plant
25 Service Taxis to Asyut, Mallawi & Cairo
26 Bus Station

Al-Minya

To Abu Qirqus
Microbus Station
& Asyut (139 km)
0   40   80 m

E£29.25/41.70; all have air-conditioning and include breakfast.

Around the corner is the *El Zahra Hotel*. It's a basic cheapie at E£10 a person. Breakfast comes for E£3.

The *Akhnaton Hotel* (☎ 325917/8; fax 326966), on the Corniche near the Beach Hotel, has 42 clean, carpeted rooms with air-conditioning on the 3rd and 4th floors, some with great views of the Nile. Get one of these rooms and in terms of value for money, this is the best place to stay. Singles/doubles are E£25.15/31.35 with breakfast, and a few pounds extra with air-con.

The *Palace Hotel* (☎ 324071/21) is on Midan Palace. It's similar to the Savoy with clean high-ceilinged rooms and a big, airy central lobby. Even if you don't want to stay there, walk in for the decorative experience. Rooms are E£11.50 with bath and E£6.75 without. The rooms with bathrooms are better and by all measures quite a good deal.

A few km north of town is the *ETAP Nefertiti & Aton* (☎ 331515; fax 326467), a four-star hotel that has rooms facing the Nile for US$72/87, or cheaper ones at US$62/77. It has three restaurants and two bars.

Camping It used to be possible to pitch a tent at the Al-Minya Stadium, which is north of the station, directly up the tracks, but the tourist office claims this is no longer so.

Places to Eat
The *Cafeteria Aly Baba – Patisserie*, on the Corniche just north of Sharia Port Said, serves a good satisfying meal of the usual favourites – kebabs or another meat dish, salad, tahina and a soft drink for about E£10. They also have a variety of typical Egyptian pastries. This is a good place to come in the morning for a cup of coffee and a pastry.

The *Restaurant al-Fairouz* is on the Corniche at the corner of Sharia Salatin. The walls inside are garishly painted with peasant farming scenes that give the place a definite character. They do a tasty meat and vegetable stew that makes a pleasant change from the standard fare.

The restaurant and cafeteria on top of the *Lotus Hotel* serve simple but filling meals. However, they tend to serve their vegetables in a pool of oil. The views of the Nile and surrounding fields are fantastic. Another place with good views to go with the food is the restaurant at the top of the *Akhnaton Hotel*.

The *Savoy Restaurant*, to the right of the hotel of the same name, serves similar dishes to the other places, again for around E£10.

The restaurant at the *Ibn Khassib Hotel* gives you a good feed for E£10 as well. This will get you chicken, potato stew, rice with bits of kidney and liver in it (not as bad as it sounds), salad, baba ghanough and an orange at the end for dessert. A local Stella beer here is E£4.50.

There are a lot of smaller places and the usual cheap stands scattered around Midan Mahatta, Midan Tahrir and along the market street stretching south off the latter. The *Savoy Café* is not a bad place for a cup of tea and a game of backgammon.

Getting There & Away

Bus Buses of differing standards and at various prices leave regularly from the bus station, which is near the Cairo and Asyut service-taxi row, for destinations north and south of Al-Minya. There are buses to Cairo at 1, 2 and 5 am, and every half an hour to one hour until about 6 pm. Buses with air-con and video cost E£8.50, those without a couple of pounds less. They all take about four hours. You can book ahead or try your luck on the day. The ticket office only seems to be open in the mornings.

Buses leave for Beni Suef every 20 to 40 minutes, and cost E£3.

Buses to Asyut (two to three hours) also cost E£3 and leave every half an hour from 6 am to 5 pm both ways.

There is one bus a day right through to Alexandria. It costs E£15.

Train At the time of writing the train station looked like a set from a war film – the whole area is being rebuilt. The temporary ticket office was a couple of hundred yards to the right of the main entrance on the square. The trip from Cairo takes about four hours and costs E£17.85 in 1st class, E£10.95 in 2nd class with air-con and E£5.20 in 2nd class without air-con.

Trains heading south depart fairly frequently, with the fastest trains leaving Al-Minya between about 11 pm and 1 am. Fares (1st class/2nd with air-con/2nd without) from Al-Minya are: Asyut E£10/6.20/2.70; Sohag E£16.05/9.90/4.60; Qena E£24.10/14.70/7.10; Luxor E£26.80/16.30/8; and Aswan E£36/21.10/10.50.

Service Taxi From Cairo, service taxis take three to four hours to Al-Minya and cost E£8. From Al-Minya, they still have departures as late as about 8 pm. Service taxis to Asyut cost E£4 and take about 1½ to two hours. The trip to Mallawi is E£1. The depot is about a five-minute walk from the train station (just past the pedestrian bridge). Microbuses also do the Mallawi run.

BENI HASAN

Beni Hasan is a necropolis on the east bank of the Nile about 20 km south of Al-Minya. More than 30 distinctive Middle Kingdom tombs of varying sizes are carved into a limestone cliff. Only a few of them are accessible.

The Beni Hasan necropolis is open from 7 am to 5 pm, but you should get there by 3 pm at the latest. It's a good idea to start earlier because it can get quite hot here towards the end of the day. Admission is E£6 (half for students). You are expected to give the guard a bit of baksheesh for unlocking the tombs, although that's his job anyway. Photography used to be prohibited inside the tombs; now you can take pictures without flash if you pay E£5 – per tomb!

There are various tombs at Beni Hasan, the best of which (and the only ones open to the public) are desribed below.

Tomb of Kheti (No 17)

Kheti was a governor of the nome, or district, of Oryx during Egypt's 11th dynasty (about 2000 BC). Wall scenes in his tomb show daily life in the Middle Kingdom, as well as two copulating cows and an attack on a fort.

Tomb of Baqet (No 15)

Baqet was the father of Kheti. His tomb has some strange wall paintings: wrestlers doing more than just wrestling with each other, gazelles doing the same, and a hunt for unicorns and winged monsters.

Tomb of Khnumhotep (No 3)

This is a beautiful tomb. Khnumhotep served as a governor under Amenemhet III (about 1820 BC). The walls show colourful scenes of Khnumhotep's family life, and above the door are some interesting scenes of acrobats.

Tomb of Amenemhet (No 2)

This has the unusual addition of a false door facing west. The dead are supposed to enter the underworld only from the west. Amenemhet was a nomarch, or governor, and commander in chief of the Oryx nome.

Getting There & Away

From Al-Minya, take the Mallawi service taxi or microbus, which costs E£1, and get the driver to let you off at Abu Qirqus. Alternatively, walk past the bus station and overpass, cross the train tracks and veer left until you find another microbus station, and take the Abu Qirqus microbus for 40 pt. It

Entrance to Beni Hasan

takes about half an hour. Once there, walk across the Ibrahimiya Canal and train tracks and on for about 200 metres. There you take a pick-up to the river (it's quite a long walk) for 20 pt.

At the river you'll find an office, where boat tickets cost E£4.50 if you want to get across and there are fewer than six people. The price drops to E£2 if there are six or more. This is for the round trip, and includes the little microbus service at the other side that takes you part of the way to the tombs. There's a great view of the Nile from the tombs further up the slope. Watch out for the baksheesh kids from the nearby village. Walking towards the village is asking to be mobbed by them.

MALLAWI

Mallawi is 48 km south of Al-Minya. There is not much in town, except for a closed museum and one hotel, but it's a convenient

Hermopolis

departure point for the ancient sights of Hermopolis, Tuna al-Gebel and Tell al-Amarna.

Archaeological Museum

The small museum in town has been closed. It housed a collection of artefacts from Tuna al-Gebel and Hermopolis, which is to be combined with the displays of the closed museum in Al-Minya to create a new museum.

Places to Stay & Eat

There is only one – the *Semiramis Hotel* on the west bank of the Ibrahimiya Canal, just north of the train station. The rooms aren't bad, but the bathrooms are a bit grimy. Beds are E£6 a head. You can get a meal in the hotel's restaurant, which is probably the best bet in the town.

Getting There & Away

A service taxi from Al-Minya costs E£1; from Asyut it's E£2 for the one-hour trip.

HERMOPOLIS

Little remains of this ancient city, eight km north of Mallawi, that was once the centre for the cult of Thoth, the ibis-headed god of wisdom, healing and writing. The Greeks associated Thoth with their own Hermes – hence the city's Hellenic name – but in ancient times the city was known as Khmunu. Khmun was one of the eight all-powerful deities of the primordial chaos that preceded creation, and this city was believed to be sited where the sun first rose over the earth. The Arabic name for the present-day village, and the area surrounding the ruined city of Hermopolis, is Al-Ashmunein – a derivation of Khmun.

Apart from a few Middle and New Kingdom remains, the only real monument at Hermopolis is a ruined Roman agora and its early Christian basilica – the largest of its type still standing in Egypt. There is a small museum near two large sandstone statues of Thoth unearthed in the area.

A Pharoah and his queen make offerings to the sun-god

Getting There & Away

To get to Hermopolis from Mallawi, take a local microbus or service taxi to the village of Al-Ashmunein for 25 pt; the turn-off to the site is one km from the main road. From the junction you can either walk the short distance to Hermopolis or coax your driver to go a bit further. Hitching around the area shouldn't be a problem, as the sight of a foreigner walking down the road is bound to attract quite a lot of attention. Admission is E£6 (half for students) and the site is open from 7 am to 5 pm.

TUNA AL-GEBEL

Tuna al-Gebel is seven km west of Hermopolis. The site is open from 7 am to 5 pm and admission costs E£6 (half for students). It gets very hot here, even in winter, so bring plenty of water, a hat and sun screen if you plan to trek across the desert to the sights.

Apart from bordering on Akhetaten, the Pharaoh Akhenaten's short-lived capital, Tuna al-Gebel was also the necropolis of Hermopolis. The oldest monument in the area is one of the six stelae that marked the boundary of Akhetaten – in this case the western perimeter of the city's farm lands and associated villages. The stela, a rock-hewn shrine and some statues show Akhenaten and Nefertiti in various poses.

To the south of the stela, which is about five km past the village of Tuna al-Gebel, are the catacombs and tombs of the residents and sacred animals of Hermopolis. A German team has been working at Tuna al-Gebel since 1979.

The most interesting things to see there are the dark catacomb galleries once filled with thousands of mummified baboons, ibises and ibis eggs – baboons and ibises were sacred to Thoth. Most of the animals have been destroyed by robbers, and in fact only one of the baboons was found fully intact by archaeologists. Most of the mummification was done in the Ptolemaic and Roman periods. The subterranean cemetery extends for at least three km, but Egyptologists suspect it may stretch all the way to Hermopolis. You definitely need a torch if you're going to explore the galleries.

Tomb of Petosiris

This is an interesting Ptolemaic tomb chapel; a sign directs the way. Petosiris was a high priest of Thoth; his family tomb, in the design of a temple, is entered through a columned vestibule. The tomb paintings show a mixture of two cultures: although they depict typical Egyptian farming scenes, the figures are wearing Greek dress.

Mummy of Isadora

In a small building behind the Tomb of Petosiris is the extremely well-preserved mummy of a woman who drowned in the Nile in about 150 AD. Isadora's teeth, hair and fingernails are clearly visible. You'll need to give the guard a bit of baksheesh to see her, though.

Well

The *sakiya*, or well, is next to a water wheel that once brought water up from its depths. The well was the sole source of water for the priests, workers and sacred baboons of Tuna al-Gebel. For a bit more baksheesh the guard will unlock the door and let you walk down to the bottom of the well. Watch out for the bats!

Getting There & Away

There's a fair amount of traffic between the Hermopolis junction and the village, so it should be fairly easy to hitch.

TELL AL-AMARNA

The scant remains of this once-glorious city, 12 km south-west of Mallawi, may be a little disappointing when compared to its fascinating, albeit brief, moment in history.

In the 14th century BC, the rebellious Pharaoh Akhenaten and Queen Nefertiti abandoned the gods, temples and priests of Karnak at Thebes to establish a new city, untarnished by other gods. There they and their followers, through their worship of Aten, god of the sun disc, developed what many scholars believe was the first known form of monotheism.

The city, in the area now known as Tell al-Amarna, was built on the east bank of the Nile on a beautiful, yet solitary, crescent-shaped plain, extending about 12 km from north to south. Except for the side bounded by the river, the palaces, temples and residences of the city were surrounded by high cliffs, broken here and there by wadis. The royal couple named their city Akhetaten, or 'horizon of the sun disc', and it served as the capital of Egypt for about 14 years.

It was abandoned for all time shortly after Akhenaten's death, when the priests of Karnak managed to regain their religious control. They desecrated the temples of Aten and generally did their best to obliterate all record of the heretic Pharaoh's objectionable new religion. Polytheism again predominated throughout the land as the Karnak priests persuaded Akhenaten's son-in-law and successor Tutankaten, or Tutankhamun as he became known, to re-establish the cult of Amun at Thebes. Akhetaten fell into ruin, and the stones of its palaces and temples were used for buildings in Hermopolis and other cities.

The Tell al-Amarna necropolis comprises two groups of cliff tombs, one at each end of the city, which feature colourful wall paintings of life during the Aten revolution. Akhenaten's royal tomb is in a ravine about six km up Wadi Abu Hasah al-Bahri, the valley that divides the north and south sections of the cliffs. He was not buried there, however, and no other tomb bearing his name has ever been found.

Due to the city's sudden demise, many of the tombs were never finished and very few were actually used.

Orientation & Information

The site is open from 7 am to 5 pm, and there is an odd admission price system in effect.

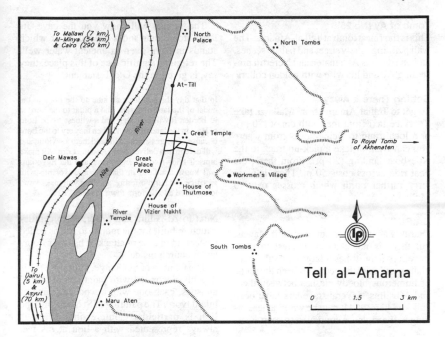

On arriving from the other side of the Nile (as most people without their own transport will), you pay a flat fee of E£1 for the feat of getting there. The E£6 (E£3 for students) fee is only charged when you get to either the south or north tombs. The ticket is valid only for the day of purchase. Because of the distance between various parts of the site, tractors have been laid on, for prices that seem to swing from E£4 to E£8. The northern tombs are about three km from the boat landing, the southern ones about five km. Other remains of temples and private and administrative buildings are scattered about a wide area. In all, there are 25 tombs cut into the base of the cliffs, numbered from one to six in the north, and seven to 25 in the south. Those worth visiting are described below.

Tomb of Huya (No 1)

Huya was the superintendent of Akhenaten's royal harem. The Pharaoh and his family are depicted just inside the entrance on the right.

Tomb of Ahmose (No 3)

Ahmose was one of the king's versatile fan-bearers; his statue is at the back of the tomb.

Tomb of Merirye (No 4)

Merirye was the high priest of Aten. The tomb paintings show the Pharaoh riding around town in his chariot and visiting the Temple of Aten.

Tomb of Panehse (No 6)

Panehse was vizier of Lower Egypt and a servant of Aten. Most of the scenes in this tomb show Akhenaten and his family attending ceremonies at the Sun Temple.

Tomb of Mahu (No 9)

This is one of the best preserved, and the wall paintings provide interesting details of Mahu's duties as Akhenaten's chief of police.

Tomb of Ay (No 25)

This is the finest tomb at Tell al-Amarna. The wall paintings show street and palace scenes, and one depicts Akhenaten and Nefertiti presenting Ay and his wife with golden collars.

Getting There & Away

To get to Tell al-Amarna from Mallawi, take a service taxi from the south depot (20 pt), or a local train to Deir Mawas from where you can walk or take a pick-up truck to the Nile boat landing (20 pt). From there, the boat ride across costs 50 pt. There is a car ferry further north which crosses over to Mallawi.

DAIRUT

Dairut is about 10 km south of Deir Mawas, but there is not a lot of interest to most travellers here. It has a large Christian population and over the years has been the scene of numerous bloody clashes between them and Muslims. Several travellers have been attacked here, and it may be wiser, at least as long as the violence continues, to keep away.

AL-QUSIYA

Just outside the small rural town of Al-Qusiya, 35 km south of Mallawi, is the Coptic complex of Deir al-Muharraq – the 'burnt monastery'. There is a large guest-house just outside the pseudo-medieval crenellated walls of the monastery and the monks sometimes allow travellers to stay there.

Deir al-Muharraq

The 100 or so monks who reside in the monastery claim that Mary and Jesus inhabited a cave on this site for six months and 10 days during their flight into Egypt – their longest stay at any of the numerous places they are said to have rested during that flight. For seven days every year (starting at different times in June), thousands of pilgrims attend feasts to celebrate the consecration of the Church of Al-Adhra, or the Virgin, the church built over the cave. Coptic Christians believe Al-Adhra to be one of the first churches in the world.

The monks will show you the cave, its large stone altar and a special pillar which stands in front over an ancient water well. The religious significance of this place, they say, is given in the Old Testament.

In that day there will be an altar to the Lord in the midst of the land of Egypt, and a pillar to the Lord at its border. It will be a sign and a witness to the Lord of Host in the land of Egypt; when they cry to the Lord because of oppressors he will send them a saviour, and will defend and deliver them. And the Lord will make himself known to the Egyptians; and the Egyptians will know the Lord in that day and worship with sacrifice and burnt offering, and they will make vows to the Lord and perform them. (Isaiah 19:19).

Next to Al-Adhra is a tower, a 5th century structure built for the monks to use as added protection in case of attack. It has four floors and a church inside.

The Church of St George, built in 1880, is lavishly decorated with paintings of the 12 apostles, each one with a wooden frame of inlaid ivory. The painting of St Mark with the lion is particularly interesting. Mark is always represented with a lion at his feet because once, when one attacked his father and Mark ordered it to go away, the great beast lay down at his feet instead.

Getting There & Away

The Asyut to Al-Minya bus will drop you at Al-Qusiya (E£1.25, about 50 minutes from Asyut), or you might take a service taxi from either Asyut or Mallawi. From there, you may be able to get a local microbus to the Deir, or the military police, worried about your welfare, may take you there themselves. It probably pays to agree with their assertions that the 'police are good' and that there are no more problems in the area.

ASYUT

Asyut, settled during Pharaonic times on a broad fertile plain bordering the west bank of the Nile, is 375 km south of Cairo and is the largest town in Upper Egypt and chief agricultural centre, dealing in camels, cotton, grain and its local speciality – carpets.

It has been an important trading town

since ancient times and was once head of the great caravan route to the Western Desert oases and across the Sahara. For several centuries, the camel caravans that travelled up the 40 Day Road from Darfur province in the Sudan ended their trip in Asyut, and as recently as 150 years ago the town boasted the largest slave market in Egypt.

Although never really politically important, Asyut was once the capital of the 13th nome – the Sycamore province – and cult centre of the wolf-god Wepwawet, the avenger of Osiris (god of the dead). In the 4th century AD Christianity became the dominant religion and today there are often confrontations in the city between the Copts and Muslim fundamentalists. The military and police presence in and around the city of Asyut can take the visitor by surprise. There are checkpoints all over town and various important points are covered by troops with machine guns squatting by sandbag emplacements. You will almost certainly have the military on your back when you arrive – remember that they see themselves as doing a job to protect you, so this is not the time to lose your cool. Generally, you'll be left to your own devices, but the simple presence of so many people under arms can be a trifle off-putting.

The Asyut Barrage was built across the Nile in the late 19th century, under British supervision, to regulate the flow of water into the Ibrahimiya Canal and assist in the irrigation of the valley as far north as Beni Suef. It's an impressive structure, but you're not allowed to walk on or around it. Photographing it would be unwise. Asyut is still a major departure point for trips to the Western Oases, or the New Valley as the region is now known.

Information

Tourist Office There is a tourist office (☎ 322400) on Sharia ath-Thawra in the Governorate building. It's on the 2nd floor, and although they are very friendly and willing to help, they don't have all that much to offer but a brochure – and a quick visit to the display of local souvenirs for sale on the 1st floor.

Money There is a cluster of banks on a square south-west of the train station. Banque Misr has two branches and the Bank of Alexandria one. Just up the road is the Banque du Caire. None offer cash advance facilities, but you can change Eurocheques at the Bank of Alexandria.

Post & Telecommunications The post office is in a street off Midan Tahrir, in front of the train station, just behind the Asyut Tourist Hotel – the same street leads on to the banks. The telephone office is beside the train station.

Museum

There is a small museum of Pharaonic and Coptic artefacts in what used to be the American College on Sharia al-Gomhurriya. The museum, which includes a mummy display and is housed in a building called the Taggart Library, was renovated in 1986, but you'll need to get there when someone is around to dig out the key to let you in. The school is now the As-Salam secondary school for girls, and the grounds are worth a quick look; it's like a very dusty college transported out of New England with palm trees attached, which is effectively probably what it was.

On the way to the museum you'll pass a Coca-Cola bottling plant. It's a bit strange to watch the mechanised bottling process through one of the front windows and then turn around and watch the donkey carts pass by.

Geziret al-Moz

'Banana Island' is in the Nile at the end of Sharia Salah Salem. The island's lush tropical forest is a pleasant place to picnic or even camp. You'll have to bargain with a felucca captain for the ride across. According to the tourist office, you need a permit from the police now, not to visit the island but to keep tabs on the felucca captains.

The town boasted an old Ottoman-era mosque, Al-Muhajideen, which was built in

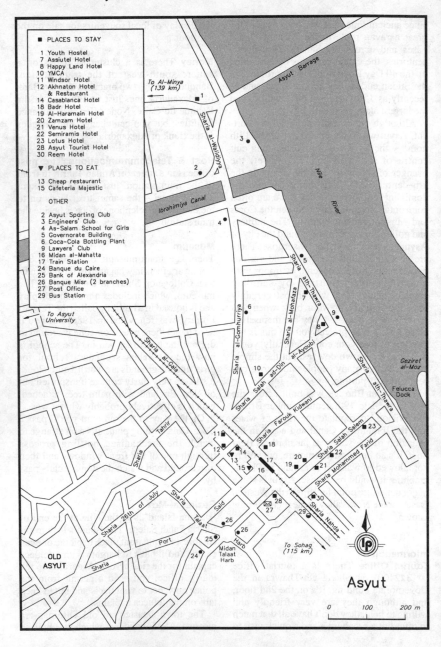

■ PLACES TO STAY

1 Youth Hostel
7 Assiutel Hotel
8 Happy Land Hotel
10 YMCA
11 Windsor Hotel
12 Akhnaton Hotel
    & Restaurant
14 Casablanca Hotel
18 Badr Hotel
19 Al-Haramain Hotel
20 Zamzam Hotel
21 Venus Hotel
22 Semiramis Hotel
23 Lotus Hotel
28 Asyut Tourist Hotel
30 Reem Hotel

▼ PLACES TO EAT

13 Cheap restaurant
15 Cafeteria Majestic

    OTHER

2 Asyut Sporting Club
3 Engineers' Club
4 As-Salam School for Girls
5 Governorate Building
6 Coca-Cola Bottling Plant
9 Lawyers' Club
16 Midan al-Mahatta
17 Train Station
24 Banque du Caire
25 Bank of Alexandria
26 Banque Misr (2 branches)
27 Post Office
29 Bus Station

To Al-Minya
(139 km)

Asyut Barrage

Sharia al-Walidyya

Nile River

Ibrahimiya Canal

To Asyut
University

Sharia al-Gala

Sharia ath-Thawra

Sharia al-Mohafaza

Sharia al-Gomhurriya

Sharia Salah ad-Din

Sharia al-Ayoubi

Sharia Farouk Kidwani

Geziret
al-Moz

Felucca
Dock

Sharia ath-Thawra

Sharia Salah Salem

Sharia Mohammed Farid

Sharia Nahda

Tahrir

Sharia 26th of July

Sharia Port

Sharia Talaat

Said

Harb

Midan
Talaat
Harb

To Sohag
(115 km)

OLD
ASYUT

Asyut

0   100   200 m

1704. It was destroyed in late 1992. When asked by whom and why, the tourist office staff said they had no idea – which all seems pretty strange.

Lillian Trasher Orphanage

Born in Jacksonville, Florida, in the USA, Lillian Trasher came to Egypt in 1910 in search of some useful work to do. The following year she founded an orphanage in Asyut, which has since grown to be the biggest and most well known of its type in Egypt. Some 650 residents of all ages live there now. Trasher never left, but died in her adopted country in 1961. The orphanage, which by a law of 1935 takes in only Christians, is something of a symbol of Christian charity in a city with a heavy concentration of Copts and a history of sectarian fighting between them and Muslims. The orphanage welcomes interested visitors, and won't say no to a donation.

Getting There & Away As the orphanage is on the east bank of the Nile, it's a bit of a hassle to get to. Microbuses run near it from the centre of town for 15 pt, but a taxi for E£2 is a lot easier. Ask for the *malga Trasher*.

Places to Stay – bottom end

The *Youth Hostel* (☎ 324846) is at Lux Houses, 503 Sharia al-Walidiya. It costs about E£2.10 for a bed in a dorm of six. They don't seem too fussed about IYHA membership cards.

The *YMCA*, about half way down Sharia Salah ad-Din al-Ayoubi, on the left, has had rave reviews from a lot of people. There are two sections, the old and new buildings. A bed in the old section costs E£6. Singles/doubles in the new section cost E£18/25. The rooms have air-con and TV.

The *Zamzam Hotel* used to be a good deal, but it seems they are not keen on foreign guests. It is not the only hotel to fall into this category, and it appears it is the police interest, and often presence in and around their places if foreigners have checked in, that causes all the ill-ease. The hotel's a little way down from the train station on Sharia Salah

Salem, and costs E£5 for a bed. Virtually across the road is the cheap-and-nasty *Venus Hotel*. There's no shower, and one shudders to think what it would be like if there were one. It costs E£2 a bed.

The *Semiramis Hotel*, just down from the Venus, is a dark, dirty place that is also probably best avoided. Single/double/triple rooms are E£6/10/15. There is hot water, but the toilets are pretty grotty.

The *Lotus Hotel* is down the Nile end of the same street. Rooms cost from E£10 for a double, but for that money, you're better off coming up with a few more pounds for a quantum leap in quality.

The *Asyut Tourist Hotel* (☎ 322615) used to be a reasonable cheap deal, but the owners seem to have been afflicted with the same reticence that has struck the Zamzam.

One of the better deals at the budget end of the spectrum is the *Al-Haramain Hotel* (☎ 320426) on Sharia Salah Salem, around the corner from the Badr Hotel. It has 18 beds in clean, carpeted rooms on two floors in a quiet apartment building. Single/double rooms are E£8.50/15, and the water is hot. The beds are of the usual rock-hard variety though.

The *Windsor Hotel* (☎ 922973), which has double rooms with bath for E£12 is noisy, but not a bad spot to stay for the money involved.

Moving up the scale, the *Akhnaton Hotel* (☎ 327723) has pretty reasonable rooms with clean linen, TV, hot water and soap in the bathrooms at E£28/35 for singles/doubles. Breakfast (they give you a choice between what they call continental and English for E£4.50 and E£6.50) is extra.

The *Reem Hotel* (☎ 326235; fax 329102), on Sharia Nahda next to the train tracks, is a medium-priced place with singles for E£37 and doubles for E£56, including taxes, TV and breakfast. It's OK, if a little overpriced. The rooms overlooking the railway are very noisy.

The *El Salam* (☎ 332256), off Sharia Port Said, is not the easiest place to find in spite of the helpful signs around the place and the touts who seem to spring up out of nowhere.

It appears to be popular with travellers, and has singles/doubles/triples/quadruples with bath for E£25.20/29.50/40.55/59. Air-con costs E£3 more. TVs and breakfasts are extra, and all up it's not that stunning for the price.

There are at least three cheapies in nearby Sharia Talaat Harb: The *Cleopatra*, *Omar el-Kaiam* and *Isis*. None of them seem to want to know about foreigners.

Places to Stay – middle & top end

The *Casablanca Hotel* (☎ 324483, 321662; fax 321662) does not have the greatest location, but it is pretty good. Good, clean rooms (the bathrooms have toilet paper, soap and towels) come at E£50/80 with breakfast.

Better located, down by the Nile, is the *Happy Land Hotel* (☎ 320444, 321944; fax 320444). Singles and doubles without breakfast cost E£50/81.

Not far away is the *Assiutel Hotel* (☎ 329022, 322713), with very comfortable rooms and amenities costing E£92/104. It's a bit overpriced, as you don't really get anything much that isn't at the Happy Land. Breakfast is extra.

Back in the centre of town, the *Badr Hotel* (☎ 329811/2) is a deluxe, Western-style hotel and an expatriate hang-out. Room rates are much the same as those of the Assiutel, but quoted in dollars. A single costs US$29 and a double US$31.50. Taxes, breakfast and so on are all extra. There's a restaurant with an à la carte menu. The hotel was started by one of Egypt's biggest construction contractors.

Places to Eat

The *Cafeteria Majestic*, opposite the train station, serves good cheap meals of shawarma, rice, salad and potatoes, among other things, from about E£7. It's a lively place with a good atmosphere.

All the bigger hotels have their own restaurants. On the cheaper end of the scale, the *Akhnaton's restaurant* does a good escalope for E£8 – with real chips. There are a few of the usual fuul and ta'amiyya stands scattered around.

Getting There & Away

Asyut, 375 km south of Cairo, 142 km northwest of Qena and 240 km north of Kharga (the nearest Western Desert oasis), is a major terminus for all forms of transport.

Bus Buses leave Cairo for Asyut and the Western Desert oases from a small station at 45 Sharia al-Azhar, near Midan Ataba. Buses to Asyut only leave Cairo from Ahmed Hilmi Station, behind Ramses train station.

From Asyut they depart for Cairo at 12.30, 8, 10 and 11 am, 2, 3, 5, 10, 11 pm and midnight every day; the cost is E£9.20/12.70/13.50/15.20, depending on whether the bus has air-con, videos and so on. The most expensive (Super Jet) tends to be quicker than the others. The trip takes about six to seven hours.

Buses depart for Al-Minya about every half an hour from 6 am to 5 pm. There are no bookings, you just grab a seat and pay the fare on the bus. The E£3 fare on the bus.

At 2 pm there's a bus for Esna and Luxor for E£12. Three buses a day leave for Qena (7 am, 1 and 5 pm). They cost E£6. A bus for Hurghada (Al-Ghardaka) leaves at 9 am for E£12.

There's a departure for Sohag about every half an hour from 6 am to 5 pm. It costs E£2.50 and takes 1½ hours.

If you are heading out to the oases, there are buses to Kharga at 7, 8 am, 1, 3, 5 and 10 pm. They take up to four hours and cost E£6, except for the last one, which is E£7.

Train Trains arrive and depart for destinations north and south of Asyut frequently. There are about 20 trains throughout the day to Cairo and Al-Minya, and about half that number to Luxor. The 1st and 2nd-class fares to Cairo are E£24.70 and E£15 (E£16.30/11.20 for students). The quicker trains take five to seven hours.

The same fares for the two to three-hour trip to Al-Minya are E£10/6.10 (E£7/4.80 for students) and to Luxor E£21/11.90 (E£14/9.70). It takes about four to six hours. There are regular trains to the next main centre down the line, Sohag. The 1st, 2nd air-con and 2nd-class fares on the fast train are E£9.70/6.90/4.80 (student E£7.50/ 5.80/ 3.70). The normal train can take hours, stopping at every possible one-donkey village.

Service Taxi Service taxis gather around the bus and train stations. You can get one all the way to Cairo for E£14. One to Al-Minya costs E£4 and takes two hours. A service taxi to Kharga costs E£8.

AROUND ASYUT
Abu Teeg
If you are particularly into mosques, there is an attractive one in the village of Abu Teeg, about 20 minutes' bus ride south of Asyut on the Sohag bus line. The tall slender minarets are elegance itself. The mosque is a centre of education in Islamic jurisprudence. At the southern end of town is a huge labyrinthine Christian cemetery.

The Western Oases

About 90% of Egypt is barren desert, lying relentlessly hot, unproductive and uninhabited on both sides of the fertile Nile Valley and Nile Delta, all the way from the Mediterranean to the Sudan border. Only about 1% of the country's total population lives in this wasteland and most of them reside in the five isolated, yet thriving, oases of the Western Desert.

Since the late 1950s, in an attempt to make use of all this spare land, the Egyptian government has been investing heavily in development projects in and around these oases. The recently opened link road between the Bahariyya Oasis and Siwa, in the north-west of the country, and another between Luxor and Kharga, are evidence of the drive to exploit this part of the country more. At the same time, to relieve the pressures of overpopulation, landless fellahin and families from crowded towns in the Nile Valley have been encouraged to resettle in this so-called New Valley Frontier District, a region centred on Kharga Oasis and covering about 376,000 sq km.

Although the oases are attracting more and more travellers, their increased popularity has not diminished the adventure of exploring this remote region. The ideal time to visit is in late autumn or early spring, because summer temperatures can soar as high as 52°C (125°F). Winter is very pleasant, but it can get quite nippy at night.

On entering the New Valley Governorate (which covers Kharga, Dakhla and Farafra oases) you must pay a one-time charge of E£4.30. The hotels will make you aware of this. Hang on to the receipt if you don't want to find yourself paying it more than once. Kharga and Dakhla oases are easily visited from Asyut; the oases of Farafra and Bahariyya are best visited from Cairo. There is no reason not to do a circuit right through the lot of them.

Although there is road access from Bahariyya to Siwa, there is as yet no public transport, so if you don't have your own transport, you'll be looking at a few hundred E£ to get a service taxi to take you out there on a special run. Otherwise, you have to go via Marsa Matruh. Siwa is described in the Alexandria & the Mediterranean Coast chapter.

If you want in-depth information on the history and archaeological sites of the oases, there is a three-volume work, published by The American University in Cairo Press, which is available at the AUC Bookstore and some hotel bookshops.

KHARGA OASIS
Kharga, the largest and most developed of the oases, lies in a desert depression about 30 km wide and 200 km long. The chief town is Al-Kharga, 233 km from Asyut; it's a boom town with a population of more than 100,000. Many of these people are Nubians, resettled from the Nubian lands inundated by the creation of Lake Nasser after the construction of the Aswan Dam. The present-day community of Berbers, however, whose ancestors were Kharga's original inhabitants, can trace their roots

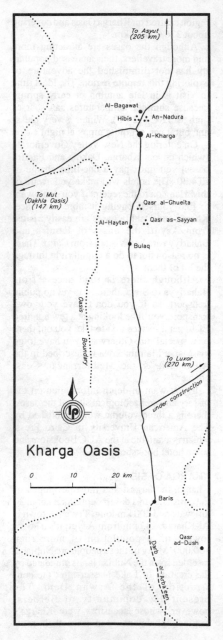

To Asyut
(205 km)

Al-Bagawat

Hibis • •   • • An-Nadura

● Al-Kharga

To Mut
(Dakhla Oasis)
(147 km)

● Qasr al-Ghueita

Al-Haytan   ● Qasr as-Sayyan

● Bulaq

Oasis Boundary

To Luxor
(270 km)

under construction

Kharga Oasis

0   10   20 km

● Baris

Qasr
ad-Dush ●

Darb al-Arba'een

back to when the oasis was a way-station on the 40 Days Road caravan route between the Sudan and Egypt.

Orientation

Most travellers will arrive in Al-Kharga (or Qasr Kharga), the main city and administrative centre of the governorate. It is a fairly faceless and uninteresting town, but there are a few things around it worth seeing. The bus station is in the south-east of the town, near what's left of the old centre, and it's a fair hike to any of the hotels. If you're coming from Dakhla, you may as well ask the driver to let you off near Sharia al-Adel.

Information

Tourist Office The office is open from 8.30 am to 3 pm every day but Friday. They speak virtually no English and, although they smile a lot, have little useful information to impart. They do post bus timetables up though. The office is up by the Kharga Oasis Hotel, at the northern end of town.

Money The Banque du Caire and Banque Misr both change cash and travellers' cheques, but credit cards are no go (in fact, you can forget credit cards altogether while in the oases).

Post & Telecommunications The post office is open at the usual times, and the imposing building housing the telephone office, on Sharia al-Adel, is open seven days a week, round the clock. Getting a line out may be a trifle difficult.

Film If you find yourself short of film, and you're heading into the oases, you'd better get some here. There's a little photography studio between the Waha Hotel and the square on Sharia al-Adel. They usually keep some Kodak film for sale in the top drawer of the office desk.

Museum

Just down a bit from the tourist office is a new museum, housing archaeological exhibits from various ancient sites around the oases.

Temple of Hibis
This 6th century BC structure dedicated to the god Amun was built mostly by the Persian emperor Darius I. The temple, a few km north of town just to the left off the main road, is undergoing restoration work. You are free to wander around the site, but cannot enter the small temple proper. If you should be able to get in, there's a great view of the surrounding palm groves from the roof.

Temple of Nadura
This small temple, to the north-east of the town, was built by the Roman emperor Antonius Pius in 138 AD. Look out for Kharga's duck farms nearby. You can't miss the ruins, as they are perched on a rise off to the right of the main road, shortly before the Hibis Temple. Follow the road to the right and scramble across the desert (it's about a 10 to 15-minute walk). There's not an awful lot to see, and the guardian will hang around expecting a tip. From here you have sweeping views of the desert and oasis, and can see the Temple of Hibis before you.

Also near the temple are the ruins of a 9th century Islamic mud-brick town, most of which was built underground so the inhabitants could escape the intense desert heat. Some of the buildings are still inhabited and the locals will gladly show you around and probably even invite you to their homes for tea.

Necropolis of Al-Bagawat
This is probably the most interesting of the three sights clustered just to the north of the town. Most of the several hundred mud-brick tombs in this Christian cemetery date from the 4th to the 6th centuries AD. They are traditional domed Coptic tombs, some of which have interesting wall paintings of biblical scenes. Admission is E£10 (E£5 for students). You will be dogged by someone anxious to become your guide; if you want to get inside some of the more colourful tombs, he's your man. The cemetery is half

a km past the Temple of Hibis, on the road to Asyut. The site is open from 8 am to 5 pm, and an hour longer in winter.

Getting There & Away If you're on foot, just cut across the desert when you see the necropolis to your left. By car, you'll have to drive a km or so up the road and take the paved lane back.

Temples of Al-Ghueita & As-Sayyan
On the road through the southern stretch of the oasis down to Baris (90 km south of Al-Kharga) are a few temple remains in an advanced state of decay. About 20 km south of Al-Kharga, and a few km off to the east of the Baris road, are the remains of Qasr al-Ghueita, a temple from the 25th dynasty dedicated to the gods Amun, Mut and Khons. Another seven km further south, and about six km east of the main road, are the fairly fragmentary remains of Qasr as-Sayyan. It dates back to the Ptolemaic period, and was a temple dedicated to Amun. Given that entry to both is E£8 (half for students), they are probably not worth the effort for most.

Getting There & Away You can take a bus heading for Baris and ask the driver to let you off at one spot or the other. If you are planning the long hike to one or the other, take lots of water. Tracks suitable for 4WD cars lead out to the ruins.

Baris & Qasr ad-Dush
Baris is the fourth town of the New Valley Governorate, but there is not much of interest here. About 24 km to the south-east is Qasr ad-Dush, a sandstone temple built about the same time as the Nadura temple. From Baris, you'll have to negotiate for a special ride out with one of the locals. There are government rest houses in Baris and along the highway between Qasr al-Ghueita and Qasr as-Sayyan. A bed in either costs E£5. Check with the tourist office in Al-Kharga that they are actually open.

Getting There & Away There are two buses a day between Baris and Al-Kharga for

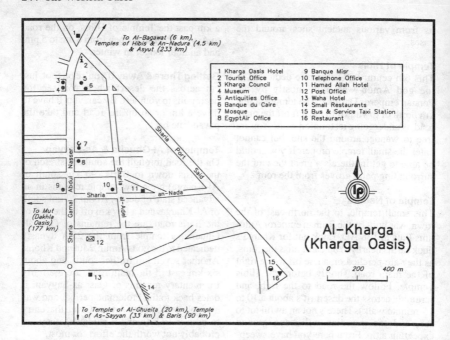

Map legend:

1	Kharga Oasis Hotel	9	Banque Misr
2	Tourist Office	10	Telephone Office
3	Kharga Council	11	Hamad Allah Hotel
4	Museum	12	Post Office
5	Antiquities Office	13	Waha Hotel
6	Banque du Caire	14	Small Restaurants
7	Mosque	15	Bus & Service Taxi Station
8	EgyptAir Office	16	Restaurant

To Al-Bagawat (6 km), Temples of Hibis & An-Nadura (4.5 km) & Asyut (233 km)

Sharia Port Said

Sharia Nasser

Sharia an-Nada

Sharia al-Adel

Sharia Abdul

Sharia Gamal

To Mut (Dakhla Oasis) (177 km)

To Temple of Al-Ghueita (20 km), Temple of As-Sayyan (33 km) & Baris (90 km)

Al-Kharga (Kharga Oasis)

0   200   400 m

E£1.35, leaving the latter at noon and 2 pm and Baris at 6 am and 3 pm. You may be able to get a pick-up there and back, but you'll have to bargain.

Al-Munira Duck Lake
If you have more than a passing interest in ducks, you can see an awful lot of them at Al-Munira, about 23 km north of Al-Kharga, where an artificial lake has been created for duck-breeding. A bus or pick-up should cost E£1 to E£2 from Al-Kharga.

Places to Stay
The *Waha Hotel* (☎ 900393) is a handily placed and reasonable cheapie. If you're coming in from Dakhla, the bus can drop you off at the entrance. Singles/doubles without bath cost E£5/8. With bath, the price shoots up to E£10.50/14. Whether you have a bath in your room or not, the water is hot and the staff are friendly. Breakfast is E£1.25.

There is supposed to be another inexpen-

sive hotel at the other end of town. If you arrive at the bus station and ask for a cheap hotel, that's probably where you'll be taken.

The *Kharga Oasis Hotel* (☎ 901500) is the town's top-of-the-range hotel. Singles/ doubles cost E£42/60.80 including breakfast and taxes. It's in a modern building at the north end of town and has 30 rooms, each with a bathroom. It's quite good, although often seems sadly empty. They have a restaurant, and a set dinner costs E£17.25.

The *Hamad Allah Hotel* (☎ 900638) has 54 rooms, with and without bathrooms. Singles/doubles with bath, breakfast and including taxes cost E£28.30/37.85. This place is popular with passing tour and overland trek groups.

Camping You may be able to camp in the grounds of the Kharga Oasis Hotel.

Places to Eat
The best places to eat are the hotels. Other-

wise, there is a chicken restaurant next to the Waha hotel, a cheap place at the bus station and several similar establishments around the square east of the Waha.

Getting There & Away

Air EgyptAir flies from Al-Kharga to Cairo at 8 am on Sunday and Wednesday. Flights from Cairo leave at 6 am on the same days. The fare is E£303 one way. Although some of these flights seem to involve trips on to or from Luxor, you cannot get down to Luxor from here. The EgyptAir office is on Sharia Gamal Abdul Nasser, just by the big mosque of the same name.

Bus There are two buses a day from Cairo to Kharga via Asyut. The first leaves at 10 am, takes about nine hours and costs E£15. The second is a Dakhla bus that leaves at 8 pm. It costs E£24 (air-con and video). Two other Cairo to Dakhla buses via Asyut and Kharga leave earlier in the evening, but according to the Upper Egypt Bus Co are direct buses for Dakhla and do not stop in Kharga to pick up or set down passengers. Check to be sure of the latest schedules.

Buses leave Cairo from the small bus station at 45 Sharia al-Azhar (near Midan Ataba). The bus stops in Giza to take on additional passengers, but it's better to board at the Al-Azhar station, where it isn't crowded. Buy a reserved seat at least a day in advance. For more details about Western Oases buses from Cairo, see the Cairo Getting There & Away section.

Two buses leave Al-Kharga for Cairo, one at 6 am for E£15 and another at 7 pm for E£18. You may be able to get on one of three other buses to Cairo from Dakhla.

From Asyut there are six buses to Kharga costing E£6 to E£7. See the Asyut Getting There & Away section for more details. There are five buses to Asyut from Al-Kharga, leaving at 6, 7, 11 am, 1 and 2 pm. Two other buses pass through from Dakhla to Asyut.

Service Taxi A service taxi is a convenient way to travel to Al-Kharga from Asyut. The trip takes from three to four hours and costs E£8 per person. To Dakhla, the trip takes three hours and costs E£7.

DAKHLA OASIS

Dakhla, about 187 km west of Kharga and 311 km south-east of Farafra, was created from more than 600 natural springs and ponds. The bus from Asyut and Kharga drops you off at Mut, the largest town in the oasis, from where you can take a service taxi to Al-Qasr, the other town of interest in the area. The bus coming from Farafra can drop you at Al-Qasr or Mut.

Information

Tourist Office Omar Ahmed (☎ 940407) must be one of the most helpful and useful tourist information officers in Egypt. He is a mine of knowledge about the oases and very obliging. His office number is shown above, but he is also happy to hand over his home number to anyone who thinks they may need his help. The office is in the same building as the Government Rest House in Mut, just by the bus station, and is open from 8 am to 3 pm and again from 7 to 10 pm.

Money The Banque Misr in Mut accepts cash and travellers' cheques only.

Post & Telecommunications The post office is behind the mosque at the bus station and is open from 8 am to 2 pm, except Friday. The phone office does not handle international traffic. If you need to make a call, go to the Mebarez Tourist Hotel, on the road to Al-Qasr.

Ethnographic Museum

This place is unfindable, and if you do stumble across it, it will be closed. If you desperately want to see displays on oasis life, ask at the tourist office to have it opened for you.

Old City of Mut

Often ignored by passing travellers, the labyrinth of mud-brick houses and winding lanes is worth exploring. Climb up to the remains of what used to be the town citadel for wonderful views of the oasis town. On the right of the street leading into the new town centre is a former medieval Islamic cemetery.

Hot Springs

There are several hot sulphur pools around the town of Mut, but the easiest to reach is the official one about three km on the road to Al-Qasr from Mut. Admission to the spring, called Mut Talata ('Mut Three') is free, and there is a dubious rest house there. The water is very hot, but relaxing. There are cold showers, but often little more than a trickle.

Sand Dunes

A few km out past the bus station you can have a roll around in the sand dunes said to have been there since Roman times. They are not the most spectacular of dunes, but easy to reach for people without their own transport.

Al-Qasr

The area just north of Al-Qasr is full of lush vegetation. The town itself is a charming little place that seems to have been barely touched by the development projects in other parts of the New Valley. The ancient architecture of this town has conserved much of its medieval character – the narrow covered streets seem to hold all sorts of secrets.

Their design is not an accident. They retain their cool in the hot summer months and also serve to protect, to some extent, their inhabitants from desert sand storms. You can see quite a few entrances to old houses that go back to Ottoman and Mamluk times, some marked by wooden beams with Qur'anic excerpts carved into them. Watch out for the mud-brick minaret built by the Ayyubid dynasty in the 12th century. It has three floors and is 21 metres high. You can still see people making mud bricks in the time-honoured way. The people are still so unaccustomed to foreigners that you'll probably find their hospitality overwhelming.

There are pick-ups to Al-Qasr from near the police station in Mut for 50 pt.

Bashandi

Another so-called 'attraction' is the village

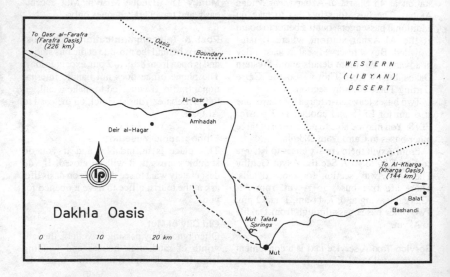

of Bashandi, 27 km from Mut, just off the road to Kharga. A sign at the crossroads near the village announces that this is the site of a development project sponsored by an Egyptian university. In the village a more descriptive sign lists the projects: 'carpets project, girl's training centre for making and embroidering old clothes, basketmaking and dressmaking'. There has also been an attempt to make this a tourist site.

From an entirely material standpoint, everything seems to have worked. The projects are alive and well. The touristic part of the village is kept clean and tidy – no garbage on the passageways between the houses and smooth, rounded mud walls. The guardian of the local monuments gladly takes you to the village's 'Pharaonic' and 'Islamic' tombs and, when it's open, to the carpet factory.

Getting There & Away Getting there from Mut is easy. There are collective pick-up trucks that go to at least the crossroads from in front of the hospital at the eastern side of town on the road to Kharga. They cost E£1. It takes about an hour to get there, as the pick-ups stop a lot on the way.

Balat
Just before Bashandi is another town that retains much of its medieval Islamic character. There is not much to do but wander around the alleyways and imagine how little has changed here over the centuries. A pick-up from near the hospital also costs E£1.

Other Sights
From Mut on the road to Al-Qasr and Farafra, there are several places that repay visiting if the traveller is in no hurry, although for some you'll need your own transport or have to bargain with locals. About 25 km out from Mut there is a turn-off to the right to **Bir al-Gebel** (signposted), where there is a pleasant spring about five km off the main road. There are good views of the surrounding area too. After passing Al-Qasr, you'll find a turn-off to the **Al-Muzawaka tombs**, which however were closed at the time of writing while a Cana-

dian team carried out research and restoration work. The cemeteries date back to Roman times. It seems that, when they open, the exorbitant E£8 entrance fee will apply. Another few km brings you to **Deir al-Hagar** (two km to the left off the main road), a sandstone temple built during the reign of Nero (45-68AD).

On another road leading back to Mut, you can visit several **tombs** near the village of Amhadah, dating from the 22nd century BC. Nearby is the Ottoman Turkish village of **Qalamun**.

Places to Stay
There are two rest houses in Mut town. The *Government Rest House* near the bus station (in the same building as the tourist office) is pretty basic, and the question of running water problematic. But it's cheap – E£3.70 a bed.

Another similar place is the *Dar al-Wafdeen Government Hotel*. It's possibly a little more basic, although the water seems to work. A bed here will set you back E£3.

Finally, there is another *Rest House* out of town at the spring and pool. A bed costs E£4.25, and plumbing problems apply. For some reason, it costs E£8.50 to pitch your tent here. They have tea and a few soft drinks for sale. The mosquitoes can be a problem in the warmer months.

The best deal in Mut is the *Gardens Hotel* (☎ 941577), where singles/doubles/triples without bath cost E£6/12/15. The showers have piping-hot water and the rooms are clean and reasonably comfortable. You can sit up on the roof or in the peaceful palm-filled courtyard out the back. Breakfast is extra. They rent bikes for an amazing E£7 – if you want a bike and are not too fussy about the state it's in, try Abu Mohammed's restaurant.

If you have a bit of money to throw around, you could do worse than the *Mebarez Hotel* (☎ 941524). It's past Abu Mohammed's on the road to Al-Qasr, and is popular with groups. A single/double with bath costs E£15.20/19 plus taxes. Breakfast is E£3.50. Without bath, the rooms come for

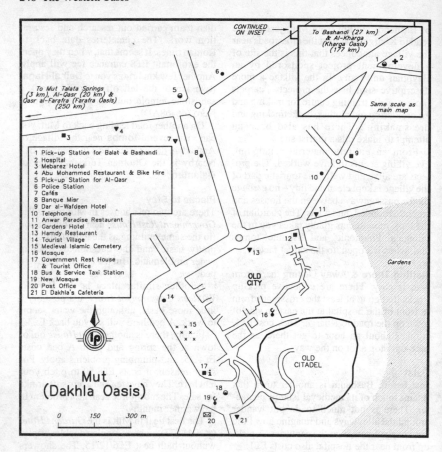

To Bashandi (27 km) & Al-Kharga (Kharga Oasis) (177 km)

Same scale as main map

To Mut Talata Springs (3 km), Al-Qasr (20 km) & Qasr al-Farafra (Farafra Oasis) (250 km)

CONTINUED ON INSET

1 Pick-up Station for Balat & Bashandi
2 Hospital
3 Mebarez Hotel
4 Abu Mohammed Restaurant & Bike Hire
5 Pick-up Station for Al-Qasr
6 Police Station
7 Cafés
8 Banque Misr
9 Dar al-Wafdeen Hotel
10 Telephone
11 Anwar Paradise Restaurant
12 Gardens Hotel
13 Hamdy Restaurant
14 Tourist Village
15 Medieval Islamic Cemetery
16 Mosque
17 Government Rest House & Tourist Office
18 Bus & Service Taxi Station
19 New Mosque
20 Post Office
21 El Dakhla's Cafeteria

Gardens

OLD CITY

OLD CITADEL

Mut (Dakhla Oasis)

0   150   300 m

E£12/14 plus taxes. They have an international phone line.

A new 'tourist village' is being painstakingly built next to the old Islamic cemetery. It will be a three to four-star establishment with restaurants, if they ever complete it.

Camping It's possible to camp in Al-Qasr, on a desert plateau just north of town, where the night sky is a spectacular field of stars; but try not to attract too much attention. You can also camp at the Mut Talata springs, but at E£8.50 to do so, it seems a pretty pointless exercise.

Places to Eat

There are not too many restaurants and cafés in Mut. *El Dakhla's Cafeteria* is on the small square where the intercity buses stop. It's a fair place for coffee, tea and pastries such as khounafa and basboosah. But the 'food' consists uniquely of fried liver. You can do better.

Another place is the *Hamdy Restaurant*, which is on the main road through town, about a 10-minute walk from the central rest house. Hamdy serves chicken, kebab, vegetables and a few other small dishes. It's pretty popular with tourists there and is a good place to get an omelette for breakfast. Try the chicken.

The *Abu Mohammed Restaurant* is the place to go for a meal that will fill you to bursting. Seemingly unending serves of soups, vegetables, rice, kebab, salads, sweets and Stella nonalcoholic beer emerge from a kitchen so clean it almost sparkles. It's not dirt cheap, however, so don't overorder if your budget is tight. The *Mebarez Hotel restaurant* is quite OK, but a little more expensive again.

Down by the Gardens Hotel is the *Anwar Paradise Restaurant*, but no-one ever seems to go there, which is hardly an encouraging sign.

Getting There & Away
Bus There are three buses a day from Cairo to Dakhla (Mut) via Asyut and Kharga. They leave at 5, 6.30 and 8 pm and cost respectively E£20/25/28. The first two are supposedly direct and do not stop in Asyut or Kharga even to set down passengers. You probably can get off – you'll just have to pay the full fare to Dakhla. The buses leave from the Upper Egypt Bus Co station at 45 Sharia al-Azhar.

At 7 am on Sunday, Tuesday and Friday, a bus runs via Bahariyya and Farafra. It takes at least 12 hours and costs E£22.

There is one bus a day to and from Farafra Oasis, except on Wednesday, but it is worth checking the latest situation to be sure of going when you want to. Buses to Farafra only leave on Sunday, Tuesday and Friday at 4 pm for E£7.50. They take about four to five hours. Buses all the way to Cairo, stopping at Farafra and Bahariyya, leave on Saturday, Monday and Thursday. Of course, if you want to go direct to Bahariyya, your choices are limited to those three days. The fare to Cairo on this route is E£22, and the trip can take anything up to 16 hours.

The services to Kharga Oasis and on to Asyut and Cairo leave every day at 6 am and 5 and, sometimes, 7 pm. The respective fares to Cairo are E£20/25/28, and the trip takes 12 to 14 hours.

Buses to Asyut via Kharga leave every day at 8.30 am and 4 pm. The morning bus costs E£5 to Kharga and E£10.50 to Asyut. The evening bus costs an extra E£1.50 for either destination.

There is a bus to Kharga alone at 2.30 pm for E£5.

Service Taxi Service taxis to Kharga leave from the bus station, and cost E£7 to Kharga, E£15 to Farafra and the same to Asyut. There are not a lot of them, so try in the morning.

Getting Around
Bus There are buses from Mut to Al-Qasr at 7 and 10 am, 2 and 4 pm. There are two buses a day to Balat, at 7 am and 2 pm. It is probably easier to get around on the pick-ups. To Al-Qasr from near the police station costs 50 pt. Most of the small towns and villages are linked by pick-up, but working out where they all go can be difficult. Theoretically, at least, it should probably be possible to get to any place mentioned with a pick-up, but it may prove simpler and less frustrating on occasion to hitch or bargain for special rides.

You can take pick-ups to Balat and Bashandi from in front of the hospital for E£1 to either.

Be warned also that they are ridiculously crowded in the early afternoons, mostly with school children.

Bicycle Abu Mohammed's Restaurant has five clattering bicycles for hire at E£3. The Gardens Hotel rents them out for E£7.

FARAFRA OASIS
The main town of Farafra, the smallest oasis in the Western Desert, is Qasr al-Farafra. Despite the relatively recent construction of a 310-km paved road linking it to Dakhla, and another 183 km stretch to Bahariyya, the 1500 people of this oasis are still quite isolated from most of the world. It is worth noting that the Bahariyya stretch is in an extremely bad state, and virtually nonexistent in parts – it makes for one dusty bus ride!

Many of the people are Bedouins and still adhere to some of the age-old traditions of

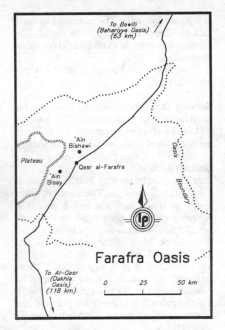

To Bawiti
(Bahariyya Oasis)
(63 km)

'Ain
Bishawi

Plateau

Qasr al-Farafra

'Ain
Bisay

Oasis

Boundary

Farafra Oasis

To Al-Qasr
(Dakhla
Oasis)
(118 km)

0   25   50 km

Museum

This is Farafra's only 'sight', so check it out. The museum consists of three stuffed gazelles, a dangerous snake behind glass, stuffed birds including an eagle and – unusually – a pelican, clay sculptures and paintings, a board game, and a catapult. The museum was built and is owned by a man named Badr, a very expressive artist who paints and sculpts not-so-subtle works of village people. His distinctive style has won him foreign admirers, and he sold all his exhibition material in two shows in Germany and the UK in 1992. At the time of writing, he was planning another exhibition in France for late 1993.

White Desert

Saad (of Saad's Restaurant) and various other locals organise overnight excursions into the White Desert for about E£25 per person. Be careful to establish whether or not food is included, and how far into the desert you'll actually go. Several travellers have reported being disappointed – driven off the main road a couple of km and left to wander around a little before eating, going to sleep and returning early the next morning. The White Desert is an otherworldly region of blinding white sand and rock formations, about 45 km from town. It may be possible to organise a similar trip on camels, and if you have your own 4WD vehicle, you can organise to have a guide accompany you.

At any rate, if you want to do such a trip, do it from here. There are some highly dubious characters organising similar trips from Bahariyya Oasis, almost 200 km away! You can see the desert on the way between the oases from the bus or your car, and some travellers simply get off the bus and take themselves off into the desert – be sure to have adequate supplies, and remember that traffic into Farafra is not overly heavy.

their culture. The small mud-brick houses of the town all have wooden doorways with medieval peg locks and the walls are painted with murals. The Bedouin women of Farafra produce beautifully embroidered dresses and shirts, although most of the work is for their own personal use and not for sale. Olives and olive oil are a speciality of the region, but the rich oasis also produces dates, figs, apricots, bananas, mangoes, guavas, oranges and apples.

The covered hot springs in town are a favourite among travellers. Women are permitted to bathe there only in the evening, but exceptions are sometimes made. It certainly makes a better bath than the showers available in the rest houses.

Especially if you are coming from Bahariyya, the calm and simplicity of this place will enchant you. There's precious little to do but wander around the town, the oasis and into the desert.

There is nowhere to change money here.

Places to Stay

The *Government Rest House* in Qasr al-Farafra has beds for E£3.50 a person. It's basic but OK. It's the building next to Saad's Restaurant, just where the buses to and from the oasis stop. Bring your own sheets, or a sleeping bag. There is electricity from 7 pm to midnight. A bit further up the road is the still more basic and cheaper *Youth Rest House* – E£2.25 per person.

Towards the end of 1992, a more expensive place, the *El Farafra Tourist Rest House*, was opened. It costs E£9.30 per person in comparatively comfortable share rooms. It's about 1 km out along the road to Bahariyya. They specifically demand you pay for your place if you want to leave luggage while going out for an overnight trip to the White Desert. Electricity seems to be a problem too.

Camping It's possible to pitch a tent at Well No 6, which is a hot spring six km west of the town. You can also go swimming in the concrete viaduct there.

Places to Eat

Saad's Restaurant is one of the few places to eat in Qasr al-Farafra. For E£4, you can get a good platter combining spaghetti, lentil soup, potato stew and beans. There are a few other little places claiming to be restaurants, but more often than not they have little more than eggs, jam and cheese.

At *Hussein's* there is an impressive menu, but ask him if he has, say, chicken, and he'll almost certainly respond: 'Tomorrow'.

There are a couple of little places in the town where you can buy some basic staples, including bottled water.

Getting There & Away

A bus leaves the Upper Egypt Bus Co station at 45 Sharia al-Azhar in Cairo at 8 am on Saturday, Monday and Thursday. It costs E£21.20 and takes 10 to 11 hours via Bahariyya. On every other day but Wednesday (when there is no bus from Cairo), the Cairo to Dakhla bus leaves at 7 am, stopping at Farafra on the way. It costs E£17.

These buses travel via Bahariyya. They depart Bahariyya at around noon and can take anything up to five hours to Farafra, because of the appalling state of the road. The three 7 am buses mentioned above con-

tinue on to Dakhla, which takes an additional three to four hours and costs E£7.50 from Farafra.

Check the latest schedules, or you may end up staying longer in one of the oases than you want.

Sometimes you can hitch a ride from Farafra to Dakhla, but don't count on this.

There is a bus to Cairo from Farafra every day except Wednesday. It leaves at 6 am on Sunday, Tuesday and Friday. To Bahariyya it costs E£6, and E£21 all the way to Cairo. On Saturday, Monday and Thursday the bus

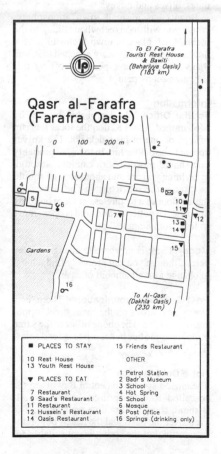

Qasr al-Farafra (Farafra Oasis)

To El Farafra Tourist Rest House & Bawiti (Bahariyya Oasis) (183 km)

0   100   200 m

Gardens

To Al-Qasr (Dakhla Oasis) (230 km)

■ PLACES TO STAY
10 Rest House
13 Youth Rest House

▼ PLACES TO EAT
7 Restaurant
9 Saad's Restaurant
11 Restaurant
12 Hussein's Restaurant
14 Oasis Restaurant

15 Friends Restaurant

OTHER
1 Petrol Station
2 Badr's Museum
3 School
4 Hot Spring
5 School
6 Mosque
8 Post Office
16 Springs (drinking only)

coming up from Dakhla leaves Farafra at about 10 am. The Cairo fare is E£18.

There is one bus a day to and from Dakhla, except Wednesday. It leaves Farafra at 4 pm on Sunday, Tuesday and Friday, and at 10 am on the other three days. The price is E£7.50.

BAHARIYYA OASIS

Bahariyya is 330 km south of Cairo and is linked to the capital by a paved road across the desert. There are several little villages spread throughout the oasis but the main one, with a population of about 30,000, is Bawiti. This prosperous oasis is renowned for its dates, olives and turkeys.

Bawiti has a small town atmosphere, which you will soon feel when talking to the locals. Each place in town seems to have a not-always-so-pretty story attached to it, and many travellers have been put off by this Egyptian soap opera.

Information

Tourist Office You'll probably be met by Mohammed Abdel Kader, the local tourism officer, or one of his sidekicks. The knives appear to be out for him in town, so probably you should proceed with caution, although everything you are told about anyone should be taken with a pinch of salt. The office is on the 1st floor of a featureless modern building opposite the police station, and is open, more or less, from 8 am to 2 pm.

Money There is nowhere to change money here, although you can probably find a local to change a small amount of cash.

Post & Telecommunications There is a sleepy post office on the main street, opposite the mosque. The phone office in the same building as the bus ticket office is for domestic calls only.

Hot & Cold Springs

The closest springs to central Bawiti are the so-called Roman springs, known as Al-Bishmu, about a 10-minute walk away. The view over the oasis and the desert beyond is wonderful, but the spring is not suitable for

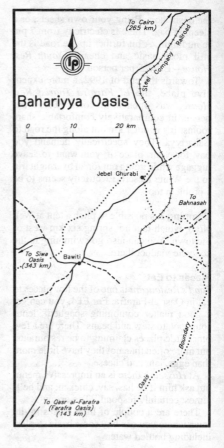

swimming in. An equally useless place for swimming is Bir al-Muftella, about three km from the centre. It's an interesting walk out through the village, but don't go for the water alone. Take the Siwa road and keep asking. If you pass a big, white conical structure (a sheikh's tomb) on your right, you'll know you're on the right track.

The hot sulphurous spring of Ar-Ramla is OK for a hot bath, but you may feel a bit exposed to the donkey traffic to and fro. Women especially should think twice. It's about a two-km walk from the centre of the town.

There's a spring at Ahmed's Safari Camp, if you choose to stay there, but the best spot is possibly Bir al-Ghaba, about 17 km away. You need 4WD transport out here, but there's nothing quite like a moonlit hot bath on the edge of the desert. The Alpenblick Hotel runs a rudimentary camping site there, so you can often get down there with them for a bath, or stay in the camp for a couple of days.

At Bir al-Mattar, seven km north-east of Bawiti, cold springs pour into a viaduct and then down into a concrete pool where you can splash.

Black Mountain

The area around Bawiti is not bad territory for walking. You can't miss Black Mountain: it's a flat-top hill with the remains of a WW I British outpost on it. Head out along the road to Cairo for a while, and turn off on to the track heading to Bir Ghaba and the Government Rest House at Bir al-Mattar. Keep the mountain in sight and follow village tracks out to it. The walk out to it takes about 1½ hours.

White Desert

The first piece of advice is simply not to do the trip to the White Desert from here, but wait until you get to Farafra (see previous section). However, if you feel you have to make an overnight trip to the desert from here, there are plenty of people trying to organise you into it, occasionally travellers themselves hoping to get a free ride for rounding up a few people.

A few years back there was a big storm about a party of Germans taken into the desert and then abandoned because they would not pay more than the agreed price. Salah Sherif (the part-owner of the Alpenblick Hotel) was accused of being the driver concerned; he claims it was a colleague of the time. Some say he ended up doing a stint in jail, but he denies it and insists he is being defamed. Whatever the truth of the story, it is an indication that it probably makes sense to ignore the whole thing and head down to Farafra yourself.

Other Attractions

Bahariyya is not renowned for its ancient sites, although in Bawiti there are the remains of a temple and settlement dating back to the 17th dynasty. There is also a special hill, south-west of the town, known as Qarat al-Firakhi, or 'ridge of the chicken merchant'. The hill features several underground galleries containing signs of bird burials. There are several ancient tombs around too. If you are interested, go to the Antiquities Office to get permission and help to see them.

Places to Stay

In spite of all the shenanigans over the years, including at one point a decision by the tourist office to close all hotels (to boost the number of people using the Government Rest House, according to some), there are a few options here. E£5 seems to be the common rate for a bed.

The *Government Rest House* is out by Bir

al-Mattar, and looks a bit like a POW camp. The facilities are not great and you need to arrange transport out there and back. Take supplies if you do go, as there is precious little out there.

The Government-run *Edelweiss Hotel* is a pretty dingy place in the centre of town. No-one seems to expect guests – you can wander in and find nobody around. It is also E£5 a bed.

For that money, you're better off taking a bed in the *Youth Hostel (beit shabab)*, which is not bad, or going out to *Ahmed's Safari Camp*, which is becoming a bit of a favourite among travellers. It's about four km out of the centre. If you can't get a cheap enough (or free) lift and want to walk, take the Siwa fork and keep asking your way there.

More expensive is the much maligned *Alpenblick Hotel*, now refurbished and owned by Salah Sherif and an Austrian-born, US-educated guy called Bakr Fahmy. He's only there in the winter months, but seems pretty straight. If the subject of Salah's questionable past comes up, Salah's protestations will be accompanied by well-meaning smiles from Bakr, who's heard the whole story so often and in so many forms that he may even sometimes wish he'd never bought into the hotel in the first place. Basic singles cost E£10, and include breakfast. The pricing system seems a little odd. A more comfortable triple costs E£20 *each*. It may be more comfortable, but not that much so. At the time of writing there was talk of getting hot water on, but for the time being you'll have to stick to cold.

The alternative is to go out with Bakr for an evening bath at Bir Ghaba, where the hotel has 15 huts with mattresses and nothing much else. The enclosure is watched by a warden, who will also help out with tea and firewood. It costs E£5 a night and is very peaceful.

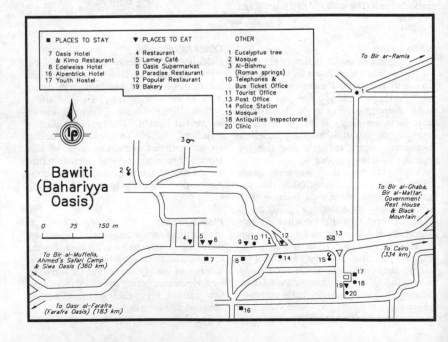

■ PLACES TO STAY	▼ PLACES TO EAT	OTHER
7 Oasis Hotel & Kimo Restaurant	4 Restaurant	1 Eucalyptus tree
8 Edelweiss Hotel	5 Lamey Café	2 Mosque
16 Alpenblick Hotel	6 Oasis Supermarket	3 Al-Bishmu (Roman springs)
17 Youth Hostel	9 Paradise Restaurant	10 Telephones & Bus Ticket Office
	12 Popular Restaurant	11 Tourist Office
	19 Bakery	13 Post Office
		14 Police Station
		15 Mosque
		18 Antiquities Inspectorate
		20 Clinic

Bawiti (Bahariyya Oasis)

To Bir ar-Ramla

To Bir al-Ghaba, Bir al-Mattar, Government Rest House & Black Mountain

To Cairo (334 km)

To Bir al-Muftella, Ahmed's Safari Camp & Siwa Oasis (360 km)

To Qasr al-Farafra (Farafra Oasis) (183 km)

0   75   150 m

There are a few other places around with signs up saying Hotel. They have all been shut down, although the *Oasis Hotel* sometimes takes people in anyway for E£5 a person.

Places to Eat

Unless you make your own meals, your food will be limited to the town's three 'restaurants', the *Alpenblick Hotel's kitchen* and grocery stores. The *Popular, Paradise* and *Kimo* restaurants all seem much of a muchness, serving a similar selection of dishes (such as chicken, rice, vegetables and a cola) for around E£7. The Kimo may be little better, and will do you a kushari if you're prepared to wait.

There are several grocery stores where you can pick up supplies for a few nights out at Bir Ghaba. The *Oasis* seems to be among the better and cheaper of them.

Getting There & Away

Bus From the Upper Egypt Bus Co station at 45 Sharia al-Azhar in Cairo, there are buses at 7 and 9 am and noon to Bahariyya (Bawiti) on Friday, Sunday and Tuesday. They cost E£9.20/10.20/11.20. The 7 am bus does not run on Wednesdays. On the other days of the week, the 8 am bus costs E£14.20 and the noon bus E£11.20. For details of which ones proceed to other destinations, see the relevant Getting There & Away sections. The trip takes about six hours.

Going to Cairo, there is a bus every day at 7 am (E£9 to E£10), one at 10 am on Sunday, Tuesday and Friday (E£14) and one at noon on Monday, Wednesday and Thursday for E£11.

You can pick up the bus from Cairo to Dakhla on Sunday, Tuesday or Friday at about noon for Farafra (E£6) or Dakhla (E£12). Otherwise, the Cairo to Farafra bus passes through at about 1.30 pm on Saturday, Monday and Thursday. The buses stop for about half an hour in front of the Lamey café. The ticket office, if you want to book (which you can only do for Cairo), is on the 2nd floor of the building housing the telephone office. Try from 9 am to 1 pm. If that fails, try again later: they seem to open up at all sorts of odd hours.

Service Taxi Supposedly, there's always a service taxi going to Sayyida Zeinab in Cairo (not far from Al-Azhar University) between 3 and 4 pm, but this could be earlier or later and not every day. If and when it does go, the taxi costs E£10 per person and takes around five hours. Ask at the Popular Restaurant.

Camel Before the paved road linked Bahariyya to Cairo, camel caravans were not uncommon. According to the local tourism representative, Mohammed Abdel Kader, the typical caravan took about 16 days. Once in a while, an intrepid foreigner organises a small caravan to make this trip.

SIWA

There is now a paved road covering the 425 km stretch between Bahariyya and Siwa, but there is no public transport link yet. Some service-taxi drivers approached over possible prices there came up with figures like E£200! So long as this is the case, the most common access route will remain that from Marsa Matruh on the Mediterranean coast. Siwa is described in detail in the Alexandria & The Mediterranean Coast section.

SOHAG

The city of Sohag, 93 km south of Asyut, is the administrative centre for the governorate of the same name and one of the major Coptic Christian areas of Upper Egypt. The only real reason to go there, however, is to see the White and Red monasteries just outside Sohag, and to visit the town of Achmim across the river. It's also not too bad as a base for the trip to Abydos, although Qena and Balyana are more convenient.

Information

Money You can change cash or travellers' cheques at the Bank of Alexandria or the Banque du Caire.

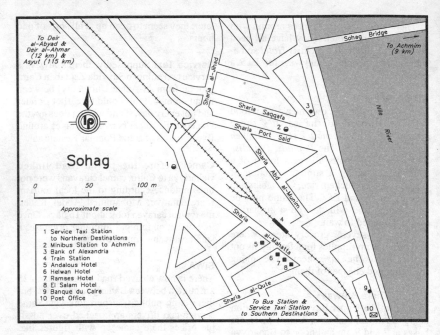

Post & Telecommunications The post office is a little way down the road from the Banque du Caire along the Nile.

White Monastery

Deir al-Abyad was built in 400 AD, by the Coptic saint Shenouda, with chunks of white limestone from a Pharaonic temple. The White Monastery, as it is called, once supported a community of 2000 monks. Its fortress walls still stand, but most of the interior is in ruins, though you can see the several types of arches used in its construction. The monastery is 12 km north-west of Sohag; there's a cafeteria across the road.

Red Monastery

Deir al-Ahmar, the Red Monastery, was founded by Bishoi, a thief who converted to Christianity, built this and two monasteries in Wadi Natrun and eventually became a Coptic saint. There are two chapels on the grounds, Santa Maria Chapel and the St Bishoi Chapel. Be sure to see the remains of a 10th century fresco on the central altar – it contains a 1000-year-old icon. There are interesting though fading frescoes on the walls, unusual pillars and old wooden peg locks on the doors.

Getting There & Away Unless you're visiting sometime during the first two weeks of July, when you can catch a bus to the monasteries for about E£1 with thousands of other pilgrims, your only option seems to be to take a taxi, which should cost about E£10 to both monasteries and back. However, some drivers said at the time of researching that there are pick-ups or service taxis all year round. A search didn't turn any up, but you may be able to do better.

Achmim

The town of Achmim, on the east bank of the Nile, is renowned for its unique woven carpets and wall-hangings. Though little of

Top: Sunrise over the fort at Sabouka, Siwa Oasis (KB)
Left: 'Allah' inscribed above doorway at Bashandi, Dakhla Oasis (KB)
Right: Mosque lit up for sunset prayers, Mut, Dakhla Oasis (KB)

Top: Camel herder and his charges, Sudan (CB)
Middle: Boy with his careta, Marsa Matruh (DS); Heavy duty biker, Cairo (RvD);
         Motorcyclist rides by a traditional lunch cart, Cairo (KB)
Bottom: The road to nowhere, Western Desert, Egypt (GB)

its past glory remains, except for an extensive, unexcavated cemetery, Achmim was once a flourishing provincial centre. There are several rockcut tombs in the area and a rock chapel dedicated to the local deity Min, the god of fertility. There's a microbus across the river to Achmim from Sohag which takes 15 minutes and costs 20 pt.

Places to Stay

There is a *Youth Hostel* at 5 Sharia Port Said. A bed costs E£2.10.

The *Andalous Hotel* is directly opposite the train station. Singles are E£7 and doubles are E£10.50. Breakfast is extra. It's quite adequate and the water is hot.

A little way down the street is the *Ramses Hotel*, which has very basic rooms, at E£5 a bed. The rooms are acceptable for the price.

The *El Salam Hotel* is next door, and has basic singles without bath for E£7 or E£10 with bath. There is hot water and there's not a lot in it between this and the Andalous.

Ignore signs for the *Sohag Hotel*. It has been converted into offices, which is probably a good thing, as it was pretty grubby anyway.

You may notice a sign for the *Helwan Hotel* near the Ramses. They won't let you stay, but it might be an interesting experience to enquire. You have to go round the corner to a parallel back street. As you walk into the darkness, a crumpled up figure crouched at a little desk tucked in under a staircase will pull a cord to turn on a light. This cross-eyed creature shrouded in his muck-grey garments will soon make you understand you are not welcome, and switch the light off again as you stumble back out into the street! There are a few other small hotels, usually with their names in Arabic, that are not interested in letting foreigners in.

Places to Eat

As well as the usual fruit and vegetable stands, there are also a few fuul and ta'amiyya places near the train station. If you follow the street south of the train station (left as you walk out the entrance) to a big square, and cross this, there is an OK kebab restaurant where a plate of the stuff will cost you E£5.

Getting There & Away

Bus The main bus station is around the corner from the big square south of the train station. It is near the city prison and service-taxi station for southern destinations. There are seven buses a day for Cairo ranging in price from E£11 to E£17. The first leaves at 7 am and the last at 10 pm. There is a bus to Luxor at 6 am for E£5.50. If you miss this, get a bus or service taxi to Qena. The bus to Asyut is E£2.50 and takes 1½ to two hours. There are departures every 30 to 40 minutes. The bus takes about an hour to Balyana (for Abydos) and costs 90 pt.

Train Trains north and south stop fairly frequently at Sohag. The 1st-class fare to Asyut is E£6.50; the 3rd-class fare is E£1. The train to Balyana generally makes a lot of stops (60 pt in 3rd class).

Service Taxi There are two service-taxi stations in Sohag. The one for Asyut and other northern destinations is north of the train station on Sharia al-Mahatta. The ride to Asyut costs E£3.50 and to Cairo it costs E£20. Service taxis for Qena and Nag Hammadi leave from the southern depot. The trip to Qena takes about 1½ hours and costs E£5. From there another taxi to Luxor costs E£2.

AL-BALYANA

The only reason to go to this town is to visit the nearby village of Al-Araba al-Madfunah. There you'll find the necropolis of Abydos and the magnificent Temple of Seti.

Abydos

The temples at Abydos served several dynasties of Egyptians and its huge necropolis was, for a long time, *the* place to be buried. Excavations indicate that it was a burial place of the last pre-dynastic kings, before 3100 BC. Seti I and Ramses II built the most important temples of the complex in the 13th

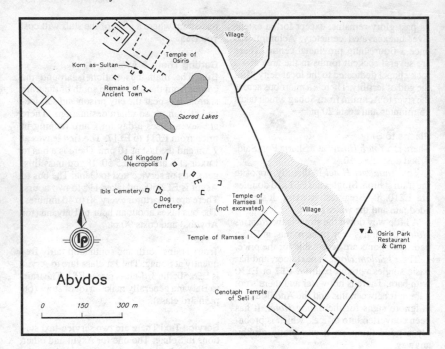

Abydos

0   150   300 m

century BC; and Abydos was still important during Roman times.

The centre of the walled town of Abydos was a mound called Kom as-Sultan; nearby was the all-important Temple of Osiris, of which little remains. Abydos maintained its importance for so many centuries because of the cult of Osiris, god of the dead.

The area was a natural shrine for the worship of this ruler of the netherworld because, according to mythology, it was here that the head of Osiris was buried after his brother Seth had murdered him, cut his body into several pieces, and scattered the bits all over Egypt. Osiris' wife and sister, the goddess Isis, searched for and found all the pieces and put him back together again, building temples wherever she found the dissected parts. Osiris and Isis then begat Horus, the falcon-god, who killed his uncle Seth. The temple at Abydos was the most important of the shrines to Osiris and became

a place of pilgrimage. Most Egyptians would make the journey there at least once in their lifetime.

Abydos is open from 7 am to 5 pm daily. The admission fee for both temples is E£6, or E£3 for students. Bring a torch.

Cenotaph Temple of Seti I The first structure you'll see at Abydos is one of Egypt's most complete temples. A cenotaph temple was a secondary mortuary temple dedicated to one or more gods and honouring the deified, deceased Pharaoh who built it. Pharaoh Seti's splendid temple honours seven gods: Osiris, Isis, Horus, Amun, Ra-Harakhty, Ptah and Seti I himself. The Osiris sanctuary was especially important; it opens into an area extending the width of the temple, with two halls and two sets of three chapels dedicated to Osiris, Isis and Horus.

As you roam through Seti's dark halls and sanctuaries a definite air of mystery, an almost tangible impression of ancient pomp and circumstance, surrounds you. The colourful hieroglyphs on the walls, describing the rituals that were carried out there, make it easy to imagine the ceremonies honouring the death and rebirth of Osiris and the great processions of cult worshippers that passed in and out of the temple.

In a corridor known as the Gallery of the Kings, to the left of the sanctuaries, a list of Egypt's Pharaohs up to Seti I was found. Though not complete, the 76 cartouches – oblong figures containing each king's name – greatly assisted archaeologists in unravelling Egypt's long history from Menes onwards.

Temple of Ramses II North-west of Seti's temple his son Ramses II built another temple dedicated to Osiris – and himself. The roof of the Temple of Ramses II has collapsed, but the hieroglyphs on the walls are interesting, though you have to get the guard to unlock the gate. The local villagers will let him know that a *khawagah*, a not-so-complimentary way of saying 'foreigner', wants to get into the temple.

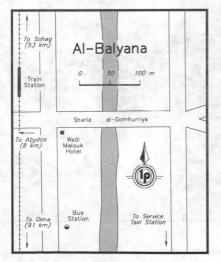

Cemetery The extensive cemetery between Kom as-Sultan and Seti's temple includes buried dogs, falcons and ibises as well as the cenotaphs or actual graves of those ancient Egyptians who wanted to lie for ever in the company of Osiris.

Places to Stay & Eat
If you really have to stay in Al-Balyana, there's the *Wadi Melouk Hotel*, which looks as if it's suffered greatly from its position right next to the train tracks. A very basic double costs E£5, and there is only cold water. There is a café below the hotel and a few basic food stands around the town.

Right in front of Abydos is the *Osiris Park Restaurant and Camp*, where a row of tents with beds has been set up. One bed costs E£10. Eating and drinking is an expensive business around here. You can be hit for E£5 just for an omelette at the Osiris, and the standard 25 pt tea somehow seems to cost E£1.

Getting There & Around
Al-Balyana is serviced by buses, trains and service taxis. The respective stations are conveniently close to each other. A 1st-class train to Asyut costs E£6.50 and 3rd class is E£1. To Sohag is 60 pt 3rd class. The buses to Sohag or Qena tend to do a circuit around the town before actually hitting the road. A service taxi to Sohag costs E£1.50, or E£5 to Asyut. There are buses between Sohag and Balyana about every half an hour from 6 am to 5 pm.

Service taxis (75 pt) and microbuses (30 pt) both go to the temple complex. There are also buses from Qena to Abydos (E£1).

QENA
Qena, a provincial capital 91 km east of Al-Balyana and 62 km north of Luxor, is at the intersection of the main Nile road and the road across the desert to the Red Sea towns of Safaga and Hurghada.

Unless you're on your way to or from the Red Sea and have not got a through connection, the only reason to stop in Qena is to visit the spectacular temple complex at Dendara, just outside the town. There are two service taxi stations quite a long way apart from one another, one for northern destinations and places across the Nile, the other for southern destinations. If you need money, there is a Bank of Alexandria not far from the bus station.

Dendara

Although it indicates the decline of a purely Egyptian style of art, the wonderfully preserved complex at Dendara is a sight to behold. Complete with a massive stone roof, dark chambers, underground passages and towering columns inscribed with hieroglyphs, the main Temple of Hathor is almost intact.

While the Dendara necropolis includes Early Dynastic tombs and evidence that Cheops and later Pharaohs built there, the temple complex, as it stands today, was built by the Ptolemys and the Romans. Its very design, however, suggests that it was built on the site of an older temple and, as was the custom of the day, reproduces the character and mythology of the original. So, despite the apparent shortcomings in the quality of its design and decoration, and the fact that it was raised during foreign occupation, it is an impressive, beautiful monument to an ancient goddess of great renown.

Hathor was the goddess of pleasure and love; she was usually represented as a cow, or a woman with a cow's head, or a woman whose headdress was a sun disc fixed between the horns of a cow. She was the beneficent deity of maternal and family love, of beauty and light; the Greeks associated her with Aphrodite.

Hathor was also the wet nurse of Horus, before becoming his mate and bearing Ihy, the youthful aspect of the creator-gods.

Temple complex at Dendara

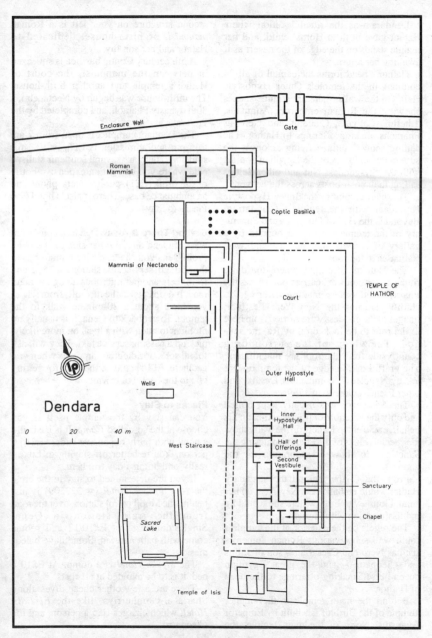

Enclosure Wall

Gate

Roman
Mammisi

Coptic Basilica

Mammisi of Nectanebo

TEMPLE OF
HATHOR

Court

Wells

Dendara

0   20   40 m

Outer Hypostyle
Hall

Inner
Hypostyle
Hall

Hall of
Offerings

West Staircase

Second
Vestibule

Sanctuary

Chapel

Sacred
Lake

Temple of Isis

Dendara was the ritual location where Hathor gave birth to Horus' child, and her temple stands on the edge of the desert as if awaiting her return.

Hathor's head forms the capital of all 24 columns in the temple's Outer Hypostyle Hall. On the walls, there are strange scenes showing the Roman emperors Augustus, Tiberius, Caligula, Claudius and Nero as Pharaohs, making offerings to Hathor. The ceiling shows vultures flying amongst the sun, moon and stars of the Egyptian zodiac, with the sky-goddess Nut and other deities sailing their solar boats across the heavens.

The hieroglyphs in the Inner Hypostyle Hall deal with the temple's foundation. Beyond is the Hall of Offerings and Sanctuary of the temple proper, surrounded by a gallery of chapels and the east and west staircases to the roof.

The Hall of Offerings, where the daily rituals of the cult were carried out, shows the Pharaoh and others making offerings to Hathor. During the New Year Festival, images of the goddess were carried from here to the roof to be looked on by Ra, the sun-god. The views of the surrounding countryside from the roof are magnificent. The graffiti on the edge of the temple were left by Napoleon's commander Desaix, and other French soldiers, in 1799.

The Sanctuary was usually kept bolted and only the Pharaoh, or priests acting on his behalf, could enter. Reliefs on the walls show the special rituals of the Pharaoh entering the Sanctuary to show his adoration for the goddess.

From the Chapel behind the sanctuary Hathor would embark each New Year on her annual journey to Edfu, where she would lie in blissful union with Horus.

The reliefs on the exterior of the temple's south wall show various Roman emperors such as Nero and Caesarian – son of Julius and Cleopatra – and the great Egyptian queen herself making offerings to the head of Hathor.

Behind the main temple is the smaller Temple of the Birth of Isis built by Emperor Augustus. North of the main temple, the second structure on your left is a Roman *mammisi*, or birth-house, dedicated to Hathor and her son Ihy.

A 5th century Coptic basilica is squeezed in between the mammisi, the court of Hathor's temple and another birth-house. The birth-house was begun by Nectanebo, a 30th dynasty Pharaoh, and completed by the Ptolemys.

The Dendara complex is open from 7 am to 6 pm and admission is E£6, or E£3 for students. There are several souvenir stalls, a café where you can get an expensive bottle of soft drink (E£1), public toilets, phone and an ambulance base. There is also a hotel (see Places to Stay).

Getting There & Away Dendara is four km west of Qena on the other side of the Nile. From Qena you can take a local microbus to the northern service taxi station for 25 pt, and from there another microbus along the main road. It drops you at the turn-off, from where you have about a 20-minute walk to the temple. To get back to Qena, it is usually no problem to hitch with a local or, more likely, pick up a passing service taxi. They will ask for all sorts of ridiculous amounts when you get there. E£1 should be the limit for getting you to the centre of town.

Places to Stay
You can stay by the temple itself if you choose at the so-called *Camp*. It is basically a hotel with fairly expensive beds – E£15 a person. You're better off staying in Luxor, really, and doing a day trip here.

If you are determined to stay in the area, the *New Palace Hotel* (☎ 322509) is just behind the Mobil petrol station, over the road from the train station in Qena. Singles/doubles cost E£10/17 and rooms come with bath and fan. Some have balconies.

The *Mekka Hotel* is a dump. At E£10 a bed, it is to be avoided at all costs.

There are a few other cheap dives along Sharia al-Gomhurriya, like the *El Fath Hotel*, which charges E£5 a person, and the *Cleopatra*.

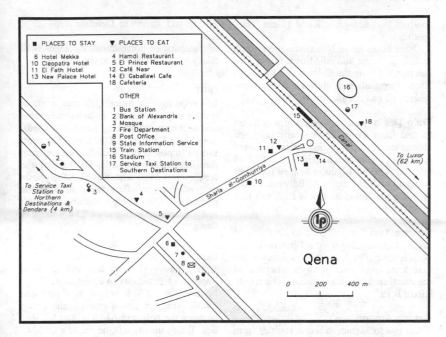

PLACES TO STAY
6 Hotel Mekka
10 Cleopatra Hotel
11 El Fath Hotel
13 New Palace Hotel

PLACES TO EAT
4 Hamdi Restaurant
5 El Prince Restaurant
12 Café Nasr
14 El Gaballawi Cafe
18 Cafeteria

OTHER
1 Bus Station
2 Bank of Alexandria
3 Mosque
7 Fire Department
8 Post Office
9 State Information Service
15 Train Station
16 Stadium
17 Service Taxi Station to Southern Destinations

To Service Taxi Station to Northern Destinations & Dendara (4 km)

To Luxor (62 km)

Sharia al-Gomhurriya

Canal

Qena

0   200   400 m

Places to Eat

Café Nasr has backgammon, tea and lots of Egyptians who stare at you because there's nothing else to do in Qena.

Restaurant Hamdi serves full meals of chicken, rice, pudding, tea, bread and beans for about E£10. The *El Prince* is similar.

Along the main street there are also several kushari, kofta and ta'amiyya places.

Things to Buy

Pottery, particularly water jugs, is the speciality in Qena; however, bear in mind that it's probably difficult to carry pottery around in your backpack.

Getting There & Away

Bus The bus station is about 50 metres northeast of the central mosque and Bank of Alexandria. From the train station you walk down the main street towards the Nile, turn right at the large intersection (the El Prince restaurant is on the corner) and the minaret

of the mosque is ahead of you. Walk past it and the station is on your left.

There are at least nine buses to Cairo from 6.15 am to 8 pm – maybe more if you get lucky with a bus coming up from further south. Fares range from E£18 for the basic bus to E£33 for the Super Jet, which has air-con, toilet and video.

At 6 am there is a bus all the way through to Alexandria – the trip takes about 14 hours.

Eleven buses go to Aswan from 6.30 am to 7.45 pm, and most stop in Luxor. A few other buses only go as far as Edfu or Luxor. The cheapest fare to Aswan is E£7. The Super Jet is E£15. To Luxor it's E£1.50, although the fare seems to rise another 50 pt after 5 pm.

There are nine buses to Hurghada; six of them go on to Suez. The flat fare to Hurghada is E£6. To Suez it's E£18, or E£22 with video and air-con. The trip takes about nine to 10 hours.

Two buses leave for Quseir, on the coast

south of Port Safaga, at 7 and 11 am. They cost E£6.

Other buses serve Nile destinations such as Sohag, Asyut and Al-Minya. Often, you can transfer from the Cairo buses for these. These buses all pass through Al-Balyana, where you can change for Abydos.

Train This is not a very practical way to get to and from Qena, as generally only the slower trains stop here. First class to Luxor is E£5.60, 2nd is E£3.50 (air-con) or E£2.40 and 3rd is 70 pt. If you're headed the other way and want to stop in Al-Balyana to visit Abydos, the 2nd-class fare is E£2, and E£1 in 3rd class.

Service Taxi Service taxis to destinations north of Qena leave from a T-junction a km outside town. For destinations south, service taxis leave from a station on the other side of the canal from the train station. The trip to Luxor is E£2.

Getting Around

There is a local microbus that shuttles from town to the north service-taxi station. You can pick it up near the train station, or, if you're coming up from the south, at the canal bridge near the south service-taxi station. It costs 25 pt. The microbus from the north

service-taxi station to Dendara costs 25 pt too.

Hantours, or horse-drawn carriages, will take you to Dendara for about E£4.

QIFT

In Greco-Roman times Qift was a major trading town on the Arabia-India trade route and an important starting point for expeditions to the Red Sea and the Sinai. The town lost its importance as a trading centre from the 10th century onwards. The harvest and fertility-god Min, who was also the patron deity of desert travellers, was considered the protector of Qift. There is nothing that can't really be missed in this town 23 km south of Qena.

QUS

During medieval times this was the most important Islamic city in Egypt, after Cairo. Founded in 1083, it served as a port and transit point for goods coming and going between the Nile and Al-Quseir on the Red Sea. Today, the town is the site of a US$246 million Egyptian-German paper mill project that converts *bagasse* – the waste product of sugar cane refining – into paper products. Beyond this, there is really nothing of great interest here.

The Nile Valley – Luxor

The sheer grandeur of Luxor's monumental architecture, and its excellent state of preservation, have made this village-city one of Egypt's greatest tourist attractions. Built on and around the 4000-year-old site of ancient Thebes, Luxor is an extraordinary mixture of exotic history and modern commercialism.

Here the fellahin work the fields as they have done since time immemorial; mundane daily business is carried on as if there weren't hordes of foreigners walking the streets; modern hotels are full of Westerners; the souqs are full of fake antiquities made just for the tourists; and modern Egyptians make a fine living out of the legacy of their ancestors.

It is one of the world's greatest open-air museums, a time capsule of a glorious long-gone era. Yet at the same time this overgrown village, with a population exceeding 100,000, thrives and bustles with life.

Its attraction for tourists is by no means a recent phenomenon: travellers have been visiting Thebes for centuries, marvelling at the splendid temples of Luxor, Karnak, Ramses II and Hatshepsut. As far back as Greco-Roman times visitors would wait in the desert to hear the mysterious voice of Memnon emanating from the colossal statues of Amenophis III; and in the past hundred years or so, since archaeology became a respectable science, curious travellers have been following the footsteps of the excavators into the famous tombs of the Valley of the Kings.

What most visitors today know as Luxor is actually three separate areas: the city of Luxor itself, the village of Karnak a couple of km to the north-east, and the monuments and necropolis of ancient Thebes on the west bank of the Nile.

Along the river, feluccas and antiquated barges compete for space with the posh hotel ships of the Hilton and Sheraton, and the many other 'flotels' plying the Nile from Cairo to Aswan.

Behind the tourist facade, the dirt streets are crowded with mud-brick tenements, pocked with mud puddles and filled with ordinary, friendly people. Unfortunately, the friendliness has developed a predictable commercial edge, and travellers in Luxor complain increasingly of the almost incessant hassle from vendors, street hawkers and felucca middlemen. In the steamy summer months, when business is slack, it can be enough to tip a temper already frazzled by the heat. In winter, it's easier to bear in mind that they are just trying to make a living.

HISTORY

Following the collapse of centralised power at the end of the Old Kingdom period, the small village of Thebes, under the 11th and 12th dynasty Pharaohs, emerged as the main power in Upper Egypt. Rising against the northern capital of Heracleopolis, Thebes reunited the country under its political, religious and administrative control and ushered in the Middle Kingdom period. The strength of its government also enabled it to re-establish control after a second period of decline; liberate the country from foreign rule; and bring in the New Kingdom dynasties.

At the height of its glory and opulence, from 1570 to 1090 BC, the New Kingdom Pharaohs made Thebes their permanent residence; the city had a population of nearly one million and the architectural activity was astounding.

Because so many kings left their mark at Thebes it can quickly become very confusing trying to keep track of who built what temples or tombs and when they did so. For detailed information on the history of Thebes, see the reference books listed in the Facts for the Visitor chapter.

ORIENTATION

There are only three main thoroughfares in Luxor, so it's easy to find your way around – as long as you don't ask for street names.

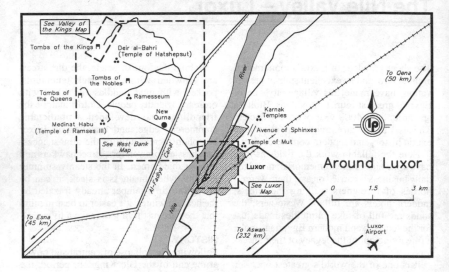

Some streets have signs, some have names but no signs and some seem to have no names at all. If you ask the locals to what the name of a particular street is they're quite likely to make one up on the spot, which is why nearly every map of Luxor is different. So, it's best to ask directions to a specific location rather than to the street or road it's on. The three main roads are Sharia al-Mahatta, Sharia al-Karnak and the Corniche. Another road you may want to know if you're looking for cheap accommodation is Sharia Television, around which are clustered many, although by no means all, of the cheap hotels.

Sharia al-Mahatta – the street directly in front of the train station – runs perpendicular to the Nile all the way to the gardens of Luxor Temple. Sharia al-Karnak runs one block in from, and parallel to, the river, from Luxor Temple to Karnak Temple. Sharia al-Karnak (or Sharia Maabad al-Karnak, 'Karnak Temple Street') meets Sharia al-Mahatta and runs around the southern end of Luxor Temple, which overlooks the Nile, to the corniche road. To confuse matters Sharia al-Karnak, where it meets Sharia al-Mahatta, is also known as Sharia al-Markaz; to the south, around the temple to the river, it's

known as Sharia al-Lokanda. The corniche road is known variously as Sharia al-Bahr, Sharia Bahr el-Nil or simply the Corniche.

INFORMATION
Tourist Offices
The main tourist office, State Information Office and tourist police are in the Tourist Bazaar on the Corniche, next to the New Winter Palace Hotel. They're open from 8 am to 8 pm and the staff can fill you in on what the official prices for various services should be, as well as the most recent schedule and prices of the sound & light show at Karnak Temple. They also occasionally have a handy booklet titled *Upper Egypt by Night & Day*. Lastly, travellers can leave messages taped to one of the columns next to the main information counter. There is another tourist office at the train station, although it hardly ever seems to be open.

A visitors' centre is also being built on the Corniche. It supposedly will have a cinema, a café and conference rooms. How much use it will be to most travellers is yet to be seen.

Visa Extensions
The passport office, open from 8 am to 1.30

pm except on Friday, is in front of the Isis Hotel, south of the town centre. Some people swear it's much easier to get a visa extension here than in the Mogamma building in Cairo. You'll need a photo, a bank receipt showing you've changed US$180 for every month you want to stay, and E£12.

Money
The Bank of Alexandria has a branch on the Corniche, a little way up from the ETAP hotel. Banque Misr is in Sharia Nefertiti, around the corner from the ETAP, and the National Bank of Egypt is down on the Corniche near the Winter Palace. Banks are usually open from 8.30 am to 2 pm and again for a few hours from 5 or 6 pm. In addition, the big hotels have various bank branches, and there is an exchange booth open quite long hours on the Corniche in front of the Tourist Bazaar.

American Express The American Express office (☎ 382862) is next door to the Winter Palace Hotel and operates from 8 am to 7 pm, although the hours seem flexible. All the usual services are available.

Thomas Cook There's also a Thomas Cook money exchange office (☎ 382196, fax 386502) across from American Express.

Post & Telecommunications
The GPO is on Sharia al-Mahatta and there's a branch office in the Tourist Bazaar.

The central telephone office is on Sharia al-Karnak and is open 24 hours; there's another, open from 8 am to 10 pm, below the resplendent entrance of the Winter Palace Hotel. Telephone numbers have undergone changes in Luxor. They are all six-digit numbers, but many places are trading in their old lines beginning with 38 and another digit and replacing them with new lines beginning with 580 or 581. There are also a lot of new lines beginning with 37. The changes still seem to be under way, so more numbers could change.

Bookshops
Aboudi's Bookshop has an excellent selection of books, guidebooks and maps and is in the same complex as the tourist office and State Information Office. A few doors down towards the old Winter Palace Hotel is A A Gaddis, where you can also find books and even aerogrammes embellished with mug shots of Tutankhamun. They also have pop-up cardboard models of Pharaonic temples. The bookshop in the ETAP Hotel has a good selection of guidebooks and books on Egypt but their prices tend to be slightly higher.

Film
Film can be bought and processed at a few shops in town, but according to some locals, most of them send their films on to Photo Queen, so you may as well go there too. It's off Sharia al-Mahatta, not far down from the train station. They charge E£28 to process a roll of 36 colour prints in a day or E£34 in an hour.

East Bank

Luxor Museum
This wonderful little museum on the Corniche, about half way between the Luxor and Karnak temples, has a small but well-chosen collection of relics from the Theban temples and necropolis. The displays, which include pottery, jewellery, furniture, statues and stelae, were arranged by the Brooklyn Museum of New York.

On the 1st floor is a well-preserved cow-goddess head from King Tutankhamun's tomb. Exhibit No 61 is a finely carved statuette of Tuthmosis III that dates from at least 1436 BC.

The most interesting exhibit is the Wall of Akhenaten on the 2nd floor, which is actually a set of 283 sandstone blocks found within the 9th Pylon of the Karnak Temple. The reliefs show the rebel Pharaoh and his queen, Nefertiti, making offerings to Aten.

Also on the 2nd floor, check out the canopic jars that once contained the internal organs of the priest of the god Montu, and King Tutankhamun's well-preserved funerary boats. There are a few other relics in the small garden outside.

To the right just after entering the museum is the entrance to a new hall, which contains 16 exhibits, some of them beautiful statues. They were found recently in Luxor Temple, but whether the extra E£10 is worth it is a moot point. A quick peek through the doorway will give you a bit of an idea of what's on offer.

The museum is open from 9 am to 1 pm and 4 to 9 pm (winter) or 5 to 10 pm (summer), seven days a week. Entry to the main museum costs E£8 (E£4 for students); the fee for the new hall is E£10 (E£5). The right to take photos costs E£10, while video is E£100.

Luxor Temple

Amun, one of the gods of creation, was the most important god of Thebes and head of the local triad of deities. As Amun-Ra, the fusion of Amun and the sun-god Ra, he was also a state deity worshipped in many parts of the country. Once a year from his Great Temple at Karnak the images of Amun and the other two gods in the local triad – Amun's wife, the war-goddess Mut, and their son, the moon-god Khons – would journey down the Nile to Luxor Temple for the Opet Festival, a celebration held during the inundation season.

Built by the New Kingdom Pharaoh Amenophis III, on the site of an older sanctuary dedicated to the Theban triad, Luxor Temple is a strikingly graceful piece of architecture on the banks of the Nile. Amenophis rededicated the massive temple as Amun's sacred 'harem of the south', and retained what was left of the original sanctuary built by Tuthmosis III and Hatshepsut 100 years earlier.

The Luxor Temple was added to over the centuries by Tutankhamun, Ramses II, Nectanebo, Alexander the Great and various Romans. At one point the Arabs built a mosque in one of the interior courts, and there was also once a village within the temple walls. Excavation work has been going on since 1885, and has included removing the village and clearing the forecourt and 1st Pylon of debris, and exposing part of the avenue of sphinxes leading to Karnak.

Fronting the entrance to the temple is the enormous 1st Pylon, about 24 metres high, in front of which are some colossal statues of Ramses II and a pink granite obelisk. There were originally six statues, four seated and two standing, but only two of the seated figures and the westernmost standing one remain. The obelisk, too, was one of a pair; its towering counterpart now stands in the Place de la Concorde in Paris. Behind the pylon, which is decorated with Ramses' victorious exploits in battle, is another of his additions to the main complex. The Great Court of Ramses II is surrounded by a double row of columns with lotus-bud capitals, more reliefs of his deeds of derring-do and

Ramses II, Luxor Temple

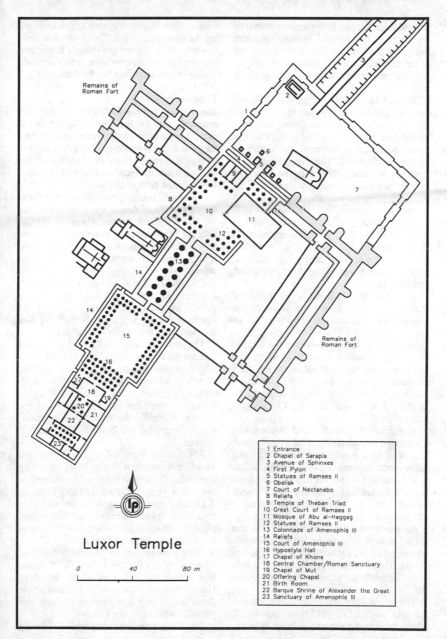

Luxor Temple

0   40   80 m

1 Entrance
2 Chapel of Serapis
3 Avenue of Sphinxes
4 First Pylon
5 Statues of Ramses II
6 Obelisk
7 Court of Nectanebo
8 Reliefs
9 Temple of Theban Triad
10 Great Court of Ramses II
11 Mosque of Abu al-Haggag
12 Statues of Ramses II
13 Colonnade of Amenophis III
14 Reliefs
15 Court of Amenophis III
16 Hypostyle Hall
17 Chapel of Khons
18 Central Chamber/Roman Sanctuary
19 Chapel of Mut
20 Offering Chapel
21 Birth Room
22 Barque Shrine of Alexander the Great
23 Sanctuary of Amenophis III

Remains of
Roman Fort

Remains of
Roman Fort

several huge statues. In the western corner of the court is the original Middle Kingdom Temple of the Theban Triad and south of that is the 13th century AD Mosque of Abu al-Haggag, dedicated to a local sheikh and holy man.

Beyond the court, 14 papyrus columns form the splendid Colonnade of Amenophis III. The walls behind the columns were decorated during the reign of the young Pharaoh Tutankhamun and celebrate the return to Theban orthodoxy. The Opet Festival is depicted in great detail, with the king, the nobility and the common people joining the triumphal procession of Amun, Mut and Khons from Karnak.

The colonnade takes you into the Court of Amenophis III. This was once enclosed on three sides by double rows of towering columns, of which the best preserved, with their architraves extant, are those on the east and west sides.

The Hypostyle Hall on the south side of the court is the first inner room of the temple proper and features four rows of eight columns each.

Beyond are the main rooms of the Temple of Amun, the central chamber of which was once stuccoed over by the Romans and used as a cult sanctuary. Through this chamber, on either side of which are chapels dedicated to Mut and Khons, is an Offering Chapel with four columns.

The interesting inscriptions in the Birth Room, to the eastern side of the chapel, show scenes of how mortal Amenophis claimed divine status by coming up with the notion that Amun had visited his mother Mutemuia in the 'guise' of his father Tuthmosis IV, with the result that he, Amenophis III, was actually the god's son.

Alexander the Great rebuilt the Barque (Boat) Shrine, beyond the Offering Chapel, adding reliefs of himself being presented to Amun. The last chamber on the central axis of the temple is the Sanctuary of Amenophis III.

The Luxor Temple is open from 6 am to 6 pm and costs E£10 (E£5 for students). It opens again in the evening, when it is lit up,

from 6.30 to 10 pm. It costs half price to visit for the evening session. This is the best time to visit, when the temperature is lower and the illuminated temple is an eerie spectacle beside the shimmering black of the Nile.

Temples of Karnak

The Amun Temple Enclosure (sometimes referred to as the Precinct of Amun) is the central enclosure of the numerous temples that make up the enormous Karnak complex; it was the main place of worship of the Theban triad. Its ancient name was Ipet-Isut, or 'the most perfect of places'.

Although the original sanctuary of the Great Temple of Amun was built during the Middle Kingdom period, when the Theban Pharaohs first came to prominence, the rest of the temples, pylons, courts, columns and reliefs were the work of New Kingdom rulers.

Karnak was built, added to, dismantled, restored, enlarged and decorated over a period of nearly 1500 years. During the height of Theban power and prosperity it was the most important temple in all Egypt.

The complex can be divided into three distinct areas: the Amun Temple Enclosure, which is the largest enclosure; the Mut Temple Enclosure, on the south side, which was once linked to the main temple by an avenue of ram-headed sphinxes; and the Montu Temple Enclosure, to the north, which honoured the original local god of Thebes.

A canal once connected the Amun and Montu enclosures with the Nile, providing access for the sacred boats in the journey to the Luxor Temple during the Opet Festival. A paved avenue of human-headed sphinxes also once linked Karnak, from Euergetes' Gate on the south side of the Amun Temple Enclosure, with Luxor Temple.

Only a small section of this sacred way, where it leaves the Great Temple of Amun and enters the forecourt of his Southern Harem, has been excavated. The rest of the three-km avenue lies beneath the city and paved roads of modern Luxor.

The Karnak site measures about 1.5 km by

Karnak Temple

0.8 km, which is large enough to hold about 10 cathedrals, and the 1st Pylon, at the entrance, is twice the size of the one at Luxor Temple. The further into the complex you venture the further back in time you go.

The oldest part of the complex is the White Pavilion of Sesostris I and the 12th dynasty foundations of what became the most sacred part of the Great Temple of Amun, the Sacred Barque Sanctuary and Central Court of Amun (located behind the 6th Pylon). The limestone fragments of the demolished pavilion, or chapel, were recovered from the foundations of the 3rd Pylon, built five centuries after Sesostris' reign, and expertly reconstructed in the open-air museum to the north of the Great Court.

The major additions to the complex were constructed by Pharaohs of the 18th to 20th dynasties, between 1570 and 1090 BC. The Pharaohs of the later dynasties extended and rebuilt the complex, and the Ptolemies and early Christians also left their mark on it.

You'll need to visit Karnak at least twice to fully appreciate the size and magnificence of the complex. A return visit in the evening for the sound & light show would complete the picture. The refreshment stand located on the map is expensive in the extreme. A cup of Coca-Cola costs E£2.

General admission to the temples of Karnak is between 6 am and 6 pm and tickets cost E£10, or E£5 for students.

Amun Temple Enclosure – main axis
From the entrance you pass down the processional avenue of ram-headed sphinxes, which once led to the Nile, to the massive 1st Pylon. You used to be able to climb the stairs on your left to the top of the pylon's north tower, from where there is an amazing view of Karnak and the surrounding country. The stairs were closed off a few years ago when a tourist fell backwards to the ground and died.

You emerge from the 1st Pylon into the Great Court, the largest single area of the Karnak complex. To the left is the Temple of Seti II, dedicated to the Theban triad. The three small chapels held the sacred barques of Amun, Mut and Khons during the lead-up to the Opet Festival.

The north and south walls of the court are lined with columns with papyrus-bud capitals. The south wall is intersected by the Temple of Ramses III, which was built before the court. Obligatory scenes of the Pharaoh as glorious conqueror adorn the pylon of this 60-metre-long temple which also features an open court, a vestibule with four columns, a hypostyle hall of eight columns and three barque chapels.

In the centre of the Great Court is the one remaining column of the Kiosk of Taharqa. A 25th dynasty Ethiopian Pharaoh, Taharqa built his open-sided pavilion of 10 columns, each rising 21 metres and topped with papyrus-form capitals.

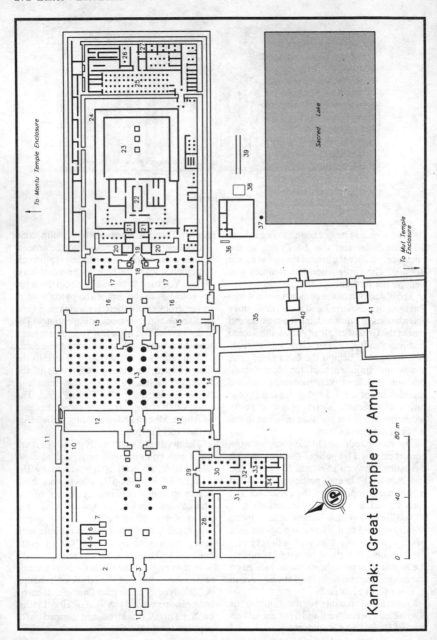

Karnak: Great Temple of Amun

The 2nd Pylon was built by Horemheb, an 18th dynasty general who headed a military dictatorship and became the last Pharaoh of his dynasty. Ramses I and II added their names and deeds to the pylon above that of Horemheb. Ramses II also raised two colossal pink granite statues of himself on either side of the entrance.

Beyond the 2nd Pylon is the awesome Great Hypostyle Hall. It was begun by Amenophis III while he was also building Luxor Temple, continued by Seti I and finished by Ramses II. Covering an area of 6000 sq metres (which is large enough to contain Notre Dame Cathedral), the hall is an unforgettable forest of towering stone pillars. It is impossible to get an overall idea of this court; there is nothing to do but stand and stare up at the dizzying spectacle. You'll notice that the papyrus-form capitals seem to sway and jostle each other for space.

Between the 3rd Pylon, built by Amenophis III, and the 4th Pylon, raised by Tuthmosis I, is a narrow court. Tuthmosis I and III raised two pairs of obelisks in front of the 4th Pylon, which was, during their reign, the entrance to the temple proper. Only

one of the four is still standing, but parts of the others lie in the court.

Beyond the 4th Pylon is the oldest preserved part of the complex, its 14 columns suggesting that it was originally a small hypostyle hall. It was constructed by Tuthmosis III in his attempt to eradicate or hide all signs of the reign of his stepmother, Queen Hatshepsut. (See the section on Deir al-Bahri further on in this chapter.) In this hall, around the two magnificent Obelisks of Hatshepsut, the vengeful king built a 25-metre-high sandstone structure. The upper shaft of one of the obelisks, which Hatshepsut raised to the glory of her 'father' Amun, lies on the ground by the Sacred Lake; the other obelisk still stands, reclaimed from the sandstone, in front of the 5th Pylon. It is the tallest obelisk in Egypt, standing 29.5 metres high, and was originally covered in electrum from its pyramidal peak to half way down the shaft.

The 5th Pylon was constructed by Tuthmosis I, with little space between it and the now ruined 6th Pylon (built at a later date). The latter, the smallest pylon at Karnak, was raised by his son Tuthmosis II

1	Avenue of Ram Headed Sphinxes	22	Sacred Barque Sanctuary
2	First Pylon	23	Central Court
3	Entrance	24	Wall of Records
4	Mut	25	Great Festival Temple of Tuthmosis III
5	Amun	26	Botanic Garden
6	Khons	27	Sanctuary of Alexander
7	Temple of Seti II	28	Colonnade
8	Kiosk of Taharqa	29	Pylon
9	Great Court	30	Court
10	Colonnade	31	Temple of Ramses III
11	Open Air Museum	32	Vestibule
12	Second Pylon	33	Hypostyle Hall
13	Great Hypostyle Hall	34	Barque Chapels
14	Reliefs of Ramses III	35	Cachette Court
15	Third Pylon	36	Fallen Obelisk of Hatshepsut
16	Central Court	37	Giant Scarab
17	Fourth Pylon	38	Refreshment Stand
18	Hypostyle Hall	39	Nilometer
19	Obelisks of Hatshepsut	40	Seventh Pylon
20	Fifth Pylon	41	Eighth Pylon
21	Sixth Pylon		

(Hatshepsut's husband and half-brother). In the small vestibule beyond the 6th Pylon are two pink granite columns on which are the emblems of Egypt carved in high relief: the lily of Upper Egypt on the north pillar and the papyrus flower of Lower Egypt on the south pillar. Nearby are two huge statues of Amun and his female counterpart Amunet, which date from the reign of Tutankhamun.

Also amongst the ruins of this area around the temple's original Central Court are a Sacred Barque Sanctuary and at least two well-preserved walls.

Hatshepsut's wall and its colourful reliefs survived the years well because once again Tuthmosis III chose to cover her structure with one of his own rather than destroy it once and for all.

Although the king was no match for his powerful though peace-loving stepmother, he made up for Hatshepsut's domination of him during his teenage years by setting out, almost immediately after her death, to conquer the known world. His reputation as a great hero and empire builder was justly deserved, as the relief work on what is known as the Wall of Records demonstrates. Though unrelenting in his bid for power, he had a penchant for being fairly just in his treatment of the people he conquered. This wall was a running tally of the organised tribute he exacted in honour of Amun from his subjugated lands.

East of the foundations of the original Temple of Amun stands the Great Festival Temple of Tuthmosis III. It contains several fine reliefs of plants and animals in the so-called Botanic Garden. Twenty of the temple's many columns are unique in Egypt in that they are larger at their peak than their base.

Between the Festival Temple and the eastern gate of the enclosure are the ruins of two other structures, a portico built by Taharqa and a smaller temple built by Tuthmosis III. The world's largest obelisk once stood on the base in front of this temple. The so-called Lateran Obelisk, which was 32.2 metres high, was removed from Karnak in 357 AD on the orders of the Roman emperor Constantine. Although it was bound for Constantinople, it ended up in the Circus Maximus in Rome and finally, in the 1580s, was re-erected in the Piazza San Giovanni in Laterano.

Against the northern enclosure wall of the precinct of Amun is the cult Temple of Ptah, started by Tuthmosis III and finished by the Ptolemies. Access to the inner chambers is through a series of five doorways which lead you to two of the temple's original statues. The headless figure of Ptah, the creator-god of Memphis, is in the middle chapel. To his left is the eerily beautiful, bare-breasted and lioness-headed, black granite statue of his goddess-wife Sekhmet, the 'spreader of terror'.

Montu Temple Enclosure A usually locked gate on the wall near the Temple of Ptah (Amun Temple Enclosure) leads to the Montu Temple Enclosure. Montu, the falcon-headed warrior-god, was the original deity of Thebes. The main temple was built by Amenophis III and modified by others. The complex is very dilapidated.

Amun Temple Enclosure – southern axis
The secondary axis of the Amun Temple Enclosure runs south from the 3rd and 4th pylons. It is basically a processional way, bounded on the east and west sides by walls, and sectioned off by a number of pylons which create a series of courts. Just before you get to the 7th Pylon, built by Tuthmosis III, is the Cachette Court, so named because of the thousands of stone and bronze statues discovered there during excavation work in 1903. Seven of the statues, of Middle Kingdom Pharaohs, stand in front of the pylon. Nearby are the remains of two colossal statues of Tuthmosis III.

The well-preserved 8th Pylon, built by Queen Hatshepsut, is the oldest part of the north-south axis of the temple. Four of the original six colossi are still standing, the most complete being the one of Amenophis I.

The 9th and 10th pylons were built by Horemheb, who used some of the stones of a demolished temple that had been built to the east by Akhenaten (before he decamped to Tell al-Amarna).

To the east of the 7th and 8th pylons is the Sacred Lake, where the priests of Amun would purify themselves before performing ceremonies in the temple. On the north-west side of the lake is the top half of Hatshepsut's fallen obelisk, and a huge statue of a scarab beetle dedicated by Amenophis III to Aten, the disc of the rising sun. There are the ruins or remains of about 20 other chapels within the main enclosure. In a fairly good state of repair in the south-west corner is the Temple of Khons, god of the moon and time, and son of Amun and Mut. The pylon faces Euergetes' Gate and the avenue of sphinxes leading to Luxor Temple, and provides access to a small hypostyle hall and ruined sanctuary. The temple was started by Ramses III, and added to by other Ramessids, Ptolemies and also Herihor. Herihor, like Horemheb, had pushed his way up through the ranks of the army to claim power, declaring himself not only Pharaoh but high priest of Amun as well.

Nearby is the small, finely decorated Temple of Opet, dedicated to the hippopotamus-goddess Opet, who was the mother of Osiris.

Mut Temple Enclosure From the 10th Pylon an avenue of sphinxes leads to the partly excavated southern enclosure – the precinct of Mut. The badly ruined Temple of Mut was built by Amenophis III and consists of a sanctuary, a hypostyle hall and two courts. The Temple of Ramses III stands south-west of the crescent-shaped lake which partly surrounds the main temple. Throughout the area are granite statues of Sekhmet, with her leonine head crowned by a solar disc.

Open-Air Museum Just before the 2nd Pylon, off to the left, is an open-air museum, which contains a collection of statuary found throughout the temple complex. A separate ticket is required for the museum, which closes at 5.30 pm. Entry is E£5 (half for students).

Sound & Light Show Karnak Temple's sound & light show easily rivals the one at the Great Pyramids of Giza. The 90-minute show recounts the history of Thebes and the lives of the many Pharaohs who built the sanctuaries, courts, statues or obelisks in honour of Amun. The show starts at the avenue of ram-headed sphinxes, passes through the 1st Pylon to the Great Court and on through the Great Hypostyle Hall to the Sacred Lake, where there's a grandstand for the show's finale.

There are two performances a night, in either English, French, German or Arabic, and the show costs E£18 (there is no student discount). The first session is at 6 pm (8 pm in summer) and the second at 8 pm (10 pm in summer). The following is the language schedule:

	1st show	2nd show
Monday	English	French
Tuesday	French	English
Wednesday	English	German
Thursday	Arabic	English
Friday	French	English
Saturday	English	French
Sunday	French	German

This schedule is subject to change, so first check with the tourist office or a hotel reception desk.

Getting There & Away To get to Karnak you can take a microbus from Luxor station or from behind Luxor Temple for 25 pt or hire a horse-drawn carriage (known as a hantour or *caleche*) for around E£3. Give the driver baksheesh if you want him to wait. It's a quick bicycle ride to the temple or you can easily walk.

Brooke Hospital for Animals
Although not really a tourist sight, the hospital, part of a worldwide UK network of clinics aiming to provide at least minimum care for animals, especially those put to work, is interesting. You might like to visit and see what they do for the horses used to pull along the hantours through the streets of

Luxor – they have a noticeboard of dos and don'ts on treatment of horses, including not tipping drivers for pushing the animals into going too fast.

If you are particularly interested in their work, they also have clinics in Cairo, Alexandria, Edfu and Aswan.

West Bank

The west bank of Luxor was the necropolis of ancient Thebes, a vast City of the Dead where magnificent temples were raised to honour the cults of Pharaohs entombed in the nearby cliffs, and where queens, royal children, nobles, priests, artisans and even workers built tombs which ranged, in the quality of their design and decor, from the spectacular to the ordinary.

During the New Kingdom, the necropolis also supported a large living population. In an attempt to protect the valuable tombs from robbers, the artisans, labourers, temple priests and guards lived permanently in the City of the Dead, their lives devoted to its construction and maintenance. They perfected the techniques of tomb building, decoration and concealment, and passed the secrets down through their own families.

The desire for secrecy greatly affected tomb design. Instead of a single mortuary monument like a pyramid, which was both a venue to worship the immortal Pharaoh and the resting place of his mummified remains, the New Kingdom Theban rulers commissioned their funerary monuments in pairs.

Magnificent mortuary temples were built on the plains, where the illusion of the Pharaoh's immortality could be perpetuated by the devotions of his priests and subjects, while the king's body and worldly wealth were laid in splendidly decorated secret tombs excavated in the hills. The prime location for the latter was an isolated canyon to the north-west, surrounded on three sides by high rugged cliffs.

However, even though there was only one way into the Valley of the Kings and the tombs were well hidden, very few escaped the vandalism of the grave robbers.

From the canal junction it is three km to the Valley of the Queens, seven km to the Valley of the Kings, and two km straight ahead to the student ticket office, past the Colossi of Memnon.

Information
What to Bring Bring a torch and, more importantly, your own water because although drinks are available at some sights, they can be relatively expensive. At the rest house just outside the Valley of the Kings, for instance, meals and drinks (including bottled water) are overpriced.

Lastly, bring plenty of small change for baksheesh. The tomb and temple guards will often try to pretend to show you something hidden or mysterious. Apparently, they want you to think that whenever they are whispering in their best tomb, temple and tourist English they are telling or showing you something special. (See the Tipping section in the Facts for the Visitor chapter.)

The best way to avoid these guys is to tag along with a group in each tomb or temple. Unfortunately, that also diminishes the aura of mystery surrounding solitary visits to these ancient sights.

Tickets If you wanted to see everything on offer in Thebes, you would end up spending more than US$30 on tickets (without student card). Add to that the cost of the various sights on the east bank and to the north and south of Luxor, and sightseeing can become prohibitively expensive for the traveller on a tight budget.

On top of the cost, the ticket system for the west bank temples and tombs is awkward and annoying. Tickets for sights other than the Valley of the Kings must be bought at either the kiosk at the downstream 'tourist ferry' landing or at the General Inspectorate/Antiquities Ticket Office (for student discounts), which is three km inland from the local ferry landing. They are sometimes reluctant to sell nondiscounted tickets at the latter office, but if they don't, it should be

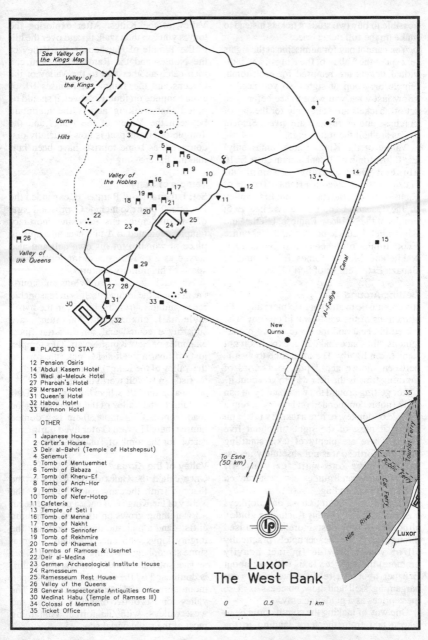

PLACES TO STAY

12 Pension Osiris
14 Abdul Kasem Hotel
15 Wadi al-Melouk Hotel
27 Pharoah's Hotel
29 Mersam Hotel
31 Queen's Hotel
32 Habou Hotel
33 Memnon Hotel

OTHER

1 Japanese House
2 Carter's House
3 Deir al-Bahri (Temple of Hatshepsut)
4 Senemut
5 Tomb of Mentuemhet
6 Tomb of Babaza
7 Tomb of Kheru-Ef
8 Tomb of Anch-Hor
9 Tomb of Kiky
10 Tomb of Nefer-Hotep
11 Cafeteria
13 Temple of Seti I
16 Tomb of Menna
17 Tomb of Nakht
18 Tomb of Sennofer
19 Tomb of Rekhmire
20 Tomb of Khaemat
21 Tombs of Ramose & Userhet
22 Deir al-Medina
23 German Archaeological Institute House
24 Ramesseum
25 Ramesseum Rest House
26 Valley of the Queens
28 General Inspectorate Antiquities Office
30 Medinat Habu (Temple of Ramses III)
34 Colossi of Memnon
35 Ticket Office

Luxor
The West Bank

0   0.5   1 km

possible to buy two student tickets instead to make up the full ticket price.

You cannot pay for admission at the sights (except at the Valley of the Kings), and individual tickets are required for each tomb, temple or group of sights, so you need to know just what you want to see before you set off. Tickets are valid only for the day of purchase and no refunds are given. Student prices are half the following:

Valley of the Kings (three tombs only) E£10 (the tomb of Tutankhamun costs E£10 alone!); Deir al-Bahri – Temple of Hatshepsut E£6; Medinat Habu – Temple of Ramses III E£6; the Ramesseum E£6; Valley of the Queens E£6; Deir al-Medina E£6; Tombs of the Nobles – Ramose, Userhet and Khaemhet E£6, Sennofer and Rekhmire E£6; Tombs of Khonsu and Benia E£6; Nakht and Menna Tombs E£6; Tomb of Babaza E£6; Temple of Seti I E£6.

Getting Around

It's unrealistic to attempt to explore all of the attractions of the west bank in one day. The incredible heat and the desolate and mountainous landscape make it an expedition not to be taken lightly. The ideal time to visit is between sunrise and 1 pm, so a series of morning trips is the best way to go about it.

For getting around the west bank, you can walk (not recommended on hot days), rent a bicycle or donkey, or hire a taxi. By taxi, you can visit most of the sights in about five hours. There are plenty of taxis shuttling back and forth so it is not absolutely necessary to have one wait for you. All transportation and guides can be arranged from the town landing.

Bicycles are E£4 to E£6 per day, donkeys cost at least E£10 per day (including guide), although it will cost more if organised through one of the cheaper hotels, practically all of which provide (in fact heavily promote) this service. Taxis will cost about E£8 per hour – it really depends on your bargaining skill and how business is. Use these prices as a guideline only.

One way of making the circuit could be to take a taxi from the ferry landing to the Valley of the Kings. After exploring the tombs you can then walk up and over the hill to the Temple of Hatshepsut, the Valley of the Nobles and the Ramesseum. You can then catch another taxi to the Valley of the Queens and the Temple of Ramses III, or even continue on foot. However, it should be noted that walking across the mountain between the Valley of the Kings and the Temple of Hatshepsut is now officially discouraged, as some tourists have been hurt making the crossing.

Temple of Seti I

Seti I, the father of Ramses II, expanded the Egyptian Empire to include Cyprus and parts of Mesopotamia. His imposing mortuary temple, dedicated to Amun, was an inspiring place of worship for his own cult and also served as a treasure house for some of the spoils of his military ventures.

Although the first two pylons and courts are in ruins, the temple itself is in reasonable repair and the surviving reliefs, in the hypostyle hall, chapels and sanctuary, are superbly executed and some of the finest examples of New Kingdom art. This temple, just off Sharia Wadi al-Melouk (the road to the Valley of the Kings), is seldom visited by tourists, so is well worth the effort.

On a barren hill, where the road from Deir al-Bahri to the Valley of the Kings meets the road from Seti's temple, there is a domed house where Howard Carter lived during his search for the tomb of Tutankhamun.

Valley of the Kings

Once called the Gates of the Kings or the Place of Truth, the canyon now known as the Valley of the Kings is at once a place of death – for nothing grows on its steep, scorching cliffs – and a majestic domain befitting the mighty. kings who once lay there in great stone sarcophagi, awaiting immortality.

The isolated valley, behind Deir al-Bahri, is dominated by the natural pyramid-shaped mountain peak of Al-Qurn, or 'the horn'. The valley consists of two branches, the east and west valleys, with the former containing most of the royal burial sites.

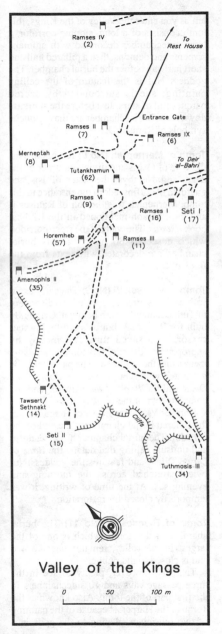

Valley of the Kings

Ramses IV
(2)

To
Rest House

Entrance Gate

Ramses II
(7)

Ramses IX
(6)

Merneptah
(8)

To Deir
al-Bahri

Tutankhamun
(62)

Ramses VI
(9)

Ramses I
(16)

Seti I
(17)

Horemheb
(57)

Ramses III
(11)

Amenophis II
(35)

Cliffs

Tawsert/
Sethnakt
(14)

Seti II
(15)

Tuthmosis III
(34)

0   50   100 m

All the tombs followed a similar design, deviating only because of structural difficulties or the length of time spent on their construction. The longer the reign of the Pharaoh, the larger and more magnificent his tomb. Two groups of workers and artisans would live, in alternating shifts, in the valley itself for the duration of the work, which usually took many years.

The tombs were designed to resemble the underworld, with a long, inclined rock-hewn corridor descending into either an antechamber or a series of sometimes pillared halls, and ending in the burial chamber. Once the tomb was cut its decoration was started; this dealt almost exclusively with the afterlife and the Pharaoh's existence in it.

The colourful paintings and reliefs are extracts from ancient theological compositions, or 'books', and were incorporated in the tomb to assist the Pharaoh into the next life. Texts were taken from the *Book of Amduat* – 'the book of him who is in the netherworld'; the *Book of Gates*, which charted the king's course through the underworld; and the *Book of the Litany of Ra*, believed to be the words spoken by Ra, the sun-god, on his own journey through the caverns of death.

The worshippers of Amun or Amun-Ra (the fusion of the two deities and king of the gods) believed that the Valley of the Kings was traversed each night by Ra, and it was the aim of those who had been buried that day to secure passage on his sacred barque.

Amun, Isis & Osiris

To do this, they had to be well equipped with a knowledge of the magic texts (hence the tomb decorations) before they could enter the boat of the god. Once aboard, they were brought to the kingdom of Osiris, god of the dead, where they were judged. Those kings who passed the ordeal would then board a second sacred barque for the journey to the east, where, having overcome the powers of darkness and death, they would live again, immortal in the company of Amun-Ra.

Tuthmosis I was the first Pharaoh to have his tomb cut in the barren cliffs, around 1495 BC, and in all 62 tombs have been excavated in the valley, although not all belong to Pharaohs.

Each tomb is numbered in order of discovery but not all are open to the public and there are often some tombs closed for renovation work. It's worth having your own torch (flashlight) to illuminate badly lit areas. Sometimes the guards have the endearing habit of switching off the lights if you won't give them baksheesh – and they wait till you're half way in to leave you in the dark.

The road into the Valley of the Kings is a gradual, dry, hot climb, so be prepared if you are riding a bicycle. There is a rest house before the entrance to the valley where you can buy mineral water, soft drinks and meals. It's expensive and usually crowded.

If you want to avoid the inevitable crowds that tour buses bring to the tombs, head for the tombs outside the immediate area of the entrance. There are many to choose from, but some good ones are the tombs of Ramses VI (No 9), Queen Tawsert/Sethnakt (No 14) and Tuthmosis III (No 34).

You can buy tickets for the tombs at the entrance to the valley itself. Note that any one ticket is for three tombs only. If you want to visit more, you'll have to buy more tickets (and if you wanted to visit, say, four tombs, you'd still have to buy two tickets). The tomb of Tutankhamun has been deemed worth a ticket on its own (E£10), but may well be closed for restoration by the time you read this.

Tomb of Ramses IX (No 6) The first on the

left as you enter the Valley of the Kings, this tomb consists of a long, sloping corridor, a large antechamber decorated with animals, serpents and demons, then a pillared hall and short hallway before the burial chamber. The goddess Nut is the feature of the ceiling painting; she is surrounded by sacred barques full of stars. Just before the staircase down to the burial chamber are the cartouche symbols of Ramses IX.

Tomb of Merneptah (No 8) Reliefs of Isis, the wife of Osiris and divine mourner of the dead, and Nepthys, the sister of Isis and guardian of coffins, adorn the entrance to this tomb. Merneptah was the son of Ramses II and the Pharaoh mentioned in the Biblical book *Exodus*. The walls of the steep corridor, which descends 80 metres to his burial chamber, are decorated with texts from the *Book of Gates*.

Tomb of Ramses VI (No 9) The early excavation of this tomb forestalled the discovery of Tutankhamun's tomb below it. Originally built for Ramses V but usurped by his successor, who saved time and money by appropriating the site, this tomb extends 83 metres into the mountain. The passageway is decorated with scenes from the *Book of the Dead* and the *Book of the Caverns* and the complete text of the *Book of Gates*.

Ramses VI's smashed sarcophagus lies in the pillared burial chamber at the end of the corridor. The burial chamber has a beautiful and unusual ceiling that details the *Book of Day & Night* and features the goddess Nut twice, stretched across the morning and evening sky. At the time of writing, it was temporarily closed for restoration.

Tomb of Ramses III (No 11) The burial chamber of this tomb, which is one of the largest in the valley, remains unexcavated and is closed to the public.

There is, however, plenty to see in the three passageways and 10 sidechambers in the first part of the tomb. Also known as the Tomb of the Harpers, because of the painting of two musicians playing to the gods in a room off the second passage, it is interesting because the colouring of its sunken reliefs is still quite vivid. The sidechambers are decorated with pictures of their former contents, while other walls depict daily happenings.

Tomb of Ramses I (No 16) Although the tomb next to Seti's belongs to the founder of the 19th dynasty, it is a very simple affair because Ramses I only ruled for a couple of years.

The tomb, which has the shortest entrance corridor of all the royal resting places in the valley, has a single, almost square, burial chamber, containing the king's open pink-granite sarcophagus. The chamber is the only part of the tomb that is decorated; it features the Pharaoh in the presence of deities such as Osiris, Ptah, Anubis and Maat set on a blue-purple background.

Tomb of Seti I (No 17) The longest, most splendid and best preserved tomb of the Theban necropolis is the burial site of Seti I, which plunges over a hundred metres down into the hillside. The detail of the enchanting, finely executed reliefs rivals even the renowned decorations in his Cenotaph Temple at Abydos.

Three long passages, intersected by decorated chambers, culminate in the large, two-part burial chamber. Colourful scenes include Seti appearing before Ra-Harakhty (god of the morning sun) beneath a ceiling of flying vultures and texts from the *Litany of Ra*.

In the first chamber Seti is shown in the presence of deities and in another passage the walls feature the Opening of the Mouth ritual which ensured that the mummy's organs were functioning.

The first section of the burial chamber is a pillared hall decorated with texts from the *Book of Gates*, while the second part, which contained Seti's magnificent alabaster sarcophagus, features texts from the *Amduat* and an astronomical ceiling. The tomb is east of the rest house.

Unfortunately, at the time of writing, this tomb was closed indefinitely for restoration.

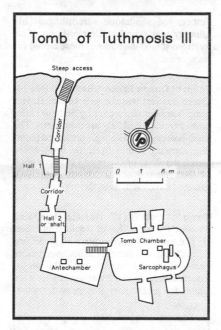

Tomb of Tuthmosis III (No 34) Hidden in the hills between high limestone cliffs and reached only via a steep staircase that crosses an even steeper ravine, this tomb demonstrates the lengths to which the ancient Pharaohs went to thwart the cunning of the ancient thieves.

Tuthmosis III was one of the first to build his tomb in the Valley of the Kings. As secrecy was his utmost concern, he chose the most inaccessible spot and designed his burial place with a series of passages at haphazard angles and a deep shaft to mislead or catch potential robbers – all to no avail, of course.

The shaft, now traversed by a narrow gangway, leads to an antechamber supported by two pillars, the walls of which are adorned with a list of over 700 gods and demigods.

The burial chamber, which is oval-shaped like a cartouche, is decorated in a fairly restrained manner. The roof is supported by two pillars, between which is the king's empty, red sandstone sarcophagus; his mummy was found at Deir al-Bahri. This tomb has joined the ranks of those closed for restoration.

Tomb of Queen Tawsert/Sethnakt (No 14)

Queen Tawsert was the wife of Seti II. Her tomb was later taken over by Sethnakt after he had trouble building his own tomb. The tomb is decorated with well-preserved paintings showing scenes from the *Book of the Dead*, the *Book of Gates* and the ceremony of the Opening of the Mouth. Sethnakt's granite sarcophagus is in the tomb.

Tomb of Seti II (15)

Adjacent to Queen Tawsert's tomb is that of her husband, Seti II. The tomb entrance starts with some fine reliefs but it was abruptly abandoned before completion. During the excavation of Tutankhamun's tomb it was used by Howard Carter for preliminary storage and restora-

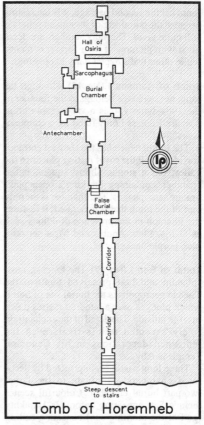

Tomb of Horemheb

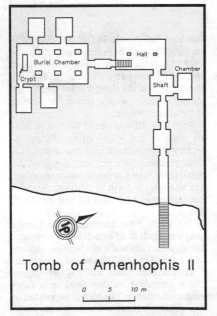

Tomb of Amenhophis II

0   5   10 m

tion work on the finds. Today the mummy of an unknown person can be seen in the tomb.

Tomb of Amenophis II (No 35)

One of the deepest structures in the valley, this tomb has more than 90 steps that take you down to a modern gangway built over a deep pit designed to protect the inner, lower chambers from thieves.

Stars cover the entire ceiling in the huge burial chamber and the walls feature, as if on a giant painted scroll, the entire text of the *Book of Amduat*. This was indeed the final resting place of Amenophis II, for although thieves did manage to make off with everything of value, they did no damage to the interior and left the king himself undisturbed.

When the huge tomb was excavated, by the French in 1898, a total of 13 mummies were found, including that of Amenophis lying *in situ* in his sarcophagus, a garland of flowers still around his neck. Nine of the other mummies, hidden there by priests, were also of royal blood, including those of Tuthmosis IV, Seti II, Amenophis III and his wife Queen Tiy.

A word of warning: this tomb can sometimes be exceedingly hot and humid; drink lots of water.

Tomb of Horemheb (No 57) Horemheb, a general of the Egyptian army in about 1320 BC, became a military dictator and eventually the last Pharaoh of the 18th dynasty.

From the entrance a steep flight of steps and an equally steep passage leads to a chamber with fine festive reliefs and then a false burial chamber supported by two pillars. This attempt to fool any potential grave robbers didn't work, as ancient thieves managed to find and uncover the stairway which leads steeply down to the real tomb; they left nothing but Horemheb's red granite sarcophagus.

The wall paintings of the burial chamber were never finished, indicating an untimely death, but are interesting because they reveal the different stages of decoration.

Tomb of Tutankhamun (No 62) The story behind the celebrated discovery of this, the most famous tomb in the Valley of the Kings, and the fabulous treasures it contained, far outshines its actual appearance, making it dubious whether or not it warrants the E£10 charged for entry (half for students). It may, in any case, be closed for restoration by the time you read this.

Tutankhamun's tomb is neither large nor

Wall paintings in the Tomb of Horemheb

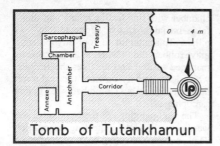

Tomb of Tutankhamun

wired Lord Carnarvon to join him immediately for the opening of what he believed was the intact tomb of Tutankhamun.

The discovery proved sceptics wrong, and the tomb's priceless cache of Pharaonic treasures, which had remained undisturbed by robbers, vindicated Carter's dream beyond even his wildest imaginings.

Sadly, in perhaps the last great irony in the history of tomb robbing in the Valley of the Kings, evidence came to light some years later to suggest that prior to the tomb being officially opened in the presence of experts from the Metropolitan Museum of Art, Carter and Carnarvon themselves broke in, stole several articles and resealed the door.

The tomb is small and for the most part undecorated. Three small chambers were crammed with furniture, statues, chariots, musical instruments, weapons, boxes, jars

impressive and bears all the signs of a rather hasty completion and inglorious burial. The extraordinary contents of this rather modest tomb built for a fairly insignificant boy-king, however, can only make you guess at the immense wealth that must have been laid to rest with the likes of the powerful Seti I or Ramses II.

For years archaeologists believed that if, in fact, Tutankhamun was buried in the valley, his tomb would contain little of interest. The nephew of Akhenaten, he was merely a puppet Pharaoh of the priests of Amun, supporting their counter-revolution against the parvenus of the late rebel king's desertion from Thebes.

During his brief reign Tutankhamun was seen to re-embrace the cult of Amun, restoring its popularity with the people, and then he died, young, with no great battles or buildings to his credit.

The English Egyptologist Howard Carter, however, believed he would find the young Pharaoh buried amongst his ancestors with his treasures intact. He slaved away for six seasons in the valley, excavating thousands and thousands of tonnes of sand and rubble from possible sites, until even his wealthy patron, Lord Carnarvon, tired of the obsession.

With his funding about to be cut off Carter made one last attempt at the only unexplored area that was left – a site covered by workers' huts just under the already excavated tomb of Ramses VI.

On 4 November 1922 he uncovered steps and then a door, its seals untouched, and

Tutankhamun's funerary mask

and food, all of which are now in the Egyptian Museum in Cairo.

The second coffin of gilded wood, the solid gold mummy case and of course the magnificent funerary mask, found on the king's body, are also in Cairo. The innermost coffin of gilded wood containing the decaying, mummified body of Tutankhamun, still lies within the carved granite sarcophagus in the burial chamber of his tomb, the walls of which are decorated with texts from the *Book of the Dead*.

Walk to Deir al-Bahri From the tombs of Seti I and Ramses I you can continue southeast and hike over the hills to Deir al-Bahri (or vice versa of course). The walk takes about 45 minutes through an amazing lunar-type landscape.

It offers various views of the Temple of Hatshepsut in the amphitheatre setting of Deir al-Bahri below and excellent views across the plain towards the Nile.

In summer you should start this hike as early as possible, partly to catch the changing colours of the barren hills as the sun rises, but also because it gets mighty hot there later in the day. If you tire on the ascent there are donkeys available to carry you to the top!

If you plan to visit the sights, however, you will need tickets, which can only be obtained when the office opens at about 6.30 or 7 am. There's also a much longer trail from the Valley of the Kings to the Valley of the Queens via Deir al-Medina.

Temple of Hatshepsut (Deir al-Bahri)
Rising out of the desert plain, in a series of terraces, the Mortuary Temple of Queen Hatshepsut merges with the sheer limestone cliffs of the eastern face of the Theban Mountain as if nature herself had built this extraordinary monument.

The partly rockcut, partly free-standing structure is one of the finest monuments of ancient Egypt, although its original appearance, surrounded by myrrh trees, garden beds and approached by a grand sphinx-lined causeway, must have been even more spectacular.

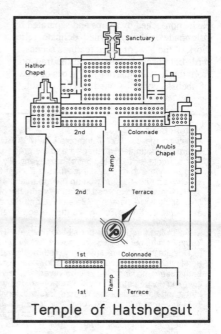

Temple of Hatshepsut

Discovered in the mid-19th century by Auguste Mariette, it wasn't completely excavated till 1896 and is still being restored. Unfortunately, over the centuries the temple has been vandalised. Akhenaten removed all references to Amun, before taking his court off to Tell al-Amarna; and the early Christians who took it over as a monastery (hence the name Deir al-Bahri, or 'monastery of the north'), also defaced the pagan reliefs.

The worst damage, however, was done out of pure spite by Hatshepsut's successor, Tuthmosis III, who developed a fairly strong hatred of the queen in the 20 years he waited to ascend the throne of Egypt. Within weeks of her death he had obliterated or covered her name or image wherever he found it. Even in her own mortuary temple, where he and Hatshepsut were always represented together, as co-rulers, he hacked out her likeness, leaving only his own.

The temple's 37-metre-wide causeway leads on to the three huge terraced courts, each approached by ramps and separated by colonnades. The renowned delicate relief work of the lower terrace features scenes of birds being caught in nets and the transport from the Aswan quarries to Thebes of a pair of obelisks commissioned by Hatshepsut.

The central court contains the best-preserved reliefs. There Queen Hatshepsut recorded her divine birth and told the story of an expedition to the Land of Punt to collect myrrh trees needed for the precious myrrh incense used in temple ceremonies. There

Hatshepsut

Following the death of Tuthmosis I in 1495 BC, a great controversy arose, between the late Pharaoh's daughter Hatshepsut and his grandson Tuthmosis III, over the rights of succession. The struggle for ultimate control was eventually won by the formidable Hatshepsut. As well as being only the third queen ever to rule ancient Egypt, Hatshepsut declared herself Pharaoh – which made her the first woman ever to reign as king.

Hatshepsut had married her father's son, her own half-brother Tuthmosis II, and she held many titles, including 'Pharaoh's wife and daughter' and of course 'queen'. She failed, however, to bear any sons, so it was Tuthmosis III, the son of one of the king's concubines, who became heir presumptive.

Following the death of her sibling/husband, Hatshepsut became regent to the new Pharaoh Tuthmosis III, but such was her power that the young boy had little chance of ruling in his own right.

Despite the backing of the army, Tuthmosis was never a match for his aunt/stepmother/co-ruler, and Hatshepsut eventually overshadowed him enough to proclaim herself absolute monarch as both queen and king. She still, however, had to win over the priesthood and this she managed by claiming divine birth (as most Pharaohs did), by assuming the dress and manner of a man and by having herself depicted wearing the traditional Pharaonic beard in reliefs.

Hatshepsut ruled for 20 years, and for Egypt it was a time of peace and internal development. It is not known how she died – whether it was of natural causes or something more sinister. Almost as soon as Tuthmosis III finally took his place on the throne he led his country into war with Palestine. ◼

Temple of Hatshepsut

are also two chapels at either end of the colonnade. At the northern end the colourful reliefs in the Chapel of Anubis show the co-rulers, Hatshepsut and Tuthmosis III (with the queen's image again disfigured by her nephew), in the presence of Anubis, the god of embalming, Ra-Harakhty, the falcon-headed sun-god, and his wife Hathor. In the Chapel of Hathor you can see (if you have a torch) an untouched figure of Hatshepsut worshipping the cow-headed goddess.

Although the third terrace is out of bounds while a Polish-Egyptian team works on its restoration, you can see the pink granite doorway leading into the Sanctuary of Amun, which is hewn out of the cliff.

In 1876 the greatest mummy find in history was made just north of the Temple of Hatshepsut. After many antiquities began showing up in the marketplace the authorities realised someone had found, and was

The Ramesseum

plundering, an unknown tomb. After investigations they discovered a massive shaft at the foot of the cliffs containing the mummies of 40 Pharaohs, queens and nobles.

It seems that the New Kingdom priests realised that the bodies of their kings would never be safe from violation in their own tombs, no matter what precautions were taken against grave robbers, so they moved them to this communal grave. The mummies included those of Amenophis I, Tuthmosis II and III, Seti I and Ramses I and III.

You can hike over the mountain to the Valley of the Kings from here (see Valley of the Kings section). It should take about 45 minutes, but be prepared for a strenuous trek on hot days. Take plenty of water. The view of Deir al-Bahri from above is spectacular. Note that climbing over the mountain is officially frowned upon.

The Ramesseum

The Ramesseum is yet another monument raised by Ramses II to the ultimate glory of himself. The massive temple was built to impress his priests, his subjects, his successors and of course the gods, so that he, the great warrior king, could live forever. Many of his other works were rather crudely constructed but in this, his mortuary temple, he demanded perfection in the workmanship so that it would stand as an eternal testimony to his greatness.

Sadly, the Ramesseum, which was dedicated to Amun, is mostly in ruins. This fact no doubt disappoints Ramses II more than it does modern-day visitors to the site. He dared all those who questioned his greatness in future centuries to gaze on the magnificence of his monuments in order to understand his power over life and death. How the mighty fall!

The scattered remains of the colossal statue of the king and the ruins of his temple prompted the English poet Shelley to cut this presumptuous Pharaoh down to size by using the undeniable fact of Ramses' mortality to ridicule his aspirations to immortality.

In the early 19th century Shelley wrote 'Ozymandias':

I met a traveller from an antique land
Who said: Two vast and trunkless legs of stone
Stand in the desert...Near them, on the sand,
Half sunk, a shattered visage lies, whose frown,
And wrinkled lip, and sneer of cold command,
Tell that its sculptor well those passions read
Which yet survive, stamped on these lifeless things,
The hand that mocked them, and the heart that fed:
And on the pedestal these words appear:
'My name is Ozymandias, king of kings:
Look on my works, ye Mighty, and despair!'
Nothing beside remains. Round the decay
Of that colossal wreck, boundless and bare
The lone and level sands stretch far away.

Although a little more elaborate than other

temples, the fairly orthodox layout of the Ramesseum, with its two courts, hypostyle hall, sanctuary, accompanying chambers and storerooms is uncommon in that the usual rectangular floor plan was altered to incorporate an older, smaller temple – that of Ramses' mother, Tuya, which is off to one side.

The 1st and 2nd pylons measure more than 60 metres across and feature reliefs of Ramses' military exploits. Through them are the ruins of the huge 1st Court, including the double colonnade that fronted the royal palace.

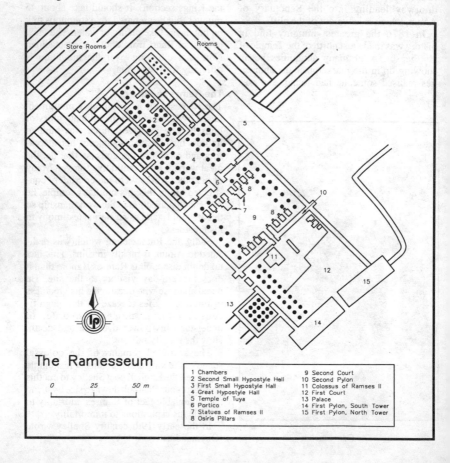

The Ramesseum

0   25   50 m

1 Chambers
2 Second Small Hypostyle Hall
3 First Small Hypostyle Hall
4 Great Hypostyle Hall
5 Temple of Tuya
6 Portico
7 Statues of Ramses II
8 Osiris Pillars
9 Second Court
10 Second Pylon
11 Colossus of Ramses II
12 First Court
13 Palace
14 First Pylon, South Tower
15 First Pylon, North Tower

Top Left: Column in Great Hypostyle Hall, Karnak, Luxor (DS)
Top Right: Collossi of Memnon, Luxor (GE)
Bottom Left: Temple of Luxor at night (GE)
Bottom Right: The Ramesseum, Luxor (GB)

Top Left: Making drums for a festival, Khan al-Khalili, Cairo (KB)
Top Right: Tamr hindi juice man washes cup for next customer, Khan al-Khalili, Cairo (K
Bottom Left: Sorting through old books & magazines to be recycled as wraps, Cairo (KB)
Bottom Right: Belly dancer and man singing to the belly rhythm, Cairo (KB)

Near the western stairs is part of the Colossus of Ramses II, the Ozymandias of Shelley's poem, lying somewhat forlornly on the ground. When it stood, it was 17.5 metres tall. The head of another granite statue of Ramses, one of a pair, lies in the 2nd Court. Twenty-nine of the original 48 columns of the Great Hypostyle Hall are still standing, and in the smaller hall behind it the roof, which features astronomical hieroglyphs, is still in place.

There is a rest house/restaurant next to the temple which is called, not surprisingly, the *Ramesseum Resthouse*. It is owned by Sayed Hussain, whose father was a friend of Howard Carter. The rest house is a great place to relax and have a cool drink or something cheap to eat.

Tombs of the Nobles

The Tombs of the Nobles are one of the best, though least visited, attractions on the west bank. Nestled in the foothills and among the houses of the old village of Qurna (Sheikh Abd al-Qurna) are at least 400 tombs that date from the 6th dynasty to the Greco-Roman period. The tomb chapels in the area date from the 18th to the 20th dynasties.

Of the hundred or so tombs that have something of interest, seven are highly recommended. They have been numbered and divided into three groups, each requiring a separate ticket, as follows: Nakht and Menna (often closed); Ramose, Userhet and Khaemhet; and Rekhmire and Sennofer.

You'll see signs to the tombs leading off the main road, opposite the Ramesseum. As you walk between the houses to the tombs, you'll be pursued by avid little salespeople, eager to sell you crudely produced handicrafts.

Tombs of Menna & Nakht (Nos 52 & 69)

The wall paintings in the tombs of Menna and Nakht (which may be closed to the public) emphasise rural life in the 18th dynasty. Menna was an estate inspector and Nakht was an astronomer of Amun. Their finely detailed tombs show scenes of farming, hunting, fishing and feasting. The

Tomb of Nakht

Tomb of Nakht has a small museum area in its first chamber. Although this tomb is so small that only a handful of visitors can

Relief in the Tomb of Ramose

squeeze in, the walls have some of the best known examples of Egyptian tomb paintings, including familiar scenes like the three musicians that grace a million T-shirts, posters, postcards and papyrus paintings.

Tomb of Ramose (No 55) This is the Tomb Chapel of Ramose, who was a governor of Thebes during the reigns of Amenophis III

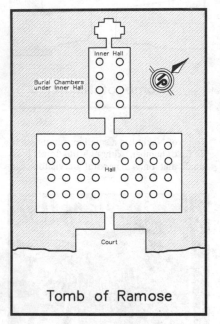

Tomb of Ramose

and Akhenaten. It's a fascinating tomb and one of the few monuments dating from that time, when the cult power of the priests of Karnak was usurped by the new monotheistic worship of Aten.

Exquisite paintings and low reliefs grace the walls, showing scenes from the reigns of both kings and the transition between the two forms of religious worship. The reliefs of Ramose, his wife and other relatives are extraordinarily lifelike and clearly show their affectionate relationships. The tomb was never actually finished because Ramose deserted Thebes to follow the rebel Pharaoh Akhenaten to his new city at Tell al-Amarna.

Tomb of Userhet (No 56) The Tomb of Userhet, who was one of Amenophis II's royal scribes, is right next to Ramose's. Its most distinctive features are the wall paintings depicting daily life in ancient Egypt. Userhet is shown presenting gifts to Amenophis II; there's a barber busy cutting hair on another wall; and there are men making wine, and hunting gazelles from a chariot.

Tomb of Khaemhet (No 57) This tomb belonged to Khaemhet, who was Amenophis III's royal inspector of the granaries and court scribe. Scenes on the walls show Khaemhet offering sacrifices; the Pharaoh depicted as a sphinx; the funeral ritual of Osiris; and images of daily country life and official business.

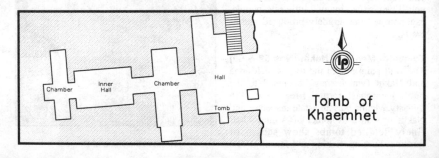

Tomb of Khaemhet

Tomb of Sennofer (No 96) Prince Sennofer of Thebes worked for Amenophis II as a supervisor of the gardens of the Temple of Amun. The most interesting parts of his tomb are deep underground in the main chamber. The ceiling there is covered with clear paintings of grapes and vines, while most of the scenes on the surrounding walls and columns depict Sennofer with his sister. The guard usually has a kerosene lamp, but bring a torch just in case.

Tomb of Rekhmire (No 100) The Tomb of Rekhmire, a governor during the reigns of Tuthmosis III and Amenophis II, is one of the best preserved in the area. In the first chamber, to the extreme left, are scenes of Rekhmire receiving gifts from foreign lands. The panther and giraffe are gifts from Nubia; the elephant, horses and chariot come from Syria; and the expensive vases come from Crete and the Aegean Islands.

Deir al-Medina

The small Ptolemaic temple of Deir al-Medina is one km off the road to the Valley of the Queens and up a short, but very rocky, road that would be difficult for bicycles. At the time of writing, however, it was closed to the public.

The temple was built between 221 and 116 BC by Philopator, Philometor and Euergetes II. It was dedicated to Hathor, the goddess of pleasure and love, and to Maat, the goddess of truth and the personification of cosmic order. However, the temple is called Deir al-Medina, which means 'monastery of the town', because it was occupied by early Christian monks.

If you have the energy and the inclination, hike southward a short distance to see the remains of a New Kingdom village occupied by the artists and workers who built some of the tombs in the area. Archaeologists have been excavating this settlement for most of this century and at least 70 houses have been uncovered.

One of the two tombs in this area which can be visited is the Tomb of Sennedjem (No 1). Sennedjem was a 19th dynasty servant in the so-called Place of Truth – the Valley of the Kings. The tomb has only one chamber, but the wall paintings are magnificent. One of the most famous scenes shows a cat killing a snake; it's above the doorway to the burial chamber.

Most of the other tombs in the area belonged to the servants, overseers and labourers who worked in the valley.

Valley of the Queens

There are at least 75 tombs in Biban al-Harim, the Valley of the Queens. They belonged to queens of the 19th and 20th dynasties and other members of the royal families, including princesses and the Ramessid princes. Only tombs Nos 43, 44, 52 and 55 are open.

The top attraction here is No 55, the **Tomb of Amunherkhepshep**. Amun, who was the son of Ramses III, was nine years old when he died. The scenes on the tomb walls show

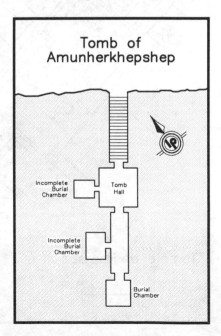

his father grooming him to be Pharaoh by introducing him to various gods.

Amun's mother was pregnant at the time of his death and in her grief she aborted the child and entombed it with Amun. A five-month-old mummified fetus was discovered there. Wall paintings also show Ramses leading his son to Anubis, the jackal-headed god of the dead, who then takes the young Prince Amun down to the entrance of the Passage of the Dead.

The Tomb of Queen Titi (No 52), who was wife and consort to one of the Ramses, is also interesting.

Medinat Habu

The temple complex of Medinat Habu was one of the first places in Thebes to be closely associated with the local god Amun. Hatshepsut, Tuthmosis III and Ramses III constructed the main buildings of the complex – which is second only to the Temples of Karnak in size and complexity – but Medinat Habu was added to and altered by a succession of rulers right through to the Ptolemys. At its height there were temples, workshops, storage rooms, administrative buildings and accommodation for the priests and officials. It was the centre of the eco-

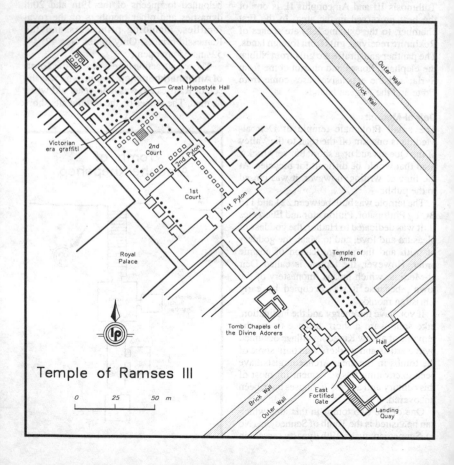

Temple of Ramses III

nomic life of Thebes for several centuries and was still inhabited as late as the 9th century AD.

The original Temple of Amun, built by Hatshepsut and Tuthmosis III, was later completely overshadowed by the enormous **Mortuary Temple of Ramses III**, which is the dominant feature of Medinat Habu.

Ramses III was inspired in the construction of his shrine by the Ramesseum of his father. His own temple and the smaller one dedicated to Amun are both enclosed within the massive outer walls of the complex.

Also just inside, to the left of the gate, are the Tomb Chapels of the Divine Adorers, which were built for the principal priestesses of Amun. Outside the eastern gate, one of only two entrances, was a landing quay for a canal which once connected Medinat Habu with the Nile.

The well-preserved 1st Pylon marks the front of the temple proper. Ramses III is portrayed in its reliefs as the victor in several wars. To the left of the 1st Court are the remains of the Pharaoh's palace; the three rooms at the rear were for the royal harem. There is a window between the 1st Court and the palace known as the Window of Appearances, which allowed the king to show himself to his subjects.

The reliefs of the 2nd Pylon feature Ramses III presenting prisoners of war to Amun and his vulture-goddess wife, Mut. The 2nd Court is surrounded by colonnades and reliefs showing various religious ceremonies.

Medinat Habu is off the road on your right as you return from the Valley of the Queens. After you have finished wandering around the complex treat yourself to a cold Stella beer at the Habou Hotel opposite.

Colossi of Memnon

The massive pair of statues known as the Colossi of Memnon are all that remain of the temple of the hedonistic Amenophis III. Rising about 18 metres from the plain, the enthroned, faceless statues of Amenophis have kept a lonely vigil on the changing landscape around them, surviving the rising

floodwaters of the Nile which gradually, through annual inundation, destroyed the temple buildings behind them.

Over the centuries, the crumbling rubble of what was believed to have been one of the most splendid of the Theban temples was ploughed into the fertile soil. A stela, now in the Egyptian Museum, describes the temple as being built from 'white sandstone, with gold throughout, a floor covered with silver, and doors covered with electrum'. (Electrum was a commonly used alloy of gold and silver.)

The colossi were among the great tourist attractions of Egypt during Greco-Roman times because the Greeks believed they were actually statues of the legendary Memnon, a king of Ethiopia and son of the dawn-goddess Eos, who was slain by Achilles during the Trojan War.

It was the northern statue that attracted most of the attention because at sunrise it would emit a haunting, musical sound that the Greeks believed was the voice of Memnon greeting his mother each day. Eos

Colossi of Memnon

in turn would weep tears of dew for the untimely death of her beautiful son.

Actually the phenomenon of the famous vocal statue was probably produced by the combined effect of a simple change in temperature and the fact that the upper part of the colossus was severely damaged by an earthquake in about 30 BC. As the heat of the morning sun baked the dew-soaked stone, sand particles would break off and resonate inside the cracks in the structure. Certainly, after a well-meaning Roman governor repaired the statue some time in the 2nd century AD, Memnon's plaintive greeting to his mother was heard no more.

The colossi are just off the road, west of New Qurna – you won't miss them.

Amenophis III had quite a reputation for high and fast living. The ruins of his amazing palace are about one km south of Medinat Habu. The royal residence featured a lake, a banquet hall, private state rooms for Amenophis, a separate residence for his beloved queen Tiy, and quarters for court officials, servants, guests and of course the Pharaoh's extensive harem, which numbered over 300. Although the palace is badly ruined, the remains are quite substantial.

ACTIVITIES
Felucca Rides
The best thing to do in Luxor in the late afternoon or early evening is to relax aboard a felucca. Local feluccas cruise the river throughout the day and cost around E£3 per person per hour or E£10 per boat per hour. In the low season, you may be able to do even better.

An enjoyable outing is the trip upriver to Banana Island. The tiny isle, dotted with palms, is about five km from Luxor and the trip takes two to three hours. Plan it in such a way that you're on your way back in time to watch a brilliant Nile sunset from the boat.

Ballooning
The UK's Abercrombie & Kent Travel (☎ (071) 730-9600) at Sloane Square House, Holbein Place, London SW1 8NS, include balloon trips over Luxor as part of one of their 10-day Nile cruise programmes, but only in the winter months. They say the balloon trip can only be made as part of the cruise, however if you go to the Hilton or Sheraton hotels in Luxor, you can organise to get on board. It costs about US$250 in Luxor – if you have that kind of money for a couple of hours' hot air!

Camel & Donkey Rides
Almost all the smaller hotels organise camel and, more commonly, donkey treks around the west bank. These trips, which start at about 7 am and finish about lunch time, cost a minimum of about E£15 a person, and may be more expensive. The hotels push these trips pretty hard, and although a lot of travellers have reported being pleased with them, you can probably organise it more cheaply yourself with some hard bargaining when you cross the river.

Some of the bigger hotels offer camel trips, including visits to nearby villages for a cup of tea.

Swimming
Several hotels have swimming pools. The Windsor and Emilio hotels and the Rezeiky Camp charge E£7, the Wena Luxor Hotel E£10. The St Joseph and Flobater hotels, next to each other on the way out to the Sheraton, have pools for use at E£10 a head. The Winter Palace and the ETAP charge E£40 and E£50 respectively for a mandatory buffet lunch with use of the pool. The Green Palace Restaurant, near the YMCA camp, sets a minimum charge on purchases of food and drink of E£15 when you use their small pool.

Organised Tours
Misr Travel and other travel agents around the Winter Palace will organise you on to half and full-day tours to the west bank in air-con buses. In summer, this might be worth considering, as they may make fairly hefty reductions. Otherwise, it's generally a pretty

expensive option (you can easily be looking at E£100 plus).

Luxor Day Festival

On April 26, festivities to celebrate Luxor's 'independence' from the Governorate of Qena in 1990 take place. There are street parades, music and other jollities, but as the festival has only been running for a few years, there is no real set tradition. In 1990, Luxor, which had been under the control of the Qena Governorate, achieved a long fought-for autonomous status.

PLACES TO STAY

Perhaps more than at any tourist destination in Egypt, the cost of accommodation here fluctuates seasonally. As the research for Luxor was done in the low season (summer), the following rates should generally be considered the minimum in the range. There is no hard-and-fast rule on how much rates might increase in winter. Some hotels double their charges, others barely alter them at all. Where only one rate is given, it is the low-season rate.

Places to Stay – bottom end
East Bank – south of Sharia al-Mahatta

Luxor is full of 'bottom end' places to stay, and more seem to be springing up all the time. Most of them are concentrated on or around the main streets south-west of the train station, and some – especially the newer ones – offer a higher standard for your money than you get in much of the rest of the country. That's the market economy in action.

Also worth noting is that many hotels boast both roof gardens and washing machines. The latter exist and you may as well make the most of them. Roof gardens vary from rooftop restaurants to concrete platforms with chunks of cement and swirls of twisted iron all over the place. This is generally the breakfast area, so you might want to check it out before you accept your room. Most hotels offer breakfast – which almost universally means bread, butter, jam, cheese and maybe an egg in one form or another, all accompanied by a cup of tea or coffee. Another common feature is the noticeboard. The quality of these varies considerably – some have a lot of useful information, others are a more token effort. Don't feel you've walked into a uniquely helpful place if the first hotel you see has one of these bulletin boards – they are becoming standard fare in the low-budget places.

If you can manage to avoid the squawking hotel touts who pounce on as many travellers as possible as they get off the train (and take a 25% to 40% cut, which goes on to the traveller's hotel bill), leave the station and you'll see the *New Karnak Hotel* on the left side of the station square.

This hotel, which is virtually on Sharia Abdel al-Moneim al-Adasi (also known as Manches St), has long been a favourite among travellers, more for its low prices and convenient location than its rooms. Hot water is available for short periods. Showers and bathrooms get flooded easily, so you may want to wear thongs. All rooms have fans, and singles/doubles cost E£8/10.

One often overlooked, and around to the left of the New Karnak, is the *Anglo Hotel*. It costs E£10 a head with breakfast, is clean and the management is friendly.

If you walk a short way down Sharia al-Mahatta, past the Ramoza, Amoun and Majestic hotels and the Hotel de la Gare (the first is no longer a budget place and the latter three don't seem to be keen on taking foreigners) and turn left at the first side street, which is Sharia al-Madrassa al-Miri, you'll find the *Happy Home*. This has long been a good place to stay for budget travellers, but at the time of writing seemed to be out of action. It might be worth trying, as locals say it is still operating.

The *Amoun Hotel*, should there be a change in policy, costs E£5 a person, and the *Hotel de la Gare* E£3. Don't expect much in these places.

Sharia Abd al-Moneim leads away from the train station to Sharia Mohammed Farid and then on to Sharia Television, which everyone seems to know as Television St. Around these two streets teems a growing

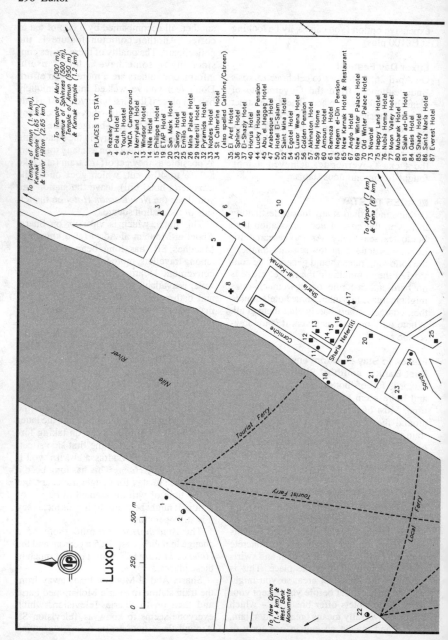

Luxor

■ PLACES TO STAY

3 Rezeiky Camp
4 Pola Hotel
7 Youth Hostel
12 YMCA Campground
13 Mersland Hotel
14 Windsor Hotel
15 Nile Hotel
16 Philippe Hotel
19 ETAP Hotel
20 San Mark Hotel
23 Savoy Hotel
25 Emilio Hotel
26 Mina Palace Hotel
29 Nefertiti Hotel
32 Pyramids Hotel
33 Nobles Hotel
34 St Catherine Hotel
   (also spelled Cathrine/Catreen)
35 El Aref Hotel
36 Sphinx Hotel
37 El-Shazly Hotel
40 Horus Hotel
44 Lucky House Pension
45 Abu el Haggag Hotel
47 Arabesque Hotel
50 Hotel El-Salam
52 Saint Mina Hotel
55 Egena Hotel
55 Luxor Wena Hotel
56 Golden Pension
57 Akhnaton Hotel
59 Happy Home
60 Amoun Hotel
61 Ramoza Hotel
63 Negem el-Din Pension
65 New Karnak Hotel & Restaurant
67 Anglo Hotel
69 New Winter Palace Hotel
70 Old Winter Palace Hotel
73 Novotel
75 Happy Land Hotel
76 Nubia Home Hotel
77 Moon Valley Hotel
80 Mubarak Hotel
81 Salah ad-Din Hotel
84 Oasis Hotel
85 Shady Hotel
86 Santa Maria Hotel
87 Everest Hotel

To Temple of Amun (1.4 km),
Karnak Temple (1.65 km),
& Luxor Hilton (2.65 km)

To Temple of Mut (300 m),
Avenue of Sphinxes (500 m),
Temple of Amun (950 m)
& Karnak Temple (1.2 km)

To Airport (7 km)
& Qena (67 km)

To New Qurna
(1.4 km) &
West Bank
Monuments

River
Nile

Corniche

Sharia al-Karnak

Sharia Nefertiti

Souqs

Tourist Ferry

Tourist Ferry

Local Ferry

0   250   500 m

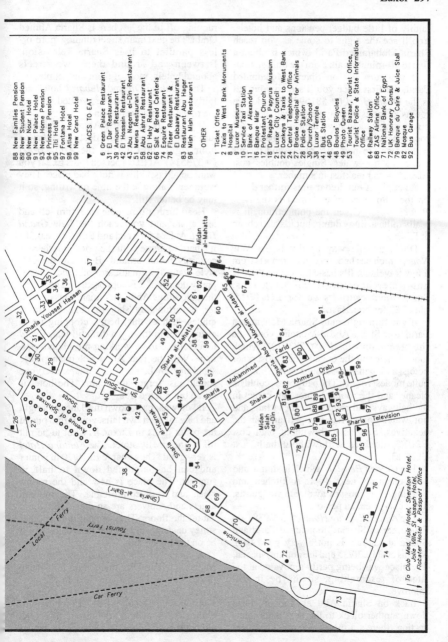

PLACES TO EAT

88 New Families Pension
89 New Student Pension
90 New Nour Hotel
91 New Palace Hotel
93 New Home Pension
94 Princess Pension
95 Titi Hotel
97 Fontana Hotel
98 Atlas Hotel
99 New Grand Hotel

▼ PLACES TO EAT

6 Green Palace Restaurant
31 El Dar Restaurant
39 Amoun Restaurant
42 El Hossein Restaurant
43 Abu Negem el-Din Restaurant
51 Mensa Restaurant
58 Abu Ashraf Restaurant
62 El Haty Restaurant
66 Salt & Bread Cafeteria
74 Esquire Restaurant
78 Fiteer Restaurant &
   El Dabaawy Restaurant
83 Restaurant Abu Hager
96 Mish Mish Restaurant

OTHER

1 Ticket Office
2 Taxis to West Bank Monuments
8 Hospital
9 Luxor Museum
10 Service Taxi Station
11 Bank of Alexandria
16 Banque Misr
17 Protestant Church
18 Dr Ragab's Papyrus Museum
21 Luxor City Council
22 Donkeys & Taxis to West Bank
24 Central Telephone Office
27 Brooke Hospital for Animals
28 Police Station
30 Church/School
38 Luxor Temple
41 Bus Station
46 GPO
48 Boulos' Bicycles
49 Phone Queen
53 Tourist Bazar, Tourist Office,
   Tourist Police & State Information
   Office
64 Railway Station
68 ZAS Airline Office
71 National Bank of Egypt
72 UK Honorary Consul
79 Banque du Caire & Juice Stall
82 Mosque
92 Bus Garage

family of little budget pensions and hotels. You'll see the signs to some as you reach Sharia Mohammed Farid, which is about a five to 10-minute walk from the train station.

If you turn left on Sharia Mohammed Farid, the first place you'll see on your left is the *Oasis Hotel* (☎ 581699). The double rooms are considerably better than the more pokey singles and have their own bath. All rooms have fans and comfortable beds. The bathrooms are new and clean, and there's plenty of hot water. Singles/doubles cost E£8/16 with breakfast in summer.

A couple of hundred metres further down on the same side of the street is the *New Palace Hotel*. Given the competition, it is really quite a dingy dump, but it's also cheap at E£4/6.

Down an alleyway nearby is the *New Nour*, which has had some good reports from a few travellers. It's basic but clean; there is hot water and the rooms have fans. Singles/doubles/triples go for E£6/12/15, plus E£2 for breakfast.

If you turn right onto Sharia Mohammed Farid from Sharia Abd al-Moneim, you'll see the *Akhnaton Hotel* (☎ 383979), which looks fancier on the outside than most other hotels and pensions around here, but has quite modest rooms. The bathrooms could be cleaner and the rooms lighter, but carpet in the hallways and rooms, overhead fans and hot water somewhat compensate for the negatives. Singles with/without bath cost E£10/8; doubles with/without bath cost E£15/13.

The *Golden Pension*, which is simple and very clean, is next door. A kitchen and washing machine are available for guests. They charge E£6 a person.

The *Abu el Haggag Hotel* (☎ 372988), on the corner of Sharia Mohammed Farid and Sharia al-Karnak, is not a very good deal. Rooms cost E£20/35 and are nothing special. The place was being partly renovated at the time of researching, so maybe it will improve.

Back on Sharia Abd al-Moneim, head down another block to the next main intersection (there's a mosque here). The street running off to the left here is Sharia Ahmed Orabi. The next main street running more-or-less parallel to it is Sharia Television. Between and around these two streets abound hotels, most of them budget places.

The *Salah ad-Din* and *Mubarak* hotels are fairly crummy, and can be avoided with all the other alternatives around.

If you walk up Sharia Ahmed Orabi and turn right into the second dusty laneway on your right, you'll find the *Atlas Hotel* (☎ 373514). At E£6 a person (plus E£2 if you want breakfast), this is not a bad place. They were renovating at the time of writing, so it may be better still.

Head further down the lane, turn left and left again and you reach the *New Grand Hotel*. At E£4 for a bed and E£1 for breakfast it's hard to argue with the price, but there is certainly better around. Beds are the old-style wafer-thin mattresses and the place is pretty decayed. It is supposedly managed by the ubiquitous Abdo Suleiman. This character, unfortunately shot to fame by travel guides such as this, began cropping up in every hotel in town – a difficult feat. Every tout claimed to be working for Abdo Suleiman. Will the real Abdo Suleiman please stand up? Or better still, perhaps everyone should just forget about him. The hotel is cheap but not too hot.

If you walk back down this lane, turn right and take the next two lefts, you'll find one of the better deals in Luxor. Try not to be put off by the smelly street. The *Fontana Hotel* is very good. They charge E£10/20 in winter and can be bargained down to half in summer. The place is new and the rooms clean and very comfortable. The modern toilets and showers are so clean you could eat off the floors. They are building another storey upstairs, and one of these days they'll be on the phone too.

A couple of blocks back down towards Midan Salah ad-Din, there are a few cheap places bunched together. Next to the now closed *New Home Pension* is the *Princess Pension*, which charges E£12/15 for doubles without/with bath in the room. It's OK, although not as good as some of the newer places. You get breakfast and they have a washing machine. Some people have reported being unhappy with the trips (eg donkey treks) organised from here.

In the lane leading away from the New Home Pension is the *New Student Pension*. It's E£5 for a bed with breakfast. The toilet/shower combinations are moderately clean, but it's a bit gloomy. Across the road, the *New Families Pension* will go E£1 lower for a similar deal.

In a lane off Sharia Television (it's blocked off though) is the *Everest Hotel*. The renovated rooms are good and come with bathrooms attached (even toilet paper is provided!), but at E£12/20 the rooms are possibly just a tad overpriced.

If none of these appeal and you find your way out of the rabbit warren, there are a whole lot more on the other side of Sharia Television. The main disadvantage is that you are getting further away from the transport and the centre of town here. The closest, a little way down from the Mish Mish restaurant on Sharia Television itself, is the *Titi Hotel*. This is another pretty good place. At E£7 a person you can't really go wrong, although the prices go up in winter. The bathrooms are outside, but are clean.

Keep going down this street, cross what passes for a main thoroughfare and you'll see the *Moon Valley Hotel* on your right. This place is new and, in summer at least, a very good deal at E£6/12. It appears they double their prices in winter. The rooms are modern and comfortable, and the adjacent showers and toilets spotless. Breakfast is included in the price.

In the next street down is the *Nubia Home Hotel*, but it was closed at the time of writing. Another street down is the *Happy Land*. Mr Ibrahim is a big man who is particularly unpopular with the railway station touts – well he would be, he does his own touting. Don't believe a lot of what he says, but his hotel is good. The cheapest rooms are E£6 a person plus E£2 for breakfast. In the low season a good single with private bath costs E£10. The sheets are changed every day, and even soap and towels are provided. It's about

a half-hour walk from the train station, and not the easiest place to find on your own. The easiest way is simply to walk to the Novotel and continue out towards the Sheraton; when you see the street with the Esquire Restaurant on the corner, head up the lane to the left of it. The hotel is about 80 metres up on your left.

East Bank – north of Sharia al-Mahatta

Just back from the Mensa Restaurant on Sharia al-Mahatta is the *Hotel El Salam*, which is deservedly a fairly popular haunt for the impecunious. At E£5/10, the prices are as cheap as they come and include breakfast and use of a washing machine. The rooms have fans. If you have a double with bath, they charge E£15.

The *Saint Mina Hotel* (☎ 386568) is a very good deal if you've got a little extra to pay. The 20-room hotel is brand new, and although the rooms are small, they are modern and clean with air-con and fans. A single with bath is E£30, but singles/doubles without bath go for E£20/35. Their prices may well go up once they are better established, but at the moment it is as good a place as some of the middle-range joints asking double or more.

Just north of the train station, virtually on the train tracks, is the *Negem el-Din Pension*. This place has hot water, awful mattresses and wonderful views of the railway lines – all for E£5.

An odd little place hidden a couple of blocks away in a private house is the *Lucky House Pension* (☎ 581172). Mr Adly Reda seems a strange old coot, but the six rooms are OK. He wants E£10/15 for his doubles/triples. Have a look at the stuffed blowfish hanging off the walls – very weird decor. Your man works at Wena Luxor Hotel and the Green Palace Restaurant and claims he can get you into the latter's swimming pool for a discount.

Down in a side street by the souqs near Luxor Temple is the *Nefertiti Hotel*. A bit on the decrepit side, it could be worse. The beds are generally fairly comfortable, but there are no fans. It's certainly a central (and noisy) location. They want E£10/19 for singles/ doubles with breakfast.

Sharia Youssef Hassan is another hotel street. Starting from the east (if you're walking from the train station) there's the *El-Shazly Hotel*. Prices seem to be for doubles, with no concession to lone travellers. A double with noisy air-con, bath and breakfast costs E£20. The same thing with a fan instead of air-con (preferable) costs E£15 and a room without bath or fan E£12. It's all right, but hardly the best deal in town.

The *Sphinx Hotel* (☎ 382830) has singles/ doubles for E£15/25 or E£18/32 with breakfast.

Across the road, the *Venus* (☎ 372625) has 25 reasonable rooms with bath. Singles/ doubles cost E£10/20 and the hotel has a restaurant and bar. This is not a bad choice at all. The food is good too.

The *Nobles Hotel* (☎ 372823) is not quite as good, but is not a terrible deal either, at E£12/20 with a fan. Breakfast is included. If you want air-con, a double costs E£30.

Just up from the Emilio Hotel is the cheap and cheerful *Pyramids Hotel* (☎ 373243). A bed here costs E£5 without breakfast. The location is good, the rooms basic but OK and the price is rock bottom.

The *Youth Hostel* (☎ 382139) is in a street just off Sharia al-Karnak. Rooms are clean and have at least two sets of bunk beds, but the showers tend to get swampy and stinky, so wear thongs. With an IYHF card they want E£8, plus E£1.50 for breakfast; E£9 plus E£1.50 without. It is a little inconvenient to stay there unless you are planning to take an early morning service taxi from the taxi station, which is about 100 metres from the hostel, and at the price there are better deals in town.

West Bank On the west bank there are only six bottom-end places to stay. The *Memnon Hotel* is across the road from the Colossi of Memnon and is basically a pit. Wild camels would not drag most right-minded people to stay here. And they want E£10/15!

Opposite the Medinat Habu temple complex is the *Habou Hotel* (sometimes spelt 'Habu'). It has dark, dingy and rather overpriced rooms (compared with what is available in Luxor). Singles/doubles cost E£10/20 in summer, and a bit more in winter. You're really paying for the great location overlooking Medinat Habu.

The nearby *Queen's Hotel* (☎ 384835) has slightly better rooms, somewhat less of a view and an interesting owner, Hajj Ali Hassan Khalifa. He charges E£10/20 for a single/double room. The roof restaurant has good views.

The *Mersam Hotel* (☎ 382403), also known as the *Ali Abd el-Rasul Hotel* or the *Sheik Ali Hotel*, is opposite the Antiquities Office. Rooms in the main building are somewhat better than the primitive mud-wall rooms in an adjacent building. Singles/ doubles with an 'English' breakfast cost E£10/20 in summer. They try to charge double in winter.

This hotel was once home to Sheikh Ali Abdul Rasul, a cantankerous old guy with a bone-cracking handshake and an aggressive sense of hospitality that kept you riveted to your seat, whether you liked it or not. Sheikh Ali actually helped discover the tomb of Seti I and if you've read Richard Critchfield's book *Shahatt*, then you'll know about this guy already. His son has now taken over the hotel.

The *Pension Osiris* attempts to charge E£20 to E£30 for its double rooms. Unless you can bargain them down further, don't bother with this place.

The *Abdul Kasem Hotel* (☎ 374835) has singles/doubles for E£20/40. This is the best of the lower budget places on the west bank, but in summer you can get better rooms still at the Pharaoh's Hotel for the same price. There's a great view from the roof. The owners, the Kasem family, also have an alabaster factory attached to the hotel and rent bicycles for E£5 a day.

To get there, follow the road inland from either of the ferry landings, turn right on the road just after the canal, which is parallel to it, and follow the signs to 'Wadi al-Melouk' (Valley of the Kings); the hotel is before the Temple of Seti I on Sharia Wadi al-Melouk.

The *Wadi el-Melouk Hotel* still exists on the east side of the canal, but excavation of the canal has almost completely isolated it. You need to bargain with someone in a row boat to get across the canal. You're really not missing much because the hotel was somewhat of a dive.

Camping The *YMCA* camping ground, on Sharia al-Karnak, costs E£3 per night, including the use of its 20 showers. This was popular with overland travel groups, but may have lost business to the new and more expensive Rezeiky Camp, further up the road towards the temple.

The *Rezeiky Camp* (☎ 581334; fax 373447) charges you E£10 to pitch a tent, for which you get access to the small pool and showers. A bed in the small mud bungalows costs E£15.

Places to Stay – middle

East Bank The *Ramoza Hotel* (☎ 581670, 372270), just down from the train station on Sharia al-Mahatta, has climbed well out of the budget bracket. Smallish rooms with wall-to-wall carpet, air-con, bath and a balcony cost as much as E£50/76 in winter. In summer they will take up to E£20 off.

On Sharia al-Karnak, about a block north of Sharia al-Mahatta, you'll see the *Horus Hotel* (☎ 372165; fax 383447). Rooms are clean and comfortable, with air-con and relatively new bathrooms. They ask E£35/45 in summer. At that rate, it's not a bad deal, and the hotel is nicely placed near the souqs and Luxor Temple. The only drawback is that a few of the rooms face a mosque, which could

Amun

mean waking up with the early morning call to prayer.

Further along Sharia al-Karnak and about half a block to the right is the *Emilio Hotel* (☎ 373570; fax 370000). This is one of the best upper-middle price range hotels in town. It was built in 1987 and has 48 rooms, all with bathrooms, air-con, TV and a hotel video channel; some rooms have Nile views. The astroturf roof terrace has plenty of shade and several reclining chairs. There is also a pool. You pay for quality though. Singles/doubles cost US$50/55, including taxes and breakfast. Reservations are essential here in winter, because it is often taken over by travel groups.

The two-star *St Catherine Hotel* (sometimes spelled 'Catreen' or 'Cathrine'; ☎ & fax 382684), 2 Sharia Youssef Hassan, is popular with German groups. Some of the bathrooms are somewhat small, but the rooms are otherwise fine. A double room for two costs E£65; for one person the cost is E£45. There is a rooftop bar. Across the road is the *El Aref Hotel* (☎ 372557), with singles/doubles for E£15/19.

The *Mina Palace Hotel* (☎ 372074) is on the Corniche, north of Luxor Temple and near the landing for local ferries to the west bank. It has singles/doubles with air-con and private bathrooms for E£54/62 in summer, but can cost quite a bit more in winter. Ask for a room with a balcony looking towards Luxor Temple.

The *Savoy Hotel* is also on the Corniche. It looks scruffy on the outside, but the bungalow rooms around the main building are quite pleasant, and in the summer of 1993 were going for a quite reasonable US$10/20. However, the hotel was in the process of shutting down at the time of writing, so it may well not be there or have taken on a new existence by the time you read this.

Virtually directly behind the Pullman ETAP Hotel on Sharia al-Karnak is the overpriced and extremely average *San Mark Hotel* (☎ & fax 373532). The small and stuffy singles/doubles cost E£50/70.

The *Windsor Hotel* (☎ 385547; fax 373447) is in a small alley just off Sharia

Nefertiti. It's a generally excellent 120-room hotel, although some of the rooms are a little shoddy and others are decidedly gloomy and dark. Most are fully carpeted and have wallpaper, modern tiled bathrooms, TV and air-con. This place is popular with European tour groups. Singles/doubles/triples cost US$14/22/30 in summer and US$29/46/63 in winter, plus taxes. This place's particular boast, aside from pretty good rooms, is the pool complex, which comes with a jacuzzi, sauna and solarium.

Just across the way is the new *Merryland Hotel* (☎ 581746). Its 32 rooms are more modest than those of the Windsor, but with TV, phone, air-con, bath and balcony, the price of E£40/55 for singles/doubles in summer is very reasonable.

The *Philippe Hotel* (☎ 372284) is on Sharia Nefertiti, between the Corniche and Sharia al-Karnak. It's an upper-middle range hotel with clean, carpeted rooms. All the rooms have powerful air-con and bathrooms with bathtubs, and there are some rooms with balconies. There's a pleasant roof garden with a small bar. Including breakfast a single/double costs E£40/50 in summer, which is quite OK. In winter, however, the rates jump to E£98/150! Reservations are recommended.

Next door to the Philippe is the newer *Nile Hotel* (☎ 382859), which has 50 double rooms of varying quality. There seem to be two hotels in the one building and the better, slightly pricier rooms are towards the front of the building. Most of them have balconies, powerful air-con and bathrooms with bathtubs. They all have TV and phone. Singles/doubles cost about E£40/50 in summer and E£60/70 in winter, altogether a much better deal than next door.

Another new place is the *Arabesque Hotel* on Sharia Mohammed Farid, just up from Sharia al-Karnak. It has modern, air-con rooms for E£40/80. The roof garden has good views over Luxor Temple and the Nile.

Down on Sharia Television, there are two middle-range places in direct competition with one another. They are both comfortable, with modern new rooms, TV, air-con and

virtually the same prices. The *Shady Hotel* (☎ 374859; fax 374859) and the *Santa Maria Hotel* (☎ 580430) offer singles/doubles for E£50/70 and, when business is slow, both are prepared to discuss discounts.

A couple of new three-star hotels have appeared just past the Club Med. The *St Joseph Hotel* (☎ 581707; fax 581727) costs about US$50 for a double. Rooms have TV, air-con, phone and bath. There is also a pool and bar. Next door, the rather oddly named *Flobater Hotel* (☎ 374223; fax 370618) is similar and more modestly priced at US$28/35 for singles/doubles in winter.

Across the road from the Rezeiky Camp there is a small place called the *Pola Hotel*.

West Bank On the west bank, *Pharaoh's Hotel* (☎ 382502) is the only middle-range place to stay, and is easily the best hotel on this side of the Nile. It's near the Antiquities Office and is the newest and best hotel in the area. There are 14 rooms, most with air-con or strong overhead fans, wallpaper and tiled floors. Three of the rooms have private bathrooms.

There's a small restaurant and bright flower garden in front. The restaurant is popular with a few tour groups and is especially renowned for its sun-baked bread. Single/double/triple rooms cost E£20/40/50 in summer. In winter, the price can easily double.

Places to Stay – top end

The hotels in this price range start at about US$50 for a single and generally have all the usual attributes of the big international hotels. Where not otherwise specified, the rates do not include breakfast or taxes of usually more than 20%.

The *Mövenpick Hotel Jolie Ville* is on Crocodile Island, four km from town. It's a Swiss-managed place with a swimming pool, tennis courts and sailboats. There are 320 modern, well-appointed rooms set out in bungalow style amidst tropical and semi-tropical gardens. Singles/doubles cost from US$85/105 to US$120/150.

A shuttle bus runs between the Jolie Ville and the Winter Palace hotels. You can also take a taxi into town for E£5 (officially set rate) or the hotel motorboat for free.

The *Pullman ETAP Hotel* (☎ 580944; fax 384912) is a four-star place where singles/doubles cost US$63/81 in summer (including breakfast and taxes) and US$73/95 in winter. The lobby is a nice cool place to hang out, and you can get a Stella (or two – there's a minimum charge) in either the bar or the so-called cafeteria. Nonresidents can go to the disco for a E£25 minimum charge – this covers you for the belly dancer at 11.30 pm too.

The *Winter Palace & New Winter Palace* (☎ 580422) on the Corniche are attached. The new side is not nearly as interesting and romantic as the old, which was built to attract the aristocracy of Europe. Rooms cost from about US$50 to US$250, and there's a swimming pool, table-tennis tables and a tennis court. The *Luxor Wena Hotel* (☎ 580018) on Sharia al-Karnak faces Luxor Temple. Singles/doubles cost US$48/60. There's a swimming pool and a variety of restaurants. Next to it is the *Egotel* (☎ 373521), with rooms starting at about US$40.

The *Novotel* (☎ 580925) has singles/doubles for US$48/60. Beyond the Novotel are the *Club Med*, the *Isis Hotel* and, near the Jolie Ville, the *Sheraton*. One km north of Karnak Temple is the *Luxor Hilton*. Prices at these are all a little below those of the Jolie Ville. The Sheraton and Hilton have occasional shuttle buses for guests into the centre of town.

PLACES TO EAT

The *New Karnak Restaurant* is next to the New Karnak Hotel. Although the portions are small, the food is good and cheap. You can eat a main meal of chicken or other meat for around E£3 to E£4. The menu includes six kinds of omelette – one wonders how different they can be. Don't get your hopes up about the ice cream – it's just a teeny bucket of vanilla whipped out of the freezer for 90 pt.

The *Salt & Bread Cafeteria* is on your left as you leave the train station. They serve many entrees, including kebab, pigeon and chicken. A full meal costs about the same as in the New Karnak next door, and there are some who insist this place is better, although really there doesn't seem to be much in it. For those who have been to Luxor before and remember the cheap fly-blown hangout *Limpy's*, it's gone.

Next to the Ramoza Hotel is a place to avoid – the *El Haty Restaurant*. Nobody seems to go here, and by all accounts it has always been like that, so how they survive is a mystery.

The *Mensa Restaurant*, on Sharia al-Mahatta, has cheap basic food. Dishes include chicken, pigeon stuffed with rice, sandwiches, and chicken with French fries and mixed vegetables. You can have almost a full meal for about E£7.

There are a few juice stands at the Luxor Temple end of Sharia al-Mahatta. This street also has a number of good sandwich stands and other cheap eats possibilities.

A little more expensive, and one of the most popular eating houses for tourists, is *El Hossein*, behind Luxor Temple where Sharia al-Mahatta runs into Sharia al-Karnak. Most main dishes cost E£6 to E£9 before they add service on. They do tasty fish in a tomato and basil sauce, and acceptable, if smallish, pizzas for E£7. The soups are sometimes good, sometimes watery.

The *Amoun Restaurant*, further up along Sharia al-Karnak, serves oriental kebab, chicken, fish and various rice and vegetable dishes for similar prices, but seems to be losing the fight for customers. You could go and sip a tea in their café.

Across the road from the El Hossein is the small and busy local hangout, the *Abu Negem el-Din*, where half a chicken will cost you E£4, and a plate of makarone E£1.50. Try the tagen, a kind of stew, with or without meat, in a clay casserole pot.

There is a huddle of small eateries and cafés in the lanes around Sharia al-Mahatta between the Amoun and the police station, where the food is cheap and the atmosphere busy. One of them, the tiny *El Dar Restau-*

Priests and Priestesses

rant, is up on the 1st floor of a building in a laneway off Sharia al-Karnak. It's not bad, and you can get a beer here.

Down on Sharia Television is another cluster of small eateries and a juice stand. There is a fiteer place, and next to it the *El Dabaawy Restaurant*. It's a pleasant enough place, and main courses cost about E£9. The only drawback is that only a few of the items on the extensive menu are actually available.

Further up Sharia Television, near the Titi Hotel, is the new *Mish Mish* restaurant. Try their Mish Mish salad – a mixed platter with hoummus and cold meats, enough to constitute a light meal, for E£4. They serve a version of pizza too.

The *Marhaba Restaurant* is an Oriental-style dining room on the roof of the Tourist Bazaar building on Sharia al-Karnak, near Luxor Temple. This place commands great views of the river, but the food is rather expensive (main courses average E£17) and nothing better than you'll find in a lot of other places.

Restaurant Abu Hager is on Sharia Abdel al-Moneim al-Adasi, just past Sharia Mohammed Farid. It serves only shish kebab and kofta (although it advertises fish and other odds and ends to attract custom) and seems to be popular with Egyptians who work in tourism-related businesses. The guy who runs it is a kebab specialist, if you believe the locals – and his is supposedly the best in town. A filling meal averages about E£9.

The *Luxor Wena Hotel* has a garden pizzeria that serves good but expensive pizzas for around E£20. They have Stella here too.

The main attraction of the *Green Palace Restaurant*, next to the YMCA camping ground, is the swimming pool – it could make a pleasant place to stop for a wet lunch after a morning visit to Karnak Temple.

Most of the middle-range hotels have their own restaurants, generally rooftop jobs of varying quality. The *San Mark*, for instance, does main courses for around E£8. The chips are good, and you can watch the goings on in the ETAP Hotel gardens below. At many of them, however, you cannot get a beer (this also applies to the bulk of the above mentioned restaurants).

The ETAP Hotel has the *Champollion* snack bar, where you can get pizza, cakes and beer. There's a minimum charge of E£15 a head. The *Winter Palace* does a reasonable open buffet breakfast for E£31.50, if you feel like splashing out. The *Novotel* has breakfast on a felucca for E£25.

If, after all this, you're hunting around for sweets, you could pop into *Twinky's*, around the corner from the New Karnak Hotel.

ENTERTAINMENT

The *Mövenpick Hotel Jolie Ville* presents a quite extravagant floor show. They will dress you up in a galabiyya, take you for a felucca ride at sunset, introduce you to 'peasants', and then feed and entertain you in a tent by the Nile.

The *ETAP* and *Winter Palace* hotels have folkloric and belly dance performances as well as discos. In the low season, the belly dancing is usually held only three or four nights a week, so check beforehand.

THINGS TO BUY

Pretty much the whole range of standard Egyptian souvenirs can be bought in Luxor, although the variety is not nearly as great as in Cairo. One exception is alabaster. You will notice a plethora of alabaster shops on the west bank. The alabaster is mined about 80 km north-west of the Valley of the Kings, and some of the handmade cups, vases and other articles make sturdy and original souvenirs. If you're interested in buying alabaster objects, this is probably the place to do it.

There's also one of Dr Ragab's papyrus museums on the Corniche, if you are interested in reasonably well made, but expensive, papyrus.

GETTING THERE & AWAY

Air

The EgyptAir office is on the Corniche, next to the American Express office. ZAS has an office not far away, in front of the New Winter Palace.

EgyptAir flies daily between Cairo, Luxor and Aswan. A one-way ticket to Luxor from Cairo costs E£283. There are frequent daily departures.

There are also daily flights from Luxor to Aswan (E£127) and Sharm el-Sheikh (E£325). ZAS has flights to the same destinations for much the same prices.

In the high season, the two airlines may also put on flights to Abu Simbel and Hurghada.

Bus

The bus station is conveniently located behind Luxor Temple on Sharia al-Karnak (the garage on Sharia Television is officially not a pick-up point).

From Cairo, the Upper Egypt Bus Co's luxury service (air-con, video and toilet) leaves from the new station near the Ramses Hilton at 8.30 pm for E£35. Book in advance.

A couple of other cheaper buses leave from the same company's station at Midan Ahmed Hilmi (see Cairo Getting There & Away for more details).

From Luxor, there are three departures to Cairo: at 6 am (E£18), 4.30 (E£21) and 7 pm (E£35). The trip takes around 10 to 12 hours.

Buses leave for Aswan about every hour from 6 am to 4.30 pm. There is one last run at 6.45 pm. These include through buses from Qena and Hurghada, so there may not always be seats. The trip takes five hours – a long time to have to stand – and costs E£6. The same buses go to Edfu for E£3.25. Don't be surprised to see 50 pt or so added to the official price when you're actually on the bus.

The trip to Hurghada on the Red Sea takes four to five hours. The first three buses leave at about 7 amd 10.30 am and noon, and cost E£7.50. The 10.30 am bus may be full, as it comes up from Aswan. The 4 pm bus costs E£10 or E£13, depending on whether or not it has air-con. It usually goes on to Suez. The 7 pm bus is the deluxe service, costing E£18.

There are 10 buses to Qena from 6 am to 4.30 pm that cost from E£1.50 to E£2. There is sometimes a late bus at 10 pm for a little more.

Train

The train station at Luxor, apart from swarming with hotel touts and irritating kids trying to sell you the *Egyptian Gazette* for E£2, has a post office, card phones, left-luggage, telex and telegraph facilities and an often closed tourist information office.

For tickets, the 3rd-class window is on your left when facing the tracks; other tickets are sold at windows on the right.

If you want a sleeper to Cairo, you can only travel on the wagon-lit trains. Berths have to be booked two or three days in advance and cost E£242 one way (from Aswan or from Luxor!). The train leaves Luxor at about 8 pm and reaches Cairo at 6 am. First and 2nd-class sitting fares to Cairo are E£38 and E£22, although for the faster trains the fares seem to be about E£3 more.

For more details on all these services, see the Cairo Getting There & Away section.

First, 2nd and 3rd-class tickets to Aswan cost E£15.30/9.40/2 (E£10.90/7.10 in 1st and 2nd for students). Heading in the other direction, fares to Al-Minya are E£30/18.40/3.50 respectively. There may be price variations for quicker trains.

Service Taxi

The service taxi station is on a street off Sharia al-Karnak, a couple of blocks inland from the Luxor Museum.

A service taxi to Aswan costs E£7.50 and takes 3½ hours; to Esna it costs E£2 and takes 45 minutes; to Edfu it costs E£4 for the two-hour trip; to Kom Ombo E£6.50 (2½ hours); to Qus E£1.25; Qena E£2; and Nag Hammadi E£4.

The drivers are always ready to bargain for special trips down the Nile to Aswan, stopping at the sights on the way – reckon with about E£100 for the car.

Felucca

You can get a felucca from here to Aswan – there's no shortage of captains and touts offering you rides, but the trip upstream can be hopelessly slow. If the wind dies, with the current against you, you can end up going backwards. For this very reason you may have trouble finding other people to join you. The great majority of travellers do the trip the other way, downstream from Aswan towards Luxor – for more details see the Aswan Getting There & Away section.

Cruise Ship

About 200 'flotels' and cruise boats ply the Nile all year round, and many of them just do the Luxor to Aswan stretch (or the other way around) as part of a package deal. If you really have hundreds of pounds (and in the case of some boats, dollars) to fling around, you could organise to get on to one of them through one of the big hotels. As a general rule, however, bookings well in advance – sometimes months – are required, entailing a lot of forethought and planning.

GETTING AROUND
To/From the Airport

The airport is seven km east of Luxor and the official price for a taxi between there and town is E£10.

Felucca

There are, of course, a multitude of feluccas to take you on short trips or day tours from Luxor. They leave from various points all along the river. See the Felucca Rides section earlier in this chapter for more information.

Ferry

A total of five ferries cross the Nile from east to west, two tourist and three local ferries, at least one of which also carries vehicles. The distinction used to be important, as the local ferry used to cost everyone only 10 pt. That's all changed, as the Luxor town council has decided that foreigners can pay E£1 regardless of which ferry they get on. Large signs by the local-ferry dock make this quite clear. If you are taking a bicycle across, or want a service taxi or to bargain on donkeys, bicycles and the like, you'll have to get one of the local ferries. It is a little galling to have to pay 10 times what the locals are paying though. Also, there is no ticket booth at the town landing. If you take the road inland for three km you'll come to the Antiquities Office, where students can purchase discount tickets to the sights (it should also be no problem to get full-price tickets there now – see the West Bank section earlier in this chapter). The local boats leave from in front of the Mina Palace Hotel, Luxor Temple and the Winter Palace (car ferry). A shuttle sometimes runs to the student ticket kiosk for 25 pt.

The tourist boats drop you off at the tourist landing, where you can buy full-price tickets to the sights, about one km north of the town landing. If you don't have a bicycle and want to haggle for a taxi on the other side, you may as well get this boat. The tourist-ferry landings are in front of the ETAP and the Winter Palace hotels. You must pay for the return trip in advance.

Motorcycle

A few hotels have started renting out motorcycles for about E£40 to E£60 a day. The New Palace Hotel is one. If you are interested, hunt around a bit. Check the condition of the bikes carefully.

Bicycle

Luxor is bursting with bicycle rent shops, and you'll get as many offers to rent one as to buy papyrus. Depending on the quality of the bike, how good business is and the determination of your bargaining, they can cost from E£3 to E£10 a day. They often ask you to leave your passport or student identification card.

Most hotels, including the ETAP and the Windsor, will also rent bicycles and it's possible to rent children's bicycles if you enquire. Bicycles can also be rented on the west bank, near the local-ferry landing, but the choice of bicycle is better in the town itself.

Hantour or Caleche

For about E£4 per hour you can get around town by horse and carriage. It's the most common means of transportation in Luxor. Rates are, of course, subject to haggling, squabbling and, sometimes, screaming!

AROUND LUXOR

An increasingly popular side trip from Luxor is a visit to the supposedly typical village of Armant, on the west bank slightly south of Thebes. It is one of the biggest villages between Luxor and Esna. To get to it, take the local ferry from the east side and a service taxi from the landing. Or you could take an Esna-bound service taxi along the east bank and get out (Armant lies on both banks). Most Luxorians can't understand why tourists would want to go. Why Armant? No particular reason, except perhaps its relative proximity to Luxor and the fact that it's a little bigger than other villages in the area.

The Nile Valley – Esna to Abu Simbel

Following the death of Alexander the Great, his huge empire was divided between his Macedonian generals. For 300 years the Greek-speaking Ptolemies ruled Egypt in the guise of Pharaohs, respecting the traditions and religion of the Egyptians and setting an example to the Romans who succeeded them.

Their centre of power tied them to Alexandria and the coast but they also pushed their way south, extending Greco-Roman power into Nubia through their politically sensible policy of assimilation rather than subjugation.

In Upper Egypt they raised temples in honour of the local gods, building them in grand Pharaonic style to appease the priesthood and earn the trust of the people. Somehow, though, these archaic imitations lost something in the translation; in many ways they were stilted, unimaginative edifices lacking the artistic brilliance that marked the truly Egyptian constructions they copied.

In southern Upper Egypt, south of Luxor, the major Greco-Roman works were a series of riverside temples at Esna, Edfu, Kom Ombo and Philae, admirable as much for their location as their actual artistic or architectural merit.

Beyond Edfu the ribbon of cultivation on the east bank gives way to the Eastern (Arabian) Desert. At Silsileh, 145 km south of Luxor, the Nile passes through a gorge, once thought to mark a cataract. In this area, there are Early Dynastic and New Kingdom ruins, including Elephantine and Abu Simbel; there's also the city of Aswan, the great High Dam and Lake Nasser, which mark the end of Egypt proper, for beyond them lie the forbidding, infertile desert lands of Nubia and the border with Sudan.

ESNA

The Greco-Roman Temple of Khnum is the main attraction of Esna, a small, busy farming town on the west bank of the Nile, 54 km south of Luxor. The post office and a branch of the Bank of Alexandria are on the street that runs next to the Nile from the bus and service taxi stations to the temple, which is about 200 metres in from the river. There is supposed to be a camel market here too.

Temple of Khnum

All that actually remains of the temple is the well-preserved Great Hypostyle Hall built during the reign of the Roman emperor Claudius. This sits, rather incongruously, in its huge excavation pit amongst the houses and narrow alleyways in the middle of town.

Dedicated to Khnum, the ram-headed creator-god who fashioned humankind on his potter's wheel, the temple was begun by Ptolemy VI and built over the ruins of earlier temples. The hall, as it stands today, was built later; it was excavated from the silt that had accumulated through centuries of annual Nile floods and is about nine metres below the modern street level.

The intact roof of the hall is supported by 24 columns decorated with a series of texts recording hymns to Khnum and relating the annual sacred festivals of Esna. The texts

Temple of Khnum

308

also refer to other temples in the area and one from the same era has in fact been excavated at Kom Mer, 12 km south of Esna. The west wall of the Roman-built hall is also the only remaining part of the original Ptolemaic temple and features reliefs of Ptolemy VI, Philometor and Euergetes II.

The ticket booth is on the river itself, about one km upriver from the main bridge across the Nile. You buy your ticket and follow the tourist bazaar through to the temple. The original quay, once connected to the temple by a processional way, is still in use. The temple is open from 6 am to 5.30 pm (an hour longer in summer) and admission costs E£4, or E£2 for students.

Places to Stay & Eat
About 500 metres south of the temple, via another covered bazaar, is the basic *Hotel Haramein*. There are a few of the usual food stands around for a cheap snack, although you should watch out for the odd rip-off in the small tourist bazaar. Esna is an easy day trip from Luxor, so there is little need to stay here anyway.

Getting There & Away
Trains are a pain, because the station is on the east bank of the Nile. There are frequent buses and service taxis from Luxor. The bus costs E£1.50, but stops a lot on the way. The service taxi (sometimes in the form of a microbus) is the quickest alternative, taking 45 minutes and costing E£2. The service taxi station is on a canal off the Nile. Follow it left from the station until you get to a small bridge spanning it near the Nile. Cross the bridge and follow the street, which soon runs up next to the Nile, down for about 20 minutes to the ticket booth. The bus stop is just by the little canal bridge.

Sometimes you can arrange for felucca trips from Aswan to finish here.

AL-KAB & KOM AL-AHMAR
Between Esna and Edfu are the scattered ruins of two settlements dating from pre-dynastic to late dynastic times. The earliest remains in the area now known as Al-Kab,

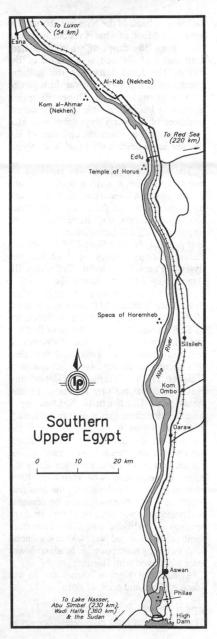

Southern
Upper Egypt

on the east bank of the Nile, are about 6000 years old. Much of what is visible, however, dates from later than that, when the ancient settlement of Nekheb was capital of the nome. The local deity was the vulture-goddess Nekhbet. Not only was she regarded as the greatest of the Upper Egyptian goddesses but, along with Edjo, the cobra-goddess of Lower Egypt, she was also guardian of the Pharaohs and one of the deities associated with royal and divine births.

The town of Nekheb was enclosed by massive mud-brick walls and still contains the remains of a Roman temple, a sacred lake and cemeteries and the ruins of the main temple of Nekhbet with its several pylons, hypostyle hall and birth-house. The temple was probably begun before 2700 BC but was enlarged considerably by 18th to 30th dynasty Pharaohs including Tuthmosis III, Amenophis II and the Ramessids.

A few km east of the town enclosure are three desert temples. At the entrance to Wadi Hellal is the rock-hewn Ptolemaic Sanctuary of Sheshmetet. To the south-east of that is a chapel built during the reign of Ramses II, restored under the Ptolemies and dedicated to a number of deities. About 3.5 km from Nekheb is the Temple of Hathor and Nekhbet; it was built by Tuthmosis IV and Amenophis III. North of Nekheb are a number of rockcut tombs with fine reliefs.

On the opposite side of the river, the remains of the ancient town of Nekhen, which predated Nekheb as capital of the nome, stretch for about three km along the edge of the desert. Now known as Kom al-Ahmar, or 'the red mound', the area features the ruins of pre-dynastic settlements and cemeteries and in the nearby wadis there are several Middle and New Kingdom tombs. The local god was Nekheny, a falcon with two long plumes on his head, who was later associated with Horus.

Al-Kab and Kom al-Ahmar are 26 km south of Esna and north of Edfu.

EDFU

The largest and most completely preserved Pharaonic, albeit Greek-built, temple in Egypt is the extraordinary Temple of Horus at Edfu. One of the last great Egyptian attempts at monument building on a grand scale, the structure dominates this west bank riverside town, 53 km south of Esna. The town and temple were established on a rise above the broad river valley around them, and so escaped the annual Nile inundation that contributed to the ruination of so many other buildings of antiquity. Edfu, a sugar and pottery centre, is also a very friendly place.

Just before you get to the temple you cross a square that appears to be the nerve centre of town. Approaching the square, the post office is along the first street off to the left. The bus station is about 100 metres in along the street to the right, past a couple of cafés and restaurants. The service taxi station is some way beyond it. The town's two hotels are also nearby (see Places to Stay & Eat).

Temple of Horus

Construction of this huge complex began under Ptolemy III Euergetes I in 237 BC and was completed nearly 200 years later during the reign of Ptolemy XIII (the father of Cleopatra) in the 1st century BC. In conception and design it follows the traditions of authentic Pharaonic architecture, with the same general plan, scale and ornamentation, right down to the 'Egyptian' attire worn by the Greek kings depicted in the temple's reliefs. Though it is much newer than the temples of Karnak, Luxor and Abydos, its excellent state of preservation fills in a lot of historical gaps because it is, in effect, a 2000-year-old replica of an architectural style that was already archaic during Ptolemaic times.

Being a copy it lacks artistic spontaneity. Where the Greek influence does penetrate, however, it produces a strangely graceful effect, which is most obvious in the fine line of the columns.

Dedicated to Horus, the falcon-headed son of Osiris, who avenged his father's murder by slaying his uncle Seth, the temple was built on the site where, according to legend, the two gods met in deadly combat.

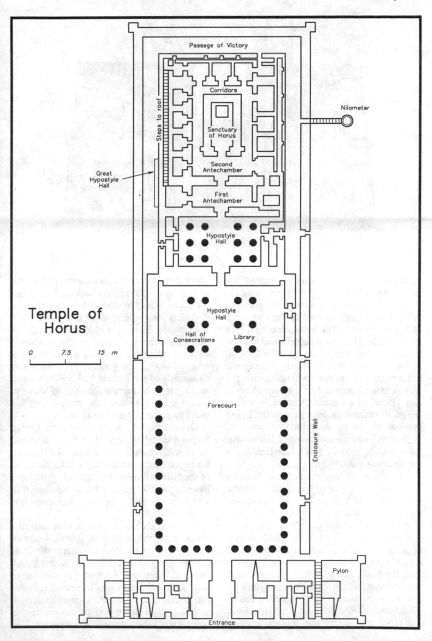

Temple of Horus

0   7.5   15 m

Passage of Victory

Corridors

Nilometer

Sanctuary
of Horus

Steps to roof

Great
Hypostyle
Hall

Second
Antechamber

First
Antechamber

Hypostyle
Hall

Hypostyle
Hall

Hall of
Consecrations

Library

Forecourt

Enclosure Wall

Pylon

Entrance

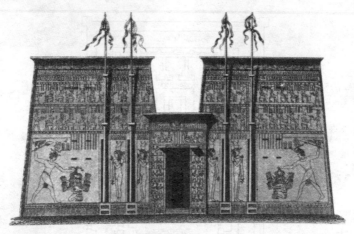

Temple of Horus

Ancient festivals at Edfu celebrated the divine birth of Horus and the living king (as all Pharaohs were believed to be incarnations of the falcon-god), as well as the victory of Horus over Seth and the yearly conjugal visit of the goddess Hathor. Another ritual was the annual recoronation of the Pharaoh to symbolise his oneness with Horus. During the proceedings, a live falcon was taken from the sacred aviary, crowned in the central court and placed in an inner chamber, where it 'reigned' in the dark for a year as the living symbol of Horus. As with the image of Hathor at Dendara, an image of Horus was taken each year to the roof of the temple for a rejuvenating sun bath.

Excavation of the temple from beneath sand, rubble and part of the village of Edfu, which had been built on its roof, was started by Auguste Mariette in the mid-19th century. The entrance to the temple is through a massive 36-metre-high pylon guarded by a huge and splendid granite falcon and decorated with colossal reliefs of Pharaoh Ptolemy XIII pulling the hair of his enemies while Horus and Hathor look on. Beyond the pylon is a court surrounded on three sides by a colonnade of 32 columns covered in reliefs.

Before you enter the temple proper,

through the 12 enormous columns of the first of two hypostyle halls, check out the areas on either side. On your left is the Hall of Consecrations where, according to the wall inscriptions, Horus poured sacred water on the king; on your right is the so-called Library, which features a list of books and a relief of Seshat, the goddess of writing. On either side of the second hall are doorways leading into the narrow Passage of Victory, which runs between the temple and its massive protective enclosure walls.

Once through the magnificent Great Hypostyle Hall there are two antechambers, the first of which has a staircase of 242 steps leading up to the rooftop and a fantastic view of the Nile and surrounding fields. You may have to pay the guard a bit of baksheesh if you want to go up because the stairs are usually closed.

The second chamber, which is beautifully decorated with a variety of scenes, leads to the Sanctuary of Horus, where the live falcon, the god and his wife reigned and received offerings. Around the sanctuary, there are a number of smaller chambers with fine reliefs and, off the Passage of Victory, a staircase leads down and passes under the outer wall of the temple to a Nilometer. The

Temple of Horus is open from 7 am to 4 pm in winter and 6 am to 6 pm in summer. Admission is E£10, or E£5 for students.

Places to Stay & Eat

The *El-Medina Hotel* (☎ 701326) is off to the right just as you leave the square on your way to the temple. This place costs about E£10 a night and has pretty basic beds in simple rooms. Several travellers have sung its praises though. The manager apparently loves a bit of song and dance, and for a pound or two will sing your favourite Christmas songs!

The other option, the *Dar El Salam Hotel*, is further down the road towards the temple, just short of the small tourist bazaar. It has similar rooms, but charges E£15 for single occupancy. The hot water is unreliable, but the rooms have fans and are OK.

Apart from the expensive cafeteria in the temple grounds, there are a couple of kebab places on the square – but ask how much they want first. One fly-blown place charged E£14 for a plate of greasy kebab that was more fat than meat.

Getting There & Away

Trains, buses and service taxis stop frequently in Edfu. However, the train station is on the east bank of the Nile, about four km from town. Buses travelling between Luxor and Aswan sometimes only stop on this side too – a real pain. Leaving is not so bad, as you can at least *take* a bus from the station in town. The fare is E£3.25 to Luxor. The bus from Aswan costs E£2. Service taxis are again the best option. From Esna, the trip takes about an hour and costs about E£2, direct taxis from Luxor take about two hours and cost E£4 and from Aswan they take 1½ hours and cost E£3.50.

If you've had enough of the Nile, tombs and temples, you can exit east and head straight for Marsa Alam on the Red Sea. The bus leaves daily at about 9 am, takes three to four hours depending on checkpoints and costs E£6. It actually goes on to Bir Shalatayn (E£12) on the disputed administrative boundary with the Sudan, but you need a military permit to travel south of Marsa Alam.

Feluccas will also stop at Edfu on their way north from Aswan. Very patient travellers who prefer to travel against the current can get a felucca heading south.

SILSILEH

At Silsileh, about 42 km south of Edfu, the Nile narrows considerably to pass between steep sandstone cliffs which are cluttered with ancient rock stelae and graffiti. Known in Pharaonic times as Khenu, which means 'the place of rowing', the gorge also marks the change from limestone to sandstone in the bedrock of Egypt. The local Silsileh quarries were worked by thousands of men throughout the New Kingdom and Greco-Roman periods to provide the sandstone used in temple building.

On the west bank of the river is the Speos of Horemheb, a rock-hewn chapel dedicated to Pharaoh Horemheb and seven deities, including the local god Sobek.

KOM OMBO

The fertile, irrigated sugar cane and corn fields around Kom Ombo, 60 km south of Edfu, support not only the original community of fellahin but also a large population of Nubians displaced from their own lands by the encroaching waters of Lake Nasser. It's a pleasant little place easily accessible en route between Aswan and Luxor but possibly best visited on a day trip from Aswan, which is 40 km to the south.

In ancient times Kom Ombo was strategically important as a trading town on the great caravan route from Nubia, and was the meeting place of the routes from the gold mines of the Eastern Desert and the Red Sea. During the Ptolemaic period it served as the capital of the Ombite nome, and elephants were brought up from Africa to Kom Ombo to train with the armies to defend the region. The main attraction these days, however, is the unique riverside Temple of Kom Ombo, about four km from the centre of town.

Temple of Kom Ombo

Kom Ombo or, more precisely, the dual Temple of Sobek and Haroeris, stands on a promontory at a bend in the Nile, where in ancient times sacred crocodiles basked in the sun on the river bank. Although substantially ruined by the changing tides of the river and by later builders who used many of its stones for new buildings, Kom Ombo is, nevertheless, a stunning sight.

It is also unusual in that, architecturally, everything is doubled and perfectly symmetrical along the main axis of the temple. There are twin entrances, twin courts, twin colonnades, twin hypostyle halls, twin sanctuaries and, in keeping with the dual nature of the temple, there was probably a twin priesthood.

The left side of the temple was dedicated to Haroeris, or Horus the Elder, the falcon-headed sky-god; the right half was dedicated to Sobek, the local crocodile (or crocodile-headed) god, who was also worshipped in Al-Faiyum.

The Greco-Roman structure faces the Nile. The entrance pylon, the outer enclosure wall and part of the court, all built by Augustus after 30 BC, have been either mostly destroyed by pilfering stonemasons or eroded by the river. The temple proper was actually begun by Ptolemy VI Philometor in the early 2nd century BC; Ptolemy XIII (also known as Neos Dionysos) built the Vestibule and Hypostyle Hall; and other Ptolemys and, after them, Romans contributed to the relief decoration.

South of the main temple is the Roman Chapel of Hathor, dedicated to the wife of Horus, which is used to store a large collection of mummified crocodiles dug up from a nearby sacred animal cemetery. Four are on display.

The temple, part of which was unfortunately obscured by layers of scaffolding for restoration in the first half of 1993, is open from 8 am to 4 pm; admission costs E£4 and half for students.

Places to Stay & Eat

The *Cleopatra Hotel* (☎ 500325) is the only accommodation option in the town, but quite adequate at E£5.25/8.70/12.75/13.80 for singles/doubles/triples/quadruples.

There's not much in the line of restaurants, just the usual ta'amiyya and kebab stands.

Getting There & Away

A service taxi or minibus from Aswan to the town of Kom Ombo takes about 30 minutes and costs E£1.50. Trains and buses also frequently stop in the town but they are slower and much less frequent.

As you approach Kom Ombo, you can ask the driver to drop you off at the road leading to the temple. Otherwise, once you are in town, take a covered pick-up truck to the boat landing on the Nile just north of the temple for 25 pt. They leave from just opposite the Cleopatra Hotel.

The road between the temple and the main highway is about a two-km walk or hitch. If you are heading back to Aswan, it shouldn't be hard to get a lift or flag down a passing service taxi or microbus once on the highway.

Horus

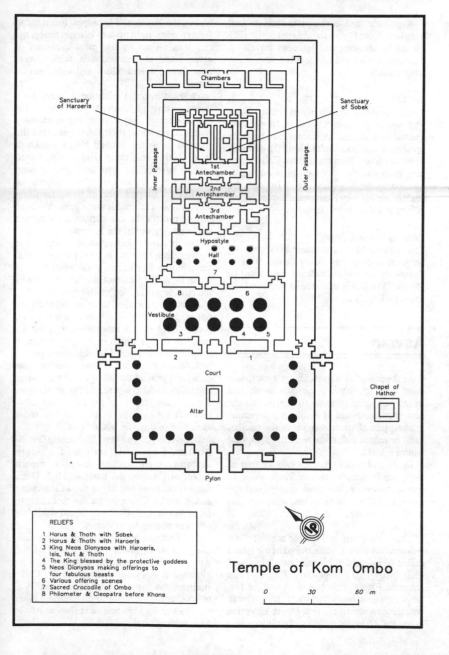

Sanctuary of Haroeris

Sanctuary of Sobek

Chambers

Inner Passage

Outer Passage

1st Antechamber

2nd Antechamber

3rd Antechamber

Hypostyle Hall

7

8   6

Vestibule

3   4   5

2   1

Court

Altar

Chapel of Hathor

Pylon

RELIEFS

1 Horus & Thoth with Sobek
2 Horus & Thoth with Haroeris
3 King Neos Dionysos with Haroeris,
  Isis, Nut & Thoth
4 The King blessed by the protective goddess
5 Neos Dionysos making offerings to
  four fabulous beasts
6 Various offering scenes
7 Sacred Crocodile of Ombo
8 Philometer & Cleopatra before Khons

Temple of Kom Ombo

0   30   60 m

A private taxi between the town and temple of Kom Ombo should cost about E£7 for the return trip; and feluccas travelling between Aswan and Luxor often stop at the temple itself.

DARAW

The main reason to stop in this small village just south of Kom Ombo is to see the Tuesday camel market. Camels are brought up in caravans from Sudan along the 40 Days Road to Daraw. Merchants from Cairo come here to buy camels for the camel market at Imbaba, a suburb of Cairo. From Imbaba, the camels are sold and shipped all over North Africa and the Middle East.

Getting There & Away

The service taxis and minibuses running between Aswan and Kom Ombo stop in Daraw (if passengers indicate they want to get off). The fare is the same as for the whole stretch – E£1.50.

Aswan

Over the centuries Aswan, Egypt's southern-most city, has been a garrison town and frontier city, the gateway to Africa and the now inundated land of Nubia, a prosperous marketplace at the crossroads of the ancient caravan routes and, more recently, a popular winter resort.

In ancient times the area was known as Sunt; the Ptolemaic town of Syene stood to the south-west of the present city; and the Copts called the place Souan, which means 'trade', from which the Arabic 'Aswan' is derived.

The main town and temple area of Sunt was actually on the southern end of the island called Yebu, which means both 'elephant' and 'ivory', and which the Greeks later renamed Elephantine Island. A natural fortress, protected by the turbulent river, Aswan was then capital of the first Upper Egyptian nome and a base for military expeditions into Nubia, the Sudan and Ethiopia. From those foreign parts, right up into Islamic times, the city was visited by the great caravans of camels and elephants laden with slaves, gold, ivory, spices, cloth and other exotic wares.

Pharaonic and Ptolemaic leaders took their turn through history to guard the southern reaches of Egypt from the customary routes of invasion; their fleets patrolled the river as far as the Second Nile Cataract at Wadi Halfa and their troops penetrated several hundred km into the Sudan. Aswan was also, to a certain extent, the 'Siberia' of the Roman Empire, one of those far-flung garrisons where troublesome generals were sent to protect the interests of the emperor while staying out of the Forum.

The modern town of Aswan, which is the perfect place for a break from the rigours of travelling in Egypt, lies at the northern end of the First Nile Cataract, on the east bank of the Nile opposite Elephantine Island.

Although its ancient temples and ruins are not as outstanding as others in the country, Aswan does have a few things to offer the traveller, one of which is the town's superb location on the river. The Nile is magically beautiful here as it flows down from the great dams and around the giant granite boulders and palm-studded islands that protrude from the cascading rapids of the First Nile Cataract. The Corniche is one of the most attractive of the Nile boulevards.

So, while you can visit Pharaonic, Greco-Roman, Coptic, Islamic and modern monuments, an excellent museum, superb botanical gardens, the massive High Dam, Lake Nasser and one of the most fascinating souqs outside Cairo, by far the best thing to do in Aswan is sit by the Nile and watch the feluccas gliding by at sunset.

The best time to visit Aswan and, if possible, to continue into the Sudan, is in winter, when the days are warm and dry, with an average temperature of about 26°C. In summer, the temperatures are around 38°C to 45°C and it's too hot to do anything other than just sit by a fan and swat flies or stay in a swimming pool.

Orientation

It's quite easy to find your way around Aswan because there are only three main avenues and most of the city is along the Nile or parallel to it. The train station is at the north end of town, only three blocks east of the river and its boulevard, the Corniche el-Nil.

The street which runs from north to south in front of the station is Sharia as-Souq (also occasionally signposted as Sharia Saad Zaghloul), Aswan's splendid market street, where the souqs overflow with colourful and aromatic wares and where merchants and traders from all over the region jostle and bargain with each other.

One block in from the Nile is Sharia Abtal at-Tahrir where you'll find the Youth Hostel, a few hotels and some pricey tourist souqs. On the Corniche itself are most of Aswan's banks, government buildings, travel agencies, restaurants and top hotels, and from there you can see the rock tombs on the west bank, as well as the islands of Elephantine (the larger one) and Kitchener.

Information

Tourist Office The tourist office is two blocks north of the Abu Simbel Hotel, which is one street in from the Corniche. The staff can give you official prices for taxis and felucca trips, but lower prices are usually obtainable with some haggling. They are generally very friendly and quite helpful, although some of their information can be a bit shaky.

The office is open seven days from 8.30 am to 8 pm, although the desk is sometimes unmanned. A second office was being planned for the train station at the time of writing.

Money The main banks have their branches on the Corniche. Banque Misr and the Banque du Caire will issue cash advances on Visa and MasterCard. The Bank of Alexandria accepts Eurocheques. Banque Misr also has a late-night booth open until about 10 pm and is the only bank where you can buy hard currency with E£.

If you're looking to buy Sudanese currency, you'll have to do so with black marketeers at the port or wait until you get to Wadi Halfa.

American Express The office (☎ 322909) is in the New Cataract Hotel. If you are heading south, this is the last American Express office where you can cash personal cheques and buy travellers' cheques until you get to Nairobi.

Thomas Cook The Aswan branch of Thomas Cook is on Sharia Abtal at-Tahrir (☎ 324011, fax 326209).

Post & Telecommunications The GPO is also on the Corniche, adjacent to the municipal swimming pool and opposite the Police Rowing Club. There's another post office on the corner of Sharia Abtal at-Tahrir and Sharia Salah ad-Din, about a block east of the Horus Hotel, but not many foreigners seem to use this branch. The crowds in the GPO may convince you to do so.

International telephone calls can be made from the telephone office, which is on the Corniche towards the southern end of town, just past the EgyptAir office. They have card phones here (and sell the cards). Alternatively, write the number, city and country on a slip of paper and hand it over the counter to the operator who places international calls. The office is open seven days from 8 am to 10 pm.

There's also a post office stamp counter that is occasionally open, and telexes and faxes can also be sent from here. Back up the road, next to Photo Sabry, is the BC Business Centre, from where you can also send faxes.

At the train station there are also a couple of the orange card phones.

Film Film is available at a few stores in Aswan. At Photo Sabry on the Corniche, it takes about one to two days to develop a roll of 36 colour prints for E£35. Kodacolor 100 (36 exposures) costs E£15, Kodacolor 400 (36 exposures) E£20 and Ektacrome 100 (36

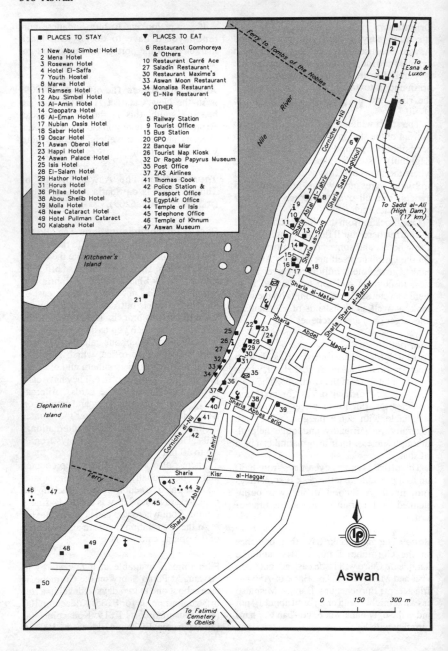

PLACES TO STAY
1 New Abu Simbel Hotel
2 Mena Hotel
3 Rosewan Hotel
4 Hotel El-Saffa
7 Youth Hostel
8 Marwa Hotel
11 Ramses Hotel
12 Abu Simbel Hotel
13 Al-Amin Hotel
14 Cleopatra Hotel
16 Al-Eman Hotel
17 Nubian Oasis Hotel
18 Saber Hotel
19 Oscar Hotel
21 Aswan Oberoi Hotel
23 Happi Hotel
24 Aswan Palace Hotel
25 Isis Hotel
28 El-Salam Hotel
29 Hathor Hotel
31 Horus Hotel
36 Philae Hotel
38 Abou Shelib Hotel
39 Molla Hotel
48 New Cataract Hotel
49 Hotel Pullman Cataract
50 Kalabsha Hotel

PLACES TO EAT
6 Restaurant Gomhoreya
   & Others
10 Restaurant Carré Ace
27 Saladin Restaurant
30 Restaurant Maxime's
33 Aswan Moon Restaurant
34 Monalisa Restaurant
40 El-Nile Restaurant

OTHER
5 Railway Station
9 Tourist Office
15 Bus Station
20 GPO
22 Banque Misr
26 Tourist Map Kiosk
32 Dr Ragab Papyrus Museum
35 Post Office
37 ZAS Airlines
41 Thomas Cook
42 Police Station &
   Passport Office
43 EgyptAir Office
44 Temple of Isis
45 Telephone Office
46 Temple of Khnum
47 Aswan Museum

Aswan

0   150   300 m

exposures) E£30. One-hour or overnight processing is also available at a few places.

Sharia as-Souq

The exotic atmosphere of Aswan's back-street souqs is definitely one of the highlights of the city. Although the fabulous caravans no longer pass this way, the colour and activity of these markets and stalls recall those romantic times. Just wander through the small, narrow alleyways off this street and you'll see, hear, smell and, if you want, taste life as it has been for many centuries in these parts. Note that there were too many of these small passageways to show on the Aswan map.

Although parts of the market have definitely risen on the hassle register in recent years, much of it still serves mainly local needs and remains a joy to explore.

Fatimid Cemetery

Just south of the city's public gardens and over a small hill is a collection of low stone buildings with domed roofs topped by crescents. Some of these early Islamic tombs also feature figures of local holy people, or the more widely revered Sayyida Zeinab, granddaughter of the Prophet.

Unfinished Obelisk

In the desert a little further south still are the northern quarries, which supplied the ancient Egyptians with most of the hard stone used in pyramids and temples, and a huge discarded obelisk. Three sides of the shaft, which measures nearly 42 metres long, were completed except for the inscriptions and it would have been the largest single piece of stone ever handled if a flaw had not appeared in the granite. So it lies there, where the disappointed stonemasons abandoned it, still partly attached to the parent rock and with no indication of what it was intended for.

The quarries are about one km from town past the Fatimid Cemetery and entry costs a rather steep E£6, or E£3 for students.

Aswan Cultural Centre

Aswan's world-famous folkloric dance troupe performs here between October and February from 9.30 to 11.30 pm. Admission is E£7. The centre also presents traditional Upper Egyptian and Nubian music performances and exhibits the instruments used in them. Whether or not there are any performances during Ramadan seems to be a matter of whim. Other exhibits in this two-storey centre on the Corniche include a few fairly sad display cases with material covering Arab-Muslim culture. There's also a library, language centre with courses in English and French, and a computer class.

Elephantine Island

Perhaps elephants once roamed the banks of the Nile here. They certainly passed through in the great caravans or with various armies, but it is more likely that Aswan's longest inhabited area was named Yebu after the numerous giant grey granite boulders, in the river around the island, which resemble a herd of elephants bathing.

Apart from being Egypt's frontier town, where the island officials were known as 'Keepers of the Gate of the South', Elephantine also produced most of the Pharaohs of the 5th dynasty and was the centre of the cult of the ram-headed Khnum, god of the cataracts and creator of humankind, and his companion goddesses Anukis and Satis.

Excavation of the ancient town, which began at the start of this century, is still being carried out by a German team and the jumbled remains of the fortress and three temples are visible. There's also a small 3rd dynasty step pyramid; a tiny chapel reconstructed from the Temple of Kalabsha, which is just south of the High Dam; and, taking up the entire northern end of the island, the deluxe and incongruous Aswan Oberoi Hotel which, most sensibly, has its own private ferry and a three-metre fence around it to keep the tourists in, and away from the local Nubians.

The inhabitants of the three colourful Nubian villages on the west side of Elephantine are friendly and the alleyways are worth exploring.

Aswan Museum On the south-east end of the island, overlooking the ruins of the original town and surrounded by an attractive flower and spice garden, this modest little museum houses a collection of antiquities discovered in Aswan and Nubia. Most of the Nubian artefacts were found and rescued before the construction of the old Aswan Dam. The weapons, pottery, utensils, statues, encased mummies and sarcophagi date from pre-dynastic to late Roman times and everything is labelled in Arabic and English. The sarcophagus and mummy of a sacred ram, the animal associated with Khnum, are located in a room by themselves to the right of the main entrance, while four mummies can be seen in the left of the museum.

The museum is open in winter from Sunday to Thursday between 8 am and 5 pm, and on Friday from 9 am to 1 pm; in summer it's open on the same days from 8.30 am to 6 pm. Admission to the museum and the ruins outside is E£5, or E£2 for students. You'll probably be shepherded around the gardens, but baksheesh will be expected at the end of the tour.

Nilometer Heavenly portents and priestly prophecies aside, the only sure indication in ancient times of the likelihood of a bountiful harvest was that given by the Nilometer. Descending to the water's edge from beneath a sycamore tree near the museum, the rock-hewn shaft of the ancient Nilometer measured the height of the Nile. Although it dates from Pharaonic times, and bears inscriptions and cartouches from the reigns of Amenophis III and Psammetichus II, it was rebuilt by the Romans and restored last century.

When the Nilometer recorded that the level of the river was high it would mean that the approaching annual flood would be heavy and therefore sufficient for the irrigation vital to a good harvest. It also affected the taxation system, for the higher the river, the better the crop season and the more prosperous the fellahin and merchants – and therefore the higher the taxes.

You can enter the Nilometer from the river or down steps from above or just view it from a felucca on the water.

Temple of Khnum Amongst the ruins of the ancient town are the remains of a large temple built by Nectanebo, a 4th century BC Pharaoh, and dedicated to Khnum, the patron of Elephantine and the god who created humankind on his potter's wheel. At the gateway to the temple Ptolemy XI Alexander II, who ruled around 80 BC, is shown worshipping the ram-god. A team of German archaeologists has been excavating and restoring the temple.

Nearby are the remains of a small portion of the Temple of Satis, dedicated to Khnum's goddess daughter. The Temple of Heqaib, an interesting stone shrine honouring a prince of the nome, is also close by. A 6th dynasty official, Heqaib was deified after his death and remained a cult figure for many centuries. A small Ptolemaic temple discovered on the tip of the island has been restored.

Getting There & Away To get to Elephantine Island you can take a felucca or row boat, for 25 to 50 pt, from the landing virtually opposite the telephone office; or catch the Oberoi ferry, although you may not be able to get beyond the hotel compound.

Kitchener's Island

One of the most delightful places in Aswan, this island to the west of Elephantine was given to Lord Horatio Kitchener in the 1890s when he was consul-general of Egypt and commander of the Egyptian army. Indulging his passion for beautiful flowers, Kitchener turned the entire island into a botanic garden, importing plants from the Far East, India and other parts of Africa. The gardens, which are perfect for a peaceful stroll, attract an amazing variety of colourful exotic birds. The hundreds of white ducks in the small out-of-bounds cove at the southern end of the island, however, belong to a biological

Top Left: Ruins at Temple of Horus, Edfu (GB)
Top Right: Temple of Philae, Agilka Island, near Aswan (GB)
Bottom Left: A view of Aswan and the Nile River (GB)
Bottom Right: Abu Simbel on Lake Aswan (CB)

Top: Side by side, a mosque and a chuch at sunset, Cairo (KB)
Left: Detail of mashrabiyya, Sultan Barsbey Mosque, Cairo (KB)
Right: Interior of a coptic chuch, Echinine, Egypt (KB)

research station. Entry is E£5 and there is no student reduction.

Getting There & Away There are no ferry services to Kitchener's Island but it's easy enough to hire a felucca for a return trip or incorporate the gardens on a river tour. The price for a felucca is negotiable and starts to come down quickly if you first show that you are interested and then begin to walk away. You would be doing well to get a felucca for an hour for less than E£5, and often you'll be looking at something closer to E£10. The official price for a two-hour tour taking in stops at Kitchener's and Elephantine islands and the Mausoleum of the Aga Khan is E£25 for the whole boat.

Dr Ragab Papyrus Museum
Dr Ragab is well known throughout Egypt for mass producing high-quality papyrus paintings. His Aswan papyrus museum/shop is actually a barge moored to the shore. Beautiful papyrus paintings of various sizes hang from the walls and are displayed in glass

Papyrus painting

cases. The cheapest painting, about the size of a paperback book cover, costs about E£10.

Tombs of the Nobles
The high cliffs opposite Aswan, a little north of Kitchener's Island, are honeycombed with the tombs of the princes, governors, 'Keepers of the Gate of the South' and other dignitaries of ancient Yebu. They date from the Old and Middle kingdoms and although most of them are in a sorry state of repair, there are a few worth visiting.

To get to the west bank tombs, you can either take the ferry from a landing in front of the train station for 50 pt or include them on a felucca tour of the river. Admission to the tombs is E£6, or E£3 for students. Hours are 8 am to 5 pm.

Tombs of Mekhu & Sabni (Nos 25 & 26)
These tombs are of rough 6th dynasty construction. The reliefs in No 26 record a tale of tragedy and triumph. Mekhu, one of the 'Keepers of the Gate', was murdered on an expedition into Africa, so his son Sabni led the army into Nubia to punish the tribe responsible. Sabni recovered his father's body and sent a messenger to the Pharaoh in Memphis to inform him that the enemy had been taught a lesson. On his return to Aswan he was met by priests, professional mourners and some of the royal embalmers, all sent by the Pharaoh himself to show the importance that was attached to the keepers of the kingdom's southern frontier.

Tomb of Prince Sarenput II (No 31) This dates from the 12th dynasty and is one of the best preserved tombs. There are statues of the prince and wall paintings depicting Sarenput and his son hunting and fishing.

Tomb of Prince Sarenput I (No 36) This tomb also dates from the 12th dynasty but it's older than No 31. On the rear wall of a columned court, to the left of the door, the prince is shown being followed by his dogs and sandal-bearer, and there are other scenes of his three sons and women bearing flowers.

Tomb of Heqaib (No 35) The Tomb of Heqaib, the deified official whose temple stood on Elephantine, has a columned facade and some fine reliefs showing fighting bulls and hunting scenes.

Kubbet al-Hawa

Also on the west bank is Kubbet al-Hawa, a small tomb constructed for a local sheikh at the top of the hill. If you climb up to it, you'll be rewarded with fantastic views of the Nile and the surrounding area. From there you can also try to rent a donkey or camel for the trek across the desert to the Monastery of St Simeon.

Mausoleum of the Aga Khan

Aswan was the favourite wintering place of Mohammed Shah Aga Khan, the 48th imam, or leader, of the Ismaili sect of Islam. When he died in 1957 his wife, the Begum, oversaw the construction of his domed granite and sandstone mausoleum, which is part of the way up the hill on the west bank opposite Elephantine Island.

Modelled on the Fatimid tombs of Cairo, the interior, which incorporates a small mosque, is more impressive than the exterior. The sarcophagus, of Carrara marble, is inscribed with texts from the Qur'an and stands in a vaulted chamber in the interior courtyard.

The Begum still lives for part of the year in the white villa, below her husband's mausoleum, which used to be their winter retreat. Every day she places a red rose on his sarcophagus; a ritual that is carried on in summer by her gardener.

The tomb is open Tuesday to Sunday from 8 am to 4 pm and admission is free (the guards are not supposed to accept baksheesh). Remember to remove your shoes.

There is a felucca dock just below the mausoleum. Negotiating a ride on a felucca or row boat to Elephantine Island can be a bit laborious. There's not much competition, so you're looking at about E£4 one way.

Monastery of St Simeon

Deir Amba Samaan is a 6th century monas-tery which, although it hasn't been used for more than 700 years, is one of the best pre-served of the original Christian strongholds in Egypt. It is not known who St Simeon was, exactly, but his monastery survived until the monks were driven out or murdered by Arabs in the 14th century.

Surrounded by desert sands, except for a glimpse of the fertile belt around Aswan in the distance, the monastery bears more resemblance to a fortress than a religious sanctuary. It once provided accommodation for about 300 resident monks plus a further 100 or so pilgrims. Built on two levels, the lower of stone and the upper of mud brick, it was surrounded by 10-metre-high walls and contained a church, stores, bakeries, offices, a kitchen, dormitories, stables and work-shops.

Getting There & Away If you don't fancy a camel or donkey ride from the Tombs of the Nobles, there is a paved pathway to the mon-astery from the Mausoleum of Aga Khan, which is, however, inaccessible when the mausoleum is closed. Camels and their owners also hang around the mausoleum in the hope of snaring people to ride up to the monastery, which is open from 9 am to 5 pm.

It is quite possible to scramble up to the desert track to the monastery from the felucca dock if the mausoleum is closed. Admission costs E£6 and half price for stu-dents.

Felucca Rides

As you will quickly discover if you spend any time near the Nile, feluccas are the tra-ditional canvas-sailed boats of the Nile. They have probably changed little in centuries. A visit to Aswan wouldn't be complete without at least an hour's ride on a felucca between the islands in the Nile.

For advice about hiring a felucca, see the following Getting There & Away section.

Swimming

Aswan is a hot place, and sometimes a swim seems just the way to escape the worst of it. Short of joining the local kids and jumping into the Nile to cool off, there are a couple of hotels with swimming pools open to the public. The cheapest by far is the Cleopatra. Its small pool is open from 9 am to 6 pm and costs E£5. The Oberoi, Isis and Cataract hotels all have pools, ranging from E£17 to E£21.

Places to Stay

The hotel rates given in this section include breakfast, unless otherwise specified. Don't expect much – usually it's just coffee or tea, two pieces of bread or rolls, jam and butter.

Places to Stay – bottom end

North of Aswan Station Square The 27-room *Rosewan Hotel* (☎ 324497) has been popular with low-budget travellers for several years. It has clean, simple, rather small doubles with shower/toilet combinations, but at E£27, they are a little expensive; singles are E£16. All rooms have fans and tiled floors, and according to some disgruntled travellers, bugs.

To get there, turn right as you leave the train station, take the first street on the left (Sharia ash-Shahid Kamal Nur ad-Din Mohammed), and the hotel is in the middle of the block, just past the Hotel El-Saffa. As with most of the hotels, the reception can organise you on to a minibus for the trip to Abu Simbel and the High Dam.

The *Hotel El-Saffa* (☎ 322173) is next to the Rosewan. Singles/doubles are E£5/10 with sinks and balconies in each room. A few rooms also have showers with hot water. The toilets could be cleaner, but at this price you can't be overly picky. The price does not include breakfast.

A few blocks north of the Rosewan and the Saffa is the partly air-conditioned *Mena Hotel* (☎ 324388). The cool, carpeted rooms have telephones, showers, toilets and balconies. A few rooms have either poor air-con or just fans. Singles are E£10, doubles E£18. The best deal in the hotel is a comfy suite with two bedrooms and a 'salon' that can sleep five people for E£35.

To get there, turn right as you leave the train station and follow the street that is parallel to the tracks for about 10 minutes. You'll see a sign for the hotel on the left. Despite being quite a way from the centre of town, it is often pretty full in high season.

South of Aswan Station Square The *Youth Hostel* (☎ 322313) is on Sharia Abtal at-Tahrir, not far from the train station. Somebody must have told them to get their act together, and at E£5 for a bed in a share double or triple, it's not a bad deal. The rooms have fans, the showers and toilets are fairly clean and the place generally empty. Small singles can be had for E£8. They make a point of keeping foreigners separate from locals.

Across the street from the Youth Hostel is the *Marwa Hotel*, which is entered from an alley on the south side of the building. The rooms are simple and a little cramped, but at E£4 a bed in a share room of three or four beds, it is fairly popular. The rooms have fans and hot water supposedly comes out of the showers, which are jammed in with the somewhat whiffy toilets.

The *Al-Amin Hotel* (also signposted as *Elamin Hotel*) (☎ 322298, 323189) is a good, inexpensive hotel that lists itself as being on Sharia Abtal at-Tahrir, but is actually on a side street just across from the Ramses Hotel and the now closed Carré Ace Restaurant. A few rooms are somewhat dusty and the toilet/shower combinations are rather small, but it's not a bad deal at E£9 for a single and E£20 for a double.

With the demise in mid-1993 of a back-packers' favourite haunt, the majestic old Continental, the *Al-Eman Hotel*, not to be confused with the Al-Amin, is left as one of the cheapest options. It's next to the Nubian Oasis Hotel and costs E£6 for a bed in a share triple. There's no breakfast, but the rooms have thick, soft mattresses and fans, and the showers are hot.

In the midst of the souq is the *Aswan Palace Hotel*. It's no palace, but at E£5/8 for singles/doubles (without breakfast), is not a bad deal – if you like noise.

Around the corner from the site of the Continental (an expensive modern hotel is to be built in its place), near the heart of the souq, is the one-star *Abou Shelib Hotel* (☎ 323051). Its central location is an advantage for exploring the souq, but the hotel is also near a mosque. If your room faces the mosque, you'll probably be shaken out of bed by the first call to prayer. Rooms are clean and simple, with fans and toilet/shower combinations (big bathrooms in some). Singles/doubles are E£15/25, but you may be able to negotiate, depending on the size of the rooms and whether or not they have showers.

The *Molla Hotel* (☎ 326540), on a side street near the souq, has similar, but less comfortable, rooms for E£15/20. Each room has a sink and there are hot showers just off the hall.

Camping There's an official, but somewhat basic, camping ground near the Unfinished Obelisk, which is a 20-minute walk from the area around the Hotel Continental. There are cold showers crammed in next to toilets. Although there are enough grassy spaces for setting up tents, and a few bushes and small trees, there really isn't any shade. Bright lamps and guards keep the place secure, but the former can make it difficult to sleep. It costs E£4 per person and so really is hardly worth all the effort.

Places to Stay – middle
Just edging out of the budget category is the recently opened *Nubian Oasis Hotel* (☎ 312126/123). It has good clean singles/doubles for E£20/30, although the staff seem to try it on a bit with some guests – try to get a look at their register to see what everyone else is paying. It's a good deal in this range.

The *Ramses Hotel* (☎ 324119), on Sharia Abtal at-Tahrir, is a good deal and, according to some travellers, is one of the best places to stay in Aswan. Doubles with showers, toilets, air-con, colour TV, mini-refrigerators and Nile views cost about E£45, singles with the same amenities E£45. During the summer, the rooms are discounted by as much as 50%. This hotel is popular with tour groups from all over Europe.

The *Happi Hotel* (☎ 314115/6) is also on Sharia Abtal at-Tahrir, a few blocks down from the Ramses Hotel, and is particularly popular with German groups. It has clean doubles with bathrooms for E£59; singles are E£45.45. The 64 rooms have fans and the tiled bathrooms are spotless. Some rooms also have balconies and TV. There is one suite containing three bedrooms and a kitchenette. The owner also runs the Cleopatra Hotel, which explains why guests can use the Cleopatra's pool for free.

Further away from the Nile is the *Oscar Hotel* (☎ 323851, fax 326066), which has become something of a travellers' favourite. Rooms are E£25/35 without breakfast (if you want their breakfast, you pay a cheeky E£10 on top!). Some of the rooms have balconies, and some even have working bedside reading lights!

The 66-room *Abu Simbel Hotel* (☎ 322888, 322327) is on the Corniche, not far from the tourist office. Doubles with showers cost E£46 for two people and E£31 for one person. There are also six rooms with big bathrooms for a little more. Although some travellers have reported being unhappy with the hotel, the view of the Nile from the balcony of each room is fantastic, and for most people makes up for the fairly decrepit state of, for instance, the bathrooms.

Just north of the Mena Hotel, the *New Abu Simbel Hotel* (☎ 326096, 312143) opened up at the end of 1991. At E£40/50, the rooms are decent but overpriced.

On the Corniche is the *El-Salam Hotel* (☎ 322651, 323649), which can be considered a fair deal for the price, without being spectacular value; singles/doubles with air-con cost E£27/35. Without the air-con, they go for E£22/30. Most rooms have fans and Nile views, as does the restaurant.

Next to the El-Salam Hotel is the 36-room *Hathor Hotel* (☎ 314580), which has some rooms with air-con and hot showers crammed in next to toilets for E£25. Singles/doubles without air-con are E£20/32.50, but some of them are a little on the small side. Rooms are clean and some have tiled floors. There's an inexpensive restaurant in the lobby.

The *Philae Hotel* (☎ 312089), also on the Corniche, is similar to the Abu Simbel, but the rooms are uncarpeted and it's altogether a bit gloomy. At E£45/55 it's not a brilliant deal, and they seem to be aware of this, as a bit of bargaining can bring the price down a bit.

Considerably better, and one of the places to aim for in this price range, is the *Horus Hotel*, also on the Corniche. Singles/doubles with bath are E£35/50. Without bath they are E£5 cheaper. The 40 rooms are comfortable, and you should try to get one with Nile views. There is a rooftop restaurant.

The *Cleopatra Hotel* (☎ 314003), on Sharia Saad Zaghloul just south of the railway station, is well situated for exploring the old market area. With singles/doubles for about E£120/150, it's out of the range of most budget travellers. All 109 rooms are clean, comfortable and air-conditioned, with private bathrooms and telephones. The pool is open to anyone for E£5 from 10 am to 6 pm.

Places to Stay – top end

The *Hotel Pullman Cataract* (☎ 323222, fax 323510) was formerly known as the Cataract or Old Cataract Hotel. It is an impressive Moorish-style building surrounded by gardens on a rise above the river, with splendid views of the Nile and across the southern tip of Elephantine Island to the Mausoleum of the Aga Khan. Singles/doubles there cost US$78/97.50 (standard room, Nile view) and US$88/110 (super room, Nile view) in the high season, plus 23% in taxes and service charges. The hotel is worth visiting just to partake of a cool Stella or a cocktail on the verandah. Sometimes a minimum charge is imposed, but this does not seem to be a hard-and-fast rule. The hotel's exterior was used in the movie of Agatha Christie's *Death on the Nile*, in part because Christie once did some of her writing here.

Everything about the Pullman Cataract bespeaks turn-of-the-century elegance, from its finely bevelled glass elevator to its large, well-furnished rooms. Both standard and 'super' rooms are equally super – high ceilings, hardwood floors, Oriental carpets, antique furniture. You can get a buffet breakfast for E£17.75 or dinner for E£48.

The *New Cataract Hotel PLM Azur* is next door. Rooms there are US$20 to US$30 cheaper than at the Pullman Cataract, largely because they have none of the style. Its swimming pool is open to the public for about E£20 per day from 9 am to 9 pm.

The four-star *Kalabsha Hotel* (☎ 322666 322999; fax 325974) nearby is another high-class affair, with an excellent view of the First Nile Cataract. Singles/doubles are US$27/33 for the back and US$37/46 for the front, plus the usual taxes. Breakfast is E£8 and the buffet dinner E£32. Guests can use the swimming pool at the Cataract Hotel for free.

The *Aswan Oberoi* (☎ 323455; fax 323485) on Elephantine Island has two hotel launches that ferry guests and visitors from the east bank. The views from the Oberoi tower are magnificent and the gardens are a pleasant place to just hang around and watch the feluccas. The swimming pool is open to the public for E£21 per day from 9 am to sunset. Rooms there, however, start at US$100 and head up to about US$300. The buffet dinner costs E£55.

Statues of Osiris

The ideally situated four-star *Isis Hotel* (☎ 315100/200/300) is between the Corniche and the Nile. The 100 rooms are more like stuccoed cabins; they are fully carpeted and have powerful air-con, large bathrooms, colour TV and telephones. There are also shops, two restaurants (one serves half-way decent Italian dishes) and a swimming pool that is open to the public for E£17. Singles cost US$74, doubles US$96 and triples US$113 including taxes. They are hoping for five-star status, which means that room rates will probably increase. In the evenings you can see belly dancing and a 'Nubian show' in their nightclub.

The same people have recently opened a five-star sibling on an island just off Elephantine and called it, funnily enough, the *Isis Island* (☎ 317401/2/3). An extremely ostentatious boat ferries guests (and outsiders wanting to use the pool and bask in reflected wealth) from in front of the Egypt-Air office. There is a Club Med on one of the neighbouring islets. More modest boats there leave from the same spot.

Places to Eat

There are a few restaurants and cafés on the south side of the Aswan Station Square including the *Restaurant Gomhoreya*, which has been recommended by some travellers. Try their grilled pigeon, when they have it. Along Sharia Saad Zaghloul (Sharia as-Souq) in the block or two from the station you pass a number of eating places with decidedly odd names. You could eat at the *Commoner Restaurant*, have a drink at *Roxy Milks* and finish up at the *Station Sweeter*.

A block back from the station on Sharia Abtal at-Tahrir is the *Carré Ace Restaurant*, long recommended by travellers but closed at the time of writing.

Next to the Youth Hostel is a good place called the *El Dar*, where they do a nice, if smallish, vegetable soup.

Back towards the station, just past the Youth Hostel, is the *Aswan Sweet Corner*, which has a good selection of honey-soaked cakes.

The *Aswan Moon Restaurant* on the Corniche remains a travellers' favourite. You can sit out on a barge on the river and get a decent main course for about E£7. The staff are mainly Nubians from Egypt and the Sudan, and the atmosphere is particularly laid back.

Nearby, the *Monalisa Restaurant* has similar food for about the same prices, but without the feel-good atmosphere. You can also get breakfast here.

The *Restaurant el-Nil* (or *El-Nile Restaurant)* is on the Corniche a few doors away from what was the Hotel Continental. A full meal with fish (carp from Lake Nasser), chicken or meat with rice, vegetables, salad, tahina and bread should cost about E£9.

A nice, bright place, extending out over the river, is the *Emy Restaurant*. They do especially nice fruit cocktail drinks and decent ice cream. They also serve the usual selection of meals. Everyone under about 40 seems to benefit from the advertised 'student discount' without even asking.

Also on the Corniche are the *Philae Restaurant*, which seems to be popular, and *Restaurant Maxime's*. The latter does not have a very savoury reputation (excuse the pun).

On the Nile side of the Corniche there are several other restaurants, all offering a similar range of dishes at virtually the same prices. They include the *Panorama* and the *El-Shati*. Another restaurant, the *Saladin*, does extremely overcooked meat dishes with salad for about E£10.

The *Medina Restaurant* on Sharia as-Souq, across from the Cleopatra Hotel, has been recommended for its kofta and kebab deals, and is often patronised by travellers. The *El Masr*, near the Marwa Hotel, has also had good reports.

In and around Sharia Saad Zaghloul is a veritable smorgasbord of small restaurants in the more lively atmosphere of the souqs. There are also plenty of cafés there and by the train station. The *Al Sayeda Naffesa*, in the souq, is also reportedly good value.

In the Isis Hotel, by the river, is the pleasant *Ristorante Italiano*, a good place to make an expensive escape from yet another meal of kofta and kebab. Pasta dishes are about

E£14, main courses E£20. The food is quite good, although connoisseurs of Italian cuisine shouldn't expect too much.

Getting There & Away

Air EgyptAir flies from Cairo to Aswan daily. The flight takes 1½ hours and costs E£393 one way (double return).

The return flight between Aswan and Abu Simbel costs E£345 and the one-way hop to Luxor E£128.

Although the private airline, ZAS (☎ 324823), was talking about setting up a service between Aswan and Khartoum in the Sudan in March 1993, it appears nothing came of it. They have an office on the Corniche.

Bus The bus station is conveniently located in the middle of town, behind and a little way to the south of the Abu Simbel Hotel on Sharia Abtal at-Tahrir.

The air-con bus to Abu Simbel costs E£30 return and leaves at 8 am daily, getting back at about 5 pm. Book in advance.

There are buses every half to one hour to Kom Ombo (45 minutes, E£1), Edfu (1½ hours, E£2), Esna (two hours, E£3.50) and Luxor (around four hours, E£6.50 or E£5.50).

The green buses are more basic, cheaper and less reliable than the green and yellow buses.

A direct bus for Cairo leaves at 3.30 pm (about 12 hours, E£45) and an hour later for E£10 less. They both supposedly have air-con and video, so what the difference is is anybody's guess.

There are also two buses going right through to Hurghada (Al-Ghardaka). The first leaves at 8 am and costs E£16; the second departs at 4.30 pm and costs E£24.

Train There are up to nine trains a day running between Cairo and Aswan, including a deluxe wagon-lit train. If you can make head or tail of them, check the timetables posted at the train station for the latest schedules.

Express trains Nos 85 and 87, from Aswan

to Luxor, Cairo and on to Alexandria, have air-con and a restaurant. They leave within 30 minutes of each other from about 3.45 pm. Both stop at Qena and then go straight through to Giza, Cairo and on to Alexandria. Train No 89 leaves 1½ hours later, has air-con, a restaurant and a 2nd-class buffet. Train No 981, which leaves at 7 am, has 1st and 2nd class, air-con and a restaurant, but makes considerably more stops.

The trip from Aswan to Cairo is scheduled to take about 16 hours but often takes more than 20.

The most expensive sleeper cars, and the only ones available to non-Egyptians and Sudanese, are the wagons-lits – E£242 to Cairo, which is the same as from Luxor; see the Cairo Getting There & Away section for more details. Reservations are needed for wagons-lits and for the faster trains.

The cheapest way to get to the High Dam, 13 km south of Aswan, is to take a train to Sadd al-Ali Station, the end of the Cairo to Aswan line. The train departs Aswan for Sadd al-Ali at 8.30 am, 1.35 and 3.10 pm. These departures seem to be about the most flexible in the whole train system, especially in Ramadan. One reason is clear – a train from Cairo that is meant to take 16 hours and ends up taking 22 will naturally be six hours late for the final leg to the High Dam. If you do get the train, it costs 85 pt.

Service Taxi The service taxi station is across the train tracks on the east side of town. Just off Sharia as-Souq, one block south of the train station, is an overpass over the tracks. Climb the overpass and walk to the end of the street on the other side (about 10 minutes). Turn right and walk about half a km to the service-taxi station. Alternatively, just follow the tracks south until you reach a point where crowds of people are crossing: the service-taxi station is just there. Service taxis (which are sometimes actually microbuses) depart regularly for Luxor (about 3½ hours, E£7 50), Edfu (1½ hours, E£3.50), Kom Ombo (one hour, E£2) and Daraw (30 minutes, E£2).

Felucca The most popular felucca trip is a three-day, two-night trip from Aswan to Edfu. From there, you take a service taxi to Luxor for about E£2.50, although some travellers have reported paying as much as E£5 each. Another alternative is a one or two-night trip to Kom Ombo, returning by service taxi to Aswan. The only problem with the latter is that you may have to walk about two km from the Nile to the main road, but it's usually easy to hitch a ride. The last option is three nights, four days to Esna, returning by service taxi to Luxor. The felucca captains are quite adamant about not continuing on to Luxor, and often will refuse to go on to Esna, even after having agreed to do so. The reasons are simple enough. The trip back upstream can take much longer, and that means lost opportunities to take out more passengers – ideally, they would do short trips down the river and turn their boats around quickly back to Aswan to get more passengers.

Officially, feluccas should carry six passengers, no more nor less, for the following prices: E£25 to Kom Ombo (plus E£5 police registration and food supplies); E£45 to Edfu (plus registration and food) and E£50 to Esna (plus registration and food). As usual, the official prices are generally inflated, and often more than six get on to the one boat. More than eight on the bigger ones is about the limit – it can get pretty cramped. In early 1993, people were still getting boats to Edfu for E£25 a person all inclusive (eight to a boat).

Finding a felucca is easy – as soon as you approach the Corniche, you will be swamped with offers. However, finding a good captain can occasionally be a problem, especially if you are a single woman or a group of women. On overnight trips, a few women travellers have reported sailing with felucca captains who had groping hands and exhibitionist tendencies.

If you are trying to assemble a group for this trip, any of the low and middle-range hotels are good sources for assembling a group. Some people leave messages at the tourist office counter.

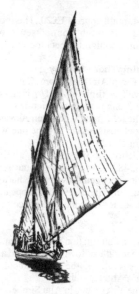

Felucca

Take plenty of bottled water for the trip; otherwise the captain will dip into the Nile for cooking and drinking water.

Bring a sleeping bag – it can get bitterly cold at night, and the supply of blankets on board won't be enough. Insect repellent is a good idea, but you can probably do without mosquito nets – it's a bit difficult to rig them up anyway! A hat is essential to protect you from the sun during the day.

When dealing with a felucca captain, be sure about a few things. Firstly, that he has what appears to be a decent, functioning boat, with some blankets and cooking implements, and something to sit on. Establish whether the price includes food and, if so, go with him to the market to do the shopping to see just what you are getting. Otherwise, set a price without food and do your own shopping. If you get a good captain, you'll probably be better off doing it with him – he'll have a good idea of the supplies needed and is less likely to pay extortionate prices for the supplies.

Don't hand over your passports. Often captains, or more likely middlemen, like to take them so that they have a couple of passengers in the bag. They then scour around for other people. With your passport in his hands, you commit yourself to him until he finds other people or gives up, all of which can be quite inconvenient. One Belgian couple handed over their passports to a middleman, who in turn was prepared to hand them over to other travellers as proof he had enough passengers! Luckily for the Belgians, no one involved actually wanted to make off with their papers, but it was a little careless! It's advisable to accompany the captain to the police when organising permission too.

Once you're off, sit back and enjoy a rare side of Egypt – quiet. No hawkers, no car horns, just the Nile lapping against the side of your boat. Often the captain will take you to visit his family in a village along the way, or drop in on other villages. As you sail down, you'll see the life of the river and the people who depend on it going on much as it has for millennia.

Boat The Nile Valley Navigation Office is next to the tourist office, one street in from the Corniche. This is the place to buy tickets to Wadi Halfa. Boat traffic has become extremely erratic over the years. It is worth keeping an eye out for activity at the office each day. Crowds of Sudanese could indicate an imminent departure. The golden rule is, if they tell you one day that there isn't another boat for two weeks, pop in again a day or two later and see what their latest story is – it's bound to be different.

Depending on whether you get the relatively new (eight-year-old) Egyptian boat or one of the older steamers, the trip south can take as few as 14 hours or as many as 24. At the time of writing, only a second vessel was running – 30 years old and without radar, making navigation at night difficult if not impossible.

You can go 1st or 2nd class, which cost respectively E£135.35 and E£85.75. On the Egyptian boat at least, 1st class means bunks in small cabins – if you want them. The most pleasant place to be on what is almost always an extremely crowded journey is outside on deck – a small area by the wheelhouse is generally set aside for foreigners, or if you're feeling more sociable you can mix it with the Sudanese elsewhere on the deck. The seating below is crowded, stuffy and uncomfortable – you can hardly breathe let alone sleep. The fare includes a meal – fuul in 2nd class or meat and rice in 1st. If you've gone 2nd class, you can still buy a 1st-class meal for E£2. Tea and soft drinks are also available on board. Bring some food yourself too.

The trip is fairly relaxing, and if you're lucky you'll sail past Abu Simbel in daylight.

As a foreigner, you should be ushered through the various customs and passport hurdles at Aswan, but remember you need E£2 as an exit tax from Egypt. Of course, this won't get you going any faster, but better to wait hours to leave on the boat than in a queue. Some of the Sudanese Immigration formalities are carried out on the boat – they will ask for your yellow fever certificate.

Coming from Wadi Halfa, the boat docks near the High Dam and passport officials check passports before the passengers disembark. Foreigners are allowed off the boat first and into the customs depot, which is adjacent to the train station (end of the line). There are taxis just outside the customs depot.

See the Sudan Getting There & Away chapter for more details of this trip.

Car & Motorbike The road south of Abu Simbel into the Sudan is closed, although some Sudanese in Aswan claim they are able to drive across.

It is possible to take your vehicle across Lake Nasser, although you'll probably have to hire a boat especially for the effort. Four people taking a car and two motorbikes across hired a boat for E£5000 in 1993. (There have been reports of plans for a new car-ferry service.) This is not a recommendation. Even with a 4WD, the going is very tough, and petrol scarce.

Getting Around
To/From the Airport The airport is 25 km from the town and the taxi fare is about E£16. If you give up on the train to the High Dam port for the steamer to Wadi Halfa, a taxi will cost about E£15, although hard bargaining might bring it down a little.

Taxi A taxi tour that includes the Philae Temple, the High Dam and the Unfinished Obelisk costs around E£25 for five to six people.

Felucca Apart from a few buses, taxis and horse-drawn carriages, feluccas are the most common form of transportation to the attractions around Aswan. There is an official government price for hiring feluccas, but with a bit of bargaining you should be able to hire a boat for five or six hours for a reasonable price. A shorter three or four-hour tour costs about E£20 to E£30, but prices vary wildly according to your bargaining and the time of year – if they're having a bad season, they may be willing to take people out for less than they would normally find acceptable.

Officially at least, a two-hour jaunt taking in Kitchener's Island and the Mausoleum of the Aga Khan should cost no more than E£20, or E£25 if you want to include Elephantine Island. A three-hour trip down to Sehel Island is E£40. An hour floating around on the Nile is E£15. This last one is well over the odds.

Ferry A ferry shuttles across the Nile from near the GPO on the town side of the river to just below the Tombs of the Nobles on the west bank. The fare is 50 pt each way. Note that the boat is divided into two sections – women up front, men in the back. The ferry to Elephantine Island (either a felucca or a row boat) costs 25 pt each way (although sometimes they jack it up to 50 pt) and leaves from in front of the telephone office.

Bicycle There are a few places at the train station end of Sharia as-Souq where you can hire bicycles for about E£4 a day.

AROUND ASWAN
The Aswan Dam
When the British constructed the Aswan Dam above the First Nile Cataract at the turn of the century it was the largest of its kind in the world. The growing population of Egypt had made it imperative to put more land under cultivation and the only way to achieve this was to regulate the flow of the Nile. Measuring 2441 metres across, the dam was built between 1898 and 1902 almost entirely of local Aswan granite.

Although its height had to be raised twice to meet the demand, it not only greatly increased the area of cultivable land but provided the country with most of its hydroelectric power. Now completely surpassed in function, and as a tourist attraction, by the more spectacular High Dam six km upstream, it is still worth a brief visit, as the area around the First Nile Cataract below it is extremely fertile and picturesque. All trips to Abu Simbel include a drive across this dam.

Sehel Island
Sehel, the large island north of the old Aswan Dam, was sacred to the goddess Anukis and her husband Khnum. As a destination for an extended felucca trip on this part of the Nile, Sehel Island is a good choice, although there isn't much to see apart from a friendly Nubian village and a great many rock inscriptions, dating from Middle Kingdom to Greco-Roman times.

One Ptolemaic inscription, on the southeastern side of the island, records the story of a seven-year famine that plagued Egypt during the much earlier time of Pharaoh Zoser. It seems that Khnum, god of the cataracts, had withheld the inundation of the Nile for seven years and Zoser finally travelled to Aswan to ask the local priests why the god was punishing the Egyptians. Apparently some land belonging to Khnum's traditional estates had been confiscated; as soon as Zoser returned the land and raised a temple to Khnum on Sehel, the Nile rose to its accepted flood level.

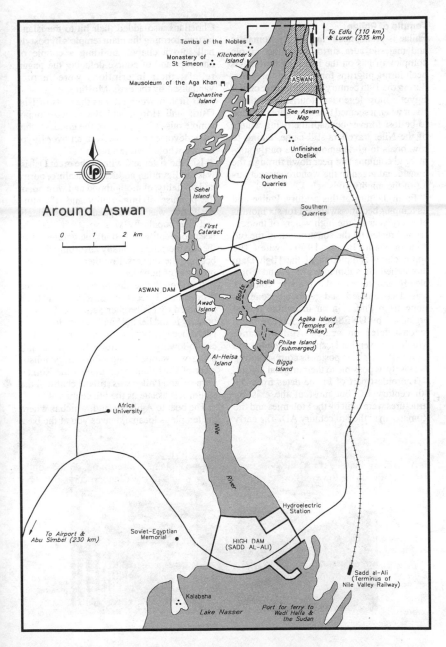

Around Aswan

0   1   2 km

To Edfu (110 km)
& Luxor (235 km)

Tombs of the Nobles
Monastery of   Kitchener's
St Simeon   Island
Mausoleum of the Aga Khan
Elephantine
Island

ASWAN

See Aswan
Map

Unfinished
Obelisk

Sehel
Island

Northern
Quarries

First
Cataract

Southern
Quarries

ASWAN DAM   Shellal

Awad
Island   Agilka Island
                             (Temples of
                             Philae)
                      Philae Island
                      (submerged)
Al-Heisa
Island   Bigga
                    Island

Nile

Africa
University

River

Hydroelectric
Station

To Airport &
Abu Simbel (230 km)

Soviet-Egyptian
Memorial

HIGH DAM
(SADD AL-ALI)

Sadd al-Ali
(Terminus of
Nile Valley Railway)

Kalabsha

Lake Nasser

Port for ferry to
Wadi Halfa &
the Sudan

Temple of Philae

Philae is pronounced 'feel-i'. The romantic and majestic aura surrounding the temple complex of Isis on the island of Philae has been luring pilgrims for thousands of years; during the 19th century the ruins were one of Egypt's most legendary tourist attractions. Even when it seemed that they were destined to be lost forever beneath the rising waters of the Nile, travellers still came, taking to row boats to glide amongst the partly submerged columns and peer down through the translucent green to the wondrous sanctuaries of the mighty gods below.

From the turn of this century, Philae and its temples became swamped for six months of every year by the high waters of the reservoir created by the construction of the old Aswan Dam. In the 1960s, when the approaching completion of the High Dam threatened to submerge the island completely and forever, the massive complex was disassembled and removed stone by stone from Philae in an incredible rescue organised by UNESCO. The temples were reconstructed on nearby Agilka Island, which was even landscaped to resemble the sacred isle of Isis, in positions corresponding as closely as possible to their original layout.

The oldest part of Philae dates from the 4th century BC but most of the existing structures were built by the Ptolemies and the Romans up to the 3rd century AD. The early

Christians also added their bit to the island by transforming the main temple's hypostyle hall into a chapel, building a couple of churches and of course defacing the pagan reliefs; their inscriptions were in turn vandalised by the early Muslims.

At first, however, it was the cults of Isis, Osiris and Horus, and the Greco-Roman temple raised in honour of the goddess, that drew devotees not only from all over Egypt but the whole Mediterranean.

Isis, the sister and wife of the great Osiris, was the Egyptian goddess of healing, purity and sexuality, of motherhood and women, of the promise of immortality and of nature itself. She was worshipped so passionately and her popularity was so great that she became identified with all the goddesses of the Mediterranean, finally absorbing them to become the universal mother of nature and protector of humans.

It was on Philae, during her search for the dismembered pieces of Osiris, who had been murdered by his brother Seth, that Isis supposedly found her husband's heart; hence the island became her most sacred precinct. Her cult following was so strong that she was still being worshipped long after the establishment of Christianity throughout the Roman Empire, and Philae was still the centre of the cult of Isis as late as the 6th century AD.

The boat to Agilka Island, which is where the temple is located, leaves you at the base

Temple of Philae

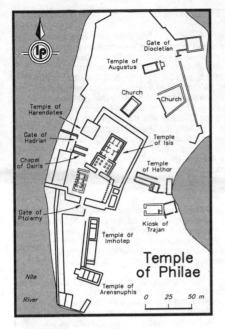

Temple
of Philae

ian; east of the 2nd Pylon is the delightful Temple of Hathor decorated with reliefs of musicians; and south of that, the elegant, unfinished pavilion by the water's edge is the Kiosk of Trajan. The completed reliefs on the kiosk feature Emperor Trajan making offerings to Isis, Osiris and Horus.

The temple complex is open from 7 am to 6 pm and admission is E£10, or E£5 for students. There is a sound & light show in the evenings which costs E£18 (no student discount) for the ticket and E£16 for the boat (eight people) to Agilka Island. There are usually three performances, at 6, 7.30 and 8.30 pm, but double-check the schedule at the tourist office or the Aswan Cultural Centre (the programme is different during Ramadan):

	1st show	2nd show	3rd show
Saturday	English	French	
Sunday	French	German	
Monday	English	Italian	German
Tuesday	French	English	Italian
Wednesday	English	Spanish	French
Thursday	Arabic	French	German
Friday	English	French	Spanish

Some travellers have reported being disappointed by their visits to the temple because of the hassles involved in first arranging the taxi and then the boat to the island. Perhaps by the time this book is published, the boats to Philae will be better regulated.

Getting There & Away The boat landing for the Philae complex is at Shellal, south of the old Aswan Dam. The only easy way to get there is by taxi or organised trip (arranged by most travel agencies and major hotels in town, but possibly for more money than you may pay otherwise). In one case, the round-trip taxi fare for a group of six cost E£30 without bargaining. It is possible, if you can get a ride to the old Aswan Dam, to walk along the water's edge to Shellal. A small motorboat to the island will cost about E£14 return for the whole boat, although this still seems to be negotiable.

of the Hall of Nectanebo, the oldest part of the Philae complex. Heading north, you walk down the Outer Temple Court, which has colonnades running along both sides, to the entrance of the Temple of Isis marked by the 18-metre-high towers of the 1st Pylon.

In the Central Court of the Temple of Isis is the mammisi, or birth-house, dedicated to Horus. Successive Pharaohs reinstated their legitimacy as the mortal descendants of Horus by taking part in the mammisi rituals, which celebrated the god's birth.

The 2nd Pylon provides access to the Vestibule and the Inner Sanctuary of Isis; a staircase, on the western side, leads up to the Osiris Chambers, which are decorated with scenes of mourners; and everywhere there are reliefs of Isis, her husband and son, other deities and, of course, the Ptolemies and Romans who built or contributed to the temple.

On the northern tip of the island are the Temple of Augustus and the Gate of Dioclet-

The High Dam

While the old Aswan Dam successfully regulated the flow of the Nile during the course of a year, it was realised, as early as the 1940s, that a much bigger dam was needed to counter the unpredictable annual flooding of the great river. However, it wasn't until Nasser came to power in 1952 that plans were drawn up for a new dam six km south of the British-built one.

The proposed construction created international political tension and focused worldwide attention on the antiquities that would be lost by the creation of a huge lake behind the dam.

In 1956, after the USA, the UK and the World Bank suddenly refused the financial backing they had offered for the project, Nasser ordered the nationalisation of the Suez Canal as a means of raising the capital. This move precipitated the Suez Crisis in which France, the UK and Israel invaded the canal region; they were eventually restrained by the United Nations. The Soviet Union then offered the necessary funding and expertise, and work began on the High Dam in 1960 and was completed in 1971.

While the old dam simply controlled the flow of the Nile, the High Dam collects and stores water over a number of years so that a high or low annual flood can be regulated at all times. The area of Egypt's cultivable land was increased by 30%; the High Dam's hydroelectric station has doubled the country's power supply and a rise in the Sahara's water table has been recorded as far away as Algeria.

On the other hand, artificial fertilisers now have to be used because the dam hinders the flow of silt that was critical to the Nile Valley's fertility, and it's estimated that in the next 40 years or so that silt will have filled the lake. In recent years, the extremely high rate of evaporation from the lake, coupled with low annual floods, has reduced the water level in the reservoir forcing a reduction in the amount of water released for irrigation and power generation. The greatest fear is that should the dam ever break or be sabotaged most of Egypt would be swept into the Mediterranean.

Another consequence of the dam's construction was the fact that a great many valuable and irreplaceable ancient monuments were doomed to be drowned by the waters of Lake Nasser.

Teams from the Egyptian Department of Antiquities and archaeological missions from many countries descended on Nubia to set in motion the UNESCO-organised projects aimed at rescuing as many of the threatened treasures as possible. Necropolises were excavated, all portable artefacts and relics were removed to museums and, while some temples disappeared beneath the lake, 14 were salvaged and moved to safety.

Ten of them, including the temple complexes of Philae, Kalabsha and Abu Simbel, were dismantled stone by stone and rebuilt on higher ground in Egypt. The other four were donated to the countries which contributed to the rescue effort; they include the splendid Temple of Dendur, which has been reconstructed in a glass building in the Metropolitan Museum of Art in New York. ■

High Dam

Egypt's contemporary example of building on a monumental scale contains 18 times the amount of material used in the Great Pyramid of Cheops. The controversial Sadd al-Ali, the High Dam, is 3600 metres across and 111 metres high at its highest point. The water contained by the dam has backed up nearly 500 km, taking it well into the Sudan and creating Lake Nasser, the world's largest artificial lake.

The rising level of this incredible reservoir has inundated the land of Nubia with waters as deep as 200 metres, forced the relocation of thousands of Nubians and Sudanese and washed away 45 villages along the banks of the Nile south of Aswan.

Most people get to the High Dam as part of an organised trip to Abu Simbel or other sites outside Aswan. For the privilege of driving part of the way along the dam to a small pavilion with a couple of displays detailing the dimensions and the construction of the dam, you pay E£2.

If you come by foot you may escape this charge, but don't bank on it. Many visitors are disappointed by the visit, expecting views more spectacular than they actually get, so perhaps you should not hope for too much if you decide to visit.

On the west side of the dam, there is a stone monument honouring Russian-Egyptian friendship and cooperation.

Getting There & Away The cheapest way to get to the High Dam, which is 13 km south of Aswan, is to take a train to Sadd al-Ali Station, the end of the Cairo to Aswan line. The station is near the docks for the boat to the Sudan and from there you can either walk for a long way or take a service taxi to the dam. The train departs Aswan for Sadd al-Ali three times a day and costs 85 pt, but the timetable is erratic at best.

If you're planning to take a taxi across the top of the dam, then you might also consider continuing on to the Temple of Kalabsha, which is another one km south, on the west side of Lake Nasser.

Kalabsha, Beit al-Wali & Kertassi

As a result of the massive UNESCO effort to rescue the doomed monuments of Nubia, these three temples were transplanted from a now submerged site about 60 km south of Aswan. Until recently the new site, on the west bank of Lake Nasser a little upriver from the dam, was considered a military area and you needed special permission to visit these monuments – which is, perhaps, one of the reasons why these temples were (and still are) seldom visited.

The Temple of Kalabsha was erected during the reign of Emperor Augustus, between 30 BC and 14 AD, and was dedicated to the Nubian god Mandulis. Isis and Osiris were also worshipped there and during the Christian era the temple was used as a church.

The West German government financed the transfer and reconstruction of the 13,000 blocks of the temple, and was presented with the temple's west pylon, which is now in the Berlin Museum. During the rescue operation, evidence was found of even older structures, dating from the times of Amenophis II and Ptolemy IX.

An impressive stone causeway leads from the lake up to the 1st Pylon of the temple, beyond which are the colonnaded court and the Hypostyle Hall, which has 12 columns. Inscriptions on the walls show various emperors and Pharaohs cavorting with the gods and goddesses. Just beyond the hall are three chambers, with stairs leading from one up to the roof. The view of Lake Nasser and the High Dam, across the capitals of the hall and court, is fantastic. An inner passage, between the temple and the encircling wall, leads to a well-preserved Nilometer.

The Temple of Beit al-Wali, which means 'house of the holy man', was rebuilt with assistance from the US government and placed just north-west of the Temple of Kalabsha. Most of Beit al-Wali, which was carved from the rocks, was built during the reign of Ramses II. On the walls of the first chamber are several interesting reliefs, including scenes of the Pharaoh's victory over the Cushites and his wars against the Libyans and Syrians. Ramses is shown pulling the hair of his enemies while women plead for mercy.

Just north of the Temple of Kalabsha are the remains of the Temple of Kertassi. Two Hathor (cow-headed) columns, a massive architrave and four columns with intricate capitals are the only pieces which were salvaged from Lake Nasser.

Kalabsha is open from 8 am to 4 pm and costs E£6 to enter (half for students).

ABU SIMBEL

While the fate of his colossal statue and the Ramesseum in Luxor no doubt gnaws at the spirit of Ramses II, the mere existence, in the 20th century AD, of his Great Temple at Abu Simbel must make him shake with laughter and shout 'I told you so!'.

The Abu Simbel temples were threatened with being swallowed forever beneath the rising water and silt of Lake Nasser. Their preservation, 280 km south of Aswan, must rank as the greatest achievement of the UNESCO rescue operation. And, hewn as they were out of solid rock, the modern technology involved in cutting, moving and rebuilding the incredible temples and statues at least paralleled the skill of the ancient artisans who chiselled them out of the cliff face in the first place.

In the 1960s, as work progressed on the High Dam, UNESCO launched a worldwide appeal for the vital funding and expertise needed to salvage the Abu Simbel monuments. The response was immediately forthcoming and a variety of conservation schemes were put forward. Finally, in 1964 a cofferdam was built to hold back the already encroaching water of the new lake, while Egyptian, Italian, Swedish, German and French archaeological teams began to move the massive structure.

At a cost of about US$40 million the temples were cut up into more than 2000 huge blocks, weighing from 10 to 40 tonnes each, and reconstructed inside a specially built mountain 210 metres away from the water and 65 metres higher than the original site. The temples were carefully oriented to face in the correct direction and the landscape of their original environment was recreated on and around the concrete, dome-shaped mountain. You can enter the dome either through a door next to the Great Temple of Ramses II or through a door across from the ticket office on the opposite side of the dome.

The project took just over four years. The temples of Abu Simbel were officially reopened in 1968, while the sacred site they had occupied for over 3000 years disappeared beneath Lake Nasser.

The Great Temple of Ramses II was dedicated to the gods Ra-Harakhty, Amun and Ptah and, of course, to the deified Pharaoh himself; while the smaller Temple of Hathor was dedicated to the cow-headed goddess of love and built in honour of Ramses' favourite wife, Queen Nefertari. They were carved out of the mountain on the west bank of the Nile between 1290 and 1224 BC. By the mid-1800s, the sandstone cliff face and temples were all but covered in sand; although they were partially cleared many times, it wasn't until the British began excavating, around the turn of this century, that their full glory was revealed.

From the Great Temple's forecourt, a short flight of steps leads up to the terrace in front of the massive rockcut facade, which is about 30 metres high and 35 metres wide. Guarding the entrance, the four famous colossal statues of Ramses II sit majestically, staring out across the desert as if looking through time itself. Each statue is over 20 metres high and is accompanied by smaller, though much larger than life-size, statues of the king's mother Queen Tuya, his wife Nefertari and some of their children.

Above the entrance to the Great Hypostyle Hall, between the central throned colossi, is the figure of the falcon-headed sun-god Ra-Harakhty. Unfortunately, the sun-god has been subjected to the trials of time and now lacks part of a leg and foot. The roof of the hall is supported by eight columns, each fronted by a 10-metre-high statue of Ramses; the roof is decorated with vultures representing Osiris; and the reliefs on the walls depict the Pharaoh in various battles, victorious as usual. In the next hall, the four-columned Vestibule, Ramses and Nefertari are shown in front of the gods and the solar barques that carry the dead to the underworld.

The innermost chamber is the sacred Sanctuary, where the four gods of the Great Temple sit on their thrones carved in the back wall and wait for the dawn. The temple is aligned in such a way that on 22 February and 22 October every year, the first rays of the rising sun reach across the Nile, penetrate the temple, move along the Hypostyle Hall, through the Vestibule and into the Sanctuary, where they illuminate the somewhat mutilated figures of Ramses II, Ra-Harakhty, Amun and Ptah. (Until the temples were moved, this phenomenon happened one day earlier.)

The other temple at the Abu Simbel complex is the rockcut Temple of Hathor, which is fronted by six massive standing statues, about 10 metres high. Four of them represent Ramses, the other two represent his beloved wife Queen Nefertari and they are all flanked by the smaller figures of the Ramessid princes and princesses.

The six pillars of the Hypostyle Hall are

crowned with Hathor capitals and its walls are adorned with scenes depicting: Nefertari before Hathor and Mut; the queen honouring her husband; and Ramses, yet again, being valiant and victorious. In the Vestibule and adjoining chambers there are colourful scenes of the goddess and her sacred barque. In the Sanctuary there is a striking statue of a cow, the sacred symbol of Hathor, emerging from the wall.

Admission (made up of various fees) for both temples is E£21, or E£12 for students – by far the most expensive monument in the country.

Places to Stay

There are two hotels at Abu Simbel. The *Nefertari Hotel* (☎ 316402/3; fax 316404) is about 400 metres from the temples. It has singles/doubles/triples for E£207/266/326, inclusive of breakfast and taxes. Organised groups generally pay less. The rooms have air-con, full carpeting and, in some, mini-refrigerators. There's also a swimming pool. A 50% discount is often available in the summer. The restaurant stays open all year. During the winter, most of the hotel's 76 rooms and suites are full, so reservations are recommended.

They will also let you camp for about E£20 – you get to use the showers, pool and mosquitoes.

The privately run *Nabalah Ramses Hotel* (☎ & fax 311660) is in the town of Abu Simbel, about 1.5 km from the temples. The 32 singles/doubles are US$31.50/60, although deals are possible. The rooms are bright and clean, come with ensuite bath and toilet and are equipped with TV, air-con and fridge. The owner, Mohammed Hassan Abdel Ghaffour, has spent E£1 million on improvements since October 1990 and hopes to expand.

The *Amun Village*, an expensive set of self-contained bungalows also in the town, was closed at the time of writing, but there were plans afoot to reopen it in 1994.

Getting There & Away

Until July 1985, when the road between Aswan and Abu Simbel was officially opened, the only way to visit the temples of Ramses II and Hathor was by flying in. (See the Aswan Getting There & Away section.)

Abu Simbel

These days the 280 km can be covered in a variety of ways.

Air-con buses leave for Abu Simbel from the Aswan bus station every day at 8 am. Tickets cost E£30 return and the trip takes about 3½ hours one way. The bus leaves Abu Simbel at about 2.30 pm, or earlier if people wish. You should buy your ticket at least one day in advance.

A slightly cheaper alternative would be to get a group together and hire a taxi or minibus for a tour of the temples at Philae and Kalabsha as well as the High Dam and Abu Simbel. A minibus should cost about E£25 per person (transportation only). But be forewarned – a visit to Abu Simbel alone is quite enough for one day.

Many hotels in Aswan band together to arrange minibus trips to Abu Simbel. The cheapest price on offer is about E£25 for the transport. Generally the trips begin between 4 and 5 am, with minibuses picking up guests from various hotels around town. They aim to get to the temple by about 8.30 am, before it gets too hot, and leave about 10 am. When you get back to Aswan depends partly on how long a sheesha break the driver decides to take at the roadside 'rest house' on the way back and how much time is spent at the High Dam. The admission fees for Abu Simbel and the High Dam (E£2) aren't included.

Abu Simbel is 50 km north of the Sudanese border but overland travel between the Sudan and Egypt is prohibited.

The Suez Canal & the Red Sea Coast

The Suez Canal, one of the greatest feats of modern engineering, links the Mediterranean with the northern end of the Red Sea.

Among the area's many highlights are the ancient monasteries of St Anthony and St Paul. The Red Sea is renowned for its spectacular marine life, and a visit to this region offers the chance to sample some of the best snorkelling and diving you'll find anywhere in the world.

The Suez Canal

The Suez Canal represents the culmination of centuries of effort to enhance trade and expand the empires of Egypt by connecting the Red Sea and the Mediterranean Sea. Although the modern canal was by no means the first project of its kind, it was the only one to bypass the Nile as a means of connecting the two seas and excavate across the Isthmus of Suez to provide a major shipping route between Europe and Asia.

The first recorded canal was begun by Pharaoh Necho, between 610 and 595 BC, and stretched from the Nile Delta town of Bubastis, near present-day Zagazig, to the Red Sea via the Bitter Lakes. Despite his oracle's prophecy that the canal would be of more use to invading barbarians than to the Egyptians, Necho persevered until, having caused the death of, it is said, more than 100,000 workers, he was forced to abandon the project.

His canal was completed about a century later under Darius, one of Egypt's Persian rulers, and was maintained by the Ptolemies. Cleopatra, in a bid to save what was left of her fleet after the Egyptian defeat at Atrium, attempted to pass up the canal to the Red Sea, failing only because of the low flood level of the Nile that year.

The canal was improved by the Romans under Trajan, but over the next several cen-turies it was either neglected and left to silt up, or dredged by various rulers for limited use, depending on the available resources.

In 649 AD it was restored by Amr, the Arab conqueror of Egypt, to facilitate the export of corn to Arabia. Twenty years later it was filled in by another caliph, to stop the supply of grain to Mecca and Medina, so he could starve the people against whom he was waging war.

Following the French invasion in 1798, the importance of some sort of sea route south to Asia was again recognised. For the first time the digging of a canal directly from the Mediterranean to the Red Sea, across the comparatively narrow Isthmus of Suez, was considered. But the idea was abandoned, however, because Napoleon's engineers mistakenly calculated that there was a 10 metre difference between the two sea levels.

British reports corrected that mistake several years later, but it was the French consul to Egypt, Ferdinand de Lesseps, who pursued the Suez Canal idea through to its conclusion.

In 1854 de Lesseps presented his proposal to the Egyptian khedive, Said Pasha, who authorised him to excavate the canal but, although de Lesseps had financial backing from private investors, the project was initially hindered by the British and French governments. Finally, in 1855, the scheme was approved and the Suez Canal Company, headed by Ferdinand de Lesseps, was formed and began issuing shares to raise the necessary revenue. Said Pasha granted the company a 99-year concession to operate the canal, with the Egyptian government to receive 15% of the annual profits.

Construction began in 1859, but it was not an easy project. At one stage, following an outbreak of cholera, all de Lesseps' workers ran away. There was also the major problem of fresh water, or rather the lack of it. Until the company built a canal to service the

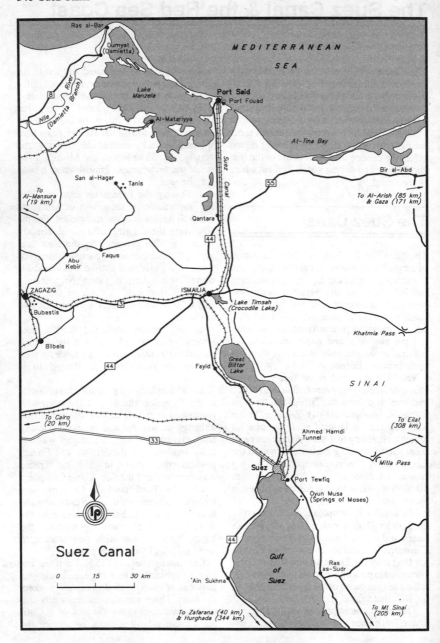

Suez Canal

0   15   30 km

construction works, 3000 camels were used to carry fresh water from the Nile.

In 1863, Said was succeeded as khedive by Pasha Ismail, who quickened the pace of construction because the American Civil War had disrupted the world cotton markets. There was increased demand for Egyptian cotton and the completion of the canal would facilitate its export.

The canal was completed amidst much fanfare and celebration in 1869. It had cost the lives of thousands of labourers and incurred several million pounds of unanticipated debt to European finance houses, a large part of which was due to the extravagant festivities Ismail had planned for the opening of the canal.

In his desire to establish Egypt as a major world power, Ismail sought to impress the kings, queens and various potentates of Europe with a four-day party to mark the completion of the new sea route between Europe and Asia.

The inauguration ceremony on 16 November 1869 was a grand affair. When two small fleets, one originating in Port Said and the other in Suez, met at the new town of Ismailia, the Suez Canal was declared open and Africa was officially severed from Asia.

In Cairo, Ismail built the Opera House and Pyramids Rd, the road from the city to Giza. The latter was constructed so that his most important guest, the French empress Eugénie, could travel to the Great Pyramids of Giza in her carriage. In Ismailia he built a new palace for the occasion, and all along the canal various special events were held. In Port Said, fireworks, feasts and the official opening ball for 6000 guests were just the start of weeks of lavish hospitality offered to the visiting dignitaries.

The celebration and resulting debts nearly finished Pasha Ismail. By 1875 he had to sell almost half his shares in the Suez Canal Company to the British government. This appeased the creditors but ushered in a period of British control over Egypt which lasted until Nasser overthrew King Farouk in the 1952 Revolution.

In 1956 Nasser nationalised the Suez Canal to raise money for the construction of the Aswan High Dam. The USA, UK and France had withdrawn financial backing for the project because of Nasser's willingness to deal with both the Soviet countries and the West.

By halting the flow of revenue from the canal to French, British and other foreign shareholders, Nasser was also making a statement about Western control in the affairs of Egypt. His move precipitated an invasion of the canal area by France, the UK and Israel; but with world opinion against them and no support from the UN, they were forced to withdraw.

After the Six Day War in 1967 – when Israel returned to the area after Egypt tried to block the Straits of Tiran, the former's only outlet to the Red Sea – the canal was closed for about eight years.

The Israelis entrenched themselves along the eastern bank of the canal by building a line of fortifications called the Bar Lev Line. In 1973 Egypt tried, but failed, to take the Sinai and Suez Canal back from Israel by blasting the Bar Lev Line with water cannons. By this time the canal was full of sunken ships and sea traffic remained paralysed until 1975, when Sadat reopened the canal.

Following the 1978 Camp David Agreement and the 1979 peace treaty signed between Egypt and Israel, the Suez Canal has been filled with a constant flow of maritime traffic. It is 163 km long but is still not wide enough to accommodate modern ships sailing in opposite directions. There are plans to widen the canal but, for now, ships can pass at only two points – the Bitter Lakes and Al-Ballah. With a depth of 19.5 metres, the canal is deep enough for most ships other than supertankers.

The canal is a prime source of hard currency for Egypt's beleaguered economy. Each ship that passes through the canal is charged a fee based on its size and weight. The average fee is about US$70,000. More than 50 ships make the 15-hour journey each day; the canal's daily capacity is 80 ships.

PORT SAID

The main attraction of Port Said, and the reason for its establishment on the Mediterranean, is the Suez Canal. Its status as a duty-free port also makes it the most flourishing of the canal cities. There are some mediocre beaches along the Mediterranean that are good for swimming and, along some of the original city streets, there are some fine old buildings with wooden balconies. This turn-of-the-century architecture, some in a pretty sad state, seems to contain all the convoluted history of this international port town in its fibre, and is well worth a wander around.

The spectacle of the huge ships and tankers lining up to pass through the northern entrance of the canal is also something to be seen.

Egyptians think of Port Said as a summer resort, and hundreds of beach bungalows line the Mediterranean coast along the city's northern edge. However, unlike Alexandria, Port Said has not yet been overrun by throngs of Egyptians seeking sun, sand and sea.

History

Port Said was founded in 1859 by its namesake, the khedive Said Pasha, as excavation for the Suez Canal began. Much of the city is an island, created by filling in part of Lake Manzela, to the west, with sand from the canal site. The city continued to grow until 1956, when much of it was bombed during the Suez Crisis. It suffered again during the 1967 and 1973 wars with Israel. Damage can still be seen but most of the city has been rebuilt.

Orientation

Today, Port Said is a city of about 400,000 people, connected to the mainland by a bridge to the south and a causeway to the west. There is also a ferry across Lake Manzela to Matariyyah (a worthwhile trip in itself), and another between Port Said and its sister town, Port Fouad, on the other side of the canal.

Most of the banks and important services are either on Sharia Palestine, which runs along the canal, or on Sharia al-Gomhurriya, which runs parallel to Sharia Palestine, a couple of blocks in.

Information

Registration & Visas If you need to register your arrival in Egypt or get a visa extension, the passport office is in the Governorate building.

Customs Port Said was declared a duty-free port in 1976, so everyone must pass through customs when entering and leaving the city. Be sure to have your passport with you, and if you are given the choice of declaring cameras, lenses, radios, cassette players and the like on entering, do so. It has not been known to happen often, but if you get unlucky, bored customs officials might slap on some tax if they think you bought any dutiable items in Port Said. If you do want to buy anything, check in the store whether or not duty must be paid on a particular item – some, including a few electrical items, can be taken out without problems. Varying rates of tax apply to others.

Tourist Office The tourist office, at 43 Sharia Palestine, has maps, some information about the Suez Canal and the port, and a fairly complete hotel list – in case the ones listed here are full. The office is open from 9 am to 1.30 pm and again from 3 to 8 pm Saturday to Thursday; it is closed on Friday.

Money There are branches of Banque Misr next to the tourist office, by the Port Fouad ferry landing and on Sharia al-Gomhurriya. You can use Visa or MasterCard for cash advances. About midway along Sharia al-Gomhurriya are branches of the Bank of Alexandria, the Banque du Caire and The National Bank of Egypt. The latter seems to be the least complicated place to change travellers' cheques.

There are also numerous moneychangers. They usually deal in cash only, but might be worth a try, as their rates are sometimes marginally better than in the banks.

Thomas Cook (☎ 227559, fax 236111), at

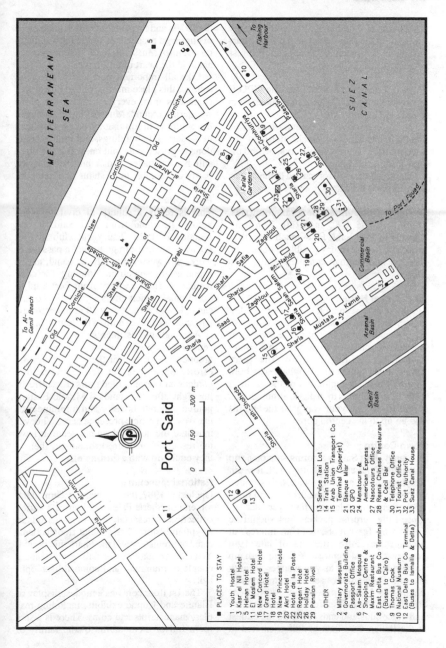

Port Said

0   150   300 m

PLACES TO STAY
■ 1   Youth Hostel
  3   Kasr el Nil Hotel
  5   Helnan Hotel
  16 New Concord Hotel
  17 Grand Hotel
  18 Hotel
  19 New Princess Hotel
  20 Akri Hotel
  22 Hotel de la Poste
  25 Regent Hotel
  26 Holiday Hotel
  29 Pension Rivoli

OTHER
  2   Military Museum
  4   Governorate Building &
      Passport Office
  6   As-Salam Mosque
  7   Shopping Centre &
      Maxim Restaurant
  8   East Delta Bus Co Terminal
      (Buses to Cairo)
  9   Thomas Cook
  10 National Museum
  12 East Delta Bus Co Terminal
      (Buses to Ismailia & Delta)

  13 Service Taxi Lot
  14 Train Station
  15 Arab Union Transport Co
      Terminal (Superjet)
  21 Banque Misr
  23 GPO
  24 Menatours &
      American Express
  27 Nascotours Office
  28 Reana Chinese Restaurant
      & Cecil Bar
  30 Telephone Office
  31 Tourist Office
  32 Port Authority
  33 Suez Canal House

MEDITERRANEAN SEA

SUEZ CANAL

To Fishing Harbour

To Port Fouad

Commercial Basin

Arsenal Basin

Sherif Basin

To Al-Gamil Beach

Farial Gardens

43 Sharia al-Gomhurriya, is conveniently situated. In the same street, in the Menatours office, is a branch of American Express (☎ 225742, 233376).

Post & Telecommunications The GPO is opposite the Farial Gardens, one block from Sharia al-Gomhurriya.

The telephone and telegraph office is on Sharia Palestine, two blocks north of the tourist office. There's another one behind the Governorate building.

You can have mail forwarded to the American Express office.

Foreign Consulates Several countries, including the UK, maintain honorary consuls in Port Said. How much help they would be in case of any trouble is uncertain. The US and German consulates have been closed.

Suez Canal House

If you've ever seen a picture of Port Said, it was probably of the striking green domes of Suez Canal House. One of the best views of the Suez Canal used to be from this white-columned building south of the ferry terminal and tourist office, which was built in time for the inauguration of the canal in 1869. It is off limits to visitors, although you might try to talk your way past the guards and go up to the central dome.

Town Centre

For many, Port Said is a boring stop on a trip through Egypt, and few bother with it at all. The five-storey buildings with their wooden balconies and high verandahs in grand turn-of-the-century style are, however, one of those little surprise packets that should be fascinating for anyone with an interest in architecture and/or the life of late 19th century colonial centres. You can turn up some odd remnants as you wander around: the old 'Postes françaises'; a sign for ship-chandlers to the pre-Soviet 'volunteer Russian fleet', another for the Bible Society and other odds and ends. Perhaps the oddest is the Italian consulate building, erected in the 1930s and resplendent with a huge piece of engraved propaganda to the Fascist dictator Benito Mussolini and 'Rome – once again at the heart of an Empire'.

Like all important port and commercial centres, this place must have had all sorts of characters from every corner of the globe wandering around. Much of the grandeur of the centre is unfortunately being sacrificed to modern ugly buildings, and little is being done to preserve the old ones. But the place still has character and a hum of activity, partly attributable to its status as a free port.

Port Fouad

This is really a suburb of civil servants, across the canal from Port Said. It was founded in 1925. The yacht club in Port Fouad is the place to go to find a passage or work on a vessel through the canal, as the captains are sometimes looking for crew members. The free ferry from Port Said to Port Fouad, which offers a great view of the canal, leaves about every 10 minutes from a terminal one block south of the tourist office.

Although not as interesting as canalside central Port Said, a short visit and stroll around the streets near the quay repays the effort. Sprawling residences with lush gardens and sloping tiled roofs are a refreshing sight after the standard Middle Eastern poured-concrete boxes – and a reminder of the West's one-time presence here. Whoever inherited the houses does not seem to have the resources or desire to maintain them – they could do with a dusting off.

National Museum

Opened in 1987, the national museum, at the top end of Sharia Palestine, houses a varied collection representative of most periods in Egyptian history. The ground floor is dedicated to prehistory and the Pharaonic period. You can see statuary, utensils, pottery and a couple of mummies and colourful sarcophagi.

The 1st floor contains a modest display of Islamic and Coptic exhibits, including textiles, manuscripts and coins. There is also a room full of memorabilia of the family of

Mohammed Ali's successors, who saw through the construction of the canal.

The museum is open from 9 am to 3.30 pm seven days a week, and admission costs E£6 (E£3 for students). Since tourists don't exactly flock to Port Said, you'll probably have the place to yourself. There's not a bad view of the canal from the 1st floor.

Military Museum
The small military museum on Sharia 23rd of July has some interesting relics from the 1967 and 1973 wars with Israel. There are captured US tanks with freshly painted Stars of David, a couple of unexploded bombs and various other unpleasant reminders of recent wars, as well as exhibits of ancient Pharaonic and Islamic conflicts. The museum costs E£2 to get in, if it is actually open. At the time of writing it was difficult to find a time when it was open – official hours are 8 am to 3 pm, seven days a week. You can see a lot of the hardware in the garden anyway.

Farial Gardens
If you get tired of watching ships cruise in and out of the canal, the Farial Gardens offer a pleasant refuge for a stroll or a picnic. They're in the centre of town next to the bus station.

Swimming
West of the Helnan Hotel, most of the shelly beaches are open to the public. They're not the greatest beaches in the world, and women will probably feel a little uncomfortable about peeling down to a swimsuit (leave the bikini at home). If that doesn't appeal, for a E£15 minimum charge you can use the Helnan's pool facilities.

Canal Cruise
The *Noras I* restaurant boat, tied up at the top of the canal, offers a 1½-hour tour of the canal for E£6, including a soft drink. They depart at 2.30, 4 and 8.30 pm. You can also have a decent seafood meal for about E£30.

Al-Matariyya Ferry
For E£2, you can chug west across shallow

lakes and lagoons to the Delta town of Al-Matariyyah, and perhaps watch as becalmed feluccas are taken in tow on the way. There's nothing to do at Al-Matariyyah but wait for the return boat.

Places to Stay – bottom end
The *Youth Hostel*, near the stadium, is the cheapest place to stay in Port Said. It costs E£3.25 with membership card and E£1 more without. It has basic bunk beds in rooms of about 20. It's OK, but in a highly inconvenient location.

The area around the canal is crawling with little dives, not all of which seem to be operating. The *Pension Rivoli*, in a lane off Sharia al-Gomhurriya, charges E£5 a night for a bed – don't expect much for your money. Nearby, the *Majestic* and *New Morandi Hotel* offer similar deals. They are next to one another in a long, low colonial building with a verandah. If you have no luck with these, there are plenty of other places like them around.

The Akri Hotel and the El-Ghazal Hotel are a couple of the better deals in town. The Greek-owned *Akri Hotel* (☎ 221013), at 24 Sharia al-Gomhurriya, has clean singles and doubles without bath for about E£9/15. The rooms have a bit of charm and are nicely furnished. The *El-Ghazal Hotel*, at 23 Sharia 23rd of July, has doubles for E£15, but tends to fill up in summer.

Out by the Military Museum, the *Kasr el Nil Hotel* has rooms for E£10, but they don't seem keen on foreigners – it's a bit of a dump anyway.

The *El Moslem Hotel* is not too far from the Delta area bus station, but not very convenient for anything else. It has big musty singles/doubles with bath for E£10/15.

The *Grand Hotel* (☎ 329730), down near the Port Authority on Sharia Salah Salem, has cramped but clean rooms, some with TV, for E£13/20. The rooms have baths and the price includes breakfast.

The *Regent Hotel*, on Sharia al-Gomhurriya, has large, charming rooms with hardwood floors, armoires, bathrooms and balconies. They cost E£14.30/23 with breakfast. Try to avoid room No 2, which looks set for demolition.

Places to Stay – middle

The *Hotel de la Poste* (☎ 229994), on Sharia al-Gomhurriya, has a fading elegance which the management has attempted to salvage through careful renovation. Singles/doubles on the street with bath and balconies cost E£26/35 without breakfast. Rooms off the street cost E£20/23. Some rooms have a TV and refrigerator. There's a restaurant, bar and patisserie downstairs. It's worth having a chat with the hotel manager, Mr Salem Sakra, if you can catch him in the evenings. One of the 'Heroes of Port Said', he fought off invading British troops in the 1956 Suez Crisis and later became city manager and governor of Sohag province.

The *Abu Simbel Hotel* (☎ 224509), 15 Sharia al-Gomhurriya, is a modern, almost European-style establishment with shower/toilet stalls, TV, fans and refrigerators in all rooms. At E£32 for a double and E£21 for a single (including breakfast), it's slightly overpriced.

Places to stay – top end

Edging into the top bracket is the *New Concord Hotel* (☎ 235341; fax 235342), a block down from the Grand. The modern, comfortable and totally characterless rooms have wall-to-wall carpet, bath, fans and TV. Some of the rooms on the higher floors have reasonable views of the canal. At E£60/80 with breakfast, it's a bit over the top.

A little further over the top is the *Holiday*, on Sharia al-Gomhurriya opposite the Hotel de la Poste, with doubles for E£110 and singles for E£93, including taxes and breakfast.

The *Helnan Port Said Hotel* (☎ 320890), on the beach front, gets a five-star rating from the tourist office, mostly because of the views. It was upgraded in 1991. Singles are US$55 and doubles US$68, plus 21% in taxes and E£8 for breakfast. You must show official exchange receipts for payment.

Places to Eat

Not surprisingly, there are plenty of fish restaurants in Port Said. One of the best and cheapest is *Galal*, on the corner of Sharia al-Gomhurriya and Sharia Gaberti, one block from the Hotel de la Poste. A big plate of delicious calamari will set you back E£10 – but they're worth it. Fish dishes start at around E£14. Outside they have a takeaway shawarma stand.

Another fish restaurant with slightly higher prices is the *Abu Essam*, across the road from the Helnan Hotel. They do a good squid casserole with salad for E£12.

In front of the *Hotel de la Poste* there's a bar, a café and a restaurant. The latter has cheap hamburgers, sandwiches, salads and what is called pizza.

Across the road, and on the corner, is *Popeye* (the sailor man), which is a pleasant place to sit on the footpath and watch the town bustle around you. The food is nothing special, but the banana splits are enormous.

If you want pizza, you could try the new *Pizza Pino*, up near the National Museum, on Sharia al-Gomhurriya.

For Chinese or Korean food, there's *Reana*, also on Sharia al-Gomhurriya. Next door is the *Cecil*, a spit-and-sawdust bar open until quite late.

For a splurge try *Maxim*, the best restaurant in town, where you can get a full fish dinner for about E£25. It's on the corner of the Old Corniche and Sharia al-Gomhurriya and has a splendid view of the ships entering the canal.

Things to Buy

Almost anything can be bought in Port Said, from the latest Western fashions to Sony Walkman personal stereos and VCRs, at duty-free prices. The best deals can be found along Sharia al-Gomhurriya, which is one of the main shopping streets. This whole business is designed mostly for people passing through on vessels headed down the canal. If you're interested in buying anything and heading out again overland, check with the store owners what you'll be liable for in duty. You may be able to get away with small items, as customs checks of foreigners seem fairly lax.

Getting There & Away
You must go through a customs check before leaving Port Said. The train and bus stations all have customs halls.

Bus There are three bus terminals. The Arab Union Transport Co runs Super Jet buses to Cairo nine times a day for E£13 from in front of the train station. They also have a bus to Alexandria at 4.30 pm for E£20. Book ahead.

The East Delta Bus Co runs buses to destinations outside the Delta (and Tanta in the Delta for some reason) from its terminal near the Farial Gardens. Remember to get there early because you must first pass through customs.

Buses to Cairo leave every hour from 6 am to 7 pm. Fares range from E£8.50 for the ordinary no-frills bus through E£9/10/11 and E£12. The latter is for this company's luxury bus, with air-con, loud video, toilet and expensive snacks. The others have varying combinations of some of these added extras. The luxury buses don't make stops, usually shaving about a half hour off the three to 3½-hour ride.

There are four buses to Alexandria, at 7, 10 am, 1.30 and 4.30 pm. Tickets cost E£11/15.

Tickets to Suez cost E£6.30 and departures are at 6, 10 am, 1 and 4 pm. The 10 am bus to Al-Arish costs E£9. There is a bus to Nuweiba, in the Sinai, at 2 pm. It costs E£23.

There are four buses to Tanta, in the eastern Delta. They cost E£7, and leave at 1.30, 2.30, 3.30 and 4.30 pm.

The other station is on Sharia an-Nasr, about a 20-minute brisk walk from Farial. It has regular buses to Ismailia from 6.30 am to 6.30 pm. Tickets range from E£3.25 to E£3.75.

Hourly departures for Damietta (Dumyat) cost E£1.50 and take about 50 minutes.

Every hour on the half hour, a bus goes south to Qantara for E£2. There are also buses to the Delta towns of Mansura (E£3.50), Zagazig (E£5) and Benha (E£3).

Train There are five trains to Cairo. This is the slowest, but can also be the cheapest, way to get there. There are no 1st-class services. The full 2nd-class air-con fare is E£10.30. Normal 2nd class is E£5 and 3rd class E£2.20. The train stops in Ismailia.

There are five other trains to Ismailia only. Tickets costs E£4.20/1.70/0.80. You can get a train to Zagazig too – it costs E£7.30/3.30/1.50.

Two trains make the long loop via Ismailia and Zagazig to Alexandria. Tickets costs E£13/6.70/1.

Service Taxi Service taxis leave from a mucky lot behind the Sharia an-Nasr bus station, and there doesn't appear to be a lot happening in the afternoon. The Cairo fare, for once, is cheaper than that of the buses – E£7.50. Others include: Ismailia (E£3.50); Suez (E£7); Qantara (E£2.25) and Zagazig (E£7).

Boat There is a twice-weekly service linking Port Said and Limassol in Cyprus, sailing with the *Princesa Cypria* or *Princesa Marissa* on Tuesday and Friday. The trip takes about 14 hours and costs E£518.90 one way – and that's the cheapest ticket. From Limassol you can connect with vessels heading on to Israel or Greece – but it's the expensive way to get around.

If you're interested, enquire at the North African Shipping Company's Nascotours office (☎ 329500) at 28 Sharia Palestine. You could also enquire at their offices in Alexandria or at Menatours in Cairo.

Unless you are a merchant sailor, getting a passage on a merchant vessel going through the canal is nearly impossible. However, you may be able to get a passage or work on a private yacht from Port Fouad.

Getting Around

The horse-drawn carriages known as hantours are the best and most enjoyable way to tour Port Said, especially around sunset. The carriage and driver can be hired for about E£4 per hour.

QANTARA

The only reason to visit the town of Qantara, 80 km south of Port Said, is so that you can cross to the east side of the canal and leave again as quickly as possible. The service taxis, which cross the Sinai to the Egypt-Israel border, leave from the east bank.

Most of Qantara was destroyed during the 1973 war with Israel and the town's buildings are still pocked with bullet holes. A free boat ferries passengers from one side of the canal to the other. Be prepared to join a stampede of people, chickens, and donkeys for a space on the boat. It can be fun if your sense of humour is still intact after trying to talk a donkey out of your seat.

ISMAILIA

Ismailia was founded by and named after Pasha Ismail, the ruler of Egypt during the construction of the Suez Canal in the 1860s. Ferdinand de Lesseps, the director of the Suez Canal Company, lived in the city until the canal was completed.

As in Port Said, a stroll around the elegant colonial streets of Ismailia can be an unexpected pleasure. Obviously we're not talking about great monuments, but it's interesting how this canal city grew in the image of the British and French masters pulling the strings in Egypt in the 19th and first half of this century.

Orientation

Ismailia is perhaps the most picturesque of the new canal towns, yet it has been quickly developing, or rather devolving, into an urban mess. The city of 544,000 people is divided in two by the railway line, which marks a boundary between well-tended streets on one side and a veritable disaster area on the other.

The streets and squares on the eastern side of the city are lined with trees and dotted with malls and parks. The Sweetwater Canal, named for its freshwater connection with the Nile, weaves through this half of Ismailia, around lush thickets of trees to Lake Timsah, or Crocodile Lake, which is the smallest of the Bitter Lakes.

Just on the other side of the tracks you'll find the main bus and service taxi stations – a microcosm of the surrounding neighbourhood, which features muddy, pot-holed streets, horn-honking maniacs and smoking piles of garbage.

In so far as Ismailia can be said to have a main street, it's probably Sharia Sultan Hussein, which runs between the railway line north of the train station and the Sweetwater Canal. The central square, Midan al-Gomhurriya, is a quiet affair, and in fact the whole eastern part of town is rather exceptional in that it is *all* comparatively peaceful. The thoroughfare beside the Sweetwater Canal is known as the Mohammed Ali Quay, the Promenade and Sharia Salah Salem.

Information

Registration & Visas Should you need to register your arrival in Egypt or get a visa extension, the passports office is on Midan al-Gomhurriya.

Tourist Office The tourist office is at the end of a 1st-floor hall, in the Governorate building on Mohammed Ali Quay. It is open from 8 am to 2 pm daily except Friday and, apart from being somewhat of an educational experience, is useless. They have a fairly hopeless glossy brochure and claim a booklet is to be published soon, but seem to have no information in their heads. No-one seems to speak any English. If you're really lucky, you'll be shunted around the corner to the so-called information and press office, where no-one knows anything and will refer you back to the tourist office. Forget it. There appear to be no maps available (they did exist once), except for the one in Arabic on the wall just outside the tourist office.

Money There's a branch of Banque Misr on Sharia Sultan Hussein where you can get cash advances on Visa and MasterCard. There's a Bank of Alexandria branch across the square from the train station, and a Banque du Caire behind the El Salam Hotel. American Express (☎ 324361) has a branch in the Menatours office at 12 Sharia ash-Shawra.

Post & Telecommunications The GPO is just up the tracks from the train station, and the phone office across the square from the station, virtually opposite the Bank of Alexandria.

Ismailia Museum
This small but interesting museum on Mohammed Ali Quay, several blocks north-east of the Governorate building, has more than 4000 objects from Pharaonic and Greco-Roman times. There are statues, scarabs and stelae, and details of the completion of the first canal, between the Bitter Lakes and Bubastis, by Darius. The 4th century AD mosaic is the highlight of the collection. It depicts some classic characters from Greek story-telling and mythology. On the top, Phaedra is sending a love letter to her son, Hippolyte – he ended up in a bad way, his father setting Poseidon on to him. Below, Dionysos, the god of wine, tags along on a chariot driven by Eros. The bottom section recounts the virtues of Heracles, demi-god and son of Jupiter. The museum is open from 9 am to 4 pm and entry costs E£3 (half for students).

Garden of the Stelae
Near the museum is a garden containing a poor little sphinx from the time of Ramses II. You need permission from the museum to visit the garden, but you can see the unremarkable statue from the street. Don't try to get into the pretty grounds of the majestic residence between the garden and the museum – it belongs to the head of the Suez Canal Authority, and the security chaps get rather on edge at the sight of unauthorised persons strolling in. The Mallaha Gardens, across the road, are nice for a quiet walk.

De Lesseps' House
The residence of the one-time French consul to Egypt used to be open to the public, but now you can only see the interior if you're a VIP of some sort, as it serves as a kind of private hotel for important guests of the Suez Canal Authority. Inside the grounds is his private carriage encased in glass, and his bedroom looks as if it has hardly been touched. Old photos, books and various utensils are scattered around the desk by his bed and on the floor. The house is on Mohammed Ali Quay near the corner of Sharia Ahmed Orabi. If you want a chance to get a peek inside, and you're alone, try going around the back and, if the gate is open, wandering in innocently.

Beaches
There are several good beaches around Lake Timsah, but using them involves paying to get into one of the clubs that dot the shore. Entrance fees vary, as some include a buffet lunch as part of the admission price, but all include access to a private swimming beach. Supposedly the lake was once full of crocodiles, but there have been no sightings for a good many centuries and certainly no record of any swimming tourists being mistaken for lunch.

According to the locals, the best beach is Le Jardin des Enfants, which is two km north of the ETAP Hotel. It belongs to the Suez Canal Authority, but is open to the public for a E£5 entrance fee. Follow the main road

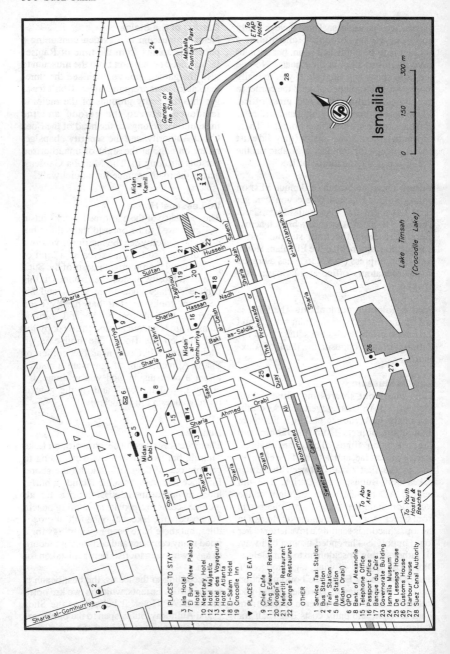

Ismailia

Lake Timsah
(Crocodile Lake)

Mahalla
Fountain Park

To
ETAP
Hotel

Garden
of the
Stelae

Midan M
Kamil

Sharia

al-Hurriya

Sharia al-Tahrir

Sharia

Sultan

Zaghloul

Hassan

Hussein

Nadh
al-Gelah

Baki as-Saldik

Midan
al-Gomhurriya

Abu

Saad

Ahmed

Orabi

Sharia Salah Salem

The Promenade or

Quay

al-Montansihat

Sharia

Mohammed Ali

Sweetwater Canal

Midan
Orabi

To Abu
Atwa

To Youth
Hostel &
Beaches

Sharia al-Gomhurriya

300 m

150

0

PLACES TO STAY

3   Isis Hotel
7   El Burg (New Palace) Hotel
10 Nefertary Hotel
12 Hotel Majestic
13 Hotel des Voyageurs
14 Hotel Atlanta
18 El-Salam Hotel
19 Crocodile Inn

PLACES TO EAT

9   Chief Cafe
11 King Edward Restaurant
20 Groppi's
21 Nefertiti Restaurant
22 George's Restaurant

OTHER

1   Service Taxi Station
2   Bus Station
4   Train Station
5   Bus Station (Midan Orabi)
6   GPO
8   Bank of Alexandria
15 Telephone Office
16 Passport Office
17 Banque du Caire
23 Governorate Building
24 Ismailia Museum
25 De Lesseps' House
26 Customs House
27 Harbour House
28 Suez Canal Authority

past the ETAP, and just before the Suez Canal ferry landing you'll find the club.

For other beaches, head south along the canal past the turn-off down to the Customs House and follow the road around the lake towards the Youth Hostel. There are a few beaches out here, just walk in and ask how much they want.

Abu Atwa

There is supposedly a war museum in this village, about five km south-east of Ismailia. The museum consists of a small crumbling memorial and five captured Israeli tanks in various stages of decay. If you have a bicycle, it's not an unpleasant ride out through some citrus groves to the village, but otherwise there's really nothing here. Follow the road on either side of the canal for a couple of km and then follow the signs leading you over a bridge to the left and on to Abu Atwa. Just keep following the main road until it hits a road in a deformed T-junction – the museum is a little way off to the left.

Places to Stay – bottom end

The *Hotel des Voyageurs*, on Sharia Ahmed Orabi, a short way in from the train station, offers basic but quite acceptable lodgings for E£5/10 for singles/doubles, or E£6/12 for a room away from the noise of the street. Bathrooms are outside.

The *Majestic*, a block south, and the *Atlanta*, across the road from the Voyageurs, both offer similar deals.

The *Isis Hotel* (☎ 227821) on Midan Orabi, opposite the train station, is about the best deal in town. Its clean and comfortable rooms with bath cost E£13/20. Breakfast is an extra E£3.

The *El Burg Hotel*, also known as the *New Palace* (☎ 326327), on the other side of the square, has musty rooms with bath for E£10/20. If you want air-con and a TV thrown in, the price rises to E£20/30. All without breakfast. It's OK, but unless you want the TV, the Isis is better.

The *Nefertary Hotel* (☎ 222822), 41 Sharia Sultan Hussein, is similar to the Isis.

Singles/doubles with bath cost E£20/26. Breakfast is E£3, and they also have a bar.

The sparkling high-rise *Youth Hostel*, out on a beach around Lake Timsah, has sparkling prices. A spot in a room with two/four/six beds costs E£18/15/8 with breakfast. The rooms are clean and comfortable and have lockers and views over the lake. The white-tiled toilets and showers blind you with their cleanliness. They don't seem too concerned about whether or not you have a membership card.

Camping There is no official camping ground in the Ismailia area; however, it is possible to camp on the beach around Lake Timsah.

Places to Stay – middle & top end

The *El-Salam Hotel* (☎ 324401), on Sharia al-Geish, has clean singles and doubles with baths ranging in price from E£24.80 for the cheapest single to E£41.90 for the dearest double, with breakfast. Some rooms have TVs.

The *Crocodile Inn* (☎ 324377), on the corner of Sharia Saad Zaghloul and Sharia Sultan Hussein, seems to have everything except crocodiles. There are various lounges and restaurants including a 24-hour coffee shop. Singles are E£35 and doubles E£45 with breakfast.

The *ETAP* (☎ 222275, 222250; fax 222220), right on the lake at Gezira al-Fursan, has all the amenities of an expensive hotel. Singles/doubles start at US$45/55 before taxes. For around E£20 you can use their swimming pool and beach, but on Friday and Sunday you have to pay for the buffet as well – E£35 all up.

Places to Eat

There are some cheap eateries in the mall near George's and the Nefertiti restaurants. The *El Gandool*, which is in among them, would like to sell you a kg of mixed meats for E£25, but you can settle for a plate of spaghetti for a couple of E£ instead.

George's and the *Nefertiti*, both on Sharia Sultan Hussein, serve fish and meat dishes for about E£10 to E£15. The fish at the Greek-run George's is particularly good.

A fairly recent and expensive restaurant is the *King Edward* (☎ 325451). They do a mixture of meat and fish dishes, all for around E£15 to E£20. The chicken curry is quite good and makes a nice change from the usual fare. You can also get a beer here.

Groppi's is just across the street from George's. It's a smaller version of the Cairo Groppi's, but with just as good a selection of pastries and ice cream.

The *Social Club* is a garden restaurant and cafeteria in Mallaha Gardens, run by the Ismailia Governorate, where you can get good, inexpensive meals.

Some of the middle-range hotels have restaurants too, and the New Palace (or El Burg if you prefer) has a fairly gloomy tearoom.

Getting There & Away

Bus You can get buses to Cairo from two stations. On Midan Orabi, the West Delta Bus Co has frequent departures for E£5 or E£5.50. At 7 am and 2.30 pm buses leave for Alexandria, costing E£8 and E£8.50 respectively.

Buses for Cairo also leave from the main station (East Delta Bus Co) on the other side of the railway line, with the same frequency and at the same price.

Port Said buses leave the East Delta Bus Co station every 30 to 45 minutes, and cost E£3.25 or E£3.75. The latter supposedly doesn't stop as often. There is a bus every 15 to 20 minutes to Suez for E£3.

To the Sinai, there is a bus every hour or so to Al-Arish from 7 am to 7 pm. It usually costs E£6.25, but prices may fluctuate for through buses from Cairo. The trip takes about three hours. At 2.30 pm there is a bus to Sharm el-Sheikh for E£15.

Train Including through trains from Port Said, there are about 10 trains to Ismailia. Tickets cost E£7.35/3.40/1.50 for 2nd class air-con, 2nd class and 3rd class. The trip can easily take three hours. To Port Said, the 1½-hour trip costs E£4.20/1.70/0.80.

There are at least nine 3rd-class trains to

Suez for 90 pt. It's a painfully slow way to go, and the station in Suez is well out of town.

Service Taxi Service taxis depart from the lot across the road from the East Delta Bus Co terminal on Sharia al-Gomhurriya. The trip to Suez costs E£3, to Port Said E£3.50, to Cairo E£4.50 and to Al-Arish E£6.

Getting Around

Ismailia's parks and tree-lined streets are good bike-riding territory. There are a few bike shops on the side streets off Mohammed Ali Quay – just ask around for the best deal. The one behind the El Gandool Restaurant wants about E£6 a day, but some tough bargaining should bring him down a bit.

SUEZ

Suez is a city going through a metamorphosis. It was all but destroyed during the 1967 and 1973 wars with Israel, although there is little obvious evidence of the devastation today. The revamped main streets, however, are mostly a facade hiding a sordid mess of back street slums. Three US-made Israeli tanks squat on the Corniche as a memorial to the wars. Slightly eerier is the sight of what appears to be an Egyptian tank (in pretty poor condition) facing the canal from Port Tewfiq – on the other side, sitting side-on in the sand, is another Israeli tank stopped in its tracks.

Suez sprawls around the shores of the gulf where the Red Sea meets the southern entrance of the Suez Canal. There is nothing much to do there except take in the best view of the ships passing in or out of the canal, and there's little in the way of tourist facilities. Suez is basically just a transit point, not only for the great tankers, cargo vessels and private yachts en route to or from the Mediterranean, but for travellers and the Muslim faithful as well. The Gulf of Suez is one of the departure points for the haj, or pilgrimage to Mecca; most other people just pass through Suez on their way to the Sinai or the Red Sea beaches.

Top: Camels at market, Cairo (GE)
Left: Camel traders shave & tattoo their animals to brand them (KB)
Right: Controlling a frisky camel, Northern Sudan (LC)

Top: Boat moored at Lord Kitchener's Island, Aswan (GB)
Middle: Loading buses for the trip to Dongola, the Sudan (DS)
Bottom: Following the poles from Wadi Halfa to Abu Hamed, the Sudan (RvD)

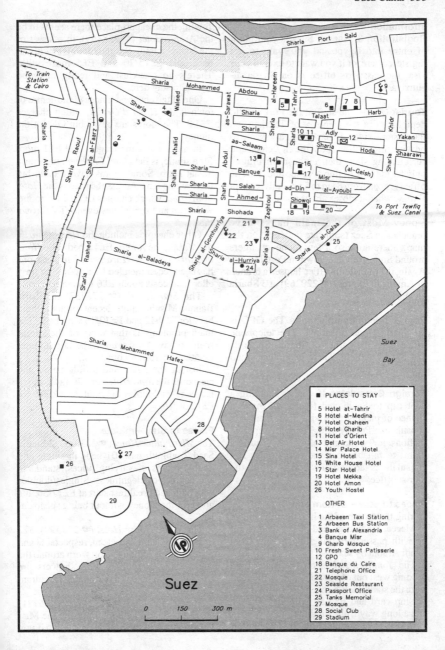

Sharia Port Said

To Train Station & Cairo

Sharia Raouf
Sharia Ataka
Sharia al-Faarz

Sharia Mohammed Waleed
Sharia
Sharia
Sharia
Sharia
Sharia
Sharia
Sharia

Sharia Khalid
Sharia Abdul

Abdou
Sharia
Sharia
as-Salaam
Banque
Salah
Ahmed
Shohada

Sharia as-Sarawat

al-Hareem
at-Tahrir

Talaat
Adly
Sharia
Hoda
(al-Geish)

Harb
Khidr
Yakan
Shaarawi

Misr
al-Ayoubi
ad-Din
Showqi

To Port Tewfiq & Suez Canal

Sharia al-Gomhurriya
Sharia
al-Hurriya

Sharia Rashed
Sharia al-Baladeya

Sharia Saad Zaghloul
Sharia al-Qalaa

Sharia Mohammed Hafez

Suez Bay

Suez

0   150   300 m

■ PLACES TO STAY

5 Hotel at-Tahrir
6 Hotel al-Medina
7 Hotel Chaheen
8 Hotel Gharib
11 Hotel d'Orient
13 Bel Air Hotel
14 Misr Palace Hotel
15 Sina Hotel
16 White House Hotel
17 Star Hotel
19 Hotel Mekka
20 Hotel Amon
26 Youth Hostel

OTHER

1 Arbaeen Taxi Station
2 Arbaeen Bus Station
3 Bank of Alexandria
4 Banque Misr
9 Gharib Mosque
10 Fresh Sweet Patisserie
12 GPO
18 Banque du Caire
21 Telephone Office
22 Mosque
23 Seaside Restaurant
24 Passport Office
25 Tanks Memorial
27 Mosque
28 Social Club
29 Stadium

Information
Registration & Visas If Suez is your point of entry into Egypt and you want to get registered here, or if you want to extend your visa, the passports office is on Sharia al-Hurriya.

Tourist Office The staff at the Port Tewfiq department of the Ministry of Tourism, on the eastern side of Suez Bay, are keen to provide information about the city, canal and surrounding sites, their enthusiasm limited only by the lack of things to see and do. The office is open from 8 am to 5 pm daily, except Friday, when it closes about noon.

Money Most of the main banks have branches in Suez (some are indicated on the map); there are also a few moneychangers around Suez itself and down in Port Tewfiq. Again, the Menatours office houses a branch of American Express (☎ 220269) at 3 Sharia al-Marwa.

Post & Telecommunications The GPO is on Sharia Hoda Shaarawi. The telephone office is on the corner of Sharias Shohoda and Saad Zaghloul. There is another small office at the bus station.

Foreign Consulates If you're planning a boat trip to Saudi and figure you have a chance of picking up a visa here, there is a consulate in Port Tewfiq. There are separate sections for work and *haj* visas. Tourism seems to fall between the two stools. The consulate is around the corner from the tourist office.

Places to Stay – bottom end
During the month of the haj, the pilgrimage to Mecca, the bottom-end places tend to fill up with passengers travelling to and from Saudi Arabia by sea.

The *Youth Hostel* is on the main road heading west out of Suez and across the road from the stadium. It's cheap (E£3 with membership card and E£3.50 without), grungy and a long way from anything.

If you have a hankering to stay in Port Tewfiq, the cheapest place there seems to be the *Arafat Hotel* (☎ 228869), in a street of the same name. Singles/doubles without bath cost E£15/20 and E£5 more with. There's no breakfast and really no good reason to stay here.

One of the cheapest places in the centre of town is the *Hotel d'Orient*, which charges E£4/8. The rooms are basic, but OK for the money.

In much the same league, and E£1 more for a single, is the *Hotel Chaheen*, on Sharia Talaat Harb. Some rooms have a bath, but there are no fans. Across the road is the *Hotel al-Medina*, which charges E£7/12 for rooms with bath and sometimes even a TV thrown in.

Other cheapies include the *Hotel Gharib*, the *Mekka*, the *Amon* (E£4 a bed), the *Hotel at-Tahrir* and the *Haramein*. This last one has been recommended by a couple of travellers and costs about E£6 a person.

The *Star Hotel* (☎ 228737) in Sharia Banque Misr has quite decent rooms without bath for E£9/12 and E£12/15 with bath. The main problems is that none of the rooms seem to have fans even in the hot summer months. There is no breakfast.

Just up the street and a little better and cleaner is the *Sina Hotel* (☎ 220394), which has singles/doubles without breakfast for E£12.30/16.

Places to Stay – middle
The *Misr Palace Hotel* (☎ 223031), 2 Sharia Saad Zaghloul, has 101 beds in single and double rooms of varying prices, standards and degrees of cleanliness. Singles/doubles with bath and breakfast start at E£17/30. It's good for the money without being spectacular.

The *White House Hotel* (☎ 227599), 322 Sharia as-Salaam, is a clean, respectable and popular place, although a bit worn around the edges. Singles/doubles with showers are E£32/40.50. There is a reasonable restaurant downstairs.

The *Bel Air Hotel* (☎ 223211; fax 225781) on Sharia Saad Zaghloul, opposite the Misr Palace, is one of the best deals in town if you have a bit money to throw around. Clean, quiet, fully carpeted rooms with phone, TV, air-con and bath cost E£41/59 with breakfast – you may be able to extract a 10% discount from them.

Places to Stay – top end

The *Green House Hotel* (☎ 223330; fax 223337) is a new joint on Sharia Port Said, on the way out of Suez to Port Tewfiq. The lobby area really is a sickly green colour. The hotel has a pool, bar and branch of the Banque du Caire. Comfortable rooms with bath, air-con, TV and balconies come for US$30/38.

One thing the *Summer Palace* (☎ 224475) is not is a palace; the rather dilapidated rooms, at E£106/145, are ridiculously expensive. You're paying for the Gulf views and the seawater pools, which you can use for E£5 if you're not a resident.

The *Red Sea Hotel* (☎ 223334/5), 13 Sharia Riad, Port Tewfiq, is Suez' premier establishment. Its 64 rooms have TV, bath, phone, radio and air-con, and are comfortable and clean. They want US$41/52 for singles/doubles, and like to see bank receipts. It's fine, but doesn't really offer anything you can't get for a lot less at the Bel Air.

Places to Eat

For the cheap old favourites like ta'amiyya and shawarma, a wander around the streets bounded by Sharias Talaat Harb, Abdul as-Sarawat, Khidr and Banque Misr will soon reveal what you're after. There are also a few juice stands and plenty of cafés and teahouses.

The *Fish Restaurant*, between the White House and Bel Air, is exactly what it calls itself. They sell the day's catch by weight and grill it. A big meal will cost around E£20, but sometimes they overcook it a bit.

A few metres further towards the Bel Air are a couple of other places. The one that has the sweets counter inside (called the *Riviera* in Arabic) serves a variety of big meat dishes and generous soups. A meal too big for most shouldn't cost much more than about E£14.

On Sharia Saad Zaghloul, not far from the telephone office, is the *Seaside*. Half a chicken costs E£6, a plate of spaghetti E£1.60 and a meal of shrimps (prawns to some) E£20.

The *Social Club*, on the Corniche, has inexpensive fish as well as hazy views of the Gulf of Suez and the surrounding mountains. It's open from 9 am to 6 pm.

For sweets, you could do worse than go for an ice cream at *Fresh Sweet*, near the Hotel d'Orient.

There is a series of cafés down in Port Tewfiq, if you happen to stumble off a boat from Saudi and want to sit down for a breather.

Getting There & Away

Bus All buses to Cairo, Ismailia, the Red Sea beaches and the Sinai leave from Arbaeen bus station on Sharia al-Faarz, near the centre of town.

Buses to Cairo (E£4.50/5, depending on mod cons) leave every half an hour from 6 am to 8 pm and take about two hours. Buses to Ismailia (E£3) leave every 15 to 20 minutes and take about an hour. There are four buses directly to Port Said, at 7, 9, 10.30 am and 3.30 pm. The ride takes a little over two hours and costs E£6.50.

Buses to 'Ain Sukhna (E£1.25 to E£1.75, depending on the number of stops they make) depart at 6, 8, 10 am, noon and 2 pm.

There are six services a day to Zafarana, Ras Gharib and Hurghada and they should be booked well ahead. The trip to Hurghada takes five hours and costs E£12. Most of these go on to Qena (E£16) via Port Safaga.

At 10.30 am there is a bus all the way to Aswan (E£26 or E£32, depending on the air-con), via Luxor (E£22 or E£30). There is another bus to Luxor at 6 pm (E£30). Book ahead. The trip to Luxor is about 10 hours, to Aswan about 14 to 15 hours.

If you want to go to Al-Arish, you can catch the bus for Nakhl at 3 pm (E£10) and try to make a connection from there. The same bus goes on to Taba and Nuweiba (E£17 and E£20). This bus is then said to head on to Sharm el-Sheikh (that would

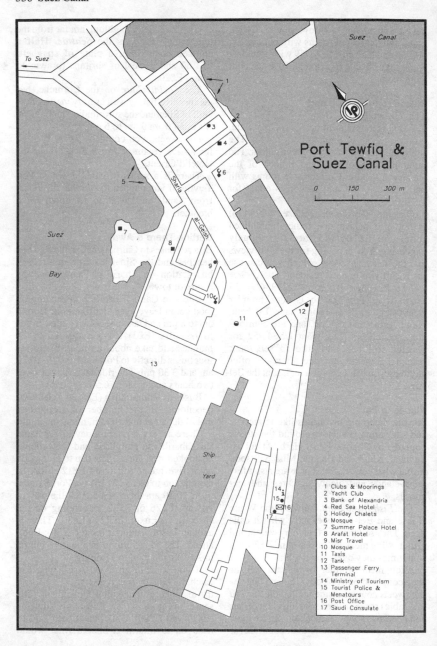

Port Tewfiq &
Suez Canal

0   150   300 m

Suez Canal

To Suez

Suez

Bay

Sharia al-Geish

Ship

Yard

1 Clubs & Moorings
2 Yacht Club
3 Bank of Alexandria
4 Red Sea Hotel
5 Holiday Chalets
6 Mosque
7 Summer Palace Hotel
8 Arafat Hotel
9 Misr Travel
10 Mosque
11 Taxis
12 Tank
13 Passenger Ferry
   Terminal
14 Ministry of Tourism
15 Tourist Police &
   Menatours
16 Post Office
17 Saudi Consulate

really be the long way!). Two buses that do go to Sharm el-Sheikh the more direct route down the Gulf of Suez leave at 10 am and 12.30 pm for E£12. They go on to Dahab for E£14, and to Nuweiba for E£17. There is a bus for St Catherine's via Wadi Feran at 2 pm for E£14.

Note that, as a rule, it is much cheaper, when travelling between Cairo and Sinai destinations, to go first to Suez and pick up something else there. Even if you found yourself paying for a night in a cheap hotel it would generally work out cheaper. Buses to Oyun Musa, Ras as-Sudr, Hammam Fara'un and El-Tor leave at odd intervals during the day. The trip takes one hour, 1½ hours and 2½ hours respectively. The 10 am, 12.30 and 2 pm services mentioned to Sharm el-Sheikh and St Catherine's can let you off at these places along the way.

Departure times are always subject to change, so remember to check them in advance.

Train Only a masochist would want to travel to or from Suez by train. The station is a good couple of km west of the Arbaeen bus station. From it depart six Cairo-bound trains that only make it as far as 'Ain Shams. Second class is E£2.60 and 3rd E£1.05.

To Ismailia there are nine very slow 3rd-class trains for 90 pt. The 3.30 pm train makes fewer stops than the others.

If you want to do this, a microbus from near Arbaeen will take you along the main road and next to the railway line out to the station for 15 pt.

Service Taxi Service taxis go from near the bus station to many of the destinations serviced by buses and trains, except in the Sinai, where no structured service-taxi system exists (which partly explains why getting a taxi there is so outrageously expensive).

The fares to Cairo, Ismailia, Port Said and Hurghada are E£4.50, E£3, E£7 and E£20 respectively. The one exception in the Sinai is El-Tor. The trip there costs E£9.

Boat It is possible to travel by boat between

Suez and Jeddah. The trip from Suez takes about three days. You can book tickets in the Misr Travel office in Port Tewfiq on boats such as the *Gowahir*, the *Zahrat Salim* and the *Fahd*. There are four classes of fare: E£255 in 1st class; E£210 in 2nd class; E£180 in Pullman and E£145 in deck class. All these are one way, and they want to see bank receipts showing you have exchanged money in a bank (an anachronism from the days when there was a black market). Apparently it's impossible to get a ticket during the haj. They won't sell you a ticket if you don't already have your visa, which, considering the difficulty of getting one, is quite sensible.

Frequency of departures seems to vary greatly – there is certainly no timetable as such, so check in advance.

Getting Around
There are regular minibus services along Sharia Salaam from the Arbaeen bus station to Port Tewfiq. They stop to pick you up or drop you off wherever you want along the route and cost 25 pt.

The Red Sea Coast

Warning There is a heavy military presence along much of the coast, and some is said to be mined. Most of the beaches are OK, but if you have any doubts, it might be worth checking with local authorities. Be prudent about where you aim your cameras, too.

'AIN SUKHNA
'Ain Sukhna, which simply means 'hot spring', is the site of springs originating from within Mt Ataka, the highest mountain on the Red Sea coast. There's not much to 'Ain Sukhna, but it is quite an attractive bit of coast. The road squeezes along between the water and the hills that slope almost down to the beach. The place is a popular resort with Egyptians.

There are five buses a day from Suez, 55 km north, so it's possible to visit 'Ain Sukhna on a day trip from the canal city. The trip costs from E£1.25 to E£1.75, apparently depending on how many stops the bus makes on the way.

If you want to stay longer there is the *Ain Sukhna Hotel*, which has 80 rooms and 30 bungalows from about E£50 for a double. A little further south is the more expensive *Mena Oasis*. At least one other resort is under construction.

ZAFARANA

This town, 62 km south of 'Ain Sukhna and 150 km east of Beni Suef on the Nile, is little more than a way-station for visits to the isolated Coptic monasteries of St Anthony and St Paul in the mountains overlooking the Gulf of Suez.

Buses running between Suez and Hurghada will drop you at Zafarana.

MONASTERIES OF ST ANTHONY & ST PAUL

The Coptic Christian monasteries of St Anthony and St Paul are open for day trips between 9 am and 5 pm; each of the monasteries has a residence in Cairo, and as a general rule permission has to be obtained from them to stay overnight. Most of the residences are around St Mark's Cathedral off Sharia al-Galaa. If the St Paul's monastery residence (☎ 900218) or that of St Anthony's (☎ 906025) cannot help for whatever reason, try the Coptic Patriarch in Cairo, at 222 Sharia Ramses, Abbassiya. St Anthony's guesthouse is for men only. St Paul's has accommodation for men and women but the monks won't take any visitors at all during Lent. There are reports that if you simply turn up, you may be allowed to sleep over anyway, but don't bank on this.

The monasteries are only about 30 km apart, but thanks to the cliffs of Gebel al-Galala al-Qibliya they're around 82 km apart by road.

Monastery of St Anthony

Hidden away in the barren cliffs of the Eastern Desert, the fortified religious community of St Anthony's represented the beginning of the Christian monastic tradi-

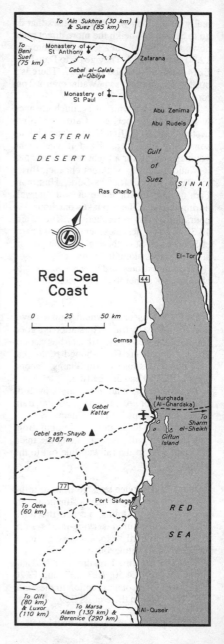

tion. Built in the 4th century AD by the disciples of St Anthony, the walled village at the foot of Gebel al-Galala al-Qibliya is the largest of the Coptic monasteries.

This founding monastic order sprang up around the son of a merchant who had given up his worldly possessions to devote his life to God. Anthony actually retreated into the desert, in about 294 AD, to escape the disciples he had attracted to his hermit's cave by the Nile. While his followers adopted an austere communal life at the foot of the mountain, Anthony took himself off to a cave, high above the developing monastery village, where he lived to the ripe old age of 105.

Despite its isolation, the monastery suffered Bedouin raids in the 8th and 9th centuries, attacks from irate Muslims in the 11th century and a 15th century revolt by bloodthirsty servants that resulted in the massacre of the monks.

Following the example set by St Anthony, St Paul and their followers 16 centuries ago, the 25 monks and five novices who live at St Anthony's today have dedicated their lives to poverty, chastity, obedience and prayer.

St Anthony's has several churches, chapels, dormitories, a bakery, vegetable garden and a spring. The oldest part of the monastery is the Church of St Anthony, built over the saint's tomb. There is a guesthouse for men only.

If you're hiking in from the main road make sure you're properly equipped, especially with water, as it's a long, hot and dry walk. If you do get this far you should also hike up to the Cave of St Anthony, which is north-east of the monastery. The medieval graffiti on the walls is fascinating and there is a breathtaking view of the hills and valley below.

Monastery of St Paul

The most fascinating part of this large complex, in the cliffs of the Gebel al-Galala al-Qibliya, is the Church of St Paul, cluttered with altars, candles, ostrich eggs (the symbol of the Resurrection) and colourful murals. It was built in and around the cave where Paul

lived for nearly 90 years, during the 4th century, after founding the monastery as a show of devotion to St Anthony. The fortress, above the church, was where the monks retreated during Bedouin raids.

Visitors are more than welcome and a couple of the monks, who speak excellent English, give guided tours. St Paul's has two guesthouses, one inside the monastery for men and one outside for women. Food and lodging are provided free of charge, so don't abuse the monks' hospitality.

Getting There & Away

Buses running between Suez and Hurghada will take you to Zafarana. Direct access to the monasteries is limited to private vehicles and tour buses from Cairo or Hurghada. The easiest way is to join one of the tours from Hurghada. Most of the hotels organise such trips, or you can ask at Misr Travel. Otherwise, it's you, your feet and, if you get really lucky, your thumb.

St Anthony's is 45 km inland from the Red Sea. To get there you follow the rather rough road which runs between Zafarana and Beni Suef. The turn-off to the monastery is about 35 km from Zafarana and from there it's a 10 km walk south through the desert to St Anthony's. Buses occasionally travel from Cairo to the Red Sea via this route across the Eastern Desert but it's really more suited to 4WD vehicles.

To get to St Paul's you can take one of the buses that run between Suez and Hurghada and get off after Zafarana at the turn-off to the monastery. Buses between Qena, north of Luxor on the Nile, and Suez go via Port Safaga and Hurghada and can also drop you at the turn-off, which is south of the Zafarana lighthouse. It's then a 13 km hike along the badly surfaced road through the desert.

Another alternative is to get a group together and take a service taxi from Suez or Hurghada to the monasteries. Beni Suef is also a departure point for the 150-km trek across the desert to the monasteries. A bus supposedly runs between Hurghada and Beni Suef, so you might be able to get it to stop for St Anthony's on the way. Otherwise you'd be better off with your own transport, preferably a 4WD, to make this journey. It might be difficult to hire a service taxi in Beni Suef for the whole trip.

RAS GHARIB

This oil workers' town, 101 km south of Zafarana, is not worth stopping for. Unfortunately, some service taxi drivers seem to think it makes the perfect rest stop on the way to or from Hurghada.

HURGHADA (AL-GHARDAKA)

The only attractions of this one-time isolated and modest fishing village are the warm and brilliant turquoise waters of the Red Sea, the amazing colours of the splendid coral and exotic creatures of the deep, and the soft white sand beaches backed up by the mountains of the Eastern Desert. There are no ancient tombs, Pharaonic temples or crumbling monasteries, just nature at its best.

While the crystal-clear waters and fascinating reefs have made Hurghada, or Al-Ghardaka as the Egyptians call it, a popular destination among diving enthusiasts the world over, if you're not into beaches, swimming or snorkelling then this developing resort town has little to offer.

The beaches near town are marred by chunks of concrete, iron rods and empty oil drums – the results of an ongoing hotel construction boom. In fact, hotels seem to be breeding. Every spare bit of dirt or sand in the town is being turned into a building site. For 20 km or more to the south, a dense band of concrete in the form of four and five-star resorts threatens the kind of disaster so often repeated on the more glamorous shores of Europe. Most of the best beaches have already been claimed by resort complexes. There appears to be little to contain the speculative boom on the area's future as a major source of tourist growth, and even towns south of Hurghada, including the far-from-beautiful Port Safaga and as far as Al-Quseir, are showing signs of going the same way. One of the few positive observations that can be made about all this is that, so far, most of the building has been low-level – no high

rises in the manner of the Australian Gold Coast. In the main town, there is a city ordinance blocking building higher than three storeys – without special permission that is, which quite a few places seem to be able to get – so, as the amount of available waterfront land dries up, buildings may start to spread up instead of out.

The beaches are not the most stunning in the world – indeed they are often quite bare and stark. But it is not so much for them that people come. Whether they take a trip in a glass-bottom boat or a yellow submarine, or go snorkelling or diving, the people who flock here come to gaze at what's going on *under* the water.

Orientation

The main town area, where virtually all the budget accommodation is located and most of the locals live, is at the northern end of the stretch of resorts that makes up the whole area. It is called Ad-Dahar, and the main road through it (the highway linking Hurghada to Port Safaga and Suez) is Sharia an-Nasr. A few km down the coast is Sigala. There are some more hotels here and a couple of decent restaurants, but apart from its proximity to the port, from where the boats to Sharm el-Sheikh leave, it has little to attract people. South of Sigala, a road winds down along the coast linking resorts down to the five-star 'tourist village' of Magawish, about 15 km south of Ad-Dahar. Here the road meets another a few km inland to head down past the incomplete shells of future pleasure domes on the way to Port Safaga.

Information

Registration & Visas You can register your arrival in Egypt or obtain visa extensions and re-entry visas at the passports section in the Passports & Immigration office at the northern end of town on Sharia an-Nasr. They are open every day except Friday from 8.30 am to 1.30 pm.

Tourist Office The tourist office is on a side street with the tourist police near the big mosque on Sharia an-Nasr. They have

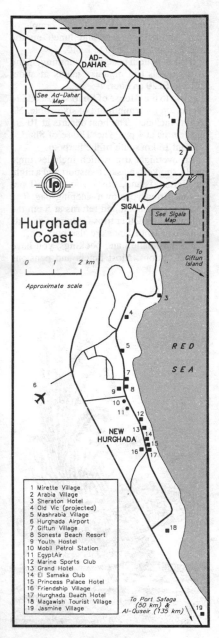

Hurghada Coast

0   1   2 km

Approximate scale

AD-DAHAR

See Ad-Dahar Map

SIGALA

See Sigala Map

To Giftun Island

RED SEA

NEW HURGHADA

1 Mirette Village
2 Arabia Village
3 Sheraton Hotel
4 Old Vic (projected)
5 Mashrabia Village
6 Hurghada Airport
7 Giftun Village
8 Sonesta Beach Resort
9 Youth Hostel
10 Mobil Petrol Station
11 EgyptAir
12 Marine Sports Club
13 Grand Hotel
14 El Samaka Club
15 Princess Palace Hotel
16 Friendship Village
17 Hurghada Beach Hotel
18 Magawish Tourist Village
19 Jasmine Village

To Port Safaga (50 km) & Al-Quseir (135 km)

nothing to offer and speak virtually no English.

Money Banque Misr, the National Bank of Egypt and the Bank of Alexandria all have branches along Sharia an-Nasr in Ad-Dahar. They are generally open seven days a week for exchange purposes, from 9 am to 1 pm and 6 to 9 pm. You can find an American Express branch at the Isis Travel office in the Grand Hotel.

Post & Telecommunications The GPO is on Sharia an-Nasr, towards the southern end of Ad-Dahar. The telephone office is about a 20-minute walk north along the same road. It's open 24 hours a day. If the queues for the card phone are too long, you could try at the bus station or the service-taxi lot, where there are also a couple of the characteristic orange phones (you can only buy the cards in the *centraal*, the telephone office.

Travel Agencies Misr Travel has an office in Ad-Dahar by the main mosque, as does one of the two companies operating boats to Sharm el-Sheikh, Spring Tours.

Bookshops & Newspapers You won't find an awful lot of brain food around here, but there is a bookshop near the bus station, the Hurghada Bookshop, with a few second-hand things of interest in various languages. A lot of the stuff is pulp novels, but it's better than nothing. You'll find a smattering of foreign newspapers, often quite old, in some of the bigger resorts.

Aquarium

If you've ended up in Hurghada and don't want to put your head under the water, you can still get an idea of some of the life teeming in the waters of the Red Sea by paying a visit to the Aquarium. They have quite a good selection of fish and various other odd-looking creatures. It's open from 9 am to 10 pm and costs E£5 (no student discount).

Marine Museum

The marine biology station, about five km north of town, has a pretty decrepit museum and mini-aquarium. If you like dusty, stuffed fish, maybe this will grab your interest. It's open only from 10 am to 1.30 pm. You can pick up a microbus from near the big mosque heading out on the highway to Suez for 50 pt.

Fishing

Fishing excursions of varying length can be organised from Hurghada. You could try Red Sea Fishing (☎ 442316), which rents out boats and equipment for all kinds of trips, including deep sea fishing. A day of fishing, with rods and tackle, costs E£40. A boat and all equipment for four people on a two-day trip costs E£1800.

Sindbad Submarine

This is one way to plumb the depths and stay bone dry. This yellow submarine can carry 46 people to a depth of 45 metres (it generally doesn't go this far down). A day trip costs US$50 a head. For more information, contact the reception of any of the big hotels or call ☎ 442166.

Water Sports

Hurghada's underwater paradise really shouldn't be missed, so if you're not interested in the Sindbad or, as at the time of writing, it's undergoing maintenance, you should take the plunge. The coral reefs are teeming with weird and wonderful exotic marine creatures that swim, float or just lie on the bottom in a variety of shapes, sizes and colours.

Although there is some easily accessible coral at the beach south of the Sheraton, the best reefs are offshore – the most popular ones are around Geftun Island – and the only way to see them is to take a boat and make a snorkelling or diving excursion of at least one day. There is a plethora of places in town that organise trips.

Swimming & Snorkelling The average day trip to Geftun Island, including transport to and from the harbour, visits to a couple of sites, snorkelling gear and lunch on the island costs from E£30 to E£40.

If glass-bottom boats are your thing, many of the hotels can organise jaunts at about E£15 to E£20 an hour.

A trip to the 'House of Sharks' costs E£20 per person for a minimum of six people. No food is included. The boat departs at 10 am and returns at 4 pm. The 'House of Sharks' is about 15 km south of the harbour.

An overnight trip, which includes three meals, snorkels, masks, transport and a night on Geftun Island, costs about E£60 per person. Bring your own sleeping bag. The boat leaves at noon and returns at 5 pm the following day. Other trips for longer periods to more distant islands are also possible.

For information and bookings, you have several options. Most hotels and pensions

can arrange these trips for you. Captain Mohammed of Happy House (see the Places to Stay section) takes people out on day trips to Geftun and Abu Ramada islands and to the 'House of Sharks'.

You will find no shortage of places offering these kinds of trips. The best advice is to shop around a little and see where you can get a deal that suits you. Simply relying on your hotel (and many of the smaller hotels work hard to get you to join the trips for which they are getting commission) may not be the best way to do things. Several people have complained of not getting everything they thought they would. Eliminating at least one intermediary might reduce the risk of disappointment.

Remember when swimming and snorkelling to use sun screen. It is probably a good idea for most people to wear a T-shirt while in the water.

Take your passport with you on any boat excursions; you may have to show it at the port. Wear tennis shoes or reef shoes while exploring tide pools and reefs. The coral is very sharp and can easily cut your feet to pieces. This applies equally to snorkellers and divers.

As pretty as they seem to be, there are some creatures that should be avoided, especially sea urchins, blowfish, fire coral, feathery lionfish, moray eels, turkeyfish, stonefish, parrotfish and, needless to say, sharks. Familiarise yourself with pictures of these creatures before snorkelling or diving, especially the latter.

If you just want to paddle about on the coastal beaches, you can go to the fairly unappetising public beach for free or pay between E£5 and E£10 to use one of the resort beaches. Some don't charge at all, or are slack about collecting the money, but if you buy anything like a drink, you'll quickly realise why you're not staying in these places.

Diving Much the same rules apply on preparing a dive trip. Blind faith in your hotel's choice of dive club may not be a good idea. There are so many dive clubs that it is difficult to recommend one over the other. The Swiss Subex outfit has a good reputation, and the operators in the bigger hotels should generally be pretty reliable. Between them, they offer the whole range of diving options, from one-off introductory dives to the most advanced certificates.

Arrange your dive the night before and be sure, if you are going through a hotel, that the proprietor of your hotel or tourist flat has correctly registered your name and passport number.

To get a rough idea of what you'll be paying, a day's diving (two dives) for people with experience costs about US$45, with equipment. An introductory dive is around US$60. A beginner's course (PADI, NAUI or CMAS, depending on the dive shop), will cost in the vicinity of US$250. The advanced PADI Open Water certificate is about US$200. Other courses, such as Divemaster, Rescue and Medical First Aid are offered by some of the dive clubs.

Most of the clubs hire out equipment. The Emperor Divers' Club at the Princess Palace Hotel, for instance, does a full equipment package for six days for US$100.

Other Water Sports Most of the bigger resorts also cater for most other tastes in water sports. Windsurfing at the Three Corners Village resort, for instance, costs E£65 an hour or E£180 a day with all equipment. If you have your own (!) they can store it for you. Jetskis are also available at some hotels.

Organised Tours
In the past few years, the range of possible organised excursions from Hurghada has become all-encompassing. Most of the bigger hotels, some small tour agents and Misr Travel all organise some or all of the following, many of them aimed at people flying in directly on charters and not planning on travelling through the country. You can do a two-day tour to Cairo for E£400, a one-day jaunt to Luxor for E£250. These are the more ambitious on offer. More feasible are some of the desert jeep safaris, which

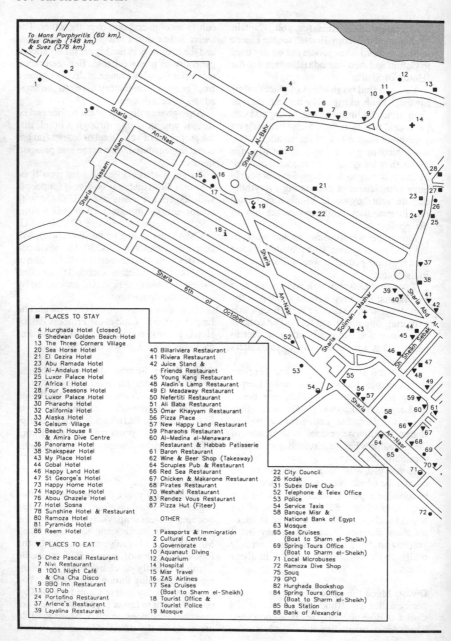

To Mons Porphyritis (60 km),
Ras Gharib (148 km)
& Suez (376 km)

Sharia
Sharia An-Nasr
Sharia Hassam Allam
Sharia Al-Bahr
Sharia An-Nasr
Sharia 6th of October
Sharia Soliman – Mazhar
Sharia Abd Al-
Sharia
Sharia An-Nasr
Sh. Sheikh Sebak

■ PLACES TO STAY

4 Hurghada Hotel (closed)
6 Shedwan Golden Beach Hotel
13 The Three Corners Village
20 Sea Horse Hotel
21 El Gezira Hotel
23 Abu Ramada Hotel
24 Al-Andalus Hotel
25 Luxor Palace Hotel
27 Africa I Hotel
28 Four Seasons Hotel
29 Luxor Palace Hotel
30 Pharaohs Hotel
32 California Hotel
33 Alaska Hotel
34 Geisum Village
35 Beach House II
   & Amira Dive Centre
36 Panorama Hotel
38 Shakspear Hotel
43 My Place Hotel
44 Gobal Hotel
46 Happy Land Hotel
47 St George's Hotel
73 Happy Home Hotel
74 Happy House Hotel
76 Abou Ghazele Hotel
77 Hotel Sosna
78 Sunshine Hotel & Restaurant
80 Ramoza Hotel
81 Pyramids Hotel
86 Reem Hotel

▼ PLACES TO EAT

5 Chez Pascal Restaurant
7 Nivi Restaurant
8 1001 Night Café
   & Cha Cha Disco
9 BBQ Inn Restaurant
11 GO Pub
24 Portofino Restaurant
37 Arlene's Restaurant
39 Layalina Restaurant

40 Billariviera Restaurant
41 Riviera Restaurant
42 Juice Stand &
   Friends Restaurant
45 Young Kang Restaurant
48 Aladin's Lamp Restaurant
49 El Meadway Restaurant
50 Nefertiti Restaurant
51 Ali Baba Restaurant
55 Omar Khayyam Restaurant
56 Pizza Place
57 New Happy Land Restaurant
59 Pharaohs Restaurant
60 Al-Medina al-Menawara
   Restaurant & Habbab Patisserie
61 Baron Restaurant
62 Wine & Beer Shop (Takeaway)
64 Scruples Pub & Restaurant
66 Red Sea Restaurant
67 Chicken & Makarone Restaurant
68 Pirates Restaurant
70 Weshahi Restaurant
83 Rendez Vous Restaurant
87 Pizza Hut (Fiteer)

OTHER

1 Passports & Immigration
2 Cultural Centre
3 Governorate
10 Aquanaut Diving
12 Aquarium
14 Hospital
15 Misr Travel
16 ZAS Airlines
17 Sea Cruises
   (Boat to Sharm el-Sheikh)
18 Tourist Office &
   Tourist Police
19 Mosque

22 City Council
26 Kodak
31 Subex Dive Club
52 Telephone & Telex Office
53 Police
54 Service Taxis
58 Banque Misr &
   National Bank of Egypt
63 Mosque
65 Sea Cruises
   (Boat to Sharm el-Sheikh)
69 Spring Tours Office
   (Boat to Sharm el-Sheikh)
71 Local Microbuses
72 Ramoza Dive Shop
75 Souq
79 GPO
82 Hurghada Bookshop
84 Spring Tours Office
   (Boat to Sharm el-Sheikh)
85 Bus Station
88 Bank of Alexandria

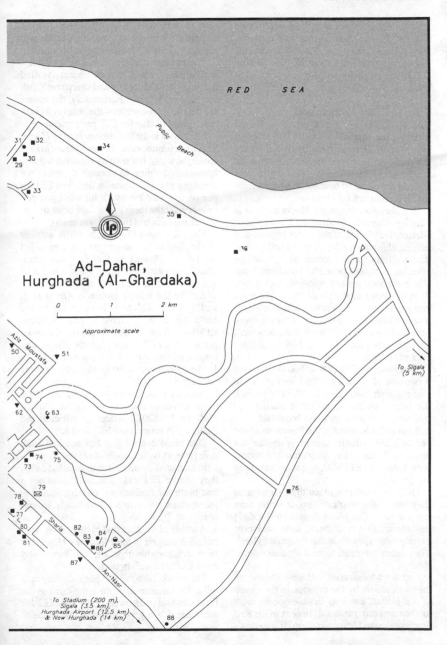

RED SEA

Public Beach

31
32
34
30
29
33
35
36

Ad-Dahar,
Hurghada (Al-Ghardaka)

0   1   2 km

Approximate scale

Aziz Moustafa

50
51

To Sigala
(5 km)

62
63

74
75
73

79
78
77
80
81

Sharia

82
83
84
86
85
87

76

An-Nasr

To Stadium (200 m),
Sigala (3.5 km),
Hurghada Airport (12.5 km)
& New Hurghada (14 km)

88

tend to include visits to at least one of two sites of Roman settlements and quarries, Mons Porphyritis and Mons Claudianus. These trips cost from about E£70 to E£100. A full-day excursion to the monasteries of St Paul and St Anthony costs about E£180.

Places to stay – bottom end

The *Youth Hostel*, if you can be bothered trekking out that way, is not a bad place to stay. The quite reasonable bunk-bed rooms are fairly well kept and the location opposite the Sonesta Beach Resort is fine if you want to hang out on resort beaches. It's E£5 a night and E£2.50 extra for breakfast.

The *Sunshine House* on Sharia an-Nasr is run by Captain Mohammed's nephew, Mohia. This is one of the better bottom-end places, although the location is a little noisy. The well-maintained rooms have window-screens, rugs and powerful overhead fans. The bathrooms are kept spotless, with water, even hot water, available 24 hours. There's a common room and a kitchen with a refrigerator available for guests. The common room becomes a sort of dorm when travellers can't find another place to stay. Mohia charges E£5 per person.

The *Ramoza Hotel* (☎ 446608) is almost a two-star place. It's not bad, and a double without/with bath costs E£10/15, although the prices are apt to go up if business is booming. The price includes breakfast.

Next to the Ramoza is the *Pyramids Hotel* (☎ 446625), which is slightly better for about the same price. Single/double rooms with baths are E£15/20; without bath they are E£10/15.

Over the road is a place that, so long as they don't hike their rates up, is better than the last two. The *Hotel Sosna* (☎ 446647) has rooms that are clean, new and cost exactly what they do at the Pyramids Hotel. They seem prepared to be bargained down too.

Captain Mohammed's *Happy House*, on the main square by the mosque in the centre of Ad-Dahar, has two double rooms with kitchen and refrigerator. It is next to his Red Sea Wonderland souvenir shop. If you don't

plan to stay here, it's still worth at least stopping by to see the souvenir store and listen to Captain Mohammed's fish stories.

The store is a study in seashore kitsch – seashell lamps and picture frames, stuffed fish with protruding lips and sharp teeth, fish nets and cork floats. Fortunately, the rooms are devoid of souvenirs – the hotel is a clean basic place to stay for E£7 per person.

Next door is the two-storey *Happy Home*. Signs, announcements and decorations cover the walls, but with an Austrian woman apparently helping to manage it, prices are sneaking up. The place is fine, but E£10 a person is a little too much for what you get, unless you take them up on their offer of free use of the beach at the Geisum resort.

Near the main Coptic church is another cheap place with a homey atmosphere called *My Place – Raoul's Budget Paradise*. Paradise is overstating it, but it's not a bad deal at E£5 a head. Breakfast is an extra E£2.

Behind the Happy House is *Africa II*. It and *Africa I*, which is down closer to the Sand Beach resort, have rooms for about E£7/14. Africa II does breakfast, the other place doesn't. They are friendly places, and may be willing to come down a little at Africa I, where, by the way, the quality of the rooms varies considerably.

Another inexpensive place that travellers have recommended is the *Luxor Palace Hotel* (☎ 447820). It's near the Africa I, and small, quiet rooms cost E£7.50/15.

One place nearby that has not had such rave reviews is the *California Hotel*. Supposedly managed by an Australian called Sally, they charge E£10/15. The rooftop is not a bad place for sunbathing, but this joint has the thinnest mattresses of the hotels around here.

Another place here that claims to be Australian-managed is the *Pharaohs Hotel*. It's more comfortable than the California and costs E£12/20 with breakfast.

The *Alaska*, around and back slightly up a hill in the same area, is much the same as the Pharaohs and charges E£12/15 plus E£2 for breakfast. It's a good, comfortable place to stay.

Also here is the *Four Seasons* hotel. The entrance is on the left side. They have very comfortable rooms, but the prices are hurtling out of the budget travellers' range. Singles/doubles with breakfast cost E£30/35.

The *St George's Hotel* in the centre of Ad-Dahar, just by the Aladin's Lamp Restaurant, is no deal at all, despite the signs posted up all over town. Exceedingly average rooms without bath or breakfast cost E£15/20, and with bath another E£5 on top.

On the road leading back into town from hotels like the California you'll find the *Abu Ramada* (☎ 440618). If they actually have a room, it'll cost E£20 a head. They seem to be reticent about letting rooms out here, so maybe they aren't so hot. Across the road, the *Al-Andalus Hotel* (☎ 442639) has OK rooms for E£15/25, but don't go out of your way to stay here. There are some great views of building sites.

A little further down the road is the *Shakespear* (☎ 446256), spelt in various ways. It has some very spacious, comfortable doubles for about E£25 – ask to see a few rooms to compare, because some are much better than others. Most come with baths and all have fans.

A couple of places in this same upper end of the budget bracket are the Gobal and the Happy Land, both in the same street. The *Gobal Hotel* (☎ 446623) has singles/doubles with breakfast, and sometimes with own bath, for E£15/25. All the rooms have fans and the bathrooms are clean with plenty of hot water.

The *Happy Land Hotel* is cheaper if there are two of you, as rooms cost E£15 whether you are alone or in twos. Breakfast is E£3 extra and the bathrooms are outside. It's quite OK.

Camping It is possible to camp in the grounds of the *Geisum* resort for E£5 per person and E£10 per vehicle. You get access to the showers and the beach. There is a *National Youth Camp* about six km north of town, but they say you need to book ahead

in Cairo – by the looks of the place, you really wouldn't want to.

Places to Stay – middle

There is a cluster of hotels in Sigala, south of the port and on the way out to the string of resorts (and Youth Hostel) that stretch about 15 km down the coast.

The *New Star Hotel* has air-conditioned singles/doubles/triples for E£25/35/50 with breakfast. The rooms are quite good and cost slightly less if you opt for a fan instead of air-conditioning.

The *White House*, a new place just up the road, has rooms for E£35/50/60, and *La Bambola* (☎ 442085), a three-star place across the road, has singles/doubles for about E£80/105. They have a disco, as does the *Golf Hotel* next door. There are one or two other pretty crummy places here. If you want to be crummy, why do it here?

The *Moon Valley Village* (☎ 442811) marks the beginning of the resort stretch. It has 30 rooms of varying quality, and a good aspect over the Red Sea. The better rooms cost E£60/75, while the simpler ones go for E£35/45. They have a private chunk of beach directly across the road. It's a bit overpriced really.

Back in Ad-Dahar, the *Sea Horse Hotel* (☎ 443704) is quite a good three-star place that, as with many of its ilk, caters mainly to tour groups. Most rooms have air-con, TV, phone, wall-to-wall carpet and their own bath. The views from some are good. In winter, rooms costs E£88/117, but come down to E£68/90 in summer.

The *El Gezira Hotel* (☎ & fax 443708) is adjacent to the Sea Horse. All the rooms have air-con, telephones, carpeting and private bathrooms. A few rooms also have TV. Single/double rooms are E£55/75 in winter and about E£15 less in summer. The same company owns the Sand Beach Hotel, so you can use their beach and pool for free.

On the beach in front of the El-Gezira and the Seahorse is the *Hurghada Hotel*, at present closed.

Up past the Three Corners Village and the Sand Beach Hotel is the *Geisum Village*

(☎ 446692; fax 447995). It's the cheapest of these places right on the beach, at US$35/40 for singles and doubles.

Places to Stay – top end

The hotels in this category, as in fact many of the middle ones already mentioned, cater mainly, if not almost exclusively, to groups, who get discounts just for being part of the organised tourism game. Travel agencies in Europe and Cairo offer reductions on these places if you book in advance. In Cairo many of the agencies along Sharia Talaat Harb and Midan Tahrir have signs in their front windows advertising special deals for these places.

The southernmost resort, about 17 km from Ad-Dahar (the main part of Hurghada), is the *Jasmine Village* (☎ 442442; fax 442441), which has 434 bungalow-style air-conditioned rooms and caters mostly to German groups. As with most of the other complexes, it has a full water-sports centre, including a diving and windsurfing centre. Singles/doubles range in price from US$33/47 to US$40/57. It is in fact only a three-star place.

New places, such as the *Coral Beach* and *Palm Beach*, are in different stages of construction further south. One km further north is the *Beach Albatross*, a Swiss-owned resort.

Next comes the four-star *Magawish Tourist Village* (☎ 442620; fax 442759). Singles/doubles here start at US$54/68. It's operated by Misr Travel, so you can get more information, particularly on possible discounts, from them.

One of this resort's distinguishing features is its dive centre – it has a decompression chamber that, at the time of writing, was up and running. This has not always been the case, due to the absence of staff able to operate it. When it is out of operation, the tendency until now has been to ship people in need of one to Eilat, in Israel, although the presence of a shiny new US-funded one in Sharm el-Sheikh should obviate the need for that.

A few km of blessed emptiness separate Magawish from the next place, which is the relatively low-grade *Hurghada Beach Hotel* (☎ 443710; fax 4422603), formerly the Hur Palace Hotel. It has a flat US$35 rate on rooms, plus taxes and breakfast. From here until you exit Hurghada on the north side, it is practically wall-to-wall hotels, resorts and construction sites. What free land there is seems bound to end up going the same way sooner or later.

Next door is the *Princess Palace Hotel* (☎ 443100/1/2/3/4; fax 443109) with 25 villas and 68 rooms at a variety of rates depending on whether you want a view of the garden or swimming pool, neither of which is spectacular. They have a diving centre offering just about every course imaginable – the Emperor Divers' Club run by Terry Simpson. Rates for single/double rooms are US$27/36.

The *El Samaka Club* (☎ 443014, 442227) is yet another group tourism place, again with a heavy German emphasis. It has a windsurfing and diving centre. Singles/doubles are US$38/60 with half board.

The *Giftun Village* (☎ 442666) has 282 bright whitewashed rooms with polished floors and air-con. There's also a diving and windsurfing centre known as the Barakuda International Aquanautic Club. Next to it is the new *Sonesta Beach Resort* (☎ 443661; fax 443660). They seem fairly slack here about letting you on to their rather nice beach. Bring something to drink and eat though; a cup of Coca-Cola here costs as much as a half dozen bottles of the stuff outside.

The *Sheraton Hotel* (☎ 442000; fax 442033), seven km south of town, has rooms ranging from US$58 for a single to US$192 for a suite. These prices are exclusive of breakfast and taxes. Check with Sheraton International for the latest rates because they are subject to change according to the seasons. If you use the Sheraton beach you'll supposedly have to pay E£5 for the privilege, but as with the Sonesta, it seems possible to sneak in.

In town along the waterfront is the *Shedwan Golden Beach Hotel* (☎ 447007;

fax 443045). Although the rooms are fine for a tourist group vacation, they are overpriced for individual travellers. The rooms have air-con, tiled floors and private bathrooms. Their single/double/triple rooms are US$67.50/95/135.

The *Three Corners Village* (☎ 447816; fax 447514) has 132 rooms and considers itself 'the best touristic resort in Hurghada'. Located on the beach in Ad-Dahar, most of the rooms have sea views. They have a good windsurfing centre and organise diving and snorkelling trips. The nearby Chez Pascal restaurant and Cha Cha Disco are part of the same group. Singles/doubles/triples cost E£111/173/236. As usual, mainly groups stay here at discounted rates. Next to it is the *Sand Beach Hotel* (☎ 447821; fax 447822), a three-star place with rooms for US$56/70.

Places to Eat
Ad-Dahar The *Baron* is a cheap and cheerful little eatery in the thick of things in Ad-Dahar. A satisfying meal of chicken, fasooliyya, rice and salad will cost you about E£4. Another cheap place nearby is the *El Meadaway*.

A few metres further down from it and in a side lane to the right is the *Aladin's Lamp*. They do a small plate of calamari for E£5.50 and chicken for E£8. It's a cosy little niche to crawl into away from the bustle outside.

Opposite the Baron is the more pretentious and expensive cheapie, if there is such a thing, called the *Al-Medina al-Menawara* and next to it the *Habbab* patisserie. A couple of doors from the Baron towards Sharia an-Nasr is a nameless chicken makarone place.

There are a few other cheap eating places around the Happy House Hotel, including one called *Zeko*, which is just across the square. You'll also find a couple of cafés around here.

Next to the fairly pricey *Riviera* Italian restaurant, which seems chronically empty, is what seems to be about the only juice stand – it's not cheap either. Behind it is the fairly unassuming *Friends* restaurant.

If you're hankering for a fiteer, you could do worse than try the unassuming little *Pizza*

Hut place across the road from the bus station, where a decent-sized fiteer costs about E£5 to E£7 depending on toppings and bargaining.

The *Omar Khayyam*, down Sharia an-Nasr towards the telephone office, has half chickens for E£8 and Stella for E£4, not a bad combination.

The *Billariviera* (sic) has a big range of pizzas, although the differences between a lot of them seem minimal. Next door to it is the *Layalina Restaurant*.

If it's Far Eastern cooking you're after, head for *Young Kang*, next door to the Gobal Hotel. The food here, although not the cheapest around, is very good. The computer printout bills are a little on the impersonal side.

It seems no small coincidence that a lot of visiting US servicemen from the Multinational Force & Observers group (MFO) across in the Sinai end up having a meal at *Arlene's*, on Sharia Abd al-Aziz Mustafa. Main courses cost around E£15 to E£20. This is one of the few places in Egypt you'll find nachos.

A little further down and across the street is another supposedly Italian place (no Italians actually run any of these joints), the *Portofino*. The food is a little expensive, but they serve Stella in nice mugs.

The *Nefertiti* Restaurant, around the corner from the Gobal Hotel on Sharia Abd al-Aziz Mustafa, serves up calamari for E£12, some casserole dishes that aren't bad at all and a limited variety of seafood. The 'milkshakes', at E£4 a pop, are not much good.

The *Nivi* Restaurant is one of several mid to upper-range places down near the waterfront. It has pizzas of a sort for around E£15, seafood, grills and a takeaway stand.

On the corner to the right of the Nivi is the *BBQ Inn*, a more expensive place than its name might suggest. To the left of the Nivi is the Belgian-run *Chez Pascal*, a posh restaurant connected to the Three Corners Village.

Just south of the Omar Khayyam, on Sharia an-Nasr, is the *New Happy Land*, which tends to concentrate on seafood. Lobster goes for E£75 a kg, if you can eat that much (smaller serves are available).

Across the road from the National Bank of Egypt is *Scruples*, which describes itself as a 'pub and steak house', so presumably you can get a Stella and a steak here.

Outside Ad-Dahar There are several fairly nondescript cheapies in Sigala, but a couple of places are worth singling out. The *El-Sakia* restaurant is right down on the water's edge. The food, a mixture of seafood and Egyptian cuisine, is good but a little expensive, with mains averaging E£20. If nothing else, it's a pleasant place to sit outside and enjoy a beer.

You'll know you've reached the turn-off for El-Sakia when you see the *Samos* Greek restaurant on the main street, which leads off to the resort strip heading south. It's not bad, with average prices. It opens for dinner at 6 pm.

A couple of km along the road, past the Moon Valley Village, is the best located *Felfela* restaurant in the country. Sitting on a rise and gentle bend in the coastline, it is a splendid place for a modestly priced meal – which is the standard fare served up by this growing chain (see Cairo Places to Eat for more on the original restaurant and its outgrowths).

The resorts all have restaurants catering to most tastes, but are generally suitably expensive and sometimes quite uninspiring.

Entertainment

Most of the bigger hotels offer belly-dancing performances in their discos, which brings us to the second form of entertainment – discos. The *Cha Cha Disco* in Ad-Dahar has a so-called reggae night on Sunday. For this kind of activity you virtually have no choice but to go to the big hotels.

The *Three Corners Village* occasionally puts on movies; ask at reception.

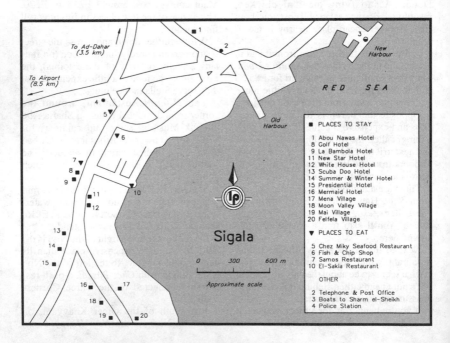

PLACES TO STAY

1 Abou Nawas Hotel
8 Golf Hotel
9 La Bambola Hotel
11 New Star Hotel
12 White House Hotel
13 Scuba Doo Hotel
14 Summer & Winter Hotel
15 Presidential Hotel
16 Mermaid Hotel
17 Mena Village
18 Moon Valley Village
19 Mai Village
20 Felfela Village

PLACES TO EAT

5 Chez Miky Seafood Restaurant
6 Fish & Chip Shop
7 Samos Restaurant
10 El-Sakia Restaurant

OTHER

2 Telephone & Post Office
3 Boats to Sharm el-Sheikh
4 Police Station

Sigala

Things to Buy

Apart from the usual run-of-the-mill tourist trinkets, you could buy an odd assortment of seashells (on sale in shops and throughout the markets in Ad-Dahar) or, even weirder, stuffed fish – even small sharks! What would you do with them though?

Getting There & Away

Air The EgyptAir office is inconveniently located seemingly in the middle of nowhere up the road from the Sonesta Beach Resort. ZAS has an office in Ad-Dahar by the main mosque. EgyptAir has a daily flight between Cairo and Hurghada. It costs E£309 one way. ZAS also has a flight to Cairo, en route from Frankfurt. At the time of writing, there were no other internal flights operating out of Hurghada, although in peak periods there may be flights to Sharm el-Sheikh.

Bus The Upper Egypt Bus Co runs at least eight buses to Cairo from Hurghada. The four ordinary buses leave at 5 and 7 am and 9.30 and 10 pm, and cost E£24. The four Super Jet buses – in other words, the comfy ones with loud videos – leave at 10 am and 1, 3 and 4 pm, costing E£30.

A couple of these set down in Suez as well, but some bypass it. There are other buses bound for Suez only. The cheapest, at E£14, leave at 9.30, 10 and 10.30 am. The 7 am bus has video (just what you need at that time of the morning) and costs E£18. So does the 9.30 pm service. The 3.30 and 5 pm buses cost E£15.

The 7 pm is the Super Jet, which usually means on-board toilet and snack service in addition to the video and air-con. It costs E£27.

There are nine buses a day to Qena starting at 6 am and finishing up at 11 pm. The rides cost E£7, except for the last one, which costs a couple of E£ more.

The Luxor buses at 6 am, noon and 3 pm all cost E£7.50. The 11 pm one costs E£11.

The 3.30 pm service to Aswan (which one would have thought would stop in Luxor) costs E£27. The 11 pm bus to Qena and Luxor goes on to Aswan for E£30.

There is a bus to Al-Quseir that goes on to Marsa Alam and Bir Shalatayn at 7 am. The fare to Al-Quseir is E£7.

There are also occasional services to Beni Suef, Al-Minya, Sohag and Asyut, and more regular ones to Qift and Qus.

This timetable should be checked, as changes are more than likely. It may be an idea to book ahead on the longer-distance rides such as Luxor and Cairo.

Service Taxi The service taxi station is near the telephone office. Taxis go to Cairo for E£30 a head (a trip of about six hours) – you'll save E£5.50 by getting a service taxi as far as Suez and getting another one from there to Cairo for E£4.50. Others go to Suez (E£20, 3½ to four hours); Qena (E£8); Al-Quseir (E£8) and Port Safaga (E£3). They don't go to Luxor or Aswan – although of course you could always try to bargain one into going. They seem to want you to pay some kind of E£10 fee for a mysterious 'ticket', in addition to the fare. Simply marching off in the direction of the bus station seems to sometimes get them to drop it. If not, keep heading for the bus station.

Boat Two companies compete for the boat trade from Hurghada to Sharm el-Sheikh. There supposedly exists a hovercraft, but it never seems to be in action. So you can take the Spring Tours *Moreen II* or the more modern *Shark II*, or Sea Cruises' *Silver Moon*. There are one or more sailings a day (except on Friday, when there are none), depending on demand, at about 8.30 am. Although it's possible to get a ticket at the port on the morning, it's safer to book ahead. You can do this in one of the offices of the companies concerned or through your hotel. The cost is E£70 however you go about it, although one or two hotels claim to be able to get tickets for less. If you book it through the hotel, they'll probably bundle you into a taxi or microbus on the morning to get you to the port, which is in Sigala.

The trip takes about five hours and as the boats are relatively small, it can be an irksome ride if the Red Sea is heaving at all.

Lie down or look up, and try to ignore the people being sick around you.

Getting Around
To/From the Airport From the airport to central Hurghada, the taxi fare is E£10.

Bus In the mornings, microbuses full of day labourers go almost all the way to the Jasmine Village for about E£1. Throughout the day, microbuses regularly run at least as far south as the El Samaka Hotel for 50 pt. This appears to be the terminus.

Taxi Taxis will take you as far south as the Sheraton for about E£8 (or more if there are plenty of tourists around). Taxi drivers here are, appropriately enough, a school of sharks.

Motorbike A little booth (☎ 443100/1) opposite the Princess Palace (aka the Princess Club) Hotel rents out motorbikes. The booth is open only from 6 to 9 pm, so you're better off calling them and fixing an appointment to see what they have to offer.

Bicycle Bicycles can be rented in town for E£4 to E£6 for the day or at an hourly rate to be haggled over.

Hitching It's sometimes possible to hitch around town or out to the beaches, but the locals seem accustomed to receiving payment from travellers.

AROUND HURGHADA
Mons Porphyritis
About 40 km into the desert, along a side track off the main coast road 20 km north of Hurghada, lie ancient porphyry quarries worked by the Romans. The precious white and purple crystalline stone was mined for use in sarcophagi, columns and other decorative work. The quarries were under the direct control of the imperial family in Rome, which had encampments, workshops and even temples built for the workers and engineers here. Evidence, albeit not much of it standing, of this quarry town can still be

seen. Tours out of Hurghada increasingly make the trip. If you want to do it yourself, make sure you have a guide or driver who knows the way. Taxi drivers eager to make a pound have been known to volunteer for the job without really knowing what they are doing. This is unpleasant territory to get stuck in without adequate water.

Sharm an-Naga
About half way down to Port Safaga, this is a fairly low-key beach resort with some tents and bungalows. Some tour companies use it.

PORT SAFAGA
Port Safaga, 53 km south of Hurghada, is first and foremost a port for the export of phosphates from local mines. It is hardly an attractive place to hang about, but there are a few small hotels at the northern end of town and some expensive resorts, some still in the throes of construction, further north still. The plague of construction around Hurghada is thus repeated on a smaller scale here.

Orientation & Information
The main waterfront road, Sharia al-Gomhurriya, has most of the services you

might need. The bus station is towards the southern end of town. Heading north there is a motley collection of small eateries and tacky souvenir stalls, and beyond them the post office. About 2.5 km north of the bus station is the service-taxi station. About 200 metres north is the main telephone and telex office. Around the telephone office are branches of Banque Misr, the Banque du Caire and the National Bank of Egypt. Further north, near the Mekka Hotel, is the Bank of Alexandria. You can catch a micro-bus up and down Sharia al-Gomhurriya for 10 pt.

Things to See & Do
There's not really much in either category, although some of the beaches are good for **swimming** and **snorkelling**. Check at the bigger hotels for some of the better possibilities.

About 40 km along the Qena road, a track breaks off south towards **Mons Claudianus**, a one-time Roman fortress complex for the protection of nearby quarries. You really need a guide for this trip, but the bigger hotels may organise excursions there. There are remains of a Roman road, columns and other evidence of the quarries and Roman military presence.

Places to Stay & Eat
There are a few cheap and basic hotels to stay in at the northern end of town. The *Mekka Hotel* costs E£10 a night and the *Amarna* is similar. Neither have all that much to recommend them. The *Cleopatra Hotel* is better, but costs about E£32/40 for singles/doubles with bath and breakfast.

Heading out of town there are at least four resorts: the *Sun Beach Camp*, the *Menaville*, *Shams Safaga* and the *Safaga Paradise*. The latter three cost about US$50 and up a night for a single before taxes. More are on the way.

As already noted, there is a whole string of cheap eats heading north from the bus station along Sharia al-Gomhurriya. Otherwise, you could try the expensive resort restaurants. They also have discos.

Getting There & Away
Bus There are buses going all over the place, many of them originating elsewhere, which goes part of the way to explaining what a piddly dump the station is. There are buses to Cairo at 3 and 6 pm. The fare is at least E£34 (the people here don't like giving out any information, so add an extra pinch of salt to these). The same buses stop in Suez for E£17. There are at least six or seven buses to Hurghada, costing from E£3 to E£5. More or less regular services to Qena cost E£5. Less regular services to Luxor and on to Aswan cost around E£6 and E£14 respectively.

Service Taxi The taxis basically do three routes. Hurghada takes about 40 minutes and costs E£3. The trip to Al-Quseir (try early in the morning) costs E£3.50, and to Qena E£8.

AL-QUSEIR
Al-Quseir, a medieval port town of 4000 inhabitants, is 85 km south of Port Safaga and about 160 km east of Qift on the Nile. Until the 10th century it was one of the most important exit points for pilgrims travelling to Mecca and was also a thriving centre of trade and export between the Nile Valley and the Red Sea and beyond. After centuries of neglect, the Ottomans cranked it up again for a while, but the opening of the Suez Canal in 1869 put an end to all that.

The place must be popular with Italians, as everyone seems to think *buon giorno* is the logical first move to make when saying hello to strangers.

Orientation & Information
A branch of the National Bank of Egypt is just north of the main roundabout on the way into town from Port Safaga. The telephone office, which is open 24 hours a day, is right on the roundabout, while the post office is off to the left, down towards the waterfront.

Things to See & Do
There are an old **fort** and a small **souq** which are worth checking out, and there's excellent **snorkelling** from various beaches around town.

One that is often recommended is **Kilo Ashara**, a small beach 10 km south of town. You can't really miss it, as it's one of the few obvious places for a swim on your way out of town – one of the many Red Sea coast military installations is up on the bluff at the southern end. If you can read Arabic numerals, follow the small yellow mileage markers out of town. It's almost exactly 10 km. You just wade in and start marvelling at the fish. Watch out for the moray eels. If you talk to the locals, they'll recommend other beaches as well, most of them seemingly placed at suspiciously convenient-sounding 10-km intervals.

Places to Stay & Eat
The obvious choice is the *Sea Princess Hotel* (☎ 430044), just south of the bus station. Singles/doubles cost E£9/14 plus taxes. Breakfast is a couple of E£ on top. They have a few masks and snorkels to rent. The toilet/shower combinations are clean, but hot water is unreliable.

Further south, right on the beach (don't get too excited, it's not at its best here) are some bungalows run by the local town hall. They're not bad at E£20 a head with your own bath and cooker. The pain is you have to head to the northern end of town to look for someone at the town hall who can give you the appropriate pieces of paper before you can actually move in – perfectly designed to make most people go to the Sea Princess.

A couple of km north of town are *Samia's* bungalows. Samia is a nice enough chap, but his bungalows are nothing special at E£15 for two.

Well, soon you won't have to worry about all that, for the biggies have discovered Al-Quseir. *Mövenpick* were due to open their five-star monstrosity, seven km north of the town, in 1994.

Foodwise, the options are limited. The people in the Sea Princess can cook you up something. Otherwise, there are a few ta'amiyya and fish joints around it and the bus station. the nicest place to have a cup of coffee is at the *Café Samir Nana*, which is right on the waterfront about half way between the bus station and the Sea Princess. The young owner hopes to have a few guest rooms ready on the 1st floor by the end of 1994.

Getting There & Away
Bus There is a bus all the way to Cairo at 8 pm. It goes via Port Safaga, Hurghada and Suez. The trip costs E£38 and takes about 11 hours. The bus south to Marsa Alam and beyond leaves at 3.30 pm and costs E£5. There are two connections for the four or so hour trip to Qena, which costs E£6. The first leaves at 7 am and the second at 12.30 pm.

Service Taxi The service-taxi station is at the southern end of town. Taxis leave when full, which doesn't always happen all that quickly. The officially prescribed fares are: Cairo E£30; Suez E£25; Hurghada E£6; Port Safaga E£3.25; Qena E£8; and Qift E£7.

Getting Around
Nasser's Baiskels has a few old bicycles for rent. He wants E£5 for the day, but can probably be bargained down. His workshop is virtually opposite the service-taxi station (and about 100 metres from the Sea Princess Hotel) near the southern exit of town.

AROUND AL-QUSEIR
One could just as easily say 'around Qena', for about half way along the road connecting the two towns is an interesting but rarely visited collection of Pharaonic graffiti. The wayward chisellings of Wadi Hammamet were first extensively examined by the Russian Egyptologist Vladimir Golenischeff late last century. The high, smooth walls of the wadi have made it an ideal resting place for travellers down through the ages, and indeed there is graffiti from post-Pharaonic times as well, right down to Egypt's 20th century King Farouk. The road runs on an ancient trade path, and remains of old wells and other evidence of the trail's long history can also be seen. You could get the early bus from Al-Quseir or Qena (one leaves each at 7 am) to drop you at Wadi Hammamet, and

try to get a lift on the next one either way about four or five hours later, or simply hitch.

MARSA ALAM
Marsa Alam is a fishing village 132 km south of Al-Quseir. A road also connects the village with Edfu, 230 km across the desert to the west. Phosphate mining is the big thing in this part of the country, and an exploration company is looking for new sources of mineral wealth in the area. The village is basically a T-junction of the road from Edfu with the coast road. South of the junction is the bulk of the village with a small, incongruous-looking shopping arcade (which has a pharmacy), a school and a telephone office, from where you can sometimes call overseas.

The main thing to do here is have a swim and snorkel. There is some good diving south of the town, and one enterprising guy brought his own inflatable boat and diving gear to explore the area. As a military pass is required for travel south of Marsa Alam, you may not be able to use what is apparently a particularly good snorkelling beach seven km south of the town. But you can still see some marine life from the beaches just north of town.

About 70 km south-west into the desert is the tomb of Sayyid ash-Shadhili, a 13th century sheikh who is revered by many as one of the more important Sufi leaders. His tomb was restored under the orders of King Farouk in 1947, but without a guide is nearly impossible to find.

Where you see loads of barbed wire, be cautious about stepping in – it appears some of the coastal area is mined, although not necessarily right on the beaches. Ask a local.

Places to Stay & Eat
About one km north of the Edfu turn-off is the mining exploration company's rest house *(istiraha)*. If the rooms aren't all occupied by employees, it's a good place to stay. At E£10 a night for a room, you get the use of a kitchen, fridge and lounge room, and have your own porch.

The only alternative, apart from simply pitching a tent somewhere on the beach, is the huddle of bungalows and tents that make up the *Beach Safari* camp about seven km north of the town. Beach Safari has an office in the town's shopping arcade, about 200 metres south of the road junction.

There are a couple of cafés at the junction, where you can occasionally get some ta'amiyya. There are a couple of grocery stores there too. That's it.

Getting There & Away
The bus across the desert from Edfu leaves at about 9 am. It takes about four hours, depending on checkpoint delays, and costs E£6. It goes on to Bir Shalatayn, but at the time of writing it was unlikely you'd get past the military checkpoint south of Marsa Alam. The bus going the other way leaves from the cafés at the junction at about 9 am. Another bus goes up to Hurghada (E£8) at about the same time, stopping in Al-Quseir (E£5) and Port Safaga. A bus coming down the other way leaves Al-Quseir at 3.30 pm. The trip takes about two hours on a patchy road that, in the unlikely event of rain, tends to become unusable.

BERENICE
The military centre and small port of Berenice, 145 km south of Marsa Alam, was founded in 275 BC by Ptolemy II Euergetes I and was an important trading post until the 5th century AD. Near the town, the ruins of the Temple of Seramis can be seen. The US Navy occasionally brings its aircraft carriers here. Apparently, this is one of the staging areas for the US Rapid Deployment Forces. As a military permit is required for travel south of Marsa Alam, it may not be possible to get this far south down the coast.

BIR SHALATAYN
This tiny village 75 km south of Berenice marks the administrative boundary between Egypt and the Sudan, although Egypt at least considers the political boundary to be another 175 km south, beyond the town of Halaib, once an important Red Sea port but long fallen into obscurity.

Alexandria & the Mediterranean Coast

On the north coast of Egypt, west of where the Rosetta branch of the Nile leaves the Delta and where the barren desert meets the sparkling waters of the Mediterranean, is the charming, although somewhat jaded, city of Alexandria, once the shining gem of the Hellenistic world. Nearby are the Mediterranean resorts of Sidi Abdel Rahman and Marsa Matruh and the famous town of El Alamein, where the tide of the African campaign during WW II was changed in favour of the Allies. The rest of this region is sparsely populated. The road westward to the Libyan border passes along an almost deserted coast that greets the sea with craggy cliffs or smooth sandy beaches.

Alexandria

History

Having conquered Greece, the Macedonian general who became known as Alexander the Great set his sights on Egypt and the Persian Empire. After leading his victorious troops south to Memphis in 332 BC, Alexander followed the Nile back to the Mediterranean and chose a fishing village as the site of his capital, Alexandria.

Alexander designed the city carefully, for he envisioned it as a naval base, a great trading port, and the political and cultural centre of his empire. Although he is said to be buried there, Alexander did not see the gift he gave the classical world, nor probably did he imagine the greatness it would achieve. Its architecture was as impressive as that of Rome or Athens, and in the last three centuries BC it attracted some of the finest artists and scholars of the time, becoming a renowned centre of scientific, philosophical and literary thought and learning.

Under the Ptolemies, who ruled Egypt after Alexander, Alexandria developed into a major port on the trade routes between Europe and Asia. The city's library once contained 500,000 volumes, and its research institute, the Mouseion, produced some of the most scholarly works of the age. The Pharos lighthouse, built on an island just offshore, was one of the Seven Wonders of the World.

During the reign of Cleopatra, the last of the Ptolemies, Alexandria rivalled Rome in everything but military power. After a brief liaison with Julius Caesar, Cleopatra married Marc Antony, who was high on the list to replace the assassinated statesman as leader of the Roman Empire. But the union of the Egyptian queen and the Roman general was not popular in Rome, especially with Caesar's nephew Octavian, whose sister was already married to Marc Antony.

In the ensuing power struggle, the Egyptian fleet was defeated at Actium in 31 BC by the superior forces of Octavian, who later

Alexander the Great

changed his name to Augustus and declared himself emperor of Rome. As Octavian led his forces towards Egypt, Cleopatra, rather than face capture, reputedly put an asp to her breast and ended the Ptolemaic dynasty.

Alexandria, the most powerful and prosperous provincial capital of the Roman Empire, remained the capital of Egypt for the next 600 years under Roman and Byzantine control. Although the original great library had been burned when the Romans had first tried to conquer Alexandria, Cleopatra had begun another collection in a new building alongside the famed Serapeum. The city was still regarded as the most learned place on earth. With nearly a million inhabitants, it was second only to Rome in size

But during the 4th century AD, Alexandria's populace was ravaged by insurrection, civil war, famine and disease, and although the city later became a centre of Christianity, it never regained its former glory. At the end of the century, the city's cultural importance was almost wiped out as Christianity became the official religion of the Roman Empire. Bishop Theophilus, Emperor Theodosius' right-hand man, had the Serapeum closed and partly destroyed. Later it was made into a church. All pagan temples were razed and learned institutes (including the Mouseion), along with the theatre, were closed.

The conquering Muslims abandoned Alexandria in the 7th century and established their new capital further south on the Nile. When the French arrived in the 19th century, Cairo had long since replaced Alexandria as Egypt's major city, and the latter was again little more than a fishing village with a population of 6000.

Napoleon's invasion, however, reinstated Alexandria's strategic importance, and it underwent a revival during the reign of Mohammed Ali when new docks, an arsenal, and a canal linking the city with the Nile were built. The stage was set for Alexandria's return as a vital Mediterranean trade centre; when the Suez Canal was completed in 1869, the city's position as a major modern port was assured.

The city also became cosmopolitan, attracting Europeans, Turks and wealthy Egyptians and providing the inspiration for Lawrence Durrell's novels known collectively as *The Alexandria Quartet*. During WW II the city was an Allied post, and part of the pivotal Battle of El Alamein was planned by Allied Intelligence from the Hotel Cecil. The revolution that brought Gamal Abdel Nasser to power in 1952 also, to an extent, struck a death knell for Alexandria's colourful European community. Probably the biggest contingent, the Greeks (there were as many as 125,000 in the city in their heyday) began to flood out of the country, many minus the properties and belongings nationalised by the new government. The Greek community in Alexandria today numbers little more than 500 – most of them seem to run restaurants (the only thing, according to one, that the government didn't nationalise).

Today Alexandria is the largest port in Egypt, a major industrial centre, and the country's unofficial summer capital, with a population of five million. Every year the perfect Mediterranean climate, the relaxed atmosphere, and the city's reputation for the best food in the country draw thousands of holiday-makers to the waterfront cafés and beautiful beaches.

The port handles about 80% of Egypt's import and export trade; more than 5000 ships call at Alexandria annually. It is cleaner and less congested than Cairo, and although it thrives to a certain extent on the romantic reputation of its past, it is still a warm and welcoming city.

Orientation

Alexandria is a true waterfront city, nearly 20 km long from east to west and only two km wide. The main port is on the western side of the Ras at-Tin (variously spelt Ras el Tin, Ras el Teen) promontory, while the Eastern Harbour, in front of the Corniche, is used mostly by fishing and pleasure craft. The tip of the promontory was once Pharos Island, where the famous lighthouse stood, but silting gradually formed the causeway

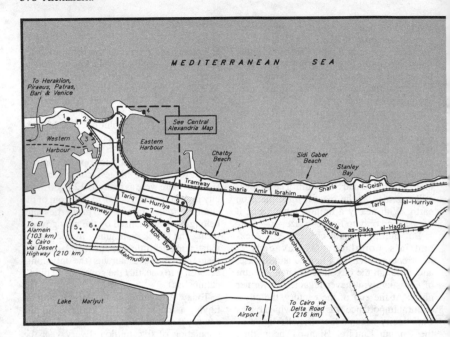

that now connects the island with the mainland.

Sharia 26th of July sweeps from the tip of the promontory east along the beaches towards Montazah Palace. Along the way its name changes to Sharia al-Geish. These two seaside streets are referred to collectively as the Corniche.

Whereas in Cairo 'sharia' is translated as 'street', in Alexandria it's French that rules and it becomes 'rue'.

The focal point of the city is Midan Saad Zaghloul, a large square running on to the waterfront. Around the midan, and in the streets to the south and west, are the central shopping area, tourist office, airline offices, restaurants, and cheaper hotels. Just east of the midan is Ramla Station, the central tram depot in Midan Ramla. In fact, with the two squares so close to each other, the whole area is generally known as Ramla. Asking for Midan Saad Zaghloul is likely to get blank expressions.

Sharia an-Nabi (or Nebi) Daniel runs approximately north-south through this area, from Midan Saad Zaghloul to Midan al-Gomhurriya, which is the square in front of Masr Station, the main terminal for trains to Cairo. The city's main east-west thoroughfare, Tariq al-Hurriya (*tariq* means road), intersects Sharia an-Nabi Daniel about half way between Masr Station and the sea.

South of the city is the Mahmudiya Canal, which links Alexandria with the Nile, and to the south-west is Lake Mariyut (or Mareotis). About 24 km east of the city centre, not far from the Montazah Palace, is the town of Abu Qir, the site of two historic battles between the French and British, and now known for its seafood restaurants.

Information
Registration & Visas If Alexandria is your first port of call in Egypt, remember that you have to register within seven days of arrival. You don't have to go through the process

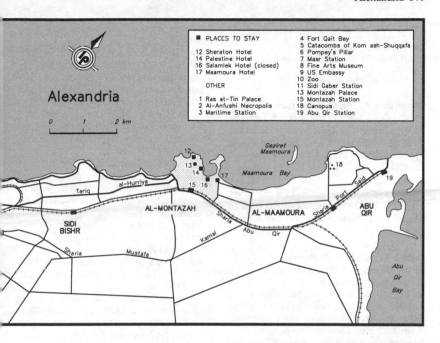

Alexandria

■ PLACES TO STAY		4 Fort Qait Bey
		5 Catacombs of Kom ash-Shuqqafa
12 Sheraton Hotel		6 Pompey's Pillar
14 Palestine Hotel		7 Masr Station
16 Salamlek Hotel (closed)		8 Fine Arts Museum
17 Maamoura Hotel		9 US Embassy
		10 Zoo
OTHER		11 Sidi Gaber Station
		13 Montazah Palace
1 Ras at-Tin Palace		15 Montazah Station
2 Al-Anfushi Necropolis		18 Canopus
3 Maritime Station		19 Abu Qir Station

0   1   2 km

yourself if you're staying in a hotel, as the management will register for you. If you do need the passport office, it's at 28 Sharia Talaat Harb. You can also get visa extensions and re-entry visas here. The office is open from 8 am to 2 pm, except Friday, when it is closed.

Tourist Office At the main tourist office (☎ 807611, 803929), on the south-west corner of Midan Saad Zaghloul, you can pick up a free copy of the pocket-size information book *Alexandria by Night & Day*, published every year for the local tourism industry by Nada Advertising Agency. The information about hotels, restaurants and things to see is sketchy, but it's not a bad publication. The office staff speak English and French, and they can give you some information about the city and transport. The central Alexandria branch of the tourist police (☎ 807611) is upstairs.

The tourist office is open from 8 am to 6 pm; 9 am to 4 pm during Ramadan. There are tourist offices at the Sidi Gaber Station (no phone, open only from 9 am to 3 pm), Masr Station (☎ 492-5985), the airport (☎ 420-2021) and the Maritime Station (☎ 803494) as well.

Money Many of the main Egyptian banks, including Banque Misr and the Bank of Alexandria, have branches along Sharia Talaat Harb, in the centre of town. Banque Misr also has a branch in the Cecil Hotel. There are several other bank branches around.

Should you have any particular problems and need an international or foreign bank, the following have branches in Alexandria:

Bank of America
    Sharia Lomomba (☎ 21257)
Banque du Caire (Bank of Cairo)
    16 Sharia Sisostris (☎ 807087)
    5 Sharia Salah Salem (☎ 32895)

Barclays International
    10 Sharia Fawotur (☎ 21307)
Chase Manhattan International
    19 Sharia Dr Ibrahim Abdel as-Said
Citibank
    95 Sharia 26th of July (☎ 806376)

American Express American Express (☎ 483-0084, 483-1275) is at 26 Tariq al-Hurriya, in the Isis Travel office. Hours are 9 am to 1 pm and 5 to 7 pm Monday to Thursday, and 9 am to 1 pm on Friday and Saturday.

Thomas Cook The main Thomas Cook office (☎ 482-7830, fax 483-4073) is at 15 Midan Saad Zaghloul and there is another (☎ 800100 ext 1360) at Ocean Terminal.

Post & Telecommunications The GPO, in Sharia Iskander al-Akbar near Midan Orabi, is open daily from 8 am to 6 pm. A more modern branch office, including poste restante, is in the post and telephone building adjacent to Masr Station. It's open daily from 9 am to 3 pm. There is another branch at Ramla Station, open from 8 am to 2 pm, and one at Masr Station, open from 8 am to 5 pm.

The telephone office at Ramla Station is open 24 hours a day. The other two branches, at Masr Station and Sharia Saad Zaghloul, are open from 8 am to 10 pm. There is an Alexandria 'yellow pages', which the bigger hotels should have.

Foreign Consulates For foreign consulates in Alexandria, refer to the Visas & Embassies sections of the Egypt Facts for the Visitor chapter.

Cultural Centres The American Cultural Center (☎ 482-4117/1009) is at 2 Sharia Pharaon, behind the consulate. The MacNeil-Lehrer Television News Hours is broadcast at noon every day but Sunday. At 2 pm, if you want news, there's CBS Evening News. If you don't even want a break from it on Sundays, you can go in at noon to watch ABC's weekly highlights. American films are occasionally shown in the evenings.

American speakers are invited here every month.

The British Council (☎ 481-0199, 482-9890) is at 9 Sharia Batalsa, Bab Sharqi. The council has an extensive library, runs language courses and occasionally shows films.

The French Cultural Centre (☎ 492-0804) is at 30 Sharia an-Nabi Daniel; hours are 9 am to noon and 5 to 7.30 pm daily, except Friday and Saturday. Films and/or videos are shown daily.

The Goethe Institut (☎ 483-9870), at 10 Sharia Ptolemy, has a busy programme of films, lectures and concerts. The institute also conducts German and Arabic language courses.

The Italian Cultural Institute (☎ 482-0258) is in the Italian Consulate building on Midan Saad Zaghloul.

Spain has a cultural centre (☎ 422-0214) at 101 Tariq al-Hurriya, which is only open from 5 to 8 pm.

If you want to take a ballet lesson or two, the Russian Cultural Centre (☎ 482-5645) at 5 Sharia Batalsa, might be the place for you. Open every day except Saturday, it also has a cinema club and a music salon.

Travel Agencies There are several travel agencies and airline representatives around Midan Saad Zaghloul and surrounding streets.

Books & Bookshops The *Guide to Alexandrian Monuments* describes the main attractions and details the city's history. It's intermittently available at the Greco-Roman Museum and some of the other sights.

Newcomers' Guide to Alexandria was written by resident Americans to help new arrivals cope with the practicalities of life in the city. It's available at some bookshops and from the American Cultural Center.

E M Forster's *Alexandria: A History & A Guide*, written during WW I, is still regarded as the best historical guide to the city. In a collection of short essays, Forster recreates the more than 2000 years of Alexandria's existence and then takes the visitor on a guided tour of the city's attractions as they were early this century. An annotated edition of the book recently published by Michael Haag Ltd brings the guide up to date for the modern traveller.

Lawrence Durrell's *The Alexandria Quartet* offers a fascinating insight into the cosmopolitan community of Alexandria before and during WW II.

You should be able to find the above publications in Alexandria in the following bookshops: Al-Mustaqbal, 32 Sharia Safia Zaghloul; Al-Ahram bookshop, on the corner of Tariq al-Hurriya and Sharia an-Nabi Daniel; and Al-Maaref on Midan Saad Zaghloul.

There is a fairly decent selection of foreign newspapers and magazines at stands outside the telephone office at Ramla Station.

Maps The best map of the city is published by Lehnert & Landrock. The *Clyde Leisure Map No 6 (Egypt & Cairo)*, published by Clyde Surveys, England, is another excellent map that includes places of interest, hotels, restaurants, and facts about the city and surrounding areas.

Medical Services & Emergency If you have a real emergency, telephone the special 'urgent help' number, 123. Other emergency services are as follows:

Fire Brigade
 (☎ 180)
Hospitals
 University Hospital, Chatby (☎ 420-1573)
 Al-Moassa Hospital, Tariq al-Hurriya, Al-Hadara (☎ 421 6664)
Police (Police Secours)
 Tourist Office, Midan Saad Zaghloul (☎ 122)
Tourist Police
 Tourist Office, Midan Saad Zaghloul (☎ 807611)
 Montazah (☎ 863804)

Ancient Alexandria

There is little left of ancient Alexandria – the modern metropolis is built over or amongst the ruins of the great classical city. A few archaeological sites, often discovered accidentally, have been excavated and preserved, but for the most part only an odd column or

two or a gateway marks the location of legendary Ptolemaic or Roman edifices.

Much of the romance of Alexandria lies in the past, not the present, and it's often a case of simply using your imagination. If you stand at the intersection of Sharia an-Nabi Daniel and Tariq al-Hurriya, for instance, you are also at the crossroads of the ancient city, then acclaimed as one of the most glorious places in the world. In those days, Tariq al-Hurriya was known as the Canopic Way, and it extended from the city's Gate of the Sun in the east to the Gate of the Moon in the west. According to a 5th century bishop, 'a range of columns went from one end of it to the other'.

Just south of this intersection, on Sharia an-Nabi Daniel, you will find what is believed to be the site of the renowned Mouseion and library, where the greatest philosophers, writers and scientists of ancient times gathered to exchange ideas.

Nearby is the modern, fairly uninteresting Mosque of an-Nabi Daniel, built on what is commonly believed to be the site of Alexander's tomb. Rumour has it that the great Macedonian still lies wrapped in gold in his glass coffin, somewhere in the unexplored cellars below.

Greco-Roman Museum

The 21 rooms of this excellent museum contain about 40,000 valuable relics dating from as early as the 3rd century BC. The museum's own guide book gives little indication of where to find anything other than the rooms and some numbered exhibits. The collection includes a splendid black granite sculpture of Apis (the sacred bull revered by Egyptians), many statues of Serapis (the fusion of Apis and Osiris, the god of the underworld and lord of the dead), and busts and statues of various Greeks and Romans. There are also mummies, sarcophagi, pottery, tiny terracotta figures, bas reliefs, jewellery, coins and tapestries.

The museum is at 5 Sharia al-Mathaf ar-Romani, just north-west of Tariq al-Hurriya and seven blocks from Sharia an-Nabi Daniel. It's open from 9 am to 4 pm daily,

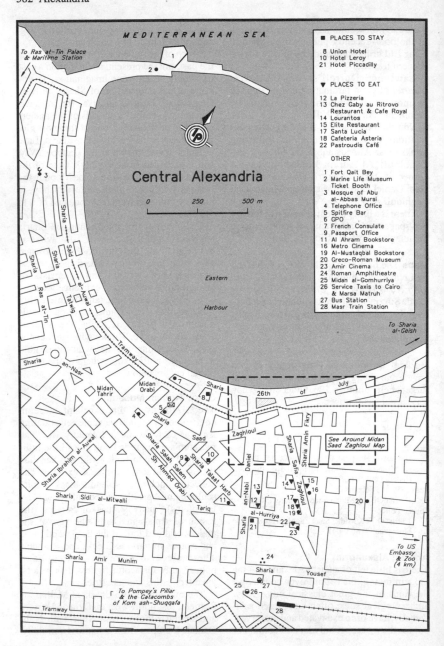

MEDITERRANEAN SEA

To Ras at-Tin Palace
& Maritime Station

Central Alexandria

0   250   500 m

Eastern

Harbour

To Sharia
al-Geish

■ PLACES TO STAY
8 Union Hotel
10 Hotel Leroy
21 Hotel Piccadilly

▼ PLACES TO EAT

12 La Pizzeria
13 Chez Gaby au Ritrovo
   Restaurant & Cafe Royal
14 Lourantos
15 Elite Restaurant
17 Santa Lucia
18 Cafeteria Asteria
22 Pastroudis Café

OTHER

1 Fort Qait Bey
2 Marine Life Museum
   Ticket Booth
3 Mosque of Abu
   al-Abbas Mursi
4 Telephone Office
5 Spitfire Bar
6 GPO
7 French Consulate
9 Passport Office
11 Al Ahram Bookstore
16 Metro Cinema
19 Al-Mustaqbal Bookstore
20 Greco-Roman Museum
23 Amir Cinema
24 Roman Amphitheatre
25 Midan al-Gomhurriya
26 Service Taxis to Cairo
   & Marsa Matruh
27 Bus Station
28 Masr Train Station

Sharia Said al-Auwal
Sharia Ras at-Tin
Sharia Talwiq

Tramway

Sharia an-Nasr

Midan Tahrir

Midan Orabi

Sharia Ibrahim al-Auwal

Sharia Sidi al-Mitwalli

Sharia Salah Salem

Sh Ahmed Orabi

Sharia Talaat Harb

Sharia Saad

Sharia Zaghloul

26th   of   July

See Around Midan
Saad Zaghloul Map

Sharia Safia Zaghloul

Sharia Amin Fikry

Sharia an-Nabi Daniel

al-Hurriya

Tariq

Sharia Amir Munim

Sharia Yousef

To US
Embassy
& Zoo
(4 km)

To Pompey's Pillar
& the Catacombs
of Kom ash-Shuqqafa

Tramway

except on Friday, when it closes at 11.30 am for two hours. Admission costs E£8, or E£4 for students.

Roman Amphitheatre

The 13 white marble terraces of the only Roman theatre in Egypt were discovered quite recently, when the foundations for a new apartment building were being dug. The terraces, arranged in a semicircle around the arena, are excellently preserved.

The area under excavation has now shifted to the north of the theatre, where a Polish team is still working. The theatre is on Sharia Youseff, east of Sharia an-Nabi Daniel. It's open from 9 am to 4 pm. Admission costs E£3, or E£1.50 for students, but it will cost you an extra E£10 to take photographs.

Pompey's Pillar & the Serapeum

This massive yet unimpressive 25-metre-high pink granite column, which the Crusaders mistakenly credited to Pompey, rises out of the disappointing remains of the far more splendid and acclaimed Serapeum. What was once an acropolis, topped by the Temple of Serapis and surrounded by subsidiary shrines and buildings, including Cleopatra's library, now merely features excavated subterranean galleries, the ruins of the Temple of Isis, a few sphinxes, a nilometer and Pompey's Pillar.

The pillar, which has a circumference of nine metres, was erected amidst the Serapeum complex around 297 AD for Diocletian, not Pompey. During the final assault on the so-called pagan intellectuals of Alexandria in about 391 AD, the Christians destroyed the Serapeum and library, leaving only the pillar.

The site is open from 9 am to 4 pm. Admission costs E£3, or E£1.50 for students. There is no fee for using your camera.

Getting There & Away To get to the pillar and the ruins of the Serapeum, which are in an archaeological park south-west of the city centre, near the Mahmudiya Canal, take yellow tram No 16 from Midan Saad Zaghloul for 10 pt. It stops right by the entrance. You can also get a local service taxi (minivan) from opposite Masr train station for 15 pt.

Catacombs of Kom ash-Shuqqafa

These catacombs, the largest known Roman burial site in Egypt, were discovered accidentally in 1900 when a donkey cart fell through a part of the roof. They consist of three tiers of tombs and chambers cut into the rock to a depth of about 35 metres. Constructed in the 2nd century AD, probably as a family crypt, they were later expanded to hold more than 300 corpses. There is even a banquet hall where grieving relatives paid their last respects with a funeral feast. In another hall, named after the emperor Caracalla, the bones of young men were found. According to the story, they ended up down here after being killed by an irate Caracalla in 215 AD for having insulted him.

The eerie nature of the catacombs is accentuated by the weird blend of Egyptian and Roman features in the sculptures and reliefs. The catacombs have been excavated, but the bottom level is usually flooded and inaccessible.

Kom ash-Shuqqafa ('hill of potsherds') is about five to 10 minutes' walk south of Pompey's Pillar. Follow the wall to the right after you leave the Serapeum and follow the street straight on. The entrance to the catacombs is on the left. The catacombs are open from 8.30 am to 4 pm. Admission costs E£6, or E£3 for students, plus E£10 for taking photographs.

Fort Qait Bey

This 15th century medieval fort guards the entrance to the Eastern Harbour. It is built on the foundations of the Pharos lighthouse, one of the ancient Seven Wonders of the World.

The lighthouse, Alexandria's original sentinel, stood about 150 metres high. It had a square lower storey with 300 rooms, a double spiral staircase leading up through the octagonal 2nd storey, and a circular 3rd storey leading to the lantern room, topped by a statue of Poseidon. It was built during the reign of Ptolemy Philadephus in about 280

BC, on what was then Pharos Island. A causeway, formed when silt blocked the channel between the island and the mainland, now connects the island with the mainland and divides the harbour in two.

It is not known exactly what reflected the firelight out to sea to guide and warn approaching ships, but writings of the time suggest it was a mysterious mirror or a lens through which the Pharos keeper could detect ships not seen by the naked eye. If the scientists of ancient Alexandria had discovered the lens, its secret was lost when the two upper storeys were wrecked. Legend has it that the Byzantine emperor could not attack Alexandria because of the lighthouse, so he instructed his agents in the city to spread rumours that it was built on top of the treasure of Alexander the Great. Before the Alexandrians could do anything to stop him, the Egyptian caliph had demolished the top half of the lighthouse, sending the mechanism into the sea.

Several Muslim leaders attempted its restoration, but the lighthouse was eventually completely destroyed by an earthquake in the 14th century, and left in ruins. In about 1480, the Mamluk sultan Qait Bey fortified the peninsula, using the foundations and debris of the Pharos lighthouse to build his fort, incorporating a castle and mosque within the walls. Mohammed Ali modernised the fort's defences in the 19th century, but the minaret and castle were severely damaged by a British bombardment in 1882.

Today, the three floors of the fort house a small naval museum. Although little progress seems to have been made in the past few years, the stated objective is to create a full museum of naval history. At the moment, there are various displays of bits and pieces recovered from Napoleon's unhappy fleet, savaged by Nelson on 1 and 2 August 1798. Having debarked his army in Egypt at Abu Qir, east of Alexandria, Napoleon left behind him a fleet of 17 ships with 1116 cannons to assure supplies while he marched on Cairo.

The fleet lined up two km off the coast, all guns pointed seaward, so Nelson, with fewer

Fort Qait Bey

ships and inferior firepower, sneaked in between the French and the coast and sent much of the French fleet, including the flagship *Orient*, to the bottom. Among the debris of this disaster on display is a collection of French republican coins.

There is also a bit of Ottoman weaponry on display. The views of the city from the fort are superb.

Getting There & Away To get to the fort and the nearby aquarium, take yellow tram No 15 from Midan Ramla or any of about six buses going to Ras at-Tin. Admission is E£6 (E£3 for students), but it will cost you an extra E£10 to take photographs inside (E£20 for video).

Aquarium & Marine Life Museum
This used to be a separate institution, but is

Top: Fishing boats & the skyline of Alexandria (TW)
Middle: The beach of Alexandria at the end of summer (KB); The British War Cemetery,
El Alamein (SW); Midan Saad Zaghloul, Alexandria (SW)
Bottom: The Mediterranean Sea at Marsa Matruh (SW)

Top: Selling oranges in the market, Dendara (CB)
Middle: Man preparing a fiteer in a small restaurant, Cairo (KB); Bedouin guide prepares
lunch for travellers, South Sinai (KB); Typical juice bar, Cairo (KB)
Bottom: Panoramic view from the restaurant atop the Ramses Hilton, Cairo (KB)

now housed in the wing of the fort you meet before getting to the main entrance. The ticket office is in an office that doesn't exactly advertise itself across the road. It has a variety of stuffed and lacquered fish, a whale skeleton, sponges and coral. All this for 20 pt, and open from 9 am to 2 pm.

Ras at-Tin Palace

The palace buildings, built by Mohammed Ali on the western side of the peninsula, are closed to the public, but the surrounding gardens are open – for an entrance fee of 25 pt. King Farouk owned the palace until 1952. The 300 rooms have been kept as they were in the '50s, and are used for state guests and other VIPs.

Necropolis of Al-Anfushi

Follow the tram tracks past the entrance to the Ras at-Tin gardens and the terminus and on the right you'll reach this necropolis, which dates back as far as 250 BC. Two of the five tombs here were discovered in 1901; the other three 20 years later. The two main tombs contain some much faded wall decoration, supposedly imitating marble, and the remains of someone's skull lurk in one of the vaults. They are not as interesting as the catacombs of Kom ash-Suqqafa. The tombs are open from 9 am to 3.30 pm and entry costs E£6 or half for students.

Mosque of Abu al-Abbas Mursi

Dominating the main square on Sharia Tatwig, about one km south of the fort, is a modern but impressive example of Islamic architecture. The original mosque on the site was built by Algerians in 1767 over the tomb of a 13th century Muslim saint. The present structure was erected in 1943 when the largely decayed original was demolished. Yellow tram No 15 from Midan Ramla stops in front of the mosque.

Synagogue

Built just over 100 years ago, this last vestige of what was once a thriving Jewish community now serves only about 70 people, but at the time of writing was closed. Before the wars with Israel there were about 15,000 Alexandrian Jews, who could trace their ancestry back to the founding of the city by Alexander the Great. The synagogue, a fabulous Italian-built structure with pink marble pillars, is at 69 Sharia an-Nabi Daniel.

Cavafy Museum

The museum dedicated to the great Alexandrian poet Constantine Cavafy has recently been moved from the Greek consulate to the apartment in which he spent the most productive and last years of his life, from 1908 until his death in 1933. Two of the six rooms have been arranged to give an idea of what the place was like while he lived and worked there. The others are being used for research. The building is at 4 Sharia Sharm el-Sheikh; this street runs off Sharia Sultan Hussein, just east of Sharia an-Nabi Daniel and two blocks north of Tariq al-Hurriya. The museum is open daily from 9 am to 2 pm except Monday, and from 6 to 8 pm on Tuesday and Thursday. Admission is free.

Hussein Sobhy Museum of Fine Arts

A limited but interesting collection of modern Egyptian art, and Alexandria's public library, are housed in this museum at 18 Sharia Menasha, east of Masr Station and south of the tracks. It's open from 8 am to 2 pm and 5 to 8 pm, except Friday. Admission is free. Yellow tram No 14 will take you part of the way to the museum from Midan Ramla.

Zoo

The surprisingly clean Alexandria zoo, on a small hill surrounded by the Nouzha and Antoniadis gardens, is a pleasant place to spend a couple of hours. There is a large outdoor café which offers light meals and refreshments. It's about 30 minutes' walk from Midan Saad Zaghloul, or you can take bus No 303 or minibus 703 from Midan Orabi. All are open from 8 am to 4 pm. Admission to the zoo is 10 pt, the Nouzha Gardens 15 pt and to the Antoniadis Gardens 25 pt.

Montazah Palace

Montazah Palace, at the eastern end of Sharia al-Geish, was built by Khedive Abbas II. It was the summer residence of the royal family before the 1952 Revolution and King Farouk's abdication. The adjacent Salamlek Hotel (now closed), also built by Abbas II, was designed in the style of a chalet to please his Austrian mistress.

The magnificent gardens and groves and the semiprivate beach (E£5 to use it) make this an ideal place to spend a relaxing day, although the palace and its museum are open only to the big nobs of the government. The grounds, which once featured a menagerie of lions, tigers and bears, include the rather tasteless but high-class Palestine Hotel, which is a little west of the Salamlek.

Admission to the palace grounds costs E£1. They get very crowded on Fridays.

Getting There & Away Bus No 260 from Midan Orabi passes the gardens on its way to Abu Qir, as does bus No 250 from Masr Station. Minibuses No 735 and No 728 go to Montazah from Ras at-Tin and Masr Station respectively. Minibuses No 220 and No 736 (from Midan Orabi) pass by on their way to Maamoura. You can also reach Montazah on the local train from Masr or Sidi Gaber stations on the way to Abu Qir.

Royal Jewellery Museum

The Royal Jewellery Museum, 27 Sharia Ahmed Yehia Pacha, Zizinia (or Zezeniya), is one of Alexandria's newest attractions. Formerly one of King Farouk's palaces, it now houses a stunning collection of jewels from the time of Mohammed Ali's early 19th century rule in Egypt until Farouk's abdication, including diamond-encrusted garden tools, jewelled watches with hand-painted miniature portraits, necklaces and a diamond-studded chess set. Check out the sumptuous bathrooms, which have been cordoned off. The not entirely tasteful tile work is as interesting as the jewels – so this is how guests of the king carried out their ablutions!

The museum is open from 9 am to 4 pm (closed for two hours on Fridays from 11.30 am). Admission is E£10, or E£5 pt for students.

Getting There & Away Take blue tram No 2 from Ramla Station or any bus on the Corniche going towards Montazah, and get off at Zizinia.

Necropolises

If you haven't had enough of tombs, there are two more sets of them. The necropolis at Chatby (across the road from St Mark's College) is considered to be the oldest found in Alexandria. It was discovered in 1904. It is open from 9 am to 3 pm and entry is E£3. Further east is the Mustafa Kamal necropolis. Two of the four tombs are interesting for the Doric columns at their centre. They are open from 9 am to 4 pm and cost E£6. Be warned that a guardian to these places will probably want some baksheesh.

Getting There & Away To get to the Mustafa Kamal necropolis, take tram No 1 or No 2 to Mustafa Kamal as-Sughayya and walk east a couple of blocks to Sharia Muaskar Rumani. Turn left here (towards the sea) and walk a couple more blocks. The necropolis is on the left.

Beaches

There are several public or semipublic beaches along Alexandria's waterfront, but most of the ones between the Eastern Harbour and Montazah are usually crowded and grubby. These include Sidi Gaber, Mandarra (not recommended) and Montazah. At most beaches you can rent chairs and umbrellas for about E£2 per day.

Maamoura Beach, about one km east of Montazah Palace, is one of the best; it even has a few small waves rolling in. You can get there on minibus No 220, which runs along the Corniche.

However, the beaches at Agami and Hannoville, about 17 km west of central Alexandria, are even better as they are cleaner and less crowded. There is nothing terribly attractive, though, about the backdrop of semi-high-rise apartment blocks.

Nor is the ride out uplifting – you get to pass steel and cement works. Buses and minibuses go there from Masr Station, Midan Orabi and Midan Saad Zaghloul (Ramla Station), and their destinations are also known as Bitash (for Agami) and Zahra (for Hannoville). Bus No 456 goes to Agami (Bitash) from Midan Saad Zaghoul. Minibuses No 750 and No 755 got to Agami (Bitash) from Midan Saad Zaghloul and Masr Station respectively. Minibuses No 720 and No 760 both go to Hannoville from Midan Saad Zaghloul.

Canopus
On Maamoura Bay, near Abu Qir, is the site of ancient Canopus, famous in Greek legends long before the founding of Alexandria. The settlement, at the end of a limestone ridge extending from the Western Desert, overlooked the Canopic mouth of the Nile (which has long since dried up), and was for a time a noted religious centre. In 450 BC, Herodotus claimed to have seen a temple to Hercules on the site, and was informed that Paris and Helen had sought refuge at Canopus during their escape to Troy. Another Greek legend claims that the district was named after a pilot of Menelaus' fleet who died there by the Nile on the Greeks' return journey from the Trojan War. Egyptian mythology, however, claims that Canopus was a god whose body was an earthenware jar!

Abu Qir
This coastal town, 24 km east of central Alexandria, is historically important for two major 18th century battles between the French and English. During the Battle of the Nile in 1798, Admiral Nelson surprised and destroyed the French fleet in the bay at Abu Qir. Although Napoleon still controlled Egypt, his contact with France by sea was effectively severed. The British landed 15,000 Turkish soldiers at Abu Qir in 1799, but the French force of 10,000 men, mostly cavalry led personally by Napoleon, forced the Turks back into the sea, drowning at least 5000 of them.

It is best to go to Abu Qir during the week to avoid the crowds of Alexandrians who flock there on the weekends. If you're into seafood, this is definitely the place to go (see the Alexandria Places to Eat section).

Getting There & Away There are plenty of buses from central Alexandria to Abu Qir every day, or you can catch a service taxi for 50 pt from in front of the Masr Station.

Work & Language Courses
Many people coming to Egypt looking for work or wanting to study Arabic simply overlook Alexandria as a possibility. The opportunities are not as abundant, but TEFL qualified teachers, if interested, should call in at the British Council to check out the demand.

Most of the cultural centres also run courses in Arabic.

Places to Stay
Summer is the high season in Alexandria. August is particularly busy, so you may have difficulty finding a hotel room even at some of the bottom-end places.

Places to Stay – bottom end
The *Hotel Piccadilly* (☎ 492-4497) is on the 8th floor, 11 Tariq al-Hurriya, three blocks north of Masr Station. Rooms plus breakfast cost from E£8.30 to E£11.90 for a single or E£11.30 to E£14.30 for a large double with bath; some rooms have balconies. It's sort of a last resort, because no-one has ever recommended it.

The *Youth Hostel*, at 13 Sharia Port Said, costs E£6.50 for members. This must be the only hostel in the country to insist on membership – and it does not issue membership cards. The price includes a bunk bed in a room of six and breakfast. The place is clean and acceptable, but not outstanding. To get there, take any blue tram from Ramla Station and get off at the Chatby Casino, in front of the College of St Mark. Cross to the waterfront side of the college and walk back west a short way along Sharia Port Said. It's open from 8 am to 11 pm.

The *Hotel Acropole* (☎ 805980), 4th floor, 1 Sharia Gamal ad-Din Yassin, is not as hot a deal as it once was. It's pleasant and centrally located, one block west of Sharia Saad Zaghloul and right next to the Hotel Cecil, but the noise from the bus station and trams below can detract from the good Mediterranean views from the more expensive rooms. The beds in some are not all that comfortable, and none of them have bathrooms. The shared bathrooms are kept clean, but hot water seems erratic at best. It costs between E£10 and E£20 for a single, depending on the location of the room and whether or not you want to take a double for yourself. The doubles range from E£20 to E£25 for two people, and there are a couple of triples. Prices include taxes and breakfast.

Across the street is the *Hotel Triomphe*, or *Nasr* in Arabic, which means the same thing. Its rooms have sagging beds but, at E£8 a person, aren't too bad. There is no breakfast and they only have cold water. Some of the rooms have sea glimpses. Some travellers reported knocking the price down to E£3.50. If you can do this, go for it!

A few doors down from the Triomphe, on Sharia Gamal ad-Din Yassin, is a building with four pensions. On the 5th floor is the *New Hotel Welcome House*, which is neither new nor very welcoming. It's an overpriced dive with nails sticking out of the floor.

The *Hotel Gamil* (☎ 815458), on the 4th floor of the same building, has seven rooms, but not all the rooms are the same, so you'll have to do some comparing. Nevertheless, the better rooms are clean and comfortable. The shared bathroom is also kept clean. It's a family-run pension, and Mustafa Gamil, the present manager, may be willing to drop his price a little. Single/double rooms are E£14/20 and breakfast is E£1 extra.

The *Hotel Normandie* (☎ 806830) is across the hall from the Gamil; some rooms have good views of the harbour. Most of the pension is furnished with French antiques, a reminder of the French lady who owned this place until her death. Although the hotel is now run by Egyptians, a 1950s photo of the lobby shows that none of the furnishings

have changed. A double costs E£16.50. Breakfast is E£2 extra.

Next to the Gamil is the *Mekka*. The prices are the same as for the Normandie, but the rooms are a little cleaner and the beds more comfortable – this is possibly the best deal in the building, but it's worth checking them all out – there's not very far to walk between them!

Around the corner from these last three pensions is the *Hotel Union* (☎ 807312/ 771/537). The hotel, on the 5th floor, is well maintained and great value. Some rooms have TVs, sparkling tiled bathrooms, balconies and fantastic harbour views. Single rooms cost between E£18 and E£20 without breakfast (which is E£3.50 extra), and doubles are between E£22 and E£25. On top of this come 22% in taxes. It's somewhat more than other bottom-end places, but if you want some comfort, it's definitely worth the extra cost. Unlike the Acropole, you don't risk ending up in a room shaken up by the noisy trams in the street below, and in any case the rooms are better quality.

Hotel Ailema (☎ 483-2916;482-7011) is on the 7th floor, 21 Sharia Amin Fikry. They have several kinds of room, and price varies according to sea views, whether or not there are bathrooms in the rooms and so on. Singles range from E£19 to E£30, and doubles from E£28 to E£42, all including breakfast. The better rooms have commanding views of the Eastern Harbour and are clean, spacious and comfortable, if not overly furnished. The staff are friendly and the only drawback is that the prices are a little overdone.

The *Hyde Park House Hotel*, on the floor above, seems to have gone out of business.

Right on the Corniche is a series of waterfront hotels worth investigating. If you're standing on the Corniche in front of the Darwish restaurant with your back to the water, you'll see the Bahrein and Philip House hotels. The entrance to the *Bahrein* is on the left side of the building, past a little shop. The hotel is on the 3rd floor and has doubles and triples for E£10. This must be one of the cheapest deals in town if there are two or three of you, as the room rate is always the same. There's no breakfast, but you can't argue with the sea views.

On the right side of the building (next to the Denis Restaurant) is the stench-ridden entrance to the *Philip House* (☎ 483-5513), on the same floor. Despite the olfactory attack on your way up, this place is a little better and more expensive than the Bahrein. Double rooms cost E£15 looking on to the street and E£20 over the sea – there is no reduction for single occupancy.

Back on the Corniche, the next building west towards Midan Saad Zaghloul contains a couple more, slightly better places again. The entrance is from the side street to the right. On the 2nd floor you'll find the *Fouad Hotel*. Singles/doubles without breakfast cost E£15/20. One floor up is the more comfortable *Misr Hotel* (☎ 482-8386), where singles/doubles cost E£22.50/26.50 with breakfast. If there are two of you, this is one of the more pleasant deals around.

Hotel Leroy (☎ 482-9224) is more or less opposite the passport office, on the top floor of an office building at 25 Sharia Talaat Harb. Most of the rooms are clean, attractively furnished and have balconies. Singles/doubles/triples range from E£19/27/35 to E£25/32/38, depending on their position and whether or not they have balconies. You get a panoramic look over the city of Alexandria, but not much in the line of sea views. There's a big restaurant. Take the special marked lift to the left of the main lift, or you'll have trouble getting into the hotel.

The *New Capri Hotel* (☎ 809310), 8th floor, 23 Sharia al-Mina ash-Sharqiyya, is in the same building as the tourist office. Singles/doubles cost around E£24/34 with bath and breakfast. The views from some rooms are almost vertiginous, but you are high enough to avoid much of the noise from Midan Saad Zaghloul below. The place is a little tatty but quite OK.

The *Holiday Hotel* (☎ 801559) on Midan Orabi is a reasonable deal. Singles/doubles cost around E£15/22 and the rooms come with showers and toilet. Some have good views of the square and Mediterranean. The staff are helpful and the place has had some good reports from travellers.

Places to Stay – middle

The *Seastar Hotel* (☎ 483-2388), 24 Sharia Amin Fikry, is just off Midan Ramla. The rooms are clean and very comfortable, but some of the singles are cramped. Singles without bath cost E£28 (including breakfast and taxes). Singles/doubles with bath cost E£38/48.

The *Salamlek Hotel*, in the grounds of Montazah Palace, once served as the guest palace for King Farouk's visitors but is now closed for renovations.

The *Semiramis Hotel* (☎ 482-6837/7837) is a tourist-class hotel on the Corniche that really should be downgraded. Walking down concrete corridors with not so much as a paint job to your dusty and tatty room is a little depressing. The rooms have TVs and if you get a corner one, the views from the balcony are as good as you'll get. The prices are ridiculous at E£70/105.

The *Agami Palace Hotel* (☎ 433-0230), Agami Beach, 17 km west of Alexandria, is well situated on the beach, although there's not much besides the beach in terms of attractions in the area. Single/double rooms are E£65/110.

The *Hannoville Hotel* (☎ 430-3138/0166), Hannoville Beach, is a little further west of the Agami Palace Hotel, and somewhat better. Single/double rooms are overpriced at E£70/92 before taxes.

The *Maamoura Hotel* (☎ 865401) is the only hotel at Maamoura Beach. It has single/double rooms for about the same price as the Hannoville.

The *Metropole Hotel* (☎ 482-1465/6/7), 52 Sharia Saad Zaghloul, is a much better deal for this kind of money. Although the rooms don't have TVs, they do have some class and some faded reminders of another age. Some rooms have sea views. There is a cosy little bar downstairs. Singles/doubles with breakfast cost about E£70/87.

There is a string of two and three-star hotels stretching along the waterfront between Montazah and the Eastern Harbour.

They are a little inconveniently located, a long way from the main transport hub and the centre of the town, but mostly well situated to benefit from views of the Mediterranean.

Places to Stay – top end

The *Hotel Cecil* (☎ 807055/463), overlooking Midan Saad Zaghloul, is a grand and elegant place and something of an institution in Alexandria. Its history is one of romance and intrigue. Its guests over the years have included Somerset Maugham, Lawrence Durrell and Winston Churchill, and during WW II it was the headquarters of the British Secret Service. These days, single rooms start at US$48 and doubles go as high as US$79, before taxes and not including breakfast.

The *Palestine Hotel* (☎ 547-3500/4033) is a five-star hotel in the Montazah Palace complex. Single/double rooms are US$88/110, but prices are higher from 1 May to 30 September. Their buffet breakfast is E£15.60. You can use their beach for E£15 or rent a cabin for the day for E£100.

The five-star *Sheraton* (☎ 548-0550/1220), across the street from the Montazah Palace grounds, is situated so that most of the rooms have decent views of the Mediterranean. The rooms, various amenities, restaurants and facilities are of a quality that you would expect from most Sheraton hotels. Their single/double rooms start at US$86.50/108.

There are a few other four-star hotels dotted along this end of the Alexandria seaside, heading west from Montazah.

Places to Eat

Around Midan Saad Zaghloul There are many places to eat along Sharia Safia Zaghloul. At the Ramla Station end of the street, close to the seafront, there are a number of cafés, juice stands, shawarma stands and bakeries. The *Trianon Café* in the Metropole Hotel, at the corner of Midan Saad Zaghloul and Sharia Safia Zaghloul, is one of Alexandria's superb cafés. Most of their ice creams and desserts cost E£3 to E£6.

There is a E£1 cover charge and 17% in taxes thrown in.

Moving up the street you come to *Al-Ekhlass* (482-4434), on 49 Sharia Safia Zaghloul, which serves very good but pricey Egyptian food. Kebab and kofta cost about E£20. There's a variety of meat dishes with Oriental rice and salad. The *Papillon* café, part of the same establishment, serves good food for about half the price.

Just across the road is a cheerful little café and an adjoining eatery, where you can get a pretty decent hamburger imitation for E£1.50.

Next is *Lourantos*, on 44 Sharia Safia Zaghloul, which serves kofta, roast beef, kibda and chicken sandwiches.

Elite, a Greek restaurant at 43 Sharia Safia Zaghloul, next to the Cinema Metro, has a bit of class and culture at reasonable prices, but not much in the way of Greek food. The walls are decorated with prints by Chagall, Picasso and Toulouse-Lautrec and originals by famous Egyptian artists such as Seif Wanly and Ahmed Moustafa. The restaurant is popular with artists, actors and journalists and the place is generally buzzing even when other places around town seem dead. The usual menu is quite long, but unfortunately the waiters prefer to give travellers the shorter, more expensive one. Look for the full menu on the wall. They serve pizza, moussaka (sometimes), espresso, or you can just sit down for a beer. Prices range from E£6 to about E£15 for simpler main meals.

Across the road from the Elite the *Santa Lucia* (☎ 482-0332) at 40 Sharia Safia Zaghloul is one of Alexandria's best restaurants. In fact, you can see the Grand Collar award it won in 1980 in Madrid declaring it 'one of the best in the world'. A full seafood meal with homemade tarama salata, calamari, side salad and drinks will cost you about E£50 – it ain't cheap, but they know how to cook fish. Next to the Santa Lucia is *Cafeteria Asteria* (☎ 482-2293) which serves good light meals. Small tasty pizzas cost E£6 and up, sandwiches are about E£1.50, and salads are about E£1. They also serve ice cream, espresso and beer. Try the chocolate mousse.

Around Midan Saad Zaghloul

■ PLACES TO STAY

1 New Hotel Welcome House,
  Hotel Gamil, Hotel Mekka
  & Hotel Normandie
2 Hotel Triomphe
3 Hotel Acropole
4 Cecil Hotel
8 Semiramis Hotel
20 New Capri Hotel
27 Metropole Hotel
34 Hotel Ailema &
  Hyde Park House
37 Admiral Hotel

▼ PLACES TO EAT

5 New Imperial Restaurant
11 Restaurant Oriental
12 Moustafa Darwish Restaurant
13 Omar el-Khayyam Restaurant
14 Darwish Restaurant
15 Monsieur Café & Nightclub
16 Athineos Café
23 Brazilian Coffee Store
24 Patisserie Delices
25 Patisserie Delices
  (2nd Entrance)
28 Trianon Café
31 Ala Kefak Pizzeria
32 Taverna Restaurant
33 Ice-cream place
36 Fuul Mohammed Ahmed
  Restaurant
41 Al-Ekhlass Restaurant

OTHER

6 West Delta Buses
7 Arab Union Transport Co
  Buses to Cairo
9 Italian Consulate
10 Athineos & Crazy Horse
  Nightclubs
17 EgyptAir
18 Hannoville Egypt Tours
19 Thomas Cook Money
  Exchange & British Airways
21 Tourist Information Office
  & Tourist Police
22 Al-Maaref Bookshop
26 National Bank of Egypt
29 Post Office &
  Telephone Office
30 Ramla Tram Station
35 Bank of Alexandria
38 St Mark's Coptic Cathedral
39 Synagogue
40 Nascotours

Turn right off Sharia Safia Zaghloul to find *Pastroudis Café* (492 9609) at 39 Tariq al-Hurriya. This is one of Alexandria's institutions, and is still a fine place to watch the passing parade while drinking Turkish coffee or fresh lemonade. Their cakes are superb.

La Pizzeria (486-4470), 14 Tariq al-Hurriya, has pizza and other cheap dishes. It's easy to miss.

Fuul Mohammed Ahmed (☎ 483-3576), 317 Sharia Shakor, is one block south of Midan Saad Zaghloul and one street east of Sharia an-Nabi Daniel; the sign is in Arabic.

You can get a simple fuul, ta'amiyya or potato chips sandwich for 20/25/30 pt.

Ala Kefak, 1 Sharia Saad Zaghloul, is a clean pizzeria. It serves good, big pizzas for E£5 to E£8, and is good value for money. Back a little up Sharia Safia Zaghloul is a small place where you can get a full meal of kofta with tahina and salad for about E£4.

Restaurant Denis (483-0457), 1 Sharia Ibn Basaam, three blocks east of Ramla Station, serves fresh seafood by weight. A kg of fish like snapper, calamari and so on costs about E£27. A kg of shrimps (prawns to some) is E£75. There's not much else on the menu, but the rice is good. The salads and tahina are average. The fish is not bad, and for people on a budget but willing to splash out a little for a decent seafood meal, this is a more realistic alternative than some of the other, better known fish restaurants.

There are a number of interesting places around Ramla Station. The *Taverna*, near the station, serves a variety of meat and fish dishes for around E£20. The salad bar is pretty good. For E£3.60 you can have as much as you want of 20 different salads and dips. The milkshakes aren't bad at all. Downstairs is a takeaway pizza and shawarma stand.

Just up from it are a couple of cafés and a terrific ice-cream parlour.

In a back lane near the Pastroudis café is *Chez Gaby au Ritrovo*, a fairly upmarket French restaurant. Next door is the *Café Royal*. It's open for lunch from 1 to 3 pm and again from 8 pm to 12.30 am.

On the waterfront are a couple of mediocre restaurants, the *Darwish*, where a main meal costs an average E£17 and a kg of fish E£42, the *Omar el-Khayyam* and the *Moustafa Darwish*. These places are OK for a drink, but you can get the same food cheaper and better elsewhere.

The *Athineos Café*, which like the Pastroudis is part of Alexandria's café history, also looks across to the station.

The *Vinous* teahouse is an Art Deco lover's dream. The tea and cakes are nothing particularly great, but the decor makes it worthwhile. It's just west of La Pizzeria.

Elsewhere in Alexandria The *San Giovanni Restaurant* (546-7774), jutting out over the sea at 205 Sharia al-Geish, Stanley Beach, is one of the best eating places in Alexandria. The food is very good, and the soft-lighted atmosphere overlooking the beach extremely pleasant, but don't bother coming if money is a problem. A main meal costs E£30, soup E£7. It's open from 1.30 to 4 pm and 8.30 pm to midnight. They also have a coffee shop, in case you arrive a bit early.

Tikka Grill, on the waterfront near the Mosque of Abu al-Abbas, has great views.

Meals cost around E£25, and you can pile your plate up with extras from the salad bar.

Alexander's Restaurant (☎ 866111), in the Ramada Renaissance Hotel, 544 Sharia al-Geish, Sidi Bishr, is a comparatively expensive but elegant restaurant. Their specialities include smoked salmon, crab and cheese soufflé, and grilled fish kebab.

The *New China Restaurant* (☎ 548-0996), in the Hotel Corail, 802 Sharia al-Geish, Mandarra Bay (near Montazah Palace), has splendid views of the Mediterranean.

The *Zephyrion* (☎ 560-1319) in Abu Qir is reputedly one of the best restaurants in Egypt. Its location alone warrants that honour. Zephyrion is Greek for 'breeze of the sea', and this restaurant, on a magnificent terrace overlooking the ocean with waves breaking below, certainly has that.

Abu Qir Coffeeshop, in the Landmark Hotel, Midan San Stefano, serves ravioli, seafood, chicken and various other dishes. It's open 24 hours a day.

Ras el-Teen Restaurant, also in the Landmark Hotel, is managed by Britons and has international food at fair prices. A plate of hoummos, tahina, baba ghanough, olives and pickles is a particularly cheap favourite.

The *Seagull Restaurant* (☎ 445-5575) is reputedly one of the best seafood restaurants in the Alexandria area. It's west of the city, on the way to Agami Beach. To get there, take the Agami bus and get off at the Al-Max bus stop. The restaurant is in a huge, castle-like building overlooking the waterfront.

There are several *Wimpy*, *Kentucky Fried Chicken* and *Pizza Hut* outlets scattered around Alexandria. A cluster of all three is out by Stanley Beach, just where most eastbound buses rejoin the Corniche on the way out towards Montazah. Other Wimpys are in Montazah, Maamoura and Rushdy, and there's a *Kentucky Fried Chicken* in Montazah and in Sharia Coptic Church, parallel to Sharia an-Nabi Daniel.

Entertainment

Most of Alexandria's major hotels have nightclubs and discos, and live music is a feature of the many clubs along the Corniche. The most popular include the *Crazy Horse* and a small Greek venue called the *Athineos* (☎ 482-0421), although you should not expect too much from them. This is not London or New York, and half the time these places are all but empty.

Some of the restaurants also have discos and nightclubs during the summer, such as the *Santa Lucia* and *Lourantos*.

If you want a drink in a tucked-away bar with low lights and decent pub music, head straight for the tiny *Spitfire Bar* just back from the GPO. Closing time is midnight, but there are plenty of good local cafés in the same street to stumble into afterwards.

Many of the waterfront restaurants and cafés from Midan Orabi all the way down to Montazah have beer available if you drink *inside*. Note that there's not much happening along the Eastern Harbour beyond the Darwish restaurant. The activity starts up again as you head east around Chatby Beach. In summer, the whole waterfront comes to life. All the cafés are overflowing, and the string of music venues on the water are jumping. These are not discos though, but good clean family fun, with lots of Egyptian music, people (usually men) getting up and dancing and general gaiety.

There are several good cinemas in Alexandria that show English-language films. They are all around Midan Saad Zaghloul and charge E£3 to E£5 admission. The best of them are the *Amir* and the *Metro*. Check with the tourist office for details of cinemas and films.

For one week every September, Alexandria hosts an *International Film Festival* of uncensored films from at least 10 countries. The tourist office will have the details.

If you don't have anything better to do with your money, there are casinos in the *Hotel Cecil* and the *Palestine Hotel*.

If you feel like a bit of a run in or around Alexandria with some of the local expatriates, followed by a social drink or two, you could try giving the Delta *Hash House Harriers* a call (☎ 848936). If this number is no good, try the Alexandria listings section of *Cairo Today*.

Getting There & Away

Air There are direct international flights from Alexandria to Athens (Olympic Airways) and Frankfurt (Lufthansa) and one or two other destinations with EgyptAir.

Air travel to Alexandria from within Egypt is expensive; the one- way fare for the 40-minute flight from Cairo is about E£168. Unless you are in a tremendous hurry, it is best to get to and from Alexandria by bus, taxi or train. And in fact, by the time you take getting to and from airports into account, you're not likely to save any time whatsoever.

Bus There are three places to get buses from, so it can get a little confusing. The West Delta Bus Co runs buses from Midan Saad Zaghloul (usually referred to as Ramla) near the Cecil Hotel, Sidi Gaber Station and from in front of Masr Station *(mahattat Masr)*. The Arab Union Transport Company runs its luxury buses from Midan Saad Zaghloul only.

Arab Union buses leave for Cairo and Cairo Airport every half hour from 5.30 am to 8 pm. The trip to Cairo costs E£15. The trip to Cairo Airport is E£20 before 4.30 pm and E£25 after. There is a daily service to Marsa Matruh (summer only) for E£20 at 7.15 am and to Port Said for the same price at 7.45 am. These buses have air-con, video, on-board toilets and a snack service.

Next to the Arab Union Transport Co is the West Delta Bus Co stand. You can buy tickets for same-day travel to Cairo and Marsa Matruh here, but if you want to book a place for later on, or for services leaving from other stations, go to the office around the corner from the New Imperial restaurant. The two windows on the right are for Cairo; the others for other destinations.

West Delta's comfy buses to Cairo and on to Cairo Airport run every hour from 5.30 am to 10 pm from Midan Saad Zaghloul and cost E£12 and E£18 respectively. They take the Desert Highway and the trip to Cairo centre takes 2½ hours, give or take. From Cairo Airport, they start from a stand in front of the old terminal at 4.45 am.

In summer, two buses leave here for Marsa Matruh, at 9 am and 3 pm. The trip takes about four hours and costs E£15.

In front of Masr Station, the blue and white buses of the West Delta Bus Co depart for a variety of destinations. These tend to be the no-frills buses, and many of them start in Sidi Gaber, so there may be some excitement in getting on and finding a seat. If you want to be sure, book ahead at Midan Saad Zaghloul.

Buses to Cairo on the Delta Highway leave hourly from 7 am to 6 pm and cost E£6 or E£8, depending on whether or not there is any so-called air-conditioning. Notice this is a lot cheaper than the luxury buses.

Buses to Marsa Matruh leave at 7 am, 1 and 5 pm, and cost E£7 or E£10, depending on the air-con. Buses to Sallum (the Libyan border) leave at 9, 10 and 10.30 am (air-con) and noon. They cost E£12.50 (E£17 air-con) and stop at Marsa Matruh.

There is a direct bus to Siwa, via Marsa Matruh, at 10 am and noon. It costs the same as the trip to Sallum.

Most of these buses stop in El Alamein, and will stop at Sidi Abdel Rahman if you want to get off there (that will cost about E£6).

There is a bus to Qena and on to Luxor at 6 am and 6 pm. The respective fares are E£34 and E£37.

A bus to Tanta costs E£3.50.

The West Delta Bus Co has four buses to Port Said from its Sidi Gaber lot. They leave at 6, 8 and 11 am and 4.30 pm. The first and last of these cost E£15, the other two E£11.

You can also book trips via Nuweiba and Aqaba (Jordan) through to destinations as far flung as Amman, Damascus, Saudi Arabia, Kuwait and Bahrein. Generally it is cheaper to do these trips in stages, paying for each leg locally as you go. The trip to Amman, the Jordanian capital, is US$59.

To/From Libya West Delta and Arab Union both run buses to Benghazi and Tripoli in Libya from Midan Saad Zaghloul. The West Delta bus leaves at 1.30 pm, costs E£90 and terminates 17 hours later in Benghazi. Another bus on to Tripoli costs LD10.

Arab Union's bus leaves at 8 am, and they demand payment in US$ from foreigners: US$53 to Benghazi and US$104 for the 32-hour trip to Tripoli.

Train Cairo-bound trains leave Alexandria at least hourly, from about 5 am to 10 pm (there's also one at 3.25 am), from Masr Station, stopping at Sidi Gaber Station, Damanhur and Tanta (and often elsewhere as well). The longest trip can take five hours. The four direct Turbo trains to Cairo, Nos 904, 916, 918 and 926, leave at 7.55 am and 1.55, 3.05 and 6.45 pm. They cost E£20.70 and E£12.40 in 1st and 2nd class.

Four trains a day leave Alexandria for Marsa Matruh and take about eight hours. Only the 10 am train leaves from Masr Station; the others from Moharram Bey. To get to the latter, you can take the No 14 tram from Midan Ramla or Masr Station. Second class costs E£6.40 and 3rd class E£2.80. The bus service on this route is faster and more comfortable.

As with all trains in Egypt, check for the latest schedules and fares before making your travel arrangements.

Service Taxi The service taxi depot is a sprawling mess opposite Masr Station. Trying to find your way to the right taxi (many of them are microbuses) can be a headache, although there is vague order. The fares are E£8.50 to Cairo and E£10 to Marsa Matruh.

To more local destinations, some sample fares are: Zagazig E£2.60; Tanta E£2; Mansura E£3; Abu Qir 50 pt; Burg al-Arab E£1 and Amariyya al-Gadeeda 65 pt.

Service taxis to Rashid leave from Midan Tahrir; the fare is E£4.

Boat Adriatica Line runs a ferry service (*Egitto Express*) between Alexandria and Heraklion (Crete), Piraeus or Patras (Greece), Bari and Venice, with departures about every 10 days, although there is no service for about two months from early

January. The ferries usually offer a choice of two or three-berth cabins, with or without private showers and toilets.

The ticket prices vary according to the cabin you choose and the time of year. High season generally runs from early July through to mid-September. There are no student or other discounts.

The approximate fares given here are representative of Adriatica Line's cheapest and most expensive berths. The boat can take a maximum of 572 passengers and 290 vehicles.

The fares from Alexandria to Heraklion range from US$190 to US$290, depending on the kind of berth and season. The trip all the way from Alexandria to Venice costs from US$540 to US$895 one way.

The prices include all meals, and if you book a round trip, there is a 20% reduction on the homeward leg.

If you are taking a car or motorcycle, that will cost more (bicycles travel for free). There are various other assorted fees and payments to take into account, depending on where you embark or land. Lone travellers pay 30% extra for single occupancy of a berth.

You can interrupt your trip at any of the stops concerned and rejoin the ship within three months, providing a berth is available. You have to notify them of your intention to do this when you buy the ticket.

You must confirm your reservation at least 48 hours in advance at the shipping agencies in Cairo or Alexandria and report to the maritime station at least three hours before the ship's departure.

Note that various embarkation and landing dues are *not* included in the ticket. These amount to E£12 in Alexandria and L10,000 in Italian ports.

Adriatica's shipping agents in Alexandria are Menatours (☎ 809676; fax 815830), Midan Saad Zaghloul. Menatours also represents other shipping lines and has an office in Cairo, at 14 Sharia Talaat Harb.

The *Egitto Express* runs to the following timetable. The full trip involves four days at sea, and the hours indicated do not include time spent in port – usually a couple of hours, but in Piraeus up to nine.

From	To	Duration
Venice	Bari	20 hours
Bari	Patras	19 hours
Patras	Heraklion	18 hours
Heraklion	Alexandria	22 hours
Alexandria	Heraklion	22 hours
Heraklion	Piraeus	10 hours
Piraeus	Bari	22 hours
Bari	Venice	20 hours

Amoun Shipping, at 71 Tariq al-Hurriya, represents a Russian vessel, the *Ivan Franko*, which runs between Alexandria, Lattakia (Syria) and destinations in Turkey. The service appears to be irregular, but the ship is said to be a good one.

The North African Shipping Company (NASCO) (☎ 483-0050), which runs ships from Port Said to Cyprus, has an office at 63 Sharia an-Nabi Daniel. It has no sailings from Alexandria. See Port Said Getting There & Away for more details.

The tourist office in Alexandria might be able to provide information on any other shipping lines and destinations, although at the time of writing, this seemed to be about it.

Getting Around

To/From the Airport To get to Alexandria Airport from the city centre you can take buses Nos 303 and 310 from Midan Orabi, or minibuses Nos 703 and 710. A taxi should cost about E£10, but don't be surprised to be hit for E£20.

Bus & Minibus Most of Alexandria's local buses leave from Ramla Station, which is actually on Midan Saad Zaghloul (the tram station is a little further east), but some leave from Midan Orabi, Ras at-Tin and Masr Station. Services operate from 5.30 am to 1 am the next morning. Single trips around Alexandria cost between 10 and 25 pt, and 50 pt out to the beaches of Agami and Hannoville.

The most important routes are serviced by the following buses: No 703, between the airport and Midan Orabi; No 260, between Midan Orabi, Montazah Palace and Abu Qir; No 250 between Masr Station, Montazah and Abu Qir; and No 456 between Ramla and Agami.

Minibus No 750 goes to Agami (Bitash) from Ramla and No 755 from Masr Station. Minibus No 760 goes to Hannoville (Zahra) from Ramla; No 720 also goes to Hannoville. No 735 goes to Montazah from Ras at-Tin, while No 728 goes there from Masr Station. No 736 goes to Maamoura from Midan Orabi.

Train The slow 3rd-class train from Masr Station to Abu Qir stops, among other places, at Sidi Gaber, Montazah and Maamoura. The fare is 40 pt.

Tram You can get to most places around central Alexandria by tram. Ramla Station is the main tram station. Yellow trams go west from Ramla Station: No 14 goes to Masr Station and Moharram Bey, No 15 goes to the Mosque of Abu al-Abbas Mursi and Fort Qait Bey, and No 16 goes past Pompey's Pillar. Blue trams go east from Ramla Station: No 2 goes about two-thirds of the way to Montazah via Zizinia. Some trams have two or three carriages, in which case one of them is reserved for women. It causes considerable amusement when an unsuspecting foreigner gets in the wrong carriage! The standard fare is 10 pt.

Taxi You can expect to pay for taxis in Alexandria what you would in Cairo. A short trip, say from Midan Saad Zaghloul to Masr Station, will cost E£1, and E£3 to E£4 is reasonable for a trip to the eastern beaches.

AROUND ALEXANDRIA
Abu Mina
St Mina is said to have fallen victim to anti-Christian feeling in the Roman Empire of the early 4th century. Born in West Africa, he did a stint in the Roman army before deserting and finally being tortured and beheaded for his faith. He was buried at a place near the present site of Abu Mina, which eventually became an object of pilgrimage. Churches and even a basilica were built, all subsequently destroyed. In the 14th century, a Mamluk army supposedly rediscovered the site and the bones of St Mina, which could not be burned (proving to the Mamluks that they belonged to a saint).

A German team has been working on Abu Mina since 1969 (excavations have uncovered the early medieval Church of the Martyr, where St Mina's remains are believed to be buried), and although the site is not officially open to visitors, it may be possible to look over it with a monk from the nearby modern monastery. The monastery (or deir) itself, built in 1976 and still being added to, is of little interest.

You can get a service taxi to the monastery from in front of Masr Station. Ask around for something going past Deir Mar Mina and you'll soon be shuffled into a service taxi heading to one of the new towns springing up off the Desert Highway between Cairo and Alexandria (E£2.50). If you have your own car, head for Amariyya al-Gadeeda (also known as Burg al-Arab al-Gadeeda). From there, it's about 12 km west to the monastery. You may also be able to get on a private bus organised from the Coptic Cathedral in Alexandria – enquire at the cathedral bookshop. The Cathedral's main entrance is a block west of Sharia an-Nabi Daniel on Sharia al-Kineesa al-Kobtiyya (Coptic Church St).

RASHID (ROSETTA)
The ancient city of Rashid, also known by its former name of Rosetta, is 65 km east of Alexandria, where the western (Rosetta) branch of the Nile empties into the Mediterranean. Founded in the 9th century, Rashid is most famous for the Rosetta stone, an inscribed stone that was unearthed by Napoleon's soldiers in 1799. The basalt slab, which dates from the reign of Ptolemy V (about 196 BC), was inscribed in Egyptian

The Rosetta Stone

hieroglyphs, demotic Egyptian and Greek. The combination of written languages enabled a Frenchman, Jean-François Champollion, to finally decipher the ancient Pharaonic language.

Rashid became one of the most important ports in Egypt when Alexandria declined between the 8th and 19th centuries. It reached its height in the 17th and 18th centuries, but as modern Alexandria began to develop, Rashid became a backwater.

Rashid has a certain charm, although its beautiful palm groves tend to shelter a city besmirched with garbage and manure. The main attractions are its fine old Ottoman-era buildings with colourful facades and superbly intricate mashrabiyyah screens. The best of these include Bait Qili, which houses a small museum, Al-Amaciali and the House of Ali al-Fatairi. The Mosque of Zaghloul, at the bottom of the main street, was founded in 1600 AD, and the Mosque of Mohammed al-Abbas, near the Nile, was built in 1809.

Getting There & Away

Although buses and trains operate between Alexandria and Rashid, the easiest way to get there and away is by hire car or service taxi. The latter should cost about E£4.

You can catch a train from Sidi Gaber Station in Alexandria to Maamoura, just east of Montazah Palace, and then another train from there to Rashid.

Buses for Rashid leave from in front of Masr Station at 7, 10 and 11 am and 12.30 pm and take about an hour.

The Mediterranean Coast

The 105 km stretch of coastline between El Alamein and Alexandria is slated for massive tourist development, and you can see the results already. Sprawling, generally ugly 'tourist villages' are spreading along the coast like a lava flow, covering everything in a layer of concrete. Places such as the Maraqiyyah and Marbella tourist villages, the Atic and Aida Beach hotels and, close to El Alamein, Dream City (!) are generally aimed at Egyptian tourists and more often than not involve long-term lets. The water out here is magnificent, but these resorts are generally not. The number of projects under way or planned seems infinite.

NOTE: Travel into the interior from the Mediterranean coast is limited to certain routes. Travelling to Siwa from Marsa Matruh, for instance, no longer entails getting a permit, but if you have plans to take a 4WD off the beaten track, say towards the Qattara Depression, or anywhere beyond about a 40-km radius around Siwa (except on the Marsa Matruh and Bahariyya roads), you'll need to arrange special permits with the Ministry of the Interior.

EL ALAMEIN

The small coastal village of El Alamein, 105 km west of Alexandria, is most famous as the scene of a decisive Allied victory over the Axis powers during WW II.

Today, El Alamein (the name literally means 'two flags', but according to locals refers more to its position between two places whose names began with 'Alam') is a busy construction area. An oil pipeline and new port facilities for shipping Egypt's oil from throughout the country are being built, and there are plans for a canal across the Qattara Depression from the Nile. The canal project is designed to open up new areas of arable land for Egypt's expanding population, but is being delayed by the many WW II minefields in the Western Desert. These unexploded mines are also a hazard to wandering travellers, so stick to the beaten tracks.

Should you need to make a phone call while you're here, there's a phone office a little way beyond the museum. The El Alamein Rest House, museum, Commonwealth cemetery and so on are actually along a side road that leaves the main highway at the Greek War Memorial and rejoins it again after passing right through the town.

The War Museum

On the western side of town, the War Museum has been brushed up a little and made more presentable, and contains a good collection of uniforms, memorabilia and pictorial material relating to the Battle of El Alamein and the North African campaigns in general. There is a huge diorama display which, in conjunction with a short tape, lights up to show the main paths of advance and retreat until the Axis forces surrendered to the Allies in Tunis in 1943. Maps and explanations of various phases in the campaign in Arabic, English, German and Italian complement the exhibits, as does a 30-minute Italian-made documentary on the battle that you can view at the end of your visit. Outside stands a collection of tanks, artillery and hardware from the fields of battle.

The museum is open from 8 am to 6 pm and admission is E£5 (E£2.50 for students). As usual, photography inside costs extra.

Commonwealth War Cemetery

The cemetery, on the eastern side of town, is a haunting place where more than 7000 tombstones cover a slope overlooking the desert battlefield of El Alamein. Soldiers from the UK, Australia, New Zealand, France, Greece, South Africa, East and West Africa, Malaysia and India who fought for the Allied cause lie here. The cemetery is maintained by the War Graves Commission, and admission is free. Outside is a small separate memorial to the Australian contingent, and a little further east is a Greek war memorial.

German & Italian War Memorials

Seven km west of El Alamein, on a bluff overlooking the sea is what looks like a hermetically sealed sandstone fortress. Inside this silent but unmistakable reminder of war lie the tombs of German servicemen and, in the centre, a memorial obelisk.

Battle of El Alamein

The massive battle of El Alamein, between the Allied tank divisions under the command of Field Marshal Montgomery and the German-Italian armoured force of Field Marshal Rommel's Afrika Korps, altered the course of the war in North Africa.

In June 1942, Rommel, nicknamed the Desert Fox, launched an offensive from Tobruk in Libya in an attempt to push his troops and 500 tanks all the way through the Allied lines to Alexandria and the Suez Canal. It was not the first attempt in what had been two years of seesaw battles, but this time the Axis forces were confident of a breakthrough. The Allies, however, thwarted their advance with a line of defence stretching southward from El Alamein to the Qattara Depression. Then, on 23 October 1942, Montgomery's 8th Army swooped down from Alexandria with a thousand tanks, and within two weeks routed the German and Italian forces, driving Rommel and what was left of his Afrika Korps back to Tunis.

More than 80,000 soldiers were killed or wounded at El Alamein and the subsequent battles for control of North Africa. The thousands of graves in the three huge war cemeteries around the town, the area's main tourist attractions, are a bleak and moving reminder of the war. ∎

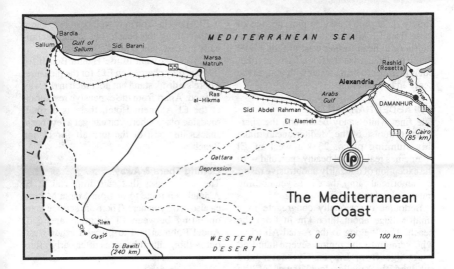

The Mediterranean Coast

Four km further on is the Italian memorial, with as its focal point a tall, slender tower. Before reaching the German memorial, you may notice on the left side of the road what seems a little like a glorified milestone. On it is inscribed 'We were short on luck, not on bravery' in Italian (mancò la fortuna, non il valore).

Places to Stay & Eat

The cheapest place to stay is the *Al Amana Hotel*. It has simple rooms that are quite adequate for E£6 a night. It also has a small cafeteria.

The *El Alamein Rest House*, however, seems to get all the passing trade. You might think twice about staying here though. Rooms cost E£17.50/23 for singles/doubles and breakfast is E£6 extra.

Hotel Atic, 15 km east of El Alamein, has double rooms and four-person bungalows for around US$50 to US$70, plus taxes. It's really part of the chain of so-called beach resorts stretching between El Alamein and Alexandria.

It may be possible to camp on the beaches, but you'll have to hunt around for the police and attempt to get a permit (tasreeh).

Getting There & Away

Bus West Delta Bus Co buses leave for Marsa Matruh and destinations beyond at regular intervals from the bus station in front of Masr Station in Alexandria. They all stop at the El Alamein Rest House and will charge E£6 for the trip. See the Alexandria Getting There & Away section for more details. You can also get a West Delta bus to Marsa Matruh from Cairo – it also stops at El Alamein. See Cairo Getting There & Away. Note that the summer-time luxury bus services to Marsa Matruh generally do *not* stop at El Alamein.

There is no reason for not doing the same from the opposite direction. Any ordinary bus to Cairo or Alexandria should generally be able to drop you at El Alamein on the way. The trip from Alexandria is about 1½ hours; from Marsa Matruh closer to 2½.

Train The train to Marsa Matruh calls at El Alamein, but it takes ages and the station is out in the desert well south of the town.

Service Taxi Service taxis leave from the lot in front of Masr Station and cost about E£6. More often than not they are of the microbus variety. It is pretty easy to pick up one of these from El Alamein to get back to Alexandria or to head further west to Sidi Abdel Rahman. Otherwise traffic is fairly regular, but remember to bring water with you, as the heat can be blistering.

SIDI ABDEL RAHMAN
The fine, white sandy beach and the sparkling turquoise of the Mediterranean make this stunning place, 23 km west of El Alamein, a real coastal beauty spot, and with the exception of one fairly unobtrusive resort and an official camp, there is, as yet, nothing much around to spoil it.

Bedouins occasionally congregate in a small village about three km in from the beach. They belong to the Awlad Ali tribe, who came into the region several hundred years ago from Libyan Cyrenaica and subdued the smaller local tribes of the Morabiteen. There are now five main tribes subdivided into clans, each of which has several thousand members. The Egyptian government has been attempting to settle these nomads, so nowadays most of the Bedouins have forsaken their tents and herd their sheep and goats from the immobility of government-built stone and concrete houses.

The spectacular beach, Bedouin village, and the expensive hotel and camping ground are about all there is to Sidi Abdel Rahman.

Places to Stay & Eat
The *El Alamein Hotel*, a semideluxe place right on the beach, has single/double rooms for E£200/305 with full board in the low season. There are also various villas and more expensive suites. The hotel has a restaurant, café and nightclub.

About three km further west down the road (the length of the village) there is another turn-off, to Hanna Beach (Shaata al-Hanna). Here you can stay in an official tent. They cost an exorbitant E£40 a night and contain two beds, but you could probably squeeze in one or two more people with sleeping bags. If you have your own tent, they'll let you pitch it here for E£8, but will want to see a permit (tasreeh) from the police

in El Alamein. You may well be able to camp further along the beach, but again, technically at least, you'll need a permit.

If you just want to use Hanna Beach for the day, they charge you E£5 for the pleasure. There's a drink stand but not much in the way of food. Apart from the expensive restaurant at the El Alamein Hotel, there is a small roadside place where you can get a few basic snacks just east of the turn-off for Hanna Beach.

Getting There & Away
The same buses that can drop you at El Alamein en route to or from Marsa Matruh ca also drop you here. There are service taxis operating between El Alamein and Sidi Abdel Rahman and to places further west, but nothing much happens after early afternoon.

RAS AL-HIKMA
About 48 km short of Marsa Matruh, this is little more than another small Bedouin village with some attractive beaches. There is supposedly an official camping site here. Ordinary buses between Alexandria and Marsa Matruh can let you off here, or you can pick up the occasional service taxi to Marsa Matruh.

MARSA MATRUH
The large waterfront town of Marsa Matruh, built around a charming bay of clear Mediterranean waters and clean white sandy beaches, is a popular summer destination with Egyptians, as yet not overly infected by the plague of resorts and beach flats spreading west from Alexandria. The water is beautiful, especially on the beaches outside town, but the town itself, with a population of about 80,000, is a bit on the grotty side.

There is a strong military presence in the area, as Libya is only 226 km away. Improving relations between the two countries does not seem to have induced the government to lower the army's profile here. At the time of writing, the road up to the Libyan border was being upgraded and traffic in both directions was heavy, so there should be no reason for not going there. Keep your ear to the ground though – relations between the two have been known to take sudden turns for the worse with little prior warning, and a few times they have seemed on the brink of fighting. If things look bad, it may be better to stay away.

Orientation

There are really only two streets in Marsa Matruh that you need to know: the Corniche, which runs right round the waterfront, and Sharia Iskendariyya (Alexandria), which runs perpendicular to the Corniche, towards the hill behind the town.

The more expensive hotels are along the Corniche. Others are dotted around the town, mostly not too far from Sharia Iskendariyya. The bulk of the restaurants and shops are on or around Sharia Iskendariyya. You'll find a market stretching south from the Corniche, a couple of blocks west of Sharia Iskendariyya.

Information

Registration & Visas The passport office is just off Sharia Iskendariyya, a couple of blocks in from the railway station. It's open from 8.30 am to 12.30 pm except Fridays, when it's closed. If you're coming in from Libya, you can register here. You can also get visa extensions and re-entry visas.

Tourist Office The tourist office, on the ground floor of the Governorate building one block west of Sharia Iskendariyya on the corner of the Corniche, is open from 9 am to 3 pm and 7 to 9 pm daily in summer. These hours are cut down in winter, and the office may not be open at all on Friday. They don't seem to be able to tell you much, although they do have a brochure with a stunningly inaccurate map.

Money There are two banks in Marsa Matruh. You can change cash and cheques at the National Bank of Egypt, a few blocks west of Sharia Iskendariyya and in from the Corniche. You *might* be able to convince the

Banque Misr branch on Sharia al-Gala'a to accept Visa or Master Card for cash advance.

Post & Telecommunications The GPO is in Sharia ash-Shaata, one block south of the Corniche and two blocks east of Sharia Iskendariyya. The hours are from 8.30 am to 2 pm except on Friday and Saturday, when it's closed. The 24-hour telephone office is across the street from the GPO – they have no card phones.

Rommel Museum

Set in the caves Rommel used as his headquarters during part of the El Alamein campaign, this pretty poor excuse for a museum contains a few photos, a bust of the Desert Fox, some ageing German, Italian and British military maps and what is purported to be Rommel's greatcoat. The museum is about three km east of the town centre, out by the beach of the same name. The turn-off to the museum and beach is signposted. The museum is open from 9.30 am to 2 pm in summer only and costs 50 pt. You can arrange to see it in winter through the tourist office or the governorate.

Rommel's Beach

This beach, a little east of the museum, is supposedly where Rommel took time off from his tanks and troops to have his daily swim. It's popular with holidaying Egyptians in summer, and women will feel uncomfortable bathing here. You can hire paddle boards for E£3 an hour.

Getting There & Away To get here you can walk right around the little bay (or hire a bike or *careta*, the donkey-drawn carts that serve as taxis here), or get a boat from the landing at the end of a road off the Corniche in front of the Radi Hotel. That costs about 50 pt. The boats also go across the bay to Shaata al-Gharam ('lovers' beach'). Like most things in Marsa Matruh, the boats only run in summer.

Other Beaches

The stunning azure water of the Mediterra-

Marsa Matruh

0   150   300 m

PLACES TO STAY	27 Radi Hotel	OTHER
	28 Adriatika Hotel	
1 Hotel Beau Site	30 Ramses Hotel &	2 Telephone Office
3 Honey Moon Hotel	Pick-up to Agiba Beach	9 Mosque
4 Semiramis Hotel	31 Families Hotel	15 National Bank of Egypt
6 Hotel New Lido	35 Mina House Hotel	17 Pick-up trucks
8 Negresco Hotel	37 Cairo Hotel	18 Tourist Office
10 Hotel Awam	39 El Dest Hotel	19 Buses to Cairo &
11 Youth Hostel	40 Hotel Ghazala	Alexandria (Summer only)
12 Reem Hotel	43 Hotel Ageba	23 Telephone Office
13 Arous el Bahr Hotel		24 GPO
14 Royal Palace Hotel	▼ PLACES TO EAT	29 EgyptAir Office
16 Dareen Hotel		34 Mosque
20 Riviera Palace Hotel	5 Pizza El-Lido Restaurant	38 Banque Misr
21 El Lido Hotel	7 Pizza Gaby	41 Service Taxis
22 Miami Hotel	32 Panayotis Greek Restaurant	42 Main Bus Station
25 Rommel House Hotel	33 Alexandria Tourist Restaurant	44 Passport Office
26 Hotel des Roses	36 Mansour Fish Restaurant	45 Train Station

nean would be even better if the town and its hotels were not here. But further away the water is just as nice and man's infringements minimal. Offshore lies the wreck of a German submarine, and sunken Roman galleys reputedly rest in deeper waters off to the east.

The Lido, the main beach in town, is no longer an attractive swimming spot, and although Rommel's Beach is OK, it is often too crowded for comfort.

The next choice is Shaata al-Gharam, on the west side of the bay, which can be reached by careta, boat or paddle board. The rock formations here are certainly worth a look.

Heading west, the first good beach is Cleopatra's, about 14 km from town. Nearby is Cleopatra's Bath, where the great queen and Marc Antony are supposed to have bathed.

Four km further on is Obayyed Beach, a resort with overpriced tent accommodation that is now undergoing reconstruction. You have to pay to use the beach, so it's probably best avoided.

Agiba means 'miracle' and Agiba Beach, about 24 km west of Marsa Matruh, is just that. It is a small but spectacular beach, accessible only by a path leading down from the clifftop. There is a café nearby where you can get light refreshments, and the hassle potential for women who actually want to strip down to a swim suit is considerably lower than elsewhere.

Places to Stay – bottom end

Accommodation prices vary greatly from winter to summer, and substantial discounts are sometimes available until early June. As the research was done in mid-June, some of the prices quoted may be borderline either way. Some of the smaller places are closed in winter.

The best deal in town is without doubt the *Hotel Awam*, down on the Corniche. It has singles/doubles for E£7/10 but for E£15 you can have a respectable if somewhat small double overlooking the Mediterranean. These rooms also have their own bath. Unfortunately they only have cold water and a mosque lurks down the road, so light sleepers will probably get the early morning call to prayer.

If it's cheap you want, you could try the *Cairo Hotel*, which has very basic doubles for E£7. They won't do singles for less though. Across the road is the similar *Mina House Hotel*.

A popular backpackers' stop over the years (there are ancient exercise books with travellers' scribblings dating to the early 1980s to prove it) is the *Hotel Ghazala*. It's off Sharia Iskendariyya, about half way between the Corniche and the railway line. They charge E£6 a head for a basic but clean bed. Most rooms have balconies (but no view to speak of) and the toilet/shower combinations are clean, if lacking in hot water.

The *Youth Hostel*, which is back in a little from the Hotel Awam, is all right. Members pay E£5.10 for a comfortable enough bunk bed in a cramped room of six or eight. They seem to have no problem with nonmembers staying. The toilets are fairly clean.

The *Hotel de Roses* is another cheap place, but it hardly ever seems to be open.

The *Matruh Hotel* (also known as the *Hamada Hotel*) is on Sharia Iskendariyya. At E£15 for a double (no singles) and with no hot water, it's not a particularly good deal.

A similar place, with doubles for E£12, is the *El Dest Hotel*, around the corner from the Hotel Ghazala.

A silly place is the *Hotel Ageba*. The rooms come with tiny toilet/shower combinations and the beds are OK, but the manager would like to see you pay E£15 a person.

There are a few other cheap and nasty places around town, some near the main bus station.

Camping Aside from the expensive camp at Obayyed Beach, the only way to use your own tent anywhere in this region is to get a permit (tasreeh) from the police. The beaches are patrolled after dark, so camping without a permit is at your own risk.

Places to Stay – middle & top end

The *Dareen Hotel* (☎ 944308), near the road to Sallum and Siwa, has reasonably comfortable rooms with own bath and breakfast for E£25/37. They seem willing to come down a bit, but the rooms have two slight problems – hot water seems an empty promise, and the mosque is very close by.

East of Sharia Iskendariyya there are three places to consider, although none can be said to be the pick of the crop. The *Radi Hotel* (☎ 934827; fax 934828), on the Corniche, offers singles/doubles without breakfast for E£46/58 plus 19% in taxes. Some of the rooms have TV, and all are fully carpeted with bathroom and fan. Were it not for the hot water, it would only be a slightly better version of the Dareen. A double with half board, by the way, costs E£142!

Heading towards the centre of town and in a couple of blocks, is the *Rommel House Hotel* (☎ 935466). Rooms with bath and breakfast cost E£60/77. Although slightly better than the Radi, this place really is overpriced.

In front of the telephone office on the Corniche is the *Miami Hotel* (☎ 935891). This 200-room three-star hotel charges E£70/90 and upwards for singles/doubles.

Possibly the worst deal in town is the *El Lido Hotel* (☎ 932248), on the corner of Sharia Iskendariyya and Sharia al-Gala'a. For US$18/36, they give you a pokey room with TV, phone, bath and breakfast.

Just across Sharia Iskendariyya is the much better value *Riviera Palace* (☎ 933045; fax 930004). You get better and bigger rooms with partial views of the bay for E£42/64. This is one of the better hotels in this price range.

There is a string of places on the waterfront heading west of Sharia Iskendariyya.

The first of them, the *Royal Palace Hotel* (☎ 933406), has reasonable rooms with bath, TV and phone for E£35/60. The price includes breakfast and most rooms have balconies looking straight out onto the sea.

Next up is the popular *Arous el Bahr Hotel* (☎ 932419). It has slightly grubbier rooms than the Royal Palace, but otherwise is much of a muchness. With breakfast, singles/doubles cost E£35/52.

The *Reem Hotel* has singles/doubles without breakfast for E£22/28.

The three-star *Negresco Hotel* (☎ 934492) has spotless rooms, but at US$36/45 in the high season, they are a bit on the expensive side.

The *Hotel New Lido* is a bit of an odd animal. It rents out what it likes to call flats for E£39.60. You get two beds, a bathroom, a kitchen area and some very large cockroaches. Or you can have much the same thing for E£36.60 about a hundred metres up the road in beach bungalows. These don't have cookers.

The *Adriatika Hotel* (☎ 935195), a little way down the road from the EgyptAir office, has acceptable singles/doubles for E£18/30. Breakfast is an extra E£5 a person.

After the *Semiramis* and *Honey Moon* hotels, you arrive at the *Hotel Beau Site* (☎ 934012). The 'luxury' rooms on the beach cost US$47/59. A suite is US$155. The rooms come with all the mod cons, without exceeding its three-star status. They have tiny rooms available above the disco with great terrace balconies but little else for US$23/29.

Places to Eat

The *Panayotis Greek Restaurant* is on Sharia Iskendariyya. Except for a short interval while Allied and Axis forces waltzed back and forward across North Africa during WW II, the restaurant has been going since 1922, when the first of the Panayotis family came over from Agios Nikolaos in Crete. They do a decent plate of fish for E£13 and calamari for E£10. You can also get a Stella beer here. In fact, from 11 to 11.30 pm, it seems to serve as the town's takeaway liquor store – you can get beer or the ouzo-style firewater, zibiba.

Across the road is the *Alexandria Tourist Restaurant*, where you can also drink a Stella, but not take it away. They do kebabs, kofta and the like, but stop serving food about 10.30 pm.

Next door is a small pizza place with a shawarma takeaway stand. The pizzas are OK, and cost E£9 with the lot, but if you really want pizza, there is better (see below). Next to this is an unassuming little fuul place. A filling meal of fuul, ta'amiyya, tahina, salad and bread costs all of E£1.70.

There are a couple of good cafés around here for a tea and sheesha.

A couple of blocks east of Sharia Iskendariyya is the *Mansour Fish Restaurant*.

Anji, to the left off Sharia Iskendariyya further up towards the railway line, serves a decent meal of hamburger patties and vegetable stew for about E£9. They also do breakfast, omelette, cheese, jam and yogurt. They claim to serve a 'very wonderful ice cream' and can organise trips to Agiba and Cleopatra's beaches.

On the corner of the same street and Sharia Iskendariyya is a juice stand.

For excellent pizza, head down to the Corniche. Just after the Negresco Hotel you'll find *Pizza Gaby*, where most of the pizzas cost around E£10. There is no beer however.

The *Beau Site Restaurant* is in the Beau Site Hotel, so it's closed in winter. The food is fairly good, but beware of the prices.

For delicious, freshly baked pastries, try *El-Sharbatly's Confectionery* in Sharia Alexandria, next to the Matruh Café and the Matruh Hotel.

Entertainment

A couple of hotels put on discos during the summer. Don't expect too much, but if you're desperate for mirror balls, try the *Hotel Beau Site* or *Disco 54* in the Radi Hotel.

Getting There & Away

Air Although you can get an EgyptAir flight between Cairo and Marsa Matruh three days a week (Thursday, Friday and Sunday) for about E£260, buses and service taxis are much cheaper and easier ways to make the trip. The EgyptAir office is on the round-about by the road to Siwa and Sallum.

Bus The West Delta Bus Co has a direct bus from Cairo at 8.45 am for E£15. It leaves from near the Ramses Hilton. In summer, West Delta and the Arab Union Transport Co put on daily luxury buses that make no stops en route. The Arab Union bus leaves at 8 am and costs E£30. The West Delta buses leave at 7.15 and 7.45 am.

Several West Delta buses leave from in front of Masr Station in Alexandria for Marsa Matruh and sometimes beyond to Siwa or Sallum, on the Libyan border. They cost between E£7 and E£10 to Marsa Matruh. In summer, West Delta has two luxury buses from Midan Saad Zaghloul (Ramla), at 9 am and 3 pm, for E£15. The Arab Union Transport Co has one bus from the same station for E£20 at 7.15 am.

From Matruh, the Arab Union bus to Alexandria leaves at 2.30 pm, and the one to Cairo at 3 pm. The West Delta luxury buses to Cairo leave at 8.30 am and 3.30 pm; and at 9 am to Alexandria. These all leave from the tourist office.

The main bus station is up near the railway. From here the daily bus to Cairo leaves at 7.30 am and costs E£15.

At least eight buses make the run to Alexandria, and cost from E£7 to E£10. Some of these are en route from Siwa or Sallum.

Buses for Siwa leave at 7.30 am and 3 pm, take about five hours and cost E£6.

A bus for Sallum (stopping at Sidi Barani on the way) leaves at 7 am and costs E£3.75 to Sidi Barani and E£5.25 to Sallum. Between 2 and 4.30 pm there are three or four more buses to Sallum, costing E£4 to E£5 to Sidi Barani and E£6 to E£8 to Sallum. The trip to Sallum takes about 3½ hours, or more depending on stops and breakdowns.

Train This is the hard way to go overland between Alexandria and Marsa Matruh. Two trains a day leave for Alexandria, at 6.45 and 10.45 am. Second class costs E£7 and 3rd E£2.80. That's the cheapest way to do the trip, which takes at least seven hours.

Service Taxi Service taxis leave Alexandria from a stand in the park in front of Masr Station. They take about the same time as the buses and cost E£8 to E£10 per person, depending on whom you talk to.

The service taxi lot in Marsa Matruh is across from the bus station. Service taxis to Siwa cost the same, if there are enough people going. The fare to Sidi Barani is E£5 and E£7 to Sallum.

If you're coming from Cairo, you may be able to get a service taxi from in front of Ramses Station, but don't count on it unless you can gather up a fair crowd of passengers yourself.

Hitching It shouldn't be too difficult to get a lift from Alexandria or Sallum to Marsa Matruh, or vice versa, but remember that the area is hot, dry, and sparsely populated. Take plenty of water and be careful about sun exposure. As you are usually expected to pay for rides, it's unlikely to work out more cheaply than simply getting a bus or service taxi.

Getting Around

Caretas, or donkey carts, are the most common form of transport around the streets of Marsa Matruh. Some are like little covered wagons with colourful canvas covers. A ride across town should cost no more than E£1. From the centre to Rommel's Museum is E£1.50.

Private taxis or pick-ups can be hired for the day, but you must negotiate and bargain aggressively, especially in the summer.

In summer there are supposedly regular buses to Cleopatra's, Obayyed and Agiba beaches. Failing this, you can get a pick-up to Agiba from in front of the Ramses Hotel for E£2 a person.

Bicycles can be rented next to the Riviera Palace Hotel for E£7 per day. They can also be rented from a place opposite the Radi Hotel for E£2 an hour or from a couple of spots along the Corniche.

SIDI BARANI

About 135 km west of Marsa Matruh on the way to Libya is this small but busy Bedouin town. There's very little of interest here, although the cool waters of the Mediterranean are temptingly close. It's a bit of a food and petrol way-station for traffic coming in from Libya, but that's about it. There's a small hotel and a few places to eat. Buses between Marsa Matruh and Sallum stop here. The fare to Sallum is E£1.75; to Marsa Matruh from E£3.75 to E£5, depending on the bus and the time of day. Service taxis also pass through.

SALLUM

Nestled at the foot of Gebel as-Sallum on the Gulf of the same name, this laid-back and friendly Bedouin frontier town is 79 km on from Sidi Barani. The lack of Western travellers coming through here means there is little sign of the hassling so common elsewhere in the country. There is a post office here and a branch of the National Bank of Egypt.

As usual, the water is crystal clear, but in town the rubbish on the beach detracts from it. Head east for a while and you can pick yourself out some secluded stretch of beach, but ask first if the spot you've chosen is OK. Some parts of the beach are government property. And remember that being on the beach without a permit after about 5 pm can get you into strife.

On the eastern entrance to the town is a WW II Commonwealth War Cemetery, a more modest version of the El Alamein cemetery.

Places to Stay & Eat

The *Hotel al-Ahram* is probably the best place to stay. It costs E£5/10 for basic rooms. When there is water, it's cold. There is a couple of *lokandas* (another name for a basic, cheap place to doss) with their names in Arabic only.

Right up at the border, 12 km further on, is the *Hotel at-Ta'un* (name in Arabic only). There are one or two modest fuul stands around, but ask first how much they want. One place seems to consider E£8 reasonable for two plates of salad, a plate of fuul mixed with tinned meat and a couple of drinks!

Getting There & Away

There are buses and the odd service taxi from Alexandria and Marsa Matruh; see the relevant Getting There & Away sections. From Sallum, buses for Marsa Matruh depart at 6 and 7 am and 1, 7 and 9 pm. Some of these go on to Alexandria. The fare to Marsa Matruh ranges from E£5.25 to E£8. The train from Marsa Matruh is apparently reserved for military purposes alone, at least for now.

To/From Libya The border crossing point of Amsaad, just north of the Halfaya Pass, is 12 km on from Sallum. Service taxis run up the mountain between the town and the Egyptian side of the crossing for E£2 to E£3. Once through passport control and customs on both sides (you walk through), you can get a Libyan service taxi on to Al-Burdi for about LD1. From there you can get buses on to Tobruk and Benghazi. There is some talk of establishing a rail link between Egypt and Libya, but that may well be pie in the sky.

Note that, at the time of writing, it was not possible to get a Libyan visa on the border.

Siwa Oasis

The lush and productive Western Desert oasis of Siwa, famous throughout the country for its dates and olives, is 300 km south-west of Marsa Matruh and 550 km west of Cairo, near the Libyan border.

The original Berber settlers were attracted to this island of green in a desolate sea of sand many centuries ago, when they discovered several freshwater springs in the area. Although Islam and Arabic eventually reached this far into the desert, Siwa's solitary location had until recently allowed the predominantly Berber-speaking inhabitants to preserve many of their ancient traditions and customs. Apart from the desert caravans of ancient times or the occasional pilgrim who journeyed there to visit the famed Temple of Amun, few outsiders ventured there.

That is all changing now, and some observers feel the onslaught of the modern age and tourists will all but drown this unique place. The road linking the oasis to Marsa Matruh has now been joined by another to the Bahariyya Oasis, to the south-east. Microwave stations link Siwa, which has about 15,000 inhabitants, to the rest of the country. What started off as a trickle of travellers venturing down the new road from Marsa Matruh has turned into something of a minor avalanche. Even tour buses get down there now. Of the population, about a thousand are Egyptians, not all of whom seem all that chuffed to be here. From about September to December, a thousand or so seasonal workers come from Upper Egypt for the harvest.

The most illustrious of Siwa's early visitors was the young conqueror Alexander, who led a small party on an eight-day trek through the desert in 331 BC to seek out the Oracle of the Temple of Amun. Alexander's goal, which he apparently attained, was to

Olive bush

seek confirmation that he was the son of Zeus, and also to uphold the traditional belief that, as the new Pharaoh of Egypt, he was also the son of Amun.

Apart from a Greek traveller who visited in 160 AD, the people of Siwa did not see another European until 1792. Then in WW II, the British and Italian forces chased each other in and out of Siwa and Jaghbub, 120 km west in Libya, until Rommel decided not to bother with it any more.

It takes about four to five hours to get to Siwa Oasis from Marsa Matruh – quite an improvement on Alexander's journey from the coast.

Information

Permits It is no longer necessary to get a permit to Siwa. However, if you're thinking of adventuring too far off the beaten track, you will need one. Mahdi Mohammed Ali Hweiti at the Siwa tourist office can advise you, although permits invariably need to be obtained from Cairo.

Tourist Office The tourist office is in the local council building, on the top floor.

Mahdi is very helpful and knowledgeable about the oasis. He can help arrange trips to some surrounding villages. The office is generally open from 9 am to noon.

Money There is no bank in Siwa, so bring enough to cover your needs, especially if you're planning to head for the other oases to the south-east.

Post & Telecommunications The post office is in the same building as the police opposite the Arous el Waha Hotel. The phone office is nearby, but you can only make domestic calls.

Bookshop Next to the telephone exchange is Hassan's bookshop. Apart from a few handicrafts, he usually has some copies of Hassan Fathy's work on the oasis.

Things to See
Siwa's greatest attraction is the oasis itself, which boasts more than 300,000 palm trees, 70,000 olive trees and a great many fruit orchards. The vegetation is sustained by more than 300 freshwater springs and streams and the area attracts an amazing variety of bird life, including quails and falcons.

Around the corner from the local council offices is a small **museum**, Siwa House, which contains a modest display of traditional clothing, implements and the like. It was inspired by a Canadian diplomat who feared the disappearance of Siwan culture and their mud-brick houses in a flood of concrete and modernity. The museum is open from 10 am to 1 pm and again in the evening from 10 to 11 pm. In the low season it's closed, but you can arrange at the tourist office to see it.

The centre of the town is dominated by the mud-brick remains of the 13th century fortress enclave of **Shali**. The chimney-shaped minaret is reputedly the only one in Egypt where the muezzin still climbs to the top and calls the faithful to prayer without the aid of loudspeaker.

On the hill of Aghurmi, four km east of the town of Siwa, are the ruins of the 26th dynasty **Temple of Amun**, built between 663 and 525 BC. The temple was dedicated to Amun, the ram-headed god of life, who was later associated with Egypt's sun-god, Ra, and the king of the Greek gods, Zeus. Nearby was an oracle supposedly used by Alexander, but there's nothing much to see now. It used to be possible to climb up the old minaret here, but it is in such an advanced state of decay that you are no longer allowed to.

Gebel al-Mawta (Mount of the Dead) is an interesting site one km north of the town. There are several tombs in the area, many of which have not yet been excavated and explored. Most of the tombs date from Ptolemaic and Roman times, and there seem to be pieces of mummies and mummy cloth scattered all over the place. You can climb the hill to see a few of the tombs, but don't take photographs of the surrounding military bases. You'll need a bit of baksheesh for the guardian here, who'll only let you in from 9 am to 2 pm.

Cleopatra's Bath, also known as the Spring of Juba, pours into a stone brick pool, which is a popular bathing hole for the locals, but the scum floating on the surface doesn't make it very appealing. Women especially should think twice about swimming here – the ogles and sometimes worse from crowds of locals is unpleasant at best. There's little point in getting upset about it. The sight of a woman, and a foreign one even more so, jumping virtually naked (in their eyes) into a well causes the kind of stir you would get if you stripped naked in Piccadilly Circus and frolicked around.

There is a similar, more secluded and more pleasant pool on **'Fantasy Island'** (Fatnas), an oasis ringed by the Salt Lake, which is accessible across a narrow causeway. The pool, about 5 km from town, is in an idyllic setting amidst palm trees and lush greenery. Although a safer place for a swim than Cleopatra's Bath, women going alone should be wary.

There are a couple of Ptolemaic tombs at **Gebel Dakrur**, about four km from town, but they are not all that interesting. Dakrur is a

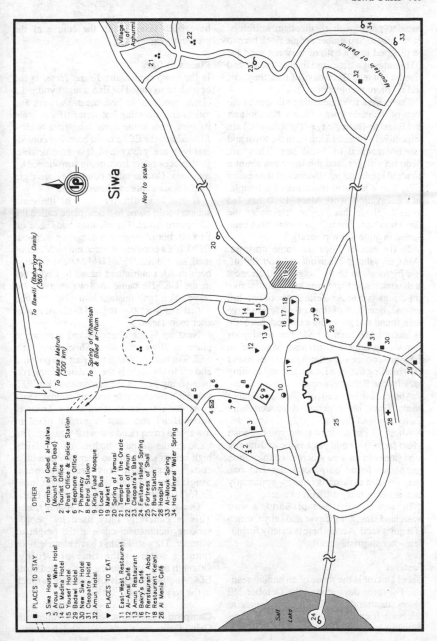

Siwa

Not to scale

To Bawiti (Baharriya Oasis) (360 km)

To Mersa Matruh (300 km)

To Spring of Khamisah & Bilad ar-Rum

Village of Aghurmi

Mountain of Dakrur

Salt Lake

PLACES TO STAY
3   Siwa House
13 Arous el Waha Hotel
14 El Madina Hotel
15 Yousef Hotel
29 Badawi Hotel
30 New Siwa Hotel
31 Cleopatra Hotel
32 Amun Hotel

PLACES TO EAT
11 East-West Restaurant
12 Al-Amai Café
13 Amun Restaurant
16 Bakry's Café
17 Restaurant Abdu
18 Restaurant Kelani
26 Al Menia Café

OTHER
1   Tombs of Gebel al-Matwa (Mount of the Dead)
2   Tourist Office
4   Post Office & Police Station
7   Telephone Office
8   Pharmacy
9   Petrol Station
9   King Fuad Mosque
10 Local Bus
19 Market
20 Spring of Tamusi
21 Temple of the Oracle
22 Temple of Amun
23 Cleopatra's Bath
24 Fantasy Island Spring
25 Fortress of Shali
27 Bus Station
28 Hospital
33 Al-Mlouk Spring
34 Hot Mineral Water Spring

popular place with rheumatism sufferers. From July to September people flock here to be plopped into a bath of very hot sand for 20 minutes at a time, and then extracted and given a hot tea. Three days of this, they say, and no more rheumatism.

There are a few interesting villages to the west of the main town of Siwa. **Kharmisah** and **Bilad ar-Rum** ('city of the Romans') are respectively 12 and 13 km from the town and can be reached by local bus. They are Bedouin villages, and the latter has about a hundred tombs cut into the rock of the nearby hills. There are also remnants of a temple, and excavation work since 1990 has led some to think that maybe Alexander the Great was buried here (he seems to have been buried in quite a few places!).

To the east of Siwa are some **springs**. 'Ain Qurayshat is 27 km out and Abu Shuruf, said by locals to be the biggest and cleanest in the oasis, a further seven km. Another five km brings you to Az-Zeitun. About two km beyond, hundreds of Roman-era tombs have been found and are being explored, but little of interest has been found. You need your own sturdy vehicle. Otherwise, Mahdi from the tourist office sometimes organises round trips heading out on a local track and coming back by the Bahariyya road.

About 120 km east of Siwa is another **oasis**, Gara, but a permit is needed from Cairo to go out this far.

About 13 km south of town you can visit a **fish farm**. This odd place is located among sand dunes in an area where oil exploration companies found only hot water and one chap decided to raise fish there – apparently they are extremely difficult to catch.

Beyond lies the **Sea of Sand**, a vast wasteland straddling Egypt and Libya, much of it quicksand. Access here is strictly forbidden – not surprising really.

Festival

Gebel Dakrur is the scene of an annual festival. For three days around the October full moon, thousands of Siwan men gather to celebrate friendship and togetherness, presumably burying all the hatchets that may have been taken up in the course of the previous year.

Places to Stay

In the town centre, the *Yousef Hotel* is the best place to stay. For E£5 a night you get a clean, comfortable bed, clean showers and toilets and steaming hot water (if you want it). Next door is the oasis' long-time hotel – *El Madina*. It's E£3 a night here, but considerably more grotty and less comfortable. Both places suffer from being surrounded by mosques. On the other hand, they are right by the restaurants and bus station.

If you head directly south of the main square you'll come to a new place called the *Cleopatra Hotel*. The cheapest beds here are E£5.60, but other rooms range up to about E£20. It's a good clean place run by Mohammed, an 'old sea dog' of HM Merchant Navy, born in Alexandria and raised in Liverpool in the UK. He came to Siwa in 1992 'to relax'. You can't mistake him – he's the one with the military bearing and the Lord Kitchener moustache.

Next up is the cheapest and scummiest place in Siwa, the *New Siwa Hotel*. It's E£2.50 a bed. A walk down past the hospital and off to the right is the *Badawi Hotel*, run by a young gent of the same name. For E£3 you get a comfortable bed and maybe a fan.

At the entrance to town is the *Arous el Waha Hotel*, the most expensive place in town, and overpriced for what you get. The basic rooms *do* have bathrooms and fairly high ceilings, helping to keep things a little cooler here than they are elsewhere. Singles/doubles/triples/quadruples cost E£15/21/28/36 and breakfast an extra E£3.

Out at Gebel Dakrur is the *Amun Hotel*. This is generally only used by people seeking rheumatism cures at the height of summer. They still didn't have electricity or running water at the time of writing, although they were on the way. A bed costs E£4. Another item missing out here is much in the way of food.

Camping The tourist office recommends Gebel Dakrur as a safe area to pitch a tent.

Places to Eat

There are eight or so restaurants/cafés in Siwa catering to tourists. The longest-standing of them is the ever popular *Restaurant Abdu*, across the road from the Yousef Hotel. They all offer a fairly similar menu, so trial and error is probably the only way of searching out any nuances in quality.

Abdu does serve a fairly tasty pizza for E£5. He also does a whole range of more traditional dishes, vegetable stews and similar items.

You can get a filling plate of couscous next door at *Bakry's Café* for E£2. Most of his meat dishes cost about E£5. Bakry came to Siwa from the Upper Nile town of Sohag in the 1970s, hence the alternative name of his place, the *Sohag Rest House*.

Across the road is the *Amun*, which does similar meals, and a pancake dripping in honey for breakfast. There is a small café further up the road opposite the El Madina Hotel.

Down to the left of the Restaurant Abdu is the *Restaurant Kelani*. Closer to the mosque, the *Al-Amal Café* seems to do smaller serves of many of the same dishes for lower prices. You could also try the *East-West Restaurant*, across the square and facing the mosque.

The Arous el Waha Hotel has its own cafeteria, and on the square facing the bus station is a fly-blown café called the *Al Menia*.

Getting There & Away

The West Delta Bus Co station is behind the Restaurant Abdu on the main square. There is a daily bus at 6.30 am to Alexandria, stopping at Marsa Matruh on the way. The fare to Marsa Matruh is E£6 and E£12.50 to Alexandria. You should book ahead for this. There is a daily service to Marsa Matruh at 1.30 pm, for which no bookings are taken. There is another bus to Alexandria via Marsa Matruh at 10 am on Sunday, Tuesday and Thursday only. The trip to Alexandria may cost as much as E£17 if the bus has air-con.

For details of getting to Siwa from Marsa Matruh and Alexandria, see the relevant Getting There & Away sections.

Although there is now a road linking the oases of Siwa and Bahariyya, there is no public transport. Occasionally you can get on to the back of a truck. Or you can hire one for E£500, taking a maximum of 10 people.

To/From Libya At the time of writing it was illegal to cross into Libya and go on to the town of Jaghbub, about 120 km away. There is, however, a customs house in Siwa, and a possible road linking the two towns is being surveyed. There is already a desert track, which presumably local Bedouins use – if they are allowed to make the crossing. Should it become possible to cross, there is a paved road from Jaghbub to the Libyan coast.

Getting Around

There is a local bus to Kharmisah and Bilad ar-Rum at 7 am and 2.30 pm from near the King Fuad Mosque. It costs E£1 and returns shortly afterwards, so it's best to catch the morning bus and come back on the afternoon bus.

Bicycles can be rented from a small shop near the El-Madina Hotel for E£3 a day, but hiring a careta can be a more amusing, if less practical, way to get around.

The Sinai

The Sinai, a region of awesome and incredible beauty, has been a place of refuge, conflict and curiosity for thousands of years. Wedged between Africa and Asia, its northern coast is bordered by the Mediterranean Sea, and its southern peninsula by the Red Sea gulfs of Aqaba and Suez. Row upon row of barren, jagged, red-brown mountains fill the southern interior, surrounded by relentlessly dry, yet colourful, desert plains. From the palm-lined coast, dunes and swamps of the north to the white-sand beaches and superb coral reefs of the Red Sea, the Sinai is full of contrasts.

In Pharaonic times, the quarries of the Sinai provided enormous quantities of turquoise, gold and copper. The great strategic importance of the 'Land of Turquoise' also made it the goal of empire builders and the setting for countless wars.

The Sinai is a land of miracles and holy places. Elijah, Jacob and Abraham, the prophets of Judaism, Christianity and Islam, wandered through its hills and deserts. It was here that God is said to have first spoken to Moses from a burning bush and, later, delivered the Israelites from the Egyptian army with the celebrated parting of the Red Sea.

And Moses stretched out his hand over the sea; and the Lord caused the sea to go back...And the children of Israel went into the midst of the sea upon the dry ground: and the waters were a wall unto them on their right hand, and on their left. And the Egyptians pursued...and the Lord overthrew the Egyptians in the midst of the sea. And the waters returned and covered the chariots, and the horsemen, and all the host of Pharaoh that came into the sea after them; there remained not so much as one of them...Thus the Lord saved Israel that day out of the hand of the Egyptians; and Israel saw the Egyptians dead upon the sea shore. (Exodus 14: 21-30)

The Sinai is the 'great and terrible wilderness' of the Bible, across which the Israelites journeyed in search of the Promised Land, and it was from the summit of Mt Sinai that God delivered his Ten Commandments to Moses:

Tell the children of Israel; Ye have seen what I did unto the Egyptians...If ye will obey my voice and keep my covenant, then ye shall be a peculiar treasure unto me above all people: for all the earth is mine. And ye shall be unto me a kingdom of priests, and a holy nation.

And Mount Sinai was altogether in smoke, because the Lord descended upon it in fire; and the whole mount quaked greatly...And the Lord came down upon Mount Sinai...and called Moses up to the top of the mount...And God spoke all these words, saying, I am the Lord thy God, which have brought thee out of the land of Egypt, out of the house of bondage. Thou shalt have no other gods before me... (Exodus 19-20)

History

In the 16th century BC, the soldiers of the Egyptian army, under Pharaoh Tuthmosis III, were far more fortunate than their biblical ancestors – they successfully crossed the Red Sea and the Sinai to conquer Palestine and Syria. Alexander the Great marched across the Sinai to conquer Egypt in 332 BC and, in 48 BC, just east of present-day Port Said, the opposing armies of Cleopatra and Ptolemy, her brother, battled for the Egyptian throne. Throughout the Sinai, holy places mark the spots where Mary, Joseph and Jesus supposedly rested during their flight into the Sinai to escape King Herod.

The Arab general Amr led his forces through the Sinai in 639 AD to conquer Egypt and bring Islam to Africa. In 1160, Salah ad-Din (known to the West as Saladin) built a fortress at Ras al-Gindi, to protect Muslim pilgrims and to guard Egypt against the invading Crusaders. In the 16th century, the Ottomans crossed the Sinai to make Egypt part of their empire.

The Ottomans' power struggle with the French under Napoleon and with the British under Allenby continued to see the passage of armies back and forth across the Sinai, right up to the beginning of this century. The

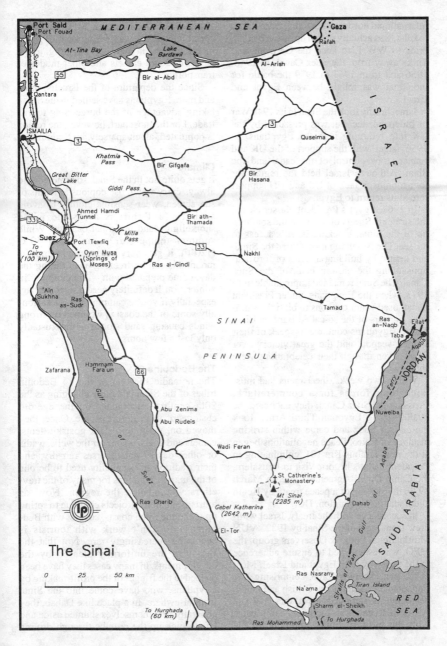

The Sinai

0   25   50 km

international border of the Sinai, from Rafah to Eilat, was actually drawn up by the British, prior to WW I, to keep the Germans and Turks away from the Suez Canal. In 1948, 1956 and from 1967 to 1979 the battle for the Sinai was fought between Egypt and Israel.

Israel briefly took the Sinai in its 1948 War of Independence, but was pressured by the UK into returning it to the Egyptians. In 1956, Israel, with the support of the UK and France, took control of the canal and the Sinai. Although Israel held the region for four months, a lack of US and UN support forced its return to Egypt.

In 1967, Egypt's President Nasser closed the strategic Straits of Tiran, at the southern tip of the Sinai, blocking Israel's access to the sea. The Israelis again captured the Sinai, and kept it by building a series of fortifications along the eastern bank of the Suez Canal. The Sinai remained impregnable until 1973, when the Egyptians, under President Sadat, used water cannons to blast the sanddune barriers of the so-called Bar Lev Line. Today, Egyptians continue to speak of their 'secret weapon' and the great victory over Israel, even though their celebrations were short-lived.

Within two weeks, the Israelis had mustered their forces for a counterattack. Crossing the Suez Canal, they encircled the 30,000-strong Egyptian Third Army, took the city of Suez and came within striking distance of Cairo. Peace negotiations began at the now-famous Km 101, culminating in President Sadat's historic visit to Jerusalem, the Camp David Agreement and, in March 1979, the signing of a peace treaty by Begin and Sadat in Washington, DC.

In accordance with the treaty, Israel withdrew from most of the Sinai by 1982. A UN Multinational Force & Observers group, the MFO, was established to ensure adherence to the treaty by both Egypt and Israel. Most of the peacekeeping force, comprising US, Canadian, French, Italian, British and Dutch personnel, is stationed at Na'ama Bay and Al-Arish to monitor Egyptian compliance with the military limits imposed by the treaty. Basically, however, MFO members spend their days either raking sand or going to the beach, in between counting jeeps, tanks, Bedouin camels and other modes of transport.

Since the departure of the Israelis, more and more Egyptians have settled in the Sinai, taking advantage of the burgeoning tourist trade. For the most part, however, the region is populated, albeit sparsely, by Bedouins.

Climate

It gets quite hot in the Sinai, so remember to always carry water, use copious amounts of sun screen, wear sensible clothes to avoid sunburn (a T-shirt is advisable while snorkelling), and use a hat or scarf. While summer temperatures can reach 50°C (120°F), it gets very cold at night and the mountains can be freezing even during the day; come prepared with warm clothing. In winter, you'll definitely need a sleeping bag, especially if you're camping out. Occasionally some of the coast is whipped by strong winds causing sand storms – they usually only last a few hours.

The Bedouins

The nomadic lifestyle of the 14 Bedouin tribes of the Sinai is rapidly changing as the 20th century encroaches on the age-old customs of these desert people. Once, they moved on, with their black goatskin tents, camels and goats, whenever the wells, wadis or other desert watercourses ran dry, and their tradition of hospitality used to be one of the major attractions for many of the travellers who visited the region. Now, as tourism and hotel projects continue to spring up along the Sinai coasts, contact with Bedouins who don't work with tourists is becoming increasingly rare. Not that the Bedouins are uniformly pleased by the developments. In many cases they have been pushed to the fringes of the profit-making by Egyptians, who have come into the Sinai from elsewhere. In a place like Dahab, they generally find themselves shunted aside and left to pick up the crumbs through driving taxis and organising camel treks, although some of the camps are still Bedouin-run.

Most of their ancestors came from the Arabian peninsula, but the Bedouins' laws, customs and religion (which blends Islam and pagan beliefs), as well as their resilience and amazing hospitality, were born of their lifestyle in the Sinai – the isolation, the harsh, dry climate and the need to keep moving on in search of water.

The wealth of a Bedouin is still measured in camels and children, but Western technology is making its presence felt. While you may see the traditional Bedouin goatskin tents and camels in the Sinai, there are also pick-up trucks and settlements of crude stone huts, or palm-frond shacks, with corrugated roofs and TV antennae.

Ever since the reign of Mohammed Ali, early in the 19th century, governments have been trying to settle the Bedouin tribes. Like the Israelis before them, the Egyptians have built schools, medical clinics and social centres for the Bedouins. They have also placed hundreds of 200-litre barrels of water strategically, at points where they wish to create stable settlements. Many of the Sinai's 50,000 Bedouins now harvest dates, cultivate grain, grow vegetables and cater to the tourists.

Information

Visas If you're entering Egypt by way of the Sinai from Israel, you will need an Egyptian visa. This can only be obtained before you get to the border. On arrival in Egypt, you must register with the police within seven days.

If you intend only to visit the coastal resorts of eastern Sinai from Taba down to Sharm el-Sheikh, you can get a 14-day pass on the border. See the Getting There & Away chapter and the Taba section for more information on crossing from Israel into Egypt.

Money Changing money in the Sinai is not a problem, unless you are staying in some of the more out-of-the-way little spots along the coast. If you are planning on this and don't want the hassle of trekking into the nearest

Bedouin woman

big town to get money, stock up on E£. The banks and hotels in Sharm el-Sheikh, Na'ama Bay, Dahab, Nuweiba, Taba, St Catherine's and Al-Arish will change travellers' cheques and occasionally accept credit cards, but otherwise you may have to try to change cash privately.

Costs Probably the majority of visitors to the Sinai come across from Israel, and so are pleasantly surprised by the apparent cheapness of the place. Those coming the other way, from Cairo or elsewhere in Egypt, are usually taken aback by how expensive it is. There is virtually no budget accommodation in the Sharm el-Sheikh and Na'ama Bay area. The backpacker havens in Dahab and along the road to Taba, where you can generally stay in basic huts for about E£5, are the exception to that rule.

Groceries are more expensive here than elsewhere in Egypt and there is an irritating tendency among shopkeepers to round up already inflated prices.

Although meals and drinks in the beachside cafeterias and restaurants are not expensive by Western standards, they are often quite a bit more than you might pay in Cairo. Drinks such as tea, coffee or soft drinks all tend to be E£1 or more, and where but here would anyone consider asking E£2 to E£3 for ta'amiyya?

Sinai buses are the most expensive in the country (and the only ones with separate, higher fares for tourists), and service taxis worse still. Travellers on a budget who intend to eat in the cafés two or three times a day should reckon with average daily costs of E£40 to E£50, although you can bring it down considerably by cooking your own food and getting lucky when hitching.

Books *The Red Sea Coasts of Egypt – Sinai & the Mainland* by Jenny Jobbins (The American University in Cairo Press) has good route descriptions of the coastal road around the Sinai.

An attractive picture book of the area is *Sinai – Guide of the Peninsula and the Red Sea*. The text is by Gérard Viant and the pictures by Ayman Taher. It is published by E. Tzaferis SA, Greece, 1992.

There is a range of books aimed at divers. *The Egyptian Red Sea – A Diver's Guide*, by Eric Hanauer (Watersport Publishing, San Diego, US, 1988), gives comprehensive coverage of what to look for and where. A more specific guide to the marine life of the area is the bilingual German-English *Red Sea Underwater Guide*, Helmut Debelius, Verlag Stephanie Naglschmid, Stuttgart, 1990.

Water Sports

Don't be completely fooled by the undeniable beauty of the Red Sea coast's blue-green waters and coral reefs – they do have their share of hazards. Always wear sandshoes or fins when you're exploring the reefs, and avoid bumping into the coral, especially fire coral, as it is extremely sharp and can cause a painful, burning sensation where it breaks your skin. Before diving or snorkelling, you should learn to recognise such potentially dangerous creatures as the stonefish, lionfish and scorpionfish. Barracuda and Moray eels are also prevalent, although seldom threaten-

---

The Rubbishing of the Sinai

Egypt is not exactly garbage free but modern litter is most evident and most sad in the Sinai. It's a combination of attitude and environment. The Bedouins were used to moving on and leaving their debris behind them. No matter, it was all biodegradable and if it took a little longer to rot away in the dry desert environment that was no problem – after all there weren't many people in the Sinai to see it. Now there are a lot more people and their modern plastic garbage doesn't decay at all. The whole Sinai is becoming covered in a scattering of plastic bags and some places are real horror stories. Moses would have no trouble at all finding his way to the top of Mt Sinai today – he could just follow the empty plastic mineral water bottles and used toilet paper. It's a pity he didn't bring down one more commandment – Thou Shalt Not Litter. On the bright side, isolated efforts are being made to resist the tide of junk. The popular budget travellers' haunt at Dahab, for instance, has somewhat cleaned up its act in the past few years. It's still far from perfect, but any sign of improvement is welcome. ■

Colourful creatures greet divers in the Red Sea
Top: (CM) Middle: (DB); (DB); (CM) Bottom: (CM)

Top: Young girls weave a complicated rug in a village school, near Cairo (KB)
Left: Young boy chisels brass plate for tourists, Khan al-Khalili, Cairo (KB)
Right: Bedouin women bargain for goods at the colourful market, Al-Arish (KB)

ing. There are sharks in the Red Sea, but it has been a long time since sharks have bothered humans in the Sinai waters. If you do see one, don't panic – nothing attracts sharks more than a terror-stricken human flailing about in their territory.

Treat the Sinai, above and below the sea, with care. Don't ruin a beautiful place by leaving garbage in the water, on the beach or in the mountains. When diving or snorkelling, do not touch the coral and plants, nor turn over rocks. Unfortunately, not enough people have respected this part of the world. On a single day in 1989, volunteers from the Cairo Divers Club collected almost a tonne of garbage from beaches near three Sharm el-Sheikh dive sites. So clean up after yourself and do what you can to preserve the natural beauty of this very special place.

Conservationists and environmentalists are also concerned that extensive tourism and related development in the area between Ras Mohammed and Na'ama Bay will upset the delicate coastal and marine ecosystems.

The National Marine Park that has been declared around Ras Mohammed was the subject of much controversy, but it appears the project is meeting with some success. Hotels cannot develop the area, and only 12 per cent of the park is accessible to visitors. In addition, a ceiling has been applied to the number of boats allowed into the area with divers. Two other protected areas along the coast, to the south and north of Dahab, were declared in 1992. They are not national parks, but designated for only limited development – what this ends up meaning remains to be seen, but it sounds promising.

Note that it is forbidden to break off coral, to fish or to harpoon along much of the coast from Ras Mohammed to Eilat. Any exceptions are intended more for the local fishing industry than for dabbling tourists.

Diving If you have never dived before, the Sinai is the perfect place to learn. The average certification course takes about five days and usually includes several dives. The total cost of a five-day open-water course leading to PADI, CMAS or NAUI certification is usually around US$300.

Na'ama Bay has the greatest concentration of dive operators but the rates are fairly similar at all the Sinai's dive centres. Daily rental costs for a mask, snorkel or fins will be around E£5 to E£10 (more like E£15 around Na'ama Bay). All other equipment is available including wet suits, regulators, buoyancy compensators, tanks and so on.

Introductory dives including equipment cost from US$45 up, advanced open-water courses including equipment cost US$200. Full-day diving trips including equipment and air fills cost US$45 to US$75 a day depending on the operator and location. From Na'ama Bay the trips to the Straits of Tiran or to Ras Mohammed are usually a little more expensive than dives at closer sites. Discounts are available on five-day and 10-day packages and can bring the daily diving cost down.

Travellers report that if you dive with Sinai Dive Club in Dahab, you can ask for a pass that allows you to dive with them in Na'ama Bay at a reduced rate.

Getting Around

The few paved roads through the desert and hills link only the permanent settlements, and transport is not as regular as elsewhere in Egypt. You can get to most places you'd be likely to want to reach by bus, but in many cases there are only a couple of connections a day, sometimes only one. Service taxis, in the organised sense of the word, do not exist. As drivers in Suez will tell you, beyond the coast route to El-Tor, you can only get hold of a service taxi by bargaining and paying far more than would be the case over similar distances elsewhere in Egypt – the reason is simple: there are not enough locals around in need of a fully built up transport system.

If you are driving yourself, you must stick to the main roads, as foreigners are forbidden to leave them.

OYUN MUSA

Oyun Musa, or the 'springs of Moses', is said to be the place where Moses, on discovering that the water there was too bitter to drink, took the advice of God and threw a special tree into the springs, miraculously sweetening the water.

Seven of the 12 original springs still exist and, around them, a small settlement has grown up. The palm trees are a bit unusual, as most have had their crowns blown off in various Sinai wars and still haven't quite returned to their previous state.

Oyun Musa is about 25 km south of the Ahmed Hamdi Tunnel, which goes under the Suez Canal near Suez (completed in 1982 and named after a 'martyr' of the 1973 war, it was undergoing repairs at the time of writing and closed from 8 pm to 6 am, causing considerable disruption to travel). Camping is possible but, as the spring water is too brackish, there is no drinkable water – and there's no sign of the special tree that Moses used.

Getting There & Away
There are half a dozen buses each way between Cairo and Sharm el-Sheikh every day, and they travel via Oyun Musa. Departures are from the Sinai Terminal (Abbassiya Station) in north-east Cairo.

The buses from Suez to Sharm el-Sheikh and St Catherine's pass through Oyun Musa. They leave Suez at 10 am, 12.30 and 2 pm, and take one hour.

RAS AL-GINDI
Eighty km south-east of the Ahmed Hamdi Tunnel is Ras al-Gindi, which features the 800-year-old Fortress of Salah ad-Din. In the 12th century AD, Muslims from Africa and the Mediterranean streamed across the Sinai on their way to Mecca. As the three caravan routes they followed all converged at Ras al-Gindi, Salah ad-Din built a fortress here to protect the pilgrims making their haj. He also planned to use the fort, which is still largely intact, as a base from which to launch attacks on the Crusaders, who had advanced as far as Jerusalem. As it turned out, Salah ad-Din managed to evict the Crusaders from the Holy City even before the completion of his fortress.

Ras al-Gindi is definitely off the beaten track and it is rarely visited. There is no public transport, so you must either have your own vehicle or hire a taxi.

RAS AS-SUDR
Ras as-Sudr, or Sudr, is about 60 km south of the Ahmed Hamdi Tunnel. The town developed around one of the country's biggest oil refineries, yet for some strange reason the Egyptians decided to build a tourist resort here, which has been followed by a couple of others.

Places to Stay & Eat
The *Daghash Land Village* and *Summer Land Village*, both on the highway around Ras as-Sudr, are the cheap end of this unlikely resort area. They both have singles and doubles ranging from about E£15 to E£25.

The *Sudr Beach Inn* (☎ 93565), and the *Sudr Tourist Village* of which it is part, have hotel rooms and self-contained villas, near the refinery and on the beach, for between US$30 and US$39 per night.

The Red Sea Club has opened its *Moon Beach Resort* in competition at Km 98 on the road to El-Tor. Its rooms are slightly more expensive.

Getting There & Away
Buses from Suez to Sharm el-Sheikh and St Catherine's pass through Sudr, as do the Sinai buses coming through from Cairo; the ones from Suez leave at 10 am, 12.30 and 2 pm. The trip takes 1½ hours going either way.

HAMMAM FARA'UN
Hammam Fara'un, or 'the Pharaoh's bath', is about 55 km south of Ras as-Sudr. The Egyptians who travel here to relax in the hot springs and streams and lie on the beautiful, isolated beach rave about the place.

Getting There & Away
The Sinai buses from Cairo and Suez or going the other way can drop you off at the turn-off to Hammam Fara'un and the beach

is not too far from the main road. The time to Suez is about three hours.

FROM ABU ZENIMA TO EL-TOR

Several of Egypt's development schemes in the Sinai are being implemented along this 90-km stretch of coastline beside the Gulf of Suez. Most of the projects relate to the offshore oil fields; consequently, the area is marred by jumbled masses of pipes, derricks and machinery.

El-Tor, the administrative capital of southern Sinai, is something of a boom town, with a broad, clean central avenue bordered by new apartment buildings. If you do decide to stay here, there are a couple of hotels in town and some impressive coral and sea life to observe virtually within wading distance of the shore. There are also several banks, and this is the nearest place for visa extensions to the resorts of Sharm el-Sheikh and beyond – go to the town's Mogamma, the main administrative building.

RAS MOHAMMED

Declared a National Marine Park in 1988, its boundaries were pushed up close to the town of Sharm el-Sheikh the following year. The actual headland of Ras Mohammed is about 30 km short of Sharm el-Sheikh, on the road from El-Tor. Vehicles are permitted to enter (US$5 per person) for the day until sundown, but access is restricted to certain parts of the park.

Officially it is not permitted to stay in the camp overnight, although some travellers have been known to get the nod from rangers. If you are going to do this, respect the environment you're in and clean up after yourselves. Don't enter areas you know to be off-limits. To get around you really need your own vehicle, or you can join a day tour by jeep or bus from Sharm el-Sheikh and Na'ama Bay. Divers are often brought in by boat instead.

Take your passport with you to Ras Mohammed. Visitors to the Sinai on Sinai-only permits supposedly cannot go to Ras Mohammed, which is beyond the Sharm el-Sheikh boundary of the permit, but should not have any problem on boat dive trips. Check with the dive clubs if you have any doubts. See Diving & Snorkelling in the following Sharm el-Sheikh & Na'ama Bay section for more details on diving in the area.

SHARM EL-SHEIKH & NA'AMA BAY

The southern coast of the Gulf of Aqaba, between Tiran Island in the straits and Ras Mohammed at the tip of the Sinai, features some of the world's most brilliant and amazing underwater scenery. The crystal-clear water, the rare and lovely reefs and the incredible variety of exotic fish darting in and out of the colourful coral have made this a snorkelling and scuba-diving paradise, attracting a growing number of divers from all over the globe.

If you've never explored the living treasures of the deep, this is the place to do it. The reefs are easily accessible and you'll find all the necessary diving equipment, as well as accommodation, restaurants, bars and public services, around Na'ama Bay and in nearby Sharm el-Sheikh.

Na'ama Bay is a resort that has grown from virtually nothing since the early 1980s, while Sharm el-Sheikh, initially developed by the Israelis during their occupation of the peninsula, is a long-standing settlement. There are more accommodation possibilities in Na'ama Bay, as well as the bulk of the dive clubs, but both are undergoing an uninterrupted building boom. There's not much on hand for budget travellers though – the cheapest place is the Youth Hostel in Sharm el-Sheikh, at E£11.60 per person. See Places to Stay for more details.

Sharm el-Sheikh is about 30 km north of Ras Mohammed and six km short of Na'ama Bay, where the coast road south from Suez and Cairo turns the corner to run north up to the Israeli border.

Information

Registration If you intend to travel beyond the Sinai coast between Taba and Sharm el-Sheikh while in Egypt, you'll need to register with the police within seven days (you also need to have entered with a visa).

You can do this at the passport office in Sharm el-Sheikh. It's to the left of the ferry harbour when you approach from the town. It's open from 8 am to 1 pm and again from 8.30 to 10 pm every day but Friday. The process takes a couple of minutes. Hotels will also do it for if you wish, but charge up to E£5.

Tourist Police There is no tourist office. The main tourist police office is up on the hill in Sharm el-Sheikh. They also have a booth in front of the Marina Sharm Hotel in Na'ama Bay.

Money Banque Misr, the Bank of Alexandria and the National Bank of Egypt all have branches in Sharm el-Sheikh (on the hill) and in Na'ama Bay. You can get cash advances on Visa card and MasterCard at the Sharm el-Sheikh and the main Na'ama Bay branches of Banque Misr.

American Express (☎ 771575) has a branch at the Ghazala Hotel, in the South Sinai Travel office.

Post & Telecommunications The post office is in the shopping centre at the top of the hill in Sharm el-Sheikh and is open from 8 am to 3 pm, except Friday. The telephone office, past the mosque on the same hill, is

open 24 hours a day. There are no card phones.

Bookshops The Sinai Book Center in Na'ama Bay has the best selection of books in the area. The bookshops in the Hilton Fayrouz and Mövenpick hotels are not bad.

Underwater Photography It is possible to rent cameras from most of the dive clubs to snap some underwater memories. You can also get them at the Photo Shop, which has stores in the Mövenpick, Hilton Fayrouz and Residence hotels. The Red Sea Diving College also has a specialist underwater photography shop.

Diving Emergency Centres A modern decompression chamber, built largely with US-government aid money, went into operation in 1993 a little way past the ferry harbour in Sharm el-Sheikh on the road to El-Tor. It has a capacity of six people.

In addition, Drs Wael and Hussam Nasef have a small one-man chamber on the premises of the Red Sea Diving Club, near the jetty in Na'ama Bay. They have a US$6 insurance scheme open to divers with any club should they end up needing the centre. Talk to your dive centre first.

The Nasef brothers also run the Cairo Underwater & Hyperbaric Medicine Centre (☎ 260-0850), 13 Sharia Seif ad-Din Barquq, Nasr City, District 1, Cairo. As they spend most of their time in Sinai, the Cairo centre is usually unstaffed.

Diving & Snorkelling
Obviously, the main attractions here are underwater and are best seen with a mask and snorkel or scuba gear. For those who don't want to get their feet wet, there are also glass-bottom boats.

Na'ama itself has no reefs, but the stunning Near and Middle gardens and the even more incredible Far Garden can be reached by foot from the bay. The Near Garden is about 45 minutes north of Na'ama, near the point at the end of the bay, and the Far

Garden another half an hour along the coast. Take plenty of drinking water with you.

The following is a list of some of the dive sites from around Tiran Island (north of Na'ama Bay) stretching down past Sharm el-Sheikh and Ras Mohammed.

Small & Large Lagoons

Off the north-west tip of Tiran Island, the Small Lagoon features a shallow reef and the wreck of the *Sangria*. The currents are strong here, and there is a mooring. The Large Lagoon, just below it, has reef and sand fish.

Jackson Reef

Midway between Tiran Island and the mainland, this reef is home to sharks and large pelagic fish. There is a 70-metre drop-off, but be warned, this is not for beginners – the currents are dangerous. The wreck of the *Lara* lies here.

Hushasha

On the south side of Tiran Island, this shallow reef ends in a sandy floor with sea grass.

Gordon Reef

Close to Ras Nasrany, this is another popular site with experienced divers. There are sharks and open-water fish here. Thomas and Woodhouse reefs also have some good diving.

Ras Nasrany

There are two sites worth noting here. One, known as The Light, has a 40-metre drop-off and pelagic fish. At The Point you can enjoy a feast of colours in the reef fish.

Shark Bay

You can just walk in off the beach here and again see a rich variety of reef fish. There is a canyon from 10 to 25 metres, and the diving site also goes by that name. See Places to Stay for details of accommodation here.

The Tower

Just south of Na'ama Bay, this is a remarkable wall dropping 60 metres into the depths just off shore.

Amphoras

Also known as the Mercury site. A Turkish galleon lies at the bottom here. Evidence of its cargo of mercury can be seen in among the coral. Other dives between here and Ras Um Sid include Turtle Bay, Paradise and Fiasco.

Ras Um Sid

Near Sharm el-Sheikh, Ras Um Sid is easily accessible. Prime diving is a 20-minute walk from the Clifftop Hotel and a simple wade from the beach. The beautiful coral garden has lots of colourful fan coral, a great variety of fish, including barracuda and at least two resident Napoleon wrasse (which love hard-boiled eggs!). It's a good dive with a deep, sloping wall.

Temple

Just around the point are three large pinnacles rising to the surface from a depth of about 20 metres.

Ras Mohammed

Ras Mohammed, the southernmost point of the Sinai is, without doubt, one of the best diving sites in the world. The splendid coral gardens, with fish of every imaginable shape, size and brilliant colour, provide a stunning visual feast. There is also a shipwreck (which scattered hundreds of toilet bowls on the bottom) and a hangout for sharks which, fortunately, don't seem to be too hungry. In an attempt to protect the various dive sites around the point and along the coast of the National Marine Park, the number of boats that can bring in divers is subject to limits. You'll have to organise dives here through the dive clubs. Popular Ras Mohammed dive sites include the Shark Observatory, Sting Ray Alley and the Eel Garden – descriptive names! Off to the south-west is the wreck of the *Dunraven*.

The following goes for diving anywhere, but particularly for Ras Mohammed: ecologists fear the number of divers visiting this area will bring permanent damage to the coral and sea life. Try to enjoy it *without touching anything*.

Dive Shops There are more than a dozen dive centres around here, most of them in Na'ama Bay. All offer similar services, trips and equipment, but it pays to shop around, especially in the low season, when some of the clubs offer cut-price deals. Another reason for being here in the low season (the blistering summer months), especially for people doing courses, is the chance of getting closer attention – it is not unknown for instructors to take classes of one!

The Aquamarine Diving Centre (☎ 600276; fax 600176), connected with the PLM hotel of the same name, offers courses and a wide variety of diving possibilities and courses through the more recently established Red Sea Diving College (☎ 600145; fax 600144). The college organises courses only, and was established in conjunction with Scuba Pro International, which provides one of the world's best diving curricula. A full-day's diving (which means two dives) costs US$40 (US$50 in the Straits of Tiran or around Ras Mohammed). A week costs US$200. All equipment can be hired – US$20 a day for the lot (less if you hire stuff for more than one day) if you are doing a dive with the centre.

Another popular place is the Aquanaute centre (☎ 600619), located in the same building as the Whitehouse restaurant. Divers have also recommended the Camel Dive Club (☎ 600700; fax 600601), next door to the Tiran Village Hotel.

The Red Sea Diving Club (☎ 600342), run by the brothers Drs Wael and Hussam Nasef, sometimes has deals a little cheaper than some of the other clubs. It is a good outfit, and the doctors are experts in hyberbaric medicine. Before you go for a cheaper deal, check out where they are going to take you. There's little point in saving a few dollars if you're going to less interesting sites than those offered by competitors.

Other clubs include the Sinai Dive Club at the Hilton Fayrouz Village, Sinai Divers, the Colona Dive Club at the Kanabesh Hotel, Oonas Divers, and Scuba Schools International (Italia) at the New Tiran Hotel.

There are three centres in Sharm el-Sheikh: Tentoria (next door to the Safety Land hotel and camp); Diving World (El Kheima Hotel); and Discover Scuba, on the beach in front of the Hilton Residence Hotel.

The Cairo Diving Club organises monthly trips, rents equipment and offers plenty of information on the dive sites. For details, see the Dive Clubs entry in the Cairo Information section.

Other Water Sports

Most of the big hotels also offer above-water sports, including sailing lessons (E£30 an hour), water skiing (E£30 an hour), windsurfing (E£30 an hour), pedalos (E£15 an hour), glass-bottom boats, banana boats (E£20 for 15 minutes) and the like. Be prepared to pay fairly hefty sums of money to participate in any of this watery frolicking. If you want to use a hotel swimming pool, you will be looking at a fee, generally, of about E£30. Most of the beach space has been taken up by hotels – a bit remains public

at the northern end. Not all the hotels seem to take much notice of nonguests using their beach.

Camel Rides

Camel rides to 'traditional Bedouin villages' for 'traditional Bedouin meals' are staged for about US$40. If you want to experience the desert from the back of a camel and in the company of the Bedouins, you're better off heading for one of the tourist spots further north, such as Dahab, and negotiating treks with the Bedouins direct.

Horse-Riding

A growing business is stables offering horse-riding. There are a couple of 'farms' around Sharm el-Sheikh and Na'ama Bay, and more are on the way. The Saheel Horse Country Club (☎ 600197/8), across the road from the Hilton Fayrouz Village hotel, offers morning or sunset rides for one/two/three hours at US$25/35/45. Lessons cost US$10 an hour and you can go for full-day 'treks' for US$75. Overnight trips cost US$125 – all pretty pricey stuff. Similar deals are offered by the Nawara Farm Country Club (contact the Sanafir Hotel).

Desert Rides

A couple of the hotels, including the Aquamarine, organise desert rides on four-wheel motorbikes ('quads') – starting at about US$60 for two hours.

Organised Tours

For those who don't want to spend all their time in or under the water, the bigger hotels are organising a growing range of other things to do. Jeep or bus trips to St Catherine's Monastery, or such desert sights as the Coloured Canyon (see Nuweiba section) are available for US$40 to US$50. For US$116 you can get on to a helicopter for a quick circuit around Mt Sinai.

For those only visiting the Sinai, quick excursions are also organised to Cairo.

Places to Stay

Sharm el-Sheikh The cheapest place to stay

in an area geared to tourists with comparatively fat wallets is the *Youth Hostel*, which is up on the hill in Sharm el-Sheikh, between the mosque and the Clifftop Hotel. A bed in a fairly standard six-bed dorm costs E£11.60 with breakfast. It's open from 6.30 to 9 am and 2 to 10 pm, and they don't seem overly fussed about membership cards.

Safety Land, just off the road to Na'ama Bay, is the next cheapest budget alternative. A bed in a big military tent costs E£15 with breakfast (standard fare – egg, bread, butter and jam, with a cup of tea or lousy instant coffee). Bungalows with fans cost E£27/35 for singles/doubles, and they also have a few more expensive rooms around the E£50 mark. They have a bit of beach to themselves, although there's no snorkelling to speak of.

The *Clifftop Hotel* (for bookings, call Cairo ☎ 393-0200) is a relic from the Israeli occupation days, and now part of the Sinai Hotels & Diving Clubs group. They have reasonable bungalows for US$10 a bed, but most of them are occupied by dive club employees. Quite pleasant singles/doubles/triples with TV, air-con, fridge, phone and bathroom cost US$42/55/65 including breakfast.

The *El Kheima Resort* (☎ 600167; fax 600166) is the first place you pass on your way down the road from the port. It has bamboo-style bungalows at E£24/48 and single/double/triple rooms for E£64/83/107, including breakfast. It's not bad, but a little inconveniently located, unless you're just going to hang about here and use the dive club next door.

The new *Hilton Residence Hotel* (☎ 770424; fax 770726) has commanding views over the Red Sea and all the usual attributes of a hotel in its class. Rates are US$87 and US$115 for rooms that can take two and three people respectively. Breakfast is extra and 21% in taxes is loaded on top.

There are several other hotels going up in the area, including the very kitsch-looking *Sandy Hotel*, with its whitewashed crenellated walls; the pseudo-Moorish style *Petra Sharm*, which will have 80 rooms, a pool and

its own dive club; the posh *Baraka Village*; and the *Delfino Tourist Village*, going up near the Clifftop Hotel.

Na'ama Bay The building boom is in full swing here too, and one can't help the feeling that between them, Sharm el-Sheikh and Na'ama Bay are going the way of Hurghada – an unending building site, spreading the blight of hotels up and down a once untouched coastline.

At the northern end of the bay, along the road heading out to Shark Bay and on to Dahab, is the cheapest option in Na'ama. The *Pigeon House* (☎ 600996; fax 600965), which opened in 1993, has comfortable huts (or bungalows, depending on what you want to call these bamboo structures) with fans and breakfast for E£25/40. Quite small rooms are not such hot value, although clean and comfortable, at E£50/60. The manager, Mr Alaa ad-Din, is a friendly fellow. Nearby, the Sonesta chain is building a big hotel complex.

Virtually across the road is *Gafy Land* (☎ & fax 600210), once the site of a cheap camp, now offering 45 modern rooms with low ceilings, TV, air-con, phone, minibar and a big bath for US$38/50 plus taxes. Breakfast is not included.

A bit further north, the Swedish-run dive centre, Oonas, has air-con rooms for US$21 including breakfast, for people diving with the centre.

Moving south, the *PLM Hotel Aquamarine* (☎ 600175; fax 600177) has singles/doubles/triples for US$74/106/128 plus taxes and breakfast. Groups can get certain discounts, and it is worth pushing for a drop in the low-season price.

Next door is the *Hilton Fayrouz Village* (☎ 760575; fax 770726), a sprawling 'village' of deluxe air-conditioned bungalows. It has almost everything you'd expect of a Hilton hotel, including high prices – singles/doubles are US$85/97 plus taxes and breakfast. Larger suites are even more expensive.

The four-star *Ghazala Hotel* (☎ 771284; fax 771349) is a medium-size complex offering rooms and cool bungalows with carpeting and polished wood-slat walls. Singles/doubles/triples cost US$68/96/111, including breakfast and all taxes.

The biggest and perhaps most awful addition to the Na'ama Bay waterfront is the outsize *Mövenpick Hotel* (☎ 600100/5; fax 600111). It has two zones – the Front Area on the promenade and the so-called Sports Area spilling back into the desert. Singles/doubles/triples in the front area are US$130/169/195, including taxes and buffet breakfast. Rooms in the other half are each about US$40 cheaper, and summer prices come down too.

Between the Mövenpick and the long-standing Marina Sharm Hotel is a small conglomeration of shops, restaurants and hotels. Among these is the *Kanabesh* (☎ 600184; fax 600185), on the promenade. It has more modest rooms at US$50/69/88/111. For an extra US$6 per person, you can get half board.

The *Red Sea Diving College* next door has air-con rooms for people taking diving courses with the college. They offer various deals depending on the season.

The *Sanafir* (☎ 600197; fax 600196) has four classes of rooms. Prices for a single range from US$22 for a hut through to US$51 for a 'superior' room. The prices include breakfast but tax has to be added. It's the Moorish-style brainchild of the dashing Adly al-Mestekawi, who is a combination of Indiana Jones and Omar Sharif. Once in a while, he rides his horse through the arched hotel entrance and into the central courtyard café, bar and restaurant area. The Sanafir's better rooms have whitewashed walls, domed ceilings, and beds raised two or three steps above the floor. The shared showers and bathrooms for the cheaper rooms are very clean.

There are two hotels by the name of Tiran. A block back from the promenade, the three-star *Tiran Village* (☎ 600221; fax 600220) is a pleasant enough place with comfortable rooms for US$54/70/85 including breakfast. You can also pay for full board, but at US$139/172/205, it's not worth it.

Across the road and on the waterfront, the 48-room *New Tiran Hotel* (☎ 600225; fax 600220) has more spacious and cooler rooms for US$60/77.40/97. The angular, rabbit-warren design of the place is unattractive, but the rooms are fine.

Overlooking the bay from the south end, the 90-room *Helnan Marina Sharm Hotel* (☎ & fax 768385) was the Israeli hotel which pioneered Na'ama Bay as a resort. The complex includes three restaurants, two cafeterias, a bakery and a ping-pong room. The cheaper domed, prefabricated, plexi-glass bungalows are not bad at US$16 for two, but they were due to be demolished at the time of writing. The more expensive rooms cost US$47/58.50/65.50; quite reasonable compared with the competition, but some people have complained that the hotel and service are a little on the shabby side.

For really sweeping views of the Red Sea, you could head up to the *Halomy Sharm Village*, further on from the Red Sea Diving Club (there is also an access track off the main road to Sharm el-Sheikh). This place offers 70 'chalets' in various categories. The cheapest are US$71/99 including breakfast and taxes, the most expensive US$95/121.

Places to Eat

Sharm el-Sheikh There is not a huge range of possibilities here, but a couple of small restaurants/cafés in the market area behind the bus station offer a few options. The *Sinai Star* does some excellent fish meals for about E£10 a person.

The nearby *Brilliant Restaurant* does a range of traditional Egyptian food at reasonable prices. A plate of kofta with salad should cost about E£7. They also have sweets. The *Fisherman's Café* does similar food at similar prices, but a smaller helping of salad it would be hard to find.

The *Aftet el-Mesk* and *El Ghazal* are much the same sort of place. More up-market and expensive is the *Restaurant Michelle*, which does calamari for E£15 and couscous for E£25. It's a lonely looking place, but as the hotels go up the restaurants might seem less out of place.

leader Anwar Sadat and his Israeli opposite number, Menachem Begin, met while the Israeli air force bombed an Iraqi nuclear power plant (an embarrassment to Sadat), has been taken over by the Helnan company and is part of the Marina Sharm Hotel. They have a range of Western and Oriental dishes. The terrace is a pleasant place for dinner, or just for tea or a beer.

The hotels have a wide range of restaurants, offering everything from seafood to Thai dishes. None of these places suits a budget traveller's pocket, but what does around here?

Dolce Vita, also in the mall, has great ice cream, but at E£2 a scoop, it's an expensive treat.

Entertainment
Discos & Bars There are a few bars and dance establishments in the hotels, including the *Cactus Disco* in the Mövenpick Hotel, another disco in the *Hilton Fayrouz Village* and *Popeye's Bar* in the Kanabesh Hotel. One of the more popular places to have a drink (Stella Export only, E£11) is the rooftop bar at the *Sanafir Hotel*.

Getting There & Away
Air Ras Nasrany, the airport for Sharm el-Sheikh and Na'ama Bay, is about eight km north of Na'ama Bay. EgyptAir has daily flights to Cairo for E£323 one way. Departures are at 11.30 am on Saturday and Thursday and 9 am every other day. There are two flights a week between Sharm el-Sheikh and Luxor for the same price.

Air Sinai flies from Cairo to Sharm el-Sheikh on Monday, for US$96 one way. These flights proceed to Tel Aviv.

There used to be EgyptAir flights between Hurghada and Sharm el-Sheikh, but at the time of writing none were running.

There are charter flights from various European cities virtually all year round. If you happen to be here and want to head off directly to Europe, it is a good idea to check around to see what charters are available for the one-way flight out.

Na'ama Bay There are a lot of places to eat here, but don't expect to dine cheaply (by the standards of the rest of the country anyway). In the El Sharm Mall, gathered around a small fountain, are a couple of places that won't tax the budget too heavily. You can get good felafel (ta'amiyya) or fuul for about E£1 at *Aida*. The *Star Light* does a good supreme pizza for E£7 and you can get a tea from *Al-Fishawy's*, a poor imitation of its Cairo namesake.

The Argentinian-run *Viva* on the promenade is a hangout popular with divers and instructors. The food is reasonable, and if they keep up their tradition of extended happy hours on drinks and a menu of four dishes at E£7, they are likely to remain popular.

Just down the road is the *Steakhouse*, which always seems empty.

There are a couple of Chinese-Korean restaurants, the *Shin Seoul* in the mall and another in the Sanafir Hotel.

The *White House*, where the Egyptian

Bus The main bus station is in Sharm el-Sheikh itself. Buses heading on to Dahab and beyond stop in the car park in front of the Marina Sharm Hotel in Na'ama Bay as well.

If you're catching a bus in the direction of Suez or Cairo, it's advisable to get it from Sharm el-Sheikh, as assurances about the buses calling in at Na'ama Bay 'about an hour before leaving Sharm el-Sheikh' seem vague at best. Seats to Cairo can and should be booked ahead.

Six buses run from the Sinai Terminal at Midan Abbassiya, Cairo, to Sharm el-Sheikh. The trip takes about seven hours. See Cairo Getting There & Away for more details. From Sharm el-Sheikh, the cheapest direct service runs at 8 am. It costs E£25 and has pitiful air-con. The 7 and 10 am and 1 pm buses cost E£10 more, and have air-con and the dubious asset of nonstop videos. The latter two have onboard toilets too, which makes for a quicker trip. The 4.30 pm bus is the same but costs E£40, while the 11.30 pm and midnight buses cost E£50.

It is much cheaper to get a bus to Suez and then another bus or service taxi from there to Cairo (the same is also true in reverse). There are two departures to Suez for E£15, at 9 and 11 am.

Six buses go to Dahab. The 6.30 am and 3 pm cost E£10; the 8 and 9 am, 5 and 7 pm buses cost E£7. The 9 am, 5 and 7 pm buses go on to Nuweiba and cost E£9. The 9 am bus goes all the way to Taba and costs E£12. There is a bus to St Catherine's Monastery at 8 am for E£12.

There is a daily bus to Mansoura at 10.30 pm for E£30. The same bus also goes to Zagazig for E£25. A second bus to Zagazig leaves at noon and costs E£20. At least one of these passes through Ismailia.

Boat Barring breakdowns and other problems, there is usually at least one daily ferry between Sharm el-Sheikh and Hurghada. There is no service on Friday. The fare for the five-hour trip is E£70 one way, and the ferry leaves Sharm el-Sheikh at 10.30 am. Tickets can be booked through most hotels or at the Spring Tours office in the Tiran

Village Hotel complex in Na'ama Bay. See also Hurghada Getting There & Away.

Getting Around
To/From the Airport A taxi to Ras Nasrany airport will cost about E£15 from Na'ama Bay.

Bus An opensided public bus, known as a *tof-tof*, runs every 40 minutes or so until about 11 pm between Sharm el-Sheikh and Na'ama Bay. It costs 50 pt for locals and E£1 for tourists, a highly irritating piece of discrimination. You can also get Toyota pick-ups for the same price, although they are less rigid about extracting the tourist rate. Other than that, it is quite possible to hitch, as there is a fair amount of traffic on the roads. The usual warnings about hitching apply.

A private bus runs between the two Hilton hotels too.

Motorbike The Sanafir Hotel rents out motorbikes at E£15 an hour or E£70 for 12 hours.

Bicycle There's probably not really much point, but you can rent a bicycle for the day from stands along the promenade in Na'ama Bay for E£5. Once you have your bike, where are you going to take it?

SHARK BAY
Also known as Shark's Bay or *Beit al-Irsh*, this low-key resort camp is about five km on from Na'ama Bay (about 2 km down a track off the main road). Located on a pebbly beach from where you can walk in to some quite good snorkelling, it is particularly popular with Germans and Israelis, most of whom dive with the Embarak dive club there.

Places to Stay & Eat
At the *Shark's Bay Camp* (☎ 600208) you can stay in clean and comfortable huts for E£31.50/42, including breakfast. Or you can pitch a tent on the beach or just sleep in the open for E£12. Put off by this price, some

people have managed to camp for free just south of the beach and camp area without any hassles. There are clean toilets and showers with hot water.

The limited lunch and dinner menu is a little expensive (minimum charge E£12), and some people prefer to hitch a ride into Na'ama Bay to eat.

Getting There & Away

The only way in and out is to hitch or bargain with taxi drivers. Trying to get there in the dead of night may well entail walking the whole way.

DAHAB

The village beach resort of Dahab is 85 km north of Sharm el-Sheikh on the Gulf of Aqaba. Dahab means 'gold' in Arabic, and the Bedouins named the beach after its glimmering sands, which resemble gold dust. There are two parts to Dahab – in the new part, referred to by the locals as Dahab City, are the more expensive hotels, bus station, post and phone offices and bank. The other part of Dahab was a Bedouin village, about 2½ km north of town. It now has more low-budget travellers and Egyptian entrepreneurs than Bedouins in residence. The part of the village where the Bedouins actually live is called Assalah, which is at the northern (lighthouse) end of what is now a higgledy-piggledy stretch of 'camps' and laid-back restaurants in among the palm trees. Accommodation virtually on the beach generally costs only E£4 to E£5 a night. The number of camps is spreading around the coast and a couple are putting second storeys on – a most unwelcome development. Dahab, like other places further up the coast, gets very crowded on Israeli holidays.

Orientation & Information

Dahab itself is off the Sharm el-Sheikh-Nuweiba-Taba road and the Bedouin village and camps are off the Dahab turn-off road. The post office and phone office (the latter is open 24 hours a day, seven days a week and has a card phone for international calls) are across the road from the main bus stop in the new town. There is a branch of the National Bank of Egypt at the PLM Azur Holiday Village (open 9 am to noon and 6 to 9 pm).

There is another fairly expensive hotel further down the coast away from town and an Assalah-style 'camp' next door.

The tourist police are near the Holiday Village. It is apparently possible to register your arrival in Egypt in Dahab.

Two middle-range hotels lie on the coast between the Holiday Village and the Bedouin village, and one of them has a dive centre. The remainder of the accommodation (the 'camps') and a tangle of cafés, bazaars and 'supermarkets', stretch along the coast up to the lighthouse. Although the area where the Bedouins live is properly called Assalah, the coast from the lighthouse to about where the long-established Mohammed Ali camp is located is known to the locals as Mazbat. From there to the Holiday Village is Mashrabat.

Just next to the Dolphin camp is an excavation site of Islamic and Coptic ruins. Just what the small site was is still unclear, but it is an intriguing diversion to think of this small town thriving in centuries gone by.

Drugs

Nothing anyone can say or write will stop people from buying and using marijuana in Dahab. It's freely available (about E£20 for a 'cup' – a small Arabic coffee cup full) and in wide use. It appears other drugs, including acid, are in limited circulation, brought in from Israel.

If you are going to indulge, at least try to be discreet. Although there is not a huge police presence, penalties for drug offences are high in Egypt, and people have been arrested here. Dealing and smuggling attract sentences of 25 years' jail or death by hanging. The first execution for such an offence took place in 1989. The rules apply equally to foreigners, and although simple possession of marijuana attracts lower penalties, there is nothing funny about Egyptian jails, even for a day.

Water Sports

After lounging around, diving is the most popular activity in Dahab. The best sites are north and south of the resort motel. Either look for the waves breaking on the offshore coral, or check the map at the dive shop. Some of the spots, from north to south, are Bells, the Blue Hole, Canyon, Little Canyon, Abu Hillal, Eel Garden, Lighthouse, Nesima Reef, 'Islands' (a collection of coral pinnacles), Lagoon, Oasis and Caves.

There are now four dive centres operating in Dahab. The first of them was the Sinai Dive Club (☎ 600890; fax 600891), located in the Holiday Village. Some divers have been put off by the state of the equipment and the lack of an alternative air source. And although they claim to run PADI courses, they have no manuals or log books. The people who used to run it, Mohammed and Ingrid Kabany, have set up their own hotel and dive centre called Inmo (no prizes for guessing why), between the Gulf Hotel and the southernmost camps along the beach. Further up, near the Dolphin camp, is the Nesima Dive Centre, the most recent addition. They say they are the only ones exploring the coast for new dive sites. Another relatively new Austrian-run place is out at the Canyon dive site north of Assalah – universally recognised, even by the opposition, as the friendliest place of the lot (E£5 in a pick-up).

The Blue Hole is an infamous deep dive, recommended only for experienced divers. The 'hole' is an 80-metre-deep pool in the reef, only a few metres out from shore. The most popular challenge is to dive to a depth of about 60 metres and swim through a tunnel to the outer edge of the reef. This is most definitely not a dive for the inexperienced. There are lurid tales of fatalities due to nitrogen narcosis or improper use of equipment (which isn't difficult at such a depth). Arman Gazeryan, the Turkish manager of the Nesima centre, described the dive as 'overrated', adding that the snorkelling is much better. 'There are a lot of good divers and equipment down there.'

An easier and probably more enjoyable approach to the Blue Hole is to dive to a much more reasonable depth and work your way around the edge of the hole to a dip in the reef known as 'the bridge'. This part of the reef seems to attract a greater assortment of bright, colourful fish, perhaps because of the noticeably warmer waters. Since this is quite close to the surface, it can also be viewed using nothing more than snorkelling gear.

The Canyon is also a popular shore dive but, to an inexperienced diver, it will seem somewhat harrowing at first. From the shore, you snorkel along the reef before diving, past a wall of coral, to the edge of the Canyon. It

is dark, narrow and seems capable of swallowing you.

The dive centres all offer a full range of diving possibilities, including night dives and beginners' courses for PADI or NAUI certification, which cost around US$300 for the five-day course, books, certification and so on. A day's diving starts at about US$45.

Many snorkellers head for Eel Garden, just north of the village.

You can hire snorkelling gear along the beach for about E£5 a day. Pedalos cost E£20 an hour and kayaks E£10 an hour.

Camel Treks

Many of the local Bedouins organise camel trips to the interior of the Sinai. In the morning, camel drivers and their camels congregate along the waterfront in the village. Register with the police before beginning the trek, and don't pay the camel driver until you return to the village. A one-day trip costs E£50. As all drivers seem to have agreed among themselves on this price, bargaining will probably get you nowhere. The price includes food. A three-day trek to Ras Abu Quluum (one day out, a day there and a day's riding back) involves some desert and coastal scenery. Another popular trek is to Wadi Gnay, where there is a small oasis and a Bedouin village. The wadi begins about four km south, along the shore from the Holiday Village.

The Inmo Hotel organises a three-day camel and dive safari to what they guarantee to be virgin dive sites. It costs US$90 a day.

Jeep Treks

Jeep trips to the Coloured Canyon, Wadi Ghazaba and the Khudra Oasis are among the treks organised from the Holiday Village. You can also negotiate similar trips in the Bedouin village. Enquire at the Palm camp for trips costing about E£50 a day.

Helicopter Rides

The truly posh can pay US$75 for a 10-minute chopper flight over St Catherine's Monastery and Mt Sinai, again organised through the Holiday Village reception.

Horse-Riding

It is also possible to hire horses. Ask around or look for the Moses Stables.

Places to Stay – bottom end

Most, if not all, low-budget travellers head straight for the Bedouin village. There is a plethora of so-called camps, which are basically compounds with simple stone and cement rooms of two or three mattresses. It is more or less useless recommending one over the other, as there is little to distinguish them. One exception is the *Mohammed Ali*, which, although it has not had rave reviews from all travellers, stands out by having two storeys and offering more expensive rooms ranging up to E£50 a double with own clean bath and shower and fat, soft mattresses.

Some others have been recommended, as much for location as anything else. These include the *Penguin*, *Dolphin* and the *Lighthouse*. The building and the changes continue, so a few things to look for to get the best deal are: hot water (some of the camps now offer hot showers), decent mattresses, electric lighting (another recent development, although candles are handy for those inevitable blackouts) and fly screens.

A warning on the *Moon Valley Camp*. One woman reported being physically assaulted by one of the camp's staff.

Outside the village, there is a similar camp called the *Canun Hotel Camp* just by the Holiday Village. A hot, sweaty bungalow in what resembles a garbage dump costs E£20 for three. Or you can pitch a tent in the dump for E£5. They sell breakfast and drinks too, but there is no earthly reason to stay.

Places to Stay – middle

The *Gulf Hotel*, south of the village and the more expensive Inmo Hotel and dive centre, has doubles of varying quality for E£28/38/48, including breakfast. Singles in the three classes are E£4 less. The cheapest of these is camp style but with comfortable beds and fan. This place has the only disco and drinking establishment (the Black Prince) in the area outside the sterile possibilities offered by the Holiday Village.

The most recent arrival in Dahab is the *Sinai Paradise Touristic Village* (☎ 600880; fax 600881), a borderline middle-category place. It has singles and doubles without breakfast for US$30 and US$50 plus taxes. The chalet-style rooms are small but comfortable, but really overpriced. The location is austere and they have no fans. It's empty, so you might be able to bargain, although they'll tell you there's no place else to stay.

Places to Stay – top end

The *Inmo Hotel* caters mainly to people on diving packages from Europe, especially Germany, and opened in December 1992. Singles/doubles/triples/quadruples are E£126.54/166.80/219.78/266.40. There are reductions for those on diving trips. The rooms are quite attractive, but with no fans or air-con they can get pretty stifling in summer.

The top of the heap is the *PLM Azur Holiday Village* (☎ 600403), with 130 rooms and five suites. Singles and doubles in various categories range from US$39 to US$92 plus taxes. They also have well-kept two-bed bungalows for E£40/85, including breakfast. Outsiders can use the beach for E£10.

Places to Eat

For those with a bit of money and the energy to go into town, the *PLM Azur Holiday Village* does a reasonable breakfast buffet for E£10.

There is a string of places to eat at along the beach in the Bedouin village. They serve breakfast, lunch and dinner and most seem to have identical menus – a meal will generally cost you about E£10 to E£15. Service is universally slow. For those sick of the usual Egyptian fare, especially at breakfast, the sweet pancakes with fruit and ice cream will be a treat. The *Sinai Rose*, out by the lighthouse, seems particularly good for these. Generally, people hang out in these places, occasionally summoning the strength of mind and soul to flop into the sparkling waters of the Gulf of Aqaba for a while and then emerge to collapse back into a state of idyllic inertia and order a tea or cola.

A few of the restaurants do some nice looking fish, displaying their wares out the front and selling by weight. The *Little Prince*, *Lucky Zone* and *Al Capone* all do this. The *Blue Hole Restaurant* doesn't do a bad imitation of a pasty. The *Oxford* seems to be a popular place to hang out, while the *Neptun* has a vaguely Mediterranean feel to it.

Breaking the mould entirely is the new Korean Chinese *Primo Restaurant* and hamburger joint by the Mohammed Ali camp. The food, both Chinese and burgers, is good and the service fast. It may be short-lived though, as it opened at the tail end of the high season and was struggling through the summer of 1993. Mains cost from E£8 to E£15.

The café in the Mohammed Ali camp has the worst sahleb in Egypt.

Entertainment

Since the MFO and Egyptian authorities combined to ban the sale of alcohol in the restaurants of the Bedouin village in 1990, Dahab's night life has concentrated itself on the *Black Prince* disco in the Gulf Hotel. An extraordinary mix of travellers, Egyptians, and the odd MFO chap make this a remarkably enjoyable dance scene. Stella local beer is E£5 and no-one seems to worry about collecting the entry charge (E£10?). And if you are sick of the dance floor, you can sway to your favourite tunes on the beach in front. The place is often open until dawn.

Getting There & Away

Bus The most regular connection is between Sharm el-Sheikh and Dahab, with up to six buses running between the two, most of them on part of other longer runs. They cost E£7 or E£10 for the 1½-hour trip. There are two morning buses to Nuweiba, at 6.30 and 10.30 am, for E£5. The latter goes on to Taba and costs E£8 for the full trip. The 9.30 am service to St Catherine's costs E£9 and takes two to three hours. It goes on to Cairo (E£55). Another bus at 8 am for Cairo that does not set down passengers in St Catherine's costs E£40. There is another bus for Suez at 8.30 am (E£20) and one at 10 am for Ismailia and Zagazig.

The bus drops incoming passengers at the Holiday Village, although the terminal is in town. When leaving, it is probably best to wait at the Holiday Village, although buses call at both stops on their way out.

Service Taxi As a rule, service taxis are much more expensive than buses – they know you're only using them because the bus doesn't suit and the hitching possibilities are limited. They have a captive market. Although a trip to, say, St Catherine's can cost as little as E£10 a person, it will often cost closer to E£20. A whole taxi (maximum seven passengers) to Nuweiba or Sharm el-Sheikh costs about E£50 to E£60. Part of the reason for the high fares is that few locals do such trips, so pricing has not been regulated at a level that Egyptians would be able to afford.

Getting Around
A taxi from the Dahab bus stop to the Bedouin village should not really cost more than a couple of pounds, but more often than not you'll find E£4 being their lowest rate.

NUWEIBA
The beach and port town of Nuweiba is 87 km north of Dahab. During the Israeli occupation, it was also the site of a major *moshav* (farming settlement), which has now been converted into a residence for Egyptian government officials.

Nuweiba is certainly not the most attractive of the Sinai beach resorts; the area has become something of a major port, with a continual flow of people and vehicle traffic on and off the ferry between Nuweiba and Aqaba.

Orientation
The town is divided into two parts. To the south is the port with a large bus station and banks and fairly awful hotels for people who get stuck waiting for a berth (this, by the way,

is rarely a problem for foot passengers). A few km further north is Nuweiba City, where the tourist resort hotels and the area's only dive centre are located, as well as a couple of places to eat. The mountain scenery, however, is beautiful and the coral reefs, for which Nuweiba is renowned, are spectacular.

Information
The post office and phone office are near the hospital on the exit road from Nuweiba City. There's another post office on the road leading into the port. At least four banks can be found on or near the same road. The tourist police are located near the Nuweiba Holiday Village (by the entrance to its camping area), and a branch of the National Egyptian Bank is open from 9 am to noon and from 6 to 9 pm inside the Nuweiba Holiday Village.

Coloured Canyon
The Coloured Canyon is between St Catherine's and Nuweiba. Few tourists visit the area, and getting there is something of an adventure. As it's about five km from the main road, you will need a 4WD vehicle. Even then, you have to park your vehicle and walk for about 1½ hours. This surrealistic place derives its name from the layers of bright, multicoloured stones that resemble paintings on the canyon's very steep, narrow walls. Total silence (the canyon is sheltered from the wind) adds to the eeriness. The canyon is sometimes known as the Blue Valley because a Swiss man painted the whole valley blue about 10 years ago.

Water Sports
Once again, underwater delights are the feature attraction and scuba diving and snorkelling the prime activities.

The Diving Camp Nuweiba (☎ 768832), run by Hartmut Janssen and Sylvia May, is on the beach just a few hundred metres to the south of the Holiday Village camping area. It offers the necessary equipment at much the same prices as in Na'ama Bay. The centre also hires out windsurfers, kayaks and pedal boats, by the hour. If you can get 10 people together, you can rent a glass-bottom boat. Fishing trips can also be organised. CMAS certificate courses for beginners are on offer as well.

Camel & Jeep Treks
Check with the reception desk of the Nuweiba Holiday Village about camel or jeep trips into the mountains. Trips by jeep to the Khudra Oasis, 'Ain Mahmed and 'Ain Furtaga can last for three days or so, or longer on camel. The trip to the Coloured Canyon can be done in a day. They charge about E£70 a day including food. Half-day excursions without food cost E£24.

Other camel trips can be arranged by talking to the Bedouins in Nuweiba or the village of Tarabin, a few km north of Nuweiba City. Trips generally cost about E£40 to E£50 a day. See under Tarabin for more details.

Places to Stay
Nuweiba Port There are three fairly unimpressive hotels you can stay in by the port if you should get stuck for any reason and want to be close to the ship. The *Al-Zahraa* is the worst and they have the cheek to ask for E£20/30. Avoid this place. Across the road is the *Al-Haramin*, which has similar prices and standards. You can't help feeling they are lifting the rate for the benefit of foreigners.

Further up the road is the *Baracuda Hotel*. It's quite expensive, but at least it is something approaching a reasonable deal. Singles/doubles with air-con and clean bathroom come for E£41/53. There is a bar downstairs, and the reception can help with bus information.

Nuweiba City There are a couple of simple camps with a few huts along the beach south of the Al-Waha Tourism Village (see below). They are called the *Sinai Star* and *Duna*. The latter has been recommended by some travellers looking for peace and nothing at all to do.

The cheapest way to stay in Nuweiba, without simply choosing a spot and pitching a tent, is to do the same in the grounds of the *Nuweiba Holiday Camp*, which is part of the Nuweiba Holiday Village. This costs E£3.15. Simply using their beach for the day would cost E£3 anyway. Otherwise you can use one of their double/triple bungalows, which cost E£30/45 a night.

Down the road a little way (heading south) is the *Al-Waha Tourism Village* (☎ 500420/1), which has tents for the same price but includes breakfast. They also have quite pleasant rooms for E£55/70.

Better value is the *City Beach Village*, just south of the dune that separates the expanding Nuweiba from the neighbouring village of Tarabin. Here single/double rooms go for E£25/38, or you can pitch a tent for E£5.

Until the *Nuweiba Coral Hilton* opens for business (it's down near the port), the *Nuweiba Holiday Village* will remain the premier establishment, catering mainly to package tourists. Rooms with breakfast range from US$32 plus taxes for the cheapest single to US$80 for a double.

Places to Eat
At one of the several places buses stop, between the Nuweiba Holiday Village and the hospital on the highway, you can try your luck at *Dr Shishkebab* or *King Fish*.

Next to the Nuweiba Holiday Camp is the *Morgana*, which specialises in seafood. The *Makondo* is another such place.

Getting There & Away
Bus Getting a bus out of Nuweiba can be a bit confusing, especially if you're staying in nearby Tarabin. Buses going to or from Taba pass down the highway and turn at the hospital to do a circuit by the Nuweiba Holiday Camp and Dr Shishkebab, before heading out again and proceeding on their way. They usually also call in at the port. You can presumably pick the buses up at any of these places (you can certainly get off).

Passengers on the boat from Aqaba should have nothing to worry about, as buses to Cairo and other destinations generally meet it. A bus from Taba to Cairo via St Catherine's stops at the hospital around 11 am (it's sometimes early). The fare is E£10 to St Catherine's and E£45 to E£50 to Cairo. There is a bus to Dahab (E£5) at 7 am and 4 pm. The bus from Sharm el-Sheikh and Dahab to Taba passes through about 12.30 pm.

From the port bus station, the 6 am bus to Suez costs E£20 and takes about six hours. There are also buses to Mansoura, Ismailia and Zagazig from the port.

There are supposedly scheduled departures for Cairo at 3 and 11 pm, as well as buses to meet the boat, but it would be wise to triple-check this (and indeed all the schedules).

Service Taxi There is a big service-taxi station by the port, and for once in the Sinai there are flat rates commensurate with what Egyptians might be prepared to pay. The fare to Suez is E£30 a person and E£40 to Midan Ulali in Cairo.

Boat Two ferries a day travel from Nuweiba to Aqaba in Jordan. The ferries are scheduled to depart at 11 am and 4 pm but, in fact, they wait for the buses from Cairo, which usually leave the Sinai Terminal (Midan Abbassiya) at 9 am and 11 pm. The ferries will also be delayed until all passport and customs formalities are completed. Tickets cost US$25, payable in dollars only. If you don't have the money, and the banks prove useless, the police will probably lead you to some money changers in the port area. Note that Jordanian currency cannot be changed in Nuweiba, although it appears to be accepted by banks in Cairo.

If you're planning to return to Egypt the same way, buy the return leg ticket in Jordan, as it's cheaper at around US$18.

TARABIN

This quiet beachside oasis offers peace, swimming and simple bamboo huts to the traveller sick of the madding crowds and for whom even the buzz of Dahab is too much. The place has been 'discovered' over the past few years, and the sight of the odd tour bus with day-trippers sitting on the beach is a horrible eyesore. The day-trippers don't hang about, and the evenings remain pretty much undisturbed, except for the Sudanese music wafting out over the Gulf from the handful of restaurants scattered in among the huts. How long the tranquillity will last is a moot point. Housing projects are moving up from Nuweiba and, as more people come here, the urge to 'develop' along Dahab lines will be difficult to resist.

The other disturbing, if inevitable, trend is the appearance of large, expensive 'tourist villages' along the coast from here to Taba, all in various stages of completion. Although most of them have been designed with at least some modesty (no skyscrapers here), they mar the wild beauty of this desert coast, as indeed will the plane and bus loads of package tourists they are hoping to attract. It's to be hoped that the development will be kept within reasonable bounds.

If you are missing monuments, have a look at the citadel of Sheikh Tarabin.

Camel Treks

If you'd like to do a trek but don't want to join something organised by the Nuweiba Holiday Village, you can simply ask the Bedouins here or enquire at the Blue Bus Restaurant by the dune.

Places to Stay & Eat

You can get a mattress in a bamboo hut for E£5 at – from north to south – *Jamia's Red Sea Camp*, The *Sea Beach*, the *Palm Beach* (which boasts a hot-water shower), *Camp David*, the *Oasis Camp* or the camp behind the *Blue Bus* restaurant. Judge for yourself which camps have the more solid huts – the differences are not too great. Note that, in the event of a sandstorm (they don't happen too often), the less perfectly constructed ones will fill with a fine yellow dust. Most of these places have cafés selling food and drinks. In some cases you simply sign for what you have in a book and pay the bill at the end – a refreshing trust system. Sudanese run a few of these places, and bring their own special laid-back touch to this laid-back place.

Getting There & Away

As Tarabin's popularity has grown, service taxis have taken to gathering around the place to take people directly out on the road north to Israel or south to Dahab, St Catherine's or Sharm el-Sheikh. To get the buses operating from Nuweiba, you need to walk the couple of km (or catch a service taxi) to one of the stops in Nuweiba City, or get down to the port (too far to walk).

MAAGANA & DEVIL'S HEAD BEACHES

Located by stunning blue waters about seven and 12 km north of Tarabin respectively, these are increasingly popular places to stop for a swim or snorkel. Both have a few huts and a café, and not much else. Without any sign of vegetation, though, they are a little on the bare side. The only way to get to them is by service taxi or hitching.

BASATA

The encampment of Basata is about 23 km north of Nuweiba. Basata, which means 'simplicity' in Arabic, is a simple, but clean, travellers' settlement of bamboo huts, very well maintained by a German-educated Egyptian named Sherif. The settlement has a common kitchen hut, an electricity generator, its own bakery and a camping ground. The kitchen is run on similar lines to some of those in Tarabin, although in a more organised way – you take whatever you want from the well-stocked cabinets and refrigerator, note it on a list bearing your name and pay for it before you leave. Sherif emphasises honesty and trusts that his guests will do the same. This friendly, carefree atmosphere attracts a variety of people, ranging from backpackers to employees of foreign embassies. You can climb the southern hill, but the one to the north is a military post.

At the time of writing, Basata charged E£20/30 for singles/doubles or E£5 to sleep on the beach. Although the huts are a little more sturdy than their counterparts further south, and the place is most pleasant, the price is a little high for travellers on a tight budget. If you simply want to use the beach, there is a E£4 day charge. Again, the only way here is by service taxi or hitching. Should you feel the need to reserve places (it can get quite crowded with groups), you can call 350-1829 in Cairo.

THE FJORD

This small protected bay is a popular sunbathing spot only about 15 km short of the Israeli border. Up on the rise to the north is a small snack and drinks stand.

PHARAOH'S ISLAND

Only about seven km short of the border-crossing town of Taba, Pharaoh's Island (*Geziret Faraun*) lies about 250 metres off the Egyptian coast. The islet is dominated by the much restored Castle of Salah ad-Din, a fortress actually built by the Crusaders in 1115, but captured and expanded by Salah ad-Din in 1170 as a bulwark against feared Crusader penetration south from Palestine. At the height of Crusader successes, it was feared they might attempt to head for the holy cities of Mecca and Medina. Some of the modern restoration is painfully obvious (concrete was not a prime building material in Salah ad-Din's time), but the island is a pleasant place for a half-day trip. Teeming with fish and coral life, the limpid aqua waters are extremely inviting, and a lot of Israeli pleasure boats carrying divers cruise down here from nearby Eilat. From the island you can see the Taba Hilton up the road and the port city of Aqaba in Jordan at the top of the gulf of the same name.

Entry costs E£8 (E£4 for students), but the boat ride there and back is an outlandish E£10.50. Because it's so close, you get a more than adequate view of it from the mainland. It's open from 9 am to 5 pm. Tickets for the boat are available in the cafeteria by the Salah el Din Hotel, and those for the island on landing. You can only get here by service taxi or hitching.

Places to Stay & Eat

The *Salah el Din Hotel* has 120 low-key rooms, where singles/doubles with half board cost E£110/157. All rooms have aircon and en suite bathrooms. Dinner is sometimes accompanied by a floor show. The only place to get a square meal is in the hotel restaurant. There is also a fairly pricey café on the island.

TABA

Until 1989, a few hundred metres of beach, a luxury hotel and a coffee shop at Taba, a place on the Israel-Egypt border, was a minor point of contention between the two countries. After several years of squabbling and formal arbitration, the land was returned to Egypt. Since 1982, when the rest of the Sinai was returned by Israel, Taba has served as a busy border crossing. The border is open 24 hours a day, except from Friday to Saturday night, the Jewish sabbath.

There is a small post and telephone office in the 'town', along with a hospital and bakery. You can change money at the Taba Hilton Hotel, or at the booths by the Egyptian passport control (if they are open). There are two possibilities for people wanting to stay here. The *Taba Hilton* has rooms beginning

at about US$70. Next door is the *Nelson Tourist Village*. The Hilton also has a diving centre.

Getting There & Away

Air Air Sinai runs a weekly flight from Cairo to Ras an-Naqb airport, 38 km away from Taba, for US$100. Tourism officials hope to start channelling charter flights of European tourists through here, perhaps keeping some of them in Taba itself.

To/From Israel The No 15 bus runs between Eilat and the border from 7 am and costs NIS5. Alternatively, you can catch a taxi for about NIS20. At the border you must first pay your exit fee (NIS31.30) and then pass through Immigration.

On the Egyptian side, you first reach Immigration. You can ask for a 14-day pass to Sinai (see Visas in Facts for the Visitor for more details) here, or have your standard visa stamped. Remember that you must register with the police within seven days if you have a standard tourist visa. You then pass through customs and have a one-km walk past the Taba Hilton (change here if you have no Egyptian money) to the border tax collection point (E£16.75) and then the bus and taxi stand.

There are three buses run by the East Delta Bus Co from Taba. The 10 am bus goes to Nuweiba (E£10), St Catherine's Monastery (E£15) and on to Cairo (E£45). Another bus to Cairo leaves at 2 pm. It costs E£65 and stops only at Nuweiba (E£10).

A more rickety bus leaves at 3 pm for Nuweiba (E£5), Dahab (E£10) and Sharm el-Sheikh (E£12).

Otherwise you are at the mercy of the service-taxi drivers. A taxi to Nuweiba is E£175 (up to seven people) and E£210 to Dahab. Your bargaining power increases if the bus is not too far off.

ST CATHERINE'S MONASTERY

Fifteen Greek Orthodox monks live in this ancient monastery at the foot of Mt Sinai. The monastic order was founded in the 4th century AD by the Byzantine empress

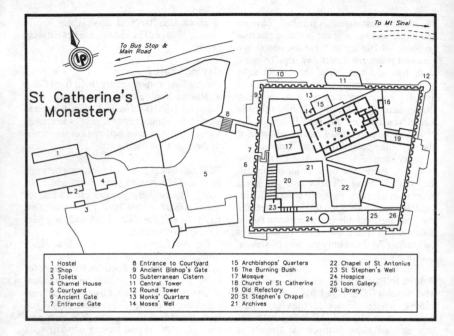

To Mt Sinai →

To Bus Stop &
Main Road

St Catherine's
Monastery

1 Hostel	8 Entrance to Courtyard	15 Archbishops' Quarters	22 Chapel of St Antonius
2 Shop	9 Ancient Bishop's Gate	16 The Burning Bush	23 St Stephen's Well
3 Toilets	10 Subterranean Cistern	17 Mosque	24 Hospice
4 Charnel House	11 Central Tower	18 Church of St Catherine	25 Icon Gallery
5 Courtyard	12 Round Tower	19 Old Refectory	26 Library
6 Ancient Gate	13 Monks' Quarters	20 St Stephen's Chapel	
7 Entrance Gate	14 Moses' Well	21 Archives	

Helena, who had a small chapel built beside what was believed to be the burning bush from which God spoke to Moses.

The chapel is dedicated to St Catherine, the legendary martyr of Alexandria, who was tortured on a spiked wheel and then beheaded for her Christianity. Her body was supposedly transported by angels to Mt Catherine, the highest mountain in Egypt, which is about six km south of Mt Sinai. There, the body was 'found', about 300 years later, by monks from the monastery.

In the 6th century, Emperor Justinian ordered the building of a fortress, with a basilica and a monastery, as well as the original chapel, to serve as a secure home for the monks of St Catherine's and as a refuge for the Christians of the southern Sinai.

Despite the isolated setting, the monastery and Mt Sinai attract a great many tourists and pilgrims, and the place can be choked with tour buses and people, especially in the mornings. When you visit, remember that this is still a functioning monastery, not just a museum piece. The only parts of the monastery to which members of the public are admitted are the chapel and a rather macabre room full of the bones of deceased monks; you are also permitted to view part of a splendid collection of icons and jewelled crosses. St Catherine's is open to visitors from 9 am to noon daily except on Friday, Sunday and holidays, when the monastery is closed.

Orientation & Information

Near the monastery there's a large roundabout where you turn east to the monastery itself, a couple of km further on. Right beside the roundabout is the large St Catherine's Tourist Village and the Al-Fairoz Hotel. Continue south from the roundabout and the road ends a couple of km further on at the village of Al-Milga, where there is a bank, phone office (open 24 hours), police station and a variety of shops and cafés. The Banque

Misr will change cash or travellers' cheques, and may accept Visa and MasterCard for cash advance. It's open from 9 am to 1.30 pm and 6 to 9 pm.

Mt Sinai

Although some archaeologists and historians dispute Mt Sinai's biblical claim to fame, it is revered by Jews, Christians and Muslims, all of whom believe that God delivered his Ten Commandments to Moses from its summit.

At a height of 2285 metres, Mt Sinai (Gebel Musa is the local name) towers over St Catherine's Monastery. It is easy to climb and there are two well-defined routes to the summit – the camel trail and the Steps of Repentance. Mt Sinai is not, however, the mountain directly up the valley behind the monastery – that one is far lower! From the top you can look across to the even higher summit of Mt Catherine.

The camel trail is the easier route and this climb takes about two hours. Along the way, you'll probably be greeted by Bedouin camel 'cowboys' anxious to put you in the saddle, although they can take you only as far as the final steps leading to the summit. Usually, there are at least four or five tea and Coca-Cola stands on the trail, catering to those in need of a caffeine fix. At the stand where the camel trail meets the steps, a full breakfast is sometimes available.

The alternative path to the summit, the taxing 3000 Steps of Repentance, was laid by one monk as a form of penance. If you want to try both routes, it's best to take the path up and the steps down, particularly if you want a great view of the monastery.

During the summer, you should avoid the heat by beginning your hike at 2 or 3 am. This way, you'll also see the sunrise. The trail can be a bit difficult in parts, so a torch (flashlight) is essential.

If you plan to spend the night on the summit, make sure you have plenty of food and water. As it gets cold and windy there, even in summer, you will also need warm

St Catherine's Monastery

clothes and a sleeping bag (there is no space to pitch a tent). Sometimes you can rent a blanket for a pound or two. As late as mid-May, be prepared to share the summit with hordes of tourists, some bearing ghetto-blasters, others carrying Bibles and hymn books. With the music and singing, and people nudging each other for a space on the holy mountain, don't expect to get much sleep, especially in the wee small hours before sunrise.

Just below the summit, along the Steps of Repentance, the small plateau known as Elijah's Hollow is dominated by a 500-year-old cypress tree, marking the spot where the prophet Elijah heard the voice of God. On the summit itself is a Greek Orthodox chapel, containing beautiful paintings and ornaments, and a small mosque. Unfortunately, they'll probably be locked. The summit also offers spectacular views of the surrounding bare, jagged mountains and plunging valleys where, throughout the day, the rocks and cliffs change colour as if they were stone chameleons.

Places to Stay

St Catherine's Monastery runs a *hostel* next door. It's open every day; although the reception is open all day, check-in may still only be between 4 and 7 pm. The hostel offers clean, basic facilities and access to a small kitchen for about E£30 per night in single-sex dorms with breakfast – not the bargain it once was. Even if you don't stay there, you can leave baggage in one of the rooms while you hike up Mt Sinai. This service will cost you about E£1 in baksheesh.

Right by the roundabout, two km west of the monastery, is the expensive *St Catherine's Tourist Village* where single/double rooms cost US$111/128 including breakfast and dinner. Beside the tourist village is the somewhat grubby *Al-Fairoz Hotel* where a dormitory bed costs E£12, a mattress in a big tent E£6.50 and one in the open E£3.50. However, if you're going to sleep in the open, you may as well climb the mountain and sleep up there, or just search out a place in the foothills.

About six km down the road to Nuweiba is the *Zeituna* camp and restaurant, followed four km further on by the *Green Lodge Camping* and restaurant, and another 10 km on, five km down the Dahab turn-off, is the *Al Salam Hotel*.

If you can, the best option is probably to come and leave on the same day, although bus timetables seem designed to make this very difficult.

Places to Eat

The modern *Al Monagah* cafeteria right by the roundabout principally caters to tour bus groups. In the village, near the bus stop, there's a bakery and a few small shops. Just behind the bakery are a few small restaurants, the most reasonable of which is the *Look Here* – try the chicken broth. Just by the bus stop you can try the *Rest House*. From here you can sip a tea and keep an eye on buses and service taxis. Across the square, near the bank, is the *Restaurant for Friends*.

Getting There & Away

Air All flights to St Catherine's were suspended in 1990. Whether or not they will be restarted at any time is unclear.

Bus You can ask the driver to drop you off at the roundabout, which is closer to the monastery. Buses leave from the square in the village, a couple of km south of the roundabout. At 1.30 pm, a bus leaves for Sharm el-Sheikh (E£12) via Dahab (E£8). The bus for Suez leaves at 6 am (there is sometimes a second at 9 am) for E£14, which is much better value than the direct Cairo bus, as you can get a bus or service taxi from Suez to Cairo for about E£4. The 1.30 pm bus from Taba to Cairo costs E£35 to E£40, seemingly depending on the mood of the bus conductor. A bus to Taba (E£15) goes via Nuweiba (E£10) at 3.30 pm.

Service Taxi Service taxis travel in and out of the village irregularly and infrequently. If you're lucky, you might be able to find a taxi driver who is willing to take you all the way to Cairo. If so, the trip could cost about

E£300 for the taxi, divided by the number of passengers up to a maximum of seven. A similar taxi to Suez will cost about E£150 to E£175 with intense bargaining. You can often find service taxis at the monastery – they wait for people coming down from Mt Sinai (not bearing the Ten Commandments) in the early afternoon. Count on at least E£10 per person to Dahab or Nuweiba.

WADI FERAN

The Bedouin outpost of Wadi Feran is between the west coast of the Sinai and St Catherine's Monastery. After many km of rough, barren desert and harsh, rocky hills, this lush date-palm oasis is certainly a refreshing sight. There is a convent on the western edge of the oasis, but you need permission from St Catherine's Monastery if you want to visit it.

AL-ARISH

Much of the north coast of the Sinai, from Port Fouad most of the way to Al-Arish, is dominated by the swampy lagoon of Lake Bardawil, separated from the Mediterranean by a limestone ridge and making the area hardly attractive for swimming. The road and former railway line that run here follow what must be one of the oldest march routes in history, used by the Pharaohs to penetrate into what is now Israel, Jordan and on to Syria, and by Persians, Greeks, Crusaders, Arab Muslims and many others coming the other way.

Al-Arish, beyond Lake Bardawil, is the capital of the Sinai peninsula and has a population of about 40,000. The water here, though perhaps not quite as stunning as along some other parts of the Mediterranean coast, still makes for very pleasant swimming. Its palm-fringed beaches, although hardly spotless, are cleaner than your average Egyptian resort beach, making it quite a pleasant place to relax. As is unfortunately so often the case, women may feel somewhat uncomfortable swimming here. On the other hand, the place is not heavily visited by either Egyptians or foreign tourists, except in the height of summer.

Although development here does not match what is happening in other parts of the country, the spread of self-contained flats and a couple of expanding tourist villages has led to a lot of wood clearing. Alarm bells are sounding for Al-Arish's greatest asset – its palm trees.

Orientation & Information

The main coastal road, Sharia Fouad Zekry, forms a T-junction with Sharia 23rd of July, which runs a couple of km south (changing name to Sharia Tahrir on the way) to the bus and service-taxi stations.

Tourist Office The tourist office is on Sharia Fouad Zekry, just down from the Sinai Beach Hotel. There's not much point in listing opening hours, because it never seems to be open.

Money The National Bank of Egypt, on Sharia Tahrir, is the closest to the bus station. Nearby, a street back from Sharia Tahrir, is the local branch of Banque Misr. The Bank of Alexandria has a branch on Sharia 23rd of July.

Post & Telecommunications The telephone office, which is open 24 hours a day, is a couple of blocks east of Sharia Tahrir. They have no card phones. The post office, open from 8.30 am to 2.30 pm except on Friday, is another block further east.

Things to See & Do

The **Sinai Heritage Museum**, on the outskirts of town (just past the UN post along the coastal road to Rafah), is one of the few attractions of Al-Arish. Established a couple of years ago to inform people about life, human and animal, in the Sinai, the museum's displays include stuffed birds and Bedouin handicrafts and clothing. It's open from 8 am to 8 pm in summer and from about 10 am to 6 pm in winter. Entry is E£1.

Next door is a fairly miserable **zoo**, among whose unhappy inmates is a young lion. This is not a place for animal lovers.

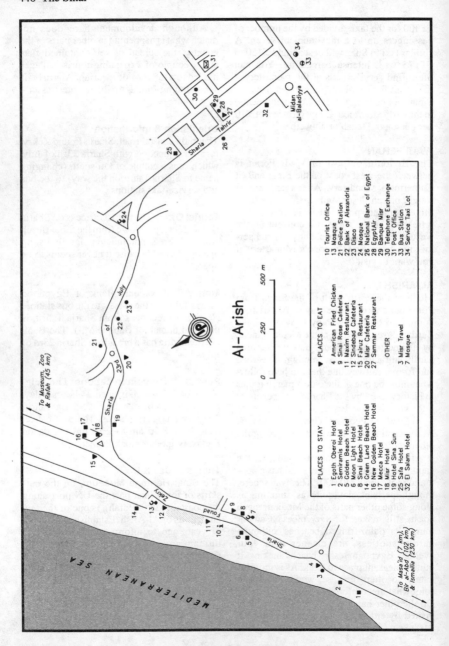

MEDITERRANEAN SEA

Al-Arish

To Museum, Zoo & Rafah (45 km)

To Masa'id (7 km), Bir al-Abd (102 km) & Ismailia (230 km)

Midan al-Baladiyya

0   250   500 m

PLACES TO STAY

1 Egoth Oberoi Hotel
2 Semiramis Hotel
5 Golden Beach Hotel
6 Moon Light Hotel
8 Sinai Beach Hotel
14 Green Land Beach Hotel
16 New Golden Beach Hotel
17 Mecca Hotel
18 Misr Hotel
19 Hotel Sina Sun
25 Safa Hotel
32 El Salam Hotel

▼ PLACES TO EAT

4 American Fried Chicken
9 Sinai Rose Cafeteria
11 Maxim Restaurant
12 Sindebad Cafeteria
15 Fairuz Restaurant
20 Misr Cafeteria
27 Sammar Restaurant

OTHER

3 Misr Travel
7 Mosque
10 Tourist Office
13 Mosque
21 Police Station
22 Bank of Alexandria
23 Disco
24 Mosque
26 National Bank of Egypt
28 EgyptAir
29 Banque Misr
30 Telephone Exchange
31 Post Office
33 Bus Station
34 Service Taxi Lot

Beyond the bus station are the remains of a **fortress**.

Every Wednesday, when the **souq** is held, the Bedouins come in from the desert with their camels. The veiled women sell silver and embroidered dresses, while the men sell camel saddles.

The main attraction is the **beach**. The parade of palms, fine white sand and clean water (even the odd small wave) make this one of the nicer Mediterranean spots in Egypt. It can get crowded in the height of summer, and there is supposedly a beach curfew after dark.

Places to Stay

There are at least three cheap places to stay on the beach which are basic but OK for the budget traveller. The *Golden Beach Hotel* has rooms with up to three beds at E£15. The rooms also have cold showers, but breakfast is not included. Just up the road is the *Moon Light Hotel*, which has singles/doubles at E£10/20. The rooms are, again, pretty basic. Further east is the equally simple *Hotel an-Nasr*.

In the same price range is the *Safa Hotel*, on Sharia Tahrir. It's a noisy place on the 2nd floor and has doubles with cold bath for E£10 a person.

Quieter and marginally better is the *El Salam Hotel*, above the Aziz Restaurant on Midan al-Baladiyya. Doubles/triples cost E£10/15. A lone guest still pays E£10. It's main advantage is being close to the bus station.

Near the junction of Sharia Fouad Zekry and Sharia 23rd of July is the *New Golden Beach Hotel*. Rooms with two beds range from E£10 to E£15 without breakfast. The better rooms have quite big comfortable beds, bathroom (cold water) and balcony. They want E£10 for breakfast.

Behind the New Golden Beach is the *Mecca Hotel* (☎ 344909), a friendly, good, clean place that has singles/doubles for E£20/30 and hot water in the showers. The *Misr Hotel*, a little place nearby on Sharia 23rd of July, was closed at the time of writing.

One of the better deals around is the *Green Land Beach Hotel* (☎ 340601), virtually on the beach. Clean and comfortable triple rooms with bathroom come for E£20, however many occupants there are. Breakfast is extra.

A little way north-east along the coast road to Rafah from the New Golden Beach Hotel is a local version of a *youth camp*, where you may be able to stay or pitch a tent, although it seems to be reserved for Egyptian youngsters.

The *Hotel Sina Sun* (☎ 341855) is a reasonable middle-level place, with rooms at US$21/25. The price does not include breakfast, but rooms come with bath, TV, phone and air-conditioning.

Slightly better but quite a bit more pricey is the *Sinai Beach Hotel* (☎ 341713). Some of the rooms, which cost E£112/125 with breakfast, have balconies looking across to the sea.

Further to the south-west are Al-Arish's two luxury establishments. The *Semiramis* (☎ 344166; fax 344168) has singles/doubles away from the beach for US$58/66. Suites facing the beach cost US$101.

The *Egoth Oberoi* costs US$70/88 for rooms alone, plus 20% taxes and E£11.25 for the continental breakfast or E£22 for a buffet breakfast. Nonresidents of the hotel can use the pool – for E£25.

There are three other hotels beyond the New Golden Beach Hotel, the *Keweder*, the *Zahra* and the *Fairuz*.

About 10 km west of the Egoth Oberoi, the developers are doing their thing, with two sprawling tourist villages, the *El Zehor*, and the *Sama*, which is still being expanded.

Dotted in and around the palm trees are *chalets*, which are often fairly mucky self-contained flats that tend to cost upwards of E£40. Some belong to Maxim's restaurant.

The disco marked on the map doesn't have much in the music line, but you can get a Stella here.

Places to Eat

There's not a huge range of places to get a meal in Al-Arish. Good cheap meals of fuul and ta'amiyya are available at the *Aziz Restaurant* on Sharia Tahrir.

At the *Sammar Restaurant*, also on Sharia Tahrir, you can get kebab and kofta.

At the junction of Sharia Fouad Zekry and Sharia 23rd of July is the *Fairuz Restaurant*. They serve kofta, kebab, fish and chicken in reasonably generous proportions. A full meal of kofta and salads costs about E£10.

Further west along Sharia Fouad Zekry is the *Sindebad*, where you can get fuul and ta'amiyya.

Right on the beach nearby is the classier *Maxim*, which specialises in fish dishes costing about E£20 to E£35. It's in a nice position among the palms and the food is good.

For something approximating Western fast food, you could try *American Fried Chicken*, on the way to the Semiramis Hotel.

There are a few places dotted along Sharia Fouad Zekry, like the *Sinai Rose Cafeteria*, which serves fish and salad.

Getting There & Away
Air EgyptAir has two flights a week between Cairo and Al-Arish. They leave Cairo at 11.45 am on Thursday and Sunday. The one-way fare is E£259.

Bus The north coast railway has long since been dismantled. There is a bus from Cairo to the Israeli border at Rafah at 8 am every day, leaving from the Sinai Terminal in Abbassiya. It costs E£35, and E£25 to Al-Arish. (Unless you are in an enormous hurry, the extra E£10 for the stretch to the border is a blatant rip-off.) The trip to Al-Arish takes about five hours, and another hour on to Rafah. Two more buses leave Cairo at 3.30 and 5.30 pm, but only go as far as Al-Arish. They both cost E£25. Buses for Cairo leave Al-Arish at 7 and 10 am and 4 pm and cost E£25.

There is a bus to Ismailia every hour or so for E£6.25. It stops in Qantara on the way (E£4.50 to E£5).

Some of the Ismailia buses go on to Mansoura (E£11) and Zagazig (E£8.50).

There is supposedly a bus from Port Said at 10 am for E£9. From Suez, you have to get a bus to Nakhl and try to hook up with another bus there, or safer still, go up to Ismailia and get a bus from there.

A bus to Tanta leaves at 8.30 am and costs E£12.

At 8.15 am there is a bus to the border for E£2. Buses to Rafah city, which can drop you about a km short of the border, leave at 7.15 am, 1 and 4 pm. They cost E£1.

Service Taxi A cheaper alternative to the expensive Sinai buses from Cairo is a service taxi from around Midan Ulali, which costs about E£12 to Al-Arish.

A service taxi to Qantara costs E£5 and E£6 to Ismailia. They like to charge anything from E£5 to E£7 to get from Al-Arish to the border or vice versa.

Getting Around
There is a pretty regular stream of buses, microbuses and service taxis – huge US limousines dating back to the 1960s at least – running between the bus station and the satellite residential area of Masa'id.

RAFAH
This coastal town virtually marks the border with Israel, lying just outside the Gaza Strip. Although town fathers apparently feel the warm Mediterranean location could make it an ideal resort, it has no hotels (there are some *chalets*). The nearest cheap hotel is in the village of Sheikh Zuweid, a few km short of Rafah.

A new road linking Rafah directly with Taba on the Gulf of Aqaba may open up new options for travelling around the Sinai. Travellers coming from Israel may be more tempted to include Al-Arish in their itinerary if bus and taxi links heading south accompany the opening of the new road, due in early 1994.

Getting There & Away
To/From Israel If you plan to cross into Egypt from Israel via Rafah, there is only the one Egged bus (No 362) from Tel Aviv to Rafah via Ashkelon. It departs Tel Aviv at

8.50 am and costs NIS19. Going the other way, it leaves at 3 pm. There are no other connections from Ashkelon and nothing from Jerusalem. Otherwise you will have to take a *sherut*, the Israeli version of a service taxi, to Rafah (Rafiah to the Israelis).

As this border crossing is in the Gaza Strip, security is heavy. The bulk of the people coming through are Palestinians or tourists on through buses to and from Cairo. The border closes at 5 pm and all day Saturday.

There is a hefty US$26 (or shekel equivalent) exit tax. Once through formalities, people are loaded on to a shuttle bus to cover the few hundred metres of trenches, barbed wire and man traps that separate the two countries. (The bus costs E£5 from the Egyptian side.)

On entering Egypt you pay a tax of E£7 (payable in E£; you can change money at one of the three or four bank booths located nearby) and then proceed through Immigration and customs. You need to have a visa, which you can obtain at the Egyptian embassy in Tel Aviv or the consulate in Eilat.

Going the other way, there is an Egyptian exit tax of E£16, but no Israeli entry fee.

Once through Egyptian customs, there is a service-taxi stand a few hundred metres down the road. The trip to Cairo should be E£15, but often is put up a few pounds. To Al-Arish the fare is E£5, also usually inflated from here.

There is a direct bus from Cairo's Sinai Terminal to Rafah at 8 am for E£35 (to save money, take it as far as Al-Arish for E£25 and arrange further transport from there).

There are a few buses between Rafah town (three km away) and Al-Arish. See Al-Arish Getting There & Away.

THE
SUDAN

Introduction

The largest country in Africa is also one of the most difficult to get across, and much of the reward for travelling through it lies in the simple achievement of getting from A to B. Civil war, famine, drought and growing isolation from the rest of the world have combined to all but bankrupt the country, and the almost complete absence of infrastructure that can make getting around such an arduous task is one visible reminder of the difficulties this country faces.

The Sudan is, for all that, a fascinating place to visit, but it is not to be taken lightly. The area south of Kosti was still off limits to travellers at the time of writing. Although the peace talks in Abuja, Nigeria, between the government of Lieutenant General Omar al-Bashir and the rebel factions in the south had produced unilateral cease-fires by Khartoum and the main rebel leader, John Garang, fighting was continuing between Garang and rebel forces opposed to him. The press in Khartoum was insisting in the early months of 1993 that 'life [was] returning to normal' in the south, but a quick word with Western aid agencies soon dispelled such illusions. By late 1993, all talk of peace had evaporated.

The fighting has uprooted millions, brought farming to a halt and caused the disintegration of whole communities and towns. Famine and disease are rampant, and few of the two million or so 'displaced people' who have fled the area talk of going back now.

Travel to the rest of the country, except the Nuba region, has been freed up, and shortly after the research in the Sudan was completed, the government lifted the requirement for travel permits to most parts of the country.

This could, of course, change at any time, and it is unlikely the good news has filtered through to all the local Security chiefs, for whom the arrival of foreigners sometimes seems to be seen as a rare opportunity to flex (slowly) the muscles of a labyrinthine bureaucracy.

The west is open to travel, but caution is the order of the day. The far west, particularly Darfur, is plagued by bandits who apparently have little compunction about robbing and sometimes torturing or killing their victims. The government is attempting – so far with only limited success – to bring these people under a measure of control. When travelling beyond Nyala, you should try to get a picture from Security and any remaining expatriates of what it is safe and not so safe to do. The west has not really recovered from the famine triggered by massive drought in the latter half of the 1980s. Many of the displaced people living around Khartoum come in fact from the west and not the south.

The Nuba region has been sealed off. What exactly is going on there has been the subject of considerable speculation, but there is little fact available. It appears that the government has embarked on a nasty campaign to remove or even exterminate the Nuba – who form a kind of black enclave on good farming ground too far north for Khartoum's liking – and replace them with Arab farmers. Whatever is happening, you can't get in.

The traditionally safest routes for travel remain open: Wadi Halfa to Khartoum by road (difficult) and train; Khartoum and Omdurman; Khartoum to Kassala and on to Port Sudan; and Khartoum to Kosti, Sennar and Dinder National Park.

The Sudan is more accessible than it has been for a while, and it is possible to enter and leave overland via Egypt, Chad, the Central African Republic, Eritrea and, through Eritrea, Ethiopia. It is nevertheless only for the hardiest and most adventurous travellers. Most of the country is as hot as hell from March to September, and the rainy season turns roads and tracks, where they exist, into thick streams of mud. It is no wonder that Sudanese Arabs are, as an age-old proverb reads, uncertain whether Allah laughed or cried when he created the Sudan. He probably did both.

The Sudan is about a third of the size of the USA. There are only 24 million people in this vast area, but they constitute more than 300 tribes and speak more than a hundred languages and dialects. Traditional culture has mostly been preserved. In Khartoum, the capital, and other towns this is evident in the dress, speech and facial scars of the people.

In the vast expanses of the Sudan, just getting from place to place is often an adventure. Whatever form of transport you end up on – train, bus (the term covers a variety of contraptions), lorry (usually a Bedford truck) or Toyota pick-up – you'll probably often find yourself wondering if you'll ever get where you're headed. In the more remote places the lorry is often the only means of transport. And yes, although all these vehicles are prone to breaking down, bursting tires and getting bogged in sand drifts or gooey mud, most of the time their ingenious drivers get them through. Even if you are temporarily stranded in some village on the edge of the world, Sudanese hospitality means you will always be offered food and shelter.

It was power and great hidden treasures that made the Sudan the object of invasion and exploration for much of its long, jumbled history. Today, a good deal of the country remains to be explored. It is one of the world's last frontiers.

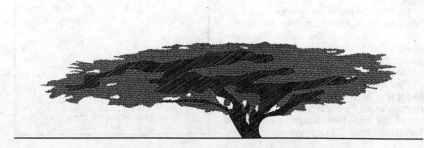

Facts about the Country

HISTORY

For historical purposes the Sudan can be divided into three regions, each made up of loosely defined kingdoms or sultanates bordered by the Nile, the mountains, the wide expanses of desert or the swamps. Most of what is known of the Sudan before the 15th century AD relates to northern Sudan, which stretches from present-day Khartoum to Wadi Halfa.

Knowledge of northern Sudan's ancient history comes from Egyptian sources. To the Egyptians of the Old Kingdom (2600-2100 BC) the Sudan was known as the Land of Cush, the source of ivory, incense, ebony, gold and slaves.

As Egyptian trading and raiding parties increased their forays into the Sudan, the imperialist designs of Egypt's Middle and New Kingdom pharaohs (2050-1085 BC) also increased. Like 20th-century European imperialists, the conquering pharaohs did their best to Egyptianise the Sudanese. Egyptian political control dominated the arts, language and religion of the Sudan. Signs of this influence can still be seen in the ruins of many Egyptian structures and temples along the Nile in northern Sudan, such as the Temple of Amun, near present-day Karima.

But, as has happened many times throughout history, the colonies that powerful kingdoms or countries create often become big headaches as they turn on their creators, or invaders, and sometimes conquer them. That is what happened with Egypt and the Land of Cush.

By the 8th century BC, Cush was a great power. Under the ruler Piankhi, the Cushites conquered Egypt, establishing the 25th dynasty (712-663 BC). Cushite control, however, was short-lived. In 671 BC, less than 50 years after Piankhi's triumph, Taharqa, the last ruler to build at Luxor's celebrated Karnak Temple, lost Egypt to invading Assyrians. By 654 BC the Cushites were back in their old capital of Napata, far to the south of Egypt, near present-day Merowe.

Historians generally believe that during the next century the capital was moved from Napata to Meroe, north of present-day Shendi, although there is some evidence to suggest that Napata and Meroe were, in fact, respectively the religious and political centres of the one empire. A new, less Egyptian kingdom arose. Temples, tombs and pyramids influenced by Greek, Roman and Indian architecture were built at Naqa and Musawwarat, and a cursive Meroitic script replaced Egyptian hieroglyphics. This writing remains undeciphered, and much of Meroe's history is mysterious.

However, it is known that marauding Romans – 10,000 infantry and 800 cavalry under Gaius Petronius – came down from Egypt in 23 BC, sacked Napata and annexed a large part of Nubia to create the Roman province of Dodecashoenus. Meroe itself was more or less reduced to the status of a client state, but in commercial terms appears to have bloomed under the Pax Romana. The Romans pulled out and redrew their southern boundary at the First Nile Cataract in 297 AD. Into the vacuum stepped the nomadic Blemmya people, ancestors of the Beja tribe, who picked away at the empire until an invasion in 350 AD by the Christian Axumite Kingdom of Ethiopia ensured the demise of Meroe.

Little is known of the subsequent period, but the bulk of the population appears to have converted to Christianity. By the 6th century AD there appear to have been three separate Christian kingdoms. Their united efforts kept out the first wave of Muslim invaders in the 7th century who, under the command of the conqueror of Egypt, Amr ibn al-As, attempted to add Nubia to the list of conversions.

In 969, the Fatimid rulers in Cairo sent a mission to Dongola, the capital of one of the

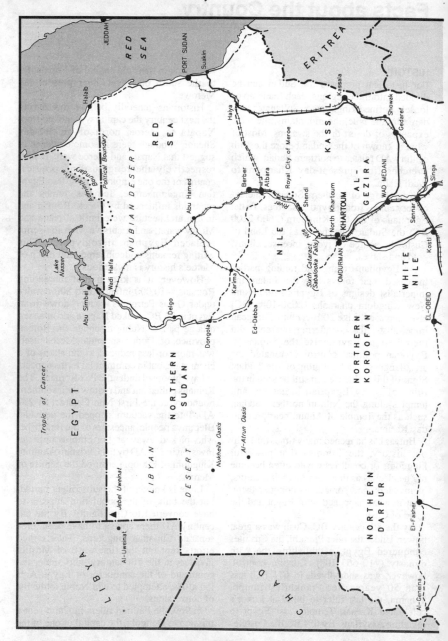

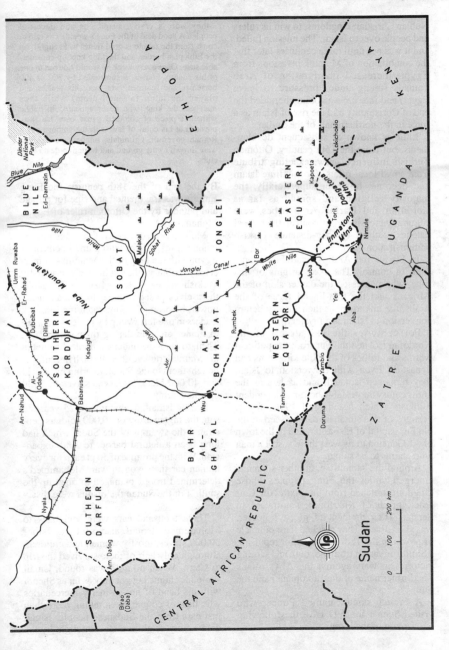

Nubian Christian kingdoms, to win its rulers and people over to Islam. The mission failed, and it was not until three centuries later that the combination of Mamluk invasions from Egypt, increased immigration of Arab nomads (many under pressure to leave Egypt) and internal squabbling heralded the end of Christianity and the rise of Islam as a force in the northern half of the Sudan.

Little is known of subsequent developments, but from the 16th century, Ottoman Turkish influence grew, exacting tribute from small local rulers. By this time Islam had become, however superficially, the majority religion and spread as far as Kordofan and Darfur. Arab tribes were coming increasingly to control their local patches, subject to long-distance Turkish administration.

In Darfur the Arab-African Fur people were in control. The exact origins of this tribe, who possessed the darker skin of the Africans and the thin-lipped faces of the Arabs, are unknown, as their history before conversion to Islam is a mystery.

For centuries the vast desert of the Kordofan isolated the Fur from the political whims and follies of the Nile kingdoms and dynasties. Even with conversion to Islam they remained isolated, and as late as the 16th century they established an independent sultanate which lasted until 1916. Today, vestiges of this sultanate can be seen in the old Fur capital of El-Fasher, and in the town of Al-Geneina to its west there is still a man who claims to be sultan.

Around the same time, another sultanate emerged under the Fung people, whose kingdom stretched from the Sixth Nile Cataract, north of Khartoum, southward to Sennar. Their moment of glory, however, was short-lived. They reached their pinnacle of power in the 18th century after repulsing a Shilluk invasion from the south and scoring victories in wars against the Abyssinians (the former name of the Ethiopians) and the Fur.

A French doctor named Poncet who visited Sennar in 1699 gave the following description of the Fung:

...they were a crafty, suspicious and deceitful people...A good deal of the Fung's wealth was said to come from the fabulous gold mines at Fazughli, on the Ethiopian border, and the king kept up considerable state. Once every week he would ride out to one of his country houses, accompanied by 300 or 400 horsemen and footmen, who sang his praises and played the tabor (a small drum) while they marched...the king, who never appeared in public without a piece of coloured gauze over his face, presided at his court of law with the authority of a Roman governor. Criminals, on being convicted, were thrown to the ground and beaten to death with clubs.

By the end of the 18th century, the Fung Empire was fragmented and ripe for pillage and plunder by the Ottoman ruler of Egypt, Mohammed Ali.

Mohammed Ali was a ruthless and power-hungry army officer who gained control of Egypt with the help of the Mamluks, a mercenary military class who were originally Turkish slaves. Later, when the Mamluks themselves posed a threat to Mohammed's power, he promptly eliminated the Mamluk leaders in one fell swoop by inviting them all to dinner and murdering them afterwards. Then, to quell the understandable disquiet in the Mamluk ranks and to furbish his coffers, he sent them to the Sudan to bring back gold and 40,000 black Sudanese slaves to build up a new army.

Led by Ismail, Mohammed's 25-year-old son, the ragtag army of 10,000 soldiers penetrated the swamps of the Sudd, which had long been a natural barrier to Arab expansion. With the promise of 50 pt each for every human ear they won in war, Mohammed's determined troops managed to open up the south. For the Sudan the results were disastrous.

Three thousand ears were sent back to Mohammed. Ismail also sent his father 30,000 slaves, mostly women and children, although only half of them survived the trip to Cairo. When no gold was found, Ismail started for home but got only as far as Shendi with his band of not-so-merry mercenaries who had, of course, been taking more than just ears from the Sudanese people. Ismail died a fiery death in a tent set alight by the locals, who had had enough of being raped, pillaged and plundered.

When Mohammed heard about his son's death, he too wanted more than ears. By 1823, as many as 50,000 Sudanese had been killed, and Mohammed Ali had control of the Sudan. Two years later, the administrative centre of Khartoum was established and the surrounding area divided into the four provinces – Dongola, Berber, Sennar and El-Obeid. More distant territory was added later.

Egypt remained in control for the next 50 years, until the time of Khedive Ismail, who ruled Egypt from 1863 to 1879. Britain and France became increasingly interested in the region, especially with the completion of the Suez Canal in 1869. This expensive project placed Egypt in heavy debt to many foreign powers and initiated European intervention in the affairs of Egypt and the Sudan.

Britain was the dominant European power in both countries, and in 1873 General Charles Gordon was appointed governor of Equatoria province. In 1877 he became governor general of all the Sudan but resigned three years later in the wake of Khedive Ismail's demise.

In the meantime, a local military leader named Mohammed Ahmad was gaining influence in the nascent world of Sudanese politics. In 1881 he joined forces with Abdullahi ibn Mohammed, of Southern Darfur, and declared himself Mahdi. Traditionally, the Mahdi is a messiah selected by Allah to lead the jihad (holy war) in defence of Islam. The Mahdi and his followers called for a return to the fundamental tenets of early Islam, and this formed the foundation of the Mahdiyya Movement, which continues to influence Sudanese politics today.

The Mahdi made the Kordofan town of El-Obeid his political centre by surrounding the town and starving the population into submission. In the process, a British colonel, William Hicks, was killed and his Egyptian army overwhelmed. The Mahdi went on to take Darfur and imprison the Austrian governor of Darfur, Rudolph Slatin.

General Gordon was sent back to Khartoum in early 1884, before the Mahdi laid siege to the city. Once the siege began, Gordon immediately requested reinforcements from Gladstone, the British prime minister. The British relief force arrived on 25 January 1885 – three days too late. (Gordon's last dispatches can be seen in the British Museum in London.) The Mahdi had already taken Khartoum; Gordon had been decapitated, and his head had been mounted on a pole to greet the arriving British troops.

The Mahdists kept control of the Sudan for more than 10 years, until Rudolph Slatin escaped from prison. Slatin wrote a book about his captivity, entitled *Fire & Sword in the Sudan*, and fired up British public opinion. By this time most of Africa had been carved up among the European colonial powers, so the British willingly pursued a campaign against the Mahdists.

Under General Herbert Kitchener, the British army marched all the way to Omdurman, meeting little resistance. They arrived on 1 September 1898. The Mahdists attacked the next day with a force of 60,000 men, many of whom were cloaked in suits of mail and long, flowing gowns, and armed with sabres and shields. The dead numbered 11,000 Mahdists and only 48 British and 92 Egyptians. On 19 January 1899 the Anglo-Egyptian Condominium Agreement was signed 'with the consent of Her Britannic Majesty's Government'. The British remained in control of the Sudan until the 1950s. On 1 January 1956 the Sudanese declared their independence from Britain. Egypt, nominally party to the administration of the Sudan until 1956 under the terms of the condominium, expected the Sudan to vote in a plebiscite for union with its northern neighbour but was to be disappointed when the Sudanese decided to go it alone.

The new Republic of the Sudan was immediately faced with problems that had both been avoided and created by British control. For the sake of stability, the British had followed a policy of isolating the predominantly African southern part of the Sudan from the predominantly Arab northern part. At one time a plan to unite the

Kitchener

southern part with Uganda had been considered. A civil war between the north and the south began even before independence had been declared.

By 1958 it was apparent that the government of the Sudan was too disunited to cope with the escalating civil war. General Ibrahim Abboud led a military coup and overthrew the government; however, he too was unable to neutralise the south. An election in 1964 saw Sadiq al-Mahdi, the great-grandson of the Mahdi, elected prime minister. But it was not until 1969, when Colonel Jafaar Nimeiri led another coup, that the southern situation began to change.

Nimeiri established a new government based on 'democracy, socialism and nonalignment' and in 1972 signed the Addis Ababa Agreement, which supposedly ended the north-south war. He granted the south a measure of autonomy, and for almost a decade northerners and southerners stopped killing each other. The situation changed for the worse, however, as Nimeiri's various economic development projects failed. He had wanted to make the Sudan the 'breadbasket of the Middle East' by encouraging Arab and Western investment in projects such as the Gezira Scheme and the Jonglei Canal.

The Gezira is a 25,000-sq-km marshy region south of Khartoum between the White Nile and the Blue Nile. Long the object of Western agricultural projects during the period of British control, much of the region is devoted to cotton. It is, however, far from being a breadbasket. The purpose of the Jonglei Canal was to divert a 560-km stretch of the White Nile that would otherwise flow into the wide marsh south of the Gezira known as the Sudd. The additional Nile water could have then been used for further irrigation and cultivation of the Gezira. But Nimeiri invested too heavily and too quickly, amassing a mountain of external debts in the process.

The International Monetary Fund and the US government pressured Nimeiri into increasing the prices of commodities such as bread, sugar and petrol. In the early 1980s he began to turn to Muslim fundamentalists for support, much to the chagrin of the predominantly Christian and animist south. For southerners, the last straw was Nimeiri's symbolic declaration of *shari'a* (Islamic law). In September 1983, a month all Nile perch will remember with drunken delight, Nimeiri dumped the capital's entire liquor stocks into the Nile.

The Civil War

The war between the Sudanese People's Liberation Movement, or SPLM, and the Sudanese government was sparked by Nimeiri's declaration of Islamic law, which the southerners interpreted as an abrogation of the Addis Ababa Agreement. John Garang, an Iowa State University alumnus and member of the southern Dinka tribe, went into self-imposed exile to reactivate the SPLM, with plenty of support from disgruntled southerners and the Ethiopian government across the border, and within a few months the government had virtually lost control of the south. Nimeiri declared a state of emergency and suspended the constitution.

In April 1985 Nimeiri was deposed in a

coup engineered by the Sudanese army. A transitional military government under General Abdul-Rahman Swareddahab took power. He set about purging the extremist Islamic fundamentalists and promised elections within 12 months.

The elections in April 1986, the first in 20 years, saw the return of the former prime minister, Sadiq al-Mahdi, who had been deposed by Nimeiri in 1969. Al-Mahdi promised to return the Sudan to a democratic and pluralist society, but he proved to be an ineffectual and disappointing leader: the shari'a was maintained, as much to curry favour with Saudi Arabia as out of any religious conviction, but by all accounts was not applied with great vigour (except with respect to alcohol); and while the leader's continued adherence to and support for shari'a placated the predominantly Muslim government and thus kept him in power, it angered the non-Muslim Dinkas and thereby helped perpetuate the war in the south.

Most of Garang's arms and supplies came from the Soviet Union and Cuba via Ethiopia before the fall there of the so-called communist leader Mengistu in 1991, although in the late 1980s some assistance also came from Israel and Kenya. About the same time, the SPLA (the army wing of the SPLM) began overrunning government army convoys. Garang himself described these victories in great detail on his daily radio broadcasts over the Voice of the Sudanese People's Liberation Movement. In one broadcast he went so far as to recite the serial numbers of the army trucks and blood types of the officers captured.

Despite pumping an estimated US$1 million a day into war efforts, the government consistently lost ground to the SPLM. By March 1989 the SPLM was estimated to have won control of about 90% of southern Sudan. Some estimates put Garang as far north as the southern base of the Nuba Mountains and the town of Malakal. Government troops were surrounded in Juba and a few other towns by SPLA troops and mined roads. Steamer traffic on the Nile south of Khartoum was stopped for seven years until

1991 because river traffic was declared fair game for target practice. Air traffic was also threatened, and a Sudan Airways passenger jet en route to Juba was shot down in 1986.

For the hundreds of thousands of southern Sudanese whose towns and villages became battlegrounds, life was totally disrupted. According to an *Economist* Intelligence Unit report on the Sudan in 1988, 'over 500,000 civilians have been killed [and] millions have been displaced'. By 1992, it was estimated that up to 750,000 had died as a result of war and human-induced famine.

Southerners have been forced to flee to Wau, Juba and even Khartoum, where sprawling refugee camps of makeshift huts and tents have sprung up. By early 1993, an estimated two million refugees from war in the south, and anarchy and famine in the west, were lodged in camps around Khartoum. Because many of them are Dinkas, who form the basis of Garang's support, the Khartoum government has resisted any temptation to turn the camps into anything more permanent, and so conditions have remained extremely basic. To make matters worse, on 4 August 1988 about a million refugees were left homeless when floods hit the Khartoum camps and most of the city.

The Coup & Its Aftermath

In June 1989 al-Mahdi was deposed and replaced by Lieutenant General Omar Hassan Ahmed al-Bashir in a military coup that was at first greeted by some as a sign of a new stabilisation of the situation in the Sudan. But although the constitution and political parties were soon abolished, and al-Bashir remains the nominal head of government, real power appears to be in the hands of Hassan at-Turabi, the leader of the fundamentalist National Islamic Front, or NIF, which has always opposed compromise on the application of shari'a law.

During the life of the military government, there have been numerous offers of peace talks. Several meetings have taken place, but little real progress has been made. Although non-Muslims in the south are supposedly exempt from Islamic law, al-Bashir's open and vigorous application of shari'a has done nothing to reduce tensions.

In the early months of 1992, sensing that the rebels' position had been weakened by bloody tribal infighting and the SPLA's loss of support from Kenya and Ethiopia's fallen Mengistu government, al-Bashir launched a dry-season offensive. Within a few months, the most optimistic reports had the government in control of 90% of the south, although Juba remained under siege. In fact, the offensive succeeded in reuniting the SPLA groups and led to an inconclusive wet-season attack. In short, although the government's position in the south appeared stronger in early 1993 than it had since the reopening of hostilities 10 years before, the war looked no more winnable. In March, both the government and John Garang declared unilateral cease-fires, but it appears Garang's motive may have been to get some room to move against rival rebel factions – particularly the one led by Reik Machar – amongst whom fighting quickly resumed. For the first time, Garang personally attended peace talks in Abuja, Nigeria, and the Sudanese press quickly hailed 'peace and victory' in the south. Too quickly. By June the talks had obviously failed and the government was claiming repeated cease-fire violations against its troops.

GEOGRAPHY

The Sudan, the largest country in Africa, is bordered by Egypt, Libya, Chad, the Central African Republic, Zaire, Uganda, Kenya, Ethiopia and Eritrea. It takes up 8% of Africa and 2% of the world's land surface. A country of contrasts, it stretches from the deserts of Nubia to the equatorial rainforests and swamps of the Sudd, just north of the great lakes and the source of the Nile.

In the north, the Nile slices through seemingly endless and lifeless stony desert plains. In some places the desert comes right up to the banks of the river, while in others a narrow band of vegetation separates the water from the barren sands. The northern desert gives way in the west to a sandier

desert, covered in what seem like waves of sand dunes.

In Khartoum, the two sources of the mighty Nile River become one. The Blue Nile flows down from Lake Tana, through the highlands of Ethiopia and via the Sudanese towns of Er-Roseires and Wad Medani, before joining the much longer White Nile, which starts from Lake Victoria on the Kenya-Uganda-Tanzania border. The White Nile loses about 60% of its water in evaporation as it passes through the Sudd on the way to Khartoum. Both rivers are fed by others as they flow north. From Khartoum, the Nile describes a long, lazy S-bend on its way to Wadi Halfa and Lake Nasser on the Egyptian border. Five of the six cataracts, or rocky outcrops, that make navigation impossible are situated between Khartoum and Wadi Halfa. The last, or first, depending on your point of view, is at Aswan.

There are several mountain ranges in the Sudan. In the far west is the Jebel Marra range – the highest in the country and a favourite hiking area among travellers. Closer to Khartoum are the Nuba Mountains – home to the intriguing and long-isolated tribes of the Nuba people. In the east are the Red Sea Hills and the mountain resort of Erkowit, which dates from British colonial days. In the south are the beautiful mountain ranges of Matong and Dongotona. Mt Kinyeti in the Immatong Mountains is the highest peak in the Sudan, at 3187 metres.

The Red Sea Hills form a rugged scarp that gives way to a narrow coastal plain. The Red Sea coast is 716 km long and teeming with rich coral and fish life that only a few divers have had a glimpse at.

CLIMATE

The climate and weather vary greatly from north to south. The northern half of the Sudan is hot and dry most of the year. South of Khartoum, the temperatures tend to be lower but the humidity and rainfall are greater.

The best time to visit the Sudan is between November and March, before the rains and after the heat. If you decide that you must go

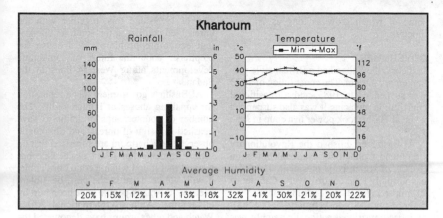

there at any other time, then be prepared for very hot weather. Temperatures of 48°C or more are not unusual in the north, and even in the cooler south the maximum temperature is up around 37°C, with humidity at 80% or more. In winter, from November to March, the temperature is still hot, but it usually gets no higher than the mid-30s, although in the north this 'cool' period really only lasts through January and the beginning of February.

Temperatures on the coast are generally milder, although the average maximum temperature will still be in the mid-30s in the winter months.

Throughout the year, but especially in the early summer period, you will encounter the infamous *haboob*, or sandstorm, in all but the mountains and tropical regions. During these sandstorms of monstrous proportions, the sun disappears from the sky as a thick curtain of sand falls over the land and the winds howl. Everything and everyone in the storm's path gets coated with fine grains of dust. A pleasant spring alternative is the khamsin, so called because it can last 50 days. It is a hot south wind that seems to suck every drop of moisture out of the air. On the other hand, for those who get to the extreme south of the country, the rainy season can last the better part of nine months.

It can get bitterly cold at night, particularly in desert areas. Up in Wadi Halfa, one of the hottest places in the country, night-time minimums of near freezing are not unusual in winter. In western Darfur, even daytime temperatures can be low in winter.

FLORA & FAUNA
Over much of the country, there is no vegetation to speak of, or merely sparse savanna-type elephant grass. Only in the south are there forests of substance.

It is perhaps in its wildlife that, to the Western mind, the Sudan is at its most 'African'. All the animals that are associated with Africa and the famous wildlife sanctuaries of African countries further south are also present in the Sudan, though mainly in the south. Elephants, lions, cheetahs, zebras, giraffes, leopards, rhinoceroses, buffaloes, hippopotamuses, antelopes, chimpanzees and baboons all have their homes in the Sudan, as do various other monkeys, crocodiles, a rich variety of birds and some very active insects, including the occasional tsetse fly.

Although all the variety is there, the animals are generally harder to find than in, say, Tanzania. A visit to Dinder National Park can be a disappointing experience for those who have visited other big-name animal reserves in Africa. If you're tramping around in the desert, watch out for scorpions, some of which grow as long as 20 centimetres.

GOVERNMENT

In theory, the Sudan had a British-style parliamentary system. The constitution of 1973 was suspended in 1985, and a transitional constitution replacing it was also suspended when al-Bashir took power in a coup in June 1989.

Al-Bashir established the Revolutionary Command Council for National Salvation (RCC), of which he is president. The RCC has virtually total control over a Cabinet of 21 ministers (al-Bashir is prime minister and defence minister). In February 1992 a 300-member transitional national assembly was established and officially given some legislative powers and the task of preparing for parliamentary elections. These have yet to materialise.

The main thorn in the side of everyone who has tried to govern the Sudan is the rift between the Muslim north and the non-Muslim south. The introduction of Islamic shari'a law in 1983 exacerbated this rift and led to the reopening of insurrection in the south. John Garang's SPLM, backed predominantly by the Dinka, wants a large degree of autonomy in a federal-style government of the Sudan. The breakaway faction, based on the Nuer people, wants complete secession for the three southern states.

The administrative structure of the country has been altered several times. Al-Bashir reorganised it all again in January 1991, creating nine *wilayat* (federal states), which were further divided into 66 provinces. The smallest division is that of the district, of which there are 217. It is apparently planned that each state should have its own legislature. The south is made up of the three traditional states of Upper Nile, Equatoria and Bahr al-Ghazal.

One of the reasons al-Bashir's coup was welcomed by some was the comparative failure of parliamentary democracy up to that point. More than 30 parties competed for power and influence prior to their suppression in 1989, and this, together with the unresolved conflict in the south and persistent economic problems, is a cause for scepticism about the future of democratic developments along Western lines in the Sudan.

Al-Bashir's government has a reputation for appalling abuses of human rights. The number of countercoups it claims to have quashed is a sign of unrest, and diplomatic observers in Khartoum are surprised that no serious uprising has taken place. One has warned that if and when a coup does come, it will, unlike those in the past, be violent because 'too many people have been hurt by this regime'. Amnesty International, Africa Watch and other groups have denounced the increasing use of torture and charged the government with embarking on a campaign of 'ethnic cleansing' of the Nuba. Claims and rumours fly around of non-Muslim families being rounded up and their children subjected to a forced Islamic education, and even of the reappearance of slavery. Atrocities are said to have been committed by all sides in the quagmire of the south. How much of all this is true is difficult to gauge, but one British journalist who went to Khartoum in early 1990 to find out was jailed for nine days and then expelled.

The government, opponents say, is ruling the whole country, not just the rebellious south, by fear. They say, for instance, that rigorous economic reforms introduced in early 1992, including the wholesale elimination of subsidies (see the following Economy section), would normally have led to far greater discontent than has been the case and attribute the subdued reaction to fear.

The Sudan's Neighbours

Winning friends and influencing people, with a few exceptions, does not seem to be the government's strong point. Relations with long-time friend Libya have cooled, partly over the vexed issue of the presence of Libyan troops on Sudanese soil for use in Chad, which in turn has not endeared the Sudan to Chad.

In 1992, the Sudan issued oil-exploration

permits to a Canadian consortium in the disputed and for-now jointly administered Halaib region on the Egyptian border. Egypt declared this illegal. There was some shooting between the two countries' police forces and mutual accusations that one side was backing terrorists (Islamic fundamentalists in Egypt and SPLA guerrillas in the Sudan) on the other's territory. The dispute heated up in early 1993, when Egypt claimed plans were afoot to allow Iran to use Port Sudan as a naval base. Egypt and Saudi Arabia made it clear that the Sudan would not be permitted this affront, and Egyptian troops were reinforced in the Halaib.

Issues of human rights have lost the Sudan kudos with the West, and its backing for Iraq in the Gulf War compounded this. (Hundreds of thousands of Sudanese working in the Gulf states found themselves forced to return home.) As recently as late 1992, there were reports that the Sudan was exporting frozen meat to Iraq in violation of the blockade of that country, raising questions about the value of food aid to the Sudan! Iraq, in return, promised help in getting the Sudan's tiny oil industry off the ground. Khartoum also denounced the US-led mission in Somalia in late 1992, although it later retracted its public opposition under pressure from Washington.

About the same time, however, Iran emerged as a big backer for the regime, buying Chinese and North Korean warplanes and tanks for the Sudanese army and purportedly even supplying some Revolutionary Guards for the fight in the south. Iran's growing influence in the area, not surprisingly, has done little to soothe feelings in the secular governments of Egypt, Tunisia, Algeria and even Libya, none of which appreciates the fundamentalist colours of al-Bashir's government. In fact, Algeria closed its Khartoum embassy in March. In late 1993, the USA put the Sudan on its list of states supporting terrorism.

ECONOMY

According to the Washington-based Population Crisis Committee, the Sudan is among five countries with the worst score on its 'human suffering index', which takes into account such factors as the availability of clean drinking water, daily calorie intakes, enrolments in secondary school, political freedom, civil rights and life expectancy.

Shortly after coming to power, al-Bashir launched the National Economic Salvation Programme, or NESP. Watched by the International Monetary Fund, the Sudanese have struggled to make a start at pulling their economy into shape – a mammoth task. Nevertheless, by early 1992 the Sudanese were announcing big improvements to incredulous outsiders. Falling output of previous years, the government announced, had been turned into growth of about 10% in 1991-1992.

Buoyed by the news and good cereal harvests (pessimists said the healthy harvests had been won in the Gezira area between the White and Blue Niles south of Khartoum at the expense of collapsing cotton production, for which growers could no longer afford imported fertilisers and equipment), the government announced a series of spectacular reforms in February 1992. These included the complete removal of several subsidies on basic commodities, including petrol. The results were spectacularly painful for the Sudanese: at the end of 1992, for example, Khartoum water rates went up 5000% in one hit. Electricity bills rise about 300% every couple of months.

The Sudanese pound was allowed to float almost unprotected and was devalued sixfold almost immediately. By April 1993, it was valued at S£135 to the US dollar, and was still falling. Unlicensed moneychangers were still offering S£50 to S£60 more and, as the government appeared to relax its penalties for operating on the black market, were again beginning to flourish. Inflation soared to anything from 150% to 200%, and the price of bread rose 500% in one year. For most Sudanese, this has sharpened the already difficult business of daily living. With an average monthly wage of US$40, the staggering rise in the cost of living is a growing burden. To combat inflation and reduce the cost of printing money, the government began introducing a 'more Islamic' currency, the dinar, at a value of SD1 to S£10, although the pound remains legal tender.

The return of up to 300,000 Sudanese from the Gulf states has cost the Sudan several hundred million dollars a year in remittances.

The Sudan is largely an agricultural and pastoral economy, although lack of irrigation schemes and other infrastructure means that the country is far from exploiting its full potential. Its main export crops, when enough can be produced, are cotton and sorghum. It also claims to be self-sufficient in wheat, but such a boast is to be taken with a pinch of salt. The south is largely pastoral, with cattle the main domestic stock.

Industry contributes as little as 4% to the national economy and is concentrated in the areas of food processing and textile, footwear and cigarette production. It will come as little surprise that tourism is not a booming industry. The last UN statistics on the matter showed that 52,000 visitors entered the country in 1987.

Potentially, the Sudan is a wealthy country. It has enough identified oil reserves to meet all its own needs for a decade, principally in south-western and north-western Sudan. Little of this is as yet accessible, although some is being mined and refined. There are also reasonable natural-gas reserves. Other mineral riches include marble, mica, chromite, gypsum, some iron ore, manganese, uranium, copper, zinc, and gold, which is found in the Red Sea Hills and has been known of since pharaonic times.

There is division among observers over how effective al-Bashir's measures will be, but with a national debt of around US$13,000 million (50% more than the gross domestic product) now a huge hindrance to development, there is a long way to go. In fact the International Monetary Fund pulled the plug in March 1993, saying it would make no more loans available because the Sudan could not even pay the interest on its debts. The trade imbalance is another depressing indicator: imports out-

weigh exports by about 20 to one. The lack of hard currency makes it difficult to get hold of even the most basic supplies. Petrol was being rationed at one gallon a week for private cars in early 1993, and rumours were rife that if new shipments didn't arrive soon from somewhere, the country would run dry. In fact, petrol for private use was cut altogether in Khartoum in April, as Khartoum accused Egypt of stopping oil tankers bound for the Sudan from passing the Suez Canal. Hopes that chumming up with Iran would lead to free oil have been dashed: Iran will sell oil at preferential rates to the Sudan, but it won't give the stuff away.

The continuing war costs up to US$2 million a day, and the burden of dealing with up to two million internally displaced people and the continued presence of hundreds of thousands of Eritrean and Ethiopian refugees is a huge strain on limited resources. The country's growing international isolation has cost it much government to government bilateral aid, and the Sudan is a long way from pulling itself out of the mess into which it has gradually been sinking since independence.

POPULATION

The sketchy statistics on the Sudan's population may be improved by the results of the April 1993 census, but at the time of writing its population was estimated at only about 26 million. The population of the Tri-City area of Khartoum is about three million, excluding refugees. It and the surrounding region is by far the most populous zone of the country.

About 70% of the population is, nevertheless, rural. Another 20% lives in cities and towns, while the remainder is nomadic. The high growth rate of between 2.8% and 3.2% does not augur well for the future. About half the Sudan's people are less than 15 years old.

Refugees & Displaced People

The rock concerts have come and gone, raising millions of dollars for relief supplies for refugees in the Sudan, and the media blitz asking for more help has long since subsided.

Yet there are still millions of people in desperate need throughout the country.

The biggest problem areas are the south, where millions of people continue to eke out an existence to a large extent cut off from the rest of the country by continued fighting; around Khartoum, where the bulk of Sudanese fleeing war in the south and famine in the west have congregated in camps; and finally in the east, where some 300,000 refugees from neighbouring Eritrea and Ethiopia still reside. According to the United Nations High Commissioner for Refugees, the east is no longer a crisis centre, and if repatriation programmes to postwar Eritrea and Ethiopia get off the ground, the problem may be reduced. Nobody believes, however, that all the refugees, some of whom have lived in the Sudan for 10 years or more, will turn around and go home.

If you are concerned about the situation and seriously interested in helping, it's possible to volunteer as a relief worker. Alternatively, you may wish to make a donation of money, food or clothing. See the list of nonprofit aid organisations in the Work section of the Facts for the Visitor chapter for details.

Although aid agencies are still active in the Sudan, some aid workers have been killed – at least one executed by the government over his supposed rebel affiliations. The government has always been suspicious of the aid agencies' work in the south, worrying that the food and medicine is actually ending up in the hands of the SPLA. Some agencies have pulled out, others have found themselves winding up and then getting involved again.

Nor has the government been keen on allowing involvement by the agencies in the displaced-people's camps around Khartoum. A campaign of forced relocation to camps well beyond the city, which often amount to little more than dust bowls with inadequate water and transport, was launched in 1990. An outcry from the UN and aid agencies in the Sudan led to a degree of grudging cooperation, but the UN Emergency Unit remained fundamentally opposed to the government's policy, which often involved bulldozing whole shanty towns on the periphery of Khartoum and Omdurman, and called for better planning and more humane treatment. As one UN spokeswoman pointed out though, its hands were tied. If it

---

Famine

The war-caused refugee crisis spawned a host of other problems throughout much of the country. Mass famine on an almost unprecedented scale – even worse than the drought-caused famine of 1985-1986 – was the chief result.

In 1984-1985 the western Sudan regions of Kordofan and Darfur and part of the eastern region near Kassala and Gedaref experienced severe drought and, subsequently, widespread famine. Six to seven million people were threatened with starvation or severe malnutrition. In Kordofan, 400,000 Sudanese were forced to leave their villages to go in search of food. The United Nations, as well as the United States Agency for International Development and other world aid agencies, rushed food and supplies to as many parts of the country as possible. During the summer months the efforts of the aid agencies were hindered by temperatures as high as 48°C and ferocious haboobs.

The west of the country has continued to be plagued by drought ever since, but in 1992 the government announced that it had become self-sufficient in cereals production and was actually able to export sorghum. Although this threw aid policy in some Western countries into confusion, there was scepticism about the claims. The UN Food & Agriculture Organization estimated that more than seven million people were threatened by serious food shortages and were in need of aid in 1992-1993, but the government retorted that this was Western propaganda to discredit the government. With at least three aid workers killed by the government or rebels in 1992, the position of aid agencies was becoming all but untenable, particularly in the south, where rebels, despite setbacks elsewhere, continued to maintain a tight siege of Juba, threatening its 300,000 population with starvation. ■

attempted to aid the people in the new camps, it appeared to be condoning government policy. If it stayed out on principle, how would that help the displaced? The UN and the aid agencies have had to accept a *fait accompli*, as the government has already completed most of the relocations.

Community Health

Officially, there are more than 200 hospitals and 400 medical centres in the Sudan, but the standard of care is generally extremely poor. Even if medicines were available, doctors and other medical personnel are in drastically short supply. According to some statistics, there are only about 4000 doctors in the Sudan, which means there is approximately one for every 6500 people. These trained medical practitioners are concentrated in or near Khartoum, so the situation in southern Sudan is even more critical. In the south there is one doctor for every 83,000 people. Wounded SPLA soldiers and others needing urgent care seek it in Kenya.

With a shortage of doctors and medicines, the Sudanese are blighted by an assortment of diseases and ailments that reads like a litany of woes. There are various strains of malaria, tuberculosis, meningitis, hepatitis, trachoma, glaucoma, bilharzia, measles, dysentery...the list goes on and on.

PEOPLE

The Sudan has more than 300 distinct tribes from more than 150 ethnic groups, and more than a hundred languages and dialects are spoken. The ethnic groups range from the predominantly Muslim Arabs, Nubians and Fur in the north and west to the predominantly Christian or animist African peoples in the south. It is interesting to travel from north to south to see the transition from Arab to African cultures.

Although northerners and southerners are often culturally distinct, some are very similar in appearance, as there has been much intermarriage between Arabs and Africans in the Sudan. Consequently, it is often possible to meet a person who looks African yet professes to be Arab. This is often as

Uduk woman

much a religious identification as anything else, and judging by the sometimes unpleasant experiences of Sudanese in other Arab countries, not all Arabs would agree with such declarations. The prevalence of decorative facial scarring also makes it hard for an outsider to distinguish between the two groups.

EDUCATION

According to UNESCO figures for 1985, there were about 37,000 students in tertiary institutions, about 500,000 in secondary school and 1.7 million in primary school. Primary and secondary education is free in the Sudan, but adult illiteracy was still estimated to be 72% in 1990, despite concerted government attempts to reduce it.

The (revised) government aim now is to achieve full primary-school enrolment by 1994, although the number of teachers and quality of schools are lamentably low in some areas.

A bone of contention is the Arabisation campaign in Sudanese schools. Examinations for high-school matriculation are now exclusively in Arabic, not in English, as was, until recently, the case. The change has caused a lot of people heartache. Many parents who were educated in English in private schools (the bulk of them Muslim Arabs, it should be noted) prefer to send their children to the same schools and, where possible, have them taught in English. Government pressure seems gradually to be putting an end to this, although one school principal in Khartoum noted that the education minister had recently congratulated his school on its English programme and hinted that some government schools would adopt similar programmes 'because English is a useful language'. The principal shrugged his shoulders in resigned disbelief at this apparent reversal and could only observe that 'perhaps the government [was] experimenting with different policies'!

Arabisation is also changing the face of tertiary education, where most instruction was, until recently, given in English. In addition to the government-controlled University of Khartoum, there is an Islamic University in Omdurman. There are also eight other universities throughout the country, as well as several private institutions and colleges.

The Sudan's continuing row with Egypt has led it to cut off its nose to spite its face. Until March, the University of Cairo had a branch in the Sudan, providing Sudanese students with a centre of excellence and the chance to get qualifications automatically recognised in Egypt and beyond. The government decided to nationalise the university (renaming it the Nilein University). More than a hundred resident Egyptian teachers were expelled, not to mention all the visiting lecturers from Cairo. Where replacements would be found is apparently something the government gave little thought to. Students halfway through degrees and worried they will end up with nothing have been offered places in Egyptian universities, but the long-term problem remains.

One of the many moves by the al-Bashir regime to anger the rebels in the south was the new national-service law of August 1992, which cancelled all exemptions under earlier legislation. All males between the ages of 18 and 33 must do at least 18 months' service; most do up to three years. Penalties for evasion include three years' jail and fines. It is not uncommon for southerners to find themselves fighting members of their own tribes in the south.

ARTS
Music
With such a racial and geographical diversity, local traditions have left their imprint on all the arts. A musician who has achieved some fame outside the Sudan is Abdel Karim al-Kabli, who seeks to reflect in his swaying but restrained music and Arabic lyrics some of his country's enormous variety. Although broadly lumped together with other 'Arab music' by many, it has a distinctly African flavour and often appeals to Western ears where more truly Arabian tones do not.

CULTURE
In the north, adherence to Islamic strictures is strong. Alcohol and pork are outlawed and clothing is conservative. The men wear long, flowing gowns called *jalabiyyas* and loosely wrapped turbans called *emmas*. The women wear *tobes*, which are nothing more than several metres of sheer, brightly coloured material wrapped around their heads and upper bodies and usually worn over their gowns.

In Khartoum, women office workers wear only white tobes because, as one woman said, 'We don't want a carnival atmosphere in our offices'. According to an article in the local press, however, more and more women are dispensing with the tobe.

In eastern Sudan, the women tend to wear brown or black tobes; some, such as the Rashaida women, also wear the ever-mysterious veils that reveal only their dark, piercing eyes and curly black fringes.

As you travel south, the people become darker skinned, culturally more African and generally less conservative than the northern Muslims. They usually wear less clothing, and some tribes, such as the Nuba from the Nuba Mountains, wear none. South of El-

Obeid you will also find a forlorn pork chop or two and a few varieties of bootleg spirits, which are definitely in short supply to the north.

The practice of facial scarring is common among Africans and Arabs of both sexes. The purposes and meanings of different scar patterns vary from group to group, although scarring is usually a sign of tribal identification or, for some women, a sign of beauty.

Another practice that crosses ethnic groups and tribes is female circumcision. Westerners find this barbaric and incomprehensible, but for many Sudanese it is still an accepted part of their culture. The government and many parents supposedly try to discourage it; they are, however, fighting an age-old tradition. An elderly woman in each village is usually assigned the role of circumcising girls when they reach the age of five. In some areas this involves the removal not only of the clitoris but also of the inner and outer labia. Despite the controversy surrounding this practice, many Sudanese women proudly claim to regard their circumcision as a sign of womanhood and a means of pleasing their husbands. It does nothing for the sex life of either side, however, and the men often resort to prostitutes, who generally belong to a class of former slaves.

The Sudanese are some of the poorest, yet most generous and hospitable, people in Africa. As you travel through the country they will welcome you into their homes to sip tea, to break bread, to chat and, sometimes, to stay for a few days. On buses, trains, ferries and even camel caravans, people will share whatever food and drink they have.

Avoiding Offence

The Muslim north is conservative. If the Sudan's Egyptian neighbours are accustomed to seeing millions of odd Westerners in every possible garb and behaving in all sorts of incomprehensible ways, the Sudanese are not. With the Islamisation of the country, strict norms are generally adhered to (although not always – there'll always be someone with some home-made hooch somewhere discreetly out of sight). If you get

your hands on a drink, keep it to yourself. The maximum penalty for Muslims caught under the influence of alcohol is 40 strokes of the rod – a high price to pay for a drink.

Dress is conservative: local men and women cover up and you should do the same. Men, let alone women, should wear long trousers. Western men do sometimes get around in shorts in, say, Khartoum without anyone saying so much as boo, but it should be borne in mind that to Muslims you are in your underwear. Most of the men wear jalabiyyas, except those in the civil service. There's probably no real reason why you shouldn't wear one too, but Westerners in local dress are not all that highly regarded.

RELIGION

More than 70% of the population is Muslim, while 20% or more adheres to various indigenous religions and 5% is Christian.

Islam

Most Sudanese Muslims, like the Egyptians, belong to the Sunni sect. Here, more so than in Egypt, however, various mystical and political currents of Islam have gained significant followings.

Generally, the mystical side of Islam is referred to as Sufism. Throughout the Sudan various Sufi orders or fraternities follow their own *tariqa* (a path or way to God). The members of a tariqa attain a closer relationship with Allah through special spiritual exercises conducted by the sheikh (leader) of the tariqa. The exercises vary from simply reciting Koranic passages to singing, dancing and whirling oneself into a state of ecstasy. The whirling dervishes of Omdurman (near Khartoum) are renowned for their weekly whirls.

The more political currents of Islam in the Sudan are not necessarily detached from mainstream Sunni Islam or the various Sufi orders; however, they can be considered as separate groups under the rallying flag of Islam.

One of the most important politico-religious movements in the Sudan is called Ansar. It has its roots in the Mahdiyya Movement of the late 19th century, and the thrust of it has not changed much since then. The members of Ansar believe that a Mahdi (a messenger of God and representative of Mohammed) will come to lead the people. The movement has become quite a political force among a variety of tribal groups ranging from the nomadic Baggara Arabs to the sedentary tribes of the White Nile.

A related organisation is the Ikhwan al-Muslimeen (Muslim Brotherhood). Essentially, this is a political organisation which seeks religious ends by encouraging the institution of Islamic society and polity based on shari'a. The organisation's popularity and influence seem to increase as economic conditions worsen, and its developing power was probably a major reason behind Nimeiri's declaration of shari'a in 1983. The brotherhood continues to be a major and, some would say, potentially destabilising influence on Sudanese politics.

In the present government, it is the National Islamic Front that carries the flag of what most hostile outsiders consider to be fundamentalism. Although technically banned along with all political parties, its leader, Hassan at-Turabi, is considered the prime force behind the government and largely responsible for its increasingly repressive character.

Accusations have been levelled at the government that non-Muslims in refugee and displaced-people's camps are being compelled to attend Muslim schools in what amounts to a concerted proselytising campaign.

Indigenous Religions

At least 20% of the population adheres to some form of indigenous or local religion, and the followers are often given the generic name of animists. The government's only (and meagre) publication about the country describes them as 'non-religious', which they would probably not appreciate. The forms vary by ethnic group and tribe, but in general, they relate to certain forces of nature and ancestor worship.

The Dinka, Nuer and other Nilotic tribes of southern Sudan, for example, see human beings as ants in relation to God, although certain men and women among them are sometimes considered to have special Godlike powers. They are often accused of being sorcerers or witches, of practising black magic and inflicting illness upon people or animals.

In the north, the notion of the 'evil eye' is prevalent among the Arabs. One who expresses too much interest in the affairs of another can be suspected of deliberately causing harm to that person. As protection against witches, sorcerers and the evil eye, each group has its versions of diviners, witch doctors and exorcists who provide amulets, medicinal concoctions and advice.

Christianity

Only 5% of the population is Christian. Most of the Christians are Roman Catholics of the Latin rite, but there are some Anglicans and a handful of several other denominations, including Copts and Greek Orthodox. Missionary incursions over the past two centuries, especially in southern Sudan, account for most of the Christian population. Missionaries continue to 'spread the word' throughout that region.

LANGUAGE

Although there are more than a hundred languages and dialects in the Sudan, Arabic is the predominant language. As well as being the lingua franca (it is vigorously promoted as such by Khartoum), it is also replacing English as the universal medium of instruction.

English is, in spite of this, spoken throughout the country and should suffice for travel in most parts of the Sudan. As in Egypt, though, knowledge of even a few words of Arabic brings instant smiles from the locals (any knowledge of local languages, especially in the south, where all things Arab are the object of considerable mistrust, would have a similar effect). Sudanese Arabic is slightly different from Egyptian Arabic.

Pronunciation

The hard 'g' sound does not exist. It is pronounced as a 'j', as by practically all Arabic speakers outside Egypt. For example, the word 'galabiyya' (the long cotton gown worn by men) is pronounced 'jalabiyya' in the Sudan.

Secondly, the 'sh' sound is generally not used at the end of a verb to negate it. Thus, the Egyptian phrase 'mafeesh' – which means 'there is not' or 'there are not' – becomes 'mafee' in the Sudan. This is closer to the standard Arabic tongue.

The Arabic 'q', as in 'qasr' (castle, palace), is often pronounced more like 'g'.

Vocabulary

There are also a few differences in vocabulary between the two countries.

How are you?	
kayf hallak?	(to a man)
	(pronounced 'haleck')
kayf hallik?	(to a woman)
	(pronounced 'halick')
What?	
shunnu? munu?	
What's your name?	
ismak shunnu/munu?	

The word lists in the Egypt section are, for the most part, applicable to the Sudan. *Khawaja* is a word which you will hear often as you travel through the Sudan. Adopted from the Persian, it is used to address foreigners and traders and generally (at least in its origins) simply means 'Mr' or 'sir'. There is little doubt that it is often used with some derogatory undertones, but don't be too quick to take offence – the word itself is not an insult.

Another feature you will notice in many people's speech is a regular clicking noise. Even many Arabs in the north have taken on this peculiarly African trait. It generally is used to say yes or otherwise indicate the affirmative or confirmation of something you say to them.

Greetings

Anyone who has visited the Arab world before will be aware of the formality and complexity of greetings between Arabs. The ceremony and repetition of questions along the lines of 'How's your health?', 'How's the family?', 'Welcome!' and so forth is always a little bewildering for Westerners more accustomed to a simple 'Hello'.

You ain't seen (or heard) nothing until you get to the Sudan. Those who understand Arabic will be mesmerised by the speed with which a seemingly endless stream of such greetings are fired between two people. Both rattle off their greetings simultaneously, apparently oblivious to what the other is saying but aware that they are doing the same. Neither wants to be the first to stop, but of course sooner or later one or the other must, if only for shortness of breath. The greeting is warm, but the words seem devoid of real meaning. Rather they are a formula to be followed. This verbal torrent is sometimes accompanied by a quite different version of the handshake: the two friends give each other a gentle shove with their right hands on each other's shoulder, *then* shake hands and embark on the oral ritual just described. An inspiring characteristic is another formula that seems to carry with it a little more depth of feeling.

People, on meeting, always carry out some form of greeting, even if relatively short, and the most common is to enquire if all is *tamam* (well). The reply is almost inevitably a beaming smile and a convincing 'tamam'! To an outsider perhaps a little oppressed by the evident difficulties of daily life for most Sudanese, it is testimony to these people's capacity to be satisfied with what life gives, however little it may seem to a Westerner.

Facts for the Visitor

VISAS & EMBASSIES

Visas are required by everyone, but the requirements vary from embassy to embassy and are liable to change at any time. Restrictions relating to South Africa and Israel, however, hold for all applicants.

Anyone whose passport contains signs of their having visited Israel, such as an Israeli stamp or an Egyptian border stamp, will be denied a Sudanese visa. If you crossed overland to or from Israel, then you are probably doomed unless both the Egyptian and the Israeli authorities put all visas and stamps on separate sheets of paper or you have a second passport. Some embassies will readily issue you a second passport, so check with your own government's passport office or embassy. But obtaining a new passport doesn't always work because the Sudanese then assume that you may be trying to hide the fact that you have been to Israel. The US embassy in Cairo, for example, issues second passports in a day or two. However, sometimes the Sudanese won't issue you a visa if your passport doesn't have an Egyptian entry stamp. South African nationals cannot obtain Sudanese visas.

Until mid-1993, visas had to be obtained from a Sudanese consulate or embassy. However, a couple of travellers have reported it is now possible to obtain them on arrival at Wadi Halfa for US$50, although this price may come down.

As a guide to what to expect when applying for visas, applications in London for a single-entry visa valid for presentation within three months, and allowing a stay of one month, take about three weeks to be processed if delivered in person. There are no multiple-entry visas. Business visas, to which the same conditions apply, can be issued more quickly if you have a sponsor in Khartoum. People of all eligible nationalities must pay UK£20, provide two passport-sized photos and fill in two application forms.

In Cairo, five forms and photos are required, along with a letter of recommendation from your embassy. It also seems to take three or four weeks for the visa to be issued. It costs US$50 (!), which must be paid in cash, and is valid for a one-month stay if presented within *one* month. The French embassy in Cairo will not issue letters of recommendation for French nationals, so French applicants should apply for Sudanese visas in France.

Sudanese visas can be obtained in Nairobi, sometimes on the same day, for Kenyan Sh 2250. Again, they are valid for a month in the Sudan.

In London, travellers' cheques amounting to UK£200 for every two weeks of your proposed visit are sometimes required as proof you can buy an air ticket out of the country. No such proof is asked for in Cairo or Nairobi.

In countries where there is no Sudanese representation, you are expected to write to the embassy in Britain or the USA. If you are planning to head there overland, it may be better to wait until you are in, say, Cairo.

Bear in mind that these requirements can change and are not absolute!

Proof of cholera and yellow-fever vaccinations is required if you're arriving from an infected area. African countries south of latitude 12°N are considered infected areas, as are many South American countries. The proof is sometimes demanded even if you are not arriving from an infected area, so a simple rule of thumb is to be sure that you at least have proof of your yellow-fever vaccination with you when you enter the country.

Registration

All visitors are required to register within three days of arrival in the country. If you enter the country at any point other than Khartoum, you must register your arrival at your point of entry *and again* when you reach Khartoum. In Khartoum, you must go to the Aliens' section of Security, in Sharia Othman Diqna, next to the Arab Institute for Agricultural Investment building. You will have to fill out a form and pay S£65.

You must present your travel permits and register with the police within 24 hours of your arrival in other towns and cities. The strictness with which these rules are enforced seems to vary, and an apparent decision to lift the requirement for travel permits to many places may make the situation even more fluid. You'll have to judge each situation on its merits, but if you are not pushed to register by officials or nervous hotel employees, you can sometimes get away with not registering.

Visa Extensions & Re-Entry Visas

Visa extensions can be obtained at the Aliens' Office of the Ministry of the Interior. Two photos are required, as are varying sums of money and some patience. Go into the office on the left of the main entrance and ask for the extension. You'll get a form to fill in, which staff will scribble on before sending you into the street to buy revenue stamps for S£75. When you go back inside, you will be shunted around for awhile until you end up at the cashier's window, where you will be expected to disburse another S£255 for a month's stay. You will be given more stamps and told to return to where you started. Eventually someone will take note of your existence, stick the stamps into your passport and tell you to come back the following day. It appears you can ask for several months' extension at a time if you want, but the time you are given is valid from the day you make the application, not from the expiry date of your previous visa.

If you want to make a foray, say, into Eritrea and Ethiopia and then return to the Sudan, you would be advised to get a re-entry visa rather than go through the hassle of applying for a new visa outside. Officials seem to make up the rules for this as they go along, but a re-entry visa valid for presentation for three months (but good for a stay of only up to a week, depending on how suc-

cessfully you beg) can be obtained in a day for S£1000.

Exit Visas

Exit visas are no longer required for people staying in the Sudan for less than three months, and according to one official, not at all. It might be an idea to check this with a travel agent or in the Aliens' Office of the Ministry of the Interior. Sudanese nationals and foreign residents *do* need them, so the rules could change.

Note that when leaving overland you must pay an exit fee of S£65, and when departing by air an airport tax of S£300 is imposed.

Sudanese Embassies

The following is a list of addresses and telephone numbers of Sudanese embassies around the world:

Australia
   No diplomatic representation
Austria
   Spittelauerplatz 4/1-4, 1090 Vienna (☎ (1) 344640)
Belgium
   12 Ave Franklin D Roosevelt, Brussels (☎ (2) 647 5159)
Canada
   457 Laurier Ave East, Ottawa, Ontario, Canada K1N 6R4 (☎ (613) 235 4000, 235 4999)
Central African Republic
   PO Box 1351, Ave de l'Indépendence, Bangui (☎ (61) 3821)
Chad
   N'Djameina (☎ 3497 2815)
Egypt
   4 Sharia al-Ibrahimy, Garden City, Cairo (☎ (2) 354 5043)
   Consulate: 1 Sharia Mohammed Fahmy as-Said, Garden City, Cairo
Ethiopia
   PO Box 1110, Kerkos Kelly, Addis Ababa (☎ (1) 516477)
France
   56 Ave Montaigne, 75008 Paris (☎ (1) 4720 0786)
Germany
   Koblenzer Str 99, 5300 Bonn 2 (☎ (228) 363074)
Ireland
   No diplomatic representation
Japan
   Yada Mansion, 6-620 Minami-Aoyama, Minato Ku, Tokyo 107

Jordan
PO Box 3305, Area No 13135, Square No 22, Jebel Amman, Amman (☎ (6) 644251/2)
Kenya
Minet ICDC Building Mamlaka, Nyerere Rd, Nairobi (☎ (2) 20770, 33707)
Libya
68 Sharia Mohammed Ali Mosadak, Tripoli (☎ (21) 32660)
Netherlands
Laan Copes van Cattenburch 81, 2585 EW The Hague (☎ (70) 605 3000)
New Zealand
No diplomatic representation
Sweden
No diplomatic representation
Switzerland
Sudan Permanent Mission, WIPO Building, 34 Ch des Colombelles, 2212 Geneva 20
Uganda
PO Box 3200, 4th Floor, Parliament Building, Kampala (☎ (41) 43518, 58971)
UK
3 Cleveland Row, St James's, London SW1A 1DD (☎ (071) 839 8080)
USA
2210 Massachusetts Ave NW, Washington DC 20008 (☎ (202) 379 8370)
Consulate: 210 East 49th St, New York, NY 10017 (☎ (212) 573 6033)
Zaire
PO Box 7347, 83 Ave des Treis, Kinshasa-Gombe, Kinshasa

Foreign Embassies in the Sudan

The addresses and telephone numbers of some embassies in Khartoum are:

Australia
See UK embassy
Canada
See UK embassy
Central African Republic
The embassy is closed, and by all accounts its representative in the Chad embassy is not very helpful. Visas are supposedly obtainable on the border.
Chad
PO Box 1514, 21 Sharia 17, New Extension (☎ 42545). The embassy is open from 9 am to noon, Sunday to Thursday. You need two passport-sized photos and S£1530 for a one-month visa, which takes a week to be issued.
Egypt
PO Box 1126, Sharia al-Gama'a, Al-Mogran (☎ (11) 77646/7, 72836)
Consulate: Sharia al-Gamhuriyya (☎ (11) 70291, 72190). This is where you get a visa. You need

one photo. A visa valid for a one-month stay will be issued on the same day for between S£1550 and S£2100. The consulate is open (except on Fridays) from 9 am to noon for applications – you pick up your passport at about 1 pm.
Consulate in El-Obeid: Al-Midan al-Kabeer (☎ (249) 4167)
Consulate in Port Sudan: Sharia Kabbashi Eissa (249) 2036, 5910)
Eritrea
39th Ave East, New Extension. The permanent delegation of the provisional EPLF government of Eritrea was converted into an embassy after the landslide independence referendum in April 1993. Visas for two weeks cost S£300 and are issued virtually on the spot.
Ethiopia
PO Box 844, Sharia 1, New Extension. Visas valid for one month cost S£1313 for people of all eligible nationalities and take 24 hours to be processed. You need two photos and a letter of recommendation from your embassy. The tricky part is that the visa bears the endorsement 'valid for air travel only'. Often a visa will not be issued without evidence of an air ticket in *and out* of Ethiopia. Officials will tell you that travelling overland via Eritrea is not permitted. The good news is that Ethiopian Airlines won't sell a ticket without a visa. Get a reservation slip from the airline and present this at the embassy. When you have the visa, throw the reservation slip away and get your Eritrean visa. There appear to be no problems crossing from Eritrea into Ethiopia overland, even with the endorsement on your visa. However, some travellers have reported difficulties trying to get out afterwards, being stuck in court for a couple of weeks and fined US$35 after trying to get an exit visa. In that case, it may be worth trying to leave without the exit visa.
France
PO Box 377, Plot No 163, Block 8, Burri (☎ 225608)
Germany
PO Box 970, Plot No 2, Block No 8DE, Sharia al-Baladaya (☎ 77990). Consular hours are from 9 am to noon, Sunday to Thursday.
Ireland
See UK embassy
Japan
PO Box 1649, 24 Block AE, Sharia 3, New Extension (☎ 44554)
Jordan
25 Sharia 7, New Extension (☎ 43264)
Kenya
PO Box 8242, Sharia 3, New Extension (☎ 40386). Consular hours are 10 am to noon, Mondays and Wednesdays only. A standard single-entry visa valid for presentation for three

months and good for a stay of varying length costs most people S£2000. Exceptions are the Dutch (S£5000) and the Japanese (S£2650). Transit visas cost S£1000. Bring three photos.

Libya
PO Box 2019, 50 Africa Rd. It seems virtually impossible to get a visa to Libya here.

Netherlands
PO Box 391, House No 47, 47th Ave East, New Extension (☎ 47271)

New Zealand
See UK embassy

Sweden
Consulate: PO Box 2206, Sharia Babika Badri (☎ 76308, 79654)

Switzerland
PO Box 1707, New Aboulela Building (☎ 40000)

Uganda
House No 6, Square 42, Khartoum East (☎ 78409). The consular window is open only on Wednesdays, from 8 am to 2 pm. Visas take a week to be issued, and two photos are required. Costs and validity seem to be decided on an ad-hoc basis.

UK
PO Box 801, Sharia 10, off Sharia al-Baladaya (☎ 70760). The embassy is virtually next door to the German embassy. Consular hours are 8 am to 2.30 pm, Sunday to Thursday.

USA
PO Box 699, Sharia Ali Abdul Latif (☎ 74700). The consular section is open for business from 7.30 am to 3.30 pm, except on Fridays and Saturdays.

Zaire
PO Box 4195, Block 12CE, 23, Sharia 13, New Extension (☎ 42424). A visa for a one-month stay costs S£8000, and it's possible to get one for longer if you want. You need three photos and a letter of recommendation from your embassy. Visas take 48 hours to be issued. The embassy is open from 8 am to noon, Sunday to Thursday.

DOCUMENTS
Travel Permits

Until very recently, permits were required for travel anywhere outside Khartoum, and were generally exasperatingly difficult to obtain. The official line as of April 1993 was that they were no longer needed except for travel south of Kosti or into the Nuba Mountains area, for which permits were not being issued to travellers anyway.

The situation seems fluid, so the following information is given in case the government changes its mind or the present decision proves in any way ambiguous. If you arrive by air in Khartoum, you can apply for travel permits when registering your arrival. You can ask to have several destinations put on the one permit, which will cost you S£350, and you'll need one or two photos. List every place you think you might want to stop at. Better still, if they let you, write them in yourself. The permits can take a couple of days to be issued (although there is really nothing to stop them handing them out on the spot).

You will need to present this permit whenever you register with the police in other towns. If, of course, the permits are no longer being issued, you can't present anything much but your passport and yourself – let's hope the local functionaries realise that!

Wadi Halfa is a pretty laid-back place, and if this is where you arrive, make an effort to get your permit done there. Officials will probably want to issue you one for travel to Khartoum, but are likely to let you fill in the destinations and then stamp the result. (Some travellers have simply added more destinations as they have gone – an example to follow only at your own risk.) The permit costs S£350, and a photo or two must be provided. (Get the photos in Egypt, as there is nowhere here to have them taken). The permit is issued while you wait, which means you may have to wait a while. Then again, there isn't much else to do in Wadi Halfa anyway.

Visiting Archaeological Sites

A permit from the Department of Antiquities in Khartoum is officially required for visits to all historical sites, and authorities seem hell bent on discouraging people from going at all. You pay US$10 (!) per site, and Meroe counts as three. The department, which is directly behind the National Museum, issues the permits on the same day. This is not much good to people travelling down from the north. If guards look like making life difficult, try flashing your travel permit or any other official bit of paperwork you can come up with – this will quite often do the trick.

Photography Permits

A fairly useless formality you need to go through is getting a photography permit, which is issued in the Tourist Information Office in Khartoum. On it you list the areas and subjects you think you'll want to photograph, and it tells you what you may not put on film – everything from bridges to 'slum areas, beggars and other defaming objects'. In Khartoum and Omdurman, just taking your camera out seems to irritate some people. The number of people marched away to have their films confiscated, in spite of waving permits around, is enough to make you want to just forget it. Outside the capital, it's generally not such a big problem.

CURFEW

In Khartoum and other cities and towns there is a curfew in force from midnight to 4 am. In most cases this doesn't matter, because there is generally little reason to be up so late anyway. It can be a pain in Khartoum, however – especially if you have an early-morning flight to catch. This means you have to get to the airport by midnight and wait for hours for your flight, or risk breaking the curfew. Expatriates caught driving after curfew have been sent back to where they came from or made to wait it out at the roadblock where they were stopped. Curfew passes are difficult to obtain, although you might get lucky if you get to know an expatriate with one. Some taxis at the airport have special curfew passes, so if you arrive late at night, you should be able to get into town. Some taxis operating from the Hilton Hotel also have curfew passes for the airport.

CUSTOMS

There is no customs or currency declaration form to be filled in now, but importing alcohol into this 'dry' country is still rigorously banned. If you have any alcohol, it will be confiscated. Electrical goods are the other problem. Computers, video cameras and the like will arouse curiosity, and you'll probably have to pay import duty on them. Your stills camera, the Sudan's particular bugbear, will be carefully examined and its serial number written into your passport. On your way out, officials will ask to see it and will compare the serial number in the passport with that on the camera.

MONEY

Drastic economic measures have been taken since the 1989 coup, including the introduction of a second currency and the loosening of exchange controls. Inflation has accelerated dramatically and will probably continue to do so. Draconian laws dealing with black marketeers have been eased, and the market is flourishing. The favoured currencies are US dollars and UK pounds, but cash in other major currencies can be changed too.

You can change cash and travellers' cheques at only a few of the myriad banks around. The Bank of Khartoum is the main one, but even at its head office in the capital, staff may look askance at travellers' cheques for anything but US dollars. With a bit of pleading, UK pounds may get past too. Cash gets a better reaction, but outside the capital even that can pose problems. The story sometimes is that the phone line is down, so they can't call Khartoum to find out the latest rate. If you are going to change money in the banks, the simplest thing to do is carry American Express or Thomas Cook cheques in US dollars, or cash.

Credit cards have only limited uses. Some of the biggest hotels in Khartoum accept

MasterCard and American Express cards for payment of bills. Visa is virtually useless. The one exception is the purchase of international air tickets, which can be done with pretty much any credit card, travellers' cheques or hard-currency cash.

The biggest hotels demand payment in hard currency, and a few others (not always the most expensive) require bank receipts if you're paying in Sudanese pounds. The latter are the exception rather than the rule, but it can't hurt to ask, before taking a room, whether receipts are required.

The black market is active in Khartoum, Port Sudan and Wadi Halfa. If you're coming overland from Egypt, you can buy Sudanese pounds at the dock in Aswan. You will probably get a marginally better rate in Wadi Halfa itself. If you haven't got any hard currency, you would be well advised to buy some US dollars at the Banque Misr before leaving Aswan.

There are divergent views on the wisdom or otherwise of using the black market, with constant rumours that some of the changers are actually planted by Security. Expatriates definitely warn against it in Khartoum. You will probably have to judge the risk for yourself. Some shopkeepers will change money at black-market rates. The black market seems most conspicuous in Wadi Halfa, while the best rates appear to be available in Port Sudan. If you wish to compare rates being offered to you on the black market with bank rates, check the latter in the following Exchange Rates section.

Currency

There are now two currencies operating side by side in the Sudan. In an attempt to reduce printing costs and rein in inflation, the Sudanese pound (S£), itself divided into 100 piastres (pt), has been joined by the dinar (SD). SD1 equals S£10. The long-term plan is supposed to be to replace the S£ entirely with SD, but that seems a long way off at the moment.

Sudanese dinar only come in SD50 and SD25 notes, which are smaller and much newer looking than the Sudanese pound.

Sudanese pound notes come in denominations of S£100, S£50, S£20, S£10 and S£5. Coins have all but dropped out of circulation, although you'll still come across S£1 coins and, very occasionally, 50 pt. Most people still talk in terms of *jinay* (pounds) so SD50 is S£500.

The Sudanese dinar notes can be a little unwieldy if you're just paying for an urban bus fare or a bottle of Pepsi, but generally shopkeepers seem to have little trouble changing them.

Exchange Rates

Here is a list of bank exchange rates on some foreign currencies:

Australia	A$1	=	S£75
Canada	C$1	=	S£103
France	F10	=	S£230
Germany	DM1	=	S£78
Japan	Y100	=	S£98
UK	£1	=	S£198
USA	$1	=	S£135

Australia	S£100	=	A$1.33
Canada	S£100	=	C$0.97
France	S£100	=	F4.30
Germany	S£100	=	DM1.28
Japan	S£100	=	Y101
UK	S£100	=	UK£0.51
USA	S£100	=	US$0.77

At the time of researching, bank rates for cheques and cash differed, but it's difficult to see any pattern in the discrepancies. By comparison, the black-market rate for US$1 hovered between S£180 and S£200. For UK£1 the rate on the streets was around S£260. In Wadi Halfa, E£1 would buy between S£50 and S£60.

Money from Home

One way to have money sent to you in Khartoum is through Citibank (☎ 452413). You need to fill out an application form at the bank and show them your passport and, if possible, your bank (key) card. You will be charged commission and made to pay for the telex to your bank. Citibank is on Farouq

Cemetery Rd, near Sharia 17 in the New Extension.

Some travellers have reported avoiding commissions by going through Sudanese banks. It partly depends on what your bank wants to do, as some have prior arrangements with certain local banks for this kind of situation. You may need to call your bank to find out what their preferences are.

American Express has an office in Khartoum but it does not offer any financial services such as cashing cheques or money transfers. (See the Khartoum chapter.)

Costs

The Sudan is a particularly cheap place to travel in. Even if you occasionally splash out a little, you can fairly easily keep daily expenses to about US$10. If you change money on the black market and stick religiously to the cheapest accommodation, you can do it for considerably less.

The cheapest beds cost from S£50 to S£100. Pepsi, Coca-Cola and similar soft drinks generally cost S£25 to S£30 for a 250 ml bottle, but can go as high as S£40 in the west (or sky high in posh restaurants). Juices like guava and lemon sold at roadside stands generally cost about S£20. A *doster*, or dozen, oranges costs around S£300, which is the price of one or two apples – a rare sight. Tinned sardines imported from Egypt cost about S£150 for 200 grams. A packet of 10 local Bringi cigarettes costs S£75.

A plate of grilled Nile perch with salad might cost about S£200; a bowl of *fuul* about S£30 to S£50. Tea is generally S£10, or S£15 with powdered milk. Sweets along the lines of *baqlawa* and *basboosah* cost about S£15 a slice. (See the Food section later in this chapter for descriptions of these items.)

WHEN TO GO

The best time to go is in winter. Although it can get pretty cold at night, especially in desert areas, the daytime heat more than makes up for this. On average, July and August are the wettest months in Khartoum; the rest of the year it is largely dry. During the rainy season, the rain is heavier and lasts longer the further south you go. And although summer includes the rainy season, it can get so hot that you'd rather be in hell: the *average* maximum in Wadi Halfa in May and June is 52°C!

WHAT TO BRING

Since it is warm (a bit of an understatement) in the Sudan throughout the year, bring light clothing. If you are planning a trek into the cooler climes of Jebel Marra, then bring a sweater or light jacket. You'll also find you need to rug up at night in the desert, particularly if you get stuck on an overnight bus or truck ride and have to sleep out.

Above all, don't be fooled by the daytime heat into not bringing a sleeping bag. Apart from the fact that it can get bitterly cold at night and, particularly in Darfur, even during the winter days, a sleeping bag has other uses: it can cushion some of the bumpier moments in the back of that old bus or lorry through the desert, because they are not built for comfort.

During the rainy season you must have a poncho or cool, loose-fitting rain jacket, although it is still warm even when it rains.

It is also a good idea to have a bandanna (the large, usually checked handkerchief often seen on the bad guys in Westerns) to cover your mouth and nose during sandstorms or wild rides on the backs of lorries.

Bring a water bottle, and a good one. There are some good lightweight ones produced for army use that are robust and can hold a couple of litres. The water in your bottle may be all you have to drink on long stretches – especially as anything you are offered en route will probably be of dubious quality.

Other suggested accessories include sunglasses, a hat, a big plastic rubbish bag to cover your pack during rain and sandstorms, insect repellent, a mosquito net, a bed sheet (often it's too hot for the sleeping bag), iodine and/or water purifier, and a nylon cord to string up your mosquito net and use as a laundry line. A bowl, a cup and some cutlery might not go astray beyond the larger centres. It would be a pity to have a load of fuul on offer and nothing to eat it with or out of!

Basic toiletries and some first-aid supplies are usually available in Khartoum and Port Sudan, but with supplies of all goods so erratic, the simplest advice is to bring whatever you need. Some hospitals don't even have aspirin! All the gismos and cleaning solutions that go with contact lenses are very difficult to come by. Condoms and other contraceptives, shaving foam in pressurised cans, the more modern cartridge-style razor blades and most other such items are virtually impossible to find, although you may get lucky in Khartoum. Toilet paper, or at least tissues, are widely available, while the old screw-on razor blades are imported from India.

TOURIST OFFICES

Getting any useful tourist information on the Sudan is difficult. There are no government tourist offices abroad, and the embassies have nothing to offer either. In the Sudan itself, you can try the Tourist Information Office in Khartoum, for what it's worth. (See the Information section of the Khartoum chapter.)

BUSINESS HOURS & HOLIDAYS

Most shops are open from 8 am to 2 pm and some from 6 to 8 pm. Government offices are officially open from 8 am to 2.30 pm. If you must visit a government office, it's better to show up after 9 am to give the busy bureaucrats enough time to have tea and read the newspaper.

Banks are open from 8.30 am to noon, Saturday to Thursday.

Fridays are holidays for Muslims; and Sundays are holidays for Christians.

Holidays & Festivals

For a rundown of Islamic holidays and festivals, refer to the Egypt Facts for the Visitor chapter. Other holidays in the Sudan are:

1 January
    Independence Day This commemorates the birth of the independent Republic of the Sudan in

1956. On this day the soldiers who are not fighting civil-war battles in the south get to line up and parade through the streets of Khartoum.

27 March
    Unity Day This commemorates the signing of the Addis Ababa Agreement, which ostensibly unified northern and southern Sudan in 1972.

25 December
    Christmas Day

CULTURAL EVENTS

It has to be said that not a lot is happening in the Sudan at the moment. Don't expect to be overwhelmed by film festivals and theatrical extravaganzas in Khartoum. Occasionally, especially around the Eid al-Fitr at the end of Ramadan (the month of fasting), Sudanese bands perform in the bigger towns. Sudanese music is a mesmeric blend of the best of Arabian and African tones and a pleasure to listen to.

In April 1993, the first ever International Camel Races to be held in the Sudan were staged in Kassala. If it becomes a regular event, it may be worth trying to get a ticket.

POST & TELECOMMUNICATIONS
Post

The GPO in Khartoum is open from 8.30 am to 1 pm and from 5.30 to 6.30 pm daily except Fridays. Mail to the USA takes about two weeks to get there, but letters from the USA can take up to a month to reach the Sudan. Mail to and from Europe takes the

same amount of time, and often does not seem to make it at all.

Ordinary letters cost S£40 to non-Arab countries, while postcards cost S£20. Letters to Arab countries cost S£30.

There is a poste restante service in the GPO of every major town and city, but the service is highly unreliable, even in Khartoum. If you want to receive mail in Khartoum, the best bet is probably to have it addressed to American Express (see the Khartoum chapter).

Telephone

Phoning anywhere in the Sudan is a trying business, and attempting to get an international line is worse. The phone office next to the GPO in Khartoum is open from 7 am to 9.30 pm, seven days a week. You might need all that time to get a call out. Bring a good book! There is a three-minute minimum. From the phone office, three minutes to the UK cost S£575, and each subsequent minute costs S£200. To Australia, the first three minutes cost S£705, while each minute after that is usually about S£250.

There are a few alternatives, but don't expect miracles from any of them. The Acropole Hotel in Khartoum is well known for having a functioning phone, fax and telex. But even it has trouble getting lines. Three minutes to the UK cost S£1200.

The other big hotels are no better, and in fact are often worse.

In Souq Two, near the New Extension in Khartoum, is a service called Hotline, which some expatriates swear by. Key International in the New Extension is another possibility. Some of the Western companies operating in Khartoum have direct outside lines or even satellite links, which cost the earth.

As a last resort, you could try Mark Wormald of DHL, at House No 10, 1/15 Sharia an-Nigomi. He has a direct international line. He can, predictably enough, also courier packages out of the country for you. Mark insists that he or his successor would be happy to help out the odd traveller in distress.

Outside Khartoum, you may as well forget

it. The chances of getting an international line in Port Sudan and Kassala, where they claim to have one, are meagre. Elsewhere you'd be lucky to get a line through to Khartoum.

Fax & Telex

The GPO in Khartoum, and in a couple of other towns, claims to have telex, fax and express-mail services. How well these function is anybody's guess, but one can only be sceptical.

TIME

There is only one time zone in the Sudan and that is two hours ahead of GMT/UTC. So, when it's noon in Khartoum it is 10 am in London; 5 am in New York and Montreal; 2 am in Los Angeles; 1 pm in Moscow; and 8 pm in Melbourne and Sydney.

ELECTRICITY

The electric current is 215 to 240 volts AC, 50 Hz. In Khartoum, Port Sudan, Kassala and some of the other bigger centres it is pretty reliable. In many places, however, the supply is provided by local generators and can be erratic. Power cuts are pretty common in towns like El-Obeid, for instance. The bulk of the country's supply is generated by hydroelectric power stations by the Sennar and Roseires dams, and another power station in North Khartoum.

LAUNDRY

Outside the big cities, you do it yourself. In Khartoum, Port Sudan and a few other places, you can generally ask your hotel to arrange to have it done.

WEIGHTS & MEASURES

The metric system is generally in use, although there are some local variations: petrol is generally sold by the gallon instead of by the litre, and fruit by the doster instead of by the kg.

BOOKS

Not many books have been written about the

Sudan but there are a few that are highly recommended.

Nick Worrall's *Sudan* (London Times Press) is an excellent summary, in words and photographs, of the diversity of cultures in contemporary Sudan.

An attractively illustrated and informative history of ancient Nubia (which covers most of the north of modern Sudan) by John H Taylor is put out by the British Museum (1991) and called simply *Egypt & Nubia*.

Winston Churchill's *The River War* is a lively, if somewhat jaundiced, view of the Kitchener campaign in the Sudan. It was one of the young Winston's first forays into war, for which he seems to have had something of a predilection.

For a detailed look at Britain's control of the Sudan, you could do worse than look at *The British in the Sudan*, edited by Francis Mading Deng & Robert Collins (Macmillan, 1984). Deng is a Dinka academic who has also done some definitive studies of Dinka mythology and collected a series of traditional stories in *Dinka Folktales*. In *Dinka Cosmology* he puts together the results of hundreds of interviews with Dinka chiefs and elders. Both books are published by Ithaca Press.

Alan Moorehead's classics, *The Blue Nile* and *The White Nile* (New English Library, 1982, and Random House, 1983), should be read by anyone planning a trip to Egypt or the Sudan. Both books are certain to whet your appetite for exploration and adventure.

Mike Asher's book *In Search of the 40 Days Road* recounts his search for the trail which Sudanese camel traders follow when taking their camels north to Aswan. It was published in 1984 by Longman Publishers and in 1987 (paperback) by Penguin Books.

The Sudan: A Country Handbook is the best general reference on the Sudan. It is published by the American University Press in Washington DC and updated every three to five years.

The London Times publication *With Geldof in Africa* recounts Bob Geldof's 1985 Band Aid trips to refugee camps. The photo-graphs are a superb and very moving presentation of the peoples of the Sudan.

Leni Riefenstahl's book *The People of Kau* (Collins, 1976) is also recommended for its photographs. This book caused a bit of controversy a few years ago because it drew a lot of attention to the Nuba people. The Sudanese government was embarrassed by the nakedness and 'primitive ways' of the Nuba people. The development-conscious government did not want the Sudan presented to the world as a country of naked tribespeople who paint themselves with red mud, wrestle and hunt with spears. Yet it is the ability of these people to continue their traditional way of life that is one of the beautiful things about the Sudan. The government's anti-Nuba campaign, however, may well put paid to that.

Tayib Saleh's books are also recommended. He writes fictionalised literary accounts of life in the Sudan. One can learn much from his books about life in northern Sudan. Some of his titles are *The Wedding of Zein & Other Stories* and *The Season of Migration to the North* (3 Continents Press, Washington DC, 1978).

Bukra, Insha'Allah, written and published by Ellen Ismail in Cologne in 1988, is the result of this German anthropologist's study of various aspects of the Sudanese way of life.

MAPS

Michelin Map No 954 of north-east Africa (scale 1:4,000,000) is excellent for the Sudan but lousy for Egypt. The map-sales section of the Survey Department, near Qasr ash-Shaab (the People's Palace) in Khartoum, sells some of the best maps on the Sudan, although most are of interest only to specialists in fields such as mineral resources or rainfall. Their map of Greater Khartoum is not bad, although not as useful for travellers as you might hope. It's available for S£300 in the Acropole Hotel and one or two bookshops.

Otherwise, there is little choice. GEOprojects in Beirut produces the *Oxford Map of Sudan*, which includes a map of

Khartoum and Omdurman. At about US$9, the map of the Sudan (scale 1:4,000,000) is not worth it, but the city maps are about the best you'll find; don't take too much notice of where they locate embassies though – most of them have moved. You can also find it in Khartoum, either in the Khartoum Bookshop or the Acropole Hotel, for S£1500.

If you're a map fanatic, have lots of money and have trouble getting a hold of British Ordnance Survey maps on the Sudan (permission for which is required from the Land Survey office or Ministry of Defence), you might think about investing in air charts, which are satellite-based maps. There are 12 on a scale of 1:500,000. In London, they come in at UK£7.50 apiece.

MEDIA
Newspapers & Magazines
If you are eager to know what's going on in the world, bring a short-wave radio. Five to six-day-old copies of the *International Herald Tribune* and week-old editions of *Time*, *Newsweek* and the *Economist* used to be available in the big hotels, but you'll be unlikely to see any of them now. Find a resident expatriate – they sometimes have weird and wonderful ways of smuggling in the latest newspapers and magazines – or go to a cultural centre for some fairly stale copies.

That leaves just the local English-language press. (If you read Arabic, don't get too excited: most locals prefer to spend double the cost of a local daily on week-old copies of Arabic-language papers from Egypt and elsewhere.)

The English-language monthly magazine *Sudanow* (S£30), published in Khartoum by the Ministry of Culture & Information, used to have a few things going for it, but it has been reduced to little more than a government rant. You'll find little in the line of balanced debate in it and not much hard news about anything in the Sudan or outside.

The four-page daily, *New Horizon* (S£5), is nothing to write home about either, although at least it carries a few wire-service briefs on what's happening in the world. (Its selection criteria seem a little weird.) The home news is, shall we say, slanted.

A slightly better alternative, but available only by subscription (there are usually a few copies lying around in the foyer of the Acropole Hotel in Khartoum), is the daily summary of news from the Sudan News Agency (SUNA). It has a lot more overseas reporting, but again, the local stuff has to be taken with a pinch of salt.

Radio & TV
The Sudan has one TV station and a few radio stations. The TV news in English is at 6.45 pm, and there are occasional English-language programmes. On Sunday nights at 10 pm there is usually an English-language movie, although at the time of writing the series *Roots* was being shown.

For the latest radio news in English, tune into the Voice of America or the BBC. Both operate on several short-wave frequencies and a couple of medium-wave frequencies at various times throughout the day and night. VOA seems to be harder to get, but the BBC comes in clear on 1380kHz. The BBC also broadcasts regularly in Arabic, and surprisingly, the broadcasts are carried on medium wave too (650kHz) – a lot of people tune into it.

FILM & PHOTOGRAPHY
Permits are required for photography in the Sudan and can be obtained free from the Sudanese Tourism & Hotels Corporation office in Khartoum (the building containing the Tourist Information Office). The permit is a formality, but as a lot of people get picked up by Security for taking photos of sensitive sights (such as beggars), mainly in Khartoum itself, it's probably better to have it than not. This won't save your film, as nine times out of 10 those people 'caught' end up relinquishing the roll of film.

Even out of Khartoum (where they seem particularly edgy about cameras), it is advisable to exercise discretion when taking photographs. Do not point your camera at anything that might be considered military or high-security related. This includes airfields, bridges, soldiers and government buildings. When taking photographs of the locals, it is always better to ask first, as some people simply don't like being photographed and others are offended by it.

Film is expensive in the Sudan, so stock up before you arrive; and outside Khartoum you'll be lucky to find anything other than colour print 100ASA – if that. A roll of Kodak colour print (36 frames) costs S£450, while Ektachrome (for slides, 36 frames) costs a pretty hefty S£1000. Processing is not too bad, at about S£800 for a roll of colour print. Slide film cannot be processed in the Sudan, and the quality of print processing is variable. The best places in Khartoum are the El Nil Kodak Studio, on Sharia al-Gamhuriyya, and the Fantastic Colour Lab, which is on the ground floor of the building that houses the French Cultural Centre.

HEALTH

Refer to the Health section in the Egypt Facts for the Visitor chapter for detailed information on the more common ailments and diseases in this part of the world and how to avoid or treat them, the suggested items for a first-aid kit and advice on travel insurance.

Medical Care

There is a severe shortage of trained medical personnel and equipment in the Sudan, and most of the country's doctors and facilities are in Khartoum. Western observers estimate that about 70% of the country's trained doctors and surgeons have left the country. This does not mean that those remaining are no good – some are very dedicated. There are doctors and hospitals in most towns, but the standard of medical care in the Sudan is a far cry from that of the West.

If you become seriously ill, first try to see a doctor from one of the relief agencies. If that doesn't work and you need to be hospitalised, try to leave the country as quickly as possible. Unfortunately, this can be a problem because the Sudan lacks the facilities for speedy medical evacuations. It may sound a bit alarmist, but expatriate workers in the Sudan don't generally think twice about being 'medevaced' straight to Europe in the event of any serious complaints. If you do want anything done in the local hospitals, you may find yourself being shunted around from pillar to post, with little result for your labour. Some hospitals, as has already been noted, do not even have aspirin. Hygiene is noticeably lacking, and outpatient care is close to nonexistent. This is one place where you'll be very glad you took out decent health insurance.

One expatriate teacher told how he was hospitalised for a knife wound (he was stabbed in the arm one night in Khartoum). He was allowed to stay in the hospital as long as he wanted because most of the ward was being emptied out. The patients who had been there were being moved to the tuberculosis ward because they had all contracted TB after entering the hospital for unrelated ailments. The teacher left the hospital as quickly as possible.

There is a clinic in the New Extension called the Khartoum Clinic, but if you need help, try your embassy first. The UK embassy, for instance, encourages people to do this and can recommend one or two doctors.

Vaccinations

The war in the Sudan has left the country with a severe shortage of doctors and medicines. Diseases such as malaria, tuberculosis, meningitis, hepatitis, trachoma, glaucoma, bilharzia, measles and dysentery are common. You must have yellow-fever and cholera vaccinations if you have come from an infected area, which includes most African countries south of the Sudan. (Travellers coming from Egypt have also been asked to present yellow-fever vaccination certificates.) Other recommended vaccinations include typhoid, tetanus and meningitis, and you should also consider either gamma globulin or the new Havrix vaccine for protection against infectious hepatitis.

Malaria is a big problem in the Sudan, and London's Travel Clinic of the British Hospital for Tropical Diseases recommends taking chloroquine *and* proguanil (brand name Paludrine in the USA and UK), as the mosquitoes here are often resistant to the former. While chloroquine-based prophylactics may be obtainable in the Sudan, proguanil and its equivalents are harder to come by. If you're travelling further into Africa, you'll need a good stock of these anyway, so bring plenty with you. It is not very hard to get malaria in the Sudan, especially from Khartoum south. A good mosquito net and strong repellent are recommended in conjunction with prophylactics. Mosquito coils are available in some stores in Khartoum. Again, refer to the Health section in the Egypt Facts for the Visitor chapter for more detailed advice.

You should check for reports of current epidemics and see a doctor for advice on vaccinations before you travel in the Sudan.

Food & Water
Unless your stomach has already been introduced to the revengeful cuisine of other developing countries, the chances are that diarrhoea will strike. For more information on how to cope, see the Egypt Facts for the Visitor chapter.

Tap water in Khartoum and Kassala generally seems safe to drink, although one British diplomat's account of how the drinking water and sewerage pipes are slowly disintegrating and their contents seeping into one another is enough to make you ill on the spot. Whatever you do in those cities, in other parts of the country you should definitely boil the water or use water-purification tablets or iodine. Sometimes the water may be so cloudy that it's definitely a good idea to filter it through a handkerchief or piece of cloth. Better still, arm yourself with a water purifier: there are several on the market, some quite compact. Some travellers rely on local advice for deciding whether to drink the water, but this is risky. What the locals think is acceptable and your body's reaction may be two entirely different things.

Foot Care
This may sound a little silly, but you should keep an eye on your feet. If you wear mainly sandals, you'll be surprised how quickly the soles of your feet – especially the heels – dry out and the skin cracks. Anyone who has spent any length of time in dry, hot countries and not worn shoes knows how painful this can become. Wear shoes every now and then – a bit of sweat works wonders, even if it does stink a little! Use a pumice stone to clean away dead skin when washing. Your feet are an important asset – look after them.

WOMEN TRAVELLERS
In some respects women are likely to have fewer problems travelling in the Sudan than in some other Arab countries. Most women who have come down from Egypt, for instance, remark on how much more at ease they feel in the Sudan. This does not eliminate the risk, and the down side is that, with so few Westerners coming through, you tend to stand out more. Women should think twice before deciding to trek overland by themselves. The sight of a lone woman travelling will so bewilder locals that it could make life a little difficult. This is particularly the case when it comes to looking for a place to stay. Many hotels are loath to have women guests and sometimes will simply turn them away. Even when accompanied by men, women can find some hotel owners saying no.

Much of what is said in the Egypt chapter on the benefits of wearing wedding rings and the like is equally valid in the Sudan.

DANGERS & ANNOYANCES
The dangers and difficulties posed by the civil war in the south have already been discussed – there is no need to repeat it all here. In the west of the country, travellers should be aware of the threat posed by armed bandits who see no less reason for attacking Whites than anybody else. Be prudent, and if travelling in the area, try to get as much local information as possible on where to go and where not to go.

Crime is not a big problem in the Sudan, but with so many people living in such grinding poverty, it obviously happens. Most people you meet will be disarmingly honest, but you should not let this lull you into a sense of total trust towards all comers; a few travellers have become incautious and then learned the hard way that you shouldn't completely drop your guard.

The police and Security forces can be a big nuisance. While the Sudanese are generally an extremely relaxed and friendly bunch, the exceptions seem to be recruited into these professions. Most often they are just irritatingly dismissive and will cheerfully leave you waiting around for something (like a stamp) for hours, but some are positively nasty. Tread carefully with these people, as they have the authority to make life unpleasant. As one traveller to the Sudan put it, among the items you need to bring is 'one sunny disposition'.

Insects & Bugs

Apart from the oft-repeated words of caution on mosquitoes, it is worth bearing in mind that other nasties, such as snakes and scorpions, are a danger. In smaller towns, they may come to you in your *lokanda* (a cheap form of Sudanese accommodation – see Accommodation later in this chapter) rather than wait for you to go to them, so keep an eye out.

WORK

Opportunities are limited, but should you want to stay in the Sudan, it is not impossible. One obvious avenue is teaching English. Two private schools in Khartoum, Unity High School and Khartoum International Preparatory High School (KIPS), sometimes need staff – generally with secondary-teaching qualifications. If recruited from outside, you can expect to be provided with lodgings, paid in local currency and given an increment in hard currency that you can probably save. If you are recruited locally, you might only get about S£15,000 to S£20,000 a month and have to pay for your own accommodation. Other schools and the universities would happily take you on, but the pay would be difficult, if not impossible, to live on.

The other alternative might be work with one of the aid agencies. This would obviously depend largely on your skills and the needs of particular organisations at any given moment. Doctors, nurses, medical technicians, mechanics and administrators, usually with experience in developing countries, are always in demand. Bear in mind, though, that some aid workers have been killed. (See Refugees & Displaced People in the Population section of the Facts about the Country chapter.)

If you want to get involved, check the situation with aid groups in the following list, keeping in mind that previous experience with refugee problems is generally a prerequisite: working in the camps of the Sudan is not for the uninitiated.

Christian Outreach
C/o Acropole Hotel, Khartoum (☎ 447110). This organisation provides medical services and sometimes joins in food distribution to refugee and displaced people's camps around Khartoum.
Concern
PO Box 3277, House 3, Block 14, Riyadh Area (☎ 222617). This is an Irish humanitarian group based in Renk, which is doing a lot of work in the Upper Nile state.
GOAL
This is another Irish group, comparable with the British VSO or the US Peace Corps. It concentrates on health-care programmes in Juba, in Al-Geneina and more recently in displaced people's camps around Khartoum.
International Committee of the Red Cross
Totally nonpolitical and nonreligious, with extensive operations in the Sudan, the ICRC has been in and out of the Sudan a few times. It recently won permission to recommence work.
International Rescue Committee
Sharia 5, New Extension, Khartoum (☎ 440367). This organisation operates 16 camps, mainly in eastern Sudan.
LALMBA Association
PO Box 233, Kassala. The objectives of this organisation are to operate and maintain a medical unit, three village clinics and dispensaries, and three feeding centres for malnourished people. The association's main centre is in the eastern Sudan town of Showak. The village clinics and feeding centres are to the east, near the Ethiopian border, in the villages of Abuda and Um Ali. The association is based at 7685 Quartz St, Golden, Colorado, 80403 USA (☎ (303) 420 1810).

Top: The jebels of Kassala, Western Sudan (SW)
Middle: Thunderstorm brews over village, Southern Sudan (RvD)
Bottom: Sunset over the Nile River, Khartoum (CB)

Top: Children at a Displaced People's Camp, near Omdurman (DS)
Middle: Dinka warrior with his young son hiding behind him, Southern Sudan (RvD);
Woman selling drinks, El-Obeid (LC); Returning from the market, the Sudan (CB)
Bottom: Lush countryside of Southern Sudan (RvD)

Médecins Sans Frontières – Holland
> Sharia Ibrahim Ahmed, Khartoum 2 (☎ 45978). The objective of this organisation is to provide emergency medical assistance to refugees. It is based at 68 Blvd St Michel, 75005 Paris, France. The French branch was expelled from the Sudan, although it was negotiating to be let back in. The Dutch branch does a lot of work in the most dangerous parts of the south, flying in medical aid and treating people with endemic diseases. It is often at loggerheads with the government, as it is suspected of being a source for a lot of the not-so-flattering news that leaks out about the war in the south.

OXFAM
> PO Box 3182, next to the UNICEF offices in Khartoum 2 (☎ 40465) This organisation has offices throughout the world and aid and development programmes throughout the Sudan.

Save the Children Fund
> (☎ 451135 in Khartoum for the British branch.) Based in Britain and the USA, this organisation is extensively involved in the Sudan. Recently it has concentrated its efforts on food distribution and long-term development projects in Darfur and Kordofan. Both the UK and US branches have offices in Khartoum.

UNICEF (UN Children's Fund)
> PO Box 1358, opposite the Farouk Cemetery in Khartoum (☎ 46381). UNICEF is a major force behind aid efforts in the Sudan.

Other Organisations
> Among the many other organisations providing assistance in the Sudan are the Adventist Development Relief Agency, Euro Action Accord, CARE, Mercy Corps International, VSO (Britain), the World Health Organization, the UN Food & Agriculture Organization and the Canadian Fellowship for African Relief (FAR).

ACTIVITIES

In the mountains of Jebel Marra, in western Darfur, **trekking** is a goal that attracts many of the Sudan's visitors out west of Khartoum. For details, see the appropriate section in the Western Sudan chapter.

Because of the difficulties intrinsic in doing anything independently in the Sudan, much may depend on your contacts with expatriates. Some of them go **water-skiing** on the Nile at weekends, others load up 4WDs and head off to such places as Dinder National Park or the Sabalooka Falls for some **swimming** or even **kayaking**.

HIGHLIGHTS

The Sudan is unlikely to become one of the great tourist drawcards. You can spend a lot of time on the road and see little to really excite the imagination. However, occasionally you do come across what seems like a fair reward for all the sweat and tears. **Jebel Marra**, as mentioned already, is a wild and beautiful mountain area providing lots of opportunities for good hiking. On the subject of jebels (hills), the bubble shaped rocky outcrops skirting the city of **Kassala** provide a dramatic backdrop and are a good spot for a bit of walking. Ask the locals where is the best place to wait to see the baboons come down at night.

For the ancient history buff, the **Royal City of Meroe** and the **pyramids at Jebel Barkal** provide two good opportunities to lose yourself among the ruins undisturbed by, well, just about anybody. No tourists, no-one selling chocolates or camel rides or otherwise pestering you.

The crumbling island town of **Suakin** is well worth a visit and can easily be reached in a morning excursion from Port Sudan. If you're lucky, you might be able to arrange some **diving** while in the Port Sudan area – if you do, you'll be looking at virtually untouched coral and sea life.

ACCOMMODATION
Youth Hostels

There are two youth hostels in the Sudan – one in Khartoum and the other in Port Sudan. At S£80 per night, they are among the cheapest places to stay. Conditions are basic but not much different from those in the cheapest lokandas. They have lots of bunk beds crammed in a room and bathrooms are dirty, but if you are on an extremely tight budget, you may not mind getting what you pay for.

Lokandas

The most common form of accommodation in the Sudan, lokandas are usually a series of basic rooms around an open courtyard. Beds tend to be closely woven rope nets stretched over a wooden frame. When it is hot – which is often – the beds are put in the courtyard.

They are simple but cheap and comfortable places to stay. Prices start at S£50 and can go up to S£200 per night.

Government Rest Houses

These are common throughout the Sudan. They are a step or two above the lokandas but are often a good deal more expensive. Outside Khartoum, Kassala and Port Sudan, these are some of the best places in which to stay. Prices and arrangements for accommodation vary from town to town, but anything below about S£600 for a room is unlikely. Many are more in the order of S£1500 to S£2000 for a double with full board.

Hotels

Khartoum has its fair share of luxury hotels, such as the Hilton and the Meridien, and like luxury hotels in any country they are comfortable but expensive. Mind you, the standards don't quite meet those of their counterparts elsewhere.

The cheaper hotels in the Sudan are usually run by Greeks or Sudanese and do not require bank receipts proving that you have changed your money officially. They have most of the amenities of semi-decent hotels, such as bugless beds, running water, maybe even rooms that have both a sink *and* a bathroom, and occasional meals. They usually have a big fan whirling over the bed or an air-conditioner that drips and circulates the air with a lot of noise. Room prices range from about S£250 to S£3000, beyond which you're heading into the top hotels bracket that is basically restricted to a handful of places in Khartoum.

Women should be aware that in some parts of the country, especially in the north, hotel and lokanda owners are reluctant to have women guests, even if accompanied by men. This can pose obvious problems, and although you'll usually be able to find something, it is worth taking into account if you are planning to travel alone.

FOOD

During Ramadan it is almost impossible to find any kind of food store or restaurant open before about 6.30 pm. Some general stores selling canned goods are the exception; they sometimes sell things like Pepsi too.

Something you'll have to get used to if you eat with locals is that people generally eat with their right hand out of a common bowl. People wash their hands, but perhaps not always terribly thoroughly. You'll have to judge each occasion on its merits, but it can be pretty difficult to be antisocial at meal times (and not much fun either), so you'll often just have to hope for the best.

Generally, you can find a reasonable assortment of basic foodstuffs in most towns. The markets are fairly well stocked with fruit (oranges, grapefruit, guava, bananas, mangoes), vegetables, dates, peanuts and spices. Meat, if you want to buy and cook it yourself, is also around. Biscuits, tinned fish, tinned fruit and other basic foodstuffs are available in the stores. In Khartoum and Port Sudan, the range is better.

Sudanese food is very simple. Few spices are used and most dishes are seasoned with only lemon juice, salt, pepper and broth. The following are some of the most common dishes, many of which you'll be lucky to find.

Vegetables

Fuul is stewed beans served in a variety of ways – sometimes with a sprinkling of cheese and mixed with salad. It is eaten by first mashing the beans with the salad and scooping the result into your mouth with a piece of pita bread. It is sometimes mixed with *ta'amiyya* – deep-fried ground chickpeas – which is similar to the Egyptian version of *felafel* and another staple in the northern half of the country.

Fasooliyya is a dish of smaller stewed beans which taste a bit like Heinz baked beans without the sauce.

Batatas are boiled potatoes. They usually come with a bit of run-off from boiled meat, making a sort of stew.

Salata is a salad of tomatoes, lettuce, onions, green peppers, and lime-juice dressing.

Sherifa is a green vegetable similar in texture to spinach.

'Aads is the ever-popular yellow lentil, one of the most common vegetables in the Sudan.

Baamiyya, also known as ladies' fingers or okra, is a long, green vegetable with red tips often used in soups and stews.

Mahshi are tomatoes or aubergines stuffed with rice and minced lamb.

Many vegetable dishes are served with a lump of meat, a splash of oil and a watery broth.

Fish

Nile perch is a speciality of Khartoum and Omdurman and is served with a coating of fried batter and red peppers. It is usually available only in the mornings.

Meat & Poultry

Kebab is stewed or skewered meat, usually lamb.

Kalawi is chopped kidney, usually served with a bit of bread and a dash of lemon juice.

Kibda is stewed or skewered liver.

Shia is strips of beef or lamb cooked on a bed of coals and served with salad.

Lahma is a large, almost indistinguishable lump of beef or lamb served in soup.

Gammonia is stewed sheep's stomach, often served with tomatoes and onions.

Chicken is usually stewed and served in a soup or broth.

Breads

Kisera is a thin unleavened bread made from *durra*, which is a type of maize.

Gurassa is a thick unleavened bread not often found in Khartoum but common elsewhere. It is often used as a soft base for very tasty meat and vegetable stews.

Dessert

Hoshab is a cold, red cocktail made from chopped bananas, figs and raisins.

A more commonly available favourite is *zabadi* (yoghurt) dripping in the syrup used in making traditional oriental sweets like *baqlawa*. The latter is widely available. For more details on varieties of these sweets, refer to the Food section in the Egypt Facts for the Visitor chapter.

DRINKS
Tea & Coffee

Laban (or *haleeb*, which is sweetened milk, sometimes hot, but often cold), is very popular with the Sudanese but is generally served only in the evening.

Shai saada is a sweet tea served in small glasses without milk and sometimes spiced with cloves, mint or cinnamon.

Shai bi-laban is sweet tea with milk, usually served only in the early mornings or early evenings.

Shai bi-nana is a sweet mint-flavoured tea.

Gahwa fransawi literally means 'French coffee' but it generally refers to Western-style instant coffee, such as Nescafé.

Gahwa turki is very strong Turkish coffee, served in very small coffee cups.

Jebbana is very strong coffee served from a tin or earthenware container with a conical spout. It is drunk from small china bowls and is often spiced with cinnamon, ginger or other spices. 'Jebbana' refers to the name of the container.

In addition to Coca-Cola, Pepsi and Fanta – widely available in the big towns but less common elsewhere – there are a few luridly coloured local varieties such as Vimto and a lime-coloured one called M&S.

Fruit Juices

A variety of freshly squeezed juices is available throughout the Sudan. Some of the best include *karkaday* (a drink made from the hibiscus plant), *limoon* (lemonade), *burtuaan* (orange juice) and *manga* (mango juice). Guava juice and grapefruit juice are also good.

Alcohol

Although alcohol is officially banned under Islamic law, it is still possible to find a few bootleg concoctions.

Aragi is a clear, strong drink made from dates. It tastes a bit like Bacardi rum and can easily knock you off your feet.

Merissa is a beer made from sorghum which looks gross but tastes fine.

Tedj is the name for a variety of wines made from dates or honey, some of which aren't too bad.

TOBACCO

About the only cigarettes available outside Khartoum are the local Bringi brand, sold in packets of 10 and, apparently, quite bearable.

ENTERTAINMENT

In Khartoum you can catch the occasional movie at one of the cultural centres, but elsewhere there's not an awful lot on offer, unless you join in with locals to listen to indigenous music or, if you're lucky, get invited to a wedding.

THINGS TO BUY

Many Sudanese men still wear daggers and swords at their sides as part of their dress, although in Khartoum they are the exception rather than the rule. You can sometimes find a variety of such dangerous trinkets in stained leather sheathes in the markets, or people may simply accost you with them: they will most likely be trying to sell them to you rather than trying them out on you.

As a form of protection, they have been superseded by more modern weaponry. However, if you're a budding Lawrence of Arabia or Mata Hari, or if you've just always wanted an exotic blade, then this is definitely the place to buy it.

Many places in Omdurman Souq sell beautiful ebony carvings. If you want some of these items but have no desire to trawl the souqs, there are a couple of small shops selling similar items around Sharia al-Gamhuriyya in Khartoum.

Gold jewellery is another item that can be worth investigating. Even relatively small towns like Dongola have a few jewellery shops selling gold necklaces, bracelets, earrings and the like.

Elephants in the Sudan and other parts of Africa are being massacred for the sake of pretty jewellery, so avoid buying ivory. Other ideologically unsound artefacts include stuffed crocodiles, and wallets or purses made from crocodile skin. The World Wide Fund for Nature would have a fit here.

In the western town of Mellit, women produce some attractive carpets and dresses and some exquisite pottery. Some of the pottery sold elsewhere is quite nice too, but carting the stuff around without breaking it is a tricky business. Plenty of other bits and bobs are sold in the markets, but little of it has souvenir value.

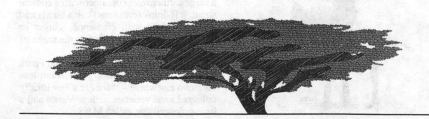

Getting There & Away

Travel to the Sudan is possible by land, sea or air, although some frontiers are closed, and the likelihood of getting a boat to the country's only sea port, Port Sudan, is slim. The civil war in the south and other internal problems, or difficulties in neighbouring countries, may close off any number of these options at any given time, so do what you can to check the present situation before embarking on journeys that you may not be able to complete.

It is highly recommended that you take out travel insurance before you leave home. Everyone should be covered for the worst, such as accidents requiring hospital treatment and possibly a flight home. For more detailed advice, refer to the Egypt Getting There & Away chapter.

AIR

For general hints on where to look for information and tickets in the USA, Europe, Asia and Australasia, as well as advice on what to watch for when buying tickets, information for air travellers with special needs and a glossary of air travel terminology, refer to the Egypt Getting There & Away chapter.

Flying is the most expensive way to get to the Sudan. Ironically, it can cost only a bit less for a one-way flight to Khartoum from Nairobi or Cairo than it does to buy a return ticket from London.

On the other hand, because the troubles in southern Sudan make travelling overland through there impossible, flying is really the only way to enter the country from any of the southern African countries.

If you buy airline tickets in the Sudan, you are generally requested to pay for them in hard currency, either by credit card, travellers' cheques or cash. For most people, that is more convenient than paying in Sudanese pounds, but if you want to pay this way, you *may* have to produce bank receipts showing you exchanged money officially. Ask first, because if this is still the case,

you'd be better off just paying in hard currency.

To/From the USA & Canada

There are no direct flights to the Sudan from the USA and Canada. It is cheaper to get a flight to London or another destination on the way to the Sudan and make your way from there. Remember that, if you want to fly, it is usually cheaper to fly return from, say, London to Khartoum, than from Cairo.

To/From the UK

Several airlines fly from London to Khartoum, including EgyptAir (via Cairo), British Airways, Lufthansa (via Frankfurt, Munich and Cairo), Aeroflot (via Moscow, but it is not the cheapest), Balkan Air (via Sofia, in Bulgaria), Kenyan Airways and Sudan Airways.

Khartoum is not exactly a favoured destination, and so there is little discounting on flights there. For more details on places in London to look for good deals, see To/From the UK in the Egypt Getting There & Away chapter. EgyptAir has 90-day excursion fares for UK£425. The same deal with Air France comes to UK£465. Sudan Airways does the same 90-day round trip for about UK£395, although it sometimes drops its fares to the bargain-basement price of about UK£220.

To/From Europe

Similar flights and fares to those available in London can be had in continental European centres. For information on travel agencies in various European cities, see the Egypt Getting There & Away chapter.

To/From Africa

Sudan Airways, Kenyan Airways, Ethiopian Airlines, Tunis Air, British Airways, KLM, Lufthansa and Air France are some of the airlines that fly between the Sudan and other African countries.

Sudan Airways flies to Asmara (Eritrea) for US$168 on Fridays and Tuesdays, while Ethiopian Airlines has two flights a week to Addis Ababa for US$257 one way or US$336 return.

All the airlines flying to Cairo do the one-way trip for US$240. Air France and KLM tend to give generous student discounts of about 40%. Sudan Airways flies from Cairo for E£1247 one way and double that return. Their youth fare is E£793 one way and double that return.

If flying to Cairo on one of the three European airlines stopping there en route to Europe (Lufthansa, KLM and Air France), you need to get a Civil Aviation Authority permit, which costs S£300. The airline or travel agent will generally look after this, but often they can't get it until the day before you fly. The permit is a result of a bilateral agreement between Egypt and the Sudan granting each other's carriers the right to carry passengers between the two. Other airlines do not automatically have this right. The permit is not required for other flights.

There used to be flights between Khartoum and Aswan, and although the private Egyptian airline, ZAS, was talking of re-establishing flights on that route, nothing had come of it at the time of writing.

Flights to Nairobi cost a staggering US$400 one way (the other way seems to be cheaper). There are no longer any direct flights to Mt Kilimanjaro. Flights to Dar as-Salam are US$525. Air Tunis will fly you to Tunis for a trifling US$615, and a one-way flight to Harare costs US$920!

To/From Australia & New Zealand

There are no direct flights to the Sudan from Australia or New Zealand. Make your way to one of the countries listed in this section and travel to the Sudan from there. The easiest and most common approach would be to get to Egypt first and then go overland (catching the steamer from Aswan to Wadi Halfa – see the Sea & River section).

Arriving & Leaving by Air

Except for the search for alcohol and record-ing the details of your camera in your passport, the passport and customs formalities on arrival are fairly straightforward. There are 24-hour banking facilities available, and if you arrive after curfew and don't want to hang about the airport, some airport taxis have special curfew passes.

There is an airport departure tax of S£300. Also, if you are flying to Cairo on any airline but EgyptAir or Sudan Airways, you must obtain a Civil Aviation Authority permit, which costs S£300. Your travel agent or airline will usually take care of this. Check also whether or not you need an exit visa. At the time of writing, people staying in the Sudan for less than three months were exempt, and some officials intimated that the exit visas were not required at all by non-Sudanese. Expatriates maintain they do need to have the visas, so there appears to be some confusion.

LAND
Your Own Transport

The number of places you are going to want to drive to will be pretty limited, unless you have a 4WD. You will need a *carnet de passage en douane* (see the Egypt Getting There & Away chapter for more details), your car's papers, insurance and an international driving permit (UK drivers' licences are sufficient). Enquire at the embassy about the paperwork involved. It is such a rare request that it may be a while before you strike anyone who has any idea at all of what to do. A special permit has to be obtained, and the Sudanese embassy in London suggested getting it in Cairo. It may be possible to arrange on the border (only a 4WD will cope with the Red Sea border crossing).

To/From Egypt

There are a few ways (at least theoretically) of going overland to the Sudan from Egypt. If you have your own 4WD vehicle, it's technically feasible to drive along the Red Sea coast, but the border will probably be closed to traffic, especially if the dispute between Egypt and the Sudan over the contested Halaib region is still on the boil.

The road to the Sudan going beyond Abu Simbel is officially closed, although some Sudanese who go to and fro between Aswan and Wadi Halfa claim they can get through overland.

It appears to be becoming more practicable to ship your vehicle from Aswan to Wadi Halfa or vice versa. In early 1993 a few people hired boats to take vehicles to Wadi Halfa. One such boat cost some people with a car and two motorbikes E£5000. Other travellers reported later in the year two regular barges were being put into service, the *Aswan* and *The 307*, costing US$150 for one car and two people.

You can try to join the camel herders on the Darb al-Arba'een (40 Days Road) from western Sudan, through the Sahara to Aswan. (See Michael Asher's book *In Search of the 40 Days Road*, published in 1987 by Penguin Books.)

For more information refer to the Egypt Getting There & Away chapter and the Aswan Getting There & Away section.

To/From Eritrea & Ethiopia

It is quite possible to cross from the Sudan to Eritrea, and this is becoming, after years of war in Ethiopia, the overland route favoured by most travellers. Buses to Asmara leave regularly from Kassala, three times a week from Port Sudan and supposedly once a week from Khartoum. From Eritrea, travellers have had no difficulty proceeding to Ethiopia, but the border to Kenya appears to be a little more difficult. Although information on that area is sketchy in the Sudan, try to find out what you can before heading off, or you may find yourself having to catch some expensive flights.

Take a fistful of Sudanese pounds to change at the Eritrean border, as hard currencies don't seem to be acceptable.

To/From Kenya, Uganda & Zaire

See the Southern Sudan chapter for more details on these crossings. At the time of writing, the civil war in the south and troubles in Zaire virtually ruled out crossing any of these borders.

To/From CAR, Chad & Libya

All three frontiers were open at the time of writing, although not very easy to negotiate. Trucks from Nyala sometimes make the trip right through to Bangui in the Central African Republic (CAR). You will more likely have to do the trip in stages. (There is a section at the end of the Western Sudan chapter that provides more information about this route.) Al-Geneina, and possibly El-Fasher, are the main jumping-off points for transport into Chad. In the past, this border has been a troublesome one, and the area is crawling with bandits, so try to find out if it is safe to cross before setting off. Judging by the amount of transport shipping in goods from Libya, it should be possible to get a lift with a truck heading north. If you have a visa and a lot of stamina, this is an option, but you'll be travelling through some of the most inhospitable desert in the world, so think carefully about it first.

SEA & RIVER
To/From Egypt

The easiest and most popular route from Egypt to the Sudan is by Nile steamer from Aswan to Wadi Halfa. The steamer (or a more modern Egyptian boat) leaves from the docks south of the High Dam at an indeterminate time, usually once a week. The journey takes from 14 hours (in the new boat) to about 24 hours and costs E£85.75 for 2nd class and E£135.35 for 1st class. The ride can be hot and uncomfortable, but it is generally a peaceful and interesting way to enter the country.

By some accounts, if you arrive on a Friday you cannot disembark until the following day because all Sudanese offices are closed on Fridays. It's not a set rule, as travellers have been let off on Fridays too, but you should be prepared for the worst.

Most of the immigration formalities are taken care of on the boat, although there are more forms to fill in and customs to get through on arrival in Wadi Halfa. The process is similar in reverse.

In Cairo you can buy steamer tickets at the Sudanese Maritime Office (also called the

Nile Valley Navigation Office) at Ramses Station: it's in the second office to your left as you walk in through the main entrance. The ticket price includes two cups of tea and a meal. It's just as easy to wait until you get to Aswan to buy your ticket, as you can't tell from one day to the next when the boat will go. (See also the Egypt Getting There & Away chapter and the Aswan and Wadi Halfa Getting There & Away sections.)

To/From Saudi Arabia
There used to be a ferry service four times a month between Jeddah (Saudi Arabia), Port Sudan and Suez, but at the time of writing it

had been indefinitely suspended. It may be possible to get a ship to Jeddah, but don't count on it. For more information, see the Port Sudan Getting There & Away section.

LEAVING THE SUDAN
Exit visas are not required for those who have stayed in the Sudan less than three months. There appears to be some confusion over whether you need one for stays of longer than three months – check with a travel agent or the Ministry of the Interior Aliens' Office.

There is an airport departure tax of S£300 and an overland exit tax of S£65.

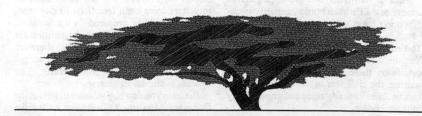

Getting Around

Whichever route you take through the Sudan, you'll end up having to use an interesting (and not very comfortable) collection of buses, lorries, riverboats, trains, international-agency jeeps, mail vans, camels, donkeys and even the occasional light plane (in which you'll travel free, as baggage). Apart from planes, all forms of transport are slow and many routes are impassable during the rainy season from June to September, so allow plenty of time to get through this country. Even the trains and planes are subject to long delays and sometimes just don't turn up at all.

AIR

Sudan 'Insha-allah' Airways is the only airline that makes internal flights and, theoretically, it flies to all of the Sudan's major cities. However, most of its planes are grounded and in need of repair.

It is difficult, if not impossible, to make reservations for any internal flights from Sudan Airways offices in other countries. Waiting lists for most flights can be as long as three weeks. You can sometimes wait for weeks to fly even on quite short routes. One Sudanese student in Karima told of waiting for more than a week to fly to Khartoum. Each day he would tramp out to the airport, ticket and bag in hand, only to be told, 'Bukra, insha-allah' ('tomorrow, if God wills it'). On the other hand, an English couple simply ignored all the dire warnings of endless passenger lists for the flight from Nyala to Khartoum and went out to the airport one morning, where they were cheerfully ushered on board. The rule? – there are no rules.

Some travellers have managed to hitch rides around the country with cargo planes, but the chances of this are fairly slim and depend entirely on the whims of the pilots themselves.

Although it's not recommended with the current political situation, we have heard of some people hopping cargo planes from Khartoum to Juba. The *only* reason to go to Juba at the moment would be the very unlikely possibility that you could get another free or cheap cargo plane out of the Sudan from there. It's not advisable to go to Juba just for the hell of it. The government holds the town and claims the area is now secure, but rebel activity is still intense in the south, even if most of the rebels' energies seem to be directed at one another now. Once, a Sudan Airways passenger jet was shot down en route to Juba.

If you do get on a flight, one cheering thing you'll notice is that they are not terribly expensive. The one-way flight from Khartoum to Nyala is S£8420, and to Port Sudan S£6220. There is no need to show bank receipts proving you exchanged money officially.

There is a domestic airport tax of S£150.

BUS

Travelling by bus is very common throughout the Sudan, even though only 2% (about 4800 km) of the country's roads are paved, and a lot of these are in need of repair.

Most buses, and many other means of road transport, such as lorries and boxes, leave from lots known as *souq shaabi*. The expression simply means 'people market' – this being the place from which you transport people, as opposed to goods. If you're wondering how to get out of a town, ask for the souq shaabi and nine times out of 10 you'll be pointed in the right direction. Unfortunately these souqs are usually a good four or five km, if not more, out of town, and you have to get a local shuttle out to them.

There are 'luxury' buses, but these only run between Khartoum, Kassala and Port Sudan. A couple of the bus lines have air-con or partly air-con buses, comfortable seats and shock absorbers. This is luxury indeed if you're going to be spending eight to 10 hours on a bus.

The more common varieties of bus are a different matter altogether. In external appearance, they all seem much the same, but there are some quite important variations on the theme. The more comfortable long-distance buses of this kind look like trucks on the outside and something like buses on the inside. They do have windows, and instead of two rows of two seats, they have one of three and one of two. What's left in terms of space for a corridor is usually filled up with extra bodies. This makes for a tight fit. Leg room is minimal and the padding on the seats is often nonexistent. These buses do not have shock absorbers. If you end up in the back row of seats, you'll feel every bump, sometimes on your head.

Many of the local buses are far more basic covered trucks with some wooden benches stuck in to accommodate people, although by the time all the goods being transported have been loaded on, there's often only room for people to squeeze in around the sacks. All that can be said about these torture chambers on wheels is that they don't cover long distances – most of them can't.

There is a special breed of bus connecting towns in the north with Khartoum. It is a cross between the awful local bus and the common long-distance job, and is equipped with huge sand tyres. There's no window at the front of the passenger cabin, and you can't see much from the barred openings that pass for windows on the sides, so in addition to being shaken like a cocktail, deafened by the clattering of metal doors in their frames, covered in swathes of dust and possibly injured on various jagged edges, you have an overwhelming feeling of sensory deprivation. The lorries may be slower, but at least they're not claustrophobic. These buses are generally voted most horrible form of transport by people travelling between Khartoum and Wadi Halfa.

As when you are travelling on lorries (see the Lorry section later in this chapter), you should take loads of water and some food with you on buses. And keep your sleeping bag with you – it makes great padding!

Note

Road transport of all descriptions is extremely tight during holidays – you may find yourself getting stuck somewhere for a few days, although it is not impossible to move around. Ticket prices can triple, especially the day before the beginning of the big feasts like Eid al-Fitr (end of Ramadan) and Eid al-Kabir at the height of the pilgrimage season.

TRAIN

Sudan Railways runs an extensive but run-down collection of trains. The 5500 km of narrow-gauge single-track railway is in bad need of an overhaul, and some projects backed by international-aid finance got under way in the late 1980s. A German group, Deutsche Eisenbahn Consulting Group GmbH, is giving them some advice – they need it. The rolling stock is in pretty bad shape too, and all up, it is reckoned that the system runs at less than a fifth of its capacity. In fact, the system is in such an appalling state that no trains run from Khartoum to the west now. (This may change if any improvements are ever made.)

The system dates back to General Kitchener's rush to clobber the Mahdi in the late 1890s. He laid track from Wadi Halfa to Abu Hamed across 370 km of harsh Nubian desert in 1897 at the rate of half a km a day. For details of this line's 'schedule' today and other train services, see the Getting There & Away sections of the relevant towns.

There are three classes on Sudanese trains – 1st, 2nd and 3rd. First-class compartments officially carry six passengers, but more passengers usually squeeze in. Second and 3rd-class compartments seem to have no limit to the number of passengers. The 2nd and 3rd classes also have subclasses called *mumtaz*, which translates as 'excellent'. So, presumably, 2nd-class mumtaz is better than regular 2nd class. The differences are usually barely noticeable though, and no distinction is made in fares.

It is also possible to ride on top of the trains for free, although this is not officially condoned because people have been known to fall off. It is often difficult to plant yourself firmly on top, and it can get quite hot and dusty, so protect yourself from the elements and tie your pack down.

Student discounts of 50% to 75% are available for those under 26 years. Permission can be obtained from the station manager in Khartoum or the area controller's office in other towns. Travellers report, however, that the discounts are not available on the train from Wadi Halfa.

The southbound train from Wadi Halfa is usually more crowded than the northbound train because it's packed with Sudanese and huge bundles of things bought in Egypt.

LORRY

Souq lorries, called *lorri* (plural *lowari*) by the locals, are big Bedford market trucks that transport goods and people between almost every town and village in the Sudan. For a minimal amount of money you get to share the back of a lorry with as many as 40 people, sacks of grain, live goats, bags of sugar and bundles of cotton or whatever else needs to be transported and sold. You never know what might be in that large, putrescent bundle next to you. West of El-Obeid, this is virtually the only available form of transport and, although excruciatingly slow, it is preferable to the desert bus in the north.

If you do travel by lorry, there are a few things to keep in mind. Take plenty of water for desert trips (you can buy large plastic Thermos jugs in Khartoum), and it's a good idea to take something to eat as well. Getting food could be a problem along the way, depending on your destination, although bread is usually available in most villages. Make sure you have a hat or something to cover your head during the day. In addition to the heat, you may have to put up with sand and dust billowing up in choking clouds if you are in the desert. The nights can be cold, so be prepared. A torch (flashlight) is also useful. Lastly, you must be in fairly decent physical and mental shape to endure travel by lorry – it can be arduous going, and the Sudanese passengers' apparent obliviousness to the discomfort can be a little deflating.

Whether you go by lorry or bus, expect breakdowns and flat tyres – they seem to be part of the pattern. Eventually the drivers and/or their crew seem to get things going again.

BOX

Relatively new and fast Toyota Hiluxes called boxes (*boksi*, plural *bokasi*) by the locals, generally serve as local transport between villages, but in northern Sudan they also do some intercity routes across the desert, notably from Dongola to Karima and Karima to Atbara. They cost a little more than lorries or buses, and will certainly only make the journey if they have a full complement of passengers – two in the cabin (who pay double) and 10 in the back – but they are fast. A driver determined to reach his goal will often do 100 km an hour – not bad in the middle of the desert!

CAR & MOTORBIKE

The only kind of car you'll want to bring into the Sudan is a 4WD. With so few of the roads paved, anything else would expire very quickly. The driving is tough on vehicles and their occupants. Make sure you are well equipped with spares, food and water, as it can be a long time between stops. If, for instance, you are coming down from the north, you can be waiting quite a while before anyone else comes by who can help. On the subject of spares, you have to assume that the small towns will not be equipped with all the latest gismos – although mechanics here have long experience in making vehicles work.

Some very determined motorcyclists have come through the Sudan from Egypt, but it is difficult to recommend. A pair of Germans took a record three hours to cover two km in the loose sand of a village on the road from Wadi Halfa to Dongola. Having started off riding during the day, they were soon beaten by the heat into riding at night. With nothing much in the way of roads, signs or anything else, you'll need to have some basic navigation skills. It can be done, but it ain't easy.

Out of Khartoum and Port Sudan, road rules do not seem to be awfully important – for the most part there are no roads. Where it counts, you drive on the right, although the number of left-hand-drive vehicles getting around is apt to confuse the newcomer.

Petrol is one of the bigger problems in the Sudan. At the time of writing, rationing for private vehicles was down to a gallon a week – you can't get very far on that. At one point, the government decided to cut private supplies altogether in Khartoum as the price shot up as high as S£2000 a gallon!

BICYCLE

Bicycles are not used much in the Sudan because most of the roads are so bad. However, in 1984 a couple of British cyclists built a contraption which allowed them to ride their bikes on the railway lines and they travelled all the way from Wadi Halfa to Khartoum. Other cyclists have been seen entering the Sudan at Wadi Halfa. Just what they did next remains a mystery. The roads are pretty difficult even for 4WDs to negotiate, so it is hard to picture bicycles getting through.

HITCHING

Hitching rides for free is uncommon in the Sudan, as most drivers will ask for some sort of compensation.

CAMEL

In western and northern Sudan camels are a common beast of burden and transport. Most of them are bred in western Sudan, so it is there that you will probably get the best deal on a camel – approximately US$150 for the latest model. But be warned if you have never ridden a camel – they can be smelly, temperamental and very difficult to handle.

DONKEY

These contrary, sometimes adorable, critters are used throughout the Sudan as a mode of transport. Souqs in most towns and villages sell them quite cheaply so you can even own your own donkey and travel at will, if you can get it to go where *you* want.

BOAT

As of mid-1986, the civil war had stopped the Nile steamers and most other Nile boat traffic, except the steamer from Aswan to Wadi Halfa and the service from Dongola to Karima. The latter does not operate from about March to June, as the river is too low to be safely navigated.

Garang had threatened to shoot at any boats moving south of Kosti, and at the time of writing, no passenger services were operating on any part of the 1435-km stretch from Kosti to Juba. Aid agencies had, however, started trying to get supplies down on barges – by all accounts a fairly grim undertaking.

The Jonglei Canal, being built in the south to win more White Nile water for irrigation from the Sudd, the huge swamp in the south, will also be navigable – if it is ever finished.

LOCAL TRANSPORT
Bus & Box

Buses, minibuses and boxes are common transport in most cities. Boxes are small pick-up trucks, usually Toyotas, with two benches in the back and sometimes a canvas covering. They usually travel prescribed routes and are much cheaper than taxis.

Taxi

Taxis are prevalent in Khartoum, Omdurman, Kassala, Port Sudan and Wadi Halfa.

Fares are subject to the whims of the drivers, the bargaining abilities of the passengers and, perhaps most importantly, the supply of fuel – which determines its price on and off the black market. Flagging down a taxi is simple – just stick your arm out and wave.

Khartoum

There is evidence that as far back as the Old Stone Age the confluence of the two Niles was inhabited by fisherfolk, but the history of the three cities only really begins with the Turkish-Egyptian domination of the country in the last century.

Khartoum is a quiet city, lacking the congestion and squalor of other Third World capitals, and the tree-lined streets near the river are a very peaceful place to stroll. But it also lacks much of the interest of those same capitals. There are none of the fascinating alleys winding between centuries of tumbledown witnesses to a long past. Until 40 years ago only ever a secondary administrative and barracks centre in one of the more far-flung corners of other people's empires, as the capital of an independent country it has expanded to accommodate a growing number of inhabitants without adding a lot to its charm. A population of just four to five million is spread among Khartoum and its sister cities, Omdurman and North Khartoum, across the Nile.

HISTORY

Established in 1821 as a military outpost by Ismail, Mohammed Ali's son, Khartoum supposedly derives its name from its site at the confluence of the Blue and White Niles on a spit of land which resembles a *khurtum* (elephant's trunk). The city grew and prospered, especially between 1825 and 1880, when many of the inhabitants made their fortunes through the roaring slave trade. The slaves were captured from regions south of Khartoum and sold to traders in Egypt, Turkey and other northern countries.

Khartoum became the capital of the Sudan in 1834 and was used as a base by many European explorers of Africa. However, during the latter part of the 19th century, the city's prosperity declined and it was ransacked twice – first by the Mahdi to oust Gordon and then by Kitchener to get rid of the Mahdi.

Cook's *Traveller's Handbook to Egypt & the Sudan*, published in 1929, had this to say about Gordon's defeat:

In 1884 General Gordon went to Khartûm to withdraw the Egyptian garrison, but very soon after the city was besieged by the Mahdi and his followers, and Gordon's position became desperate; famine, too, stared him in the face, for he distributed daily among the destitute in the city the supplies which would have been ample for the garrison...During the whole of January Gordon continued to feed all the people in Khartûm; 'for that he had, no doubt, God's reward, but he thereby ruined himself and his valuable men'...On the night of 25th January (1885) Gordon ordered a display of fireworks in the town to distract the people's attention, and in the early dawn of the 26th the Mahdists crossed the river, and, swarming up the bank of the White Nile where the fortifications had not been finished, conquered the Egyptian soldiers, who made but feeble resistance, and entered the town. Numbers of Egyptians were massacred, but the remainder laid down their arms and, when the Mahdists had opened the gates, marched out to the enemy's camp. The Dervishes rushed to the palace, where Gordon stood on the top of the steps...and in answer to his question, 'Where is your master, the Mahdi?' their leader plunged a huge spear into his body. He fell forward, was dragged down the steps, and his head having been cut off was sent over to the Mahdi in Omdurmân. The fanatics then rushed forward and dipped their spears and swords in his blood, and in a short time the body became 'a heap of mangled flesh'.

The Mahdi professed regret at Gordon's death, saying that he wished he had been taken alive, for he wanted to convert him...Khartûm was given up to such a scene of massacre and rapine as has rarely been witnessed even in the Sudan.

Thirteen years later, Sir Herbert Kitchener and his troops recaptured the city, raising the British and Egyptian flags 'amid cheers for Her Majesty Queen Victoria, and the strains of the Khedival Hymn'. Kitchener began rebuilding Khartoum in 1898, designing the streets along the lines of the Union Jack so that the city would be easier to defend. At about the same time, North Khartoum, on the other side of the Blue Nile, was developed as an industrial area.

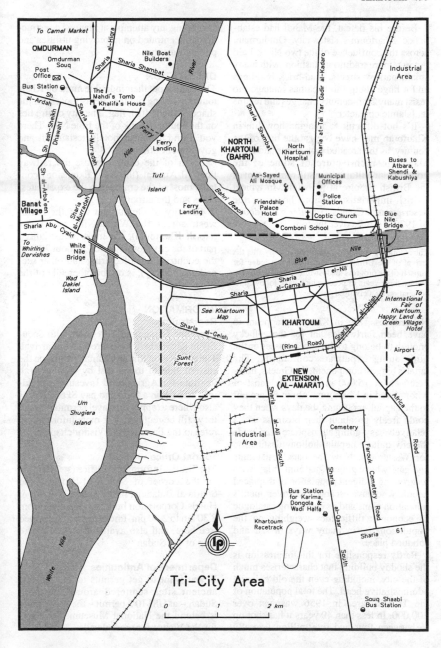

Tri-City Area

0   1   2 km

Before his defeat, the Mahdi had established Khartoum's sister city, Omdurman, across the confluence of the two Niles. Laid out in a more traditional fashion, with many small, narrow streets, mud-brick buildings and a huge souq, this area has managed to resist many 20th-century changes and retains its Islamic character.

It's not difficult to imagine how life in Khartoum may have been at the turn of the century, as the arcaded pavements and colonial-style architecture of some of the government buildings are still reminiscent of the British Empire at its height. In typical British-imperialist fashion, however, the description in Cook's *Traveller's Handbook* of 1929 is a little over the top:

The rebuilding of the city began immediately after the arrival of the British, and the visitor can judge for himself of the progress made in this respect during the twenty-three years of peace which have followed its occupation by a civilised power.

Nevertheless, life in Khartoum appears to have been fairly pleasant for those lucky enough to belong to the upper classes or the burgeoning expatriate community. The latter's biggest component, the Greeks, numbered about 15,000 in the 1960s, most of whom lived in Khartoum. About 80 are left in the capital, mourning the days when they could freely go about their business and a relatively easy-going atmosphere even made the city quite a popular holiday destination for Westerners. Now the bars, restaurants and gaiety have gone. Khartoum today, with its growing indigent population of displaced people who have escaped the government's relocation plans and its expanding catalogue of economic difficulties weighing on the population, is, in many ways, a sad and subdued place.

Partly responsible for this impression is the shoddy building that characterises much of the city, including even the old colonial administrative heart. The total population of the Tri-City area in 1956 was just over 200,000. In less than 40 years it has shot up to between four and five million – totally swamping any attempts at planned construction concentrated on improving utilities and public transport.

ORIENTATION

The British put their indelible mark on Khartoum by laying out the streets loosely in the shape of the British flag. The city centre lies on the southern bank of the Blue Nile. There you'll find the cheap hotels, restaurants and government offices.

South of the centre, across the railway line, Al-Amarat (the New Extension) contains most of the embassies, the expatriates' clubs and the airport.

The city of Omdurman is to the northwest, across the White Nile, and Bahri (North Khartoum), the most industrialised part of the city (responsible for about 70% of the country's manufacturing and other secondary industry), is on the other side of the Blue Nile.

INFORMATION

Registration

Everyone is required to register with Security in Khartoum within three days of arrival. The office is on Sharia Othman Diqna, on the eastern side of town, just by the big Arab Institute for Agricultural Investment building. You fill in a form and pay S£65. This is also where to apply for travel permits, should they still be required. For more information, refer to the Facts for the Visitor chapter.

Tourist Office

The Tourist Information Office (☎ 74664) is on the corner of Sharia al-Huriyya and Sharia al-Baladaya in the Sudan Tourism & Hotels Corporation building. It's open from 8.30 am to 2.30 pm. Photo permits are issued free here, and also available is a colourful map of the Sudan.

Department of Antiquities

If you want to get permits to see the few ancient sites scattered around northern Sudan – at US$10 a permit – the department is behind the National Museum. See Facts for the Visitor for more details.

Money

Banks Khartoum is teeming with banks. What they all do is anyone's guess, but changing money does not seem to head the list. Your best bet is to go to the Bank of Khartoum, which has several branches around the city centre. The banks generally open from about 8.30 am to 1 pm. Even in the head office on Sharia al-Qasr, staff seem to balk at changing anything but cash or US$ travellers' cheques, although UK pounds get through with a little friendly persuasion. There is a 1% commission on travellers' cheques. Ask for a receipt.

Black Market This is not a recommendation, but if you want to use the black market, the most common place to find changers is along Sharia al-Gamhuriyya. It is widely believed that some of these people are Security stooges. Some shops may also discreetly change money. Ask expatriates for advice.

American Express The American Express office is opposite the British Airways office on a small side street just off Sharia al-Gamhuriyya, between Sharia at-Taiyar Morad and Sharia al-Khalifa. The office is upstairs, above the KLM office, and is open from 8.30 am to 1.30 pm and from 5.30 to 7.30 pm daily except Fridays and Sunday evenings. This American Express office does not offer any financial services (such as cheque cashing or cash exchange).

Mail can be collected from the box on the front counter; after-hours access to the box is sometimes possible because American Express shares an office with Contomichalos Travel.

Post & Telecommunications

Postal, telegraph, telephone, telex, fax and express-mail services are all in a building on the corner of Sharia al-Gama'a and Sharia al-Khalifa.

Post The GPO is open from 8.30 am to 1 pm daily except Fridays. It costs S£40 for ordinary international letters, and S£20 for postcards. Poste restante is located here. The office also purportedly opens for an hour in the late afternoon, but this seems unreliable. If you just want to buy envelopes and stamps, you can do so from street vendors just outside the GPO. They charge a little extra, so a S£20 stamp will cost S£25.

Telephone, Telex & Fax The telephone office is open from 7 am to 9.30 pm, seven days a week. Calls should be booked several hours or even a day in advance.

The telegraph, telex and fax office is open 24 hours a day, seven days a week, including holidays.

Phoning in Khartoum has always been fraught, but many of the numbers have been or are being changed. This has sometimes involved adding one or two digits to the front of the number, but in other cases the whole number has been altered. In any case, this doesn't appear to have greatly improved the system. Many foreign organisations in Khartoum telex each other when trying to communicate.

The big hotels are a better bet when trying to phone out of the country, but there are no guarantees. Most people agree the Acropole Hotel is the most reliable. It has phone, fax and telex.

Two other possibilities are Hotline, in Souq Two, and Key International, on Sharia 5, in the New Extension. Both have their defenders and detractors, which indicates that neither is completely reliable. If you're in dire straits, go to the DHL offices (☎ 73956, 84590), on Sharia an-Nigomi, or on Sharia 9, in the New Extension, and ask to use its phones. You will be charged about what the Acropole would charge you, but you'll have a direct line out and so will not have to play cat and mouse with temperamental operators.

If you want to make a local call in Khartoum (more often than not a waste of time), newspaper kiosks and some shops and offices will let you use their phones.

Foreign Embassies

For information on foreign embassies in Khartoum, refer to the Visas & Embassies

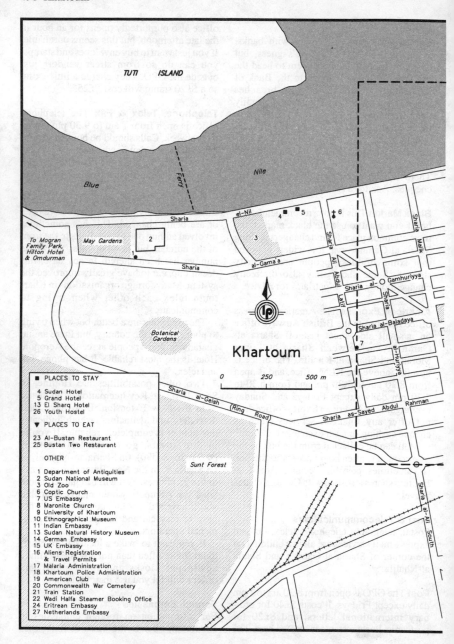

Khartoum

TUTI ISLAND

Nile

Blue

Ferry

To Mogran
Family Park,
Hilton Hotel
& Omdurman

May Gardens

Sharia   el-Nil

Sharia   al-Gama'a

Botanical
Gardens

0   250   500 m

Sharia al-Geish (Ring Road)

Sharia as-Sayed Abdul Rahman

Sunt Forest

PLACES TO STAY

4 Sudan Hotel
5 Grand Hotel
13 El Sharq Hotel
26 Youth Hostel

PLACES TO EAT

23 Al-Bustan Restaurant
25 Bustan Two Restaurant

OTHER

1 Department of Antiquities
2 Sudan National Museum
3 Old Zoo
6 Coptic Church
7 US Embassy
8 Maronite Church
9 University of Khartoum
10 Ethnographical Museum
11 Indian Embassy
13 Sudan Natural History Museum
14 German Embassy
15 UK Embassy
16 Aliens Registration
   & Travel Permits
17 Malaria Administration
18 Khartoum Police Administration
19 American Club
20 Commonwealth War Cemetery
21 Train Station
22 Wadi Halfa Steamer Booking Office
24 Eritrean Embassy
27 Netherlands Embassy

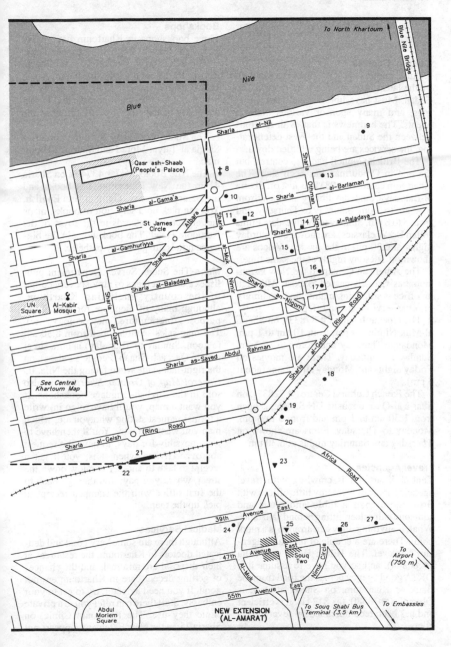

section in the Sudan Facts for the Visitor chapter.

Cultural Centres

Cultural centres are great places to catch up on the latest news and learn more about the Sudan. Most have libraries and film showings, and many sponsor various cultural events. The bad news is that, with relations between the Sudan and the West deteriorating, the services are being whittled down.

The British Council had two centres, but the one in Omdurman has been shut. The Khartoum centre (☎ 80817) is just off Sharia al-Baladaya, and the library is open from 8.30 am to 2 pm, Saturday to Thursday, and from 5 to 8 pm, Sunday to Wednesday. Films (often B&W classics) are shown on Saturday nights at 6.30 pm in the garden. Videos are shown on Tuesday nights at the same time.

The American Center, in the New Extension, has virtually ceased to exist. Although an office is still being maintained, no library or other services are on offer.

The Goethe Institut (☎ 77833), on Sharia al-Muk Nimir, is open from 10 am to 1 pm, Monday to Thursday, and from 5 to 7.30 pm, Sunday to Thursday. There are movies on Friday nights and Monday afternoons (about 3 pm).

The French Cultural Centre (☎ 72837), on Sharia al-Qasr, opposite UN Square, is open from 8.30 am to 1 pm and from 5 to 8 pm, Monday to Thursday. Films are shown on Thursday and Saturday nights at 6.30 pm.

Travel Agencies

Central Khartoum is crawling with travel agencies, most of them tiny little offices with little more than a table and chair and someone half asleep sitting behind said table. What, if anything, they can arrange is a moot point. There are a couple of reputable agencies however. The Hilton Hotel uses Julia (☎ 80844), and so you have to assume it is OK. A good agency across the road from the Bank of Khartoum, on Sharia al-Qasr, is Olympia (☎ 78580; fax 81241). It is efficient and has been recommended by several travellers.

Bookshops

Three bookshops in Khartoum have fairly good selections of English-language books.

The Khartoum Bookshop, on Sharia Zubeir Pasha, one block from the Araak Hotel towards Sharia al-Qasr, is possibly the best, but it is only open sporadically. In fact a cloud was hanging over its future at the time of writing.

The Sudan Bookshop is on the corner of Sharia at-Taiyar Morad and Sharia al-Barlaman.

The Nile Bookshop (☎ 43749), on Sharia 41 in the New Extension, has books and magazines in French, German, and English. You can pick up a selection of books, maps and attractive postcards in the foyer of the Acropole Hotel. The bookshops in the big-name hotels are generally pathetic.

Maps The Sudan Survey Department publishes excellent maps of almost every corner of the country, including Khartoum, although many of them are for specialised purposes (agriculture, meteorology, etc). The map-sales section (open from 8.30 am to noon, Sunday to Thursday) is on a street next to Qasr ash-Shaab (People's Palace), on the right-hand side when facing the Nile. Its *General Map of Greater Khartoum* is also sold in the English-language bookshops. If you want a map, you'll have to go in, write a formal request stating who you are, which map you want and why. You'll then have to wait, possibly for days, to have the request approved. If and when it is, you'll get a receipt to take to another window down the street, where you pay; you then go back to the first office with the stamped receipt to pick up the map.

Medical Services

Although there are some very good and dedicated doctors in Khartoum, the resources at their disposal are minimal, and the chances of getting decent care in Khartoum are not good. If you need a doctor, try to get to your embassy. Staff there can refer you to a private clinic they use. The Khartoum Clinic, on Sharia 25, in the New Extension, appears not to be too bad. If the problem is serious, the only course of action that can be recommended is to get out of the country as quickly as possible.

Emergency

The following numbers are subject to the vagaries of Khartoum's on-again, off-again phone system. The police can supposedly be contacted on ☎ 73333, and the fire brigade on ☎ 72035. There doesn't appear to be much of an ambulance service.

THINGS TO SEE
National Museum

The National Museum is the best of Khartoum's four museums. The 1st-floor exhibits feature artefacts and antiquities from prehistoric Sudan and later periods, including the kingdoms of Cush and Napata. You can see glassware, pottery, bronze figurines, statuary and stelae made of black granite, some of it from the Hellenistic period – evidence of the southernmost expansion of the Mediterranean powers in Africa.

On the 2nd floor there are colourful frescoes and murals depicting the Holy Family and saints and dating from the 8th century to the 15th century. Little is made of the Christian period of northern Sudan's history, but these reminders from the ruins of churches scattered across ancient Nubia are tangible evidence that Christianity survived for 700 years before Islam finally swept it aside.

In the garden outside are the reconstructed temples of Buhen and Semna, salvaged from parts of Nubia that were flooded by Lake Nasser.

The Temple of Buhen, built by Egypt's Queen Hatshepsut in about 1490 BC and dedicated to the god Horus, contains very colourful hieroglyphs and some interesting graffiti left by passing Greeks in the 3rd century BC.

The Semna West Temple was built by Hatshepsut's successor, Pharaoh Tuthmosis III, and dedicated to the Nubian god Dedwen.

The temple closest to the National

Museum was built in Semna East to the god Khnum. Hatshepsut, Tuthmosis II and III and Amenhotep II all had a hand in its construction. Like the Semna West Temple, it belongs to the period of the 18th dynasty (1536-1308 BC).

To protect the temples from humidity during the wet season, corrugated iron shells were built around them and designed to be rolled back in the dry season. They have rusted into place.

The museum is open from 8.30 am to 6.30 pm, Tuesday to Sunday. On Fridays it closes from noon to 3.30 pm. You can get there from the centre of town on an Omdurman bus. Admission is S£20; there are no student concessions for museums.

Ethnographical Museum

The museum's small but interesting collection relates to Sudanese village life. Clothing, musical instruments, and hunting, cooking and fishing implements are on display. The museum is on Sharia al-Gama'a and is open from 8.30 am to 1.30 pm, Tuesday to Sunday. On Fridays it closes at noon. Unfortunately, these hours tend to be quite erratic – the place seems to be closed more often than it's open. Admission is S£20.

Natural History Museum

This museum features stuffed birds and model replicas of crocodiles, snakes and other reptiles. It's also on Sharia al-Gama'a and supposedly open at the same times as the Ethnographical Museum, although at the time of writing it was closed altogether.

College of Fine & Applied Arts

The students occasionally hold public exhibitions of their work, which provides a unique opportunity to gain an insight into aspects of Sudanese culture and society. The college is part of the University of Khartoum.

Mogran Family Park

Khartoum's mini-Disneyland features a roller coaster, carousel, ferris wheel and other typical amusement-park attractions. It's near the tip of the 'elephant's trunk' peninsula, a short distance from the National Museum, and is open until 11 pm daily. The entrance fee is S£30 and rides are S£25 each. You can get there on an Omdurman bus from the centre of the town. With the string of new restaurants nearby on the river bank, this is the hub of nocturnal Khartoum, a whir of activity and a blur of bright lights.

Khartoum Zoo

The old zoo, just past the Sudan Hotel, has entrances on Sharia el-Nil and Sharia al-Gama'a. There are a few healthy-looking animals, but overall, it's fairly depressing and not a place for animal lovers. There are a couple of crocodiles, a disconsolate elephant, some vultures, a hippopotamus, a panther and a tiger, but none of them have very inspiring quarters. At the time of writing, the animals were being moved to another park just east of the National Museum – the monkeys and gorillas were already there, but looked no happier than their confrères in the old zoo, which may well have closed down completely by the time you read this. Entrance to either is S£10. Take the Omdurman bus from the centre of town.

Tuti Island

The inhabitants of this island, at the confluence of the Blue and White Niles, are descendants of the Mahas people from northern Sudan.

One of the most interesting aspects of a visit to Tuti Island is the ferry ride across the Blue Nile. The ferry (S£3) leaves from the Khartoum side of the river near the National Museum, and the landing procedure is quite an amusing spectacle. As the ferry hits the shore, men, boys and donkeys always scramble off first; the women wait until they're absolutely certain that the ferry's metal gangway is firmly planted in the mud on the bank before they tiptoe off the boat.

At the Tuti Island landing, a minibus sometimes picks up passengers for the short

trip to the small brick village in the centre of the island. It offers nothing much of interest.

A 10-minute walk from the village is the landing from which, for S£5, a small, leaky rowing boat will take you across the other branch of the Blue Nile to Bahri Beach in North Khartoum, not far from the Friendship Palace Hotel. Ask someone in the village for directions.

A couple of young people work on the boat, but often the passengers like to get involved in the rowing too, much to the consternation of some of the more elderly women passengers, who obviously aren't very confident the boat will make it anyway. If you happen to fall into the Blue Nile, you needn't worry about bilharzia. There might be crocodiles, but bilharzia is confined to the White Nile.

If you survive the boat trip, and most people do, the beach in front of the Friendship Palace Hotel is a good place to go swimming.

Racetrack

Khartoum's racetrack is south of the city, near the souq shaabi. There are supposedly races on Fridays, but no-one much seems to know anything about them. Boxes for the souq shaabi and the racetrack leave from Sharia at-Taiyar Zulfa near UN Square.

Commonwealth War Cemetery

Just across the road from the American Club, near the railway line, is the Commonwealth War Cemetery, containing the graves of all Commonwealth and Empire servicemen killed in action in the Sudan since the campaigns of the late 19th century. More than half the buried died during WW II. The most intense campaign, fought against the Italians based in Ethiopia in 1940-1941, is explained in a plaque by the entrance.

Comboni (verona) Fathers

The Comboni Fathers is an Italian-based missionary order that has been been working in the Sudan for about a hundred years. The order is sometimes known to Anglo-Saxons as the Verona Fathers, as Verona is where their founder, Daniel Comboni, came from. The order operates a secondary and private school in Khartoum, on Sharia al- Qasr, near the Meridien Hotel, and also helps run schools in several displaced-people's camps on the outskirts of the city.

The Fathers don't mind having visitors. They sometimes present BBC video shows on various aspects of the Sudan, such as the construction of the Jonglei Canal.

OMDURMAN

Across the confluence of the two Niles is Khartoum's sister city, a world apart from the capital. At first, Omdurman has the appearance of a large, scattered village. There is no skyline of gleaming high-rise offices (most of the buildings are mud constructions), the streets are narrow and goats wander the dusty alleys between the houses. Little seems to have changed here since the Mahdi made Omdurman his capital after decapitating General Gordon and defeating the British in 1885.

Souq

Omdurman Souq, the Sudan's largest market, attracts people from all over the country to sell an amazing variety of wares. In the shops and stalls, craftspeople carve and shape pieces of ebony and ivory into candlesticks and statuettes, goldsmiths and silversmiths crouch over glimmering bits of metal pounding and cutting out jewellery, and other merchants hang shrivelled crocodiles and zebra heads in their shop windows. Some of the jewellery is nice, but Cairo's Khan al-Khalili Bazaar is more extensive. The Omdurman buses from the centre of town terminate at the souq. Friday mornings are the best time to be there. The traders have come to expect expatriates to visit then and display the best of their wares at that time.

Camel Market

There is a daily camel market about two km north of the main souq in Omdurman. Most of the animals are from the eastern and western parts of the country, but some are also brought in from as far away as Somalia.

Other beasts have to pursue the trek along the Darb al-Arba'een (40 Days Road) into Egypt and then on to Cairo, finally to be sold at the Imbaba Market there.

Whirling Dervishes

Every Friday afternoon, about an hour before sunset, a group of dervishes, dressed in jalabiyyas and brightly coloured patchwork gowns, gathers in front of the Hamed an-Niel Mosque in Omdurman. These men come together to venerate, in a most unusual way, a 19th-century sheikh who was the head of their tariqa, or path of Islam.

The various tariqas have their origins in 16th-century Sufism and their members follow an ascetic, more mystical form of Islam. The sheikh of each tariqa teaches its members his own particular path to Allah, which may involve simply studying the Qur'an or taking part in a frenzied ceremony called a *dhikr*. As most Sudanese Muslims today belong to an order of some sort, you may see quite a variety of dhikrs as you travel through the Sudan.

The whirling dervishes of Omdurman follow the teachings of the late Sheikh Hamed an-Niel. He is venerated as a saint because it is believed that he was, and still is, able to perform miracles and act as an intermediary between the members of the tariqa and Allah.

As a show of respect for the sheikh, some of the men who have gathered at the mosque begin beating steadily on big drums. This is a signal for the dervishes to begin their march across the field to the mosque. They enter the circle of observers which forms in front of the mosque and begin chanting and walking slowly around a pole. As the drum beat and chanting speed up they, and anyone who wants to join them, attempt to whirl themselves into a detached state of mind. The object of this dhikr is 'oneness with Allah', and it lasts until sunset or complete dizziness, whichever comes first.

Some of these guys are pretty advanced in years and do not always seem as enthusiastic about their whirling as observers might wish.

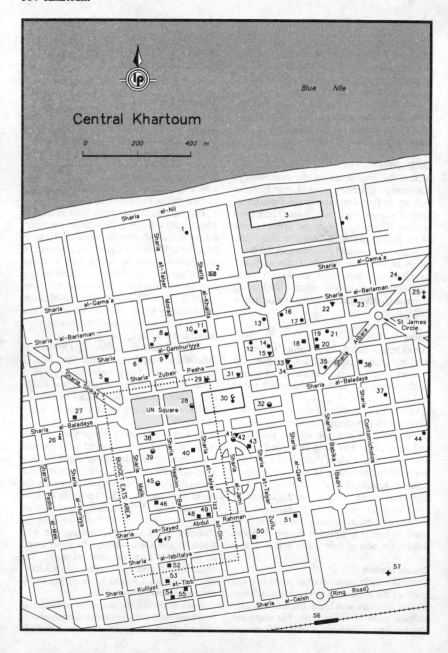

Central Khartoum

Blue Nile

0   200   400 m

Sharia el-Nil

Sharia at-Taiyar

Sharia al-Khalifa

Sharia al-Garna'a

Sharia al-Barlaman

Sharia al-Garna'a

Sharia al-Barlaman

Sharia Sinkat

Sharia al-Baladaya

Sharia al-Gamhuriyya

Sharia Zubeir Pasha

UN Square

Sharia al-Baladaya

Atbara

Sharia Babika Badri

Sharia al-Qasr

Sharia Contomicholos

Sharia at-Taiyar

Sharia al-Taiyar

Sharia Izz ad-Din

Sharia al-Jami

Sharia Hashim Bey

Sharia Malik

BUDGET EATS AREA

Sharia al-Huriyya

Sharia Pasha

Sharia al-Mek

Abdul Rahman

as-Sayed

Sharia al-Isbitalya

Sharia Kulliyat

at-Tibb

Sharia al-Geish (Ring Road)

Zuftu

St James Circle

Even without too much dancing, it remains a spectacle worth seeing.

As dervishes begin their initiation into the ways of the tariqa at the age of 10, there are usually a few young boys mimicking their elders outside the circle of whirling men.

The easiest way to get to the Hamed an-Niel Mosque is by taxi, or you can take the Omdurman bus across the White Nile and get off before it turns up Sharia al-Murradah. From there it is about a half-hour walk. Ask for the Hamed an-Niel Mosque. The dervishes do *not* gather during Ramadan.

Sometimes, you can also see a display of Nuba wrestling nearby. Unfortunately both events take place at about the same time.

The Mahdi's Tomb

The Mahdi and his 50,000 warriors were responsible for instigating the first uprising against the British in the 1880s. After capturing Khartoum from the British in 1885, however, the Mahdi apparently retired to a life of amazing decadence and grew tremendously fat, while his harem of 30 women attended to his every whim. The only interruptions he allowed were the occasional councils of war.

The Mahdi died on 22 June 1885, only five months after General Gordon was beheaded, and was entombed in a mosque with a shiny silver dome. The Khalifa Abdullahi, who had taken over the Mahdi's

■ PLACES TO STAY	
5	El-Sawahli Hotel & Restaurant
18	Sahara Hotel
20	Acropole Hotel
27	Safa Hotel
29	Araak Hotel
36	Falcon Hotel
40	Nakiel Hotel
43	Haramein Hotel
46	Bahr al-Ghazal Hotel
47	Salli Hotel
48	Badr Tourist Hotel
49	Tourist Hotel
50	Sharazad Hotel
51	Meridien Hotel
52	Wadi Halfa Hotel
53	Dana Hotel
54	Port Sudan Hotel
55	Hotel Medinet al-Manura

▼ PLACES TO EAT	
9	Sandwich Stand
15	Dun Doon
22	Casa Blanka
31	Maxim's Burgers
33	Dac Burger
41	Flash Fantastic Foods

OTHER	
1	Ministry of the Interior (Visa extensions)
2	GPO
3	Qasr ash-Shaab (People's Palace)
4	Map Sales Section of Survey Department
6	Egyptian Consulate
7	Bank of Khartoum
8	Lufthansa
10	American Express & KLM Airlines
11	British Airways
12	El Nil Kodak Studio
13	Bank of Khartoum
14	Sudan Airways (International & Domestic)
16	Olympia Travel Agents
17	Ethiopian Airlines
19	Swedish Consulate
21	Belgian Consulate
23	Former Sudan Club
24	Sudan Airways (International)
25	Greek Church
26	Tourist Information Office
28	Buses to Omdurman
30	Al-Kabir Mosque
32	Minibuses to North Khartoum (Bahri)
34	French Cultural Centre
35	ZAS Airlines
37	British Council
38	Sudan Airways (Domestic) (Industrial Bank of Sudan Building)
39	Minibus to Saganat
42	Minibuses to Souq Two, New Extension
44	Ugandan Embassy
45	Souq al-Arabi - Minibuses to Souq Shaabi (& past Saganat)
56	Train Station
57	Civic Hospital

residence after his death, declared that Omdurman was the 'sacred city of the Mahdi' and that a pilgrimage to the Mahdi's tomb was an obligation of Sudanese Muslims, in place of the haj to Mecca (which was prohibited).

General Kitchener destroyed the mosque when he recaptured Khartoum in 1898. Cook's 1929 *Traveller's Handbook to Egypt & the Sudan* described the desecration as 'necessary':

The tomb was badly injured in the bombardment of Omdurmân on the 22nd, and after the capture of the town it was destroyed by the British, the Mahdi's body being burnt in the furnace of one of the steamers and his ashes thrown into the river. This was considered to be necessary as the building had become a symbol of rebellion and fanaticism, the goal of pilgrimages and the centre of fraudulent miracles.

The mosque and tomb were rebuilt in 1947 by the Mahdi's son. Foreigners are not permitted to enter, but the Omdurman bus from central Khartoum passes right by the mosque and the Khalifa's house nearby. The tomb is the building with the more conical dome.

Beit al-Khalifa

This house was built in 1887 as the home of the Mahdi's successor. The mud and brick building has changed little from the time when the Khalifa Abdullahi lived there, before his defeat at the hands of General Kitchener's forces in the 1898 Battle of Omdurman.

The house is now a museum featuring relics from the Mahdi's various battles and the British occupation of the Sudan. The steel boat used by the French leader General Marchand to 'occupy' Fashoda in 1897 and the Arrol motor car of Sir Wingate, governor of the Sudan in 1902, are on display in the courtyard. There is even a 'water room', where there were facilities for hot baths. Interesting suits of mail from the Battle of Atbara in 1898 and numerous Mahdiyya war banners and guns can also be seen. Also, there is an interesting collection of photos from Khartoum at the time of the Mahdi's

revolt and the return of the British under Kitchener.

Beit al-Khalifa is opposite the Mahdi's tomb, so you can take the same bus to visit both. At the time of writing, however, it was officially closed. You might be able to convince the caretaker to let you in if you offer a bit of *baksheesh* (tip).

Nile Boat Builders

On the Omdurman side of the Nile, just north of the Shambat Bridge, a group of workers can be seen sawing and hacking at long planks of wood. They are building the broad-sailed boats which are seen up and down the Nile.

Kereri Battlefield

If you have access to private transport, you can drive a few km north of Omdurman to the site of the battle which saw the end of the Mahdist revolt. Part of the area is closed off because it is a military zone, but you can see a monument to the 21st Lancers (to which the young reporter Winston Churchill was seconded) and poke around looking for spent cartridges and mess kit. Take a copy of Churchill's *The River War* up onto Sorghum Hill and you can get an idea of how the battle unfolded.

ACTIVITIES
Cruises

Most of the major hotels used to operate two to three-hour cruises on the Nile, but the majority have stopped doing so due to lack of interest.

There is at least one local operation, however, which does what is described as a disco cruise. For S£500 you tour around on the Nile, munch on some food and sip on soft drinks while listening to the music – perhaps not the most relaxing way to experience the two Niles. The *Arous* leaves the jetty near the Sudan Hotel at 2 pm on Fridays and returns at 5 pm. Tickets should be bought the day before.

A couple of places out by the string of restaurants near the Hilton also advertise river cruises for about S£100 per head, presumably with no trimmings.

Swimming

There are several places to go for a swim if you're dying of heat exhaustion. The cheapest is the German Club, where you pay S£100 to get in for the day, but sometimes staff insist on your being accompanied by a club member. Next up is the Meridien Hotel, where use of the pool costs S£500 a day. Bring your own drinking water though, as the drinks are ridiculously expensive. The Hilton and Friendship Palace hotels also have pools, but the former requires you to become a member of its health club and the latter is inconveniently located.

Hash House Harriers

Where there is even a handful of expatriates of the British persuasion, there seems to be Hash. This is a loose association of people ostensibly interested in keeping up a small degree of fitness by going for a run somewhere in the city – usually to a different location each time. The more pressing motive is the party afterwards. The Harriers usually get together on a Monday night. If you're interested, inquire at the British embassy.

PLACES TO STAY
Places to Stay – bottom end

The *youth hostel* is in Khartoum 2, on 47th Ave East, near the eastern end of Al-Muk Nimir Circle, about halfway between the Dutch ambassador's residence and the restaurants and markets of Souq Two. It's relatively clean and not bad value at all for the money, but there have been too many reports of theft for it to be warmly recommended. A bed costs S£80 a night.

Slightly cheaper, but not in nearly as pleasant a location, is the *Port Sudan Hotel*, on Sharia Kulliyat at-Tibb, about five minutes' walk from the train station. It has beds for S£75 in rooms or in the courtyard.

The *Bahr al-Ghazal Hotel*, near Souq al-Arabi off Sharia Malik (the sign is in Arabic), is also fairly cheap at S£190 a bed in a room

of four or five, but don't expect much from this place. The windowless rooms are a bit dark and gloomy, but as the showers and toilets are combined in the same stall, they at least are kept fairly clean. During the summer, you can sleep on the roof. If you are just looking for a place to sleep, this is certainly one of the cheaper joints.

The *Hotel Medinet al-Manura*, the *Wadi Halfa* and the *Salli Hotel* are just three of a whole collection of cheap hotels situated between Sharia as-Sayed Abdul Rahman and the railway line. However, many are often either full or unwilling to take in Westerners.

The Hotel Medinet al-Manura has beds for S£310. The nearby Wadi Halfa (the name is in Arabic only) has similar rooms, and its singles cost S£340. The Salli Hotel, at S£475 for a double, is quite reasonable value. Other cheapies scattered around here include the *Khartoum* and the *El-Aman*.

The *Asia Hotel* is popular with travellers. It's next to the Safa Hotel, on Sharia al-Baladaya, around the corner from the Tourist Information Office. Dusty doubles cost S£680 per night; the rooms on the roof are the best and have good views of UN Square. There is no sign: just go up the stairs marked Abdel Jack Trading & Contracting.

The *Safa* (☎ 79985/6) itself is pretty reasonable. Rooms (singles or doubles) cost S£570 without bath, S£690 with one bath shared between two rooms and S£810 with your own bath. The rooms without bath generally are windowless and a bit gloomy, but all are clean and quite OK. The toilet/shower combinations are usually, but not always, kept passably clean.

The *El-Sawahli Hotel* has 24 clean, simply furnished rooms with air-con and overhead fans. Doubles cost S£580, and showers and toilets are shared on each floor. The hotel is on Sharia Zubeir Pasha, about a block north-east of UN Square. It seems to be a little difficult to get in there sometimes.

Right in the middle of things is the *Haramein Hotel*, also popular with travellers. At S£340 a bed, it's not bad.

The *El-Sharq Hotel* is a much overpriced place of last resort. You'll pay S£650 for a single bed in a dark, grimy room with peeling walls, stained sheets, a sink and an overhead fan. Doubling the pleasure costs S£755. The smaller front rooms share a common bathroom in which it's a good idea to wear shoes or sandals. The rooms surrounding the courtyard at the rear each have bathrooms that resemble medieval torture chambers, but the doors do have locks. Be insistent if you have a preference for one of these rooms.

If you feel you'd prefer to stay in Omdurman, there is a couple of small hotels on Sharia al-Murradah, not far from the bridge from Khartoum.

Places to Stay – middle

The *Nakiel Hotel* is not a bad choice at the lower end of the middle price bracket and is popular with Sudanese honeymooners. It's centrally located in a lane near Souq al-Arabi, a couple of blocks from UN Square. It can get a bit noisy, being in the midst of a district of artisans. Singles/doubles cost S£900/1400. The rooms have air-con, overhead fans and typically dungeon-like toilet stalls. The lobby is furnished with a TV and fuzzy sofas.

Two similarly named places on Sharia as-Sayed Abdul Rahman are OK without being amazingly good value. The *Tourist Hotel* (☎ 81108/9) has singles/doubles for S£880/1890. This might be all right, if the manager were not one of the few left to request a bank receipt showing legal exchange for payment.

The *Badr Tourist Hotel* (☎ 80795) is next door. The rooms have air-con and fans and are clean, as are the toilets outside. But its singles/doubles really aren't worth the S£1007/1390 charged.

Slightly more expensive, but good value, is the nearby *Dana Hotel* (☎ 83092/3/4/5). The place is bright and new, the rooms modern and comfortable. Staff claim international telephone lines are available. There is also a restaurant.

The *Gulf Palace Hotel*, on Sharia al-Huriyya, a little way south of the Tourist Information Office, is well overpriced at S£945/1890 for singles/doubles. Only stay here if no alternative presents itself.

There are a few possibilities in the upper-middle range, one of the better ones being the *German Club*, out by the airport, on Sharia 1, in the New Extension, which has good rooms with hot showers for S£2000/3000. It has a swimming pool and tennis courts, and a restaurant serving a limited range of filling meals.

One of Khartoum's institutions, the *Sudan Club*, also had rooms until it was forced to close in March 1993. The club's members were divided over whether to search for new premises or accept defeat and simply join the German Club. With expatriate numbers dropping, the latter option looked all but a certainty, despite the rather bigoted opposition of a few die-hards in both clubs. It may be worth inquiring to see if it has been resurrected.

The *Falcon Hotel* (☎ 72195, 74614) is a spotlessly clean and comfortable choice. The rooms are modern, with telephone, TV and sparkling bathrooms. The price of S£3935/5920/7755 for singles/doubles/triples including a big breakfast is good without being a steal. You do at least get what you pay for.

The same cannot be said for the *Sahara Hotel* (☎ 75240). At S£3290/4640, the dusty and tatty rooms only seem worse because of the reluctant service. If you want to spend this amount of money, go to the Falcon.

Places to Stay – top end

A block away from the Meridien, which is hard to miss, is the fairly new *Sharazad Hotel* (☎ 83575/7, 70965). Its rooms come with bath, are clean and bright, and have TV and air-con. A single costs S£4000 (or S£5100 for single occupancy of a double room) and a double S£6400, which includes breakfast. Staff insist on seeing receipts proving you have changed money in the bank, and so really you'd be better off in something like the Falcon, or going a bit further upmarket to the Acropole.

The *Acropole Hotel* (☎ 72860, night calls on 72026; telex 22190 ACROP SD) is run by a Greek family that continues to host a good proportion of the development aid and refugee relief workers passing through the Sudan. It is nearly always full of expatriates, although even this hotel is feeling the pinch as the Sudan manages to isolate itself from the rest of the world. The family has greatly assisted several international agencies in expediting communications and providing information. Singles/doubles cost S£6035/8470, including full board. Staff don't seem to require you to produce bank receipts, although many guests tend to pay in dollars, so check beforehand at what exchange rate you'll be expected to pay if you are asked for dollars.

If you are not staying here, it's worth stopping by for tea and a chat with some of the guests. Everybody here seems to have an interesting story to tell about some part of the Sudan.

Of Khartoum's top five hotels, the *Sudan* and the *Grand* (☎ 72782, 77756), virtually next door to one another, on Sharia el-Nil, are the cheapest, although the Sudan was closed at the time of writing. The Grand charges US$82/98.

Next up is the *Meridien* (☎ 75970), which falls a fair way behind its international stablemates. It charges US$120/160, plus 20% in taxes.

The cavernous and seemingly empty *Friendship Palace Hotel* (☎ 78204) charges US$130/160 plus taxes. It's inconveniently

located in North Khartoum – next door are farms and crops. There are good views of the Nile from the roof though.

The top of the tree is occupied by the *Hilton*, where a single starts at US$155 plus taxes.

PLACES TO EAT

Most restaurants in Khartoum are simple, nameless places which serve a single dish or a small variety of dishes. When you eat in these places, you first buy tokens at the cash register for the dishes you want. Then you take the tokens to the kitchen window and hand them to the 'cooks'. The Sudanese use bread to scoop up their food, so you won't be offered eating utensils.

There are a few Eritrean restaurants, mostly run by refugees. Most of the restaurants are small rooms hidden behind unmarked metal doors. Furthermore, many disappear as quickly as they appear, and as they don't advertise, you must ask Eritreans to show you the way. They usually sell *ngira* – a spicy vegetable and meat concoction served with soft, flat bread.

Budget Eats

Just by the Haramein Hotel is *Flash Fantastic Foods*, where a half a deep-fried chicken costs S£225. It also serves small liver, fish or meat rolls for S£35. Outside is an ice-cream stand.

Just across the road is another stand selling two kinds of roll, meat (S£30) and fuul (S£15). There are a few juice stands around here as well.

Just back from the Meridien Hotel, towards the railway line, is a shop that sells kebabs for S£40 and soft drinks. Just in by the bus station for North Khartoum is a busy little place selling kibda (liver) rolls, ice cream and guava juice.

On Sharia al-Qasr, you can get *sujuk* (a kind of sausage burger) and an odd sweet drink made with Quakers white oats at *Dun Doon*, outside the Sudan Airways office. Across the road is *Dac Burger*, which serves small burger-like items and a pretty decent impression of small pizza slices (S£25).

South of UN Square there is a whole string of juice stands on Sharia Hashim Bey. All around this area are people who have simply set up coffee and tea stands in the street. There is little in the line of cafés.

In a side street on the western side of the US embassy is an excellent fuul place. You get big serves of a really tasty version of this staple.

Not far away, but hard to find, is a Coptic club. It does good fuul, salad and some meat dishes. Ask around, as it's well tucked away in a side lane.

North-east of UN Square, near the Araak Hotel, *Maxim's Burgers* is Sudan's first attempt at Western-style fast food. The S£45 hamburgers are meagre but tasty if you drown the meat in ketchup.

On the corner of Sharia al-Gamhuriyya and Sharia at-Taiyar Morad is another coke and sandwich stand.

There is a collection of small eateries in Souq Two, very handy to the youth hostel. One of them – a pizzeria of sorts – is just behind the usually empty *Bustan Two* restaurant.

For a change from all of this go to the *Casa Blanka* and treat yourself to a big ice-cream sundae for S£80. It also serves a pretty good espresso coffee for S£40 and a less convincing cappuccino for S£50.

Restaurants

Along the river front by the Nile Hilton and stretching up to the Mogran Family Park is a series of new local restaurants. They all serve much the same food – a few meat and fish dishes for around S£500. Their location makes them pleasant places to eat at or just sit in and sip a coffee or juice.

There is a Chinese restaurant on Sharia 21, in the New Extension, near the airport. A complete typically Chinese meal costs more than S£1000.

Nearby, a Korean restaurant serves traditional Korean food, including octopus. It's in the *Africa Hotel*, just past the entrance to the airport road. Look for the hotel sign and red lantern.

You can also get a meal at the *German Club*. The menu is fairly limited (soup, a couple of meat dishes and fish), but for S£300 to S£500, you can have a very satisfying meal. Now that the Sudan Club looks like joining forces with the Germans, the range of food might improve.

Some of the big hotels have Western-style restaurants. The *Meridien* has a pizza restaurant that is well patronised by expatriates.

At the Hilton Hotel, the *Ivory Room*'s S£2250 all-you-can-eat Friday buffet brunch is hardly cheap, but it's very good. The chic thing to do is to browse around Omdurman Souq in the morning and retire to the Hilton for brunch at about 11 am. The Ivory Room also has several different buffet dinners, depending on the evening. Reckon on paying around S£3000 for a full meal.

The Friendship Palace Hotel serves club and tuna-fish sandwiches in the *Tuti Cafe*. A fairly decent burger with chips costs S£180. There is also a nightly buffet in the restaurant.

ENTERTAINMENT
Clubs

Various ethnic, religious and national clubs form the backbone of Khartoum social life, especially for the city's expatriate residents. Although entry to all clubs requires membership, it is sometimes possible to arrange temporary membership or enter with a member. The clubs' activities vary from music, film presentations and athletics to serving food, conducting tours and providing accommodation.

The old British Empire establishment, the Sudan Club, died an ignominious death in March 1993 when the former owners of the premises, a powerful Greek family, won a court battle to have the property restored to them, 20 years after it had been seized by the state and made over to the club, which itself had been turfed out of its one-time lodgings. At the time, dwindling funds and waning enthusiasm made it unlikely it would reopen, although at least some of its committee were casting around for a new home.

The German Club (☎ 42438), on Sharia 1, in the New Extension, found itself being flooded with new members. It has none of the old imperial atmosphere (or pompousness) of the old Sudan Club, but you can get a good meal, go for a swim or even play tennis. The club also has rooms. Day membership costs S£100, but staff sometimes insist you be accompanied by a member.

The American Club (☎ 70114) is just opposite the Commonwealth War Cemetery. To get there, cross the railway line at Sharia al-Muk Nimir and follow the tracks about 100 metres. The cemetery is on your right, the club on the left. Here the rules about being accompanied by a member are stricter still, and the day rate is S£100. If you end up in Khartoum for a protracted period, two weeks' membership (which may not require that you be accompanied) costs S£700.

The Syrian and Armenian clubs, opposite each other in the New Extension, are all but ignored by the expatriate community, but they may be worth a try. Call the Syrian Club (☎ 42660) or the Armenian Club (☎ 43165) for details of what's on.

If you're an inveterate socialiser, there are also the Hellenic Club (☎ 43757) and the Italian Club (☎ 42322).

GETTING THERE & AWAY

In 1993 the travel situation was extremely fluid. Reports from travellers after research was completed showed that an easing of the hassles involved in getting travel permits to move beyond the capital had resulted in the permits being dropped altogether, except for restricted regions, for which permits would not be granted anyway. At the time of writing, it was, as has been the case for many years, virtually impossible to venture south of Kosti and Dinder National Park. The Nuba Mountains area was also off limits. With or without permits, travel west, east and north was possible, although a legacy of famine and growing banditry made parts of the west extremely dangerous.

With peace talks between the government, John Garang and rebel factions opposed to him having failed in Abuja, Nigeria, the situation could again change. Expatriates spoke of a 'charm offensive' on the West at the time of the talks. If the charm wears off, the permits may well be back.

Air

For details of flights into, around and out of the Sudan, refer to the Getting There & Away and Getting Around chapters at the start of the Sudan section. See also the respective Getting There & Away sections of each town or city entry. Sudan Airways has flights, of greatly varying reliability, to most main towns throughout the country.

If you're arriving in Khartoum on an international flight, the entry procedure is simple. Before going through passport control, you have to fill out two arrival registration forms, which you'll find on the side counters next to the tourist-information booth. Sometimes, the booth has maps and information about Khartoum.

The Sudan is a 'dry' country. The customs officials are strict about alcohol and will confiscate any liquor you have.

After clearing customs, you can change money at the bank window on your right if you can't wait until you get into town.

Airline Offices Sudan Airways has several offices in Khartoum. The office in the Industrial Bank of Sudan building on UN Square books only internal flights. The offices on Sharia al-Qasr and Sharia al-Barlaman book international flights, although the office on Sharia al-Qasr opens for about an hour at 5 pm for international and domestic bookings.

Most international airline offices are on or near Sharia al-Gamhuriyya and Sharia al-Qasr. Some of the airlines operating in and out of Khartoum are:

Air France
    Meridien Building, Sharia al-Qasr (☎ 76606)
Alitalia
    87 Sharia al-Barlaman (☎ 80526)
Balkan Airlines
    Sharia at-Taiyar Morad (☎ 76234)
British Airways
    3241 Sharia al-Barlaman (☎ 74577)
EgyptAir
    New Aboulela Building, Sharia al-Qasr (☎ 70259)

Ethiopian Airlines
    Sharia al-Gamhuriyya (☎ 70866)
KLM
    Al-Fayehaa Building, off Sharia al-Gamhuriyya
    (☎ 81662)
Kenya Airways
    Sharia al-Qasr (☎ 73429)
Kuwait Airways
    Sharia al-Gamhuriyya (☎ 81826)
Lufthansa
    Sharia at-Taiyar Morad (☎ 71332)
Swissair
    Morhig Building, Sharia al-Gamhuriyya
    (☎ 80196)
Saudia
    (☎ 71633)
Tunisair
    Sharia al-Gamhuriyya (☎ 81739)
ZAS Airlines
    Sharia Atbara (☎ 84178)

Permits for Air Travel Any traveller flying to Egypt with Air France, Lufthansa or KLM must have a Civil Aviation Authority permit. You may need an exit visa – for more details see the Getting There & Away chapter. The travel agency or airline office at which you finalise your ticket can arrange your Civil Aviation Authority permit (S£300) and give you the latest information about these matters.

Bus

For the excruciating bus ride north to Dongola, Karima or all the way to Wadi Halfa, you need to get to the Saganat bus lot in south Khartoum. It's on the way to the main bus station at the souq shaabi – look out for the blue, yellow and white contraptions that pose as buses. There is usually a bus a day to Karima and Dongola – they can take 30 hours or more, and are no fun. The Dongola bus usually goes on to Wadi Halfa. See the Getting There & Away sections for these destinations for details. It is advisable to check out schedules, to the extent that there are any, before attempting to travel.

Buses to all destinations en route to Port Sudan and to those places in the south you are permitted to get to, and to many destinations in the west, all leave from the huge and eminently confusing souq shaabi in south Khartoum.

There is an enormous range of buses to choose from, but tracking the company ticket booths that match the varying categories is far from easy, especially if you don't speak Arabic.

There are three companies that run what are unreservedly recognisable as buses in the modern accepted meaning of the term – Safina, Taysir and Arrow, of which the first is said to be marginally the better. They have windows, reasonably comfortable seating, shock absorbers and don't break down too often. You would be lucky to get a seat on one of these without a prior booking.

Buses generally serve one destination, so if you get a Port Sudan bus but only want to go as far as Kassala, you will probably have to pay the full fare and will simply be dropped on the main highway.

Buses to Port Sudan and Kassala tend to leave between 6 and 7 am. The fare to Port Sudan is about S£2000, and the ride takes 16 hours at the very least. Sometimes the driver hauls up for a few hours' kip short of his destination. The trip to Kassala takes about nine hours and costs S£935.

The cheaper, less comfortable buses look and feel more like lorries. They leave about the same time and cost S£1730 to Port Sudan and S£735 to Kassala.

Buses of all descriptions leave throughout the day for Wad Medani (S£175 to S£205; 3½ hours), Kosti (S£465; four to five hours), Sennar (S£450; about four hours) and Gedaref (S£395 to S£590; about six hours). There are no bookings for these routes.

Heading west, there are a few services to El-Obeid (S£580; one day) and to Er-Rahad (S£830). Book ahead for this last route, as not many buses travel it. There are occasionally buses to other destinations, including Kadugli in the Nuba Mountains area, but travel there is prohibited.

Some buses also leave for El-Obeid from the souq shaabi in Omdurman. They may not run during the rainy season. Because the road is bad, you may find they stop overnight en route.

Buses north to Shendi and on to Atbara via Kabushiya (Meroe) leave in the morning

Top: Tomb of the Mahdi, Khartoum (CB)
Left: Ruins of coral buildings, Suakin, Eastern Sudan (DS)
Right: Women in front of a mosque, Khartoum (LC)

Top: Men on the desert track from Dongola to Karima, Northern Sudan (DS)
Middle: Arab man in traditional dress, the Sudan (CB); A whirling dervish, Omdurman (HF
Weary traveller, Wadi Halfa, Northern Sudan (LC)
Bottom: Colourful market scene, Babanusa, Western Sudan (RvD)

from a lot in North Khartoum, just east of the railway line about 500 metres north of the bridge over the Blue Nile. For more details on tickets, see the Getting There & Away sections for the respective towns.

Train

The increasingly miserable rail system in the Sudan offers only a few services heading north and north-east. All trains to destinations west and south have been pulled out of service.

There is a train a week to Wadi Halfa, which actually appears to leave more or less when it's supposed to – on Sunday. It takes about two days. Sleepers cost S£3610, 1st-class seats S£2165, 2nd-class seats S£1445 and 3rd-class seats S£870. Once every two weeks there is a train for Karima via Atbara and Abu Hamed. It is excruciatingly slow. Apart from this, there are two trains to Port Sudan via Atbara. For details, see the Port Sudan, Atbara and Karima Getting There & Away sections.

You should book all tickets at least a day ahead.

Student discounts are possible. Before buying your ticket, go to the station master's office, further down the line from the ticket office (which is just west of the extension of Sharia al-Qasr). Get a letter of approval from him, then go back and buy your ticket.

Lorry

Lorries to all eastern and north-eastern destinations leave from the souq shaabi in Khartoum.

Lorries for destinations in western Sudan leave from the souq shaabi in Omdurman – to get there take a local bus from the main souq in Omdurman.

Boat

You can book the Wadi Halfa boat to Egypt at the train station. The office is tucked away about 100 metres west of the ticket window. The tickets cost S£4850 for 1st class and S£3350 for 2nd class.

GETTING AROUND
To/From the Airport

The airport is 10 to 15 minutes' drive from central Khartoum, and the ride there costs about S£300 by taxi, depending on the price of increasingly rare petrol. If you arrive or want to leave during curfew hours (midnight to 4 am), there are taxis with special curfew passes from the airport into town and from the Hilton Hotel to the airport. Otherwise you'll have to hang around the airport for a while.

There are also buses to town from the main road – just flag one down. The trip costs S£8, but the buses are often full by this point because they are coming from the outlying suburbs.

Bus & Minibus

Buses, minibuses and taxis are the main modes of transport around Khartoum. Most buses and minibuses begin and end their trips in and around UN Square.

Minibuses to North Khartoum (which you will want if heading to Shendi, Meroe or Atbara by bus), leave from a lot just east of Al-Kabir Mosque (the Grand Mosque), and cost S£8 (S£10 if no-one has any change; this seems to be standard treatment for everyone).

Buses and minibuses to the souq shaabi in south Khartoum (for all bus and lorry connections south and east, and some buses west) leave from Souq al-Arabi and cost S£8. Some leave from in front of the Haramein Hotel too. They also pass by Saganat, where you can get buses north to Dongola and Karima. Minibuses to Saganat only leave from a lot a block west of the Nakiel Hotel.

Minibuses for Souq Two and the New Extension depart from just by Flash Fantastic Foods. They pass by many of the embassies on their way to the southern perimeter of the city.

Buses for Omdurman leave from the eastern side of UN Square and cost S£5.

Occasionally you will see boxes (Toyota pick-up trucks) zipping around town, but they don't appear to serve any destinations useful to travellers that can't be done on buses and minibuses.

Taxi

If you're in a hurry (and that's a difficult state of mind in the Sudan) or just frustrated, take one of the battered yellow taxis. At S£200 for a ride across town, they're relatively cheap. The fare to the airport is usually about S£300 to S£400. These fares can increase greatly if petrol is scarce and, hence, expensive.

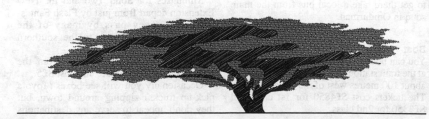

Northern Sudan

The 1628-km stretch of Nile between Wadi Halfa and Khartoum is often overlooked by travellers, yet the bulk of the ruins of ancient Sudan are to be found along this route. The kingdoms of Cush, Meroe and Napata all rose in this region, and for centuries the fluid frontier between Egypt and its southern neighbours moved back and forth with the ebbing and flowing fortunes of empires and their rulers. Thus was set a pattern that has lasted until the modern day. Seeing the Sudan as the gate to Black Africa, ancient Egyptians, Turks and people of several other European powers penetrated its interior with greater or lesser success in the hope of opening up and dominating trade routes – for gold and slaves, among other items – into central Africa. Egypt and the Sudan still contest control of the Halaib region that straddles the border.

Although the pyramids, temples and palaces left behind by the Sudan's ancient empires don't rival those of Egypt, they are untouched by the commercialism that surrounds the Egyptian monuments and are well worth visiting. You are left alone to wander, undisturbed by anxious guides and con artists selling trinkets and camel rides. It is this opportunity for solitary exploration that makes these sites so appealing. Unfortunately, they are equally untouched by restoration and protection, and are, in a sense, being worn away by the sands of time – or, at least, being sandblasted by haboobs.

Northern Sudan is also home to the distinctive people of Nubia and several Arab tribes. As much of Nubia was submerged by the waters of Lake Nasser (which was created by the construction of the Aswan High Dam), the Nubian people now live throughout Upper Egypt and northern Sudan. About 50,000 were resettled at Khashm al-Girba, on the Atbara River, when the dam was being built. Many others from the original town of Wadi Halfa, which disappeared under the rising waters of the lake,

were sent to New Halfa, not far from Kassala. Along with all the psychological trauma of a forced mass move came the tragedy of illness. Many of the newcomers succumbed to malaria, against which the locals appear to have some immunity. Others spread out to towns and settlements further up and down the river. Despite the diaspora, the Nubians have retained their unique language and many of their traditions.

The two predominant Arab tribes in northern Sudan are the Shaiqia and the Ja'alyeen. The town of Shendi is the main centre of the Ja'alyeen, who are scattered across the region from Atbara to the Sixth Nile Cataract. The Shaiqia are dispersed throughout northern Sudan amongst the Nubians, the Ja'alyeen and other tribes.

To truly experience this part of the Sudan, you have to forgo the comparative comforts of the train trip for the rigours of lorry or bus travel through barren desert plains and meagre oases on roads that are seldom more than faint tracks in the sand. Between Dongola and Karima, however, you can take a break from bouncing around in the back of a lorry to cruise up or down the Nile on an old steamer for a few days – if you arrive at the right time of year.

WADI HALFA

Wadi Halfa is a sobering introduction to the Sudan for those arriving on the boat from Aswan. For burned-out trans-Africa travellers heading the other way, it is variously seen as yet another painful obstacle or, more optimistically, the beginning of the end of the rigours of budget trekking through Africa – after all, the beauty of Aswan is just a boat ride away.

Wadi Halfa, to judge by a collection of pictures left over in the Nile Hotel, must have been quite a pleasant little place before Lake Nasser destroyed it. What has replaced it is a pretty cheerless, hot transit point. All anybody here wants to do is leave. This is

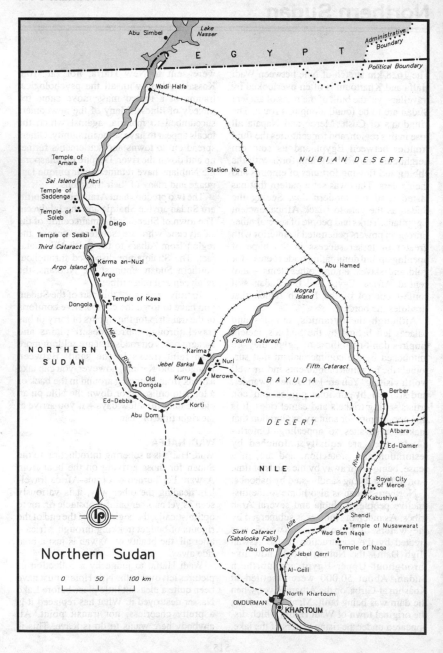

EGYPT

Abu Simbel

Lake Nasser

Administrative Boundary

Political Boundary

Wadi Halfa

NUBIAN DESERT

Station No 6

Temple of Amara

Sai Island
Abri
Temple of Saddenga
Temple of Soleb

Delgo

Temple of Sesibi

Third Cataract

Kerma an-Nuzl

Argo Island
Argo

Temple of Kawa

Abu Hamed

Mograt Island

Dongola

NORTHERN SUDAN

Karima
Nuri

Fourth Cataract

Nile River

Jebel Barkal
Old Dongola
Kurru
Merowe

Fifth Cataract

BAYUDA

Ed-Debba
Korti
Abu Dom

DESERT

Berber

Atbara

Ed-Damer

NILE

Royal City of Meroe

Kabushiya

Shendi
Temple of Musawwarat

Wad Ben Naqa
Temple of Naqa

Sixth Cataract
(Sabalooka Falls)

Abu Dom
Jebel Qerri

Al-Geili

North Khartoum

OMDURMAN
KHARTOUM

Northern Sudan

0   50   100 km

where you can pick up a train, bus or lorry heading south to Khartoum and stops in between. Near the dock, there is an ice plant and cold-storage house built by the People's Republic of China in the 1970s for a then, and still, nascent fishing industry. The Chinese even provided 35 two-tonne fishing boats.

Information

Customs & Registration If you arrive from Aswan, some of the formalities will have been taken care of on the boat. Don't wait to be told you can get off: when you see some movement on the dock (it takes the officials a while to set up the various tables and the like that serve as the various customs and passport-control points), shuffle politely to the nearest exit, look gormless and try to get off. Just waiting patiently in line could leave you stuck for up to two days! You then fill in a registration form (this does not take the place of registering with the police) and submit your bags to a customs check. The officials' main concern is alcohol, closely followed by cameras, the details of which they will scribble into your passport. There are no customs or currency declaration forms.

The police station and passports office are near the TV mast. Here you can register with the police and get travel permits, if they are still required, for travel to other towns. Exploit this opportunity. More often than not you'll be allowed to write as many destinations as you like on the permit and be given the official stamp of approval for them all. Quite a few travellers have cheerfully added destinations to the list as they have gone, but if you choose to follow their example, do so at your own risk. There are three forms to fill in, and although no photos seem to be needed, it is a good idea to come equipped with some from Egypt – there is nowhere to get them here. The total cost is S£350.

If you arrive overland and are heading to Egypt, this is where you get your exit stamp – it costs S£65. Don't lose the little strip of paper they slip into your passport, as you'll need it later on the boat.

Money Travellers will be eagerly met at the quay by moneychangers, who will happily change your Egyptian pounds or hard currency. Wadi Halfa's biggest business seems to be black-market currency exchange, and the number of people wandering around the place with fistfuls of money seems to dispel any fears of official retribution. If you are going to use the black market, this is probably the place to do it. Change a little so you can get a box into the town proper, and then shop around for the best rate.

There are a few banks, but only the Bank of Khartoum will change money, and then perhaps only cash. Staff will probably wonder why you're doing it in the bank in the first place.

Post If you have something you're eager to post now and are not too perturbed by the thought of it taking quite a while to get through, there is a small post office by the train station.

Places to Stay & Eat

The best place to stay without a shadow of a doubt is the *Onatti* (Nubian for 'moon') *Motel*. Mohammed Salah and his German wife have created a little oasis of fruit trees, grass, water well and windmill right on the lake, about three km away from the town. They are setting up camp facilities for people with 4WDs, tents, etc. Just ask around for Mohammed. He charges about US$4 per night plus US$1 more for breakfast. If you get stuck in Wadi Halfa, this is the place to do it.

Otherwise, the town's three better hotels are near the train station. The best of them is the *Boheira Hotel*, which costs S£150 per person. This is probably where you'll be dropped by the box. If it's full, as it often is, try the *Nile Hotel*, which costs S£120 per bed. The main problem here is water: if there's any at all, it's just a trickle. The *Wadi el-Nil Hotel* seems permanently booked out by companies in Khartoum.

There are a couple of other lokandas by the Khartoum and Dongola bus stop. At these

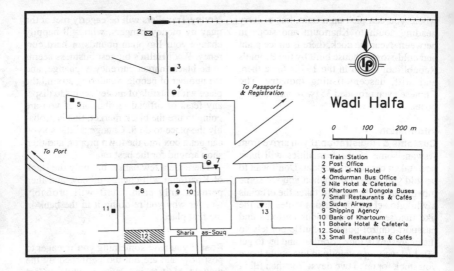

you can get a bed for about S£60, but there is usually no water for washing.

The Boheira and Nile hotels have cafeterias where they occasionally sell tea, and small bowls of fuul (S£30), fasooliyya (S£40) or egg (S£60). Depending on how much the swarms of people passing through have exhausted supplies in the market, it is possible to get fuul, ta'amiyya, salad and sometimes fish in the small cluster of restaurants near the Khartoum bus stop. Tea and baqlawa can sometimes be found. There are a few shops selling some basic tinned staples.

Getting There & Away
For information on getting to Wadi Halfa from Egypt or Khartoum, refer to the following Boat section or the Getting There & Away sections for Aswan and Khartoum.

Bus If the train isn't due for a while and you're in a hurry, there is usually at least one so-called bus heading to Khartoum (from the stop near the Wadi el-Nil Hotel they supposedly go to Omdurman, not Khartoum) and all points south each day. If you want to follow the Nile down to the capital and make

some stops on the way, which is certainly more interesting than simply sitting on the train through the desert, this is your only real option, unless you can get a lorry.

Be warned, however, that this is a pretty rugged trip through the desert – a lot of it fairly unpleasant stony stuff. Although some of the journey takes you along the Nile, much of it is well inland. The bus – a metal cage on a truck chassis – is highly uncomfortable and usually jammed with people and their chattels. Many travellers have said they would prefer to take a lorry, no matter how much slower, so they could ride on top and at least avoid the claustrophobia and sensory deprivation of being shut up inside the bus.

Prices seem to vary, but the trip to Khartoum costs from S£2100 to S£2600. Often you have to pay the full fare, even if you only want a fare to, say, Dongola, which should really be about S£1500. The buses stop at most towns of any significance on the way. You will probably be told the bus takes 12 hours to Dongola and two days to Khartoum. Don't believe any of it. Even without breakdowns, blown tires and the like, which appear to be par for the course, it is likely to take you about 24 hours to get to Dongola, and at least another 40 to get from there to Khartoum. If you are told the bus is leaving at 6 pm, it will probably leave at 10 pm. You know the rules: there are none.

Train The train station is the only building of any stature at the northern end of town. Trains, like the boats, have become quite erratic. One is supposed to leave for Khartoum every Wednesday, but don't bank on this. The 1st-class fare to Khartoum is S£2165. Second and 3rd class are bad but cheap (S£1445 and S£870 respectively). You can get a sleeper for S£3610. Travelling on top of the train is free, but as one traveller reports, 'You have to jump on out of sight of the conductor when the train is already in motion and there are few handholds...with your stuff it's impossible. That must be left inside for fellow travellers to watch.'

Tickets must be purchased at least a day in advance, but this will probably pose no problems. On the day the train actually goes, hundreds of people crowd around the gate and then scramble for a seat. Even if you get one, you still have to sit and wait for several hours until the train is ready to leave.

The trip to Khartoum can take anything up to three days, and there have been reports of it taking longer. The train stops at the 10 numbered stations in the Nubian Desert. At Station 6, tea and sometimes food can be purchased. Local untreated water, which the Sudanese are content to drink, is available throughout the trip, except at Abu Hamed. Most compartments do not have windows, there are no lights and sand swirls in, coating everything (including passengers) with dust. By nightfall, everybody looks ghostly. The train also stops frequently to clear sand from the tracks or for repairs.

Lorry Because there does seem to be a bus every day, the number of lorries heading south with passengers does not seem all that great. The souq lorry is even slower than the bus, but again, sitting in the open on top may be preferable to being stuck on the bus. Fairly frequent stops are made, so if you

don't bring your own food, you shouldn't starve on the way.

Boat You can buy a ticket for the boat (whether it be the old steamer or a more modern Egyptian boat) to Egypt in Khartoum or in Wadi Halfa – the ticket office is in the middle of town. First and 2nd-class tickets should cost S£4850 and S£3350 respectively. (Lower fares have been quoted, but these prices sound about right, as they more or less correspond to the Egyptian prices.) As for when the boat goes, there is little point in making any claims: gaps between departures of two weeks are not uncommon. For more details of the trip, see the Aswan Getting There & Away section.

SAI ISLAND

Sai Island, 190 km south of Wadi Halfa, contains the ruins of a small Egyptian temple built by the Egyptian Pharaoh Tuthmosis III in about 1460 BC.

On the western bank of the Nile, opposite Sai Island, is the **Temple of Amara**. Superseding a fort built there by Seti I in about 1300 BC, the temple was one of a series commissioned around 1270 BC by Ramses II and is one of the most complete constructions surviving from his reign.

On the eastern bank, where once also stood a Meroitic temple, is the little town of Abri, where it is possible to stay in a small lokanda, the *Nile Hotel*, for S£50. The Security people here seem a little on the nasty side – one group of travellers recounted sitting in a café and having its game of dominoes taken from it by twitchy (and probably bored) Security officials one night.

SADDENGA & SOLEB

Twenty km further south are the ruins of the Temple of Saddenga, built in about 1370 BC by Pharaoh Amenophis III for his consort Queen Tiy. As it's on the western bank, the temple is a bit difficult to visit.

The Temple of Soleb, a few km to the south, is also difficult to visit. It too was built by Amenophis III, to commemorate his victories over local tribes. It is considered the most interesting of the Egyptian colonial sites in the Sudan.

DELGO

Delgo is 68 km south of Soleb. There is a rest house here and the village is a popular lorry stop. Lorries from Wadi Halfa sometimes end their trips at Delgo, but other lorries and boxes cover the 110 km to Dongola.

Across the Nile are the subterranean ruins of the **Temple of Sesibi**, built by Amenophis IV (Akhenaten) around 1360 BC. The temple was part of a walled city, the remains of which were excavated in 1937.

KERMA AN-NUZL

Although there is not much for the casual visitor to see today, since 1913 archaeologists have had rich pickings in the royal Nubian graveyards around the modern town. The discovery of large quantities of Egyptian handicrafts suggests Egyptian craftspeople oversaw the production of the wares for their Nubian masters. There is evidence that some of the Nubian princes buried here were accompanied by their slaves into the next life, the difference being that the slaves were buried alive.

A box to Dongola costs S£150 per person.

DONGOLA

Dongola, the heart of ancient Nubia, is famous for its palm groves, which are a welcome sight after hundreds of km of desert. The date harvest in September is quite a show. Young boys from the town scale the palms, knives clenched between their teeth, and cut down clusters of dates.

There's a colourful fruit and vegetable market behind the town's central box lot, and occasionally nomads come in from the desert to buy and sell camels, sugar, tea and other goods.

On the eastern bank there are the ruins of the **Temple of Kawa**, which was the repository of gifts for the Cushite ruler Taharqa. Taharqa was king of the Land of Cush from 688 to 663 BC and was also the last Pharaoh of Egypt's 25th dynasty. (He lost the country to invading Assyrians.) A ferry takes you across the river, from where you must negotiate with a box driver to get out to the site. Not a lot of the original temple is still standing.

Information

Registration The police station where you must register (have your permit with you) is outside the town centre, a couple of blocks south of the main bus station.

Money There seems to be no black market here at all. If you have to change money, there is a Bank of Khartoum in the centre of town. Don't take it for granted that staff will change money. Sometimes they claim they need to call Khartoum for the latest rates but that they can't get a line!

Post There is a small post office in the souq.

Places to Stay & Eat

About the best place to stay is the *Al-Manar Hotel*, although its staff seem a little reticent about letting women stay, a problem throughout the town. Beds in clean rooms with fans cost S£135. The shower/toilet combinations are pretty clean, and there is plenty of water (which will come as a welcome change for travellers coming down from Wadi Halfa).

The next best place is the *Ash-Shimal Palace*, but it seems even harder to get into. Between the two, and across the road, is a cluster of three lokandas, the *Haifa*, the *Mecca & Jeddah* and the *Semiramis*. The latter is the worst of the three, but none is too hot. The Mecca & Jeddah charges S£125 per bed, but the Al-Manar is much better.

Near the lokandas is a good little fish place, where they grill up the day's catch from the Nile and chuck in a bit of salad too. Otherwise, there's not an awful lot around, aside from an ice-cream stand and a shop where you can buy yoghurt and baqlawa. The *Riyadh Restaurant* doesn't seem to have any food. There are one or two places where you can sit down for a cup of coffee or tea, and on the way out to the bus station there is

Dongola

0   50   100 m

■ PLACES TO STAY

1 Al-Manar Hotel
2 Haifa Hotel
3 Semiramis Hotel
4 Mecca & Jeddah Hotel
6 Ash-Shimal Palace Hotel

▼ PLACES TO EAT

5 Fish Restaurant
8 Juice & Ice-Cream Stand
9 Pepsi Stand
12 Riyadh Restaurant

OTHER

7 Civic Hospital
10 Satellite Dish
11 Box Lot
13 Bank of Khartoum
14 Souq
15 Sudan Airways

To Ferry

To Bus
Station

To Police
Registration

a shop that sells Pepsi. The bustling market is well stocked.

Getting There & Away

Air There is, maybe, a weekly flight to Khartoum with Sudan Airways; it costs S£5000.

Bus The main bus station is west of town. There are supposedly five departures a day for the gruelling cross-desert trip to Khartoum. Tickets cost S£1500, and the buses stop in Ed-Debba. A bus goes to Wadi Halfa on Sundays, Tuesdays, Wednesdays and Fridays for S£1000 (prices are rather arbi-

trarily set). The vague instruction is to be at the ferry (the 'road' to Wadi Halfa is on the right bank) by 6 am. What happens then is anyone's guess. If you're coming down from Wadi Halfa and you arrive too late to get the ferry across to the left bank and town, you get to sleep rough on the river bank and finish the trip the next day. There is meant to be a bus to Karima on Saturdays, leaving from the right bank at 9 am. It purportedly takes eight hours and costs S£800. You can also get to Karima the long way, following the Nile and going first to Ed-Debba, but transport on to Karima from there is hard to find.

Lorry Occasionally you can get onto a souq lorry from the main bus station, but if you're trying to get out to Karima this way, you could be in for a long wait. A lorry to Ed-Debba costs S£300 per person.

Box The fastest and possibly most comfortable way to get straight across the desert to Karima is by box – if one will go. Drivers want S£1000 for each passenger and won't leave until they have enough passengers to make it worthwhile. If you're in a hurry, you can try offering more. The alternative could be to wait for days. You have to go to the right bank to pick up the box – there's a little booth; just ask for the *boksi li Karima*. Once it actually leaves, you embark on an exciting cross-desert race against sunset, gliding over sand dunes and occasionally getting stuck in them. For most of the way there is no track at all – the driver just seems to know where to go.

Boat A more civilised and certainly more leisurely way to Karima must be by steamer, stopping at places like Ed-Debba and Old Dongola on the way. However, the vessels have an erratic schedule; they usually don't run at all from March to June, when the level of the Nile is low. If you do get on, the calm four-day journey to Karima is perfect for recuperating from the lorry or bus trip.

Getting Around

To/From the Airport There are special boxes marked 'airport' in Arabic.

Ferry The river ferry, which you will probably use a few times if you hang around the area at all, runs from dawn until early evening. It costs S£5 per head for foot passengers.

OLD DONGOLA

The first Dongola was the centre of power of medieval Nubia, and the remains of a once-proud city have been under excavation by a Polish-led team since 1964. The central structure is thought to have been a royal palace, upon which a mosque was built in 1317. Elsewhere, a church, possibly dating back to the 8th century, has also been closely studied. The Nile steamer often stops here.

ED-DEBBA

There's not much to this lorry and bus-stop town, and travellers wanting to pursue their trip up the Nile to Khartoum have found this place to be a bit of a stumbling block, as traffic towards Karima from here is slight. You might have better luck if you can push on to the road-junction town of Abu Dom, through which traffic from Khartoum also passes. There is nowhere to stay in Abu Dom, but a small lokanda in Ed-Debba has beds for S£50. There is no running water and the loos are merciless to sensitive noses. There are a few fuul and tea stands around.

KARIMA

Karima is a dusty market town with a population of over 15,000. The market is held twice a week and attracts people from the surrounding villages, but apart from the souq and a Pepsi shop offering a brief respite from midday summer temperatures of 50°C, there is little of interest in the town itself. Outside town, however, there are several important archaeological sites dating from the ancient Egyptian and Napatan kingdoms.

Information

Registration It's difficult to know where you are supposed to register here. There is a big police station in Merowe (on the southern side of the river), where the officers claim you must register for Merowe and Karima. However, a few travellers have been hauled into a small building by Security officials in Karima (virtually opposite the post office) for a compulsory registration.

Money Although there are a few banks in Karima, don't count on being able to change money in any of them. If the Bank of Khartoum's staff can get a phone line to the capital, they may change US dollars in cash or, with luck, sterling. Travellers' cheques don't seem to get much of a reaction here.

Post There is a post office on the road leading down to the train station.

Jebel Barkal Pyramids & Amun Temple

By far the most impressive site around Karima is also the most accessible. Two km south of Karima, Jebel Barkal rises 100 metres. It was considered sacred by the 18th-dynasty Egyptians. In the 13th century BC, Ramses II started work on the Temple of Amun at the foot of the hill, and it remained a religious centre for the next thousand years. The temple was the second longest after the Temple of Karnak, and the area was once

surrounded by at least half a dozen smaller temples. You can see columns, statuary and well-worn hieroglyphics carved into the stone walls of what has been described as the 'spiritual centre of the Cushites'. This was, in fact, part of one of the nerve-centres of the classical Cushite Empire – Napata, which stretched as far to the south-west as Kurru and to the south-east as Nuri.

Just to the west of the Amun Temple lies a series of slender pyramids in a style similar to that found further to the south-east, in Meroe. You are technically supposed to have a permit from the Department of Antiquities,

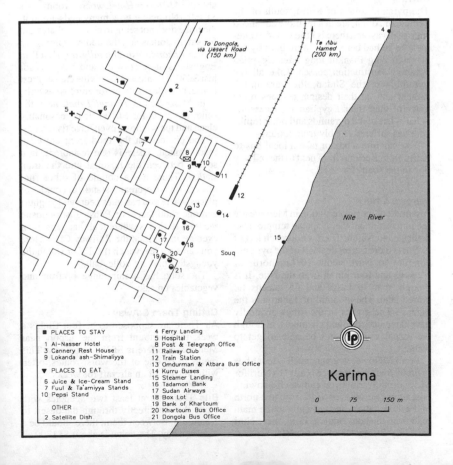

PLACES TO STAY

1 Al-Nasser Hotel
3 Cannery Rest House
9 Lokanda ash-Shimaliyya

▼ PLACES TO EAT

6 Juice & Ice-Cream Stand
7 Fuul & Ta'amiyya Stands
10 Pepsi Stand

OTHER

2 Satellite Dish

4 Ferry Landing
5 Hospital
8 Post & Telegraph Office
11 Railway Club
12 Train Station
13 Omdurman & Atbara Bus Office
14 Kurru Buses
15 Steamer Landing
16 Tadamon Bank
17 Sudan Airways
18 Box Lot
19 Bank of Khartoum
20 Khartoum Bus Office
21 Dongola Bus Office

To Dongola, via Desert Road (150 km)

To Abu Hamed (200 km)

Nile River

Souq

Karima

0   75   150 m

and a caretaker will almost definitely accost you. If you have no permit, try showing your travel permit – that often seems to work wonders. Have a heart for the guy – he's only doing his job: there's a sign over his little 'office' requesting people to 'cooperate in the maintenance' of the site by reporting to the police the absence of the caretaker.

If you get out early in the morning, the hill itself makes a nice spot for a bit of climbing; there is a commanding view of the Nile from the top.

Kurru

The pyramid tombs of Kurru, south of the Temple of Amun, are in a far more advanced state of decay, and there is little visual excitement to be had here. They were built by the Napatan king Piankhi long after Egyptian pyramid construction ceased. Like all the pyramids in the Sudan, they are much smaller and, in their design, perhaps more graceful than their Egyptian predecessors. What is left of the pyramids and other tombs here has suffered terribly from looting.

You can hire a box or take a local bus to Kurru from Karima (from next to the railway line in the souq) for S£30.

Merowe & Nuri

Just north of the police station in Merowe are the remains of another Napatan temple, also dedicated to Amun. There's not much left of it. Nor is there a great deal left of the pyramid complex at Nuri, about 10 km north of Merowe and four km in from the Nile. It is thought that 19 kings and 53 queens lie buried here. The pyramid of Taharqa is the biggest. The graves of the kings generally have three underground chambers, although the casual visitor won't be able to get to them.

From Merowe, you can catch a local bus (a pretty awful experience really) to Nuri for S£50. From Karima you can catch a rowing boat across the Nile for S£10 from just north of the train station, and get a box to the main road from the boat landing. From there Nuri is a fairly short walk off to the left.

Deir al-Ghazali

About 15 km south of the Nile and about 10 km further on from Nuri lie the rarely visited ruins of Deir al-Ghazali, a site comprising church, monastery and fortress. It is one of only three positively identified ancient monasteries in the Sudan; the other two lie below the waters of Lake Nasser. The site lies on the once-important road from Napata to Meroe.

Places to Stay & Eat

Accommodation in Karima and Merowe is limited. In the former, the best deal is probably the *Al-Nasser Hotel*, where a room costs S£350. (No matter how many beds are in it, the price does not seem to change. Watch out for smelly toilets and the odd scorpion.)

The *Lokanda ash-Shimaliyya* ('Hotel' in English) is more crowded and has beds for just S£50. The nicest place is the cannery rest house, but it seems to be for employees only.

In Merowe, the *Tirhagi Hotel*, near the souq, has beds for S£100. It is reasonably clean and the windows even have flyscreens.

The choices on the food front are even more limited. There is one restaurant, in a square between the hospital and the train station. There are a couple of other fuul places, one ice-cream stand, a couple of places where you can get sweets and yoghurt and one shop that sells Pepsi. Just opposite the train station is where it all happens of an evening in Karima: the Railway Club. Here you can sip a tea, watch the TV or watch the youngsters playing volleyball.

The souq has a fair range of fruit and vegetables on sale.

Getting There & Away

Air There are supposed to be four flights a week to Khartoum from the airport near Merowe. The fare is S£3820 one way. This seems to be one of the worst routes, often with no sight of an aircraft for weeks.

Bus There are at least two agencies with buses that go directly through the desert to Khartoum. Between them, there should be a service a day. The ticket is about S£1700.

The agency behind the Tadamon Bank has a bus to Port Sudan via Atbara at 7 am on Sundays. It costs S£750 to Atbara. A separate agency has a weekly bus to Dongola which costs S£800. It takes about nine hours at best.

Train Once every two weeks, a train leaves for Khartoum on a Sunday. It takes about three days, and the fare is S£1640 in 1st class, S£1100 in 2nd class and S£660 in 3rd class. It stops in Atbara and is meant to link up with a Wadi Halfa-bound train in Abu Hamed.

Lorry Lorries to Atbara cost S£400 per person. They leave from Merowe, or from Tangasi, about 20 km south-west of Merowe along the Nile.

Box Again, the fastest way to get across the desert from Karima either to Dongola or Atbara is by box. The hard part is finding one with enough people wanting to go. A box to Atbara from the souq in Karima – ask around to find out if there is one about – is S£1000. From the souq in Merowe, a place in a box to Atbara is S£1200. If the box can't round up enough passengers, it'll head to Tangasi, where it'll wait, for days if necessary, for enough passengers to make the trip worthwhile – unless of course you are willing to pay enough to make up the shortfall.

Boat There are three steamers that do the run to Dongola, if the Nile is not too low (as it usually is from March to June). The trip down the river is quicker than the trip the other way.

Getting Around

There are regular minibuses that clatter from the souq in Karima to a boat landing about eight km south, from where you can cross to Merowe. The minibus costs S£25, the boat S£10. The ferry linking Karima and Nuri leaves from a landing north of the train station. It also costs S£10. From the landing you need to take a box. The bus fare from Nuri to Merowe is S£50. Buses for Kurru leave from the souq in Karima and cost S£30; they seem fairly infrequent.

ABU HAMED

There is very little reason for getting stuck here, unless you get off the Karima train in the hope of making a connection for Wadi Halfa. You would probably be better off staying on until you got to Atbara, a more pleasant place to be waiting for connections.

Next to the train station is a government *rest house* with a huge verandah and showers. To stay there, you need to obtain prior permission from police at the station near the mosque.

The arrival of a train at night is an interesting sight. A market, illuminated by little kerosene lanterns, suddenly materialises out of nowhere around the train. You can usually buy fruit, vegetables and bread.

There is also an hourly ferry to the former Christian stronghold of Mograt Island, the largest island in the Nile.

ATBARA

The Atbara River flows down from the Ethiopian highlands to meet the Nile here, although prior to the rains it is barely more than a series of pools. Atbara is also the junction of two of the Sudan's major train routes: the line from Khartoum to Wadi Halfa and the line from Atbara to Port Sudan.

The railway dominates life in this city of 75,000 people. It's not surprising then that Atbara is a major centre for the Sudanese railway unions and was the scene of an attempted coup by pro-Communist army officers in 1971.

The city figured prominently in the Sudan's colonial history. The 1898 Battle of Atbara was the first major battle between the British and the Mahdists since the defeat of Gordon. In April of that year, the Mahdist army marched down the Nile to meet Kitchener's Anglo-Egyptian expedition at Atbara. The Mahdists were completely routed; 2000 of them were killed when Kitchener and his army attacked, with superior modern artillery, to the rousing music of Scottish pipes and English flutes, drums and brass instruments. The young Winston Churchill, who witnessed the battle as a war correspondent, later wrote a book about his experiences called *The River War*.

After the victory, Kitchener marched on to take Khartoum. British officials settled in Atbara, expanding the railway and building several large colonial-style houses which can still be seen – they now house government offices or belong to the Wadi an-Nil University. The Anglican church in Atbara is one of the few in northern Sudan.

Atbara is of particular interest to railway buffs because it's something of a graveyard for the steam locomotives that died during Nimeiri's rule. Perhaps more indicative of the neglect of the railways are the locomotives built in the 1960s that have also ended up here through lack of maintenance. Nimeiri supposedly ignored the railways, the railway unions and the city itself because the Communist Party was, and still is, very strong in Atbara.

An interesting **camel and crafts market** is held on Saturdays at nearby Ed-Damer. To get there, take a box from Atbara.

There are ferries from town across the confluence of the Atbara and Nile rivers.

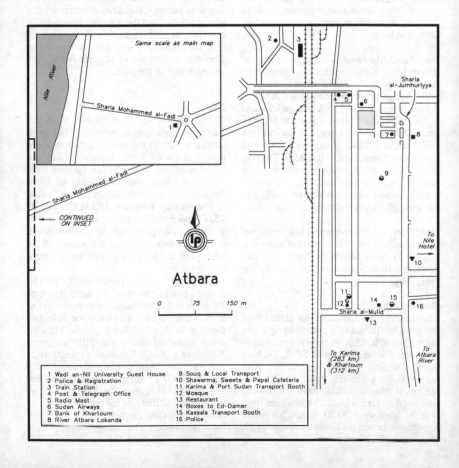

Atbara

0   75   150 m

1 Wadi an-Nil University Guest House
2 Police & Registration
3 Train Station
4 Post & Telegraph Office
5 Radio Mast
6 Sudan Airways
7 Bank of Khartoum
8 River Atbara Lokanda
9 Souq & Local Transport
10 Shawarma, Sweets & Pepsi Cafeteria
11 Karima & Port Sudan Transport Booth
12 Mosque
13 Restaurant
14 Boxes to Ed-Damer
15 Kassala Transport Booth
16 Police

When the rivers are low, you can wander along the river bed of the Atbara to the Nile.

Information

The police station for registration is near the train station. The Bank of Khartoum is virtually opposite the River Atbara Lokanda, the only cheap place in town. The post and telegraph office is by the radio mast and bridge over the railway line.

Places to Stay & Eat

The *River Atbara Lokanda* is a cockroach-infested dump. However, at S£150 a bed, it is the cheapest place in town, and the most conveniently located.

If money is no object, you could try living in something of a relic of faded colonial elegance at the *Wadi an-Nil University Guest House*. It costs S£2600 per person with full board. The rooms are big and cool, with high ceilings. The showers and sit-down toilets are outside, but they're a little grubby. It really is overpriced, in spite of the pleasant gardens and peaceful setting.

The only other option is the government-run *Nile Hotel*. At S£2130 per person for full board, it is a marginally better deal than the guesthouse, although the location – about one km east of town – is pretty much a wasteland. The rooms have air-con and there is even hot water.

A hunt around the souq will turn up a few places serving fuul, ta'amiyya and sometimes even fish. On Sharia al-Jumhuriyya is a bright place selling shawarma, which you don't see so often in these parts, as well as sweets and Pepsi. Buy a token for what you want first and take it to the guy looking after the meat on the spit. Not far from the mosque is a place that does a pretty good omelette. There are also a couple of juice stands around. The alternative is to go and try out the food at the two expensive hotels.

Getting There & Away

Air Three days a week there is a flight to Khartoum costing S£3520. On Saturdays you can fly, insha-allah, to Port Sudan for S£4420.

Bus To get to Khartoum by road, you first have to get a box down to Ed-Damer, which costs S£15, and then line up for whatever is going. The bus leaves at between 5 and 6 am and costs S£600. It's a bone-jarring and exhausting eight-hour trip.

If you don't want to stay overnight at Meroe, the buses generally pass fairly close to the pyramids – maybe you could get your driver to stop briefly.

From the booth near the mosque in Atbara, a bus from Karima proceeds to Port Sudan at a cost of S£750. A bus going the other way (to Karima) also leaves on the same day, costs the same and supposedly takes about 12 hours to get through. Much faster is a box, if you can get onto one (see the following Box section).

It is apparently possible to get a bus from Atbara direct across to Kassala via New Halfa.

Train Because no trains actually originate in Atbara, it might be a little more difficult here than elsewhere to get on one. Don't pay too much attention if you are told that it's necessary to book two weeks ahead for any train. The two weekly trains from Port Sudan and one from Wadi Halfa pass through here on the way to Khartoum, as does the train every two weeks from Karima. Fares are S£745 in 1st class, S£500 in 2nd class and S£300 in 3rd class. The fares are a little more if you get the 'super' train from Port Sudan. Reckon on 24 hours or more travel time.

To Port Sudan, the fares on the normal train are S£1620 for the sleeper, S£985 in a 1st-class seat, S£645 in a 2nd-class seat and S£390 in a 3rd-class seat. There is no sleeper on the 'super' train. First class costs S£1280, 2nd S£1070 and 3rd S£700. Both trains are supposed to pass through some time on Tuesdays.

On the weekly train passing through from Khartoum, a sleeper from Atbara to Wadi Halfa costs S£2380; in 1st class it's S£1430, in 2nd class it's S£955 and in 3rd class it's S£570. The trip usually takes 24 hours or more.

To Karima, the prices from Atbara are

S£1680 in the sleeper, S£1030 sitting in 1st class, S£680 in 2nd class and S£410 in 3rd class. The service runs once every two weeks. The painfully slow trip lasts about 30 hours.

Lorry Lorries leave from Ed-Damer later in the morning than the buses. They cost S£500 to Khartoum, S£250 to Shendi and S£200 to Kabushiya. The trip takes about 12 hours and is every bit as exhausting as the bus ride. Like buses, lorries pass fairly close to the pyramids.

Lorries occasionally go to Karima or Port Sudan, at a cost of S£400. It is apparently possible to get a lorry from Atbara to Kassala via New Halfa.

Box If you can get onto a box to Karima or Port Sudan, it will get you to your destination in half the time taken by the bus at a cost of S£1200.

Getting Around

There are old Peugeot taxis that will take you around town, should you need them to.

ROYAL CITY OF MEROE

The ruins of the capital of the ancient Kingdom of Meroe are about 100 km south of Atbara.

Between the Nile and the railway line stands the Temple of Amun and traces of the nearby royal palaces and swimming pool.

The ruins of another temple are about 1½ km east of the Temple of Amun, and the royal pyramids, where the Meroites buried their dead, are in the desert, five km to the east.

To get to the ruins, take the train, bus or lorry to Kabushiya, then local transport to Bagrawiya, the village near the site. There is a *rest house* nearby.

SHENDI

The town of Shendi is 70 km south of the Royal City of Meroe and is the starting point for visits to the Meroitic temples of Musawwarat and Naqa. In 1988 a group of US aid workers set out to explore this area in two Land Rovers. While stuck on a soft, sandy part of the road, they were approached by a group of camel riders, faces covered by long scarves, who pulled out daggers and swords and stole all they could carry from the Americans and their vehicles.

Such incidents are rare, but when looking for a driver, try to make sure you get someone who knows the territory and the best way to the sites. At the time of writing, it was difficult to get anyone to go out to both and bring you back for under S£5000. Most of the box drivers who'll go hang out at the western end of the souq. There is no public transport to either Naqa or Musawwarat.

Information

This town seems to have a particularly vigilant Security apparatus – or maybe the

---

The Royal City of Meroe

The kings of Meroe lived here from 592 BC to 350 AD and gained fame in the Greco-Roman world for their prosperous iron industry and agricultural development. Their architecture was highly developed and reflected extensive Egyptian influence. Hieroglyphic inscriptions on the ruins of pyramids, palaces and temples in the area show that the Meroites worshipped Egyptian deities. The Meroites also developed their own script, which has been only partly deciphered.

The Kingdom of Meroe ended in 350 AD with the rise of King Ezana of the Abyssinian Kingdom of Axum and his armies' subsequent invasion of Meroe.

In the 1820s, the Italian explorer Ferlini arrived in what was left of the royal city with the Turco-Egyptian forces of Mohammed Ali. Ferlini was specifically looking for treasure but managed to find only a single cache of gold in Pyramid No 6, which he smuggled back to Milan for auction. In his greedy search, Ferlini hacked the tops off 40 pyramid tombs! Although his vandalism is still evident, these pyramids are in better shape than those at Jebel Barkal and Nuri. ∎

officers have so little to do that the sight of a foreigner sets them all off. At any rate, they like you to register, which you do in their office, about two km south along the railway line. If you are on foot, you pass the soccer field on your left and take the next street on your left. Ask for *al-amn*, which means 'Security'. A taxi will cost about S£100, which is OK if you want to see inside an old Russian Volga, the predominant make in this town. There is a Bank of Khartoum in the town centre.

Temple of Musawwarat

The site of the Temple of Musawwarat, about 20 km south of Shendi, features a reconstructed temple complex and the remains of a palace. Statues of elephants and lions are scattered in the sand near the *hafirs* (reservoirs) that the Meroites dug to provide the area with water.

Temple of Naqa

The Temple of Naqa is 40 km east of the Nile and 55 km south-west of Shendi. A kiosk at the temple reflects the extent of Roman influence in the Sudan – on the back wall of the temple, carvings show that the Meroites worshipped Apedemek, a lion-god.

Places to Stay & Eat

There's very little choice here. The *Shendi National Hotel*, a basic lokanda by the train station, has beds for S£85 per night, and does not always welcome Westerners with open arms. The *Funduq Siyaha* (Tourism Hotel) costs S£500 for a room with two beds. It's in a quiet spot with lots of greenery around. The rooms have fans and flyscreens. The main problem is it's about 2½ km out of town, and about 3½ km away from the bus and lorry station!

Getting There & Away

Bus The bus station is inconveniently located about one km east of the train station. It can be a real dogfight trying to get on a bus in the morning. It's a good idea to be there by 6.30 am. The trick then is knowing which bus belongs to which booth: even if you read

Kiosk at the Temple of Naqais, Naqa

Arabic, this is far from clear. When a bus appears, there is a mad scramble for the appropriate booth. First in, first served. If you miss out, you have to keep your eyes open for where the next queue might form for another bus – not a good way to start the day. The fare is usually S£270. The ride in either direction is bad, but worse going north. The last 20 km or so into Khartoum is actually paved, and an effort seems to be being made to extend the paving some way north towards Shendi.

Train The train, if you can get on it, costs S£355 in 1st class to Khartoum, S£250 in 2nd class and S£190 in 3rd class.

Lorry Lorries leave later than the buses, both for Atbara and Khartoum, and cost S£250 either way.

SABALOOKA FALLS

These beautiful but seldom-visited waterfalls are at the Sixth Nile Cataract, about 50 km north of Khartoum. If you enjoy kayaking and just happen to have a kayak with you, this place is recommended. A British expatriate kayaker in Khartoum visits Sabalooka regularly and has somehow avoided getting bilharzia. If you're not worried by the possibility of getting bilharzia, there's also a spot here where you can go for a swim. Nearby, the hills provide a decent place for a bit of climbing. To get there, leave the bus at Jebel Qerri or Abu Dom and persuade a local to take you the rest of the way.

Western Sudan

Travel through western Sudan is rough, tough and absolutely fascinating. This diverse region covers an area of 549,579 sq km, from the deserts and plains of Kordofan to the mountains and hills of Darfur, and is populated by more than six million people from as many as 23 tribes and ethnic groups. These include the Arab Baggara tribes of Northern Kordofan, the African Nuba people of the Nuba Mountains and the Black Saharan nomads of the Zaghawa tribe of Northern Darfur.

Most of the land is harsh desert nurturing only thorny heskanit grass and acacia bushes. The tiny heskanit thorns stick to your skin and clothes, and the grass is brutal to extract. In the midst of this apparent bleakness, however, there are beautiful lakes, mountains, hills and lush palm groves.

Little is known of the early history of the provinces of Kordofan and Darfur because the region has no ruins of ancient palaces and temples from bygone kingdoms and dynasties.

Until Islam was introduced here in the 16th century, most of the scattered tribes and groups were isolated from each other. By 1596 the dynasty of Sultan Suleiman Solong had established itself in Darfur and united the Fur people, converting them to Islam. The Fur Sultanate thrived for the next 320 years, fending off challenges from the Fung Sultanate and from the Abyssinians to the east. In 1916 it was overthrown by Anglo-Egyptian forces.

El-Obeid, the capital of Kordofan, was the Mahdi's first political centre. It was there that he decimated the smaller, weaker forces of Colonel Hicks in 1883 and consolidated his political and military forces before marching to Khartoum.

Today the towns and villages of Kordofan and Darfur are still strongholds for Mahdiyism. Until the June 1989 coup, the Umma Party, one of Sudan's foremost political groupings, was headed by the great-grandson of the Mahdi, Sadiq al-Mahdi; the party has a big following in western Sudan.

Over the past few years, drought and famine in Kordofan, Darfur and neighbouring Chad have displaced or killed hundreds of thousands of people. The United Nations estimated that more than 400,000 Sudanese had to leave their villages in search of food and water in the late 1980s. At the same time, thousands of refugees swarmed into the Sudan, fleeing war and hunger in Chad. In 1985 and 1986, food and medical aid was rushed into the area from all over the world.

Even in the face of such persisting problems, numerous travellers and expatriate relief workers speak of the incredible hospitality and friendliness of the Sudanese. The people in this region, suffering such severe hardship, still share what little food and drink they have with visitors. Do not abuse the privilege of experiencing Sudanese hospitality. Give your host at least a token of thanks, such as a small gift. The gesture alone means a lot.

EL-OBEID

El-Obeid, a city of 200,000 people, is surrounded by inhospitable desert. Once the Mahdi's capital, El-Obeid is also famous as the 'gum arabic capital of the world'; as well, it has the second and third-best football teams in the Sudan.

For those yearning to know, gum arabic is used in the manufacture of ink and food thickeners. It's also one of the ingredients in the soluble capsules of some pain killers and other drugs. The gum arabic is extracted from little balls hanging from the branches of acacia trees.

Information

There's an Egyptian consulate (☎ 249 4167) in the main square.

The British Council used to run a small library where films were occasionally shown. As relations between Britain and the

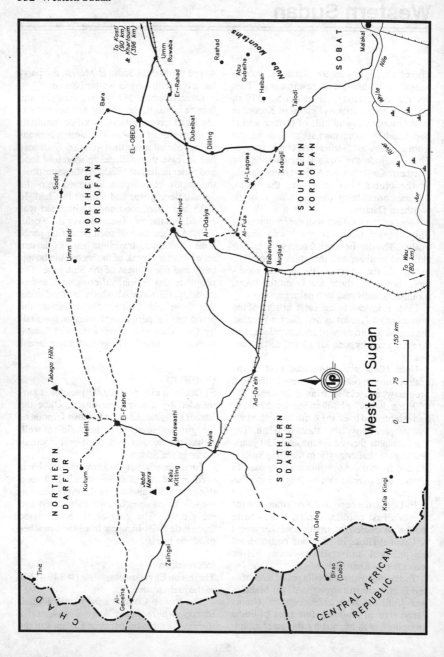

Sudan have deteriorated in the 1990s, most direct aid and other UK projects have been suspended, and the council is one of the victims.

El-Obeid's only electricity is provided by private generators, and power cuts are common. The city's water supply also fluctuates. When it dries up completely, water has to be trucked in.

For those travellers who cannot exist without TV, the Syrian and Coptic clubs have TV sets and generators.

Things to See

The town's small **museum** has displays on the Sudan's ancient history and Colonel Hicks' defeat at the hands of the Mahdi's forces. Outside El-Obeid, a **monument to Hicks** marks the site of the battlefield, but it's well off the beaten track, and you'll need a guide if you really want to see it.

El-Obeid's **cathedral**, one of the largest in Africa, is the result of extensive missionary efforts in the area, catering to the town's large African Catholic community. The drums and xylophones that accompany Sunday services have a distinctly African beat, and it's worth going to church just to hear the music.

There are two **souqs** in El-Obeid. One deals predominantly in meat and vegetables, but cloth and clothing are also sold, and you can have a shirt or pair of pants made in a day. At the other, older market, produce prices tend to be lower and some local crafts are available.

Places to Stay

There are not many places to stay in El-Obeid. The *International Hotel* has beds in a lokanda-style arrangement near the main souq for S£150. It's not great. In a similar vein is the *Al-Medina Hotel*, which is OK. The *John Hotel*, which used to be patronised by Westerners a lot, has closed.

The best place, if you can afford it, is the *Kordofan Hotel*, near the airport. It has good, clean doubles for about S£700. Also good value is a small place in the same square. It has no name in English and describes itself

as a 'business hotel'. It has very acceptable rooms for S£300.

Places to Eat

There are several good cafés and tea stands near the souqs, as well as a takeaway restaurant selling fish and chicken, and an old ice-cream shop that also sells beef burgers. The best place to eat Sudanese food is the *Banker's Club*.

Getting There & Away

Air There are four flights a week between El-Obeid and Khartoum, and a one-way ticket costs S£4020. There are also flights to Nyala.

Bus Buses arrive daily in El-Obeid from the souq shaabi in Khartoum. They cost S£580 and can take a full day to get here. The rainy season can double travel time. From Kosti, the bus costs S£600 and takes about eight hours on a mostly paved road.

A daily bus travels south to the railway-junction villages of Dubeibat, Dilling and Kadugli. It takes between four and seven hours to get to Kadugli on a road that is paved most of the way. Note that, at the time of writing, all access to the Nuba Mountains area was closed.

Train There is no longer any train service to the west of the Sudan from Khartoum, a measure of the state the railways are in.

Lorry Souq lorries travel in and out of El-Obeid every day. Lorries from the main souq go to virtually every town and village in the area. The journey to El-Fasher takes two to three days; to Nyala, four to five days; to Khartoum, 24 hours; and to Umm Ruwaba, three hours. These trips are all unscheduled and subject to frequent fuel shortages. The hike to Nyala costs about S£2000, but just as departures are affected by fuel shortages, so are fares.

The El-Obeid fuel situation was a problem for an elderly British couple who had driven their beaten-up Land Rover all the way from South Africa. Their ages were difficult to ascertain because they looked as worn and rugged as their vehicle. On arrival in El-Obeid, they had to change money at the bank in order to buy diesel fuel for the Land Rover. However, there wasn't any fuel, so two of the bank managers took a rubber tube and siphoned fuel out of the bank's supply for them. The couple also said that when they were camping out, the lorry drivers would stop, toot their horns and ask if they were OK.

UMM RUWABA

This little town is 135 km east of El-Obeid along a terrible road but can also be reached by train from Khartoum. Umm Ruwaba has a small but interesting **camel market** at which members of the Arab Baza'a tribe sell their camels. The town is also home to some of the more African Jawa'ama tribe. The two groups seem to stay away from each other.

NUBA MOUNTAINS

Everyone who has travelled in this region raves about the beautiful scenery and the fascinating Nuba people. That may all be in the process of changing. The entire area has been sealed off to foreign travellers, and rumours abound of massacres of the Nuba being carried out at the instigation of the government. One Western diplomat said, 'Genocide is the word that springs to mind'. Most observers, working with scanty information, say that whatever is happening and

for whatever reasons, the Nuba culture has already been all but destroyed. It is rumoured that the government, wanting to secure the comparatively good land for Arabs (not just Muslims) as part of its struggle with the predominantly Black Christian or animist south, has armed local Arab tribes historically antagonistic to the Nuba and sent them in to kill or expel them. One observer claimed that, to lend the operations a little more bite, helicopter gunships were occasionally sent in.

There are a few obvious points to take into consideration if you do manage to visit this region, the most important of which is to show respect for what's left of the traditional ways of these people. This is a rather contentious issue for travellers because the influx of inquisitive Westerners has already had its effect: at last report, it was not uncommon for the younger men to paint themselves and perform their dances for dollars.

If you wish to take photographs, always ask first and remember that the Nuba are people, not museum pieces or circus performers to be gawked at.

The following information should be helpful if it again becomes possible to travel in the region.

Er-Rahad

The town of Er-Rahad, although relatively commercialised and not particularly noteworthy, is a good starting point for treks into

---

The Nuba

Scattered throughout the mountain villages where they practised terrace farming, the Nuba remained isolated from the modern world until quite recently and managed to retain most of their traditional ways. Body painting and scarring, female circumcision and bloody wrestling matches were still common. What is left of all this is anybody's guess.

The photojournalist Leni Riefenstahl assembled a beautifully photographed account of the Nuba called *The People of Kau*. Her photographs of the naked Nuba and their wrestling matches and courting dances piqued the curiosity of many travellers and accelerated the Nuba's exposure to the outside world.

The Sudanese government, ever mindful of its development and modernisation efforts and embarrassed by this display of traditionalism, attempted to impede visits to the Nuba Mountains by insisting that foreigners obtain travel permits and leave their cameras in Kadugli. The government had embarked on a programme to clothe the Nuba until it apparently decided it was easier to kill or disperse them. ■

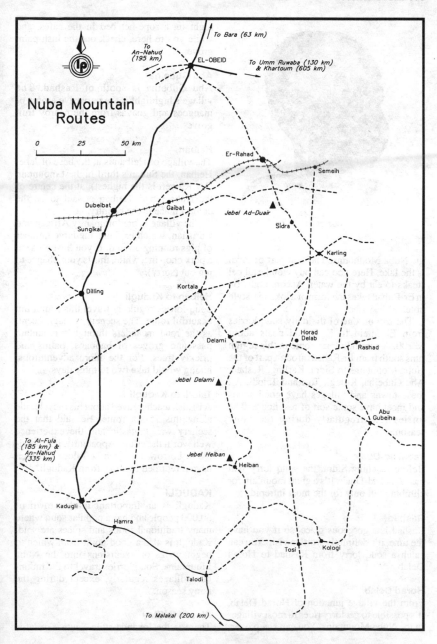

To Bara (63 km)

To
An-Nahud
(195 km)

EL-OBEID

To Umm Ruwaba (130 km)
& Khartoum (605 km)

**Nuba Mountain
Routes**

0   25   50 km

Er-Rahad

Semeih

Dubeibat

Gaibat

Jebel Ad-Duair

Sidra

Sungikai

Karling

Dilling

Kortala

Horad
Delab

Delami

Rashad

Jebel Delami

Abu
Gubeiha

To Al-Fula
(185 km) &
An-Nahud
(335 km)

Jebel Heiban

Heiban

Kadugli

Hamra

Tosi

Kologi

Talodi

To Malakal (200 km)

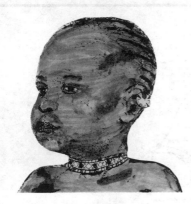

Nuba child

the Nuba Mountains. The best part of town is the lake. Here you can buy wonderful eel steaks to eat by the water. Accommodation in Er-Rahad takes the form of a lokanda-style hotel.

The trip on one of the daily souq lorries from El-Obeid to Er-Rahad costs about S£200. A common lorry route in this region runs south from Er-Rahad through part of the Nuba Mountains to Sidra, Karling, Rashad, Abu Gubeiha, Kologi, Tosi and Talodi. All these towns and villages have good souqs and most have some sort of rest house. The lorries run irregularly during the rainy season.

Jebel ad-Duair
Before reaching Sidra, the souq lorry will pass Jebel ad-Duair. It's a great mountain for climbing but only for the most intrepid.

Rashad
Rashad is a gorgeous place, so if you have the time, it's definitely worth a visit. You can catch a souq lorry from Rashad to Horad Delab.

Horad Delab
From the village junction of Horad Delab, it's possible to get lorry rides to most villages in the Nuba Mountains. You can sleep over-

night on a rope-net bed in the cafés, and while you're here, check out the lush palm grove.

Abu Gubeiha
Abu Gubeiha is south of Rashad. The village's highlight is the pervasive aroma of mangoes and guavas from the nearby fruit groves.

Heiban
The village of Heiban is at the base of Jebel Heiban, the Sudan's third-highest mountain (Mt Kinyeti is the highest), at the centre of the Nuba range. Heiban is said to be the coldest place in the country.

The village is predominantly African and Christian, which explains the large number of pigs running around. If you haven't seen a pork chop in a while, this is your chance to pig out (sorry).

Heiban to Kadugli
Souq lorries regularly travel this rough but beautiful route. The scenery is magnificent, as the road meanders through a mountain pass and groves of baobabs, palms and prickly trees. For the more adventurous, hiking would take two to three days.

Talodi to Kadugli
A British teacher raved about his bicycle ride along this 75-km route. He said that the scenery was fantastic and the experience well worth the effort. Apparently, it is possible to borrow a bicycle in Talodi and then have it returned by lorry from Kadugli.

KADUGLI
Kadugli is an important market town of 30,000 people and has a popular souq where many traditional foods and spices are sold. Kadugli is also a good point from which to begin walks or excursions into the Nuba Mountains. Souq lorries travel to the mountain villages regularly, except during the rainy season.

Places to Stay
There is the lokanda-style *South Kordofan*

Hotel or, alternatively, the government rest house called *The Palace Resthouse*.

Getting There & Away
There is usually a daily bus from El-Obeid to Kadugli, but at the time of writing foreigners were not permitted to catch it. It takes from four to seven hours.

Two buses a day to El-Obeid leave Kadugli from in front of the cinema. Between Kadugli and Dilling, you pass through sorghum and sesame country.

The souq-lorry route from Kadugli to Al-Lagowa, Al-Fula and Nyala has been highly recommended for its scenery.

AN-NAHUD
The noteworthy feature of the Southern Kordofan town of An-Nahud, 215 km south-west of El-Obeid, is its unique limestone architecture. The government *rest house* is the only place to stay.

AL-ODAIYA
The beautiful town of Al-Odaiya is 83 km south of An-Nahud. There are lots of trees and green hills, especially after the rains, and the 145-km lorry ride to Babanusa is another which has been recommended for its scenery.

BABANUSA
Babanusa is a railway-junction village where you used to be able to catch trains to Nyala, Er-Rahad and Khartoum.

MUGLAD
A few km south of Babanusa is Muglad, which was basically an oil-exploration base, complete with an airstrip and a large compound full of foreigners. Today, this erstwhile Texas-style boom town is full of refugees who, in 1988, were starving and dying at an appalling rate (see the introduction to this chapter).

BARA
There is not much to this oasis town, just north of El-Obeid, except a lot of vegetable gardens. Buses going between Khartoum and El-Obeid stop at Bara.

SODIRI
Sodiri is a very bleak place in the middle of the desert, 167 km north-west of Bara. It used to be the site of a large camel market, but the market and the people of Sodiri suffered greatly during the 1985 famine.

UMM BADR
This mere dot on the map, seemingly in the middle of nothing but desert, is apparently quite a surprising little place. One traveller who ventured there described it as 'a very beautiful, very green lake area where a lot of camel nomads hang out'. It is a two to three-day lorry trip from El-Obeid.

AD-DA'EIN
Ad-Da'ein is a railway village almost 200 km west of Babanusa, and the 'capital' of the nomadic Rizeigaat tribe. It's a very laid-back place, with a lokanda-style hotel and friendly, hospitable people.

NYALA
Nyala was the Fur Sultanate's capital from the late 16th century. With the Fur people united under the banner of Islam, the sultanate thrived and prospered for more than 300 years, partly because of Nyala's isolation from the rest of the Sudan. With the railway line no longer in use, the town remains an isolated outpost on the edge of the desert, at the base of a mountain range dominated by the Sudan's second-highest mountain, Jebel Marra.

Information
The staff at the government tourist office in Nyala can help you plan a trek to Jebel Marra, including the purchase of a donkey, camel or horse from the souq. The tourist office is just past the radio mast. Immigration, where you register, is between the hospital and the stadium, while Security is out by the airport. Sometimes you may find you have to go to both.

Another good source of information about

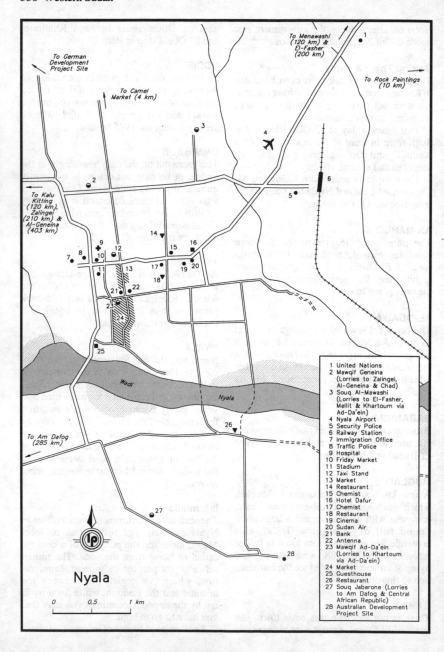

To Menawashi
(120 km) &
El-Fasher
(200 km)

To German
Development
Project Site

To Camel
Market (4 km)

To Rock Paintings
(10 km)

To Kalu
Kitting
(120 km),
Zalingei
(210 km) &
Al-Geneina
(403 km)

Wadi

Nyala

To Am Dafog
(285 km)

Nyala

0   0.5   1 km

1 United Nations
2 Mawqif Geneina
   (Lorries to Zalingei,
   Al-Geneina & Chad)
3 Souq Al-Mawashi
   (Lorries to El-Fasher,
   Mellit & Khartoum via
   Ad-Da'ein)
4 Nyala Airport
5 Security Police
6 Railway Station
7 Immigration Office
8 Traffic Police
9 Hospital
10 Friday Market
11 Stadium
12 Taxi Stand
13 Market
14 Restaurant
15 Chemist
16 Hotel Dafur
17 Chemist
18 Restaurant
19 Cinema
20 Sudan Air
21 Bank
22 Antenna
23 Mawqif Ad-Da'ein
   (Lorries to Khartoum
   via Ad-Da'ein)
24 Market
25 Guesthouse
26 Restaurant
27 Souq Jabarone (Lorries
   to Am Dafog & Central
   African Republic)
28 Australian Development
   Project Site

treks to Jebel Marra are the few remaining expatriates still working in Nyala (down to eight at the time of writing).

Nyala has at least four souqs scattered around, but because of the drought and famine in the region, the main market is now only a quarter the size it was in 1985.

Places to Stay

Camping Nyala has two unofficial camping sites. Although the land is privately owned, it is sometimes possible to camp along Wadi Nyala, among the mango trees and monkeys. The other site is under the mango trees of the Kondura Forest, about four km further down the wadi (watercourse). Some travellers have had the distinct feeling the authorities do not approve.

Hotels The *El-Ryan Hotel* has been recommended by travellers. It's next to the central souq and costs S£520 for a double.

The cheap and basic *Darfur Hotel* has mattresses on rusty springs. It's difficult to store your gear there though and it's not very clean.

Other hotels which have been recommended by travellers include the *Deenobee Hotel*, *Hotel Zaire* and the *Andafusu Hotel*. You could try to check out the government *rest house*.

Places to Eat

Topping the list of eating places is the *Camp David*, near the Darfur Hotel. They serve delicious cakes, tea and milk. At a hole-in-the-wall near the mosque in the centre of town you can get veal cutlets.

Fresh food is easily purchased in the souq. Tinned food is available in town, although it is expensive. In fact most items are more expensive here than elsewhere in the country, reflecting the cost of transporting goods from Port Sudan and Khartoum. A bottle of Pepsi that would cost S£25 in the capital costs S£40 in Nyala.

Getting There & Away

Air Most days there are flights between Nyala and Khartoum. A one-way ticket costs S£8420. Make a booking at the airline office in the centre of town, but don't take too much notice of the passenger lists. The best way to find out whether or not you are going to get on is to turn up at the airport and try your luck. There are occasional flights to El-Obeid and El-Fasher as well.

Train Nyala is the railway terminus, but at the time of writing there were no train services west of Khartoum. If they are reinstated, the trip can take four to six days.

Lorry Souq lorries travel to practically every imaginable destination, petrol supplies permitting, including the Central African Republic, Khartoum, the villages near Jebel Marra, El-Fasher and Al-Geneina. From the souq south of the wadi there are occasional lorries to Am Dafog and even on to Bangui in the Central African Republic. Other lorries leave for Khartoum from the souq in the centre of town and from another in the north, not far from the airport. From here, the popular trip to El-Fasher takes 1½ days. Lorries to Al-Geneina and possibly on into Chad leave from a fourth market directly north of the hospital. Prices depend more than anything on the availability of fuel and what it costs on the black market. One Westerner reported paying S£700 a gallon in March 1993.

HAMI ROTOKI

On the way to the village of Kass, you might consider making a stop at the medicinal hot springs of Hami Rotoki, near Jebel Marra. The locals claim that the water there is hot enough to make tea, yet not too hot to bathe in.

JEBEL MARRA MOUNTAINS

This beautiful mountain region of rivers and orchards is fine, hilly walking country. No two people share the same experience here, but travellers agree that the hospitality in these mountains is unrivalled.

Nyala is the starting point for a visit to Jebel Marra, the crater of an extinct volcano which, at 3071 metres, is the second-highest mountain in the country and the feature attraction of this area. Before doing anything else, you need to get a special permit from Security. Again, you may have to go both to Security and Immigration. Bandit activity is rife throughout westernmost Sudan, and you will not always be granted a permit. If the Security officers feel your life is in danger, take their advice. If you insist on going, they will ask you to sign forms absolving them of any responsibility.

Food and water are no problem and you can't really get lost because the local people are always pointing you in the right direction. The locals also insist that you visit their houses and will fill your arms with fruit. If you want to get a guide, which could save time, be careful. Some travellers have reported being put into the hands of a guide at the El-Ryan Hotel who took them *away* from where they wanted to go and ended up costing them the aim of their trek – the crater.

Jebel Marra Trek
Route 1 To get to Jebel Marra, take a lorry from Nyala to Nyatiti, then begin your walk – just head towards the mountains. Halfway to Quaila, just past the first village, is an excellent **waterfall** and **pool** where you can camp and swim. The teacher in Quaila may

---

A Second View of the Jebel Marra Trek
A British teacher, who made the trek after working in Ad-Da'ein, Southern Darfur, reported:
The Jebel is probably the most beautiful place in that part of Sudan not affected by war...For those hiking on the higher slopes above the villages...[this] is an area that I think is a potential death-trap...It can be a problem finding food, water and people to ask the way...I hiked on Jebel Marra from Nyatiti to the crater and back again. I've never heard of anybody starving to death, but I can assure you that of the six teachers I met on the mountain who were hiking in three groups, all of them had been lost between the crater rim and Quaila and two of them had run out of water and would very likely not have come down alive if they hadn't luckily met a local man who showed them the way. As for me, I ran out of water too and was in a pretty desperate state for a while. Once you run out of water and are lost, panic can set in very quickly. Furthermore, the mental and physical deterioration your body suffers when it's dehydrated is alarmingly quick! None of us were hiking novices at the time so the difficulties we had are likely to be shared by many if not most other people...

December is more than two months into the dry season, so water is not going to be over-abundant outside the villages...take as much as you can carry. My advice to anyone walking from Nyatiti to the crater and then to the Hot Springs: for those based in Nyala, the best place to start your hike is Nyatiti. There is a paved road from Nyala to Zalingei and all buses to Zalingei will stop at Nyatiti. The rest house is situated beyond the village on the way to Quaila about half an hour's walk from the main road. Don't go straight there though, as you need to get a letter of permission which can be obtained from the centre of the village. Nyatiti has at least one restaurant, and shops where you can buy food for the walk and even saucepans.

Before going further, I would suggest that, when in Al-Fasher or Nyala, you find out from a knowledgeable foreigner or Sudanese when the village souq days are. It is a good idea to time your hike in accordance with them. On these days, the villages are much more lively and colourful and you should be able to get hot meals...Furthermore, there are more people walking to and from the villages on these days...

If you're hiking from Nyatiti to Quaila, you should leave soon after sunrise so you can laze around Quaila during the hottest part of the day – very enjoyable on souq days. If you want to get to the crater the following day, you can either just walk up to the waterfall above the village and camp there or continue on to the hot springs. The springs aren't too hard to find as the path is fairly easy to follow. Beyond the waterfall there's a long narrow passageway in the rocks near the stream. The path then crosses the stream several times but the last part of the walk is quite an exhausting ascent from the right bank of the stream. If you are a little anxious about getting your bearings and your Arabic isn't too good, take heed of the following: as you look towards Jebel Marra, you will see a flat-topped mountain not far ahead of you to the left of Marra. This is Jebel Idwa, and provided you keep it to your left, you won't go far wrong. For directions, you should ask

be able to find accommodation for you and point you in the direction of the crater. From Quaila, you walk to the **hot springs** and up to the crater of Jebel Marra. Once at the edge, you go halfway round the rim before heading down again, to the crater floor. From here you walk out through the canyon to Taratonga to catch the weekly lorry to Nyala.

If you have the time, stay in Taratonga and visit some of the nearby villages. Three worth a look at are Sunni to the north and Gandator and Kalu Kitting to the south-west. From Kalu Kitting, you can get back onto the main road at Nyama, between Nyala and Nyatiti. Here, there's a camp for the German

construction gang who have been building the road. They often have transport going to Nyala and some travellers have reported that they were allowed to use the camp swimming pool.

It is also possible to trek to Jebel Marra in the opposite direction. One couple suggested the easiest way to go is to take a lorry from Nyala to Nyama. From here there is a drivable track to Taratonga, from where you can hike to the crater. Return via Quaila and Nyatiti. The exact route you take will naturally depend on your objectives and the available time, but the following is one other possibility.

for Deriba, which is the local name given to the crater lakes. At the hot springs, the place to fill your water bottle is the stream just beyond them (straight ahead from the Quaila path) where you can see some palm trees. This is the last place you'll find water before you get to the crater bottom. From here onwards, the path is often quite hard to find, as the terrain is first stony and very steep and then ashy with stones and lots of ash ravines to fall into or get lost in. So take care! From the springs upwards there are no villages and few people around to help if you're in trouble.

The hardest part of the walk comes first, so start early when it's still cold and you won't have to drink much water. Looking at the springs coming from Quaila, the path is on the steep slope on your right (with Jebel Idwa straight ahead). It's very heavy going but it levels out and then you have to do a lot of clambering (sometimes on all fours) across the rocks. You need to concentrate hard, as it's a long way down in places.

After a couple of hours, the path starts to run parallel with the crater rim. The highest point of the mountain is on your right, but you'll probably be too tired to even contemplate the idea of attempting the very steep and probably dangerous ascent. Your first view of the crater takes about three hours from the hot springs as the path runs along the rim. It's a breathtaking sight. On the right is a green sulphur lake which fills a crater within the main crater, below almost vertical cliffs rising to the summit. On the left are two salt lakes. The grassy crater bottom is a startling contrast with the grey ash ravines below you on the other side. Apart from the livestock grazing on the crater pasture there are also baboons which live in the crater sides as well as in the ash ravines. I only heard one screaming above the green lake, but the other teachers spotted them in the ravines.

Assuming you want to get downhill, you'll have to be patient, as the path down is nearer to the far end of the crater. By the time you get to the bottom (about five hours after leaving the hot springs), you'll probably be running short of water. Fortunately, you won't have to go far, as you'll soon come to a muddy area where the cattle drink. If you look carefully, you'll find a spring very near the path where fresh, sulphur-free water flows out of the muddy ground. As far as I know, this is the only source of fresh water on the crater, although you can drink from the green lake if you're really desperate.

Those travelling in the opposite direction from the crater and/or Taratonga to Quaila are very likely to get lost unless they keep Jebel Idwa to their right and don't start descending towards the ravines. If the path you're on seems to be leading you down towards Idwa, it's better to retrace your steps towards the crater rim again. Otherwise, you'll probably get lost in the ravine without much water. You could come seriously unstuck. Coming from this side, Jebel Idwa is easy to spot. Looking ahead on the Quaila path, it's below you a little to the right. Once you get down to Nyatiti, you have the choice of going down the main road and taking a bus or lorry, or staying at the rest house. However, if you choose to stay there you must get permission, so you, or a representative of your group, will have to go down to the village and come back again. If you are in a hurry, it is possible to walk from the crater rim down to Nyatiti in a day as long as you start early. ∎

Route 2 Take a lorry from Nyala to Menawashi, which is basically just a lorry stop where several people sell food. Menawashi has no rest house, but the locals may offer you accommodation in their huts.

From Menawashi, it's a two-hour walk over flat, scrubby land to Marshing. There's usually an empty hut or two there; ask the village teacher where you can sleep. At the café in Marshing, you can get soup and bread and tea. There's also a market on Wednesdays and Sundays.

A five-hour walk from Marshing brings you to the beautiful village of Melemm. The *rest house* is next to the police station and the very friendly police will probably supply you with firewood, water and other necessities. Melemm's market takes place on Mondays and Fridays.

The all-night lorry ride from Melemm to Deribat takes you through beautiful hills, some of which are so steep that it may be necessary to winch the lorry up. There's no rest house in Deribat, but the village does have several tea houses, a café and a Monday market.

Jawa is a two-hour walk from Deribat. You may be able to find accommodation in the huge hospital. Market day in Jawa is Thursday.

About 1½ hours away is Sunni, one of the Jebel Marra's most scenic settlements. Sunni's large, old *rest house* has four beds. There's no souq, but a small shop sells rice, nuts, dates, cigarettes and the occasional chicken. Don't miss the 35-metre-high **waterfall** behind the power station.

From Sunni, it's a five-hour walk or scramble to Lugi. The views en route are beautiful but it gets very cold, especially at night, and there are only a few huts in the fields along the way. There's no rest house or market at Lugi, but there is a small shop with basic supplies.

The next leg is the 2¼-hour walk to Taratonga through a landscape of conifers and heather which is very similar to the Scottish highlands. Taratonga itself is a picturesque little village set on wooded, grassy slopes. It has a market on Saturday and a shop that sells

basic supplies. The *rest house* is in disrepair, so if you're there during the rainy season, it's better to look for an empty hut or try the schoolhouse. The village teacher speaks English and can arrange guides to the crater for you.

It's a good idea to get a guide up to the crater. The walk usually takes three hours with a guide but could take five to eight hours if you go it alone. The same applies between the crater and the next village of Kronga (also known as Kuela), which you can walk to in about five hours with a guide but much longer if you get lost.

The walk from Kronga to the village of Khartoum takes 1½ hours. Khartoum has a Saturday market. It's another 3½ hours to Nyatiti, with its well-stocked market, cafés, *rest house* and transport back to Nyala.

If you lack camping equipment and/or don't fancy walking, it's possible to buy donkeys and sell them again when you're ready to leave.

DAGU JEBELS

These hills are a two-day hike from Nyala and feature **prehistoric rock paintings**. This is beautiful walking country, especially after the rains, but watch out for the heskanit burrs which are very thick and sticky in this area.

KAFIA KINGI

This village, in the south-western corner of Southern Darfur, is most interesting for the people who live in the area. The Fallata Umboro, members of a non-Arab nomadic group, are descended from the Fulani people of West Africa and are famous for their *fakis*. A faki is usually a teacher, but the Fallata give their teachers the status of magicians. These fakis travel around, for one month each year, collecting roots and herbs. When they return, people come to them for spells and secret potions. The fakis' love potions are popular, especially among old women. The women pour the potion into the tea of the men whose attention they are trying to attract.

The Sudanese government has declared

the area around Kafia Kingi a national park. The park is barely accessible, but souq lorries occasionally travel into the region.

EL-FASHER

El-Fasher first gained prominence in the early part of the 18th century as a principal centre of the Fur Sultanate. It was also the starting point for one of Africa's most famous caravan routes, the Darb al-Arba'een (40 Days Road). Incredibly wealthy camel caravans laden with ebony, spices, ivory and beautiful cloth, as well as hundreds of slaves captured from other parts of Africa, regularly made the long trip across the desert to the great bazaars of Aswan and Asyut in Egypt.

In the early 19th century, as if slavery itself wasn't horror enough, Mohammed Ali commissioned two Coptic priests in Asyut to carry out castrations on most of the young male slaves who survived the arduous journey.

Although Mohammed had managed to extend his military might into other parts of the Sudan, his ambition to conquer El-Fasher and gain control of Darfur and the great caravan route was never realised. It was not until 1874, long after his death, that Darfur became a province of Egyptian Sudan. Egyptian control lasted until the time of the Mahdi and the subsequent downfall of the Khalifa in 1898. A religious zealot named Ali Dinar then established an autonomous sultanate based in El-Fasher. The sultanate lasted until 1916 when, on 6 November, a couple of British planes flew in and shot Sultan Ali Dinar dead from the air. This was the price he paid for joining the Turks in the war against the Allies. The locals of El-Fasher revere the sultan as a martyr, and his crest – three stars within a crescent moon – can still be seen today.

During WW II, El-Fasher was a small but important airbase for US C-47 cargo planes. It was basically a refuelling stop for planes flying the supply route from Miami to north Africa, but little then or since has encroached on the traditions of this pleasant old town – you may well see a sheikh galloping off into the country on his camel, a falcon perched on his wrist for the afternoon's sport. The camel is, indeed, still the preferred mode of transport. Souq lorries and aid workers' cars are the only petrol-driven vehicles to be seen.

As with much of Darfur, it can get bitterly cold at night, and in winter during the day too, so be prepared.

Things to See

The sultan's former palace now houses a small museum, where you can see the ruler's throne room, coffee house and some general exhibits on the Sudan. In the gardens are some exotic birds along with trees brought back from pilgrimages to Mecca and Medina.

Places to Stay & Eat

The government *rest house*, in the building next to the palace, is a good place to stay. It was once the British commissioner's residence. Some of the locals rent out rooms in their houses. Otherwise, approach aid workers in the area who may be able to put you up or suggest a place.

Buji's, one of the few restaurants in town, is on Palace Rd and serves decent roast beef and chips. Opposite Buji's is the only place in El-Fasher where you can get ice cream.

Getting There & Away

There are occasional air connections to Nyala. Souq lorries and a few buses travel to most destinations near El-Fasher. There is a weekly bus to Mellit and a twice-weekly bus to Kutum. There are also daily buses and lorries to Nyala. There is regular traffic into Libya, and the souqs often have wares brought in from Libya, which is cheaper than hauling them all the way across from Port Sudan.

MELLIT

This village, north of El-Fasher, is home to a large number of camel breeders and salt traders from the semi-nomadic Zaghawa tribe who, until recently, spoke only their own Saharan languages. They have now been Arabised, and today most Zaghawa also speak some form of Arabic and profess

Islam. The landscape between El-Fasher and Mellit is dominated by high perpendicular rock formations rising out of the desert floor, many of them topped by eagles' nests.

The salt traders of Mellit travel 140 km north by camel through the Tabago Hills to the village of Malha, where they meet the salt miners who come down from the Meidob Hills. The salt is then taken back to Mellit and on to El-Fasher.

Mellit's camel traders take a much more arduous route. They travel for 27 days, north from Mellit through the Tabago and Meidob hills, across the Sahara Desert to the oases of Al-Atrun and Nukheila and on to Jebel Uweinat on the Libyan border, where they sell their camels. If you dare, you may accompany the Zaghawa on this trek, but they do tend to lose camels and a few people along the way! The traveller and writer Wilfred Thesiger shot game in this area, but there's not much to be seen today.

In addition to a busy camel market, there is also a women's handicrafts centre, where you can buy clothes, carpets and some beautiful pottery.

According to some Westerners who have worked out this way, the Zaghawa have little time for the central Sudanese government, and may move to set up some sort of breakaway state. Whatever the truth of this, there is little doubt that banditry has been stepped up in recent years, making travel in the region a hazardous undertaking. There is a curfew for Whites in vehicles from 10 pm to 5 am. As one observer said, 'The best way to acquire a new 4WD is to take one from Whites'. Western travellers are also advised not to be seen in a vehicle with police, who tend to be the object of bandits' special attentions.

KUTUM

This small and quite old town, not far from El-Fasher, is probably not a good place to visit. The bandits seem to be particularly thick around here, and some of the stories about what they get up to with anyone unlucky enough to be in their path are bloodcurdling to say the least.

AL-GENEINA

Al-Geneina, the Sudan's westernmost town, is little more than a principal border post for crossing into Chad. Once the centre of a powerful sultanate, Al-Geneina ('garden'), is now the seat of the 'powerless' Sultan of Massalit, the son of a ruler installed by the British in the first half of this century. Although his kingdom is divided between Chad and the Sudan, the sultan still holds court every day in a courtyard at the base of his palace. With a bit of diplomacy, you might be able to talk your way into the palace for an official audience. The town is surrounded by citrus and mango groves. There is a small colony of refugees from Chad, and goods from as far away as Nigeria are traded in the souq. Just outside the town is a small village of blacksmiths, where you can buy an authentic desert dagger for about S£500.

There is a government *rest house* in town. Souq lorries from El-Fasher travel regularly to Chad.

TINE

The village of Tine is a two-day lorry ride north of Al-Geneina. It used to be possible to cross into Chad from here, but the war in Chad may have put an end to that, as well as causing increased banditry in the Sudan. To combat this, the Sudanese government formed a camel corps of armed nomads who have been quite effective in tracking down these bandits. Their presence has given the place a sort of Wild West atmosphere.

TO/FROM THE CENTRAL AFRICAN REPUBLIC

Lorries from Nyala sometimes go all the way to Bangui in the Central African Republic, via the Sudanese village of Am Dafog and the Central African Republic border town of Birao. The cost of the trip will depend partly on the driver and also on the availability of fuel; it can take from four to 17 days, as the lorry drivers often spend a couple of days selling their wares in souqs along the way.

Between August and December, the rains prevent lorries from operating between Nyala and Bangui. The police also refuse to grant travel permits allowing visitors to head west at that time.

An alternative way of travelling this route involves taking a lorry from Nyala to Rahad al-Berdi, where you can stay at the police station. The trip takes at least 12 hours.

Once in Rahad, ask around for a guide and animal transport to Am Dafog. Donkeys and guides are available, but camel trains are the usual choice. The 160-km trip through shallow swamps and coarse grass is tough, but shouldn't take longer than five days.

The police station at Am Dafog provides accommodation; food is available at a café. An interesting souq straddles the border between the Central African Republic and the Sudan, and the lake here has water even at the end of the dry season.

Birao, a town often referred to by the Sudanese as Daba, is a 1½-day journey from Am Dafog. You can hire camels for this trip in Am Dafog. Along the way, you will ford at least five deep wadis and meet nomadic cattle herders. The nomads are usually very helpful and hospitable. You stay with them, eat with them – prime steak, fresh milk and yoghurt – and, if you're lucky, share some of their music with them.

One British couple who drove this route in the opposite direction, seeing no other vehicles for three days, could only say, 'What a horrible track of sand'.

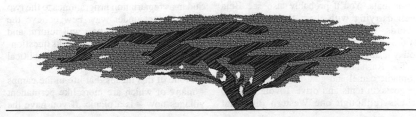

Eastern Sudan

Eastern Sudan is one of the country's most accessible regions. A 1200-km stretch of reasonable paved road links Khartoum with Kassala and Port Sudan, travelling through terrain that is basically flat, except in the Red Sea Hills area south of Port Sudan. The road, which was completed in 1980, has greatly facilitated the transport of goods and people. It was built in this region because much of the Sudan's sorghum, an important staple, is grown here. The road was beginning to crumble along certain stretches in the early 1990s, but some attempt is being made to upgrade the worst stretches.

In the late 1980s, drought and pestilence resulted in poor crops and increased the great hardship faced by the locals and the thousands of refugees crowded into the region, but in the past couple of years crops have been more successful – to the point where the Sudan surprised many countries involved in aid programmes by announcing it was in the position to export sorghum in 1992.

There is a great diversity of people in eastern Sudan. In the Red Sea Hills are the nomadic Beja people. They speak Bedawiya, a language without script; according to some experts, they bear a close resemblance to the ancient Egyptians. Divided roughly into five tribes, for a long time they defied attempts by the central government to bring them under control. Only in the 1920s did the British-run administration have any luck in extracting taxes from them. The vault-shaped tents you may see in parts of eastern Sudan are peculiar to the Beja: on two-layered wooden frames are stretched smoked palm mats. You'll probably also see Beja men carrying with them their traditional swords – the sheath widens towards the point of the sword; what they get up to with these today is anyone's guess.

The Rashaida people, near Kassala, are nomadic camel and goat breeders who live in goatskin tents and drive Toyota pick-up trucks (although one Western diplomat claims the government has confiscated the vehicles because they were primarily used for gun-running). The Rashaida are relative newcomers, having migrated from Saudi-Arabia about 150 years ago, and they still maintain close links with their kin across the Red Sea.

In the Gedaref area, the Shukriya Arabs predominate, and throughout the region there are Eritrean and Ethiopian refugees, who, after fleeing drought, famine and war in Eritrea and Tigre, have in many cases become more or less permanent residents.

The refugee situation in eastern Sudan has long since been overtaken in urgency by the question of internally displaced people resulting from the years of civil war in the south. More than 300,000 refugees live in camps and settlements along the 439-km stretch of road from Wad Medani to Kassala. From the road, you cannot really see how bad conditions are in the camps. As many as 20% of the refugees – mainly women and children – are malnourished, disease is rife, and there are shortages of shelter, water and clothing. On the other hand, many have moved into the towns and found work. According to one observer, relations between the local people and the refugees are fairly good. As a matter of tradition, many people used to cross over from Eritrea as seasonal farm labour – the only difference is that now they stay for the rest of the year. With war behind them and Eritrea and Ethiopia attempting to haul themselves back onto their feet, the United Nations High Commissioner for Refugees hopes to wind down the operations in eastern Sudan as repatriation programmes to the two countries get under way. Few believe the whole refugee population will return, and even the definition 'refugee' looks questionable now in the light of the new political status quo.

None of this means that life in the camps – many of which are more like permanent villages now – is a picnic. If you have the

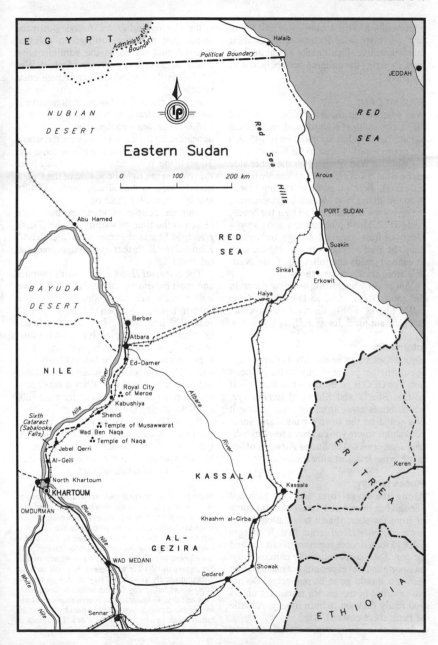

opportunity to visit a camp, you will see in just what straitened circumstances their inhabitants live. Don't make a 'sightseeing' visit, though – the refugees need help, not an audience.

WAD MEDANI

Wad Medani, on the Blue Nile, is the first major city south of Khartoum along the road to Port Sudan. It has a population of 145,000 but not much of interest to the visitor.

Opposite Wad Medani, on the other side of the Blue Nile (which is supposedly free of bilharzia), there's a good swimming beach. A box from the Wad Medani vegetable souq to the village of Hantub, just near the beach, costs S£10. Hantub has quite a good souq – plenty of fruit, vegetables, eggs, turkey and duck. In Wad Medani various staples, such as canned goods and toilet paper, are available from small grocery shops.

You can buy interesting wedding drums in the souq. Sharia Seif ad-Din Sharfa (also called Sharia el-Nil), the river-side avenue, is a pleasant place for a stroll.

Information

Nobody seems to be terribly bothered here about whether you register with the police or not. The GPO is on the corner of Sharia Seif ad-Din Sharfa and Sharia al-Jumhuriyya, which heads away from the river. Along it you will find the town's banks, and some bookshops where you can buy a few English-language books. The Sudan Airways office is off to the left, just after the banks.

Places to Stay

Along the river front are two pleasant enough but overpriced hotels. As you come in from the souq shaabi bus station out of town, the *Nile Hotel* is the first. It charges S£1835 for a double room with bath, fan and air-con. Staff seem extremely curious about passports and travel permits but make no hint that you should go to be registered. Do not eat or drink in the garden restaurant unless you really do want to burn money. A bottle of Pepsi there costs S£71!

In much the same vein, but a little cheaper,

is the *Continental Hotel*, further down the street, just past the lurid-green colonial remnant that serves as the administrative centre for the Gezira province, of which Wad Medani is the capital. A double here costs S£1690.

A much cheaper and simpler alternative is the *Central Hotel*. It costs from S£400 to S£500 for a room with three beds. As so often appears to be the case, you pay for the whole room, no matter how many of you there are. To get to this hotel, take the street away from the river on the right-hand side of the Continental. Walk to the railway yards and turn left; it's about 50 metres on.

Another couple of cheapies that were closed at the time of writing are the *Gezira Hotel*, on Sharia al-Jumhuriyya, and the *Al-Khawad Hotel*, further up the same street and off to the right.

The *Imperial Hotel* is the town's premier and most expensive establishment. It's on a traffic circle near the Nile, but if you're coming in from the souq shaabi, you won't see it. The Imperial is a favourite with Sudanese honeymoon couples. It's also one of the few places in town with regular supplies of Pepsi and ice cream. The hotel is fairly new, with a TV in the lounge and air-con and flush toilets in the rooms, and it has a small rose garden in front. The rates can increase substantially during holidays.

If you stay at this hotel, you will probably see many Sudanese newlyweds with intricate henna tattoos on their feet and arms. A US aid worker who got tattooed described this traditional Sudanese practice:

Sudanese brides arrive at the hotel with henna designs on their feet and arms; the men have similar decorations, but only on their left hands. After a paste is made from the henna leaves and painted on the skin, it is left to dry and then scraped off. Then you are seated over a smoking hole and covered up for 'curing'. You are supposed to stay over the hole as long as possible. Foreigners usually can't last more than half an hour, although ideally you should stay at least an hour. It takes about half a day for the tattoos to completely cure and dry. To maintain the brown-maroon colouring of the designs, you should spread oil over the tattoo about two or three times a day. The result, of course, is continually slippery skin.

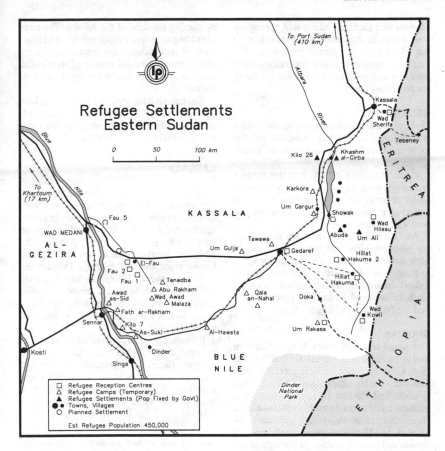

Refugee Settlements Eastern Sudan

Est Refugee Population 450,000

□ Refugee Reception Centres
△ Refugee Camps (Temporary)
▲ Refugee Settlements (Pop Fixed by Govt)
●● Towns, Villages
○ Planned Settlement

Places to Eat

The *Gulinar Restaurant*, near the GPO, serves good Ethiopian curries, chicken & chips, yoghurt and salads. Each table is painted with the name of a different African country.

The park behind the GPO is a pleasant place to sit in during the evening. You can get fuul (S£40), omelettes, ice creams (S£25) and tea, or smoke on a *sheesha* (waterpipe). Behind the park is a place where you can sometimes get quite a decent serve of kebab, potato stew and salad. There are a few Pepsi stands around the market.

Getting There & Around

There are buses and lorries from the souq shaabi (a few km out of town) to Khartoum (S£175, about 3½ hours), Sennar (S£135, two hours), Gedaref (S£250, about three hours), Kassala (S£620, six hours) and Port Sudan. The fare will be more if you get one of the more comfortable buses. A red share taxi between the souq shaabi and town costs S£30 a head.

EL-FAU

There are numerous refugee camps and settlements along the road between Wad

Medani and Gedaref. Many that sprang up over the years around El-Fau have taken on the air of more permanent settlements. El-Fau is a common rest stop for traffic on the road to and from Kassala. You can get food, tea and Pepsi here.

GEDAREF

Gedaref is a dirty semi-industrial city with a population of 30,000. It is renowned only for its sesame seeds, huge quantities of which are auctioned daily.

If you somehow get stuck in this sesame centre and need a place to stay, try the *Amir Hotel* or approach an expatriate. The souq and grocery stores are well stocked, so you won't go hungry.

As Gedaref is along the main road, there are frequent lorry and bus connections in both directions – west to Khartoum or north to Kassala and Port Sudan. The main road is a short distance from town. If you choose to hitch, be aware of the dangers, particularly if you are female.

SHOWAK

The small town of Showak is the eastern Sudan headquarters for the United Nations High Commissioner for Refugees, and for a Colorado-based charity called LALMBA (pronounced 'la-lum-ba'). They operate a medical clinic and a nationally renowned eye clinic that brings in visiting ophthalmologists. LALMBA also runs small medical clinics and feeding centres in the villages of Abuda and Um Ali, near the Ethiopian border.

KHASHM AL-GIRBA

Khashm al-Girba is a relatively uninteresting town 62 km north of Showak. Several thousand Nubians have been resettled in the area, after being displaced from their own lands by the creation of Lake Nasser when the Aswan High Dam was built.

A dam, built on the Atbara River just outside town, has proved a classic example of a development project whose impact was miscalculated and underestimated. The dam caused a range of environmental problems by altering the flow of the Atbara. The river banks began to erode more quickly and large areas of date palms were destroyed. As the dates were a principal source of livelihood, many people were forced to migrate to other towns.

You can visit the area and swim in the lake that was created by the dam. However, this is supposedly a military area, so you can't stay overnight.

KASSALA

Kassala, a city of 150,000 people, is famous for its fruit and its jebels. The bizarre sugar-loaf jebels can be seen on the horizon from several km away and add a certain mystical beauty to the place. The city, which lies on the Gash River, is the centre of power of the Khatmiya Brotherhood, a rival to the Mahdi family since the last century. Despite the arrival in power in 1989 of al-Bashir and his NIF backers, these and a couple of other traditional families that have long held sway in the Sudan retain much of their financial and social clout.

Kassala's souq is considered to be one of the best in the Sudan and sells grapefruit, oranges, dates, pomegranates, melons and bananas, as well as cloth, local crafts and jewellery. A lot of the silver jewellery is made by the veiled women of the Rashaida tribe.

Most, if not all, of the Rashaida live in the goatskin tents which you will see by the road as you approach Kassala and Port Sudan. The women wear unique veils and thick silver bracelets and necklaces. Silver is a status symbol for the Rashaida.

A Rashaida girl announces her eligibility for marriage by wearing an intricately woven silver veil and several necklaces. When the girl finds a man she likes, she expresses interest by lifting the veil to expose her chin to him. (The Rashaida consider chins erotic!) If the man accepts the invitation to marry her, he then has to come up with a hundred camels for her family before the wedding. Take advantage of any opportunity you have to attend one of the interesting Rashaida wedding ceremonies. The big wedding season is after Ramadan.

Kassala is also a favourite destination for

honeymoon couples from other parts of the Sudan.

Information

Registration You are required to register with the police upon arrival in Kassala. The police can also assist you with obtaining permission to visit the huge Wad Sherifa refugee camp nearby. The office is to the north-east of town, about 600 metres from the central minibus and box lot.

Money There seems to be a dearth of banks

here, so changing money could pose a problem.

Post & Telecommunications The GPO is on the north-western side of the souq. It claims to have an express-mail service and international telephone (good luck!) available from 8 am to 8 pm.

Things to See & Do

You can walk into the hills a few km from town (see the following Khatmiya section); go in the late afternoon for a respite from the

PLACES TO STAY
5 El-Sharq Hotel
8 Safa Hotel
9 Qasr el-Nur Hotel
10 Qasr el-Sharq Hotel
13 Ryad Hotel
14 Medina Hotel
15 Kassala Hotel
16 Toteel Hotel
17 Hipton Hotel
18 Bashair Hotel
20 Taka Hotel
21 El-Salam Hotel
23 El-Nil Hotel
24 El-Nekhil Hotel

OTHER
1 GPO & Radio Mast
2 Kassala Fantastic Food
3 Minibus to Souq Shaabi
4 Sudan Airways
6 Tea Shops
7 Minibus & Box Lot
11 School
12 Mosque
19 Drop-off Lot for Late Buses
22 Shell Service Station

To Police & Registration

Main Street

Street of a Thousand Fools

To Souq Shaabi

Kassala

0   50   100 m

To Khatmiya

stuffy heat of the town and a possible look at the **baboons**.

In April 1993 the first **International Camel Races** to be held in the Sudan were staged at Kassala. This may not become a regular event, but it might be worth checking out. The Tourist Information Office in Khartoum will know if anything of the kind is happening.

Places to Stay

The *Taka* and *El-Salam*, opposite the Shell service station, are cheap lokanda-style hotels. The first charges S£80 for a bed, while the latter, which several travellers have recommended, charges S£120.

The *Khartoum Hotel* is the cheapest place in town; beds there only cost S£50.

A pretty bad deal is the *Kassala Hotel*, where a bed costs S£200. The fans are so noisy you'd probably rather bathe in sweat than try to sleep with one on. If there is ever any water in the stinking showers and toilets, it just seems to excite the cockroaches. Next door, the *Medina* is little better.

In the middle price range, the two best deals in town are the *Toteel* and *Safa* hotels. The former has rooms with three beds, air-con and fan for S£700. The shower and toilet combinations are outside. It is a cool, clean and friendly place. The Safa is a brighter place, and its showers and toilets positively sparkle. A small room with two beds and a fan costs S£700, something bigger with air-con thrown in is S£1100, and the same with ensuite bath is S£1500.

Kassala mosque

The *Ryad Hotel*, pretty well in the centre of the souq, is not a bad, if you can get in.

Another pretty reasonable place, the *Qasr el-Nur Hotel*, just down from the Safa, has rooms with fan for S£450 and others with noisy air-con for S£750. It's often full. A little way down from it, the *Qasr el-Sharq Hotel* has doubles with fan for S£590 and with air-con for S£990. However, they always seem to be in the midst of building works and consequently don't apparently have any rooms.

The most expensive place in town is the *Hipton* (it's hard not to believe the inspiration for the name came from a similarly named international chain of hotels). For S£2030 you can have a double room with fan, air-con, TV, sitting room and new shower.

Places to Eat

The *Hipton cafeteria* on the roof is not a bad place to get a filling meal of kebab, kofta, sausages or kofta with salad for about S£400.

At more down-to-earth prices, you can get a range of food at *Kassala Fantastic Food*. It has fish, fuul, some meat, sweets and, to drink, sweetened milk (laban or haleeb). On the western side of the market is a good tea shop, where you can also smoke a sheesha if you want.

Getting There & Away

Air The weekly flight to Khartoum is supposed to leave on Wednesdays and costs S£4120.

Bus Several buses a day leave both Khartoum and Port Sudan for Kassala, the bulk of them early in the morning. As usual they take you to a station a few km out of town. If your bus happens to arrive late at night, you'll probably be dropped at an old lot near the Shell service station closer to town.

The Sunshine Express bus company operates buses to Port Sudan. Tickets for the eight-hour trip cost S£645. Tea and iced water are served en route, but bring your own cup – sharing the public cup is not recommended.

The Taysir, Arrow and Safina companies have daily buses to Khartoum. Tickets with these companies cost around S£930. Tickets on the less comfortable buses (that look more like trucks) are about S£200 cheaper. The trip takes eight to nine hours. The fare to Wad Medani is S£620 for the six-hour journey. Minibuses run regularly to Gedaref and cost S£240.

To/From Eritrea There are several buses a week from Kassala to the Eritrean capital, Asmara. They cost S£1700 and spend an eternity going from one security check to another. It might be better to take a box to Tesany and then a bus from there on to Asmara (29.25 Birr). The best exchange rate you'll get will be on the border at Tesany, from Sudanese pounds into Birr. Hard currencies don't seem to excite anyone much there, so you may want to stock up a little on S£.

Getting Around
Minibuses leave from in front of the Sudan Airways office for the souq shaabi (the intercity bus station) and cost S£15.

Buses to the village of Khatmiya leave the main bus and box lot and cost S£10. You can also get a bus to the refugee camp of Wad Sherifa from the same lot.

KHATMIYA
You can begin a climb into the hills from the village of Khatmiya, at the base of the jebels. In the early evening, bats appear in the sky and baboons come down from the jebels to drink from the village well. On moonlit nights, the effect is quite eerie.

Married couples come to Khatmiya to drink from a well here. This is supposed to bring them good luck and help women become pregnant.

The village is mainly made of thatched huts, although the mosque is a more solid structure, dating back a few hundred years.

WAD SHERIFA
East of Kassala, near the Ethiopian border, the Wad Sherifa refugee camp must be one

of the largest in the world. With a population of 60,000, it is a city in itself. If you want to visit the camp, you must first obtain permission from the police and the Sudanese Commissioner of Refugees in Kassala.

HAIYA
Haiya is a railway-junction town 351 km north of Kassala. From here, you can catch the train westward to Atbara.

ERKOWIT
This beautiful, isolated resort is in the Red Sea Hills, 30 km off the main road between Kassala and Port Sudan. The hotel is surrounded by picturesque hills, streams and vegetation. Whatever truth there is to claims of it being converted into a Palestinian training camp, it is definitely closed and out of bounds to foreigners.

SUAKIN
The small island of Suakin, 58 km south of Port Sudan, is linked to the mainland by a short causeway. Once a major trading centre, Suakin today is noteworthy for its unique, but crumbling, architecture. Many of the buildings are made from coral.

Suakin's history is cloaked in myth and legend. One legend concerns the origin of the name Suakin, which translates as 'land of Ginn'. Apparently, Queen Balgies, of the Sabaa Kingdom of Yemen, sent seven virgin maidens to King Solomon in Jerusalem. On the way to the Holy City, however, a storm drove the ship off course to Suakin, and by the time it arrived in Jerusalem, all the girls were pregnant. They claimed that they had had sexual relations with the Ginn, a demon of Suakin.

As early as the 10th century BC, Suakin was an important commercial centre and was used by Ramses III as a port for his trade with the lands across the Red Sea. In subsequent centuries, it declined in importance and it was not until the 19th century, under Ottoman rule, that Suakin again prospered, this time as a slave-trading centre. In 1881, the Mahdi restored the coral buildings. Today the buildings are again crumbling, for with the establishment of Port Sudan in 1905, Suakin was superseded and deserted.

It used to be necessary to get special permission in Port Sudan to go to Suakin, but that requirement seems to have fallen by the wayside.

Places to Stay & Eat
The best place to stay is the *Amir el-Sharq Hotel*, which is on the main highway from Kassala to Port Sudan, by the turn-off to Suakin. Singles/doubles cost S£382/547. You can get decent meals in the restaurant and they will take care of the registration formalities, if they are still a problem.

There are three lokandas along the road into Suakin. The first, the *Ibad el-Rahman*, is off to the right, a short way in from the highway. A little further on, to the left, is the *Ar-Rasheed*, and further on again, also on the left, is the *As-Sahilein*. All have beds for S£150 and are much of a muchness.

Getting There & Away
There is a frequent minibus service running between Suakin and Port Sudan, terminating at the bus lot near the Omyia Hotel. The one-hour ride costs about S£70. The other option is to get a share taxi, which costs S£200 per person.

PORT SUDAN
The harbour city of Port Sudan has a population of more than 200,000. It was established by the British in 1905 as a sea port to facilitate the export of raw commodities such as cotton, sorghum and sesame. The city has fallen into disrepair and decay – even the carefully planned parks are now defoliated – but the beautiful lattice woodwork on the windows of many of the older buildings is one of the signs of a more elegant past. The main attractions in and around Port Sudan are the trip to Suakin and the possibility of Red Sea diving.

This is Sudan's export and import window to the world, but as the country's international political isolation has grown, activity has slowed to a trickle. What does come in, however, is cheaper here than elsewhere in the country, and you even come across a few things that don't seem to make it past Port Sudan – Egyptian bottled water, Baraka, for instance.

Information
Registration The Red Sea Province Headquarters is on the waterfront, but the office for registration is actually in a narrow lane behind the main building. Officials seem to take this quite seriously here, demanding a photocopy of your travel permit. They keep your passport and make you pick up everything in the afternoon. They even insist that you check with them before leaving Port Sudan, although it seems more sensible to ignore this: the bureaucratic hassle is a pain, and once you've left, who cares?

Tourist Office The local tourist office has been closed and its functions usurped by the fairly useless Ebonus travel agency. Staff there can give you some vague information about diving (see the following Diving section).

Money There are several banks in Port Sudan. The Bank of Khartoum is in the centre of town, next to the Sudan Shipping Line building. There is something of a black market too and, if anything, the rates seem better here than in Khartoum or Wadi Halfa. Use your common sense if you are considering changing money this way.

Post & Telecommunications The GPO is on Sharia ash-Sharfa, and the telephone, telex and express-mail services are all here too, for what that's worth. A better bet might be the CMSB office next to the Bohein Hotel, which claims to offer international phone and fax connections.

Diving
Hamido travel agency and Red Sea Enterprise (run by Captain Halim) can help arrange diving trips in the area.

You can also try Ebonus travel agency, which is an agent for a German team organising diving trips from Arous, north of Port

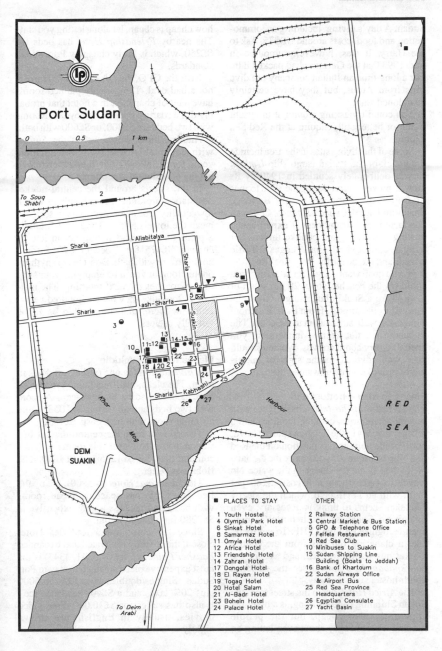

Port Sudan

0   0.5   1 km

To Souq
Shabi

To Deim
Arabi

DEIM
SUAKIN

Khor
Mog

Harbour

RED
SEA

Sharia Alisbitalya

Sharia

ash-Sharfa

Sharia

Sharia Kabhashi

Sharia Suakin

Eissa

■ PLACES TO STAY

1 Youth Hostel
4 Olympia Park Hotel
6 Sinkat Hotel
8 Samarmaz Hotel
11 Omyia Hotel
12 Africa Hotel
13 Friendship Hotel
14 Zahran Hotel
17 Dongola Hotel
18 El Rayan Hotel
19 Togag Hotel
20 Hotel Salam
21 Al-Badr Hotel
23 Bohein Hotel
24 Palace Hotel

OTHER

2 Railway Station
3 Central Market & Bus Station
5 GPO & Telephone Office
7 Felfela Restaurant
9 Red Sea Club
10 Minibuses to Suakin
15 Sudan Shipping Line
   Building (Boats to Jeddah)
16 Bank of Khartoum
22 Sudan Airways Office
   & Airport Bus
25 Red Sea Province
   Headquarters
26 Egyptian Consulate
27 Yacht Basin

Sudan. A day's diving, including accommodation and food, costs around US$75. Ask to see Harry. It was, however, rumoured in mid-1993 that the Germans had packed it in. For a long time an Italian company ran dive trips from Arous, but they have certainly abandoned ship.

You could try asking around at the yacht basin, or better still, enquire at the Red Sea Club.

Some of the diving sites in the area include the wreck of the Italian cargo ship *Umbria* (it was deliberately scuttled in 1940 by its crew to prevent surrendering the 3000 tonnes of bombs it contained to the British); Shaabrumi Reef (where Jacques Cousteau conducted his Precontinent II experiments, leaving behind a giant podlike underwater hangar and several shark cages); Turtle Island; and the beautiful Dolphins' Reef.

If you just want to go for a swim, you could try the beaches about 20 km south of town. Take a Suakin bus and get out at the turn-off to the airport. From there it's about a three-km walk straight out to the coast. The Sudanese are not keen swimmers, so you needn't worry about crowds. Women should keep well covered, as the sight of bikinis might provoke some unwanted hostility.

Places to Stay – bottom end

The 50-bed *youth hostel* is a basic place with several dormitories, cooking facilities and a refrigerator. It's in the Salabona part of town, north of the port, and its position on the Red Sea is picturesque – if you ignore the garbage on the beach and the sludge in the water. No waves to catch though. It costs S£80 per night with an IYHF card, which the sleepy caretaker seems to think is necessary, even though no Sudanese youth hostel is now even recognised by the IYHF. To get there, take a clattering old bus from the central market bus station for S£5, and ask for the *beit shabab*. You should see the standard youth-hostel signs anyway.

The *Africa Hotel*, down the street from the Sudan Shipping Line building, is a dive. It's apparently also cheap, but the people running it seem cagey about even letting on

how cheap is cheap, let alone letting you stay. The nearby *Friendship Hotel* has beds for S£250, which is fairly cheap by Port Sudan standards.

Near the GPO, the *Olympia Park Hotel* is not a bad deal. The garishly painted rooms have a bit of character, in a hotel that probably did a roaring trade in its heyday. Rooms with two beds are S£400, or S£600 with bath.

Another block north-east is the *Sinkat*, with acceptable singles/doubles/triples going for S£380/640/780. It takes a while to get the attention of reception.

In the streets around the central-market bus station are quite a few hotels in which low quality does not necessarily seem to mean the lowest prices. The *Hotel Salam* is a place of last resort if you get in late. It charges S£475 for a bed or S£915 for a double room with bath. Don't leave anything on the floor, or you'll be emptying your stuff of cockroaches the next morning. The mattresses look like they have a hundred years' grime in them, and are so thin as to be virtually useless.

Places to Stay – middle

The *Bohein Hotel* is one of the best deals in town. The clean, well-maintained rooms all have fans and some have air-con. A room with two beds and no bath is S£1055, while a similar room with bath costs S£1990.

The *Omyia*, near the central-market bus station, has quite reasonable rooms with air-con and bath for S£1275 and S£1890. The Bohein is better.

The *Samarmaz Hotel* (☎ 5800), out by the Red Sea Club, has spacious, clean rooms with baths and fan. It's a mite expensive at S£2280 for a double room.

Since the colonial-era Red Sea Hotel closed, the recently renovated and expanded *Baasher Palace Hotel* (☎ 3341, 3343) is the most expensive place at which to stay in Port Sudan. Singles/doubles cost S£3750/5000 plus 20% taxes and a S£40 'residence fee'. It also has suites for S£10,000. Free video movies, usually in English, are shown nightly.

Places to Eat

The restaurant at the *Baasher Palace Hotel* serves some very good meals. Try the succulent chicken curry & rice for S£350 (if you're in the mood to splash out a little).

Another posh place to eat is the *Red Sea Club* (not to be confused with the Red Sea Hotel). Take your passport along and you can take out temporary day membership, which entitles you to use the swimming pool and snooker tables and to eat whatever the cook feels like serving. This is also a good place to meet divers and arrange a diving trip.

At the end of Sharia Suakin, by the yacht basin, is a good little kebab joint where you can sit by the water. Next door is a drink stand that sells, among other things, pretty revolting alcohol-free beer.

Not far from the Sinkat Hotel is a branch, believe it or not, of the Egyptian ta'amiyya chain *Felfelas*, although it's a pretty poor cousin. In the central market you'll find a whole collection of fuul, ta'amiyya, meat and juice stands.

Getting There & Away

Air There are occasional international flights from Port Sudan to Cairo and Jeddah. There are also twice-daily connections to Khartoum, at S£6220 one way.

Bus Buses terminate at the souq shaabi, a few km to the north-east of town. There are daily buses between Kassala and Port Sudan. They cost S£645 (but can go up to S£900 or more on holidays or when availability is low) and take around eight hours. Sunshine Express is one of the better companies.

Buses to and from Khartoum take at least 16 hours, and sometimes, if they are running

particularly late, pull in at a highway rest stop for the night before pushing on to their destination. You'll be grateful for your sleeping bag if that happens. Buses leave between 6 and 7 am as a rule, aiming to complete the trip in one hit. Fares vary according to the company and the comfort factor. A ticket on the cheaper buses is S£1730.

There are three buses a week to Asmara, the Eritrean capital.

Train The 'super' train is the Sudan's 'nice' train. It leaves Port Sudan on Thursdays, as indeed does the ordinary train – or at least that's what the timetable says. It takes a minimum of 30 hours to get to Khartoum, stopping only at Atbara and Shendi. Fares to Khartoum are: 1st class, S£2005; 2nd class, S£1510; and 3rd class, S£865. To Atbara the fares are: 1st class, S£1280; 2nd class, S£1070; and 3rd class, S£700.

The ordinary train is considerably slower – at least 2½ days by the admission of rail officials – and makes more stops. The fares to Khartoum are: sleeper, S£2670; 1st class, S£1600; 2nd class, S£1075; and 3rd class, S£640. The sleeper to Atbara is S£1620, while 3rd class is S£390.

Book a couple of days in advance for sleepers and 1st class.

Lorry The souq-lorry parks are in Deim Arabi, just south of the city's outskirts.

Boat It used to be possible to get a boat to and from Jeddah (Saudi Arabia), Port Sudan and Suez, but there is virtually no passenger traffic at all now. Occasionally a service runs to Jeddah, at a cost of S£10,000. The agent's office is in the Sudan Shipping Line building (see the Port Sudan map).

If you're desperate for the seafaring experience, the only other way might be to get passage on one of the freight ships moored in the harbour – not many success stories have been reported on that front either.

Getting Around

To/From the Airport An airport bus takes

you from the Sudan Airways office in town to the airport, about 18 km south.

AROUS

Arous, 50 km north of Port Sudan and once an overpriced tourist resort run by an Italian company, has recently hosted a small German dive firm called Tommy's. To arrange diving with them, see the Ebonus travel agency in Port Sudan. It was rumoured in mid-1993 that the Germans had decided to close shop. There is, however, excellent diving in the colourful coral reefs offshore. If you have all your own equipment, you might be able to go it alone; bring your own food and water supplies.

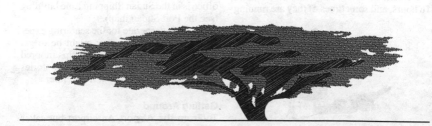

Southern Sudan

WARNING Southern Sudan is a war zone and is closed to travellers. Travel in this region at your own risk.

At the time of writing, travel south along the White Nile from Kosti to Juba, either overland or by steamer, was impossible for foreigners. The Sudanese People's Liberation Movement (SPLM) Anya-nya 2 rebels have been waging a guerrilla war against the government since 1983, when rebel leader John Garang went into hiding to reactivate the SPLM. Although a cease-fire was called by the government and John Garang in March 1993, fighting was continuing between rival rebel factions.

The main reason for the rebellion in the south was the then prime minister Nimeiri's declaration of shari'a, which made Islamic law applicable to the entire country. The SPLM, which represents the predominantly Christian and animist southerners, kept up the hostilities even after the 1985 coup that ousted Nimeiri and brought in the one-year rule of the Transitional Military Council (TMC). The rebels continued their fight against the government of Sadiq al-Mahdi because, although the new leader regularly announced the 'imminent abrogation of shari'a', he did not implement this promise. The 1989 coup that brought Lieutenant General al-Bashir, and through him an Islamist government, to power only served to exacerbate matters. The government's comparative military success in its 1992 dry-season offensive was due partly to the open factional fighting between rebels loyal to John Garang and at least two other groups, and the loss of support from such sources as the toppled President Mengistu of Ethiopia.

The central government lost control of the south when the railway line between Babanusa and Wau was sabotaged, the Nile steamer travelling between Kosti and Juba was blown up (in February 1984) and roads throughout the region were mined. Chevron-sponsored oil-exploration projects in the Bentiu area were abandoned due to rebel attacks, and French engineers were forced to stop work on the building of the Jonglei Canal. Although the government has now re-established a measure of control in the towns, fighting between rival rebel factions and the apparent failure of peace talks in Abuja, Nigeria, combine to make the area as risky to travel in as ever.

Travel to all southern towns and villages, including Juba, Torit and Wau, is unsafe and illegal. At the time of writing, travel permits were not being issued for these and most other southern destinations.

Travel to Kosti, and beyond to Sennar, Dinder, Dinder National Park, Ed-Damazin and Er-Roseires, however, poses no problems.

If the civil war is resolved, the roads cleared of mines, autonomous Arab tribal militias placated and the south reopened for travel, the following information will again be applicable.

KOSTI

Kosti, a relatively small city along the White Nile, was named after a Greek shopkeeper. There's not much of interest here except, perhaps, the Kenana sugar plant. The plant is a significant development project for the Sudan. The post office is across the road from the Abu Zayd Hotel, a small phone office is further along Sharia Markaz (away from the river), and a branch of the Bank of Khartoum is by the radio mast.

Places to Stay & Eat

The lokanda-style *Tabidi Hotel*, built around a courtyard, has been recommended by travellers. A bed in a room of three costs S£150. To get to it, walk right down Sharia Markaz, the main street, towards the river and turn right one block before the end. Take the next left, and it's on your right. It's a short walk away from the river bank.

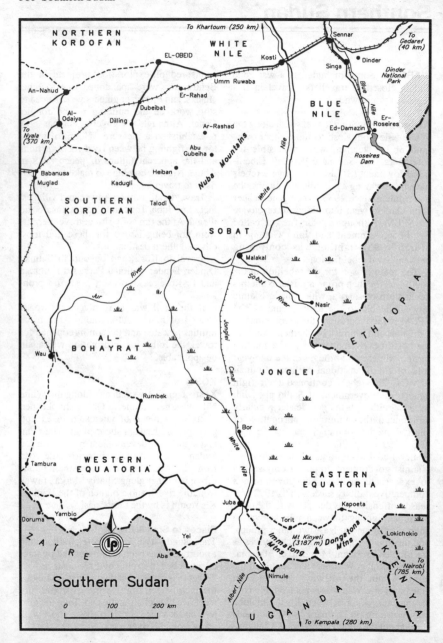

Southern Sudan

0   100   200 km

A few blocks further along the river and back a bit is another small place, the *Hotel Kosti*, which has beds for S£80.

The *Abu Zayd Hotel*, on Sharia Markaz and virtually in the middle of the town, is basic but clean enough and costs S£200 for a two-bed room. The shower is on the roof, and if you feel like having a hot one, just wait until the middle of the day for a solar-heated splash.

Off to the west, near the railway line, is the *Lokanda al-Medina* (the sign is in Arabic only), where a bed costs S£100.

The *Kosti Province Rest House*, about half a km south-east of the Abu Zayd (to your right when looking at the river), is the expensive joint, costing S£1100 per person with full board. The old and somewhat shabby colonial relic is set in unkempt gardens.

There are a few small food and juice stands scattered around the railway line.

Getting There & Around

The souq shaabi is, as usual, a few km out of town. A shuttle takes you there from near the railway line for S£10. Frequent buses leave for Khartoum and Sennar. They cost S£465 (five hours) and S£145 (two hours) respectively. There is a daily bus to El-Obeid which costs S£600. The trip takes about eight or nine hours.

For details of the boat trip between Kosti and Juba, refer to the Juba Getting There & Away section. No passenger boats were in service at the time of writing.

SENNAR

Sennar is a convenient transit point, from which it is easy to make a lorry connection to Suki, Singa or the village of Dinder. The town is right on the banks of the Blue Nile, but apart from the river there's not much to see. There are a few banks clustered around the modest souq in the middle of town.

Places to Stay & Eat

The best place to stay is the *El-Rasheed Tourism Hotel*, which is near where the shuttle bus from the souq shaabi stops. It has good, clean rooms with fan and spotless

toilets and showers outside, and costs S£560 for a double.

Cheaper but less attractive alternatives include the *Lokanda al-Jumhuriyya*, just up from the river, and the *Funduq Medina*, on the main road from the centre of town to the souq shaabi. The signs for both of these are in Arabic only.

Food-wise there's not much to choose from, but you might like to try the *Gulf Cafeteria*, near the El-Rasheed.

Getting There & Around

There are minibuses to Kosti for S£145, which take a couple of hours. If nothing is going to Kosti, get a minibus to Rabak for S£110 and another connection from there to Kosti for S£25. Minibuses to Singa cost S£100; to Wad Medani they cost S£135. The bus to Khartoum costs S£450. The shuttle bus between the centre of town and the souq shaabi, which is about four km out of town, costs S£10.

DINDER

Dinder's extremely friendly and hospitable people are the main attraction of this dusty little village. You will constantly be followed by a parade of kids, all wanting to shake your hand. The villagers will overwhelm you with invitations to share food and drink with them in their homes. Dinder is a good base for visiting the Dinder National Park.

Places to Stay

If there's room, you can stay at the national park rangers' *rest house*. To get to it, walk a short distance out of the village, up the street past the mosque and huts, and you'll see the yellow buildings of the rest house on your left. Accommodation costs S£100 per person; there are three beds to a room and warm-water showers are available. It also has a refrigerator and crockery. It's a very peaceful place, and the walk through the forest, from the rest house to the Nile, is beautiful. You might be able to camp by the river, although it's discouraged.

DINDER NATIONAL PARK

One of the Sudan's 14 game reserves, this park features many animals, including giraffes, lions, buffaloes, kudus, waterbucks, baboons, other monkeys and crocodiles. The park does not compare with game reserves further south in Africa, although the bird life is abundant. The main attraction is the wildness of the place. The best time to visit is between December and May, when you'll usually have the place to yourself.

Very few people manage to visit the park at any time of year, and it's no wonder – the fees you are officially supposed to pay are enough to deter most. They include US$50 admission to the park, US$50 per night in the camp and US$100 per day for tours inside the park. If you go along to the Wildlife Service in Khartoum, on Sharia el-Nil, next to the old zoo, you might be able to arrange for some sort of reduction on these ridiculous prices. There are actually two camps in the park. Galegu is the main one. The camp there is equipped with grass huts, showers and latrines. The second camp, Atabia, is in a remote corner of the southern end of the park. The 10 or so park rangers there are all but cut off, fighting an uphill battle against poachers. Migrants from nearby Ethiopia tend to wander into the park – borders have a fluid meaning here.

There is no food in either camp, so bring your own. Expatriates who occasionally drive down take their own water supplies too, as the local water is full of all sorts of goodies, including Guinea worm. If you have to use the local water, use a filter and iodine or purification tablets. Malaria is also a problem, so bring a good mosquito net and lots of repellent.

Getting There & Away

If you don't have your own transport, hitching is the only way to get to the park. The best bet is to try to get a ride with a park ranger from Dinder town – they occasionally drive into the park with supplies. From Khartoum, you can get buses to Sennar and then on to Singa, from where you'll have to cross the Blue Nile on an unreliable ferry. Alterna-tively, you might be able to get a bus from Sennar directly to Dinder. If you do get a lift into the park, remember that it may be days before another vehicle comes into the park, so you could be stuck for a while.

ER-ROSEIRES

At the head of a lake created by the Er-Roseires Dam is the town of Er-Roseires, a beautiful place with lots of trees, green hills and tall savanna grasses. Swimming is possible downstream from the dam; your bag will be searched when you cross the bridge.

There's a *youth hostel* in town.

WAU

You can sleep in the Wau police-station yard for free, as long as you don't mind bedding down in the dust along with the mosquitoes and a bunch of interesting criminals.

If you don't fancy that, the *Catholic mission* sometimes dispenses a little Christian charity, and the *youth hostel* offers accommodation.

The *El-Nilein Hotel* and the *Riverside Hotel* are relatively cheap options.

The best place to eat in Wau is the *Unity Restaurant*.

Getting There & Away

There is really only one route from Wau to Juba. What appears to be the direct route on the maps – Wau to Juba via Rumbek – is almost impassable these days, with virtually no traffic along it. Apart from that, it goes too close to the fighting, and the Anya-nya 2 guerrillas have warned that they will kill all White people on sight.

The road that you must take is Wau to Juba via Tambura, Yambio, Maridi and Yei. You'll need to get rides on lorries from Wau to Yei, but you have the choice of lorry or bus from Yei to Juba. There are daily buses in either direction between Yei and Juba; they leave Juba between 6 and 7 am.

The stretch between Wau and Tambura is pretty bad, but the section from Juba to Yambio is much better. Between Maridi and Yei, there are incredible views into the Nile and Zaire river basins.

The best people to approach for lifts along this route are the international aid agencies like UNICEF and the UN's Food & Agriculture Organization (FAO), Sudanese government departments and the Sudanese Council of Churches – but keep in mind that their first priority is to assist local inhabitants. If you find yourself stuck in Wau, there is a weekly mail truck to Juba that takes three to five days – but there's a lot of competition for seats.

YAMBIO & YEI

You may be able to spend a night at Yambio's beautifully located *Protestant mission*. From Yambio, you can cross the border into Zaire via the market village of Gongura. Lorries to Isorio are available in Gongura. If you want to stay in Yei, ask at the *Agricultural Research Station* for a place to stay.

Shilluk man

JUBA

With the government's comparatively successful 1992 dry-season offensive, its hold on Juba and the surrounding country has become more secure. Nevertheless, rebel activity and fighting between the rebels' various factions would make travel in the area, even if it were permitted, extremely hazardous. Many travellers do grow to like this 'one-horse town'. At the moment, however, it seems to have little to recommend it. Why go there?

If you do, you must register with the police on arrival. If you're heading south, you must get an exit permit before you leave. These permits are obtainable from the Immigration office, which is in the same building as the police. Get this permit before you start looking for a lift. Photography permits can be obtained from the Ministry of Information, but they have to be countersigned by the police.

Malakia

Much of the life of Juba actually takes place here, in the traditional village of Malakia. If life returns to normal, the market may again be well worth visiting, especially if you're about to take the boat north to Kosti. Among other things, you may be able to get your hands on portable stoves and charcoal.

Malakia is two km from Juba. The main Juba lorry park is near the souq.

Immatong Mountains

Dominated by the Sudan's highest mountain, Mt Kinyeti (3170 metres), the Immatong Mountains were developed as a hill station resort by the British colonial authorities.

If you have time for a detour, it's worth visiting this region, east of Juba and south of Torit. Make your way to the Gilo Guest House in Gilo; although it was looted in the civil war, the guesthouse retains a lot of old-world charm. There are no mosquitoes or tsetse flies in these hills, and it's wonderfully cool. You can forget about this place in the rainy season, however, when the road is impassable.

Places to Stay

For many years, the most popular hotel in Juba has been the *Hotel Africa*, where you can get a bed or simply sleep on the floor. Because of its popularity, however, this hotel, at last report, was often full, and the management had allowed it to run down. One traveller said it was 'no better than the boat', and another drew attention to the 'cholera-style toilets'. The hotel food was good, but not the cheapest in town.

If you don't like the Africa, or can't get in, try the *Medical Training Centre* (MTC), behind the football stadium, or the *Juba Hotel*.

You may also be able to stay on the verandah of the Immigration office free of charge.

Places to Eat

For food, go to the *People's Restaurant* or the *Greek Club*. The latter has been recommended by many travellers. The *Unity Garden* on May St is also very popular.

Most of the tap water in Juba comes straight from the Nile and is not filtered. If you drink it, you'll get sick.

Getting There & Away

Air There are no scheduled flights to Juba, but aid organisations sometimes fly in and out. If you have a pressing reason for getting there, you may be able to hitch a lift. It may be possible to do the same from Juba to Kenya.

Bus There are daily buses between Juba and Nimule. These take about six hours.

Lorry Going south from Juba, you have the choice of crossing into either Uganda or Kenya. Until Idi Amin was deposed in Uganda, the main route south went directly into Kenya via Torit, Kapoeta, Lokichoggio and Lodwar. If you're looking for a rugged trip, you can still go this way, but you should allow at least a week for the journey. It's not possible during the rainy season. The section between Lodwar and Kapoeta was being upgraded, but the civil war has probably put an end to this.

These days, most travellers take the road into Uganda via Nimule. To make this trip, you need to obtain a permit in Juba. Most days, lorries travel from Malakia, two km from Juba, to Kenya, via Uganda. You can pay in Kenyan currency, or even in US dollars or UK pounds.

The journey takes about 1½ days, with many army/police checkpoints en route, at which you will be thoroughly searched. Ugandan army and police officers will pressure you into giving them certain items of your baggage. A polite but firm refusal and a little humour may do the trick; otherwise, leave something you can do without in the top of your pack. As they seem to be particularly fond of medical supplies, they may take these and leave the rest of your pack alone. It's best to go through in the morning, when they're more likely to be sober.

Boat The following information about the Nile steamer from Kosti to Juba refers to the period before the civil war flared up again. It should still give you a good idea of what to expect if the political situation permits travel in the region in the future, but for now, apart from the occasional barge carrying emergency relief, there is no traffic on the river at all.

The steamer that used to do the run from Kosti to Juba was sunk by SPLM rebels in February 1984. It was replaced by two new boats, the *Juba* and the *Nimule*, which make the journey in far less time than the old boat used to take. They have 1st and 2nd class only.

The steamer trip should take six to eight days travelling upstream, and about four days going downstream. There used to be departures in either direction two or three times a week, and it was essential to book a berth in advance.

At the time, meals could be bought on the boat, but they were not cheap. If you want to keep costs down, take some food and a portable stove. Putting your own food together also helps pass the time. Water comes straight from the Nile and is not boiled. The toilets get sluiced down once a day, but they don't stay clean for long. You will also need insect repellent.

If you're heading north from Juba, it may be worth hanging around the harbour for awhile and talking to the crew members of boats docked there. Some travellers have managed to get free lifts as far north as Malakal. You can save a lot of money this way.

Depending on how you take to slow boats, this journey can be very interesting – there are plenty of tribal villages and lots of wild-life en route – or very boring. If it turns out to be the latter, you could always pass some time by writing us a letter and telling us about the latest developments. Be careful about taking photographs of tribespeople on the river banks. The boat crew, too, are espe-cially sensitive to being photographed, and many travellers have had their film ripped from their cameras.

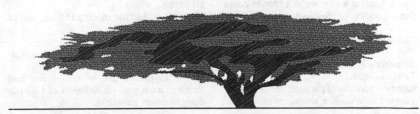

Egyptian Gods & Goddesses

Amun – one of the deities of creation and the patron god of Thebes. Amun, his wife Mut and their son Khons formed the Theban triad.
Amun-Ra – king of the gods; the fusion of Amun and the sun-god Ra.
Anubis – jackal-headed god of embalming and of the dead.

Anubis

Anukis – wife of Khnum; wears a white crown flanked by two gazelle horns.
Aten – the disc of the rising sun, worshipped as the sole deity by Pharaoh Akhenaten and Queen Nefertiti.
Atum – god of the rising sun, identified with Ra.

Bastet – cat-goddess; local deity of Bubastis in the Nile Delta.

Edjo – cobra-goddess of Lower Egypt; she was the protector of the Pharaoh and was represented on his crown as a rearing cobra.
Eos – goddess of the dawn.

Geb – god of the earth and husband of Nut.

Haroeris – Horus the Elder, a form of Horus the falcon-god.
Hathor – goddess of pleasure and love. Represented as a cow, a woman with a cow's head, or a woman with a head-dress of a sun disc fixed between the horns of a cow. She was the wet-nurse and lover of Horus, and the local deity of Dendara in the Nile Valley.
Horus – falcon-god; the offspring of Isis and Osiris. Identified with the living Pharaoh.

Ihy – the youthful aspect of the creator-gods.
Isis – powerful goddess of healing, purity, sexuality, motherhood and women. The sister and wife of Osiris and mother of Horus, she was also the divine mourner of the dead. She was worshipped so passionately that she became identified with all the goddesses of the Mediterranean, finally absorbing them to become the universal mother of nature and protector of humans.

Isis

Khnum – ram-headed god of the Nile cataracts and local god of Elephantine Island. He was often shown moulding humankind on his potter's wheel.
Khons – god of the moon and time; son of Amun and Mut.

Maat – goddess of truth and the personification of cosmic order.
Min – ithyphallic god of the harvest and fertility; local god of Achmim and patron deity of desert travellers.

Montu – falcon-headed war-god; the original patron deity of Thebes.

Mut – vulture or lioness-headed war-goddess; wife of Amun.

Neith – goddess of war and hunting, and protector of embalmed bodies.

Nekhbet – vulture-goddess of Nekheb; guardian (along with Edjo) of the Pharaohs and a deity associated with royal and divine births.

Nekheny – local falcon-god of ancient Nekhen, later associated with Horus.

Nepthys – guardian deity and sister of Isis.

Nut – sky-goddess, often depicted as a woman or a cow stretched across the ceilings of tombs, swallowing the sun and creating night. Each morning, she would give birth to the sun.

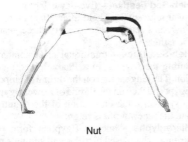

Nut

Opet – hippopotamus-goddess; the mother of Osiris.

Osiris – ruler of the Underworld. Osiris was murdered by his brother Seth and brought back to life by his sister Isis to rule as the judge of the dead.

Ptah – creator-god who formed the world with words from his tongue and heart; local deity of ancient Memphis.

Ra – the great sun-god. He was creator and ruler of other deified elements of nature and was often linked with other gods.

Ra-Harakhty – falcon-headed god, the fusion of Ra and Horus.

Sacred Animals – Apis bulls of Memphis, cats of Beni Hasan, crocodiles of Kom Ombo, cobra or uraeus, baboons, hippopotamuses, ibis, monkeys, rams, cows, goats, leopards, jackals, snakes and lizards.

Satis – daughter of Khnum and Anukis. This family was the triad of the First Nile Cataract and was worshipped at Elephantine Island (Aswan).

Sekhmet – lioness-headed goddess; the 'spreader of terror' and wife of Ptah.

Serapis – Greco-Egyptian god; the fusion of Osiris and Zeus.

Seshat – goddess of writing.

Seth – evil brother and murderer of Osiris.

Shu – god of the air.

Sobek – crocodile or crocodile-headed god; local deity of Al-Faiyum and Kom Ombo.

Thoth – ibis-headed god of wisdom, healing and writing; local god of ancient Hermopolis in the Nile Valley.

Wepwawet – wolf-god and avenger of Osiris; local god of Asyut in the Nile Valley.

Glossary

Bab – gate.

Book of the Dead – ancient theological compositions, or hymns, that were the subject of most of the colourful paintings and reliefs on tomb walls. Extracts from these so-called books were believed to assist the deceased person safely into the afterlife via the Kingdom of the Dead. The texts were sometimes also painted on a roll of papyrus and buried with the dead.

Canopic Jars – pottery jars which held the embalmed internal organs and viscera (liver, stomach, lungs, intestines) of the mummified Pharaoh. They were placed in the burial chamber near the sarcophagus.

Capitals – in Pharaonic and Greco-Roman architecture the top, or capital, of a column was decorated with plant forms, such as the papyrus, palm or lotus, or other motifs, like the human face and cow's ears of the goddess Hathor.

Hathor and Lotus capitals

Caravanserai – large inn enclosing a courtyard, providing accommodation for caravans.

Careta – donkey cart.

Cartouche – oblong figure enclosing the hieroglyphs of royal or divine names.

Cenotaph – symbolic tomb, temple or place of cult worship that was additional to the Pharaoh's actual burial place.

Electrum – alloy of gold and silver used for jewellery, ornaments and decorating buildings.

Fellahin – the peasant farmers or agricultural workers who make up the majority of Egypt's population.

False Door – fake, seemingly half-open ka door in a tomb wall which enabled the Pharaoh's spirit, or life force, to come and go at will.

Galabiyya – full-length robe worn by men.

Haj – pilgrimage to Mecca. All Muslims should make the journey at least once in their lifetime.

Hantour – horse-drawn carriage.

Heb-Sed Festival – five-day celebration of royal rejuvenation, held after 30 years of a Pharaoh's reign and then every three years thereafter.

Heb-Sed Race – traditional re-enactment, during the festival, of a Pharaoh's coronation. The king sat first on the throne of Upper Egypt and then on the throne of Lower Egypt to symbolise the unification of the country and the renewal of his reign.

Hieroglyphs – ancient Egyptian form of writing, which used pictures and symbols to represent objects, words or sounds.

Hypostyle Hall – hall in which the roof is supported by columns.

Iconostasis – screen with doors and icons set in tiers, used in eastern Christian churches.

Ithyphallic – denoting the erect phallus of a Pharaoh or god (usually used in reference to the god Min); a sign of fertility.

Iwan – vaulted hall, opening into a central court, in the madrassa of a mosque.

Ka – spirit, or 'double', of a living person which gained its own identity with the death of that person. The survival of the ka, however, required the continued existence of the body, hence mummification. The ka was also the vital force emanating from a god and transferred through the Pharaoh to his people.

Khedive – Egyptian viceroy under Ottoman suzerainty (1867-1914).

Kiosk – open-sided pavilion.

Kuttab – Qur'anic school for boys.

Lotus – white waterlily regarded as sacred by the ancient Egyptians, who likened their land to the lotus – the Nile Delta was the flower, Al-Faiyum the bud, and the Nile and its valley the stem. The lotus was specifically identified with Upper Egypt.

Madrassa – theological college that is part of a noncongregational mosque.

Mammisi – birth-house. In these small chapels or temples, erected in the vicinity of a main temple, the rituals of the divine birth of the living king were performed. All Pharaohs were believed to be incarnations of the falcon-god Horus.

Mashrabiyyah – ornate carved wooden panel or screen; a feature of Islamic architecture.

Mastaba – Arabic word for 'bench'; a mud-brick structure above tombs from which the pyramids were developed.

Midan – town or city square.

Mihrab – niche in the wall of a mosque that indicates the direction of Mecca.

Minbar – pulpit in a mosque.

Mortuary Complex – a Pharaoh's last resting place. It usually comprised: a pyramid which was the king's tomb and the repository for all his household goods, clothes and treasure; a funerary temple on the east side of the pyramid which served as a cult temple for worship of the dead Pharaoh; pits for the solar barques; a valley temple on the banks of the Nile, where the mummification process was carried out; and a massive causeway from the river to the pyramid.

Muezzin – mosque official who calls the faithful to prayer five times a day from the minaret.

Natron – whitish mineral of hydrated sodium carbonate that occurs in saline deposits and salt lakes and acts as a natural preservative. It was used in ancient Egypt to pack and dry out the body during mummification.

Nilometer – pit descending into the Nile and containing a central column marked with graduations. The marks were used to measure and record the level of the river, especially during the inundation.

Nome – administrative division or province of ancient Egypt.

Obelisks

Obelisk – monolithic stone pillar, with square sides tapering to a pyramidal top, used as a monument in ancient Egypt. Obelisks were usually carved from pink granite and set up in pairs at the entrance to a tomb or temple. A single obelisk was sometimes the object of cult worship.

Opet Festival – celebration held in Luxor (Thebes) during the Nile inundation season, when statues of the Theban triad – Amun, Mut and Khons – would be transported by river from Karnak Temple to Luxor Temple to join in the festivities.

Papyrus – plant identified with Lower Egypt; writing material made from the pith of this plant; a document written on such paper.

Pylon – monumental gateway at the entrance to a temple.

Pyramid Texts – paintings and reliefs on the walls of the internal rooms and burial chamber of pyramids and often on the sarcophagus itself. The texts recorded the Pharaoh's burial ceremonies, associated temple rituals, the hymns vital to his passage into the afterlife and, sometimes, major events in his life.

Sabil – covered public drinking fountain.

Sarcophagus – huge stone or marble coffin used to encase other wooden coffins and the mummy of the Pharaoh or queen.

Sarcophagi

Scarab – dung beetle regarded as sacred in ancient Egypt and represented on amulets or in hieroglyphs as a symbol of the sun-god Ra.

Serapeum – network of subterranean galleries constructed as tombs for the mummified sacred Apis bulls; the most important temple of the Greco-Egyptian god Serapis.

Serdab – hidden cellar in a tomb, or a stone room in front of some pyramids, containing a coffin with a life-size, lifelike, painted statue of the dead king. Serdabs were designed so that the Pharaoh's ka could communicate with the outside world.

Sharia – Arabic for 'road' or 'way'.

Shari'a – Islamic law, the body of doctrine that regulates the lives of Muslims.

Solar Barque – wooden boat placed in or around the Pharaoh's tomb. It was the symbolic vessel of transport for his journey over the sea of death to the Kingdom of the Dead to be judged before Osiris, and for his final passage to the eternal afterlife.

Souq – market.

Speos – rockcut tomb or chapel.

Stele (plural: stelae) – stone or wooden commemorative slab or column decorated with inscriptions or figures.

Ulama – group of Muslim scholars or religious leaders; a member of this group.

Uraeus – rearing cobra with inflated hood, associated with the goddess Edjo. This was the most characteristic symbol of Egyptian royalty and was worn on the Pharaoh's forehead or crown. The sacred fire-spitting serpent was an agent of destruction and protector of the king.

Wakala – inn for travelling merchants. It was built around a courtyard, with living quarters above the warehouses and stables.

Index

TEXT

576

Thanks

We greatly appreciate the contributions of
the many people who put so much effort into
writing and telling us of their weird and
wonderful experiences. Writers (apologies if
we've mis-spelt your name) to whom thanks
must go include:

Jurgen Ammann (B), Hilary Anderson (UK), Juliette
Arde (SA), Ian Arscott (UK), Tina Asplund (S),
Borsos Balazs (H), Amanda Banton (UK), Anthony
Barnes (UK), Janet Barnett (Aus), Miss Barnett (UK),
Lucy Bates (UK), Robert Belcher (UK), Ewen Bent
(UK), Karl Beringhs (B), Michael Birch (Aus), Helen
Body (UK), Tad Boniecki (Aus), Sheree Boore (UK),
Thor M Bostad (N), Marjoke Brachel (NL),
Annemarie Breukels (NL), Jan Brown (Aus), Peter
Brown (UK), Robert Brown (USA), Kevin Bruce
(UK), George Burles (UK), Monique de Bussy (NL),
Ian Buttenshaw (UK), Prof Brooke Cameron (USA),
Leigh Carey (UK), Maya Catsanis (Aus), Sarah
Challis (UK), Peter Christensen (Dk), Glen Christian
(NL), Michael Citrino, Therese Clason (S), Mary
Colfer (UK), David Corbett (NZ), Leslie Dann
(USA), Ron Dar-Ziv (Isr), Phil Davis, Michael Davis
(USA), Sharon Dray (Aus), Chrisna Du Plessis (SA),
Alison Dunning (UK), V Eichholtz (NZ), Michele
Einert (USA), Carolyn Elliot-Stevens (C), Matthias
Ernst (CH), Daniel Fascione (UK), Michael Fasman
(USA), Michael Ferck (D), Jim Fisher (Aus), Soren
Fisker (Dk), Henrik Frank (Dk), Ian Fraser (UK), J
Freedland (USA), Matt Fry (USA), J S Funk (USA),
Nathanial Gibson (USA), WJ & EA Gregory (UK),
Marieke Groen (NL), P Haddacks (UK), Glen Harbott
(UK), J Casserly Haskell (USA), Susan Hawker
(UK), Mr R Hawkins (UK), K Heaney (USA), Chris-
tina Henning (USA), Ivo Hens (NL), P Hessard (C),
Bronwyn Hill (Aus), Phil Hitchings (UK), Camilla
Holmgren (S), Bryan Howard (UK), Alice van Hoye
(NZ), Bert Hughes (NZ), Miss P C Hunt (UK),
Richard Ingle (UK), Paul Israel (UK), Anita Jackson
(UK), Mr M James (UK), Berj Jamkojian (A), Azza
Jeena (C), Scott Jenkinson (Aus), Leonie Joordens
(NL), Arlene Joy (USA), Tal Kahana (USA), Ashraf
Kamal, Ruth A Karl (USA), Zoe Keel (UK), Tim
Kelleher (UK), Nick Kemp (UK), Eric Kendell (UK),
Miriam Keulers (NL), Barbara Key (Aus), Angeline
Khoo (Sin), Margaret Kikkert (NL), Mr A F Kilbey
(UK), Lorelle Kilpatrick (Aus), N Kingma (NL), Alan
Kinnaman (USA), Lewis Kinnear (UK), Eva Kirsch-
ner (Dk), Ruth & Drew Klee (USA), Susan Kosurala
(UK), Dimitri Kotzamaris (USA), Maarten
Krabbendam (NL), Sebastian Krug (D), Sebastian

Larcher (A), Judith Large (UK), Joanne Law (UK),
Florence Lawson (UK), Rozanna Lee (Aus), Robin
Leigh (UK), Steve & Suzie Lemlin, David Lewis
(UK), Han Ing Lim (NL), David C Lipfert (USA), Iain
Lobban (UK), Turid Lovskar (N), Mr Derek Lowe
(UK), Mattias Ludvigsson (S), Dieter Marchl (D),
Andy Matkin (UK), Marlon Maus (USA), Jane
Maycock (UK), J McCarthy (Aus), Keri McCormick
(NZ), Mrs M A McLoughlin (Ire), Lucy Meek (NZ),
Henrika Mensah (Fin), Roger Miles (UK), Leslie
Miller (USA), Patrick Miller (Aus), Kelvin Moody
(NZ), L Morgan (UK), Klaus G Muller (D), Hazel
Mullinger (UK), Louise Murray (Aus), C B Nisker
(USA), Gamal Ahmed Noor, Nelle Norbart (NL),
Libor Novak (CZ), Rick Olderman (USA), J Owen
(UK), J W Owen (UK), Julie Parker (UK), Nisha Parti
(UK), Hamish Paterson (UK), Tim Penney (NZ),
Jerry Perichon (USA), Helen Phillips (Aus), Jenny
Pickles (Aus), Kevin Pilley (UK), Jonathan Poon
(HK), Henry Posner (USA), Rolf D Potthoff (D),
Michael Powell (UK), Nick Quantock, Abdelsalam
Ragab (USA), Nicholas Redeyoff (USA), Vincent G
Reidy (UK), Susan Rhodes (UK), Mr & Mrs A Rice
(UK), John Roberts (C), Bradley Robinson (USA),
Marcus Rodrigues (Aus), Julian Rota (UK), Caitlyn
Ryan (Aus), Sonja Ryckewaert (B), Susan Sabo
(USA), Sarah Sammons (USA), Dr Ravi Sandhu
(NZ), A & O Sarti (I), G Scheibmair (Aus), Rolf
Schenker (CH), Jim Schoot (USA), Gitte Schwartz
(Dk), John Seidel (USA), Mohamed el Shafie (Egy),
Peter & Flo Shaw (Aus), Jon Sidaway (UK), David
Sidders (UK), Mrs G Snook (UK), Abdo Solieman
(Egy), Kate Spalding (UK), Jochen Stegmaier (D),
Elisa Stivanello (I), Jo Anne Strubeel (C), Katalin
Sztankovits (UK), Mrs K Talbot (UK), Matt Taylor
(UK), Jeremy Taylor (UK), Elaine Telford (Aus), I
Tierlinck (NL), Lisa Jane Travell (UK), Paul van der
Snyspen (NL), L Vellacott (UK), Astrid Venterogel
(NL), Michael Wach (USA), Kathryn Ward (UK),
Susan Wastie (UK), Greta Watson (USA), Alan
Westrup (UK), Veronica Wiles (USA), Erik Wilke
(NL), David Williams, Yolanda Wisewitch (NZ),
Hartmut Wolgberg (D), Stuart C Wright (UK)

A – Austria, Aus – Australia, B – Belgium, C –
Canada, CH – Switzerland, Cz – Czech Republic, D
– Germany, Dk – Denmark, Egy – Egypt, Fin –
Finland, H – Hungary, HK – Hong Kong, I – Italy, Ire
– Ireland, Isr – Israel, N – Norway, NL – Netherlands,
NZ – New Zealand, S – Sweden, SA – South Africa,
Sin – Singapore, UK – United Kingdom, USA –
United States of America

Keep in touch!

We love hearing from you and think you'd like to hear from us.

The Lonely Planet Newsletter covers the when, where, how and what of travel. (AND it's free!)

When...is the right time to see reindeer in Finland?
Where...can you hear the best palm-wine music in Ghana?
How...do you get from Asunción to Areguá by steam train?
What...should you leave behind to avoid hassles with customs in Iran?

To join our mailing list just contact us at any of our offices. (details below)

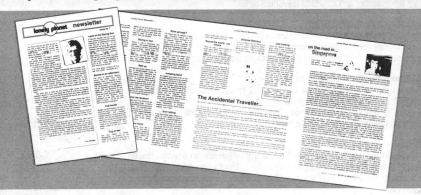

Every issue includes:

- *a letter from Lonely Planet founders Tony and Maureen Wheeler*
- *travel diary from a Lonely Planet author - find out what it's really like out on the road*
- *feature article on an important and topical travel issue*
- *a selection of recent letters from our readers*
- *the latest travel news from all over the world*
- *details on Lonely Planet's new and forthcoming releases*

Also available Lonely Planet T-shirts. 100% heavyweight cotton (S, M, L, XL)

LONELY PLANET PUBLICATIONS
Australia: PO Box 617, Hawthorn 3122, Victoria (tel: 03-819 1877)
USA: Embarcadero West, 155 Filbert Street, Suite 251, Oakland, CA 94607 (tel: 510-893 8555)
UK: Devonshire House, 12 Barley Mow Passage, Chiswick, London W4 4PH (tel: 081-742 3161)

Guides to the Middle East

Arab Gulf States
The Arab Gulf States are surprisingly accessible and affordable with an astounding range of things to see and do – camel markets, desert safaris, ancient forts and modern cities to list just a few. Includes concise history and language section for each country.

Iran - a travel survival kit
The first English-language guide to this enigmatic and surprisingly hospitable country written since the Islamic Revolution. As well as practical travel details the author provides background information that will fascinate adventurers and armchair travellers alike.

Israel - a travel survival kit
Detailed practical travel information is combined with authoritative historical references in this comprehensive guide. Complete coverage of both the modern state of Israel and the ancient biblical country.

Jordan & Syria - a travel survival kit
Two countries away from the usual travel routes, but with a wealth of natural and historical attractions for the adventurous traveller...12th century Crusader castles, ruined cities, the ancient Nabatean capital of Petra and haunting desert landscapes.

Turkey - a travel survival kit
This acclaimed guide takes you from Istanbul bazaars to Mediterranean beaches, from historic battlegrounds to the stamping grounds of St Paul, Alexander the Great, the Emperor Constantine, King Croesus and Omar Khayyam.

Trekking in Turkey
Explore beyond Turkey's coastline and you will be surprised to discover that Turkey has mountains with walks to rival those found in Nepal.

Yemen - a travel survival kit
The Yemen is one of the oldest inhabited regions in the world. This practical guide gives full details on a genuinely different travel experience.

West Asia on a shoestring
Want to cruise to Asia for 15 cents? Drink a great cup of tea while you view Mt Everest? Find the Garden of Eden? This guide has the complete story on the Asian overland trail from Bangladesh to Turkey, including Bhutan, India, Iran, the Maldives, Nepal, Pakistan, Sri Lanka and the Middle East.

Also available:
Arabic (Egyptian) phrasebook, **Arabic (Moroccan)** phrasebook and **Turkish** phrasebook.

Guides to Africa

Africa on a shoestring
From Marrakesh to Kampala, Mozambique to Mauritania, Johannesburg to Cairo – this guidebook has all the facts on travelling in Africa. Comprehensive information on more than 50 countries.

Central Africa - a travel survival kit
This guide tells where to go to meet gorillas in the jungle, how to catch a steamer down the Congo...even the best beer to wash down grilled boa constrictor! Covers Cameroun, Central African Republic, Chad, The Congo, Equatorial Guinea, Gabon, São Tomé & Principe, and Zaïre.

East Africa - a travel survival kit
Detailed information on Kenya, Uganda, Rwanda, Burundi, eastern Zaïre and Tanzania. The latest edition includes a 32-page full-colour Safari Guide.

Kenya - a travel survival kit
This superb guide features a 32-page 'Safari Guide' with colour photographs, illustrations and information on East Africa's famous wildlife.

Morocco, Algeria & Tunisia - a travel survival kit
Reap the rewards of getting off the beaten track with this practical guide.

South Africa, Lesotho & Swaziland - a travel survival kit
Travel to southern Africa and you'll be surprised by its cultural diversity and incredible beauty. There's no better place to see Africa's amazing wildlife. All the essential travel details are included in this guide as well as information about wildlife reserves.

Trekking in East Africa
Practical, first-hand information for trekkers for a region renowned for its spectacular national parks and rewarding trekking trails. Covers treks in Kenya, Tanzania, Uganda, Malawi and Zambia.

West Africa - a travel survival kit
All the necessary information for independent travel in Benin, Burkino Faso, Cape Verde, Côte d'Ivoire, The Gambia, Ghana, Guinea, Guinea-Bissau, Liberia, Mali, Mauritania, Niger, Nigeria, Senegal, Sierra Leone and Togo.

Zimbabwe, Botswana & Namibia - a travel survival kit
Exotic wildlife, breathtaking scenery and fascinating people...this comprehensive guide shows a wilder, older side of Africa for the adventurous traveller. Includes a 32-page colour Safari Guide.

Also available:
Swahili phrasebook.

Lonely Planet Guidebooks

Lonely Planet guidebooks cover every accessible part of Asia as well as Australia, the Pacific, South America, Africa, the Middle East, Europe and parts of North America. There are five series: *travel survival kits*, covering a country for a range of budgets; *shoestring guides* with compact information for low-budget travel in a major region; *walking guides*; *city guides* and *phrasebooks*.

Australia & the Pacific
Australia
Bushwalking in Australia
Islands of Australia's Great Barrier Reef
Fiji
Melbourne city guide
Micronesia
New Caledonia
New Zealand
Tramping in New Zealand
Papua New Guinea
Bushwalking in Papua New Guinea
Papua New Guinea phrasebook
Rarotonga & the Cook Islands
Samoa
Solomon Islands
Sydney city guide
Tahiti & French Polynesia
Tonga
Vanuatu
Victoria

South-East Asia
Bali & Lombok
Bangkok city guide
Cambodia
Indonesia
Indonesia phrasebook
Laos
Malaysia, Singapore & Brunei
Myanmar (Burma)
Burmese phrasebook
Philippines
Pilipino phrasebook
Singapore city guide
South-East Asia on a shoestring
Thailand
Thai phrasebook
Vietnam
Vietnamese phrasebook

North-East Asia
China
Beijing city guide
Mandarin Chinese phrasebook
Hong Kong, Macau & Canton
Japan
Japanese phrasebook
Korea
Korean phrasebook
Mongolia
North-East Asia on a shoestring
Seoul city guide
Taiwan
Tibet
Tibet phrasebook
Tokyo city guide

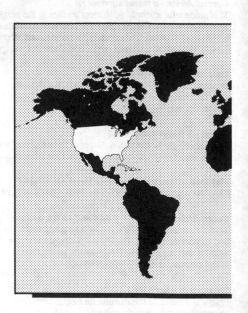

West Asia
Trekking in Turkey
Turkey
Turkish phrasebook
West Asia on a shoestring

Middle East
Arab Gulf States
Egypt & the Sudan
Arabic (Egyptian) phrasebook
Iran
Israel
Jordan & Syria
Yemen

Indian Ocean
Madagascar & Comoros
Maldives & Islands of the East Indian Ocean
Mauritius, Réunion & Seychelles

Mail Order

Lonely Planet guidebooks are distributed worldwide. They are also available by mail order from Lonely Planet, so if you have difficulty finding a title please write to us. US and Canadian residents should write to Embarcadero West, 155 Filbert St, Suite 251, Oakland CA 94607, USA; European residents should write to Devonshire House, 12 Barley Mow Passage, Chiswick, London W4 4PH; and residents of other countries to PO Box 617, Hawthorn, Victoria 3122, Australia.

Indian Subcontinent
Bangladesh
India
Hindi/Urdu phrasebook
Trekking in the Indian Himalaya
Karakoram Highway
Kashmir, Ladakh & Zanskar
Nepal
Trekking in the Nepal Himalaya
Nepali phrasebook
Pakistan
Sri Lanka
Sri Lanka phrasebook

Africa
Africa on a shoestring
Central Africa
East Africa
Trekking in East Africa
Kenya
Swahili phrasebook
Morocco, Algeria & Tunisia
Arabic (Moroccan) phrasebook
South Africa, Lesotho & Swaziland
Zimbabwe, Botswana & Namibia
West Africa

Central America
Baja California
Central America on a shoestring
Costa Rica
La Ruta Maya
Mexico

North America
Alaska
Canada
Hawaii

South America
Argentina, Uruguay & Paraguay
Bolivia
Brazil
Brazilian phrasebook
Chile & Easter Island
Colombia
Ecuador & the Galápagos Islands
Latin American Spanish phrasebook
Peru
Quechua phrasebook
South America on a shoestring
Trekking in the Patagonian Andes

Europe
Dublin city guide
Eastern Europe on a shoestring
Eastern Europe phrasebook
Finland
Hungary
Iceland, Greenland & the Faroe Islands
Ireland
Italy
Mediterranean Europe on a shoestring
Mediterranean Europe phrasebook
Poland
Scandinavian & Baltic Europe on a shoestring
Scandinavian Europe phrasebook
Switzerland
Trekking in Spain
Trekking in Greece
USSR
Russian phrasebook
Western Europe on a shoestring
Western Europe phrasebook

The Lonely Planet Story

Lonely Planet published its first book in 1973 in response to the numerous 'How did you .do it?' questions Maureen and Tony Wheeler were asked after driving, bussing, hitching, sailing and railing their way from England to Australia.

Written at a kitchen table and hand collated, trimmed and stapled, *Across Asia on the Cheap* became an instant local bestseller, inspiring thoughts of another book.

Eighteen months in South-East Asia resulted in their second guide, *South-East Asia on a shoestring*, which they put together in a backstreet Chinese hotel in Singapore in 1975. The 'yellow bible' as it quickly became known to backpackers around the world, soon became *the* guide to the region. It has sold well over half a million copies and is now in its 7th edition, still retaining its familiar yellow cover.

Today there are over 120 Lonely Planet titles in print – books that have that same adventurous approach to travel as those early guides; books that 'assume you know how to get your luggage off the carousel' as one reviewer put it.

Although Lonely Planet initially specialised in guides to Asia, they now cover most regions of the world, including the Pacific, South America, Africa, the Middle East and Europe. The list of *walking guides* and *phrasebooks* (for 'unusual' languages such as Quechua, Swahili, Nepalese and Egyptian Arabic) is also growing rapidly.

The emphasis continues to be on travel for independent travellers. Tony and Maureen still travel for several months of each year and play an active part in the writing, updating and quality control of Lonely Planet's guides.

They have been joined by over 50 authors, 54 staff – mainly editors, cartographers, & designers – at our office in Melbourne, Australia, 10 at our US office in Oakland, California and another three at our office in London to handle sales for Britain, Europe and Africa. In 1992 Lonely Planet opened an editorial office in Paris. Travellers themselves also make a valuable contribution to the guides through the feedback we receive in thousands of letters each year.

The people at Lonely Planet strongly believe that travellers can make a positive contribution to the countries they visit, both through their appreciation of the countries' culture, wildlife and natural features, and through the money they spend. In addition, the company makes a direct contribution to the countries and regions it covers. Since 1986 a percentage of the income from each book has been donated to ventures such as famine relief in Africa; aid projects in India; agricultural projects in Central America; Greenpeace's efforts to halt French nuclear testing in the Pacific and Amnesty International. In 1993 $100,000 was donated to such causes.

Lonely Planet's basic travel philosophy is summed up in Tony Wheeler's comment, 'Don't worry about whether your trip will work out. Just go!'